NINTH EDITION

TECHNIQUES OF FINANCIAL ANALYSIS

A Modern Approach

Erich A. Helfert, D.B.A.

IRWIN

Chicago • Bogotá • Boston • Buenos Aires • Caracas
London • Madrid • Mexico City • Sydney • Toronto

THE IRWIN SERIES IN FINANCE, INSURANCE AND REAL ESTATE

Stephen A. Ross
Sterling Professor of Economics and Finance
Yale University
Consulting Editor

FINANCIAL MANAGEMENT

Block and Hirt
Foundations of Financial Management
Eighth Edition

Brooks
PC FinGame: *The Financial Management Decision Game*
Version 2.0—DOS and Windows

Bruner
Case Studies in Finance: *Managing for Corporate Value Creation*
Second Edition

Eun and Resnick
International Financial Management

Fruhan, Kester, Mason, Piper and Ruback
Case Problems in Finance
Tenth Edition

Helfert
Techniques of Financial Analysis: *A Modern Approach*
Ninth Edition

Higgins
Analysis for Financial Management
Fourth Edition

Levich
International Financial Markets

Nunnally and Plath
Cases in Finance
Second Edition

Ross, Westerfield and Jaffe
Corporate Finance
Fourth Edition

Ross, Westerfield and Jordan
Essentials of Corporate Finance

Ross, Westerfield and Jordan
Fundamentals of Corporate Finance
Third Edition

Stonehill and Eiteman
Finance: *An International Perspective*

White
Financial Analysis with an Electronic Calculator
Second Edition

INVESTMENTS

Bodie, Kane and Marcus
Essentials of Investments
Second Edition

Bodie, Kane and Marcus
Investments
Third Edition

Cohen, Zinbarg and Zeikel
Investment Analysis and Portfolio Management
Fifth Edition

Hirt and Block
Fundamentals of Investment Management
Fifth Edition

Lorie, Dodd and Kimpton
The Stock Market: *Theories and Evidence*
Second Edition

Morningstar, Inc. and Remaley
U.S. Equities OnFloppy
Annual Edition

Shimko
The Innovative Investor
Version 2.0 - Lotus and Excel

Comments about Erich A. Helfert and *Techniques of Financial Analysis* . . .

"Dr. Helfert's book and his teachings go a long way toward removing the mystery from the financial workings of an enterprise. His approach allows managers from all areas of the business to understand how their decisions impact shareholder value."

Stephen E. Frank
President and Chief Operating Officer
Florida Power & Light Co.

"Erich Helfert's writing and teaching have become a mainstay in our 'Renewal Series' at AMOCO. This series, in its third year and directed at the top 3,500 leaders/managers in AMOCO worldwide, is an aggressive approach at helping to transform our culture through the use of early educational interventions that cascade through the organization. Erich's business and strategic sense have been recognized as valuable guides to our process."

William H. Clover, Ph.D.
Manager of Training and AMOCO Learning Center

"Erich Helfert has played an instrumental role in teaching HP managers of both financial and nonfinancial backgrounds in our longstanding Functional Management Program. His excellent financial overviews and simplified models effectively broaden our managers' understanding and ownership of their fiscal reponsibility to HP and our shareholders."

Robert P. Wayman
Executive President/Chief Financial Officer
Hewlett-Packard Company

"Erich Helfert has a great style of weaving the theory and practice of capital investment into a very interesting story. He has a solid corporate background that translates into high credibility concerning capital investment decision-making processes."

Professor James Gentry
University of Illinois—Urbana–Champaign

"The strengths of *Techniques of Financial Analysis* are its readability and accessibility to most groups of potential users. It does a very thorough job of explaining how management decisions rely on more than just financial strategy."

Professor Andrew Terry
University of Arkansas—Little Rock

"Over the past 30 years, thousands of managers and managers-in-training have read *Techniques of Financial Analysis*. For most, it was the first exposure to understanding the relationship between finance concepts and daily decisions. It remains, for many, a valuable reference called upon for day-to-day performance. I am confident you will also utilize this great resource for years to come."

Michael W. Junior
Publisher
Richard D. Irwin

FINANCIAL INSTITUTIONS AND MARKETS

Flannery and Flood
Flannery and Flood's BankMaster:
A Financial Services Simulation

Rose
Commercial Bank Management:
Producing and Selling Financial Services
Third Edition

Rose
Money and Capital Markets: *Financial Institutions and Instruments in a Global Marketplace*
Sixth Edition

Rose and Kolari
Financial Institutions: *Understanding and Managing Financial Services*
Fifth Edition

Santomero and Babbel
Financial Markets, Instruments, and Institutions

Saunders
Financial Institutions Management:
A Modern Perspective
Second Edition

REAL ESTATE

Berston
California Real Estate Principles
Seventh Edition

Berston
California Real Estate Practice
Sixth Edition

Brueggeman and Fisher
Real Estate Finance and Investments
Tenth Edition

Lusht
Real Estate Valuation: *Principles and Applications*

Smith and Corgel
Real Estate Perspectives: *An Introduction to Real Estate*
Second Edition

FINANCIAL PLANNING AND INSURANCE

Allen, Melone, Rosenbloom, and VanDerhei
Pension Planning: *Pensions, Profit-Sharing, and Other Deferred Compensation Plans*
Eighth Edition

Crawford
Law and the Life Insurance Contract
Seventh Edition

Crawford
Life and Health Insurance Law
LOMA Edition

Hirsch
Casualty Claim Practice
Sixth Edition

Kapoor, Dlabay and Hughes
Personal Finance
Fourth Edition

Kellison
Theory of Interest
Second Edition

Skipper
International Risk and Insurance

⊓⊤⊐ Times Mirror
⋈ Higher Education Group

Irwin Book Team
Publisher: *Michael W. Junior*
Sponsoring editor: *Gina Huck*
Editorial coordinator: *Wendi Sweetland*
Marketing manager: *Katie Rose*
Senior project supervisor: *Mary Conzachi*
Production supervisor: *Pat Frederickson*
Assistant manager, desktop services: *Charlene Perez*
Designer: *Keith McPherson*
Compositor: *Shepard Poorman Communications Corp.*
Typeface: *10/12 Times Roman*
Printer: *R.R. Donnelley & Sons*

Library of Congress Cataloging-in-Publication Data

Helfert, Erich A.
    Techniques of financial analysis: a modern approach / Erich A.
Helfert. -- 9th ed.
      p. cm.
    Includes bibliographical references and index.
    ISBN 0-7863-1120-7 0-256-14611-X
      1. Corporations--Finance.   2. Cash flow.   3. Financial statements.
4. Ratio analysis.   I. Title.
HG4026.H44 1997
658.15'1—dc20 96-20988   96–20988

Printed in the United States of America
1 2 3 4 5 6 7 8 9 0 DO 3 2 1 0 9 8 7 6

To Anne

For the past 34 years, the eight previous editions of this book have provided the student, analyst, or business executive a concise, practical, usable, and up-to-date overview of key financial analysis tools. The presentation is carefully designed to help the reader understand the linkage between management decisions and their impact on the financial performance and economic value of the business. The concept that any business is essentially a financial system of cash flows provides the foundation on which the presentation is built. This book helps the reader to interpret financial reports, develop basic financial projections, evaluate capital investment decisions, assess the implications of financing choices, and derive the value of a business or a security. Every technique and measure is described and demonstrated in the context of important underlying financial and economic concepts, but without delving into theoretical abstraction.

All analytical tools and related financial concepts are discussed from the perspective of the three basic *types of decisions* made continuously by the management of any ongoing business: *investment, operating, and financing.* The presentation is also structured around the *viewpoints* of the major parties interested in the analysis and performance of a business: *managers, owners, and creditors.*

In all this, however, practicality is paramount. Any issues and concepts going beyond what is essential are left to the more specialized textbooks and articles identified in the references. Self-study exercises and problems are provided after each chapter so the reader can practice applying the analytical tools and check the results against solutions in Appendix V.

The book has consistently maintained a unique appeal for both students and practitioners because of its clarity and commonsense approach. Originally an outgrowth of the compact technical briefing materials used in the MBA program at the Harvard Business School, which supplement practical case study discussion with essential background, the book has been regularly updated and modified approximately every four years. This ninth edition reflects not only the latest practice in the use of the various financial techniques, but also the experience gained over eight editions from the widespread use the book has enjoyed in university finance courses, both graduate and undergraduate, and from hundreds of executive development seminars and in-company programs in the United States, Canada, Latin America, and overseas, including the author's own numerous Fortune 100 client companies. Translated into seven foreign languages over the years, the book has transcended the confines of American business practice on which it is built, because the way in which the analytical methods are described makes them almost universally applicable.

The current edition has been refined and updated in its logical, integrated flow of the materials beginning with an overview of the "business system" and the financial analysis concepts, all the way to the development of business valuation and the meaning of shareholder value. The various graphics supporting the materials were tested in numerous executive development courses over the past 10 years.

The first five chapters form an integrated set, built around the conceptual overview of the business system, its decisional context, and its relationship to financial statements and analytical tools as presented in Chapter 1. The coverage of analytical methods begins in Chapter 2 with funds flow analysis, moves on to financial performance analysis, covers financial projections, and culminates in a discussion of the financial dynamics useful in modeling financial conditions.

The last four chapters deal with more specialized topics such as business investment analysis, the cost of capital, financing choices, and valuation of securities and businesses, as well as the creation of shareholders value.

The existing appendixes were also updated and solutions to all problems were again included in Appendix V, making the book truly self-contained for individual study.

The revision process has not, however, affected the book's primary focus on the doable and practical—in effect an "executive briefing" concept—and on building the reader's basic ability to grasp financial relationships and issues. As before, the book only presupposes that the user has some familiarity with basic accounting concepts.

I would again like to express my appreciation to my former colleagues at the Harvard Business School for the opportunity to develop the original concept of the book. My thanks also go to my business associates and to my colleagues at universities and in executive development programs here and abroad, too numerous to mention individually, for their continued extensive use of the book and for the many expressions of interest and constructive suggestions that have supported the book's evolution.

I am grateful to Michael Madaris, University of Southern Mississippi; James A. Gentry, University of Illinois, Urbana-Champaign; S. William Yost, University of California-Los Angeles; Michael Atchison, University of Virginia; Michael J. Fishman, Northwestern University; Andy Terry, University of Arkansas-Little Rock; James T. Murphy, Tulane University; James McNulty, Florida Atlantic University; Allan Young, Syracuse University; M. B. Humber, George Washington University; Dan Laughhunn, Duke University; and Marvin E. Camburn, Illinois Benedictine College for their constructive inputs.

Finally, I continue to be most gratified by the positive responses from so many individual users, past and current, who have found the book helpful in their studies and a supportive resource in their professions.

Erich A. Helfert

CONTENTS

Chapter 7

The Cost of Capital and Business Decisions   245

Chapter 8

Analysis of Financing Choices   273

Chapter 9

Valuation and Business Performance   303

Introduction

When a student, analyst, or business executive is dealing with a financial problem or wishes to understand the economic trade-offs related to business investment, operations, or financing decisions, a wide variety of analytical techniques—and sometimes rules of thumb—are available to generate quantitative answers. Selecting the appropriate tools from these choices is clearly an important part of the analytical task. Yet, experience has shown again and again that developing a proper perspective for the problem or issue is just as important as the choice of the tools themselves.

Therefore, this book not only presents the key financial tools generally used, but also explains the broader context of how and where they're applied to obtain meaningful answers. To this end, the first chapter provides an integrated conceptual backdrop both for the financial/economic dimensions of business management and for understanding the nature of financial statements, data, and processes underlying financial analysis techniques—all viewed in the context of creating shareholder value.

While the tools and techniques covered in this book are discussed and demonstrated in detail, the user must not be tempted to view them as ends in themselves. It's simply not enough to master the techniques alone! Financial and economic analysis is both an analytical and a judgmental process which helps answer questions that have been carefully posed in a managerial context. The process is at its best when the analyst's efforts are focused primarily on structuring the issue and its context, and only secondarily on data manipulation. We can't stress enough that the basic purpose of financial analysis is to help those responsible for results to make sound business decisions within a relevant framework.

Apart from providing specific numerical answers, the "solutions" to financial problems and issues depend significantly on the points of view of the parties involved, on the relative importance of the issue, and on the nature and reliability of the information available. In each situation, the objective of the analysis must be clearly understood before pencil is put to paper or computer keys are touched—otherwise, the process becomes wasteful "number crunching."

Management has been defined as "the art of asking significant questions." The same applies to financial analysis, which should be targeted toward finding meaningful answers to these significant questions—whether or not the results are fully quantifiable. In fact, the qualitative judgments involved in finding answers to financial/economic issues can often count just as heavily as the quantitative results, and no analytical task is complete until these aspects have been carefully spelled out and weighed.

The degree of precision and refinement to which any financial analysis is carried also depends on the specific situation. Given the uncertain nature of many of the estimates used in calculations, it's often preferable to develop ranges of potential outcomes rather than precise answers. At the same time, it's wasteful to further refine answers that clearly suggest the choice of particular alternatives—there's no need to belabor the obvious! Moreover, common sense dictates that most of the analytical effort should be directed at areas where the likely payoff from additional analysis is largest—to match the amount of energy expended with the significance of the results.

The following points are a suggested checklist for review and consideration before any financial analysis task is begun. This list should be helpful to the person actually doing the work as well as to the manager who may have assigned the question or project to an associate:

1. What's the exact nature and scope of the issue to be analyzed? Have the problem and its relative importance in the overall business context been clearly spelled out, including all the relevant alternatives to be considered?

2. Which specific factors, relationships, and trends are likely to be helpful in analyzing the issue? What's the order of their importance, and in what sequence should they be addressed?

3. Are there possible ways to obtain a quick "ballpark" estimate of the likely result to help decide (1) what the critical data and steps might be, and (2) how much effort should be spent on refining these?

4. How precise an answer is necessary in relation to the importance of the problem itself? Would additional refinement be worth the effort?

5. How reliable are the available data, and how is this uncertainty likely to affect the range of results? What confirmation might be possible, and at what degree of effort?

6. Are the data to be used expressed in cash flow terms—essential for economic analysis—or do they represent unadjusted accounting information?

7. What limitations are inherent in the tools to be applied, and how are these likely to affect the range of results? Are the tools chosen truly appropriate to solving the problem?

8. How important are qualitative judgments in the context of the problem, and what's the ranking of their significance? Which analytical steps might be made unnecessary by such considerations?

Only after having thought through these questions should specific analytical work on a problem proceed. The amount of care and effort expended on taking this critical first step at the beginning of the task will pay off in much more focused and meaningful work and results. In effect, we're talking about using a rational approach to problem solving in financial/economic analysis. In the end, this is what effective support of decision making involving a company's investments, operations, and financing is all about. Shareholder value creation is the logical result of sound decisions carefully analyzed and successfully implemented.

CHAPTER 1

A Financial Systems Context for Business

Any business, large or small, can be described as a system of financial relationships and movements of cash, activated by management decisions. This concept has gained particular importance in the 90s, as creation of shareholder value has emerged as the critical performance challenge. Creating shareholder value depends on bringing about a positive pattern of cash flows in excess of investor expectations—and a business that is successfully managed as a system will generate such cash flows over time and well into the future.

If the basic purpose and value of business activity amounts to cash flow generation, then it is necessary for us to understand in broad terms how the dynamics of the business system work. Moreover, we must relate the various analytical concepts and tools we'll discuss in this book to the business system, for they should be applied to making decisions that support cash flow generation and shareholder value creation. Finally, we must provide an appropriate context within which such analytical activity should take place.

This introductory chapter therefore covers three conceptual overviews for understanding the context and meaning of financial analysis and the economic trade-offs involved—thus going beyond mere technical methodology:

- A graphic representation of the business system, showing the relationships and dynamics of the three basic management decision areas:
    Investment decisions.
    Operations decisions.
    Financing decisions.

- A broad perspective of the nature and meaning of published financial statements and their relationship to the business system:
    Balance sheets.
    Operating (income) statements.
    Cash flow (funds flow) statements.
    Statements of changes in owners' (shareholders') equity.

1

■ A general overview of the key analytical processes used in interpreting the performance of the business system, grouped by major analytical viewpoints:

Financial accounting.
Investor analysis.
Managerial economics.

In all of our discussions, we'll differentiate between purely financial analysis on the one hand, and economic analysis and trade-offs on the other. The first is largely based on financial statements and accounting data, while the second focuses on cash flows. We make this key distinction because the task of analyzing, judging, and guiding a firm's activities is far broader than the mere manipulation of reported financial data. Ultimately, the performance and value of any business must be judged in economic terms, that is, expressed in cash flows achieved and future cash flows expected.

Yet, much of the available data and many of the analytical techniques used are based on financial accounting and its special conventions, which by their nature don't necessarily reflect current and future economic performance and value. Therefore, the analyst must carefully interpret and even translate the available data to properly match the context and purpose of the analysis. It's the analyst's duty to make sure that the process used and the results obtained in any analysis clearly fit the desired objectives.

A DYNAMIC PERSPECTIVE OF BUSINESS

Decision Context

Successful operation, performance, and long-term viability of any business depend on a continuous sequence of sound individual or collective decisions made by the management team. Every one of these decisions ultimately causes an economic impact, for better or worse, on the business. In essence, the process of managing any enterprise amounts to making an ongoing series of economic choices. These choices in turn activate specific movements of the financial resources supporting the business.

For Example

Hiring an employee means incurring a future series of salary or wage payments for useful services provided. Selling merchandise on credit releases goods from inventory to the customer and creates a documented obligation by the customer to remit payment 30 or 60 days hence. Investing in a new manufacturing facility causes, among other effects, a potentially complex set of future financial obligations to be fulfilled. Successful negotiation of a line of credit with a lender brings an inflow of cash into the business, to be repaid in future periods. ■

Some decisions are major, such as investing in a new manufacturing plant, raising large amounts of debt, or adding a new line of products or services. Most other decisions are part of the day-to-day processes through which every functional area of a business is managed. Common to all, however, is the basic concept of economic trade-offs, that is, before every decision the manager must weigh the cash benefits obtained against the cash costs incurred.

In normal day-to-day decisions, these underlying trade-offs may be quite apparent. In complex situations, however, managers must carefully evaluate whether the resources committed directly or indirectly by the decision are likely to be profitably recovered. The combined effect of all these trade-offs and decisions ultimately impacts both the performance and value of the business. These are judged periodically, either by means of financial statements or with the help of special economic analyses.

Fundamentally, managers make decisions on behalf of the owners of the business. Managers are responsible to deploy available internal and external resources in ways that create an economic gain for the owners—a gain reflected over time in the combination of dividends and capital appreciation received by owner/shareholders. This so-called *total shareholder return* (TSR) is one of the key criteria for measuring the success of the company, as we'll discuss in Chapters 3 and 9.

Despite the great variety of issues faced every day by managers of different businesses, their tasks are sufficiently similar in principle that we can effectively group all business decisions into three basic areas:

- The investment of resources.
- The operation of the business using these resources.
- The proper mix of financing that funds these resources.

Figure 1–1 reflects the continuous interrelationship of these three areas.

Today's business world has infinite variety. Enterprises of all sizes engage in activities such as manufacturing, trade, finance, and myriad services, using widely different legal and organizational structures, and often involving international

FIGURE 1–1

The Three Basic Business Decisions

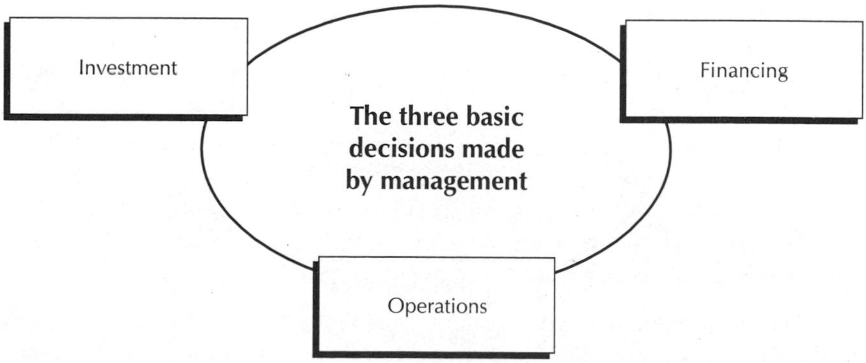

Investment

Financing

The three basic decisions made by management

Operations

operations and far-flung investments. Common to all businesses, however, is the following definition of the basic economic purpose of sound management:

> Planned deployment of selected resources in order to create, over time, economic value sufficient to recover all of the resources employed while earning an acceptable return on these resources under conditions that match the owners' expectations of risk.

Over the long run, therefore, successful resource deployments should result in a net improvement in the economic position of the owners—including their ability to make further resource investments if they choose. Only if such an improvement is achieved has additional shareholder value been created, as we'll discuss in more detail in later chapters. The primary effect will normally be a higher valuation of the business. If the company's stock is traded publicly, its value is judged by the securities markets. If the company is privately held, value creation will tend to be reflected in the price offered by potential buyers of the business. If no value increment is achieved over time, the firm's economic viability may be in doubt.

Creating shareholder value, therefore, ultimately depends on properly managing the three basic decisional areas common to all organizations:

- Selecting, implementing, and monitoring all *investments* with sound economic analysis and effective management.

- Guiding all *operations* of the business profitably through proper trade-offs and effective use of all resources employed.

- Prudently *financing* the business by consciously trading off the rewards expected against the risks encountered when using external financing.

Making successful economic trade-offs in these decisions is fundamental to driving the value creation process. The trade-offs must be explicitly managed in a consistent way to achieve long-run success, instead of occasional short-term

FIGURE 1–2

The Process of Value Creation

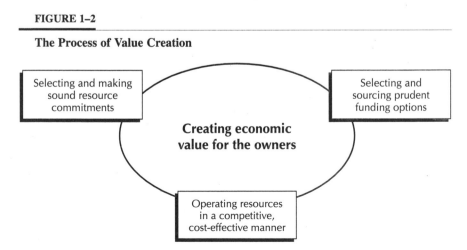

FIGURE 1–3

The Broad Context of Financial/Economic Analysis

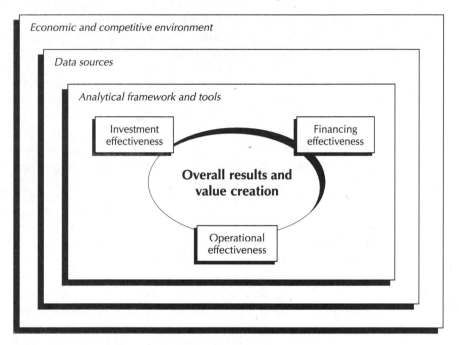

gains that cannot be sustained. Figure 1–2 depicts the interrelationship of the three decision areas.

The basic task—and the challenge—of financial/economic analysis lies in constructing a reasonably consistent and meaningful set of data and relationships that will support the decision-making process. If this is done well, the chosen frameworks and tools should enable the analyst and the manager to judge economic trade-offs, financial conditions, operational effectiveness, and the outlook for the enterprise's economic performance and value.

Figure 1–3 adds, in the form of background layers, the analytical framework and tools, data sources, and the general backdrop of competitive and economic conditions to the three decision areas. Now we have a picture of an integrated set of concepts for the ideal interplay of management decisions and the interpretation of results.

The Business System

As we said earlier, the daily decisions made by managers impact the resources under their control in one way or another in a dynamic interrelationship. Decisions cause resource movements of various types that ultimately result in changing the cash flow pattern of the business. The process may involve some intermediate steps before cash movements occur, as we'll discuss in Chapter 2, but increases or decreases in cash will always follow any decision made. In a successful business, the balancing of cash uses and sources over time generates positive cash flow patterns that lead to the desired buildup of economic value and long-term viability. The creation of shareholder value and overall cash flow patterns, both achieved and expected, are inseparable.

In fact, as we'll see, the simple principle of relating "cash in" to "cash out" is the key to any economic analysis that focuses on creating shareholder value, such as judging a new facilities investment, or evaluating the performance prospects of a product line or service. In Chapter 2, we'll discuss formal ways of tracking and analyzing overall resource flow patterns and their cash impact, while in Chapters 6 and 9, we'll show how the specific cash flows associated with an investment project or a business proposition can be established, analyzed, and valued.

Let's now develop a conceptual view of how a typical business operates. With the help of a simplified systems diagram, we can show the basic cash flow patterns, the key relationships, and the key decisions involved. Then we can relate the major financial analysis measures and key business strategies to the business system. Every one of these measures and concepts will, of course, be discussed in greater depth in the appropriate chapters of this book.

Figure 1–4 presents a basic flow chart containing all major elements necessary to understand the broad cash flow patterns of a typical business. The arrangement of boxes and arrows is designed to show that we're dealing with a system in which all parts are interrelated with each other—and which has to be managed as a whole. The system is organized into three segments that match the three major decision areas: investment, operations, and financing.

- The top segment represents the three components of business investment: the *investment base* already in place, the addition of *new investments,* and any *disinvestment* (divestment) of resources no longer deemed necessary or effective.

- The center segment represents the operational interplay of three basic elements: *price, volume,* and related *costs* of products and/or services. It recognizes that costs usually are partly fixed and partly variable as volume changes.

- The bottom segment represents the basic financing options open to a business in two parts:
  1. The normal *disposition of the operating profit* that has been achieved for a period. It's a three-way split among dividends paid to owners, interest paid to lenders, and earnings retained for reinvestment in the business.
  2. The available choices for a company's long-term capital sources. It shows ownership (shareholders') *equity* (augmented by any retained earnings) and *long-term debt* held by outsiders. Trade-

FIGURE 1–4

The Business System: An Overview

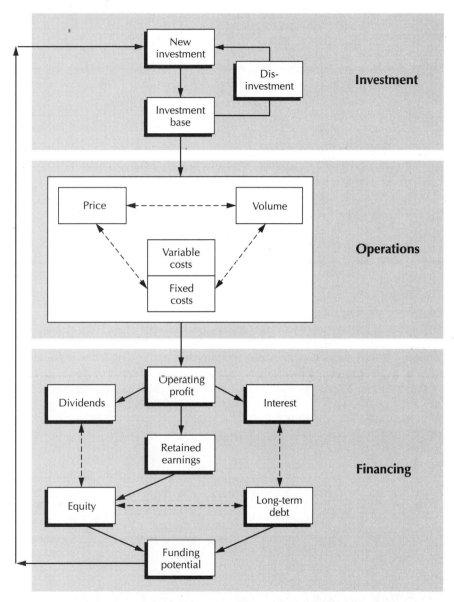

offs and decisions that affect the levels of equity, retained profits, or long-term capital sources impact the company's *funding potential,* which, as the arrow on the left indicates, governs the amount of new investment to be added to the investment base at the top.

We'll now examine each part of the business system in some detail to highlight the types of decisions and the various interrelationships among them.

Investment Decisions

Investment is the basic driving force of business activity. It's the source of growth, supports management's explicit competitive strategies, and is normally based on plans (capital budgets) for committing existing or new funds to three main areas:

■ Working capital (cash balances, receivables due from customers, and inventories, less trade credit from suppliers and other normal current obligations).

■ Physical assets (land, buildings, machinery and equipment, office furnishings, laboratory equipment).

■ Major spending programs (research and development, product or service development, promotional programs, acquisitions, etc.).

Note that investment is broadly defined here in terms of resource commitments to be recovered over time, not by the more narrow accounting classification which would, for example, categorize most spending programs as ongoing expenses. Figure 1–5 shows the investment portion of the systems diagram, accompanied by major yardsticks and key strategies that can be identified in this area.

During the annual planning process when capital budgets are formulated, management normally chooses from a variety of options those new investments that are expected to exceed or at least meet targeted economic returns. The level of these returns is generally related to shareholder expectations via the cost of

FIGURE 1–5

The Business System: Investment Segment

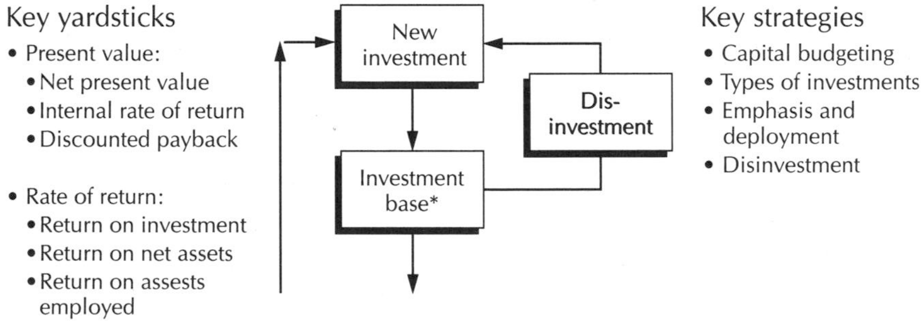

Key yardsticks
- Present value:
  - Net present value
  - Internal rate of return
  - Discounted payback

- Rate of return:
  - Return on investment
  - Return on net assets
  - Return on assests employed

New investment

Dis-investment

Investment base*

Key strategies
- Capital budgeting
- Types of investments
- Emphasis and deployment
- Disinvestment

* Assumes that an amount equal to depreciation and amortization of assets is continuously reinvested here, in order to maintain all existing facilities and equipment in good operating condition; but cost increases in such replacement assets may, of course, actually require a greater amount of reinvestment.

capital calculation, to be described in Chapter 7. Making sound investment choices and implementing them successfully—so that the actual results in fact exceed the cost of capital standard—is a key management responsibility that leads to value creation. New investment is the key driver of growth strategies that cause enhanced shareholder value, but only if expectations are met or exceeded. At the same time, successful companies periodically make critical assessments of how their existing investment base (portfolio) is deployed, to see if the actual performance and outlook for the individual products, services, and business segments warrant continued commitment.

If careful analysis demonstrates below-standard economic results and expectations about a particular market or activity, the opposite of investment, *disinvestment,* becomes a compelling option. As we'll see, such poorly performing activities destroy shareholder value, and disposing of the assets involved or selling the operating unit as a going concern will allow the funds received to be redeployed more advantageously elsewhere. Also, the sale of any equipment being replaced by newer facilities will provide funds for other purposes. Shareholder value creation thus depends on a combination of ongoing successful performance of existing investments, and the addition of successful new investments—a continued reassessment of the company's portfolio of activities.

Yardsticks helpful in selecting *new* investments and disinvestments are generally based on present value concepts, which measure the economic trade-off between investment funds committed now and the expected stream of future operational cash flow benefits. These cash flow tools are detailed in Chapter 6. In contrast, yardsticks that measure the effectiveness of the *existing* investment base generally are accounting rates of return, as will be described in Chapter 3. We'll show that there's a disconnect between the economic measures for new investments and the accounting-based measures for existing investments, a problem of comparability that has to be bridged in order to achieve a consistent approach to shareholder value creation.

Operations Decisions

Here key strategies and decisions should focus on effective utilization of the funds invested. This requires selecting target markets and setting appropriate pricing and service policies that are competitive in filling customers' needs, and that rely on the core competencies of the company. These choices invariably amount to economic trade-offs, in which management must balance the impact of changing prices and competitors' actions on sales volume and on the profitability of products or services. At the same time, all operations of the business must be made cost effective and maintained as such to achieve competitive success. Figure 1–6 highlights key elements of the operations segment of the financial system.

Sound operating results depend in part on understanding and exploiting *operating leverage,* that is, the effect on the company's profitability of the level and proportion of fixed (period) costs committed to the operations, versus the

FIGURE 1–6

The Business System: Operations Segment

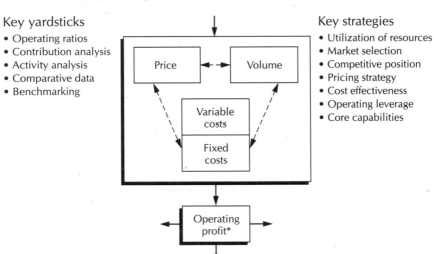

Key yardsticks
- Operating ratios
- Contribution analysis
- Activity analysis
- Comparative data
- Benchmarking

Key strategies
- Utilization of resources
- Market selection
- Competitive position
- Pricing strategy
- Cost effectiveness
- Operating leverage
- Core capabilities

* Assumes that all legally required income taxes have been paid after deducting interest, and therefore operating profit is shown here net of such income taxes.

amount and nature of variable (direct) costs incurred in manufacturing, service, or trading operations. This concept will be discussed in detail in Chapter 5. The interplay of all these forces and decisions results in the net operating profit for a period.

The key yardsticks in the operations segment include a variety of operating ratios that measure the effectiveness with which revenues and costs are managed, as well as specific expense and profit indicators. The relative profit contribution margins of different products and services are also measured, along with a variety of comparative operating expense ratios useful for benchmarking the cost effectiveness of particular operations, both of which are detailed in Chapters 3 and 4.

The distinction between accounting ratios and economic analysis is again important in the operations segment, because the answers provided by each can vary significantly. This problem has led to the evolution of a relatively recent concept that directly addresses the need for economic answers, namely, *activity-based analysis*. This process essentially amounts to a step-by-step identification of the physical activities involved in a specific function of the company, or the activities required to support a product line, followed by a careful economic analysis of the costs and benefits incurred in each step and in total. Because it amounts to an economic assessment, activity-based analysis has become an important technique supporting the current emphasis on corporate reengineering and value-based management.

Financing Decisions

Here we must deal with the various choices available to management for funding the investments and operations of the business over the long term. Note that the financing section includes the operating profit, which normally is a key source of funds for a company. Two key areas of strategy and trade-off decisions are identified:

■ The disposition of profits.

■ Shaping of the company's capital structure.

Normally this set of trade-offs and decisions is made at the highest levels of management and endorsed by the board of directors of a corporation because the choices are crucial to the firm's long-term viability. Figure 1–7 displays the relationships, yardsticks, and strategies in the financing segment.

The first area, the disposition of profits, amounts to a basic three-way split of aftertax operating profit among:

FIGURE 1–7

The Business System: Financing Segment

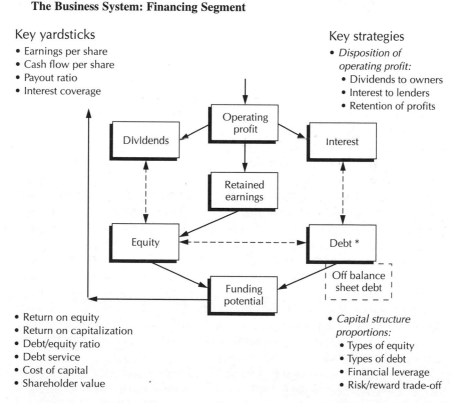

Key yardsticks
- Earnings per share
- Cash flow per share
- Payout ratio
- Interest coverage

Key strategies
- *Disposition of operating profit:*
  - Dividends to owners
  - Interest to lenders
  - Retention of profits

- Return on equity
- Return on capitalization
- Debt/equity ratio
- Debt service
- Cost of capital
- Shareholder value

- *Capital structure proportions:*
  - Types of equity
  - Types of debt
  - Financial leverage
  - Risk/reward trade-off

* Assumes a continuous rollover of debt (refinancing), that is, there is no reduction in existing debt levels from repayments, as new funds are raised to cover these. It does not specifically provide for off-balance sheet debt, such as leases.

■ Owners.

■ Lenders.

■ Retention for reinvestment in the business.

Every one of these choices is affected by current or past management policies, trade-offs, and decisions. For example, payment of dividends to owners is made at the discretion of a corporation's board of directors. Here, the critical trade-off choice is the relative amount of dividends to be paid out versus the alternative of retaining these funds to invest in the company's growth.

Payment of interest to lenders is a matter of contractual obligation. The level of interest payments incurred relative to operating profit, however, is a direct function of management policies and actions regarding the use of debt. The higher the proportion of debt in the capital structure, the greater the demand will be for profit dollars to be used as interest expense, and the greater the firm's risk exposure will be, that is, its potential inability to meet interest obligations and/or repayment during a downturn.

Retained earnings represent the residual aftertax profit for the period, which remains in the company after payment of interest and dividends. This usually represents a significant part of the funding potential for additional investment and growth. Additional funding potential can be found in new funds provided by lenders and investors, depending on the company's policies governing the use of such long-term sources.

Key measures in the area of earnings disposition are both earnings and cash flow (aftertax profit plus depreciation), calculated on a per-share basis, which are viewed as broad indicators of the company's ability to compensate both lenders and owners. In addition, specific ratios are used that measure the proportion of dividends paid out, the degree to which earnings cover the current interest on debt, and how well total debt service requirements are covered. These measures are discussed in Chapter 3.

The second area, the planning of capital structure proportions, involves selecting and balancing the relative proportions of funds obtained over time from ownership sources and long-term debt obligations. The chosen combination, after taking into account business risk and debt service requirements, is intended to support an acceptable level of overall profitability while matching the degree of risk exposure deemed appropriate by management and the board of directors. A key concept in choosing funding methods is the impact of financial leverage (see Chapter 5). It can be defined as the prudent use of funds obtained from fixed-cost debt obligations for financing opportunities that promise potential earnings higher than the interest cost on the borrowed funds—the difference benefiting the owners of the company.

Again, this process requires a series of economic trade-offs, which include weighing the rewards obtained versus the risks involved in the different alternatives open to management. Numerous types of equity, ranging from straight common equity to convertible shares and preferred stocks, can be used for new ownership funding while, conversely, existing ownership funds can also be returned through repurchase of the company's shares in the open market. The latter has become an important aspect of capital structure management, for repurchasing stock with corporate cash flow reduces the number of shares outstanding, making each remaining share proportionately more valuable. At the same time, no dividends need be paid on the purchased shares. The trade-off is between adding value through new investment and adding value through reduced ownership claims.

The choices of debt instruments are even more varied, as we'll discuss in Chapter 8. These also include leases and similar long-term obligations, which are called off-balance sheet debt because they are not listed on the balance sheet and only impact the operating statement as annual expenses.

Major measures in the area of capital structure strategy include ratios that measure the return on equity and the return on capitalization (equity and long-term debt combined), various debt service coverage ratios (Chapter 3), ratios for relative levels of debt and equity (Chapter 5), measures of the cost of various forms of capital as well as the combined cost of capital for the company as a whole (Chapters 7 and 8), and, finally, shareholder value creation concepts (Chapter 9). As we'll see, one of the fundamental principles of running a successful business system is that the returns from the investments supported by the capital structure must exceed the cost of the capital employed in this structure in order to create shareholder value. Returns just matching the cost will leave value unchanged, while returns below the cost of capital will destroy value. As we'll discuss in Chapter 9, the analyst again must carefully distinguish between accounting-based and cash flow-based measures in this area.

Internal Assumptions

Our highly simplified model of the business system contains three key assumptions, as stated in the footnotes to Figures 1–5, 1–6, and 1–7. They cover the following areas:

- Depreciation.
- Taxes.
- Rollover of debt.

Depreciation expense isn't recognized as such anywhere in the system because we've assumed that an amount equal to the annual depreciation write-off made against operating profit will be automatically reinvested each year in the investment base in order to maintain the firm's productive capacity, but without providing any incremental profits.

This is why the diagram shows operating profits as the ultimate operating result. The assumption reflects a common rule of thumb used in financial analysis, namely, that an ongoing operation needs to spend approximately an amount equivalent to depreciation to keep operations functioning at current levels. Normally, a growing business will require investments in excess of depreciation

(Chapter 2 discusses the funds aspects of depreciation), while a declining business will need to spend less.

Next, we assume that required income taxes for every period have been calculated, paid, and subtracted in arriving at operating profit, and that all appropriate deductions have been taken, including the interest expense shown in the systems diagram.

Finally, we assume that the chosen proportion of long-term debt outstanding remains unchanged; that is, no provision was made for paying off this debt as long as the business is operating and growing. Instead, a continuous "rollover" of debt is assumed: New financing is arranged as repayments of existing blocks of debt become due, leaving the desired proportion of debt and equity unchanged.

Normally, as the amount of owners' equity grows with every period of profitable operations, management will likely wish to match, in proportion, such incremental retained earnings with an incremental amount of new debt—unless management decides that a change in debt policy is appropriate for a variety of reasons. In that case, specific assumptions would have to be made about the pattern of repayments planned, which, of course, would change the relative proportions of debt and equity outstanding.

Interrelationship of Strategy and Value Creation

It should be obvious by now that our concept of the basic business system (Figure 1–4) forces us to recognize and deal with the many dynamic interrelationships of the key management strategies, policies, and decisions, and the major cash movements they cause. In effect, the system amounts to a basic financial model which displays the interplay of key variables in support of the ultimate goal—value creation through positive cash flows over time. Achieving consistency in the choices and decisions about these variables is critical to managing a firm's long-term success and shareholder expectations.

For Example

It would be ineffective for a company to set aggressive growth strategies for its operations while at the same time restricting itself to a set of rigid and conservative financial policies. Similarly, paying out a high proportion of current operating profit in the form of dividends, or repurchasing significant amounts of the company's shares, while at the same time maintaining a restrictive debt policy would clash with an objective to hold market share in a rapidly expanding business that requires substantial funding. Under such circumstances, adequate funds for new investment simply wouldn't be available, unless new equity is raised in the market. The company's strategic position could be at risk, and the stock market would adversely assess future cash flow expectations and thereby lower the valuation of the company. ∎

The basis for successful management, therefore, is to develop and maintain a consistent set of business strategies, investment objectives, operating goals, and financial policies that reinforce each other rather than conflict. They must be chosen through conscious and careful analysis of the various economic trade-offs involved, both individually and in combination. They must also be targeted toward a long-term pattern of performance that will establish and reinforce positive shareholder expectations about current and future cash flows from successful existing investments and sound new investments—or from divestments of underperforming parts of the company. As we'll demonstrate in later chapters, understanding the dynamics of business strategies and financial policies is essential, whether involving operational cash flow management, key drivers of financial performance, investment and divestment analysis, or capital structure planning. Our simplified systems diagram has provided a way to recognize the main interrelationships in a broad context of management decisions and cash flows.

THE NATURE OF FINANCIAL STATEMENTS

To apply the insights gained from the conceptual overview of the business system, we must now look for information that will:

- Allow the manager or analyst to track the financial condition and operating results of the business.
- Assist in understanding the funds flow patterns in more specific terms.

In the process of financial/economic analysis, a great variety of formal or informal data are normally reviewed and tested for their relevance to the specific purpose of the analysis. The most common form in which basic financial information is available publicly, unless a company is privately held, is the set of financial statements issued under guidelines of the Financial Accounting Standards Board (FASB) of the public accounting profession and governed by the U.S. Securities and Exchange Commission (SEC). Such a set of statements, prepared according to generally accepted accounting principles (GAAP), usually contains balance sheets as of given dates, operating statements for given periods, and cash flow statements for the same periods. A special statement highlighting changes in owners' equity on the balance sheet is commonly provided as well.

Since financial statements are the source for much of the analytical efforts, we must first understand their nature, coverage, and limitations before we can use the data and observations derived from these statements for our analytical judgments. Financial statements reflect the cumulative effects of all of management's past decisions. However, they involve considerable ambiguity. Financial statements are governed by rules that attempt to consistently and fairly account for every business transaction using the following conservative principles:

- Transactions are recorded at costs prevailing at the time.
- Adjustments to current values are made only if values decline.
- Revenues and costs are recognized when committed to, not when cash actually changes hands.

- Periodic matching of revenues and costs is achieved via accruals, deferrals, and accounting allocations.

- Allowances for negative contingencies are required in the form of estimates that reduce profits and recorded value.

These rules leave reported financial accounting results open to considerable interpretation, especially if the analyst seeks to understand a company's economic performance and the basis for shareholder value results.

The Balance Sheet

The balance sheet, prepared as of *a specific date,* records the categories and amounts of assets employed by the business (i.e., the funds committed) and the offsetting liabilities incurred to lenders and owners (i.e., the funds obtained). Also called the *statement of financial condition* or *statement of financial position,* it must always balance, because by definition, the recorded value of the total assets invested in the business at any point in time must be matched precisely by the recorded liabilities and owners' equity supporting these assets. Liabilities are specific obligations that represent claims against the assets of the business, ranking ahead of the owners in repayment priority. The recorded owners' equity in effect represents a residual claim of the owners on the remaining assets after all liabilities have been subtracted.

The major categories of assets, or funds committed, are:

- Current assets (items that turn over in the normal course of business within a relatively short period of time, such as cash, marketable securities, accounts receivable, and inventories).

- Fixed assets (such as land, mineral resources, buildings, equipment, machinery, and vehicles), all of which are used over a longer time frame.

- Other assets, such as deposits, patents, and various intangibles, including goodwill that arose from an acquisition.

Major sources of the funds obtained are:

- Current liabilities, which are obligations to vendors, tax authorities, employees, and lenders due within one year.

- Long-term liabilities, which are a variety of debt instruments repayable beyond one year, such as bonds, loans, and mortgages.

- Owners' equity, which represents the recorded net amount of funds contributed by various classes of owners of the business as well as the accumulated earnings retained in the business after dividends.

Balance sheets are *static* in that, like a snapshot, they reflect conditions on the date of their preparation. They're also cumulative because they represent the effects of all decisions and transactions that have taken place since the inception of the business and have been accounted for up to the date of preparation.

As we indicated earlier, financial accounting rules require that all transactions be recorded at costs and values as incurred at the time, and retroactive adjustments to recorded values are made only in very limited circumstances. As a consequence, balance sheets (being cumulative) display assets and liabilities acquired or incurred at different times. Because the current economic value of assets can change, particularly in the case of longer-lived items (such as buildings and machinery) or resources (such as land and minerals), the costs stated on the balance sheet are likely not reflecting true economic values. Moreover, changes in the value of the currency in which the transactions are recorded can, over time, distort the balance sheet.

Ultimately, the book value of owners' equity is affected by all of these value differentials. There generally is quite a divergence between this residual value and the current economic value of the business as reflected in share prices or in valuations for acquisition. In fact, the shares of successful companies are usually traded at price levels far above their recorded book value (see Chapter 9).

Finally, a number of relatively recent accounting rules require the estimation and recording of contingent liabilities arising from a variety of future obligations, such as pensions and health care costs, further introducing a series of value judgments. These are frequently shown as "other liabilities," listed just ahead of owners' equity, and, in effect, amount to a reclassification of part of the owners' residual claims into liabilities.

The accounting profession's FASB is expending a great deal of effort to resolve these and other issues affecting the meaning of the balance sheet, but with only partial success. Accounting standards continue to evolve, and a manager or analyst must be aware of the underlying issues and processes when reviewing and analyzing this statement. We'll discuss the most important of these specifically as we examine analytical techniques in later chapters.

In our decisional context of investment, operations, and financing, the balance sheet can be viewed as a cumulative listing of the impact of past investment and financing decisions, and the operational results from using these resources. It's a historical record of all transactions that affected the current business. The net effect of operations in the form of periodic profit or loss is reflected in the changing ownership equity account. Figure 1–8 is a simple conceptual picture of the balance sheet as it relates to the three areas of management decisions.

Only the major categories normally found on the balance sheet are listed here, which is an oversimplification. In actual practice, the analyst encounters a large variety of detailed asset, liability, and net worth accounts because balance sheets reflect the unique nature of a given company and the business sector to which it belongs. But the actual accounts can always be grouped into the basic categories listed.

To provide an example of the balance sheet of a major corporation, Figure 1–9 shows the consolidated balance sheets for December 31, 1995, and December 31, 1994, of TRW Inc., as published in its 1995 annual report, but presented here without accompanying notes. (These are reproduced in Chapter 3, Figure 3–6).

FIGURE 1–8

Balance Sheet in Decisional Context

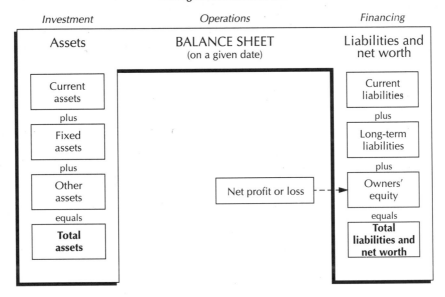

TRW Inc. is a global manufacturing and service company headquartered in Cleveland, Ohio. It's strategically focused on providing products and services with a high technology or engineering content to the automotive, space and defense, and information systems markets. TRW holds leading positions in most of its market segments. Founded in 1901, the company employs about 64,000 people in 24 countries, and ranks 126th in sales in the 1995 Fortune 500 listing. We'll use TRW's published financial statements as examples in Chapters 2 and 3 and demonstrate the use of analytical techniques on their data.

The Operating Statement

The operating statement reflects the effect of management's operating decisions on business performance and the resulting accounting profit or loss for the owners of the business *over a specified period of time.* The profit or loss calculated in the statement increases or decreases owners' equity on the balance sheet. The operating statement is thus a necessary adjunct to the balance sheet in explaining this major component of change in owners' equity, and it provides a variety of performance assessment information.

The operating statement, also referred to as the *income statement, earnings statement,* or *profit and loss statement,* displays the revenues recognized for a specific period, and the costs and expenses charged against these revenues,

FIGURE 1–9

TRW INC. AND SUBSIDIARIES
Consolidated Balance Sheets
December 31, 1995 and 1994 ($ millions)

	1995	1994
Assets		
Current assets:		
Cash and cash equivalents	$ 59	$ 109
Accounts receivable	1,428	1,338
Inventories	534	470
Prepaid expenses	78	59
Deferred income taxes	237	239
Total current assets	2,336	2,215
Property, plant, and equipment at cost	5,866	5,556
Less: Allowances for depreciation and amortization	3,303	3,067
Total property, plant, and equipment—net	2,563	2,489
Intangible assets:		
Intangibles arising from acquisitions	483	477
Capitalized data files and other	488	441
Other	92	69
Total intangible assets	1,063	987
Less: Accumulated amortization	405	331
Total intangible assets—net	658	656
Other assets	333	276
Total assets	$5,890	$5,636
Liabilities and Shareholders' Investment		
Current liabilities:		
Short-term debt	$ 133	$ 122
Accrued compensation	385	346
Trade accounts payable	807	737
Other accruals	545	541
Dividends payable	36	33
Income taxes	26	50
Current portion of long-term debt	80	157
Total current liabilities	2,012	1,986
Long-term liabilities	779	796
Long-term debt	541	694
Deferred income taxes	313	269
Minority interests in subsidiaries	73	69
Shareholders' investment:		
Serial preference stock II	1	1
Common stock	40	40
Other capital	398	354
Retained earnings	1,688	1,383
Cumulative translation adjustments	76	66
Treasury shares—cost in excess of par	(31)	(22)
Total shareholders' investment	2,172	1,822
Total liabilities and shareholders' investment	$5,890	$5,636

Source: Adapted from 1995 TRW Inc. annual report.

including write-offs (e.g., depreciation and amortization of various assets) and taxes. Revenues and costs involve elements such as:

- Sales for cash or credit.
- Purchases of goods or services for resale or manufacture.
- Salaries and wages.
- Research and development costs.
- Marketing expenses.

The operating statement represents the best effort of the firm's accountants to match the relevant items of revenue with the relevant items of cost and expense for the period, a process which involves accrual accounting and extensive use of allocation of revenues and costs.

Among the judgmental areas involving costs are:

- Depreciation of assets being used over more periods than the current reporting period.
- Cost of the goods purchased or manufactured in previous periods.
- Proper allocation of general expenses to a specific period.

We'll take up the more critical of these elements and choices as we apply the analysis techniques in later chapters.

When viewed in our decisional context, the operating statement in the center column of Figure 1–10 expands the details of the transactions and allocations that make up one of the key performance elements, profit or loss.

Again, we are providing an actual example of an operating statement in Figure 1–11, the consolidated statement of earnings for TRW Inc. for the years ending December 31, 1995 and December 31, 1994.

The Cash Flow Statement

Because we are interested in the combined effects of investment, operating, and financing decisions, analyzing both the operating statement for the period and the balance sheets at the beginning and the end of the period together provides more basic insights than either statement alone. Management decisions affect not only the profit for the period, but cause accompanying changes in most assets and liabilities, particularly in the accounts making up working capital, such as cash, receivables, inventories, and current payables. The statement that captures both the current operating results and the accompanying changes in the balance sheet is the *cash flow statement, statement of cash flows,* or *funds flow statement.* It gives us a dynamic picture of the ultimate changes in cash resulting from the combined decisions made during a given period.

The statement is prepared by comparing beginning and ending balance sheets and using key items of the operating statement for the period, all interpreted in terms of uses and sources of cash:

FIGURE 1–10

Operating Statement in Decisional Context

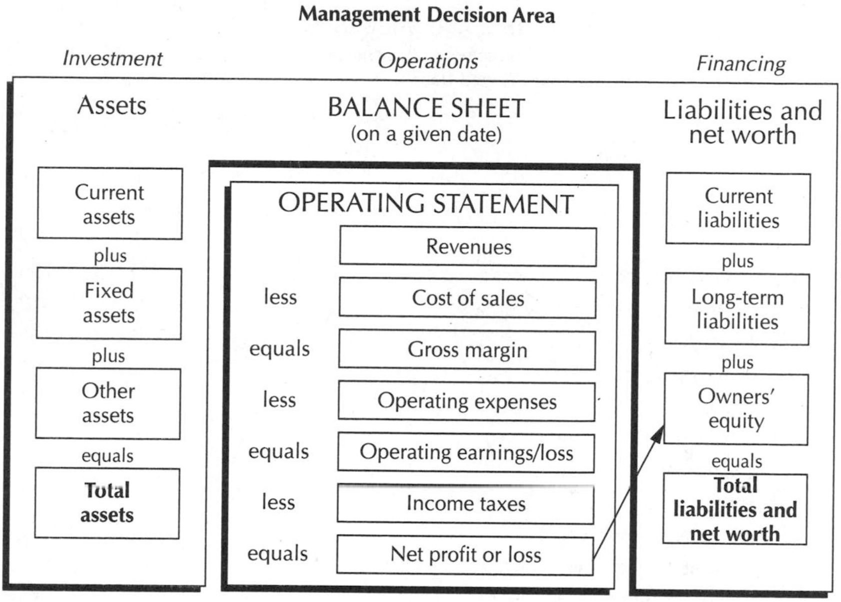

Management Decision Area

Investment	Operations	Financing

| Assets | BALANCE SHEET (on a given date) | Liabilities and net worth |

OPERATING STATEMENT

Current assets		Revenues		Current liabilities
plus				plus
Fixed assets	less	Cost of sales		Long-term liabilities
plus	equals	Gross margin		plus
Other assets	less	Operating expenses		Owners' equity
equals	equals	Operating earnings/loss		equals
Total assets	less	Income taxes		**Total liabilities and net worth**
	equals	Net profit or loss		

- Commitments of cash to invest in assets or to repay liabilities.
- Raising of funds through additional borrowing or by reducing asset investments.
- Cash generated by profitable operations or drained by unprofitable results.
- Adjustments for accounting allocations, write-offs, and other noncash elements in the income statement and the balance sheets.
- Net impact of the period's cash movements on the company's cash balance.

The statement thus offers a ready overview of the combined cash impact of all management decisions during the period. The user can judge both the magnitude and the relationships of these cash movements, such as the company's ability to fund investment needs from operational results, the magnitude and appropriateness of financing changes, and disproportional movements in working capital needs. Observing the cash flow patterns can stimulate questions about the effectiveness of management strategies as well as the quality of operational decisions. The amount of detail can vary widely, depending on the nature of the business and the different types of movements emphasized.

In the past, basic formats for these statements used to differ widely as well. In more recent times, the FASB and SEC required that all published cash flow

FIGURE 1–11

TRW INC. AND SUBSIDIARIES
Statement of Earnings
For the Years Ended December 31, 1995 and 1994

	1995	1994
Sales	$10,172	$ 9,087
Cost of sales	8,190	7,270
Gross profit	1,982	1,817
Administrative and selling expenses	747	756
Research and development expenses	422	412
Interest expense	95	105
Other expenses (income) net	10	9
Total expenses	1,274	1,282
Earnings (loss) before income taxes	708	535
Income taxes	262	202
Net earnings (loss)	$ 446	$ 333
Per share of common stock:		
Average number of shares outstanding (millions)	67.4	66.4
Fully diluted net earnings per share	$ 6.62	$ 5.01
Primary earnings per share	$ 6.62	$ 5.02
Book value per share	$ 32.97	$ 27.91
Other data ($ millions):		
Depreciation of property, plant, and equipt	$ 433	$ 402
Amortization of intangibles, other assets	77	74
Capital expenditures	485	506
Dividends paid	134	126

Source: Adapted from 1995 TRW Inc. annual report.

statements follow a common format, listing uses and sources by the familiar three decision areas: operations, investments, and financing. This rule recognized the usefulness of this arrangement in understanding the dynamics of the business system, as described earlier. Figure 1–12 shows how the cash flow statement fits into our management decision context.

One aspect of the cash flow statement that requires some explanation is the treatment of accounting write-offs. From a cash flow standpoint, write-offs such as depreciation and amortization merely represent bookkeeping entries that have *no* effect. The reason is simply that the assets being amortized by these entries represent cash committed in *past* periods. Consequently, the write-off categories, insofar as they had reduced net profit, must be added back here as a positive cash flow, thus restoring the cash generated by operations to the original level before

FIGURE 1–12

Cash Flow Statement in Decisional Context

Management Decision Area

Investment	*Operations*	*Financing*

FUNDS FLOW STATEMENT		
Investments	**Operations**	**Financing**
Investments (increases) in all types of assets are uses of cash; disinvestments (reductions) in all types of assets are sources of cash.	Profitable operations are a source of cash; losses drain cash from the system. Accounting write-offs or write-ups do not affect cash; their profit impact must be adjusted for.	Trade credit and new financing (increases in liabilities and equity) are sources of cash; repayments of liabilities, dividends, and returns of capital are uses of cash.

the write-off was made. Handling of this adjustment will be illustrated more specifically in Chapter 2.

The cash flow statement has the same inherent limitations as the balance sheet and the operating statement, because it's derived from the accounting data contained in these statements. However, because it focuses on the *changes* incurred during the period, limitations due to historical valuation are usually not significant. But we must remember that by displaying the net change from the beginning to the end of the chosen period in each asset, liability, and ownership account reported, the statement may "bury" major individual transactions that occurred during the period and perhaps offset each other. Normally, however, material transactions of this kind (such as major investments, acquisitions, or divestitures) are noted specifically in the company's cash flow statement. The statement therefore affords the user the most detailed picture of the impact of major events of the period.

TRW's consolidated cash flow statement for the years ended December 31, 1995, and December 31, 1994, in Figure 1–13 shows how the various elements are listed in practice. A number of adjustments based on information only internally available have been made by TRW to show more clearly the nature of cash movements during the periods covered.

The Statement of Changes in Owners' (Shareholders') Equity

The fourth financial statement commonly provided by a business is an analysis of the main changes, during a specific period, in the owners' capital accounts, or net worth. We know from the earlier discussion that one of these changes is the profit or loss for the period, as displayed in the operating statement. But other management decisions may have affected owners' equity.

FIGURE 1–13

TRW INC. AND SUBSIDIARIES
Statement of Cash Flows
for the Years Ended December 31, 1995 and 1994

	1995	1994
Operating Activities:		
Net earnings (loss)	$446	$333
Adjustments to reconcile net earnings (loss) to net cash provided by operating activities:		
Depreciation and amortization	510	476
Restructuring	—	(23)
Deferred income taxes	46	8
Other—net	33	26
Changes in assets and liabilities, net of effects of businesses acquired or sold:		
Accounts receivable	(75)	(112)
Inventories and prepaid expenses	(71)	(33)
Accounts payable and other accruals	31	262
Other—net	(51)	35
Net cash provided by operating activities	869	972
Investing Activities:		
Capital expenditures	(485)	(506)
Proceeds from divestitures	9	22
Investments in other assets	(78)	(81)
Proceeds from sales of property, plant, and equipment	20	16
Other—net	(12)	7
Net cash used in investing activities	(546)	(542)
Financing Activities:		
Increase (decrease) in short-term debt	(47)	(270)
Proceeds from debt in excess of 90 days	36	176
Principal repayments in excess of 90 days	(207)	(154)
Dividends paid	(134)	(126)
Other—net	9	9
Net cash used in financing activities	(343)	(365)
Effect of exchange rate changes on cash	(30)	(35)
Increase (decrease) in cash and cash equivalents	(50)	30
Cash and cash equivalents at beginning of year	109	79
Cash and cash equivalents at end of year	$ 59	$109
Supplemental Cash Flow Information:		
Interest paid (net of amount capitalized)	$ 88	$112
Income taxes paid (net of refunds)	239	93

Source: Adapted from 1995 TRW Inc. annual report.

FIGURE 1–14

Statement of Changes in Owners' Equity in Decisional Context

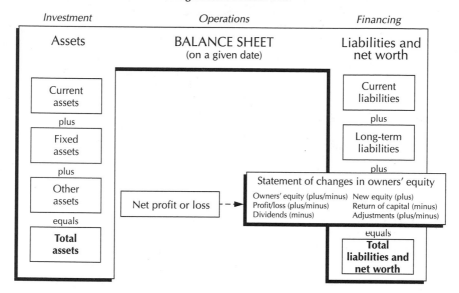

Management Decision Area

For example, most corporations, including TRW, pay dividends on a quarterly basis. Such dividends are normally paid in cash, reducing both the cash balance and retained earnings, the latter being part of owners' equity. Another decision may be to provide additional capital through sale of new shares of common stock, or conversely, the repurchase of shares in the open market using excess cash balances—some of which may be resold to employees under stock purchase or option plans. A third area may involve write-offs or adjustments of asset values connected with disposition of assets or with business combinations. A fourth area relates to the complex adjustments related to the exchange of foreign currencies by companies doing business internationally.

The net change in owners' equity may thus be selectively split into its major components to highlight the impact of these decisions. Figure 1–14 provides a conceptual view of this special analytical statement. Its imitations largely depend on how much the issuing company chooses to disclose beyond what's legally required.

Again TRW's consolidated statement of changes in owners' (shareholders') equity for the years ended December 31, 1995, and December 31, 1994 is given as an actual example in Figure 1–15. The format used by the company displays the changes in each of the key areas involved, by type of stock, ownership equity, retained earnings, currency translation effects, and treasury stock (repurchased shares).

In this portion of the chapter, we have provided an overview of the nature and relationships of the four major financial statements as the background for

FIGURE 1–15

TRW INC. AND SUBSIDIARIES
Statement of Changes in Shareholders' Investment
For the Years Ended December 31, 1995 and 1994

	1995		1994	
	Shares (millions)	Millions of Dollars	Shares (millions)	Millions of Dollars
Serial Preference Stock II:				
Series 1:				
Balance at January 1 and				
December 31	.1	$—	.1	$—
Series 3:				
Balance at January 1 and				
December 31	.1	1	.1	1
Common Stock:				
Balance at January 1	64.9	40	64.1	40
Sale of stock and other	.7	—	.8	—
Balance at December 31	62.9	40	64.9	40
Other Capital:				
Balance at January 1		354		293
Sale of stock and other		44		61
Balance at December 31		398		354
Retained earnings:				
Balance at January 1		1,383		1,178
Net earnings (loss)		446		333
Other		(3)		—
Dividends declared:				
Preference stock		(1)		(1)
Common stock ($1.84 and $1.80				
per share)		(137)		(127)
Balance at December 31		1,688		1,383
Cumulative Translation Adjustments:				
Balance at January 1		66		36
Translation adjustments		10		30
Balance at December 31		76		66
Treasury Shares—Cost in Excess of Par Value:				
Balance at January 1		(22)		(14)
ESOP funding		17		—
Purchase of shares		(26)		(8)
Balance at December 31		(31)		(22)
Total shareholders' investment: . . .		$2,172		$1,822

Source: Adapted from 1995 TRW Inc. annual report.

FIGURE 1–16

Generalized Overview of Financial Statements

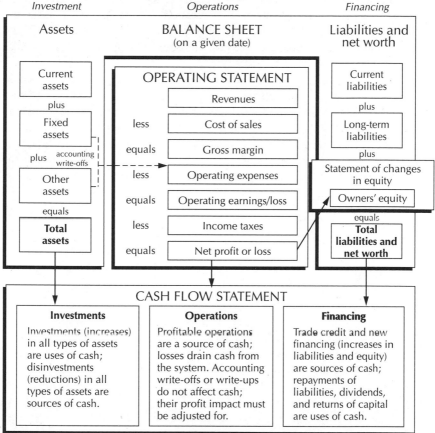

analysis of the results of management decisions and their impact on funds movements. Within our decisional framework, these four statements can be combined
to help us visualize their coverage and relationship as an integrated whole. Note
that the generalized overview in Figure 1–16 displays not only what the four
statements cover in terms of key information, but also how they are related, being
derived from the same basic information. The dotted lines indicate the impact of
any accounting write-offs.

    To summarize, the balance sheet describes the financial condition of a bus-
iness at a point in time. It shows the cumulative effect of previous decisions and
includes the profits or losses for preceding periods. The operating statement
matches revenues and expenses for a specific period, including write-offs
allocations. It provides more detail about the elements making up the afte

net profit and loss that was recorded in arriving at the owners' equity on the balance sheet.

In contrast to the two previous statements, the cash flow statement is a *dynamic* representation in that it highlights the *net changes* in assets, liabilities, and ownership accounts over a specific period. It reflects the pattern of cash uses and sources that resulted from management's decisions concerning investments, operations, and financing. The statement corrects for the fact that write-offs and amortization of assets acquired in the past are bookkeeping entries and not cash movements.

Finally, the statement of changes in owners' equity gives more details concerning the change in ownership accounts as recorded on the beginning and ending balance sheets. Within the limitations of GAAP rules and the accountants' judgments, financial statements are an effort to reflect, with reasonable consistency, all business transactions that, over time, result in a net improvement or worsening of the recorded value of owners' equity. But as we'll discuss in the ensuing chapters, the manager or analyst must carefully interpret their meaning, and apply standard techniques as well as explicit judgments in evaluating the financial, and more importantly, the economic, performance of the company under review.

THE CONTEXT OF FINANCIAL ANALYSIS

Now that we've explored the broad background of business system dynamics and the nature of financial statements that describe performance and values, it's useful to provide one more context that allows us to put the materials of the book into proper perspective. It will reinforce a number of the references we have made earlier to the judgmental aspects involved in financial analysis.

Managers or analysts performing various kinds of financial analysis normally do so with a specific purpose in mind. During the process of analysis, financial statements, special analyses, data bases, and other information sources are used to derive reasonable judgments about past, current, and prospective conditions of a business and the effectiveness of its management.

We must recognize that not only the person performing the analysis and interpretation has a purpose and viewpoint, but so do the preparers and providers of the various types of data and information on which the analysis is based. During our discussion of financial statements, we referred to the accounting rules and principles governing the compilation of these documents, and to the need to allow for the specific biases introduced by them. This isn't to say that financial statements are right or wrong in an absolute sense, but rather that the information may have to be adjusted in some cases, or discarded in others, in order to suit the purpose of the analysis.

Figure 1–17's descriptive overview presents the key objectives of three major financial/economic processes as a context for understanding the differences in data generation and analytical orientation involved in each. The table identifies:

FIGURE 1–17

The Different Objectives of Financial/Economic Processes

Financial Accounting	*Investor Analysis*	*Managerial Economics*
Profit Determination	**Financial Information**	**Activity Economics**
■ Revenue recognition	■ Adjustment process	■ Task analysis
■ Expense recognition	■ Trend analysis	■ Economic allocation
■ Cost allocation	■ Profit projection	■ Contribution analysis
■ Profit definition	■ Cash flow projection	■ Trade-off determination
Value Determination	**Comparative Data**	**Resource Effectiveness**
■ Historical costs	■ Industry analysis	■ Investment base
■ Conservatism	■ Competitor analysis	■ Capital investments
■ Equity as residual value	■ Economic conditions	■ Capital divestments
■ Contingency recognition	■ Adjustment areas	■ Human resources
Tax Determination	**Market Analysis**	**Shareholder Value**
■ Legal data requirements	■ Share price patterns	■ Cash flow patterns
■ Income/expense timing	■ Market trends	■ Cost of capital
■ Tax management issues	■ Value drivers	■ Investor expectations
■ Statement adjustments	■ Market models	■ Ongoing business value

■ Financial accounting.

■ Investor analysis.

■ Managerial economics.

as processes whose objectives differ, but which frequently have to draw on each other for information and data. We must consider the orientation and focus of these processes when information is shared between them, or exchanged for use by any one of them. Our ultimate aim is to analyze and judge business problems, company performance, and shareholder value in *economic* terms, which requires careful adjustment of data and analyses that often were prepared with different objectives in mind.

When we speak of basic financial analysis within the scope of this book, we put more emphasis on the objectives of the left column (financial accounting) and to some extent on the middle column (investor analysis). When we refer to economic analysis, the focus is on the right column (managerial economics) and also on a number of the areas in the center column. Despite the obvious differences in the three areas, the majority of the available data are originated on the left, by financial accounting, while some are obtained from the right, from internal data bases on which managerial economics depends. In addition, databases covering the stock market and economic activity come into play in the center column.

There are three major objectives in *financial accounting,* as governed by professional standards and SEC regulations:

■ Profit determination

■ Value determination

■ Tax determination.

Profit determination focuses on recognizing when revenue is earned during a period, and how to determine the matching costs and expenses. A clear distinction must be drawn between the recording of a revenue or expense transaction, and the actual receipt or disbursement of cash, which may lag by days or months. Similarly, costs incurred in the past are allocated to current or future periods with the objective of determining a profit figure that matches only "recognized" revenue and expense elements. A similar allocation process may apply to anticipated future costs that are apportioned to current periods. These allocations have significant implications for cash flow analysis, as we'll see in Chapter 2.

Value determination rests firmly on the principle of historical costs, a conservative concept which uses only actual transaction evidence as the value criterion. When economic values of assets acquired in the past change, adjustments to values are made only if they decline. This is commonly done for accounts receivable that have become uncollectible, or inventories where market value has declined below cost. Increases are recognized (realized) only when assets are sold, not while they're being held. The residual value of the business, that is, its recorded ownership equity (book value), therefore may over time bear little resemblance to the equity's market value (economic value). In addition, the growing emphasis on recording contingencies of all kinds in the liability section of the balance sheet introduces a negative bias in value, because only potential liabilities are established, not potential gains. Examples are long-term pension and benefit obligations, and potential liabilities arising from all types of operational, legal, and contractual issues.

Meanwhile, appreciation of assets like land, buildings, natural resources, technologies, and patents is left unrecognized until they're disposed of. As the wave of corporate takeovers in the past decade demonstrated, careful analysis of the target companies' balance sheets uncovered massive amounts of unrecorded potential gains, which could be turned into cash from the eventual breakup of the acquired companies, and used in part to pay for the acquisition.

Tax determination is governed by the legal requirements of the current tax code, which often involves modified principles of income and expense recognition, including disallowance of certain costs and expense—in effect amounting to a different set of books. Tax rules tend to speed up the timing of revenue recognition compared with financial accounting rules, and at the same time, delay expense recognition. These rules are clearly designed to enhance current tax receipts for the government. Differences between financial accounting for reporting purposes and for tax accounting give rise to tax management issues (legally minimizing taxes) in companies and industries where the amounts involved may be significant enough to affect actual decisions on investments, operations, and financing.

From the standpoint of financial analysis, the important question is what effect tax accounting has on the financial statements used for analysis. As we'll see, the amount of taxes actually paid versus the amount shown on the operating statement can differ materially, and adjustments made on the balance sheet to compensate for this situation may involve significant funds movements.

Investor analysis in this context has three objectives:

- Interpretation of financial information.
- Use of comparative data.
- Analysis of financial markets.

Interpretation of financial information essentially amounts to analyzing financial statements and other financial data about a company in order to assess and project its performance and value. The key judgments focus on the adjustment process through which reported accounting data are modified or converted into information that permits economic and cash flow assessments to be made. Only rarely can financial data, as generally provided, be used in their exact form to derive analytical judgments. Applying the various ratios and relationships discussed in Chapter 2, for example, often leads to significant questions and actual adjustments during the analysis.

Trend analysis uses various series of adjusted past data to look for and analyze significant changes in magnitudes and ratio relationships over time, and becomes one of the bases of profit projection. Finally, the ultimate adjustment leads to understanding the pattern of net cash flows generated by the business, and the projection of these cash flows as an indicator of expected economic performance and value.

Comparative data are an essential part of financial analysis, as they help put judgments about a particular company or business in perspective. By implication, all judgments made about performance and value are relative to the standards and perceptions of the analyst; comparable data assist in confirming these judgments. Industry analysis involves the selection of relevant groupings of companies and compiling appropriate data and ratios (often available in data bases) against which to measure the attributes of the company being studied. The important issue here again is the need to interpret and adjust the financial data so that they match the data used for the original company.

Competitor analysis applies the same process to individual companies or divisions of those companies that compete directly with the business. Economic conditions and the competitive dynamics of the markets served are brought into the analysis as a backdrop for explaining past variations, and as a guide to projecting future performance and value.

Market analysis involves the study and projection of the pattern of share prices of the company and its competitors relative to stock market trends. It is here that financial analysis becomes a bridge between published financial statements and the market trends that reflect the economic value of a company. The analyst focuses on the value drivers behind the market value of the shares, which are basic economic variables like cash flow generated and the relative cost effectiveness of the business, along with judgments about the expected impact of known strategies. Market models range from simple relationships of key variables and share price to complex computer simulations, in an effort to determine the current and potential shareholder value created by the expected cash flows of the business.

Managerial economics encompasses three basic objectives:

- Determining activity economics.
- Determining resource effectiveness.
- Calculating shareholder value.

All three areas deal with economic insights management can use to make decisions that will enhance shareholder value. In that sense, the orientation of managerial economics is very closely allied to the basic purpose of economic analysis as we define it here. In fact, the third objective directly supports the ultimate question: Is the business creating value for its owners? In later chapters, we'll address the most important aspects of these areas.

Activity economics is a summary term for various types of analysis that define and establish economically relevant data to describe and judge the relative attractiveness of any operational aspect of a business and its subdivisions. Among these, task analysis amounts to determining the true economic cost of a task. This is done by identifying and measuring the series of steps required to provide a service, or the phases of a manufacturing process, and the resources used directly or indirectly in each case. This kind of analytical process goes far beyond cost accounting principles, which often fall short of a proper economic allocation of jointly used resources or often don't recognize all aspects of a task or an activity.

Contribution analysis refers to measuring the difference between revenues created and the economic costs involved in a given line of business or a particular product or service. Such information on economic contribution helps management plan which combination of activities will create the most economic value. The choices always require economic trade-offs based on economic data, not accounting information. As we mentioned, the new field of *activity-based analysis,* which supports both operational and strategic decisions, is gaining wide acceptance as a means of developing data relevant to this purpose.

Resource effectiveness addresses the important question of how well, from an economic standpoint, the resources employed by a business are currently being utilized or will be utilized in the future. The process includes measuring the returns from the existing investment base, gauging the economic justification of new capital investments or capital divestments, and measuring the returns from human resources. As we mentioned earlier, these questions will be discussed in more detail in Chapters 2 and 6, and we'll highlight again the need to develop an economic basis for these judgments.

Shareholder value creation, management's ultimate goal, is measured by a combination of past and projected cash flow patterns, the cost of capital of the particular company, and the overall return expectations of investors for this type of business. In essence, shareholder value creation becomes a tangible expression of the risk/reward trade-off the investor has to judge when investing in the equity of a company. Management has to assess at all times whether cash flow expectations from the strategies, policies, and decisions employed are likely to serve the investors' interest by creating additional shareholder value. The approach will be discussed in detail in Chapters 7 and 9.

SUMMARY

First, we provided a conceptual overview of the business system to show the dynamic interrelationship of cash flows activated by management decisions. Three basic decision areas were recognized—investment, operations, and financing—that underlie all business activity. The cash impact of decisions in any or all of these areas on the system was shown. The systems' view also demonstrated how decisions in each area were affected by key strategies and policies, and how consistency was essential in optimizing the system to achieve the ultimate goal— enhanced shareholder value. The overview also provided a first look at major areas of financial and economic analysis, and how these were related to management strategies and decisions.

Second, we gave an overview of the major financial statements commonly prepared by companies, and their relationship both to each other and to the three decisional areas defined earlier. We also indicated how the origin, rationale, and limitations of financial statements affect the potential for analyzing performance and value, and how important the cash flow statement was as a useful dynamic view of the changing cash flow patterns in the system.

Third, we reinforced the context within which financial analysis takes place, and provided an overview of the various objectives of analysis and data preparation. This was done to highlight the need for building a bridge between accounting-oriented data and the ultimate objective of financial/economic analysis, that is, judging business performance and shareholder value creation in economic terms. Adjustment areas were suggested as prerequisites for developing useful information, and the analyst's judgmental role was emphasized.

The chapter serves as a contextual preview of the various analytical concepts explored in the remainder of the book. It's intended to reinforce the point that financial/economic analysis is not a freestanding activity or an end in itself, but rather an effort to understand and judge the characteristics and economic performance of a highly interrelated system of financial relationships.

SELECTED REFERENCES

Hackel, Kenneth S. and Joshua Livnat. *Cash Flow and Security Analysis.* Burr Ridge, Ill.: BusinessOne Irwin, 1992.
McTaggart, James M., Peter W. Kontes, and Michael C. Mankins. *The Value Imperative: Managing for Superior Shareholder Returns.* New York: The Free Press, 1994.
Rappaport, Alfred. *Creating Shareholder Value.* New York: The Free Press, 1986.

Johnson, H. Thomas and Robert S. Kaplan, *Relevance Lost: The Rise and Fall of Management Accounting.* Boston: Harvard Business School Press, 1987.

Porter, Michael E. *Competitive Advantage: Creating and Sustaining Superior Performance.* New York: The Free Press, 1985.

Stewart, B. Bennett. *The Quest for Value.* New York: Harper Business, 1990.

Managing Operating Funds

We now turn to the key issues surrounding the flow of funds through a business, that is, how to properly manage funds inflows and funds requirements for day to day operations on an ongoing basis. Managers must understand the specific cash movements within the business system caused by their daily decisions on investment, operations, and financing, and by the many external circumstances affecting the business. These decisions and events, in one form or another, affect the company's ability to pay its bills, obtain credit from suppliers and lenders, extend credit to its customers, and maintain a level of operations that matches the demand for the company's products or services, supported by appropriate investments. In the end, the combined effect of these decisions is the creation of shareholder value—but only if the net cash flows achieved by the business exceed the market's expectations over time.

As we've said, every decision has a monetary impact on the ongoing pattern of uses and sources of cash. Management's job is to maintain at all times an appropriate balance between cash inflows and outflows, and to plan for the cash impact of any changes in operations—whether caused by their own decisions or by outside influences—that may affect these flows. Properly managing operating cash flows is therefore fundamental to successful business performance.

The principle is quite simple: Obtain the most performance over time with the least commitment of resources. In practice, however, leads and lags in receipts and payments, unexpected changes from planned conditions, delays in receiving cash from funding sources, and myriad other factors can make cash flow management a complex challenge. New businesses often find that balancing operating funds needs and sources is a continuous struggle for plain survival. Yet, even well-established companies need to devote considerable management time and effort to balance the funding of their operations as they strive for optimal economic results.

In addition to managing working capital, balancing operating funds flows requires dealing with changing cash flow patterns from periodic profits and losses, and with the ultimate cash impact of current decisions on both new investment and new financing choices.

As we'll demonstrate, managing operating funds requires a thorough understanding of the combined systems effect of investment, operating, and financing decisions. This includes recognizing the impact on funds uses and sources caused by various basic operating patterns, such as seasonal peaks and valleys, cyclical variations, rapid growth, or gradual decline. The resulting cash flow patterns will behave in quite different ways.

For Example

Managing working capital soundly is a major operating cash flow challenge. The key components of working capital, accounts receivable, inventories, and accounts payable often represent significant funds commitments and sources for a business. In fact, the basic level of working capital (commonly defined as the difference between current assets and current liabilities) with which a business operates represents a long-term investment supported by long-term capital sources. Each component, however, must be carefully managed to match the changing requirements of operations—with the objective of minimizing the resources committed at any point in time while meeting all operational needs, such as ensuring smooth production and customer service goals.

Fluctuations in working capital should be planned in line with changing conditions, rather than become surprises in the form of soaring inventories or overextended supplier credit. As in all business decisions, economic trade-offs apply here: Is the cost of carrying extra inventory outweighed by better service to customers? Is the cost of granting higher discounts for early payment offset by the reduction in receivables likely to be outstanding? What is the real cost of not meeting the credit terms extended by the company's vendors? ■

In Chapter 3, we'll examine a variety of performance measures drawn from financial statements, which we know to be periodic summaries of financial condition and operating results. As we'll see, these summaries often mask peaks and valleys of funds movements—for example, a seasonal buildup causing critical near-term financing needs—because these points may lie within the period spanned by the statements. Obviously, managing a business is an ongoing day-to-day process, which must deal with peaks and valleys of funds flows as they occur.

In this chapter, we'll describe how operating funds cycle through a business, what the implications of these movements are, and how to identify the critical financial variables that must be weighed in making daily operating decisions. We'll demonstrate how significantly different types of operations impact a company's funds movements, and also highlight key accounting issues, such as inventory costing and methods of depreciation. Then we'll return to the interpretation of cash flow statements, using our sample of TRW's 1994 and 1995 financial data, and demonstrate how to use cash flow statements in a meaningful

FIGURE 2–1

Ice Cream Vendor

Initial Cash Investment to Start the Day

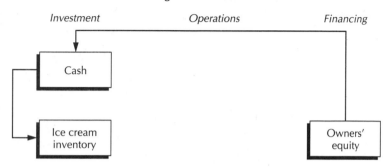

way. Finally, we'll discuss the key levers available to managers with which to minimize funds needs, moderate the impact of fluctuations, and generally optimize the management of operating funds as part of shareholder value creation.

FUNDS FLOW CYCLES

Businesses vary widely in orientation, size, structure, and products or services, but they all experience operating funds cycles that in the end affect cash needs and availability. To illustrate the simplest of circumstances, let's observe a solitary ice cream vendor who sells cones from his cart for cash. To carry on the business, he has to provide an inventory on wheels which he slowly converts into cash as the day progresses. Let's also assume that he has invested his own cash at the beginning of the day to purchase the ice cream from his supplier. He obviously hopes to recoup these funds as well as pocket a profit by the end of the day.

Our vendor's decision to commit his own cash to inventory can be visualized in Figure 2–1, which traces the funds movements in a simple diagram. Note that the layout reflects the three decision areas we discussed in Chapter 1.

The initial cash investment is financed from owners' equity, and in turn, the cash is used to invest in the first day's inventory. If our vendor was short of cash, he could decide to sign an IOU at the supplier's, promising to pay for the inventory the next morning, using the day's cash receipts as funding. This assumption modifies the diagram, as shown in Figure 2–2. Here, the creditor's funds effectively supplant the owner's funds, if only for a single day.

In any event, our vendor's funds cycle is very short. The initial investment in inventory, funded either with his own cash or with credit from his supplier, is followed by numerous individual cash sales during the day. These receipts build up his cash balance for the following day's operations.

Next, we've represented the first day of operations—assuming the vendor financed the inventory himself—in Figure 2–3, where cash on hand is built up by

FIGURE 2–2

Ice Cream Vendor
Initial Use of Credit to Start the Day

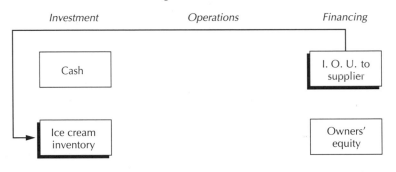

Management Decision Context

FIGURE 2–3

Ice Cream Vendor
Profitable Operations During the First Day

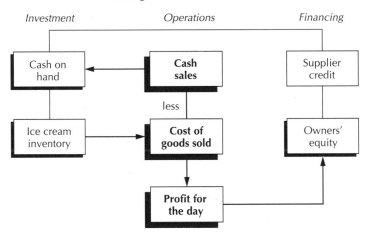

Management Decision Context

sales receipts, inventory is drawn down during the day, and where the difference between sales revenue and the cost of the ice cream sold represents the profit earned. This profit increases ownership equity, reflecting the value created during the day.

The following morning, our vendor uses the accumulated cash either to replenish his inventory, or to pay off the supplier so that he'll be extended credit for another day's cycle. Any profit he has earned above the cost of the goods sold will, of course, be his to keep, or to invest in more inventory for the next day.

FIGURE 2–4

Ice Cream Vendor
Repayment of Credit After Profitable First Day

Management Decision Context

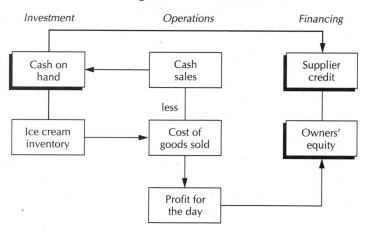

Figure 2–4 shows the alternative funds movements that would arise had our vendor used supplier credit for the first day. He would find that the amount of cash left after repayment of the initial supplier credit—the amount of his profit for the first day—would purchase only a portion of the next day's inventory. To continue operating on the second day he would have to decide whether to

- Ask for renewed credit from his supplier, or
- Provide the additional funds from any resources of his own that aren't yet committed to the business.

Funds cycles of larger and more structured businesses differ from this simple situation only in complexity, not in concept. Even for the most complex international conglomerate, the ultimate form of settlement of any transaction is cash. Meanwhile, however, such a company's operational funds cycle usually involves a great variety of partially offsetting credit extensions, changes in inventories, transformations of assets, etc., that precede the cash collections or payments.

In essence, any funds cycle arises because of a series of lags in the timing of business transactions. Our ice cream vendor has a lag of only a few hours between the purchase of his inventory and its conversion into cash through many small transactions. In contrast, a large manufacturer may have a lag of months between the time a product is made in the factory and the ultimate collection of the selling price from customers who purchased on credit. A service company may have a lag of weeks between the time salaried or contract professionals are paid for their work and the ultimate collection of service fees.

Management must plan for and find financing for the company's funds tied up because of these timing lags. This is important because these funds will remain committed for the foreseeable future, unless there are significant changes in the company's operations. As with any type of investment, management should attempt to minimize this resource commitment while maintaining operational effectiveness. Ways to reduce the funding required include methods such as "just-in-time" delivery of materials or parts in manufacturing, or purchasing merchandise on consignment in retailing.

To illustrate the nature of the concept further, we'll explore in some detail the following two processes:

- The funds cycle of a simplified manufacturing operation.

- The funds cycle for selling the manufactured products.

We've separated these processes for purposes of illustration and discussion, even though the two cycles are always intertwined in any ongoing business which both produces and sells products. The sales cycle alone, of course, applies to any retail, wholesale, or trading operation that purchases goods for resale.

The Funds Cycle for Manufacturing

To keep the illustration simple, let's assume that the Widget Manufacturing Company has just begun operations and is going to produce widgets for eventual sale. Figure 2–5 shows the company's funds flow cycle in the form of an overview, using only a minimum of detail. We've again arranged the diagram to reflect the three management decision areas.

As is readily apparent, the company was initially financed through a combination of owners' equity, long-term debt, and three kinds of short-term debt:

- Accounts payable due vendors of materials and supplies.

- Some short-term loans from banks.

- Other current liabilities, such as accrued wages and taxes.

The initial investments involve fixed assets (such as plant facilities), other assets (such as patents and licenses), and three kinds of current assets:

- Cash.

- Raw materials inventory.

- Finished goods inventory.

Of course, the last of these won't appear until the plant actually starts producing widgets. We can assume that long-term debt and owners' equity are the logical sources of funds for investing in plant and equipment, because they match the long-term funding commitment involved. In contrast, the short-term loans most likely provided the ready cash needed to start operations. Materials and supplies were bought with short-term trade credit extended by the company's vendors.

FIGURE 2–5

Funds Flow Cycle for Manufacturing

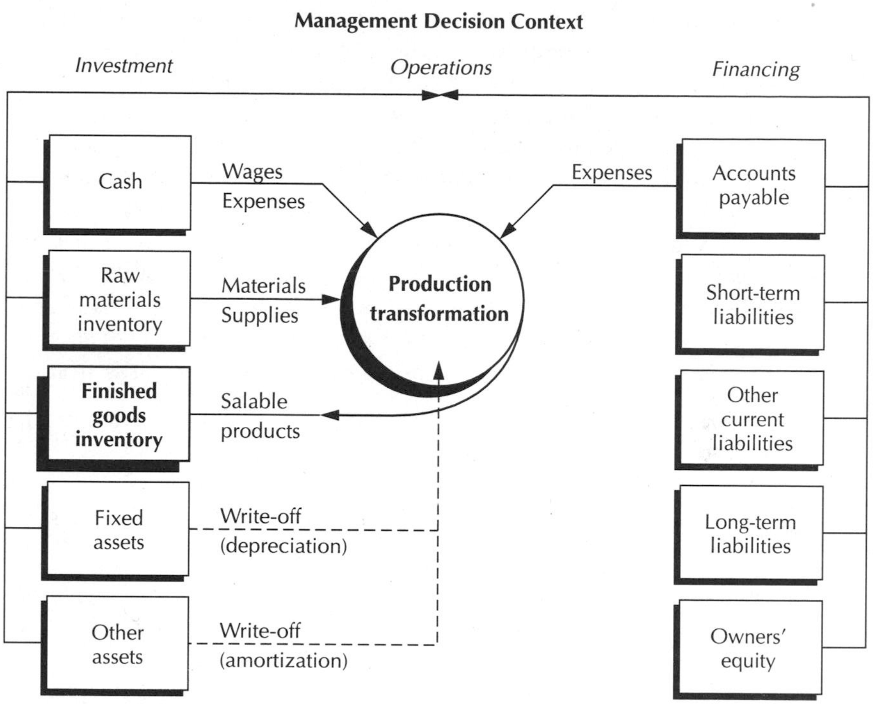

Management Decision Context

Investment	*Operations*	*Financing*

As production begins, a basic transformation process takes place. Some of the available cash is used to pay weekly wages and various ongoing expenses. Materials and supplies are withdrawn from inventory and used in manufacturing widgets, and inventories are replenished with additional credit. Some operating inputs, like power and fuel oil, are obtained on credit, and are temporarily financed through accounts payable.

Use of the plant and equipment is reflected in the form of a depreciation charge, which becomes part of the cost of the transformation process. Any patents and licenses are similarly amortized and charged to the production cost. As widgets are finished on the factory floor, they're moved into the warehouse and their cost is added to the growing finished goods inventory account.

In the absence of any widget sales, the production process continuously transforms cash, raw materials, expense accruals, and trade credit into a growing buildup of finished goods inventory. A fraction of the original cost of the building, machinery, and other depreciable assets used has now become part of the cost of finished goods via the depreciation charge—even though no cash is actually moved by this allocation process. This accounting write-off merely affects the company's books by transferring a portion of the recorded cost of the assets into the cost of the inventory. Remember, the only time cash actually changed hands was when the assets were originally acquired.

What are the funds implications of this transformation? The operational funds flows, which occurred after the business was established, so far only affected working capital components. The major sources of funding for the production process largely came from drawing down cash and raw materials, which were among the initial funds committed. An additional source was found in increased trade credit and in expenses accrued but not yet paid.

The major use of these funds was in the buildup of finished goods inventory. Unless the company can eventually turn finished goods into cash through successful sales to its customers, the continued inventory buildup will eventually drain both the cash reserves and the stores of raw material. These would have to be replenished by new infusions of credit or owners' equity, or both. Adding to the cash drain is the obligation to begin, at some point, the repayment of accounts payable for trade credit incurred, on normal terms like 30 or 45 days from the invoice date.

From a funds flow standpoint, several timing lags are significant in our example:

- A supply of raw materials sufficient for several days of operation has to be kept on hand to ensure uninterrupted manufacturing.

- The physical lag in the number of days required to produce a widget causes a buildup of an inventory of work in process, that is, widgets in various stages of completion.

- A sufficient number of widgets must be produced and kept at all times in finished goods inventory to support an ongoing sales and service effort.

The combined funds commitment caused by these lags has to be financed on a *continuous* basis through resources provided by owners and creditors, as long as the pattern of lags remains unchanged.

Offsetting this funding requirement, but only in part, is the length of time over which credit is extended by the company's suppliers. This is a favorable lag, because purchases of raw material and supplies, as well as certain other expenses, will be financed by vendors for 30 or 45 days, or for whatever length of time is common usage in the industry. New credit will continue to be extended as repayments are made of the accounts coming due.

Another significant favorable lag is the temporary funding provided by the employees of the company whose wages are paid periodically. In effect, employees are extending credit to their employer for a week, two weeks, or even a month, depending on the company's payroll pattern. Such funding is recognized among current liabilities as accrued wages. Other expense accruals, such as income taxes currently owed, will similarly provide temporary funds.

As we observed before, however, the buildup of finished goods in the warehouse cannot go on indefinitely, and at some point, revenues from the sale of the widgets become essential to replenishing cash in order to meet the company's obligations as they become due. To complete the picture, we must next examine the funds implications of the selling process.

The Funds Cycle for Sales

The funds flows caused by selling the widgets can be examined within our decisional framework, as shown in Figure 2–6. The operations segment in the center of the diagram now includes the main elements of an operating statement:

- Sales revenue.
- Cost of goods sold.
- Selling expenses.
- General and administrative expenses.
- Net income.

The selling cycle is based on a major timing lag, which arises from the extension of credit to the company's customers. If the widgets were sold for cash,

FIGURE 2–6

Funds Flow Cycle for Sales

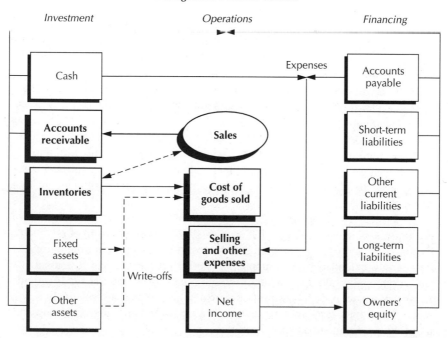

Management Decision Context

collection would, of course, be instantaneous. If the company provides normal trade credit, however, the collection of accounts receivable will be delayed by the terms extended to customers, such as 30, 45, or whatever number of days is common practice in the industry.

This sales lag, like the lags incurred during the production cycle, has to be financed *continuously*, because for any given volume of sales, the equivalent of 30, 40, or 50 days' worth of sales will always be outstanding. As accounts becoming due are collected, new credit will be extended to customers on current sales—just as was the case with the vendors supplying materials and other items to the company itself.

Cost of goods sold represents the value of the widgets withdrawn from finished goods inventory, each of which contains a share of the labor, raw material, overhead, and other costs expended in its manufacture, including apportioned depreciation for the use of the facilities and a share of the amortization of any patents or licenses involved.

Selling expenses, which consist of the salaries of the sales force, the marketing support staff, and advertising and promotional costs, will be paid partly in cash, partly with funds obtained from creditors. General and administrative expenses will be paid in a similar fashion. Once all these costs and expenses have been subtracted from sales revenue, the resulting net income (or loss), after allowing for state and federal income taxes, causes an increase (or decrease) in owners' equity.

What are the funds flow implications of this picture? First of all, assuming that the company is maintaining a level volume of sales and manufacturing operations, management must plan for a continuous long-term commitment of funds to support the necessary amount of working capital. This means that sufficient funds must be provided for inventories of raw materials and work in process to carry on production. In addition, funds are needed to maintain a proper level of finished goods to support smooth sales and deliveries, and to allow for sufficient accounts receivable balances to permit normal credit extension to customers. Also, a minimum cash balance must be maintained for punctual payment of currently due obligations.

Beyond these working capital requirements, additional funds are likely needed for any investment outlays on fixed and other assets with which to support growing operations. Finally, arrangements have to be made for payment of declared dividends, any scheduled repayment of debt, or for refinancing long-term obligations.

The sources of this financing will come only in a relatively small part from accounts payable outstanding, which can usually support a portion of raw materials, supplies, and ongoing operating expenses in line with the normal number of days' credit extended by the suppliers. The difference between the amount of funds continually tied up in inventories and receivables, and the funds provided by current accounts payable, must come from sources that are relatively permanent, such as long-term debt and owners' equity—the latter augmented by after-tax profits or diminished by net losses.

The dynamics of the system are such that once desired conditions and relationships have been reached, the requirement for operating funds will be constant as long as the business operates on a sustained level. As we shall see next, however, the level of funding requirements will change significantly when operation conditions themselves change.

VARIABILITY OF FUNDS FLOWS

Unless there are significant changes in the company's internal conditions or in its markets, the level of ongoing financing needed to support operations will mainly depend on effective inventory management, sound management of customer credit, and prudent use of supplier credit, as well as reliable relations with other lenders, such as banks. Also, profitable operations will generate cash that can be used as part of the funding pattern. The company's continuous funding needs will be increased if collections from customers worsen, credit terms extended by suppliers or lenders tighten, or if profits decline.

Rarely does a company enjoy the steady state conditions that made financing the company's operations so predictable in our simple example. In reality, several internal and external factors can affect any business. Major internal forces include management's ability to seize growth opportunities, its effectiveness in managing all activities, or its inability to stem a decline in the company's volume of operations. Major external forces include the competitive interplay in the industry, as well as seasonal variations and cyclical movements in the economy, which go beyond the impact of specific actions taken by the company's competitors. Each of these conditions has its own particular cash flow implications, and we'll illustrate the most important of these now.

Growth/Decline Variations

Growth   A pattern of steady growth in a business brings with it the need to fund the underlying expansion of all financial requirements. Successful growth can't be achieved without providing for appropriate increases in working capital, longer-term investments, and other expenditures. These growing funds commitments will be permanently tied up as long as growth continues or as long as operations remain at a given level. Normal profits earned from successful operations usually supply only a portion of these funding needs.

Consider the following rules of thumb:

■ If the business sells on 30-day credit, the value of each incremental layer of sales will be added to accounts receivable for 30 days and must be funded continually, because as prior sales are collected, new and larger current sales are added.

■ Similarly, if the business turns over its inventory nine times per year, the value of the incremental cost of the goods sold will have to be

added to inventories in the form of 40 days worth of inventory
(360÷9), which must also be funded continually.

■ Offsetting this additional use of funds, but only in part, will be the
incremental growth in accounts payable and other minor accruals. The
credit from the company's vendors will amount to an equivalent value
of the additional purchases for, say, 30 days, if that is the usual credit
pattern.

Because the required investment in accounts receivable and inventories is
normally much more than twice the credit obtained from current payables and accruals, it should be clear that successful growth requires extensive funding of additional working capital. To this must be added funds required for any expansion of
physical facilities or for contractual arrangements to support the growth in sales.

For Example

Let's take the simple example of a wholesaling company, which sells on
average terms of 45 days, buys on terms of 40 days, and turns over its
inventory every 30 days (twelve times per year). Its cost of goods sold is
72 percent of sales, and its profit after taxes is six percent of sales. As the
company grows, the funding consequences of every *incremental* $100 in
annual sales are as follows:

■ Accounts receivable increase by $12.50 ($100 × 45/360)

■ Inventories of goods purchased increase by $6.00 ($72 × 30/360)

■ Accounts payable to vendors increase by $8.00 ($72 × 40/360)

The net effect is a funds increase of $10.50 in additional working
capital ($12.50 + $6.00 − $8.00), assuming no other changes take place in
the company's financial system. At the normal level of aftertax profits of
6 percent, the company could provide $6.00 of this funding need—if no
other uses of these profits existed, such as paying dividends to shareholders, or expansion of the warehouse and associated equipment to support
the growth trend. Thus, a minimum of $4.50 would have to be continu-
ously financed for every $100 in additonal sales. ■

The pattern of sales, operating assets (working capital plus fixed assets), and
profits of the typical growing company will look something like in Figure 2–7,
where growth requires additional working capital every single year as receivables
and inventories expand, only partially offset by growing accounts payable. Periodically, new investments must be made in expanded facilities, as is indicated by the
jump in the operating assets in 2001 and again in 2004. The asset column continues
to grow as long as volume growth persists, and constant funding of this increase
will be necessary through a combination of profit and other sources.

The dotted funding line indicates the total need for funds required to finance
growing operating assets, reduced by total aftertax profits in every year. An amount
equal to depreciation is assumed to be spent on maintaining the facilities, the same

FIGURE 2–7

Typical Growth Pattern

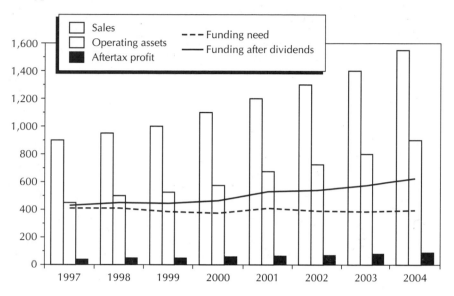

concept we used in the financial system discussion in Chapter 1. No dividend payments have been allowed for in this line, which therefore understates the actual funding need. Note that growing profits in the later years are able to gradually reduce the total funding requirements.

When dividend payments are provided for, however—in this case rising gradually from $20 in 1997 to $40 in 2004—what was essentially a level funding need becomes a steadily growing requirement for permanent funding, as shown in the solid line. By now it should be clear that successful growth typically requires an ongoing, and more than likely growing, funding commitment, which must be financed over the long term through the use of additional owners' equity and long-term debt. Frequently, reinvestment of profits alone is not a sufficient source, because in a high growth business, the contribution from the profit margin may be far outweighed by the cumulative funding demands (as Chapter 5 details).

Decline   In the opposite case, when a business declines in volume and is deliberately managed to achieve such shrinkage efficiently—a difficult assumption not always realized—the company will in fact turn into a strong generator of cash. Here the reverse of the growth situation prevails. As sales decline, management must carefully seek to reduce operations, working capital, and other operating assets to match the decline in volume, thus releasing the funds that had been tied up over time.

This idealized situation is demonstrated in Figure 2–8. Note the dramatic decline in the basic funding needs, which turn into positive funds generation during the last two years. When dividend payments of as much as 50 percent of aftertax

FIGURE 2–8

Managed Decline Pattern

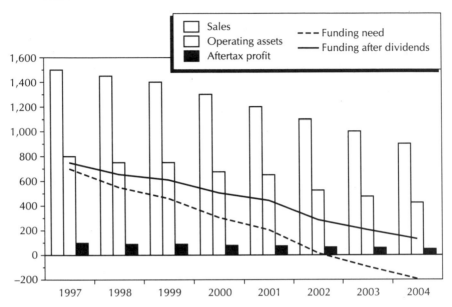

profits are assumed in every year, the funding requirements decline more slowly, but represent still only a fraction of the level at the beginning of the period.

Basically, the ability of the business system to release cash depends on the careful removal of all layers of activity that no longer need to be supported. A proportional shrinkage of receivables and inventories, partly offset by declining payables, becomes the major potential cash source, apart from the disposal of other assets no longer needed. If the decline pattern becomes precipitous or cannot be managed properly, however, the specter of inventory markdowns, operating inefficiencies, and emergency actions will seriously impede the release of funds. Under these conditions, real difficulties can arise and the expected cash flow may not materialize.

Seasonal Variations

A fairly large number of industries experience distinct seasonal operating patterns (specific months or weeks of high sales, followed by an often dramatic decline in demand). These ups and downs repeat themselves quite predictably. Examples are most common in retailing operations, many of which are geared to special holiday periods or specific customer segments with seasonal style or gift requirements. Producers of seasonal items, like snowmobiles or bathing suits, will experience high fluctuations in demand, unless they can sell into global markets that have offsetting climates. Similar patterns impact canneries that process specific crops or other seasonal foods.

FIGURE 2–9

Typical Seasonal Pattern

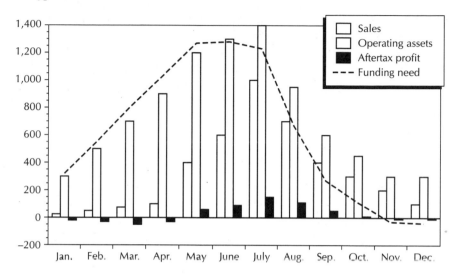

Common to all seasonal businesses is a funds cycle with large short-term swings during the period of a year or less. The financial implications of such a pattern are quite obvious. During the low point of demand, ongoing operations have to be supported with cash from internal or external sources, unless the business can be shut down, as are some seasonal resorts. In many seasonal manufacturing businesses, inventories are gradually built up, either through production or through purchases from suppliers.

As was the case in our earlier simple example, funding for this buildup must come from credit, loans, and owners' equity. Once the selling activity begins, growing amounts of receivables due from customers buying on normal credit terms have to be funded by the company. It is not until the first receivables are actually collected that cash starts flowing back into the business. The financial lags are usually such that collection of the receivables from peak sales will occur well after the peak of funding requirements has occurred.

Figure 2–9 demonstrates a typical seasonal pattern on a month-by-month basis which reflects the dramatic rise and fall in funding needs over the year, before any dividends are even considered. In this case, management must make several critical decisions, among them the size of the buildup of inventories needed to support anticipated demand, the level of operating and other expenditures to be made during the different phases of the operating cycle, and the nature of the funding to finance the bulge in requirements. Contingencies must be allowed for, such as lower-than-expected demand or prices, or both, delays in collections from customers, or the time involved in arranging for short-term financing with banks and other lenders. Otherwise, the business could find itself strapped because its own financial obligations must be met well before collections are made.

We'll discuss applying turnover relationships and the aging of receivables as a means of judging the effectiveness of asset use by management in Chapter 3. Under highly seasonal conditions such relationships become unstable, because lags and surges in the accounts within the period spanned by financial statements make most ratio comparisons difficult.

As we'll see in Chapter 4, a more direct evaluation of a seasonal business is possible through a month-to-month (or week-to-week) analysis of funds movements and a careful assessment of changes in the funds cycle of the company from peak to peak or trough to trough, instead of comparing quarterly or year-end financial statements.

Cyclical Variations

A variant of the seasonal picture is the cyclical pattern of funds movements. It mainly reflects external economic changes that impact the company over a period of several years. Economic variations and specific industry cycles are generally long-term and not as regular and predictable as seasonal variations. Economic swings that affect a business or industry tend to bring many more variables into play, such as changes in raw materials prices and availability, competitive conditions in the market, capital investment needs, etc. Nevertheless, the cash flow principles we observed in dealing with the seasonal pattern apply here as well.

Funds lags during a cyclical upturn or downturn tend to be magnified by a mostly unavoidable lag in decision making. As conditions begin to change, it is usually very difficult for management to gauge, from its day-to-day experience, whether the economy or the market is undergoing a long-term shift and what the specific timing is likely to be.

A cyclical downturn thus brings significant challenges: First, management must recognize, with reasonable confidence, that a turning point has indeed arrived. Next, it must prevent inventories from rising by curtailing purchases and production. This is usually followed by reducing staffing levels, and by cutting ongoing costs wherever possible. Careful management of credit, both extended and used, becomes critical as well. Meeting these challenges is easier said than done, because data on current economic trends available at any one time tend to lag significantly behind actual conditions, while economic forecasts often fall short of predicting both the timing and degree of economic change.

For Example

A gradual downturn in housing construction will leave many producers and wholesalers of building materials with inventories in excess of declining demand. As the sales slump accelerates, and prices of lumber, plywood, and other commodities fall, management faces a funding crisis. Continuing normal production will transform raw material into products that cannot be sold; thus, production must be curtailed. Lower volume and prices also decrease the eventual cash flow generated from current sales, while the stream of collections from past higher sales begins to run out. ■

FIGURE 2–10

Typical Cyclical Pattern

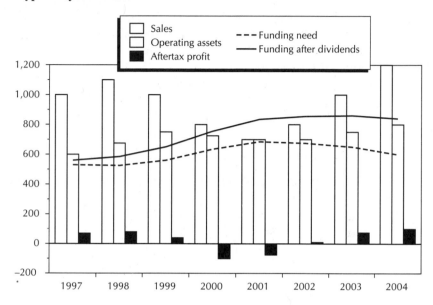

Figure 2–10 demonstrates a typical cyclical pattern, where sales volume and prices swing with economic conditions, but where operating asset levels and their accompanying funding needs lag behind the volume changes due to the factors we've just mentioned. Note the steady increase in funding required during the decline phase, brought about by a combination of rising investment (mostly a buildup of working capital) and plummeting profits. If dividends are maintained at the level of $30, and if we assume that these are paid every year, the funding line rises to a new high, indicating that the company isn't able to make up for the funds drain of the cyclical decline.

In the cyclical upswing, lags in decision making may cause inventory and production levels to be insufficient as sales volume begins to surge. To compensate, extra shifts or outside purchases might be used, even though the costs incurred with these alternatives are typically higher than normal and will depress profitability. Growing sales will also raise the amount of receivables credit extended to customers.

Thus, a cyclical boom will likely require the infusion of additional funds to provide the increased working capital needed and to finance increased physical operations. The latter may involve additional investment in plant and facilities. Overall, it may be said that a cyclical upswing will usually require an increase in medium- to long-term financing to support added levels of working capital and other financial requirements, while a downswing will first result in rising inventories—until management can adjust its operations—and then begin to release cash, which can be used to repay credit obligations. The latter condition, however, will hold only if both working capital and production levels are carefully managed downward.

In summary, variability in funds flows is caused by management actions, by external conditions, or both. We know that a business operating in a steady state must maintain a permanent stock of working capital, as well as properties, facilities, equipment and other assets. As a general rule of thumb, the amount of funds tied up in current assets far exceeds trade credit sources and normal short-term borrowings. Therefore, when significant variability in the level of operations is introduced, major shifts in the company's financial condition may be caused by changes in working capital alone. Funding for other needs, such as capital investments and major spending programs, must be superimposed on this pattern. In Chapter 4, we'll discuss these issues in the context of the techniques of forecasting funds requirements.

Generalized Cash Flow Model

At this point, it's useful once again to examine the overall relationships of funds movements in a generalized framework, as shown in Figure 2–11. The diagram is applicable to any business, large or small. We have added flow lines, which show the potential funds movements and linkages between the main accounts of the balance sheet and the operating statement. A summary of sources and uses of

FIGURE 2–11

Generalized Cash Flow Diagram

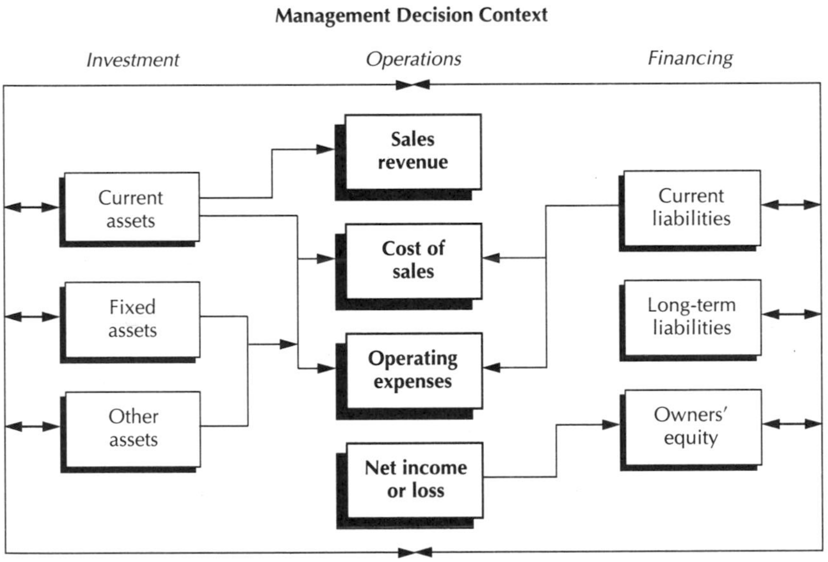

Management Decision Context

| Investment | Operations | Financing |

| Investments (increases) in all types of assets are uses of cash; reductions in assets are sources of cash. | Profitable operations are a source of cash; losses drain cash from the system. **Note:** Accounting write-offs do not affect cash and must be adjusted for (reversed). | Trade credit, new financing (increase in liabilities), and new equity are sources of cash; repayments, dividends, and returns of capital are uses of cash. |

cash in terms of our familiar management decision context is given at the bottom of the diagram. This representation will be a useful reference when we discuss the interpretation of cash flow statements next.

INTERPRETING FUNDS FLOW DATA

We are now ready to examine in somewhat more detail the use and implications of a company's funds flow information, as normally represented in its cash flow statements. As we discussed in Chapter 1, companies that are publicly held and publish regular financial statements are required by the SEC to provide a statement of cash flows along with balance sheets and operating statements. Where such statements aren't readily available, however, or in situations where the analyst wishes to project future funds movements, it's relatively straightforward to develop meaningful cash flow statements. With the help of the cash flow statement, we can develop many insights about the actual funds changes that took place, and also obtain clues for further analysis of the nature and quality of management decisions in operations, investments, and financing.

In this section, we'll illustrate how to quickly draw up a basic cash flow statement from available balance sheets and operating statements and discuss the major principles involved in transforming this accounting information into the funds flow pattern we are interested in. For this purpose, we'll again use the 1995 and 1994 TRW Inc. financial statements originally shown in Chapter 1 as Figures 1–9 and 1–11. We'll work back from these to develop a derived cash flow statement, which we can then compare to the more detailed one published by TRW. Not having access to the detailed records of the company, we'll find that our own version of the cash flow statement will approximate, but not be identical to, the key funds movements shown in TRW's statement.

We'll begin with a look at the differences in the key balance sheet items between the two dates, and sort these into funds sources and uses as a convenient way of identifying positive and negative cash flows. Then we'll turn to the operating statement to obtain additional details necessary to expand our insights into the operational aspects of funds movements. The objective is not accounting refinement, but simply an understanding of the principles involved in transforming key data into funds flow patterns.

TRW's consolidated balance sheets are reproduced as Figure 2–12, showing changes in the accounts between the two balance sheet dates. To develop a cash flow statement, these changes must be classified as either funds uses or sources. We've done this in Figure 2–13, where increases and decreases in assets and liabilities are assigned to the appropriate categories, following the rules we developed earlier. However, some of the balance sheet categories are too broad for our purpose. As a result, several of the funds flows cannot be specifically delineated:

■ Net profit (or loss) from operations is not recognized as such, but is part of the net change in retained earnings.

FIGURE 2–12

TRW INC. AND SUBSIDIARIES
Consolidated Balance Sheets at December 31 ($ millions)

	1995	1994	Change
Assets			
Current assets:			
Cash and cash equivalents	$ 59	$ 109	−$ 50
Accounts receivable	1,428	1,338	+ 90
Inventories	534	470	+ 64
Prepaid expenses	78	59	+ 19
Deferred income taxes	237	239	− 2
Total current assets	2,336	2,215	+ 121
Property, plant, and equipment at cost	5,866	5,556	+ 310
Less: Allowances for depreciation and			
amortization	3,303	3,067	+ 236
Total property, plant, and equipment—net	2,563	2,489	+ 74
Intangible assets:			
Intangibles arising from acquisitions	483	477	+ 6
Capitalized data files	488	441	+ 47
Other	92	69	+ 23
	1,063	987	+ 76
Less: Accumulated amortization	405	331	+ 74
Total intangible assets—net	658	656	+ 2
Other assets	333	276	+ 57
Total assets	$5,890	$5,636	+$ 254
Liabilities and Shareholders' Investment			
Current liabilities:			
Short-term debt	$ 133	$ 122	+$ 11
Accrued compensation	385	346	+ 39
Trade accounts payable	807	737	+ 70
Other accruals	545	541	+ 4
Dividends payable	36	33	+ 3
Income taxes	26	50	− 24
Current portion of long-term debt	80	157	− 77
Total current liabilities	2,012	1,986	+ 26
Long-term liabilities	779	796	− 17
Long-term debt	541	694	− 153
Deferred income taxes	313	269	+ 44
Minority interests in subsidiaries	73	69	+ 4
Shareholders' investment:			
Serial preference stock II	1	1	0
Common stock	40	40	0
Other capital	398	354	+ 44
Retained earnings	1,688	1,383	+ 305
Cumulative translation adjustments	76	66	+ 10
Treasury shares—cost in excess of par	(31)	(22)	− 9
Total shareholders' investment	2,172	1,822	+ 350
Total liabilities and shareholders' investment	$5,890	$5,636	+$ 254

Source: Adapted from 1995 TRW Inc. annual report.

FIGURE 2–13

TRW INC. AND SUBSIDIARIES
Statement of Balance Sheet Changes
For the Year Ended December 31, 1995
($ millions)

Sources:

Decrease in cash and cash equivalents	$ 50
Decrease in deferred income taxes	2
Increase in allowances for depreciation	236
Increase in accumulated amortization	74
Increase in short-term debt	11
Increase in accrued compensation	39
Increase in trade accounts payable	70
Increase in other accruals	4
Increase in dividends payable	3
Increase in deferred income taxes	44
Increase in minority interests in subsidiaries	4
Increase in other capital	44
Increase in retained earnings	305
Increase in cumulative translation adjustments	10
	$896

Uses:

Increase in accounts receivable	$ 90
Increase in inventories	64
Increase in prepaid expenses	19
Increase in property, plant, and equipment	310
Increase in intangibles arising from acquisitions	6
Increase in capitalized data files	47
Increase in other intangibles	23
Increase in other assets	57
Decrease in income taxes payable	24
Decrease in current portion of long-term debt	77
Decrease in long-term liabilities	17
Decrease in long-term debt	153
Increase in treasury shares	9
	$896

- Cash dividends are also immersed in the net change in retained earnings.
- Depreciation and amortization are buried in the changes in the respective accounts for accumulated depreciation and amortization.
- New investments in facilities, as well as acquisitions, disposals, and divestments are similarly netted out in the balance sheet accounts.

TRW's statement of earnings, reproduced in Figure 2–14, provides us with information on the first three elements, while we have to rely on separate information from the company about the amount of new investments, acquisitions, disposals, and divestments. We've provided some summarized data at the bottom of the operating statement.

The simple sources and uses statement in Figure 2–13 is an indication of the broad financial implications of growth to record sales volume and profits, after having completed the restructuring begun by TRW in 1991. The major funds uses were:

- An increase in property, plant, and equipment supporting TRW's growth.
- A net reduction of long-term debt, as well as of the current portion of this debt, in line with one of the announced purposes of the restructuring.
- Changes in working capital accounts reflecting the growth of the company.

The key net funds sources were:

- An increase in retained earnings reflecting the net effect of record profits.
- An increase in allowances for depreciation and accumulated depreciation.
- Increases in accounts payable, deferred income taxes, accrued compensation, and other capital, as well as a reduction in cash and cash equivalents.

The period's depreciation and amortization, which we would expect to be major sources, are so far hidden in the overall changes of the accumulated allowances shown on the balance sheet.

Although we do, at this point, have a broad picture of TRW's sources and uses of funds, we can make a few modifications, using what information is readily available to us:

1. The net change in retained earnings can be separated into profit or loss from operations and cash dividends paid. In the case of TRW, we know from the operating statement that there was net income for 1995 of $446 million. This amount must have been added to retained earnings. The operating statement further indicated that cash dividends paid were $134 million, which was subtracted from retained earnings. The net of these two amounts is $312 million, very close to the change in retained earnings of $310. The remainder is due to a minor difference between dividends declared and dividends actually paid, and to other small adjustments.

2. The amount of depreciation and amortization charged against income during the period should be shown as a positive funds movement. The largest of

FIGURE 2–14

TRW INC. AND SUBSIDIARIES
Statement of Earnings
For the Years Ended December 31, 1995 and 1994
($ millions)

	1995	1994
Sales	$10,172	$9,087
Cost of sales	8,190	7,270
Gross profit	1,982	1,817
Administrative and selling expenses	747	756
Research and development expenses	422	412
Interest expense	95	105
Other expenses (income) net	10	9
Total expenses	1,274	1,282
Earnings (loss) before income taxes	708	535
Income taxes	262	202
Net earnings (loss)	$ 446	$ 333
Per share of common stock:		
Average number of shares outstanding	67.4 million	66.4 million
Fully diluted net earnings per share	$ 6.62	$ 5.01
Primary earnings per share	$ 6.62	$ 5.02
Book value per share	$ 32.97	$27.91
Other data ($ millions):		
Depreciation of property, plant, and equipment	$ 433	$ 402
Amortization of intangibles, other assets	77	74
Capital expenditures	485	506
Dividends paid	134	126

Source: Adapted from 1995 TRW Inc. annual report.

these normally is depreciation of plant and equipment, followed by amortization of patents, licenses, and other intangibles. In some cases, depletion of mineral deposits and standing timber is charged. We remember that such write-offs reflect the apportionment of past expenditures, and therefore do not involve current funds movements. They must be added back to income for cash flow purposes. This practice, however, results in a common misconception—to view depreciation and amortization as actual sources of cash. Remember that depreciation and amortization as such do not create any cash—they are only accounting entries that reduce reported income and thus understate the actual cash flow obtained. They do, of course, directly affect the amount of income taxes paid, but this positive funds impact has already been recognized in the income tax charge which was deducted before arriving at net income. In TRW's case, depreciation and amortization were shown at the bottom of the operating statement as $433 million and $77 million, respectively. These amounts should be listed as sources, because their addition in effect restores net income to its prewrite-off level.

3. Capital expenditures for new investment are often provided as a line item in published statements. If we did not have direct information about new investments, acquisitions, disposals, and divestments made during the period, we would have to approximate the amount of funds used by arguing that the net change of the property, plant, and equipment account was affected by two main elements:

■ The amount of depreciation charged during the year.

■ All the other transactions combined.

Because we know that the net change in TRW's property, plant, and equipment was $74, we can derive the net effect of all the other movements by adding back the amount of depreciation of $433, for a net change in investments of $507. This result suggests, at the very least, that the actual new investments of $485 shown below the operating statement in Figure 2–14 must have been offset by divestments of $22. As we'll see, the published cash flow information provided by the company shows the details of the positive and negative movements in this area. We can use the same approach to approximate the net change in intangible investments by adding back the amortization charge of $77 to the balance sheet change of $2.

Now we can assemble a modified cash flow statement from the information displayed earlier in Figure 2–13. The statement will be improved somewhat by the adjustments we've discussed in owners' equity, net income, and plant and equipment. In Figure 2–15, we've rearranged the derived TRW data both in terms of our three familiar areas of management decision: operations, investment, and financing, and also by sources and uses to highlight the specific impact of each element. It provides a picture of the effect of TRW management decisions in 1995.

We observe that operational decisions resulted in a net funds sourse of $971 million, which represents 1995 net income of $446 million, adjusted for depreciation ($433 million), amortization ($77 million), and reduction in deferred taxes ($46 million). The smallest item is the net increase in working capital of $31 million (a $123 million increase in current assets offset by a $92 million increase in current liabilities).

Funds required for investment amounted to $643 million, which included our derived capital investment figure of $507 million, plus a similarly derived investment of $79 million in intangible assets, and the decrease in other assets of $57 million.

Funds from financing decisions were most significant in debt modification, with long-term debt reduced by $230 million, and short-term debt increased by $11 million. There was also an increase in long-term liabilities of $17 million, and other capital grew by $44 million, while dividends paid amounted to $136 million. The remaining items are minor.

A check of the company's annual report reveals that, as we know, actual 1995 capital investment for property, plant, and equipment was $485 million,

FIGURE 2–15

TRW INC. AND SUBSIDIARIES
Derived Funds Sources and Uses Statement
For the Year Ended December 31, 1992
($ millions)

	Sources	Uses
Funds from Operations:		
Net income	$ 446	
Depreciation (noncash item)	433	
Amortization (noncash item)	77	
Change in deferred income taxes (net)	46	
Increase in current liabilities (payables, accruals)	92	
Increase in current assets (cash, receivables, inventories, less increase in prepaids)		123
Total operational funds flows	1,094	123
Net funds from operations	971	
Funds for Investment:		
Capital investments (adjusted for depreciation of $433)		507
Investment in intangible assets (adjusted for amort. of $77) . .		79
Increase in other assets		57
Total investment funds flows		643
Funds from Financing:		
Increase in short-term debt	11	
Decrease in long-term debt (including current portion)		230
Increase in long-term liabilities		17
Decrease in minority interests	4	
Increase in other capital	44	
Increase in treasury shares		9
Currency translation adjustments	10	
Dividends paid		136
Adjustments to retained earnings		5
Financing funds flows	69	397
Net funds used in financing	—	328
Totals	971	971

while proceeds from divestitures and the sales of property, plant, and equipment were $9 million and 20 million, respectively. The actual investment in other assets was 78 million, offset in part by other proceeds. Thus, we've slightly overstated capital investments and understated divestiture proceeds and investments in other assets because of our simplifying assumptions.

When we compare TRW's actual cash flow statement, reproduced in Figure 2–16, to our derived statement in Figure 2–15, we find that, apart from differences in presentation, many of the figures we have developed are reflected there as

FIGURE 2–16

TRW INC. AND SUBSIDIARIES
Statement of Cash flows
For the Years Ended December 31, 1995 and 1994
($ millions)

	1995	1994
Operating Activities:		
Net earnings (loss)	$ 446	$ 333
Adjustments to reconcile net earnings (loss) to net cash provided by operating activities:		
Depreciation and amortization	510	476
Restructuring	—	(23)
Deferred income taxes	46	8
Other—net	33	26
Changes in assets and liabilities, net of effects of businesses acquired or sold:		
Accounts receivable	(75)	(112)
Inventories and prepaid expenses	(71)	(33)
Accounts payable and other accruals	31	262
Other—net	(51)	35
Net cash provided by operating activities	869	972
Investing Activities:		
Capital expenditures	(485)	(506)
Proceeds from divestitures	9	22
Investments in other assets	(78)	(81)
Proceeds from sales of property, plant, and equipment	20	16
Other—net	(12)	7
Net cash used in investing activities	(546)	(542)
Financing Activities:		
Increase (decrease) in short-term debt	(47)	(270)
Proceeds from debt in excess of 90 days	36	176
Principal repayments in excess of 90 days	(207)	(154)
Dividends paid	(134)	(126)
Other—net	9	9
Net cash used in financing activities	(343)	(365)
Effect of exchange rate changes on cash	(30)	(35)
Increase (decrease) in cash and cash equivalents	(50)	30
Cash and cash equivalents at beginning of year	109	79
Cash and cash equivalents at end of year	$ 59	$ 109
Supplemental Cash Flow Information:		
Interest paid (net of amount capitalized)	$ 88	$ 112
Income taxes paid (net of refunds)	239	93

Source: Adapted from 1995 TRW Inc. annual report.

well. The various items on which the statements disagree all require more detailed knowledge than is normally available in published statements. This is particularly true with details in the financing section, which reflect much information not available to us. Also, a number of minor funds movements have been netted out. In broad terms, however, our derived statement reasonably approaches the overall magnitude of funds movements in the three decision areas.

To summarize, in this section we constructed a cash flow statement that goes beyond simply listing the changes readily observed in a comparison of beginning and ending balance sheet accounts. We achieved this by making some broad adjustments in several of the accounts. The purpose of the refinements was to highlight significant results that reflect management decisions involving investments, operations, and financing. If a company's cash flow statement is not made available as a matter of course, the analyst can usually approximate the statement, which an insider could prepare by going through the basic adjustment process we have demonstrated.

FUNDS MANAGEMENT AND SHAREHOLDER VALUE

It'll be useful to reflect once more on the nature of funds movements in the context of shareholder value creation. We've demonstrated the complex interrelationship of funds movements, driven by management decisions as well as by external forces and the intrinsic nature of a company's business. We've further shown how to determine and illustrate the impact of funds movements on cash flows.

The overriding principle for successful management of operating funds is constant attention to the economical use of the resources these funds represent. The best managed companies tailor their information systems and management incentives to minimize funds use relative to the level of each activity. If the foundation of shareholder value creation is to earn returns on the resources employed at levels above shareholder expectations, the notion of a "scarcity" approach to resource deployment should be a natural consequence. Such thinking must not be limited to funding new capital outlays alone, as we'll discuss in Chapter 6, but reach into all aspects of the business, including working capital management, employment practices, funding of research, product and service development, and marketing and promotional programs, etc. We'll now briefly discuss some of the key elements involved in managing operational funds.

Cash Management

As we've stated before, all management decisions and the funds movements caused by them eventually materialize in the form of a cash impact. But we must also realize that company's cash balance at any one time represents a resource commitment, even though its movements are more frequent and extensive than those of other investments. The principle which applies to this resource is the same as with any other resource:

> Minimize its size relative to the needs it supports, and obtain the greatest possible return by investing cash balances in ways that reflect its unique characteristics.

The economics of sound cash management therefore require that time lags in cash receipts be minimized, and that disbursements be made no sooner than required by commercial and legal terms. Ways to achieve time compression range from the use of lockboxes, to which remittances from customers are mailed for speedier processing, to the growing use of electronic funds transfers, which allow immediate collection of amounts due without the delays of paperwork. Effective banking relationships are a great assist in this process, and companies with widespread locations will attempt to concentrate cash management into regional processing arrangements.

Minimization of cash balances can be achieved by transferring any excess cash into marketable securities of short maturities, including U.S. treasury bills, commercial paper issued by corporations, and certificates of deposit issued by banks. While returns from these temporary investments will not approach the returns from a company's normal business activities, the trade-off between leaving cash idle versus earning a modest return until the cash can be used for longer-term investments, dividends, or repurchase of shares, will be positive and in the shareholders' interest.

Working Capital Management

Investments in customer credit in the form of accounts receivable, and in inventories of goods or materials, are long-term resource commitments, as we discussed earlier. Minimization of these investments relative to the level and pattern of a company's operations is a crucial element in the total management of operating funds. The key to successful management of customer credit and inventories is a clear understanding of the economic trade-offs involved.

Credit terms are a function of the competitive environment as well as of a careful assessment of the nature and creditworthiness of customers. For example, the issue may be whether extended credit terms, and the resulting rise in receivables outstanding, are compensated for by the contribution from any incremental sales gained. Similarly, extending normal credit to marginal customers has to be judged in terms of the risk of late payment or default versus the contribution from the sales gained. Techniques in the customer credit area include constant updating of credit performance, aging of accounts receivable into time categories, and developing sound criteria for credit extension.

Inventory management in successful companies has evolved into a rigorous process of asset minimization. Information technology has permitted a general reduction in inventory levels, whether in manufacturing, wholesaling, or retailing. In an effort to push inventories as low as possible, techniques such as just-in-time deliveries by suppliers to manufacturing locations of their customers, and carefully scheduled restocking triggered by instantaneous purchase data from major wholesales and retailers have become widespread. In effect, these techniques have woven a very close relationship between major suppliers and major customers, allowing timely coordination of schedules and helping to minimize inventories on both sides.

Offsetting receivables and inventories in part is normal trade credit from suppliers in the form of accounts payable. Here the appropriate principle is to make use of the credit terms extended, but to watch for potential favorable trade-offs such as discounts for early payment. Accounts payable are one form of financing working capital, and therefore, maximum use of trade terms is appropriate. If discounts offered for early payment are attractive—for example, 2 percent for paying in 10 days instead of 30 days amounts to a sizable interest rate of 36 percent per year (2 percent gained for a 20-day speedup in payment), there is an obvious advantage in using less expensive bank credit in order to remit to the vendor in 10 days. Exceeding the credit terms makes the interest trade-off more favorable, of course, but at the same time, there is the risk of affecting the company's credit standing if delays beyond the terms granted become habitual. Sound management of supplier credit, as was true with customer credit, relies on current up-to-date information on accounts and aging of payables to ensure proper payment.

As we discussed earlier, funding of working capital must be considered a long-term commitment, unless the business is characterized by significant seasonal or cyclical fluctuations. Given that even tightly managed receivables and inventories require long-term financial support, successful management of operational funding requires a combination of reinvested earnings and long-term debt, augmented as needed by temporary short-term funding.

Investment Management

Funding of operations also involves periodic investments in facilities, programs, and other long-term resource commitments beyond working capital needs. As we'll discuss in Chapter 6, the principles of sound investment management are no different in terms of shareholder value creation—the need to minimize funds needs relative to the expected benefits is paramount. The main complications arise because of the generally longer time frame and greater degree of uncertainty surrounding the expectations. The techniques of analysis are somewhat more involved, but still are based on the notion of cash flow trade-offs. The funding for such commitments will also tend to have a longer time horizon.

SUMMARY

In this chapter, we've demonstrated the funds flow cycle involved in any business, large or small, and its implication for management. We began with a simple illustration of basic funds movements, and then discussed operating funds cycles from a manufacturing and sales standpoint. We observed the nature and behavior of working capital, highlighted the impact of variability of operations, and demonstrated the effect of funds lags on the nature and duration of financing required to support a business. The insights gained included the need to consider the permanence of basic working capital requirements, the financial drain of even successful growth, and the potential funds release from decline in volume.

Several key questions arise as funds movements are analyzed. Most relate to the types of funds commitments (uses) made compared to the sources of funds available. Have enough long-term funds been provided to fund ongoing growth in working capital and fixed asset expansion? Are most sources of funds temporary loans and credit extension? Is the business counting on profits to fund peak needs that may exceed such expectations?

In essence, funds flow analysis is a broadbrush dynamic view of the financial management of the business, that relates changes in conditions to the key financial implications by reconstructing the cash implications of major transactions during the period. The techniques are simple, requiring only some basic accounting knowledge to provide this extra dimension in assessing balance sheets and operating statements. The transformation into cash flow thinking achieved by funds flow analysis matches the dynamics of the systems concept we discussed in Chapter 1.

SELECTED REFERENCES

Anthony, Robert N. *Essentials of Accounting.* 5th ed. Reading, MA.: Addison Wesley, 1993.
Brealey, Richard, and Stewart Myers. *Principles of Corporate Finance.* 4th ed. New York: McGraw-Hill, 1991.
Garrison, Raymond H. *Managerial Accounting: Concepts for Planning, Control, Decision Making.* 5th ed. Burr Ridge, Ill.: Richard D. Irwin, 1988.
Ross, Stephen; Randolph Westerfield; and Jeffrey Jaffe. *Corporate Finance.* 4th ed. Burr Ridge, Ill.: Richard D. Irwin, 1996.
Weston, J. Fred, and Thomas E. Copeland. *Managerial Finance.* 10th ed. Hinsdale, Ill.: Dryden Press, 1992.

SELF-STUDY EXERCISES AND PROBLEMS

(Solutions in Appendix V)

1. Develop a funds flow statement from the balance sheets and income statements of the CBA Company for the year 1997. Make appropriate assumptions and comment on the results.

CBA COMPANY
Operating Statements for 1996 and 1997

	1996	1997
Net sales	$1,133,400	$1,147,700
Cost of goods sold*	740,500	813,300
Gross margin	392,900	334,400
Expenses:		
Selling expense	172,500	227,000
General and administrative	65,500	71,800
Other expenses	22,200	25,000
Interest on debt	9,700	14,300
Total expenses	269,900	338,100
Profit (loss) before taxes	123,000	(3,700)
Federal income tax	56,600	(1,700)
Net income (loss)†	$ 66,400	$ (2,000)

*Includes depreciation of $31,500 for 1996 and $32,200 for 1997.

†Dividends paid were $30,000 for 1996 and $15,000 for 1997.

CBA COMPANY
Balance Sheets
December 31, 1996 and 1997

	1996	1997
Assets		
Current assets:		
Cash	$ 39,700	$ 27,500
Marketable securities	1,000	11,000
Accounts receivable (net)	81,500	72,700
Inventories	181,300	242,000
Total current assets	303,500	353,200
Fixed assets:		
Land	112,000	112,000
Plant and equipment (net)	445,200	464,800
Total fixed assets	557,200	576,800
Other assets	13,300	21,500
Total assets	$874,000	$951,500
Liabilities and net worth		
Current liabilities:		
Accounts payable	$ 71,200	$ 83,000
Notes payable	50,000	140,000
Accrued expenses	33,400	36,300
Total current liabilities	154,600	259,300
Long-term debt:		
Mortgage payable	106,000	90,800
Net worth:		
Common stock	225,000	230,000
Retained earnings	388,400	371,400
Total net worth	613,400	601,400
Total liabilities and net worth	$874,000	$951,500

2. Work the following exercises:

   a. The following data about the ABC Company's operations and conditions for the year 1997 are available from a variety of sources:

Depreciation for 1997	$21,400
Net loss for 1997	14,100
Common dividends paid	12,000
Amortization of goodwill, patents	15,000
Inventory adjustment—write-down	24,000
Investments in fixed assets	57,500
Loss from abandonment of equipment	4,400
Balance of retained earnings 12-31-96	167,300

   Which of the preceding items affect retained earnings during 1997 (the only surplus account of the company), and what's the balance of retained earnings as of December 31? Which of the preceding items are funds sources, and which are funds uses? Can depreciation be considered a funds flow item if the operating results are negative? What would be different if the $4,000 loss from abandonment had been a gain from sale of assets instead? Discuss.

b. The following items, among others, appear on the funds flow statement of DEF Company for the year 1997:

Outlays for properties and fixed assets . . .	$1,250,500
Profit from operations after taxes	917,000
Funds from depreciation	1,613,000

The only other information readily available is:

Gross property and fixed assets, 12-31-96	$8,431,500
Gross property and fixed assets, 12-31-97	8,430,000
Accumulated depreciation, 12-31-97	3,874,000

Determine the change in the *net* properties and fixed assets accounts from this information, and spell out your assumptions. How significant would be the likely effect on the results if you used some possible alternative assumptions? Discuss.

c. The XYZ Company experienced the transactions and changes listed below, among many others, during 1997. These affected its balance sheet as follows:

Fixed assets recorded at $110,000 were sold for $45,000 (gain reflected in net income).

Accumulated depreciation on these specific assets was $81,000.

Accumulated depreciation for the company as a whole decreased by $5,000 during 1997.

Total depreciation charged during 1997 was $78,500.

Balance of gross fixed assets was as follows: 12-31-96, $823,700, and 12-31-97, $947,300.

From this information, determine the amount of new investment in fixed assets for 1997 that should be shown in the funds flow statement. What was the amount of change in the *net* fixed assets account during 1997? Which other items shown above or derived from these should be shown on the funds flow statement? What assumptions are necessary? Discuss.

3. Develop a funds flow statement from the balance sheets, income statements, and retained earnings statements of the FED Company, shown below, for the year 1997. Make appropriate assumptions and comment on the results. If you net out changes in working capital accounts into one figure, will significant information be obscured?

Will it be helpful to assign uses and sources to key management decision areas? Discuss.

Other data you may need include: (1) sold fully depreciated machinery for $4,000, (2) issued $20,000 of common stock ($1 par) to reduce note payable, and (3) issued $4,000 of preferred stock to outsiders.

FED COMPANY
Balance Sheets, December 31, 1996 and 1997
($ thousands)

	1996	1997	Change
Assets			
Current assets:			
Cash	$ 12	-0-	–$12
Marketable securities	18	-0-	– 18
Accounts receivable—net	68	73	+ 5
Notes receivable	30	50	+ 20
Inventories	131	138	+ 7
Total current assets	259	261	+ 2
Fixed assets:			
Land	25	25	-0-
Plant and equipment	268	283	+ 15
Less: Accumulated depreciation	157	160	+ 3
Net plant and equipment	111	123	+ 12
Total fixed assets	136	148	+ 12
Other assets:			
Prepaid expenses	12	14	+ 2
Patents, organization expense	30	27	– 3
Total other assets	42	41	– 1
Total assets	$437	$450	+$13
Liabilities and net worth			
Current liabilities:			
Bank overdraft	$ -0-	$ 4	+ $4
Accounts payable	73	97	+ 24
Notes payable	100	70	– 30
Accrued expenses	13	22	+ 9
Total current liabilities	186	193	+ 7
Long-term liabilities:			
Secured notes payable	40	20	– 20
Net worth:			
Deferred income taxes	25	27	+ 2
Preferred stock	35	39	+ 4
Capital surplus	90	109	+ 19
Retained earnings	51	51	-0-
Common stock	10	11	+ 1
Total net worth	211	237	+ 26
Total liabilities and net worth	$437	$450	+$13

FED COMPANY
Operating Statement for 1996 and 1997
($ thousands)

	1996	1997
Sales	$1,115	$1,237
Cost of goods sold:		
Material	312	345
Labor	274	341
Depreciation	24	26
Overhead	158	210
Cost of goods sold	768	922
Gross profit	347	315
Expenses:		
Selling and administrative expense	268	297
Interest on debt	9	7
Total expenses	277	304
Profit before taxes	70	11
Income taxes	32	5
Net income	$ 38	$ 6

FED COMPANY
Statement of Retained Earnings for 1997
($ thousands)

Balance 12-31-96		$51
Additions:		
Net income from 1997 operations	$6	
Gain from sale of fixed assets	4	10
		61
Deductions:		
Preferred dividends	2	
Common dividends	5	
Patent, other amortization	3	10
Balance, 12-31-97		$51

4. The ZYX Company, a vegetable packing plant, operates on a highly seasonal basis, which affects its financial results during various parts of its fiscal year and forces a financial planning effort in tune with these fluctuating requirements. From the company's nine quarterly balance sheets (covering two fiscal years of the ZYX Company), develop a funds flow analysis that appropriately reflects the funds requirements and sources as balanced by company management.

Additional data you may need include (1) purchases of machinery, $48,000 in April 1997 and $50,000 in April 1998; (2) depreciation charged at $6,000 per quarter through April 1997, at $7,000 through April 1998, and at $8,000 through July 1998, and (3) dividends paid at $15,000 per quarter through October 1997 and at $18,000 per quarter through July 1998.

Comment on the various alternative ways this analysis can be developed, and state your reasons for your choices. What are your key findings?

ZYX COMPANY
Balance Sheets by Fiscal Quarters
July 31, 1996 to July 31, 1998
($ thousands)

	1996		1997				1998		
	7-31	10-31	1-31	4-30	7-31	10-31	1-31	4-30	7-31
Assets									
Cash	$ 21	$ 30	$ 74	$ 91	$ 7	$ 28	$ 90	$103	$ 16
Accounts receivable	114	247	319	128	141	293	388	151	103
Inventories	231	417	315	131	271	467	351	98	310
Net plant and equipment	239	233	227	269	262	255	248	291	283
Other assets	15	16	16	15	15	14	18	18	17
Total assets	$620	$943	$951	$634	$696	$1,057	$1,095	$661	$729
Liabilities and net worth									
Accounts payable	*$ 68*	*$297*	*$121*	*$103*	*$ 79*	*$ 314*	*$ 188*	*$ 97*	*$ 84*
Notes payable . . .	35	126	294	—	63	178	342	—	80
Mortgage payable	80	80	75	75	70	70	65	65	60
Preferred stock . .	100	100	100	100	100	100	100	100	100
Common stock . .	100	100	100	100	125	125	125	125	125
Retained earnings	237	240	261	256	259	270	275	274	280
Total liabilities and net worth	$620	$943	$951	$634	$696	$1,057	$1,095	$661	$729

Assessment of Business Performance

When we wish to assess the performance of a business, we are looking for ways to measure the financial and economic consequences of past management decisions that shaped investments, operations, and financing over time. The important questions to be answered are whether resources were used effectively, whether the profitability of the business met expectations, and whether financing choices were made prudently. Shareholder value creation ultimately requires positive results in all these areas—bringing about favorable cash flow patterns.

As we'll see, there are wide choices among many individual ratios and measures, some purely financial, some economic, and no one ratio or measure can be considered predominant. In this chapter, we'll discuss the analysis of business performance based largely on published financial statements. These represent the most common data source available for the purpose, even though they are not designed to reflect economic results and conditions. We'll also discuss the more important measures that help assess economic performance aspects. Our focus will be on key relationships and indicators that allow the analyst to assess past performance and also to project assumed future results (as discussed in Chapter 4). We'll point out their meaning as well as the limitations inherent in them.

RATIO ANALYSIS AND PERFORMANCE

Because there are so many tools for doing performance assessment, we must remember that different techniques address measurement in very specific and often narrowly defined ways. One can be tempted to "run all the numbers," particularly given the speed and ease of computer spreadsheets. Yet normally, only a few selected relationships will yield the information the analyst really needs for useful insights and decision support. By definition, a ratio can relate any magnitude to any other—the choices are limited only by the imagination. To be useful, both the meaning and the limitations of the ratio chosen have to be understood. Before beginning any task, therefore, the analyst must define the following elements:

- The viewpoint taken.
- The objectives of the analysis.
- The potential standards of comparison.

Any particular ratio is useful only in relation to the viewpoint taken and the specific objectives of the analysis. When there is such a match, the ratio can become a standard for comparison. Moreover, ratios are not absolute criteria: They serve best when used in selected combinations to point out changes in financial conditions or operating performance over several periods, and help illustrate the trends and patterns of such changes, which, in turn, may indicate to the analyst the risks and opportunities for the business under review.

A further caution: Performance assessment via financial statement analysis is based on past data and conditions from which it may be difficult to extrapolate future expectations. Yet, decisions made as a result of such performance assessment can affect only the future—the past is gone, or sunk, as an economist likes to call it.

No attempt to assess business performance can provide firm answers. Any insights gained will be relative, because business and operating conditions vary so much from company to company and industry to industry. Comparisons and standards based on past performance are especially difficult in large, multibusiness companies and conglomerates, where specific information by individual line of business is normally limited. Accounting adjustments of various types present further complications. To deal with all of these aspects in detail is far beyond the scope of this book, although we'll point out the key items, but the reader should be aware of them and always be cautious in using financial data.

To provide a coherent structure for the many ratios and measures involved, the discussion will be built around three major viewpoints we can take in financial performance analysis. While there are many different individuals and groups interested in the success or failure of a given business, the most important are:

- Owners (investors).
- Managers.
- Lenders and creditors.

Closest to the business from a day-to-day standpoint, but also responsible for its long-range performance, is the management of the organization, whether its members are professional managers or owner/managers. Managers are responsible and accountable for operating efficiency, current and long-term profitability, and for the effective deployment of capital, human effort, and other resources, all within the context of sound business strategies.

Next are the various owners of the business, who are especially interested in the current and long-term profitability of their equity investment. They usually expect growing earnings, cash flows, and dividends, which in combination will bring about growth in the economic value of their "stake."

Finally, there are the providers of "other people's money," lenders and creditors who extend funds to the business for various lengths of time. They are mainly concerned about the reliability of the interest payments due them, about the ability of the business to repay the principal, and about the availability of specific residual asset values that will give them a margin of protection against their risk.

Other groups such as employees, government, and society have, of course, specific objectives of their own—the business' ability to pay wages, the stability of employment, the reliability of tax payments, and the financial wherewithal to meet various social and environmental obligations, for instance. Financial performance indicators are useful to these groups in combination with a variety of other data.

The principal areas of financial performance of interest to management, owners, and lenders are shown in Figure 3–1, along with the most common ratios and measures relevant to these areas. We'll follow the sequence shown in the table and discuss each subgrouping within the three broad viewpoints. Later, we'll relate the key measures to each other in a systems context.

MANAGEMENT'S POINT OF VIEW

Management has a dual interest in the analysis of financial performance: To assess the efficiency and profitability of operations, and to judge how effectively the resources of the business were used. Judging operations is largely done with an analysis of the operating (income) statement, while resource effectiveness is usually measured by reviewing both the balance sheet and the income statement. In order to make economic judgments, however, it's often necessary to modify the available financial data to reflect current economic values and conditions.

For purposes of illustration, we'll again use appropriate information from the sample statements of TRW Inc. for 1995 and 1994, which were reproduced in Chapter 1. The same statements are shown as Figures 3–2 and 3–3 on pages 75 and 76, and we'll use this information for the remainder of this chapter. For added convenience, we've also expressed the various items on the operating statement as a percent of sales, a common way of highlighting the relative magnitude of the various categories in relation to the base of net sales.

In addition, Figure 3–6 at the end of this chapter contains several selections from the "Notes to Financial Statements," as published in TRW's 1995 annual report. They are provided as explanatory background for the company's key accounting policies, recent restructuring, income tax provisions, deferred income taxes, postretirement benefits accounting change, debt, and industry segments. Because these items affect the development of many of the ratios in this chapter, the notes will help to understand some of the choices an analyst must make in using financial statement information.

Operational Analysis

An initial assessment of the operational effectiveness for the business as a whole or any of its subdivisions is generally performed through a "common numbers" or percentage analysis of the operating statement. Individual costs and expense

FIGURE 3–1

Performance Measures by Area and Viewpoint

Management	Owners	Lenders
Operational Analysis	**Profitability**	**Liquidity**
Gross margin	Return on total net worth	Current ratio
Profit margin	Return on common	Acid test
Operating expense	equity	Quick sale value
analysis	Earnings per share	Cash flow patterns
Contribution analysis	Cash flow per share	
Operating leverage	Share price appreciation	
Comparative analysis	Total shareholder return	
	Shareholder value	
	analysis	
Resource Management	**Disposition of Earnings**	**Financial Leverage**
Asset turnover	Dividends per share	Debt to assets
Working capital	Dividend yield	Debt to capitalization
management	Payout/retention of	Debt to equity
■ Inventory turnover	earnings	Risk/reward trade-off
■ Accounts receivable	Dividend coverage	
patterns	Dividends to assets	
■ Accounts payable		
patterns		
Human resource		
effectiveness		
Profitability	**Market Indicators**	**Debt Service**
Return on assets (total or	Cash flow analysis	Interest coverage
net)	Price/earnings ratio	Burden coverage
Return before interest	Cash flow multiples	Cash flow analysis
and taxes	Market to book value	
Return on current value	Relative price	
basis	movements	
Investment project	Value of the Firm	
economics		
Cash flow return on		
investment		
Free cash flow		

items are normally related to net sales, that is, gross sales revenues adjusted for any returns and allowances. The common base of net sales permits a ready comparison of the key costs and expenses from period to period, over longer stretches of time, and against competitors and industry databases.

Expense to sales ratios are used both to judge the relative magnitude of selected key elements and to determine any trends toward improving or declining performance. However, we must keep in mind the type of industry involved and

FIGURE 3–2

TRW INC. AND SUBSIDIARIES
Consolidated Balance Sheets at December 31
($ millions)

	1995	1994
Assets		
Current Assets:		
Cash and cash equivalents	$ 59	$ 109
Accounts receivable	1,428	1,338
Inventories	534	470
Prepaid expenses	78	59
Deferred income taxes	235	239
Total current assets	2,336	2,215
Property, plant, and equipment at cost	5,866	5,556
Less: Allowances for depreciation and amortization	3,303	3,067
Total property, plant, and equipment—net	2,563	2,489
Intangible assets:		
Intangibles arising from acquisitions	483	477
Capitalized data files and other	488	441
Other	92	69
Total intangible assets	1,063	987
Less: Accumulated amortization	405	331
Total intangible assets—net	658	656
Other assets	333	276
Total assets	$5,890	$5,636
Liabilities and Shareholders' Investment		
Current liabilities:		
Short-term debt	$ 133	$ 122
Accrued compensation	385	346
Trade accounts payable	807	737
Other accruals	545	541
Dividends payable	36	33
Income taxes	26	50
Current portion of long-term debt	80	157
Total current liabilities	2,012	1,986
Long-term liabilities	779	796
Long-term debt	541	694
Deferred income taxes	313	269
Minority interests in subsidiaries	73	69
Shareholders' investment:		
Serial preference stock II	1	1
Common stock	40	40
Other capital	398	354
Retained earnings	1,688	1,383
Cumulative translation adjustments	76	66
Treasury shares—cost in excess of par	(31)	(22)
Total shareholders' investment	2,172	1,822
Total liabilities and shareholders' investment	$5,890	$5,636

Source: Adapted from 1995 TRW Inc. annual report.

FIGURE 3–3

TRW INC. AND SUBSIDIARIES
Statement of Earnings
For the Years Ended December 31, 1995 and 1994
($ millions)

	1995	Percent of Sales	1994	Percent of Sales
Sales	$10,172	100.0%	$9,087	100.0%
Cost of sales	8,190	80.5	7,270	80.0
Gross profit	1,982	19.5%	1,817	20.0%
Administrative and selling expenses	747	7.3	756	8.3
Research and development expenses	422	4.2	412	4.5
Interest expense	95	0.9	105	1.2
Other expenses (income) net	10	.1	9	.1
Total expenses	1,274	12.5%	1,282	14.1%
Earnings (loss) before income taxes	708	7.0	535	5.9
Income taxes	262	2.6	202	2.2
Net earnings	$ 446	4.4%	$ 333	3.7%
Per share of common stock:				
Average number of shares outstanding (millions)	67.4		66.4	
Fully diluted earnings	$ 6.62		$ 5.01	
Primary earnings (as above)	6.62		5.02	
Dividends paid	2.05		1.94	
Other Data ($ millions):				
Depreciation of property, plant, and equipment................	$ 433		$ 402	
Amortization of intangibles, other assets	77		74	
Capital expenditures	485		506	
Dividends paid	134		126	

Source: Adapted from 1995 TRW Inc. annual report.

its particular characteristics, as well as the individual trends and special conditions of the company being studied. For example, the gross margin of a jewelry store with slow turnover of merchandise and high markups will be far greater (50 percent is not uncommon) than that of a supermarket, which depends for its success on low margins and high volume (gross margins of 10 to 15 percent are typical). In fact, comparing a particular company's ratios to those of similar companies in its industry over a number of time periods will usually provide the best clues as to whether the company's performance is improving or worsening.

   Many published annual overviews of company and industry performance use such ranking approaches, such as the annual Fortune 500 listings. Individual companies usually develop their own comparisons with the performance of comparable units within the organization or with relevant competitors on the outside. It is also often useful to depict graphically a series of performance data over time, a process now easily achieved with the ubiquitous availability of computer spreadsheets and databases.

Gross Margin and Cost of Goods Sold Analysis

One of the most common ratios in operational analysis is the calculation of cost of goods sold (cost of sales) as a percentage of net sales. This ratio indicates the magnitude of the cost of goods purchased or manufactured, or the cost of services provided, in relation to the gross margin (gross profit) left over for operating expenses and profit.

   The ratios calculated from our TRW sample statements appear as follows:

$$\text{Cost of goods sold} = \frac{\$8,190}{\$10,172} = 80.5\% \ (1994:\ 80.0\%)$$

$$\text{Gross margin} \quad = \frac{\$1,982}{\$10,172} = 19.5\% \ (1994:\ 20.0\%)$$

The cost of goods sold of 80.5 percent and the gross margin of 19.5 percent indicate the margin of "raw profit" from operations. Remember that gross margin reflects the relationship of prices, volume, and costs. A change in gross margin can result from a combination of changes in:

■ The selling price of the product.

■ The level of manufacturing costs for the product.

■ Any variations in the product mix of the business.

   In a trading or service organization, gross margin can be affected by a combination of changes in:

■ The price charged for the products or services provided.

■ The prices paid for merchandise purchased on the outside.

■ The cost of services from internal or external sources.

■ Any variations in the product/service mix of the business.

The volume of operations can also have a significant effect if, for example, a manufacturing company has high fixed costs (see Chapter 5 for a discussion of operating leverage), or a small trading company has less buying power and economies of scale than a large competitor.

   In the case of TRW, the cost of goods sold and the gross margin shown in the annual report represented a consolidation of the three major product lines, that is, the income statement combined space and defense, automotive, and information systems. We note a margin shrinkage of one half of a percentage point from the prior year, which is typical of the competitive pressures encountered by industry in general during the 90s. For a more detailed insight, it would be desirable to calculate the gross margins for the individual business areas, if this information were available.

In its annual report, TRW provided a selective breakdown, by major product line, of sales, operating profit, identifiable assets, depreciation and amortization, and capital expenditures, which allows the analyst to make some overall comparisons. (See p. 127.) These data would have to be supplemented by additional internal information, however, to be able to perform a detailed ratio analysis—something routinely done within the company.

There are particular complications in the analysis of manufacturing companies. The nature of manufacturing cost accounting systems governs the specific costing of products for inventory and for current sale. Significant differences can exist between the apparent cost performance of companies using standard full cost systems (all costs, fixed and variable, are allocated to each unit of production based on an estimate of normal cost levels) and those using direct costing (fixed manufacturing costs are not allocated to individual products but charged as a block against operations). The charges against a particular period of operations can be affected to some degree by the choice of accounting methods. Increasingly, however, companies are turning to various forms of activity-based accounting for internal purposes, which provides a more precise basis for judging the real costs of products and services. Inflation, which affects the prices of both cost inputs and goods or services sold, or currency fluctuations in the case of international businesses, further distort the picture. We'll take up some of these issues later in this chapter.

Any major change in a company's cost of goods sold or gross margin over a relevant period of time would call for further analysis to identify the cause. The relevance of the time period depends on the nature of the business. For example, as we demonstrated in Chapter 2, many businesses have normal seasonal fluctuations, while others are affected by longer-term business cycles. Thus, the ratio serves as a signal rather than an absolute measure, as is the case with most of the measures discussed.

Profit Margin

The relationship of reported net profit after taxes (net income) to sales indicates management's ability to operate the business with sufficient success not only to recover the cost of the merchandise or services, the expenses of operating the business (including depreciation), and the cost of borrowed funds, but also to leave a margin of reasonable compensation to the owners for putting their capital at risk. The ratio of net profit (income) to sales (total revenue) essentially expresses the overall cost/price effectiveness of the operation. As we'll demonstrate later, however, a more significant ratio for this purpose is the relationship of profit to the amount of capital employed in generating it.

At this point, we should note that earnings can be significantly affected by mandated changes in accounting methods issued from time to time by FASB.

There may be sizable adjustments, as occurred in the early 90s, when future employee medical benefits had to be recognized as a liability with an offsetting charge to earnings. For purposes of ratio analysis and for period-to-period comparisons, extraordinary adjustments should be excluded, along with any other extraordinary gains or losses a company might encounter in a particular period. In most cases, significant items of this kind are highlighted in the company's financial statements, allowing the analyst to choose whether to include them in the analysis.

The calculation of the net profit (net earnings) ratio is simple, as the figures from our TRW example show:

$$\text{Profit margin} = \frac{\$446}{\$10,172} = 4.4\% \ (1994: 3.7\%)$$

Note the increase of three quarters of a percentage point from 1994, which is the result of both record volume and aggressive cost containment.

A variation of this ratio uses net profit *before* interest and taxes. This figure represents the operating profit before any compensation is paid to debt holders. It's also the profit before the calculation of federal and state income taxes, which are often based on modified sets of deductible expenses and accounting write-offs. The ratio represents a somewhat purer view of operating effectiveness, undistorted by financing patterns and tax calculations. Referred to as earnings before interest and taxes (EBIT), this pretax, pre-interest income ratio for TRW appears as follows:

$$\text{EBIT} = \frac{\$708 + \$95}{\$10,172} = 7.9\% \ (1994: 7.0\%)$$

A sound argument can be made, however, for considering income taxes as an ongoing expense of being in business. The formula can therefore be modified by using profit *before* interest but *after* taxes, which requires a tax adjustment for the interest amount. Again, the intent is to focus on operating efficiency by leaving out any compensation to the various holders of capital.

Using the TRW figures, this modified result appears as follows:

$$\text{EBIAT} = \frac{\$446 + (1 - .37)\ 95}{\$10,172} = 5.0\% \ (1994: 4.4\%)$$

For convenience in removing the effect of interest from aftertax profit, we usually assume that the interest paid during the period was fully tax deductible. Thus, we simply add back to the stated profit figure the aftertax cost of interest. We obtain the latter by multiplying pretax interest by a factor of "one minus the tax rate," employing either the effective (average) tax rate paid on earnings (37.0 percent in TRW's case) or, ideally, the marginal (highest bracket) corporate tax rate for the firm in question.

The choice of tax rates depends on the complexity of the company's taxation pattern. TRW operates worldwide, and therefore is subject to a variety of

taxes which are combined in the provision for income taxes on the income statement. It's most straightforward to rely on the effective overall rate paid, which
for TRW approximated the marginal U.S. corporate tax rate prevailing in 1995.
Chapter 7 contains a specific discussion of the cost of debt and the nature of the
necessary tax adjustments to be made to interest cost.

As a general rule, when there are unusual or nonrecurring income and expense elements not directly related to ongoing operations, the analyst should adjust the ratios by excluding these items when measuring operating effectiveness.
The adjustment should be done on the same basis as we demonstrated for interest,
that is, the tax effect of revenue or expense items must be calculated if aftertax
comparisons are desired.

Operating Expense Analysis

Various expense categories are routinely related to net sales. These comparisons
include such items as administrative expense, selling and promotional expenses,
and many others typical of particular businesses and industries.

The general formula used to calculate this expense ratio is:

$$\text{Expense ratio} = \frac{\text{Various expense items}}{\text{Net sales}} = \text{Percent}$$

There are relatively few expense categories shown in the abbreviated operating statement of TRW, but the ratio to sales was calculated for each item in
Figure 3–3. In practice, a much finer breakdown is generally desirable. Many
trade associations collect extensive financial data from their members and com-
pile published statistics on expense ratios, as well as on most of the other ratios
discussed in this chapter. These publications help provide standards of comparison and the basis for trend analysis. References to such information sources are
listed at the end of the chapter and also in Appendix II.

To make such comparisons reasonable, however, businesses should be
carefully categorized within an industry by size and other characteristics, to reduce the degree of error introduced by large-scale averaging. Moreover, companies with complex product or service offerings, or companies with many
international operations, may be hard to categorize. Yet, even without specific
comparative data available, a skilled analyst will scan the revenue and expense
categories on an income statement as a matter of course over a number of time
periods to see if any of them seem out of line or are trending adversely within the
particular company's experience.

Contribution Analysis

This type of analysis has been used mainly for internal management, although
it is increasingly applied in broader financial analysis. It involves relating net
sales to the contribution margin of individual product groups or of the total business. Such calculations require a very selective analysis or estimate of the fixed
and variable costs and expenses of the business, and take into account the effect
of operating leverage (see Chapter 5). Only directly variable costs are usually

subtracted from net sales to show the contribution of operations toward fixed costs and profits for the period.

The contribution margin is calculated as follows:

$$\text{Contribution margin} = \frac{\text{Net sales} - \text{Direct costs (variable costs)}}{\text{Net sales}} = \text{Percent}$$

Significant differences can exist in the contribution margins of different industries, due to varying needs for capital investment and the resultant cost-volume conditions. Even within a particular company, various lines of products or services may contribute quite differently to fixed costs and profits.

As we mentioned before, a great deal of effort has been expended in recent years on so-called activity-based accounting analysis. This approach can be used for an assessment of the relative economic contribution of various parts of a company, thereby going beyond the limitations of existing cost accounting systems. During this process, a specific financial/economic allocation is made of all resources, direct or indirect, internal or external, which support a particular activity, product line, operation, or line of business. The result serves as the basis for periodic strategic assessment of the current and prospective relative economic contribution of the area under study. The insights gained often differ from a straight accounting analysis, because the activity-based process is much more precise in defining and allocating relative effort, cost, and support capital required. The techniques involved go beyond the scope of this book, and the reader is directed to the references at the end of the chapter.

Contribution margins as derived from financial statements are useful as a broad, if limited, tool in judging the risk characteristics of a business. The measure suggests the amount of leeway management enjoys in pricing its products and services, and the scope of its ability to control costs and expenses under different economic conditions. Analysis of break-even conditions and pricing strategies as they relate to volume achieved become important in this context. Chapter 5 contains a more extensive discussion of these points.

Resource Management

Here we are interested in judging the effectiveness with which management has employed the assets entrusted to it by the owners of the business. When examining a balance sheet, an analyst will draw company-specific conclusions about the size, nature, and value of the assets listed, looking at relative proportions, and judging whether the company has a viable asset base. Clues such as high accumulated depreciation relative to recorded property, plant, and equipment may suggest that aging facilities are in need of upgrading. Similarly, a significant jump in cash balances may suggest lagging new investment and an accumulation of excess funds. Surges in working capital may signal problems with inventory management or customer credit policies.

In a more overall sense, a few ratios are used to judge broad trends in resource utilization. Such ratios essentially involve turnover relationships and express, in various forms, the relative amount of capital used to support the volume of business transacted.

Asset Turnover

The most commonly used ratios relate net sales to gross assets, or net sales to net assets. The measure indicates the size of the recorded asset commitment required to support a particular level of sales or, conversely, the sales dollars generated by each dollar of assets.

    While simple to calculate, overall asset turnover is a crude measure at best, because the balance sheets of most well-established companies list a whole variety of assets recorded at widely differing cost levels of past periods. These stated values often have little relation to current economic values, and the distortions grow with time, with any significant change in the level of inflation, or with the appreciation of assets such as real estate. Such discrepancies in values can attract corporate raiders intent on realizing true economic values through the breakup and selective disposal of the company, as we'll discuss in Chapter 9.

    Another distortion is caused by a company's mix of product lines. Most manufacturing activities tend to be asset-intensive, while others (like services or wholesaling) need relatively fewer assets to support the volume of revenues generated. Again, wherever possible, a breakdown of total financial data into major product lines should be attempted when a company has widely different businesses.

    Basically, the turnover ratio serves as one of several clues that, in combination, can indicate favorable or unfavorable performance. If gross assets are used for the purpose, the calculation for TRW's turnover ratios appears as follows:

$$\text{Sales to assets: } \frac{\text{Net sales}}{\text{Gross assets}} = \frac{\$10,172}{\$5,890} = 1.73 \ (1994: 1.61)$$

or

$$\text{Assets to sales: } \frac{\text{Gross assets}}{\text{Net sales}} = \frac{\$5,890}{\$10,172} = 0.58 \ (1994: 0.62)$$

If net assets (total assets less current liabilities, representing the capitalization of the business) are used, the calculations are either:

$$\text{Sales to net assets: } \frac{\text{Net sales}}{\text{Net assets}} = \frac{\$10,172}{\$5,890 - \$2,012} = 2.62 \ (1994: 2.49)$$

or

$$\text{Net assets to sales: } \frac{\text{Net assets}}{\text{Net sales}} = \frac{\$3,878}{\$10,172} = 0.38 \ (1994: 0.40)$$

    The difference between the two sets of calculations lies in the choice of the asset total, that is, whether to use gross assets or net assets. Using net assets eliminates current liabilities from the ratio. Here the assumption is that current liabilities, which are mostly operational (accounts payable, current taxes due, current repayments of short-term debt, and accrued wages and other obligations), are available to the business as a matter of course. Therefore, the amount of assets employed in the business is effectively reduced by these ongoing operational credit relationships. This concept is especially important for trading firms, where the size of accounts payable owed suppliers is quite significant in the total balance sheet.

Working Capital Management

Among the assets of a company, the key working capital accounts, inventories and accounts receivable, are usually given special attention. The ratios used to analyze them attempt to express the relative effectiveness with which inventories and receivables are managed. They aid the analyst in detecting signs of deterioration in value, or excessive accumulation of inventories and receivables. The amounts as stated on the balance sheet are generally related to the single best indicator of activity levels, such as sales or cost of sales (cost of goods sold), on the assumption that a reasonably close relationship exists between assets and the indicator.

Inventory levels cannot be judged precisely, short of an actual count, verification, and appraisal of current value. Because an outside analyst can rarely do this, the next best step is to relate the recorded inventory value to net sales or to cost of goods sold, to see whether there is a shift in this relationship over a period of time. Normally *average* inventories are used to make this calculation (the average of beginning and ending inventories). At times, it may be desirable to use only ending inventories, especially in the case of rapidly growing firms where inventories are being built up to support steeply rising sales.

Furthermore, it's necessary to observe closely the method of inventory costing employed by the company—such as last-in, first-out (LIFO), first-in, first-out (FIFO), average costing, etc.—and any changes made during the time span covered by the analysis, as these can significantly affect the amounts recorded on the balance sheet. (We'll discuss inventory costing and other key accounting issues later on.)

While the simple relationship of sales and inventories will often suffice as a broad measure of performance, it's usually more precise to relate inventories to the cost of goods sold, because only then will both elements of the ratio be stated on a comparable cost basis. Using net sales causes a distortion, because recorded sales include a profit markup that is not included in the stated cost of the inventories on the balance sheet.

The difference in the two methods of calculating the size of inventory relative to sales or cost of sales is reflected in the equations below:

$$\text{Inventory to sales:} \quad \frac{\text{Average inventory}}{\text{Net sales}} = \frac{.5(\$534 + \$470)}{\$10,172} = 4.9\% \ (1994 \text{: } 4.8\%)$$

or

$$\text{Inventory to cost of sales:} \quad \frac{\text{Average inventory}}{\text{Cost of sales}} = \frac{\$502}{\$8,190} = 6.1\% \ (1994 \text{: } 6.1\%)$$

In the sample calculations, we've used total TRW sales and total cost of goods and services. The fact that TRW has three rather different major businesses and numerous product lines again suggests that a more refined analysis is desirable. TRW's inventories essentially relate to manufactured products of the automotive (64 percent of sales) and space and defense (30 percent of sales) businesses. In contrast, the information systems and services business (6 percent of sales) provides credit data services to its customers.

Given the different nature of the three businesses, it would be useful to develop separate ratios for each, if detailed inventory information were available to the outsider. As we'll see later, the line of business breakdown generally presented in annual reports does not provide sufficient detail for this insight.

When dealing with any manufacturing company, we must also be particularly aware of the problem of accounting measurements—so often encountered when using other analytical methods—because the stated value of inventories can be seriously affected by the specific cost accounting system employed.

In assessing the effectiveness of a company's inventory management, it's more common to use the number of times inventory has turned over during the period of analysis.

The TRW inventory turnover figures appear as follows:

$$\text{Inventory turnover: } \frac{\text{Net sales}}{\text{Average inventory}} = \frac{\$10,172}{\$502}$$
$$\text{(Sales)}$$
$$= 20.3 \text{ times (1994: 20.6 times)}$$

or

$$\text{Inventory turnover: } \frac{\text{Cost of sales}}{\text{Average inventory}} = \frac{\$8,190}{\$502}$$
$$\text{(Cost of sales)}$$
$$= 16.3 \text{ times (1994: 16.5 times)}$$

These calculations reflect the frequency with which the inventory was turned over during the operating period. In TRW's case, turnover remained relatively high due to a combination of inventory management and change in the mix of products. Generally speaking, the higher the turnover number the better, because low inventories often suggest a minimal risk of unsalable goods and indicate efficient use of capital.

However, inventory turnover figures which are well above prevailing industry practice may signal the potential for inventory shortages, resultant poor customer service, and thus the risk of suffering a competitive disadvantage. The final judgment about what a desirable turnover goal should be depends on the specific circumstances.

The analysis of accounts receivable again is based on net sales. Here, the question is whether accounts receivable outstanding at the end of the period closely approximate the amount of credit sales we would expect to remain uncollected under prevailing credit terms. For example, a business selling under terms of net/30 would normally expect an accounts receivable balance approximating the recorded sales of the prior month. If 40 or 50 days' sales were reflected on its balance sheet, this could mean that some customers had difficulty paying or were abusing their credit privileges, or that some sales had to be made on extended terms.

An exact analysis of accounts receivable can only be made by examining the aging of the individual accounts recorded on the company's books. Aging involves classifying accounts receivable into brackets of days outstanding, 10 days, 20 days, 30 days, 40 days, and so on, and relating this pattern to the credit terms applicable in the business. Because this type of analysis requires access to detailed inside information about individual customer accounts, financial analysts assessing the business from the outside must be satisfied with the relatively crude overall approach of restating accounts receivable outstanding in terms of the number of days' sales they represent.

This is done in the following two steps, using TRW's figures:

$$(1) \text{ Sales per day: } \frac{\text{Net sales}}{\text{Days in the year}} = \frac{\$10,172}{360} = \$28.26/\text{day} \quad (1994: \$25.24/\text{day})$$

and

$$(2) \text{ Days outstanding: } \frac{\text{Accounts receivable}}{\text{Sales per day}} = \frac{\$1,428}{\$28.26}$$
$$= 50.5 \text{ days} \quad (1994: 53.0 \text{ days})$$

TRW is showing a significant improvement in the management of its receivables.

A complication arises when a company's sales are normally made to different types of customers under varying terms, or when sales are made partly for cash and partly on account. If at all possible, cash and credit sales should be separated. If no detailed information is available on this aspect and on the terms of sale used, the rough average calculated above must suffice to provide a broad indication of trends.

A similar process can be used to judge a company's performance regarding the management of accounts payable. The analysis is a little more complicated, because accounts payable should be specifically related to the purchases made during the operating period. Normally purchase information is not readily available to the outside analyst, except in the case of trading companies, where the amount of purchases can be readily deduced by adding the change from beginning to ending inventories to the cost of goods sold for the period. In a manufacturing company, purchases of goods and services are buried in the cost-of-goods-sold account and in the inventories at the end of the operating period. We can make a crude approximation in such cases by relating accounts payable to the average daily use of raw materials, if this expense element can be identified from the available information.

In most cases, we can follow the approach used for analyzing accounts receivable, if it's possible to approximate the average daily purchases for the period. The number of days of accounts payable is then directly related to the normal credit terms under which the company makes purchases, and serious deviations from that norm can be spotted.

Optimal management of accounts payable involves remitting payment within the stated terms, but not sooner—yet taking discounts whenever offered for early payment, such as 2 percent if paid in 10 days versus remitting the full amount due in 30 days. Credit rating agencies can be a source of information to the analyst because they will express an opinion on the timeliness with which a company is meeting its credit obligations, including accounts payable.

The ultimate issue in interpreting working capital conditions is the flow of cash through the business, as we discussed in detail in Chapter 2. Over time, all working capital elements are converted into cash, and the analyst must assess the nature and quality of the company's *cash conversion* cycle (CCC). Excessive lags in receivables and payables, and a steady buildup in inventories, for example, can significantly affect the normal cash conversion patterns and lead to distortions in the company's financial system performance.

Human resource effectiveness has been gaining increased attention in recent years. Ratios used in measuring this complex area go beyond purely financial relationships, and are based on carefully developed statistics on output data, such as various productivity indicators. They also extend to managing human resources, such as costs of employment, training, and development, and the whole complex job of compensation and benefits administration. Examples of broad measures are units of output per employee, dollars of investment per employee, costs of hiring and training per employee, benefits costs per employee, etc.

Profitability

Here the issue is the effectiveness with which management has employed both the total assets and the net assets as recorded on the balance sheet. This is judged by relating net profit, defined in a variety of ways, to the assets utilized in generating the profit. The relationship is used quite commonly, although the nature and timing of the stated values on the balance sheet and the accounting aspects of recorded profit will again tend to distort the results. As we'll see later, the approach can be refined to reflect the cash flow concepts underlying shareholder value creation.

Return on Assets (ROA or RONA)
The easiest form of profitability analysis is to relate reported net profit (net income) to the total assets on the balance sheet. Net assets (total assets less current liabilities) may also be used, with the argument (already mentioned earlier) that current operating liabilities are available essentially without cost to support a portion of the current assets. Net assets are also called the *capitalization* of the company, or *invested capital*, representing the portion of the total assets supported by equity and long-term debt. Whether total or net assets are employed, it's also appropriate to use *average* assets for the period, instead of ending balances. Using average assets allows for changes due to growth, decline, or other significant influences on the business.

The calculations for both forms of return on assets for TRW, in this case using ending balances, appear as follows:

$$\text{Return on total assets: } \frac{\text{Net profit}}{\text{Assets}} = \frac{\$446}{\$5,890} = 7.6\% \text{ (1994: 5.9\%)}$$

or

$$\text{Return on net assets: } \frac{\text{Net profit}}{\text{Net assets (capitalization)}} = \frac{\$446}{\$5,890 - \$2,012}$$
$$= 11.5\% \text{ (1994: 9.1\%)}$$

While either ratio is an indicator of overall profitability, the results can be seriously distorted by nonrecurring gains and losses during the period, changes in the company's capital structure (the relative proportions of interest-bearing long-term debt and owners' equity), significant restructuring and acquisitions, and changes in the federal income tax regulations applicable for the period analyzed. It's usually desirable to make further adjustments if some of these conditions prevail.

Return on Assets before Interest and Taxes

As we stated before, net profit (net income or net earnings) is the final operating result after interest and taxes have been deducted. It's therefore affected by the proportion of debt contained in the capital structure through the resultant interest charges deducted from profit before taxes. A somewhat more meaningful result can be obtained when we eliminate both interest and taxes from the profit figure and use EBIT (earnings before interest and taxes), which was demonstrated earlier. Moreover, it'll again be generally useful to eliminate any significant unusual or nonrecurring income and expense items.

The revised return ratio expresses the gross earnings power of the capital employed in the business, independent of the pattern of financing that provided the capital, and independent of changes in the tax laws.

The calculation of return on assets before interest and taxes, based on average assets, is as follows for TRW:

Return on average total assets before interest and taxes:

$$\frac{\text{Net profit before interest and taxes (EBIT)}}{\text{Average assets}} = \frac{\$803}{\$5,763} = 13.9\% \text{ (1994: 11.7\%)}$$

or

Return on average net assets before interest and taxes:

$$\frac{\text{Net profit before interest and taxes (EBIT)}}{\text{Average net assets (capitalization)}} = \frac{\$803}{\$3,764} = 21.3\% \text{ (1994: 17.4\%)}$$

If we accept the argument that income taxes are a normal part of doing business, this result can be modified by using net profit before interest but after taxes. We can again employ the simple adjustment shown earlier to add back to net profit the aftertax cost of interest and the aftertax effect of any nonrecurring income and expense items.

When there is reason to believe that income taxes paid were modified for any reason and the effective tax rate does not reflect normal conditions, the marginal income tax rate should be used to calculate the net effect of interest and other items added back by determining the earnings before interest, after taxes (EBIAT).

The calculations for TRW are as follows:

Return on average total assets before interest, after taxes:

$$\frac{\text{Net profit after taxes, before interest}}{\text{Average assets}} = \frac{\$510}{\$5,763} = 8.8\% \ (1994: 7.3\%)$$

or

Return on average net assets before interest, after taxes:

$$\frac{\text{Net profit* after taxes, before interest}}{\text{Average net assets (capitalization)}} = \frac{\$510}{\$3,764} = 13.5\% \ (1994: 11.1\%)$$

Note that the results of the last two sets of more refined calculations show a significant improvement in TRW's overall effectiveness of asset utilization, as did the first calculation, which was based on net profit alone. Again, it would be useful to break down these results into major product lines, but in most cases there's not enough information to make all the adjustments from published data.

Another refinement used at times is the relationship of profit, defined in the various ways we have described, to the net assets of the business restated on a *current value* basis. This requires a series of very specific assumptions about the true economic value of various assets or business segments of a company, and it is employed particularly by analysts developing a case for the takeover of a company that may be underperforming on this basis. At this writing, the Financial Accounting Standards Board is engaged in developing new rules that are designed to take some changes in value into account.

As we'll discuss in Chapter 6, profitability also depends on the economic analysis and successful implementation of new *investment projects*. Here it's critical to define and develop the relevant cash flow changes brought about by the investment decision, and to judge the results through an economic appraisal process based on discounted cash flow techniques. In recent years, this methodology has been expanded to measure the *cash flow return on investment* on both existing and new investments, in effect treating the company as a whole or its major parts as if they were a series of investment projects. This calls for a number of specialized techniques, and we will return to this subject as we discuss valuation concepts in Chapter 9.

The concept of *free cash flow* will also be discussed in Chapter 9. It is the basis for cash flow valuation techniques that help establish the value of a company

---

*before cumulative effect of accounting changes.

or its parts. In its simplest form, free cash flow is the net amount of (1) reported profit, adjusted for depreciation, depletion, and other noncash accounting elements, less (2) new investment in facilities, and plus or minus (3) changes in working capital. Free cash flow comes closest to a cash-in, cash-out concept of performance, and is used in valuing current and prospective cash flow as the driver of a company's value.

In summary, the various ratios available for judging a business from management's point of view deal with the effectiveness of operations, the effectiveness of capital deployment, and the profitability achieved on the assets deployed. These measures are all affected to some degree by uncertainties involving accounting and valuation methods, but together they can provide reasonable clues to a firm's performance, and also suggest areas for further analysis.

OWNERS' POINT OF VIEW

We now turn to the second of the three viewpoints relevant in analyzing performance, that of the owners of a business. These are the investors to whom management is responsible and accountable. So far, we have not mentioned owners directly, even though it should be quite clear that the management of a business must be fully cognizant of, and responsive to, the owners' viewpoint and expectations in the timing, execution, and appraisal of the results of operations. This is the basis for shareholder value creation, as we've said before. Similarly, management must be alert to the lenders' viewpoint and criteria.

The key interest of the owners of a business, the shareholders in the case of a corporation, is profitability. In this context, profitability means the returns achieved, through the efforts of management, on the funds invested by the owners. The owners are also interested in the disposition of earnings which belong to them, that is, how much is reinvested in the business versus how much is paid out to them as dividends, or, in some cases, through repurchase of outstanding shares. Finally, they are concerned about the effect of business results achieved—and future expectations about results—on the market value of their investment, especially in the case of publicly traded stock. The key concepts related to this last aspect are taken up in detail in Chapters 7 and 9, and we will only make brief reference to them here.

Profitability

The relationship of profits earned to the shareholders' stated investment in a company is watched closely by the financial community. Analysts track several key measures that express the company's performance in relation to the owners' stake. Two of these, return on net worth and return on common equity, address the profitability of the total ownership investment, while the third, earnings per share, measures the proportional participation of each unit of investment in corporate earnings for the period.

Return on Net Worth

The most common ratio used for measuring the return on the owners' investment is the relationship of net profit to net worth (equity or shareholders' investment). In performing this calculation, we don't have to make any adjustment for interest, because the net profit available for shareholders has already been properly reduced by interest charges, if any, paid to creditors and lenders. However, we do have to consider the impact of nonrecurring and unusual events, such as restructuring and major accounting changes and adjustments.

Net income for purposes of this calculation is the residual result of operations and belongs totally to the holders of common and preferred equity shares. Within the shareholder group, only those holding common shares have a claim on the residual profit after obligatory preferred dividends have been paid.

The ratio is calculated for TRW's shareholders' investment as follows:

$$\text{Return on net worth: } \frac{\text{Net profit}}{\text{Net worth (equity)}} = \frac{\$446}{\$2,172} = 20.5\% \ (1994: 18.3\%)$$

Here we have used the ending shareholders' investment (net worth). It's quite common, however, to use the average net worth for this calculation, on the assumption that profitable operations build up shareholders' equity during the year, and that therefore the annual profit should be related to the midpoint of this buildup.

The ratio for TRW is calculated as follows:

$$\text{Return on average net worth: } \frac{\text{Net profit}}{\text{Average net worth}} = \frac{\$446}{.5\ (\$2,172 + \$1,822)}$$
$$= 22.3\% \ (1994: 19.8\%)$$

A possible distortion must be mentioned here. Frequently, questions arise about the way a particular liability account on the balance sheet, "deferred taxes" should be handled in this analysis. Less frequently, there is even a deferred taxes account on the asset side of the balance sheet. As we mentioned before, deferred taxes represent the accumulated difference between the accounting treatment and the tax treatment of a variety of revenue and expense elements. Essentially, they are tax payments deferred (or advanced) due to a timing difference in recognizing tax deductions allowable under prevailing Internal Revenue Service (IRS) rules.

A larger issue involves so-called long-term liabilities, which are generally shown before interest-bearing long-term debt on the liability side of the balance sheet. These growing amounts ($779 in the case of TRW) represent mostly the results of changes in accounting rules designed to establish estimated liabilities—and corresponding reductions in profit—for such obligations as postretirement benefits, which previously had been paid as incurred. Such liabilities are noninterest-bearing estimates, and in effect, represent set-asides of shareholder equity.

Some analysts argue that such liabilities should be treated as owners' equity, while others argue that they represent a form of long-term debt. Because there is no consensus on the analytical treatment, deferred income taxes and long-term liabilities often are not included in any of the ratio calculations. As this accumulation on the liability side of the balance sheet may be quite large, material differences can result if they are considered in the calculations.

Return on Common Equity (ROE)

A somewhat more refined version of the calculation of return on owners' investment is necessary if there are several types of stock outstanding, such as preferred stock in different forms. The goal is to develop a return based on earnings accruing to the holders of common shares only. The net profit figure is first reduced by dividends paid to holders of preferred shares and by other obligatory payments, such as distributions to holders of minority interests. Net worth is likewise reduced by the stated amount of preferred equity and any minority elements, to arrive at the common equity figure. TRW in effect has only common stock outstanding, since its Serial Preference Stock II is reflected at the very nominal value of just $1.0 million. Thus, we will merely show the formula for the calculation, because the results will be the same:

$$\text{Return on common equity: } \frac{\text{Net profit to common}}{\text{Average common equity}} = \text{Percent}$$

Return on common equity is a widely published statistic. Rankings of companies and industry sectors are compiled by major business magazines and rating agencies. The ratio is closely watched by stock market analysts and, in turn, by management and the board of directors. Because the ratio focuses only on the ownership portion of the capital structure, however, the ROE of companies with widely different uses of long-term debt is not directly comparable. As we observed before, successful use of leverage will boost the owners' return and make it higher than that of an otherwise identical company that uses no debt. Moreover, the accuracy of recorded balance sheet values and earnings calculations is an issue in this ratio as well, and adjustments may be necessary if the analyst is aware of major inconsistencies, such as assets with sizable economic values that are not reflected on the balance sheet and thereby leave owners' equity understated.

Earnings per Share

The analysis of earnings from the owners' point of view usually centers on earnings per share in the case of a corporation. This ratio simply involves dividing the net profit to common stock by the average number of shares of common stock outstanding:

$$\text{Earnings per share: } \frac{\text{Net profit to common}}{\text{Average number of shares outstanding}} = \text{Dollars per share}$$

Earnings per share is a measure to which both management and shareholders pay a great deal of attention. It is widely used in the valuation of common stock, and is often the basis for setting specific corporate objectives and goals as part of strategic planning. Yet, the rise of shareholder value concepts during the past decade is causing a reassessment of the importance of earnings per share which, as a pure accounting measure, does not adequately reflect cash flow performance and expectations that drive shareholder value creation. Chapter 8 contains more background on the uses and limitations of this measure. Normally, the analyst does not have to calculate earnings per share because the result is readily announced by corporations large and small.

In TRW's 1995 annual report, earnings per share were reported as $6.62 for 1995, and $5.01 for 1994 (see Figure 3–3). Earnings per share are available on both an annual and a quarterly basis, and are a matter of record whenever a company's shares are publicly traded.

A recent requirement by the Financial Accounting Standards Board and the Securities and Exchange Commission calls for the calculation of earnings per share on two bases: The first is the so-called primary earnings per share, which uses average shares actually outstanding during the period. The second basis makes the assumption that all shares *potentially* outstanding be counted in addition to actual shares outstanding, that is, shares which would result from the conversion of preferred and debt securities that are convertible into common shares under various provisions, as well as rights, warrants, and stock options outstanding.

The result is referred to as "fully diluted" earnings per share, and reflects the reduced earnings per share that would result from any overhang of such potential shares—putting the investment community on notice that such a dilutive effect is possible. In TRW's case, there is no significant potential dilution, and fully diluted earnings per share are practically identical to primary earnings in both years.

Even though the earnings per share figure is one of the most readily available statistics reported by publicly held corporations, there are some complications in their calculation. Apart from possible unusual elements in the quarterly and annual net profit pattern, the number of shares outstanding varies during the year in many companies, either because of newly issued shares (new stock offerings, stock dividends paid, options exercised, etc.), or because outstanding old shares are retired (purchase of treasury stock). Therefore, the *average* number of shares outstanding during the year is commonly used in this calculation. Moreover, any significant change in the number of shares outstanding (such as would be caused by a stock split, for example) requires retroactive adjustments in past data to ensure comparability.

A great deal of interest among analysts is focused on past earnings per share, both quarterly and annual. Future projections are frequently made on the basis of past earnings levels. Fluctuations and trends in actual performance are compared to the projections and watched closely for indications of strength or weakness. Again, great caution is advised in interpreting these data. Allowances must be made for unusual elements both in the earnings figure and in the number of common shares outstanding.

Cash Flow per Share
A calculation to approximate the cash flow per share from operating results, this measure is frequently used as a very rough indicator of the company's ability to pay cash dividends. It is developed from the net profit figure to which accounting

write-offs such as depreciation, amortization, and depletion have been added back. We recall from our earlier discussion of the funds flow statement that such write-offs do not represent cash movements. Adding back these bookkeeping entries restates the net profit in a form that partially reflects the cash generated by operations, but leaves out many other significant funds movements, such as changes in working capital, investments in new assets, etc.

The calculation parallels the earnings per share ratio:

$$\text{Cash flow per share:} \ \frac{\text{Net profit to common plus write-offs}}{\text{Average number of shares outstanding}} = \text{Dollars per share}$$

In the case of TRW, we know that depreciation and amortization amounted to $433 million and $77 million, respectively. The average number of shares outstanding was given in the annual report as 67.4 million for purposes of calculating primary earnings per share. Write-offs thus amounted to $7.57 per share, which when added to the primary earnings per share of $6.62, results in a cash flow per share of $14.19 in 1995, and $12.48 in 1994.

Because the use of all funds in a business is largely at the discretion of management, the limited cash flow per share concept is at best only a crude indication of the potential to pay dividends. A more extensive analysis of funds flows is required to judge the total pattern of sources and uses, including dividend payment, as we demonstrated in Chapter 2.

Share Price Appreciation

Apart from current earnings generated for the shareholders, some of which will be received as dividends, investors expect an appreciation in the value of their common shares in the stock market over time. The main driver for this appreciation is the creation of additional economic value, that is, the generation of more positive cash flows than outlays in the long run through the combined effect of sound investment, operating, and financing decisions. We'll discuss shareholder value creation more fully in Chapter 9, but suffice it to say here that the analyst will look for movement in the share prices that at least matches and hopefully outperforms the trend in the stock market as a whole. Similarly, the performance trend of particular business segments in a large company will be related to the share price trends of relevant composites of comparable companies.

Total Shareholder Return (TSR)

The return to investors holding shares in a company is a combination of share price appreciation (or decline) and cash dividends received over appropriate time periods selected for analysis. Since only part of the earnings belonging to shareholders are paid out in the form of dividends, the relevant positive inflow to the shareholder is the stream of dividends received, not the announced earnings per share. The full economic benefit received by the shareholder is the sum of this stream of dividends plus any change in the price of the stock. The calculation simply involves taking the market price of stock at the beginning of the period, summing the quarterly dividends for the period, determining the change in price at the end of the period, and calculating the annualized return this pattern represents on the initial market price (the present value techniques of Chapter 6 are helpful in this process).

The results of this process are published annually in April by Fortune magazine for publicly held companies in the Fortune 500 listings. The previous year's TSR and the annual rate for the prior ten-year period is provided for companies in each major segment. TRW was listed among 24 companies in the motor vehicles and parts segment, even though a large portion of its operations involve space and defense and information services. Its TSR for 1995 was 20.7 percent (−2.0 percent for 1994), while the more meaningful long-term return from 1985 to 1995 was 9.5 percent. Comparable figures for the median of the segment were 8.0 percent for 1995 (−12.0 percent for 1994), and 10.0 percent for the decade.

The TSR concept is critical to assessing the relative performance of a company within the market as a whole, compared with its peers, and within broad industry groupings. We'll discuss TSR in relation to *shareholder value analysis* in Chapter 9.

Disposition of Earnings

The periodic split of earnings (net profit) into dividends paid and earnings retained for reinvestment is closely watched by shareholders and the financial community, because the retained residual builds up the owners' equity recorded on the balance sheet and is a source of funds for management's use.

As we discussed in Chapter 1, earnings—after payment of any interest— are either reinvested in the business to support further growth, or are paid out in part or full as dividends. Cash dividends are the most common form of payment, although stock dividends are also frequently used. In the latter case, no cash is involved. Instead, additional fractional shares are issued to each holder of record. If there is a normal cash dividend paid as well, stock dividends result in fractionally higher cash dividends, of course.

Dividends per Share

Dividends are generally declared on a per share basis every quarter by a corporation's board of directors, the elected representatives of the shareholders. Therefore no calculation is necessary. Dividend policy is the prerogative of the board, which has legal authority to set payments at any level it deems appropriate. Because the market value of common stock is in part influenced both by dividends paid and dividends anticipated, the board generally deals with this periodic decision very carefully. TRW Inc. paid dividends of $2.05 per share in 1995 and $1.94 in 1991.

Dividend Yield

Annual dividends paid per share can be related to current or average share prices to derive the dividend yield:

$$\text{Dividend yield:} \frac{\text{Annual dividend per share}}{\text{Average market price per share}} = \text{Percent}$$

This is a measure of the return on the owners' investment from cash dividends alone. In the case of TRW, the 52-week range of stock prices from January 1995 to December 1995 was 82⅝ to 61¾, with an average of approximately 72¼. The dividend yield at $2.05 per share thus amounts to 2.8 percent on the average price. The ratio falls short as a basis for comparison with other companies, however, because dividend policies differ widely. As we stated earlier, the more important measure is TSR, a combination of dividends and market appreciation (or decline) of the stock.

Payout/Retention

A ratio commonly used in connection with dividend policy is the so-called payout ratio, which represents the proportion of earnings paid out to the shareholders in the form of cash during any given year:

$$\text{Payout ratio: } \frac{\text{Cash dividend per share}}{\text{Earnings per share}} = \frac{\$2.05}{\$6.62} = 31.0\% \ (1994: 38.7\%)$$

Because most boards of directors tend to favor paying a fairly stable dividend per share, adjusted only gradually, the payout ratio of a company may fluctuate widely in the short run in response to swings in earnings performance. Over a period of several years, however, the payout ratio can often be used to indicate the tendency of directors to reinvest funds in the business versus paying out earnings to the shareholders.

There are no firm standards for this ratio, but the relationship is significant in characterizing the style of the corporation. High-growth companies tend to pay out relatively low proportions of earnings because they prefer to reinvest earnings to support profitable growth. Stable or moderate-growth companies tend to pay out larger proportions. Some companies pay no cash dividends at all, or provide stock dividends only. Many more factors must, of course, be considered in making judgments in this area, and the reader is directed to the references at the end of this chapter for further insight into both concepts and practices.

Dividend Coverage

Owners are also interested in the degree to which their dividends are covered by earnings and cash flow. Furthermore, they are concerned about the degree to which the proportion of debt in the capital structure and its associated interest and repayment requirements will affect management's ability to achieve reasonably stable and growing earnings, and to pay dividends commensurate with the owners' expectations. A variety of coverage ratios can be calculated, but they hardly differ from the ones we'll take up in the discussion of the lenders' point of view.

Dividends to Assets

Finally, it is sometimes useful to relate the annual dividends paid by a company to the total assets or net assets involved in generating them. The rationale is similar to the dividend yield discussed earlier, except that in this case, it is not the market value of the shares, but the book value of the assets they represent, which is used as the denominator. It can be argued that market valuation is a more current indicator for the yield relationship than the historical basis of the asset values as recorded on the balance sheet. Nevertheless, dividends to assets is often found as part of an analytical set of performance data.

Market Indicators

We'll only briefly mention two ratios which are commonly used as indicators of stock market values: the price/earnings ratio and the market to book ratio. The subject of market valuation will be covered in detail in Chapters 6 and 8.

Price/Earnings Ratio

The simple relationship between current or expected earnings per share and the current market price of the stock is often quoted by both management and owners. The ratio is also called the earnings multiple, and it is used to indicate how the stock market is judging the company's earnings performance and prospects. The calculation is quite straightforward, and relates current market prices of common shares to the most recent available earnings per share on an annual basis:

$$\text{Earnings multiple (Price/earnings ratio): } \frac{\text{Market price per share}}{\text{Earnings per share}} = \text{Factor}$$

The result is a simple factor. If fully diluted earnings differ significantly from primary earnings per share, the calculation can be done on both bases. The earnings multiple is used quite commonly as a rough rule of thumb in valuing companies for purposes of acquisition.

Earnings multiples vary widely by industry and by company, and are, in effect, a simple overall approximation of the market's current judgment of industry and company risk versus past and prospective earnings performance. They are tracked by various investor services and related to total market averages, as well as to average price earnings multiples for selected industry groups, to assess the relative performance of a particular company. Earnings multiples will tend to be higher in emerging industries, such as high technology companies or biotechnology firms, than in more established industries, such as public utilities or basic manufacturing. The reason for this divergence lies in the collective expectations of the market about the ability of an industry to achieve superior growth, technological breakthroughs with above average earnings, and cash flow potential, and other ways of achieving shareholder returns well above average through sustainable differentiation. The same is true for individual companies in their respective industry classifications—standouts like innovative Wal-Mart within the mature retailing field come to mind.

The reverse of the earnings per share formula is the so-called earnings yield, which relates earnings per share to the market price. Although it is sometimes used to express the current yield the owner enjoys, the measure can be misleading, because earnings are not normally paid out in full as dividends. Thus, the earnings yield cannot be compared to, for example, the yield on a bond where interest payments are contractual cash remittances. As we already know, the real economic return to the shareholder is a combination of the dividends received and the appreciation (decline) of the stock.

Cash Flow Multiple

A variant of relating current earnings performance to current market value is the use of cash flow per share, as discussed earlier. (TRW's cash flow per share in 1995 was $14.19.) Usually the definition of cash flow for this purpose is aftertax profit plus depreciation and amortization, divided by the average number of shares outstanding. We know from the discussion in Chapter 2 that this represents only a limited view of the actual cash generation of the business, but the measure is widely used and quoted as a rule of thumb that relates operating cash flow to share values.

Market to Book Ratio

This indicator relates current market value on a per share basis to the stated book value of owners' equity on the balance sheet, also on a per share basis. TRW's December 31, 1995, book value per share was $32.97, while the average market value for 1995 at $72¼ was more than twice this figure. The market to book ratio leaves much to be desired as a measure of performance for many of the reasons mentioned in earlier discussions of other ratios. It's not an economic measure of performance, because it relates accounting earnings to stated historical accounting values. In addition, while in a given company the relationship between stated balance sheet values and market values may be favorable, the ratio does not truly help the analyst judge what comparable expectations should be for other firms. Thus, the measure can only be a beginning step in the appraisal of long-term performance and outlook.

Relative Price Movements

While the typical investor is interested in the absolute change in the value of the shares held, the insights from the relative performance of the stock to the market as a whole and to appropriate averages for specific industries can be useful to assess the trend of a particular company. These movements can be expressed in absolute dollar terms, or in several of the ratios mentioned above. In view of the growing importance of cash flow thinking, fueled by the acquisition and leveraged buyout boom of the past decade, services like Value Line provide cash flow multiples as an additional indicator of relative price movements (see Appendix V).

Value of the Firm

This is a common concept which recognizes that the two main components of a company's capital structure, equity and debt, are valued separately in the marketplace. At any time, the market value of the firm is the sum of the market values of its shares and its debt:

$$V_F = V_S + V_D$$

where V_S is the market price per share times the number of shares outstanding, and V_D is the market value of the various classes of long-term debt the company has outstanding. The formula can, of course, be restated to show that the value of the company's shares is a function of the total value of the firm less the value of its debt:

$$V_S = V_F - V_D$$

We'll return to a more detailed discussion of valuation principles and shareholder value creation in Chapter 9.

In summary, the ratios pertinent to the owners' view of a company's performance are measures of the return owners have earned on their stake and the cash rewards they received in the form of dividends. These results depend on the earning power of the company and on management policies and decisions regarding the use of financial leverage and reinvestment. Ultimately, they affect the economic value of the owners' capital commitment, as reflected in stock market prices. The concepts and issues are taken up in more detail in Chapter 9.

LENDERS' POINT OF VIEW

While the main orientation of management and owners is toward the business as a going concern, the lender—of necessity—has to be of two minds. Lenders are interested in funding the needs of a successful business that will perform as expected. At the same time, they must consider the possible negative consequences of default and liquidation. Sharing none of the rewards of success other than receiving regular payments of interest and principal, the lender must carefully assess the risk of recovering the original funds extended—particularly if they have been provided for a long period of time. Part of the assessment must be the ultimate value of the lender's claim in case of serious difficulty.

The claims of a general creditor rank behind federal tax obligations, accrued wages, and the claims of secured creditors, who lend against a specific asset, such as a building or equipment. Thus, caution dictates that lenders look for a margin of safety in the assets held by the company, a cushion against default.

Several ratios are used to assess this protection by testing the liquidity of the business. Another set of ratios tests the relative debt exposure, or leverage of the business, in order to weigh the position of lenders versus owners. Finally, there are so-called coverage ratios relating to the company's ability to provide debt service from funds generated by ongoing operations.

Liquidity

One way to test the degree of protection afforded lenders focuses on the short-term credit extended to a business for funding its operations. It involves the liquid assets of a business, that is, those current assets that can readily be converted into cash, on the assumption that they would form a ready cushion against default.

Current Ratio

The ratio most commonly used to appraise the debt exposure represented on the balance sheet is the current ratio. This relationship of current assets to current liabilities is an attempt to show the safety of current debt holders' claims in case of default. The calculation is shown using TRW's relevant totals from Figure 3–2:

$$\text{Current ratio:} \frac{\text{Current assets}}{\text{Current liabilities}} = \frac{\$2,336}{\$2,012} = 1.16: 1 \ (1994: 1.12 : 1)$$

Presumably, the larger this ratio, the better the position of the debt holders. From the lenders' point of view, a higher ratio would certainly appear to provide a cushion against drastic losses of value in case of business failure. A large excess of current assets over current liabilities seems to help protect claims, should inventories have to be liquidated at a forced sale and should accounts receivable involve sizable collection problems.

Seen from another angle, however, an excessively high current ratio might signal slack management practices. It could indicate idle cash balances, inventory levels that have become excessive when compared to current needs, and poor credit management that results in overextended accounts receivable. At the same time, the business might not be making full use of its current borrowing power.

A very common rule of thumb suggests that a current ratio of 2 : 1 is about right for most businesses, because this proportion appears to permit a shrinkage of up to 50 percent in the value of current assets, while still providing enough cushion to cover all current liabilities. The problem with this concept is that the current ratio measures an essentially static condition and assesses a business as if it were on the brink of liquidation. The ratio does not reflect the dynamics of a going concern, which should be the top priority of management. A lender or creditor looking for future business with a successful client should bear this in mind, and will likely turn to the type of cash flow analysis described in Chapter 2 to judge the viability of the business as a client.

Acid Test

An even more stringent test, although again on a static basis, is the acid test or quick ratio, which is calculated using only a portion of current assets—cash, marketable securities, and accounts receivable—which are then related to current liabilities as follows:

$$\text{Acid test:} \frac{\text{Cash + marketable securities + Receivables}}{\text{Current liabilities}} = \frac{\$59 + \$1,428}{\$2,012}$$
$$= .74: 1 \ (1994: .73 : 1)$$

The key concept here is to test the collectibility of current liabilities in the case of a real crisis, on the assumption that inventories would have no value at all. As drastic tests of the ability to pay in the face of disaster, both the current ratio and acid test are helpful.

From an operational standpoint, however, it is better to analyze a business in terms of the expected total future cash flow pattern, which projects inflows and outflows over the period for which credit is extended. The proportion of current assets to current liabilities normally covers only a small part of this picture.

Quick Sale Value

Another stringent test that can be applied to the business as a whole is testing through a series of assumptions what cash value the various assets of the company would bring in a hurried sale, and relating this total to the liabilities of the business. Again, this is a liquidation point of view that does not allow for the ongoing cash flow patterns.

Financial Leverage

As we'll discuss in greater detail in Chapters 5 and 8, successful use of debt enhances earnings for the owners of the business, because the returns earned on these funds—over and above the interest paid—belong to the owners, and thus will increase the return on owners' equity. From the lenders' viewpoint, however, when earnings do not exceed or even fall short of the interest cost, fixed interest and principal commitments must still be met. The owners must fulfill these claims, which might then severely affect the value of owners' equity. The positive and negative effects of leverage increase with the proportion of debt in a business. With higher leverage, the risk exposure of the providers of debt grows, as does the risk exposure of the owners.

From the lenders' point of view, a variety of ratios that deal with total debt, or long-term debt only, in relation to various parts of the balance sheet, are more inclusive measures of risk than leverage alone. These ratios measure the risk exposure of the lenders in relation to the available asset values against which all claims are held.

Debt to Assets

The first and broadest test is the proportion of total debt, both current and long-term, to total assets, which is calculated as follows:

$$\text{Debt to assets:} \quad \frac{\text{Total debt}}{\text{Total assets}} = \frac{\$1,633^*}{\$5,890} = 27.7\% \ \% \ (1994: 31.2\%)$$

This ratio describes the proportion of "other peoples' money" to the total claims against the assets of the business. The higher the ratio, the greater the likely risk for the lender. It is not necessarily a true test of the ability of the business to cover its debts, however, because as we've already observed, the asset amounts recorded on the balance sheet are not necessarily indicative of current economic values, or even liquidation values. Nor does the ratio give any clues as to likely earnings and cash flow fluctuations that might affect current interest and principal payments.

---

*includes long-term liabilities and deferred income taxes.

Debt to Capitalization

A more refined version of the debt proportion analysis involves the ratio of long-term debt to capitalization (total invested capital). The latter is again defined as the sum of the long-term claims against the business, both debt and owners' equity, but doesn't include short-term (current) liabilities. This total also corresponds to net assets, unless some adjustments were made, such as ignoring deferred taxes.

The calculation appears as follows, when long-term liabilities and deferred taxes are included in the debt total:

$$\text{Debt to capitalization: } \frac{\text{Long-term debt}}{\text{Capitalization (net assets)}} = \frac{\$1,967}{\$3,446}$$
$$= 57.1\% \ (1994\text{: } 52.1\%)$$

If deferred taxes are excluded from debt, the ratio changes to 50.6 percent and 40.1 percent, respectively.

The ratio is one of the elements rating companies like Moody's take into account when classifying the relative safety of debt. Another definition of debt is sometimes used, which includes (1) short-term debt (other than trade credit), (2) the current portion of long-term debt, and (3) all long-term debt in the form of contractual obligations. In this case, long-term liabilities like representing potential employee benefit claims and deferred taxes are not counted as part of the capitalization of the company, which is (1) the sum of debt as defined above, plus (2) minority interests, and (3) shareholders' investment (equity). In TRW's case, the debt total thus becomes $754 ($133 + $80 + $541), and the capitalization becomes $2,999 ($754 + $73 + 2,172), resulting in a ratio of 25.1 percent for 1995 and 34.0 percent for 1994.

A great deal of emphasis is placed on the ratio of debt to capitalization, carefully defined for any particular company, because many lending agreements of both publicly held and private corporations contain covenants regulating maximum debt exposure expressed in terms of debt to capitalization proportions. There remains an issue of how to classify different liabilities, and how to deal with accounting changes, such as most companies, including TRW, experienced in having to establish long-term liabilities for future employee benefits.

As we shall see later, however, there is growing emphasis on a more relevant aspect of debt exposure, namely, the ability to service the debt from ongoing funds flows, a much more dynamic view of lender relationships.

Debt to Equity

A third version of the analysis of debt proportions involves the ratio of total debt, normally the sum of current liabilities and all types of long-term debt, to total owners' equity, or net worth. The debt to equity ratio is an attempt to show, in another format, the relative proportions of all lenders' claims to ownership claims, and it is used as a measure of debt exposure. The measure is expressed as either a percentage or as a proportion, and in the example shown below, the figures again were taken from TRW's balance sheet in Figure 3–2:

$$\text{Debt to equity: } \frac{\text{Total debt}}{\text{Net worth (equity)*}} = \frac{\$3,645}{\$2,245} = 162\% \ (1994: 198\%)$$

In preparing this ratio, as in some earlier instances, the question of deferred income taxes and other estimated long-term liabilities is often sidestepped by leaving these potential long-term claims out of the debt and capitalization figures altogether. We have included all of these elements here. One specific refinement of this formula uses only long-term debt, as related to net worth, ignoring long-term obligations and deferred taxes.

$$\text{Debt to equity: } \frac{\text{Long-term debt}}{\text{Net worth (equity)*}} = \frac{\$541}{\$2,245} = 24.1\% \ (1994: 36.7\%)$$
$$\text{(alternate)}$$

The various formats of these relationships imply the care with which the ground rules must be defined for any particular analysis, and for the covenants governing specific lending agreements. They only hint at the risk/reward trade-off implicit in the use of debt, which we'll discuss in more detail in Chapters 7 and 9.

Debt Service

Regardless of the specific choice from among the several ratios we just discussed, debt proportion analysis is in essence static, and does not take into account the operating dynamics and economic values of the business. The analysis is totally derived from the balance sheet, which in itself is a static snapshot of the financial condition of the business at a single point in time.

Nonetheless, the relative ease with which these ratios are calculated probably accounts for their popularity. Such ratios are useful as indicators of trends when they are applied over a series of time periods. However, they still don't get at the heart of an analysis of creditworthiness, which involves a company's ability to pay both interest and principal on schedule as contractually agreed upon, that is, to service its debt over time.

Interest Coverage

One very frequently encountered ratio reflecting a company's debt service uses the relationship of net profit (earnings) before interest and taxes (EBIT) to the amount of the interest payments for the period. This ratio is developed with the expectation that annual operating earnings can be considered a basic source of funds for debt service, and that any significant change in this relationship might signal difficulties. Major earnings fluctuations are one type of risk considered.

No hard and fast standards for the ratio itself exist; rather, the prospective debt holders often require covenants in the loan agreement spelling out the number of times the business is expected to cover its debt service obligations. The ratio is simple to calculate, and we can employ the EBIT figure developed for TRW earlier in the management section:

---

*includes minority interests.

$$\text{Interest coverage: } \frac{\text{Net profit before interest and taxes (EBIT)}}{\text{Interest expense}}$$

$$= \frac{\$803}{\$95} = 8.5 \text{ times (1994: 6.1\%)}$$

The specifics are based on judgment, often involving a detailed analysis of a company's past, current, and prospective conditions.

Burden Coverage

A somewhat more refined analysis of debt coverage relates the net profit of the business, before interest and taxes, to the sum of current interest and principal repayments, in an attempt to indicate the company's ability to service the burden of its debt in all aspects. A problem arises with this particular analysis, because interest payments are tax deductible, while principal repayments are not. Thus, we must be on guard to think about these figures on a comparable basis.

One correction often used involves converting the principal repayments into an equivalent pretax amount. This is done by dividing the principal repayment by the factor "one minus the effective tax rate." The resulting calculation appears as follows, if we take as repayments the $207 million in principal (due in over 90 days) TRW paid in 1995, as indicated in the funds flow statement in its 1995 annual report (see Chapter 2):

$$\text{Burden coverage: } \frac{\text{Net profit before interest and taxes (EBIT)}}{\text{Interest} + \dfrac{\text{Principal repayments}}{(1 - \text{tax rate})}}$$

$$= \frac{\$803}{\$95 + \dfrac{\$207}{(1 - .37)}}$$

$$= \frac{\$803}{\$95 + \$329} = 1.89 \text{ times}$$

An alternate format uses operating cash flow (net profit after taxes plus write-offs), taken from Figure 3–3, to which aftertax interest has been added back. This is then compared to the sum of aftertax interest and principal repayment, and the calculation for 1995 appears as follows:

$$\text{Burden coverage: } \frac{\text{Operating cash flow} + \text{Interest} (1 - \text{tax rate})}{\text{Interest} (1 - \text{tax rate}) + \text{Principal repayments}}$$

$$= \frac{\$956^* + \$95 (.63)}{\$95 (.63) + \$207} = \frac{\$1,016}{\$267} = 3.81 \text{ times}$$

Cash Flow Analysis

Determining a company's ability to meet its debt obligations is most meaningful when a review of past profit and cash flow patterns is made over a long enough period of time to indicate the major operational and cyclical fluctuations that are

---

*$446+$433+$77.

normal for the company and its industry. This may involve financial statements covering several years or several seasonal swings, as appropriate, in an attempt to identify characteristic high and low points in earnings and funds needs. The pattern of past conditions must then be projected into the future to see what margin of safety remains to cover interest, principal repayments, and other fixed payments, such as major lease obligations. These techniques will be discussed in Chapter 4.

If a business is subject to sizable fluctuations in aftertax cash flow, lenders may be reluctant to extend credit when the debt service cannot be covered several times at the low point in the operational pattern. In contrast, a very stable business would encounter less stringent coverage demands. The type of dynamic analysis involved is a form of financial modeling that can be greatly enhanced both in scope and in the number of possible alternative conditions explored by using computer spreadsheets or full-fledged corporate models.

RATIOS AS A SYSTEM

The ratios discussed in this chapter have many elements in common, as they are derived from key components of the same financial statements. In fact, they are often interrelated and can be viewed as a system. The analyst can turn a series of ratios into a dynamic display highlighting the elements that are the most important levers used by management to affect operating performance.

In internal analysis, many companies employ systems of ratios and standards that segregate into their components the series of decisions affecting operating performance, overall returns, and shareholder expectations. Du Pont was one of the first to do so almost a century ago. Early on, the company published a chart showing the effects and interrelationships of decisions in these areas, thus presenting a first "model" of its business.

We'll demonstrate the relationships between the ratios discussed by using two key parameters segregated into their elements. *Return on assets*, which is of major importance for judging management performance, and *return on equity*, which serves as the key measure from the owners' viewpoint. We'll leave aside the refinements applicable to each to concentrate on the linkages. As we'll show, it's possible to model the performance of a given company by expanding and relating these ratios. Needless to say, careful attention must be paid to the exact definition of the elements entering into the ratios for a particular company to achieve internal consistency. Also, it's important to ensure that the ratios are interpreted in ways that foster economic trade-offs and decisions.

Elements of Return on Assets

The basic formula for return on assets (ROA) was:

$$\text{Return on assets} = \frac{\text{Net profit}}{\text{Assets}}$$

We also know that net profit was related both to asset turnover and to sales. Thus, it is possible to restate the formula as follows:

$$\text{Return on assets} = \frac{\text{Net profit}}{\text{Sales}} \times \frac{\text{Sales}}{\text{Assets}}$$

Note that the element of sales cancels out in the second formula, resulting in the original expression. But we can expand the relationship even further by substituting several more basic elements for the terms in the equation:

$$\text{ROA} = \frac{(\text{Gross margin} - \text{expenses})(1 - \text{tax rate})}{\text{Price} \times \text{Volume}}$$
$$\times \frac{\text{Price} \times \text{Volume}}{\text{Fixed} + \text{Current} + \text{Other assets}}$$

Note that the relationships expressed here serve as a simple model of the key decision levers management can employ to improve return on assets. For example, improvement in gross margin is important, as is control of expenses. Price/volume relationships are canceled out, but we know they are essential factors in arriving at a satisfactory gross margin, as is control of cost of goods sold. (We could have substituted "price/volume less cost of goods sold" for gross margin in the first bracket.)

All along we have said that asset management is very important. The model shows that the return on assets will rise if fewer assets are employed and if all the measures of effective management of working capital are applied. Minimizing taxes within the legal options available will also improve the return.

Elements of Return on Equity

A similar approach can be taken with the basic formula for return on owners' equity (ROE), which relates profit and the amounts of recorded equity:

$$\text{Return on equity} = \frac{\text{Net profit}}{\text{Equity}}$$

If we use some of the basic profit and turnover relationships to expand the expression, the following formula emerges:

$$\text{Return on equity} = \frac{\text{Net profit}}{\text{Assets}} \times \frac{\text{Assets}}{\text{Equity}}$$

Note that in effect, the formula states that return on equity (ROE) consists of two elements: the net profit achieved on the asset base and the degree of leverage or debt capital used in the business. "Assets to equity" is a way of describing the leverage proportion.

We can expand the formula even more to include the key components of return on assets:

$$\text{ROE} = \frac{\text{Net profit}}{\text{Sales}} \times \frac{\text{Sales}}{\text{Assets}} \times \frac{\text{Assets}}{\text{Assets} - \text{Liabilities}}$$

Now we can again look for the key decision levers that management should use to raise the return on owners' equity. As before, improving profitability of sales (operations) comes first, combined with effective use of assets that generate sales. An added factor is the boosting effect from successful use of debt in the capital structure. The greater the liabilities, the greater the improvement in return on equity—assuming, of course, that the business is profitable to begin with and continues to earn more on its investments than the cost of debt.

Using other people's money can be quite helpful—until the risk of default on debt service in a down cycle becomes significant. The analyst can use this simple framework to test the impact on the return on equity from one or more changed conditions, and to test how sensitive the result is to the magnitude of any change introduced.

A more inclusive format of the relationship of key ratios to each other and to the three major decision areas is displayed in Figure 3–4. We've added the major drivers behind the ratios on the left, as an indication of the levers management can use in managing the company. Note that in this diagram, we have included the cost of interest on debt as part of the "net contribution from leverage" in the financing area, while defining operating earnings as excluding the cost of interest.

This representation can be viewed as a simple model of a business in financial ratio format. It can be useful in tracing through the ultimate effects from changes in any of the drivers that are brought about by management decisions. For example, note that an increased level of inventories will reduce working capital turnover, which lowers the return on investment, and in the end, the return on equity. Or take an increase in debt (leverage), where the funds obtained are successfully invested with a rate of return higher than the interest cost—this will make a positive contribution to the return on equity. The latter example also illustrates that different degrees of leverage employed by companies being compared can affect the comparability of the return on equity measure.

There should be a word of caution, however. The neat precision implied in this arrangement must not blind us to the fact that while accounting ratios are commonly used indicators, the ultimate driver of TSR and shareholder value is the pattern of cash flows achieved and, more importantly, expected by the stock market. This represents an economic viewpoint which transcends the short-comings of accounting statements and relationships, and expresses market valuation as a cash flow mechanism—which has been confirmed by many empirical studies.

Does this mean that we cannot really use the various tools and relationships we've discussed in this chapter? Not at all. The challenge to analysts and managers is to be constantly aware of the cash flow implications of their decisions in addition to any accounting-based analysis. Accounting ratios and data will at times conflict in the near term with economic choices, and some will not be useful for a particular decision. Over the long run, measures such as return on equity and return on net assets will converge with cash flow results. The rule to observe at all times is that true economic trade-offs must be based on cash flows, and if decisions are consistently analyzed and executed in this manner, positive accounting results will follow in due course.

FIGURE 3–4

A Systems View of Key Ratios and their Elements

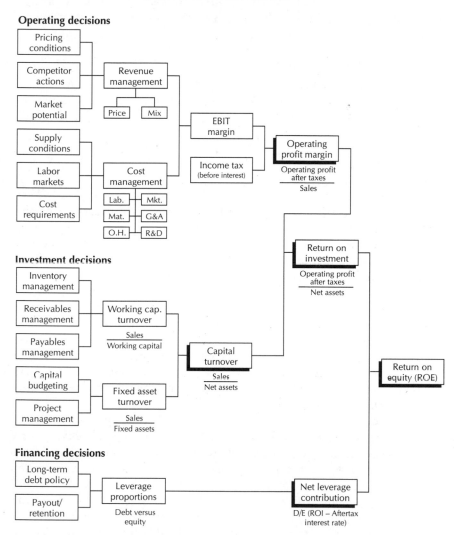

We'll return to the subject of business modeling again in Chapters 4 and 5, and highlight economic cash flow trade-offs in Chapters 6 through 9.

INTEGRATION OF FINANCIAL PERFORMANCE ANALYSIS

We've discussed the great variety of financial ratios and measures available to anyone wishing to analyze the performance of a company, its various units, or of an individual business. We've also grouped the measures by points of view and shown their many interrelationships as well as the key management drivers that impact them.

At this point, it'll be helpful to provide a few practical guidelines for structuring the process of using the measures. We'll briefly address the following key points:

- Careful definition of the issue being analyzed.
- Combination of primary and secondary measures and tools.
- Trending performance data over time, both historical and prospective.
- Finding comparative indicators and supplementary information.
- Identifying key "value drivers" that affect performance.
- Past performance as a clue to future expectations.
- Systems issues and optimal performance.

First, there is nothing more important in any kind of financial/economic analysis than a clear *definition of the issue* to be addressed. For example, when a banker ponders whether to extend a short-term loan to a business for working capital needs, the key issue is the company's ability to repay within a relatively short time period. Immediately, the analysis focuses on past and prospective cash flow patterns, supplemented by measures on working capital management and profitability. When a security analyst wishes to assess the quality of a company's management, the focus will be on past and prospective strategic direction, competitive position, and investment effectiveness. Measures of profitability benchmarked against comparative industry data will be important, as will be indicators of shareholder return and value creation. The point is that every type of analysis, complex or simple, should be preceded by an issue definition that will naturally lead to a focused choice of measures to be applied.

Second, it should be obvious that most financial/economic analysis has to use a *combination of primary and secondary measures* to be effective. Rarely will a situation require only a single measure or indicator, for as we saw, all ratios are limited to some extent both by the nature of the data and the relationship underlying them. Looking only at the return on equity as a measure of profitability, for example, falls far short of the insights gained when it is combined with key measures of operating earnings, investment turnover, and contribution from leverage, as we saw earlier. It's good practice to decide which key indicators best fit the specific issue, and which subsidiary ratios can provide additional insight or verification. The analytical results should then be expressed in these terms.

Third, it's an axiom of good analysis that *trends in financial/economic performance* be judged in a time frame befitting the nature of the business and its industry, including the aspects of cyclicality, seasonality, growth, and decline we discussed in Chapter 2. This calls for developing data series that cover at least several years, in order to judge the trends affecting various aspects of the company's performance. Sound analysis uses the perspective gained from positive or adverse trends in the primary and secondary performance indicators, and carefully weighs their relative importance to the issue being addressed. Remember also that performance analysis is not just an exercise in historical assessment—rather, it's most likely the basis from which future expectations are developed. Trend analysis becomes especially important in this context, for the analyst often needs to project future conditions and must decide whether the trends observed are likely to continue, or change, because of foreseeable events.

Fourth, the results of performance analysis are much more meaningful when placed in the *context of comparable data* about the industry, key competitors, or intracompany comparisons of organizational units. It's here that both the level of performance and key trends can be judged in relative terms. While it's often hard to find truly comparative data, the notion of benchmarking results whenever possible has grown in the past decade as management began to focus on improving competitive effectiveness. The references at the end of this chapter and in Appendix IV contain published sources of industry data and ratios, which companies often supplement with special efforts to develop even more specific data. Depending on the importance of the issue being analyzed, the industry/competitive context for viewing performance results can be critical.

Fifth, sound analytical practice includes *identifying the key value drivers* underlying the performance of any business. Whether production-oriented, such as the yield in producing electronic chips, or service-based, such as call volume by sales personnel, performance ratios and measures are usually directly affected by variations in these key drivers. While one can find many kinds of value drivers, varying greatly between types of business, there are generally just a few in each organization that really make a difference. The effective analyst makes it a practice to understand what these drivers are, how they affect the broader financial/economic measures used, and how trends in the drivers themselves impact both past and prospective performance. It's good practice to test the sensitivity of key measures chosen to varying value driver conditions, and to include critical value drivers as part of the combination of measures chosen to address the performance issue under review.

Sixth, viewing past performance as a *clue to potential future expectations* is a common practice in financial/economic analysis. We've already touched on this aspect in our discussion of trend analysis. A word of caution is needed, however. While it's proper to identify past trends in both value drivers and the broader ratios and measures, and to extrapolate them into the future, this can only be a first step. As we'll see especially in Chapter 4 and also in later chapters, historical conditions are merely an indication that may not fit the outlook. Past performance trends have to be carefully tested against expectations about future conditions, both internal to the company and external in the broader context of business, competitive, and economic conditions. It may very well be true that recent actions taken by management, or discernible changes in the environment, require a different set of assumptions about the future.

Finally, performance analysis in the broadest sense has to be viewed in the *context of the business system*, as described in Chapter 1. When the issue selected is an overall assessment of a company or a major business unit, it's good practice to test the results and trends of the various measures not only in the form of absolute and relative performance against proper benchmarks, but also in relation to each other. As we pointed out in Chapter 1, sound economic/financial performance requires optimizing the systems results over time. This simply means that policies and strategies in the areas of investment, operations, and financing should reinforce each other. The skilled analyst will put performance analysis into this broader context, and view the historical results as well as the projected expectations as indicators of systems balance. Are growth policies matched by appropriate financing plans? Are operating results in cash flow terms sufficient to support dividend policies and investment plans? Do the results reflect sound trade-offs over time? Many of these points will be discussed in more detail in later chapters.

SELECTED SPECIAL ISSUES

The impact of accounting practices and decisions on the management of funds was briefly mentioned in Chapter 1, where accounting write-offs and deferred taxes were identified as aspects to be considered. At this point, it will be useful to refine our understanding of these issues a little further because possible alternative treatments of these matters at times significantly affect the assessment of operations as well as understanding the patterns of cash flows. Figure 3–6 at the end of this chapter reproduces the notes to TRW's financial statements to illustrate the many accounting and tax considerations underlying the reported financial data of any large U.S. corporation. Appendix IV contains some of the more specialized issues of interpreting performance statements in an *international setting*, especially the problem of judging the profitability of parts of a multibusiness company operating in different countries.

We'll limit ourselves to a review of the key choices available to management in the areas of *inventory costing and depreciation methods* to help the reader in forming his or her own judgments when faced with interpreting financial statements and funds flows. We'll also briefly mention the effects of *inflation*, although no satisfactory methods of dealing with that issue have been established so far.

Inventory Costing

One accounting challenge present at all times is the proper allocation of a portion of the costs accumulated in the inventory account to the actual goods being sold. We can visualize *layers of cost* built up over time in the inventory account, which correspond to the physical movement of raw materials, work in process, and finished goods into storage. The accountant wants to *match revenues and expenses* in keeping track of the inventory account, yet from a physical standpoint, it is just as possible to ship the oldest unit on hand as it is to ship the most recent arrival. The warehouse supervisor can even pick the goods at random.

If unit costs never changed, matching costs to revenues would not be a problem, because the accountant would simply track the number of units shipped and multiply them by the unchanged unit cost, regardless of the actual physical choices made by the warehouse supervisor. In real life, however, several problems arise. A manufacturing company may experience fluctuations that affect the unit cost of the products inventoried. This effectively results in different layers of cost recorded in the finished goods inventory account. Further, the prices of raw materials and other inputs may be positively or negatively influenced by supply and demand. The materials inventory account will therefore reflect different layers of cost. A merchandising company will similarly encounter variations in the cost of inventory items, as supplier prices change. Most cost accounting systems allow for variances to the extent they are predictable, but larger swings do affect costs that are charged to periodic operating statements.

Finally, there is the impact of general inflation, or, more rarely, deflation. The impact of inflation on inventories generally is a steady rise in the cost of the more recent additions, resulting in successive layers of escalating costs.

The accountant is therefore faced with a real problem in the effort to match costs and revenues. If unit costs are growing significantly from period to period, deciding which costs to charge against the revenues for a period can have significant effects on the financial statements. If the more "logical" method of removing the oldest units first is used, the oldest, and presumably lowest, unit costs will be charged against current revenues. Depending on how quickly the inventory turns over, such costs may *lag* current conditions by months and even years. Therefore, under rising price levels, first-in, first-out (FIFO) inventory costing causes the profit on the income statement to be higher than it would be if current unit costs had been charged. At the same time, the balance sheet will reflect inventory values that are reasonably current, because the oldest, lowest cost units are being removed.

If the opposite method is employed, that is, last-in, first-out (LIFO) costing, the income statement will be charged with current costs and thus reflect lower but more realistic profits. The balance sheet, however, will show inventory values that in time, will be highly *understated*, because only the oldest and lowest layers of cost remain.

We could argue that the choice of methods does not really matter, because one of the two financial statements will be distorted in *either* case. The question then simply becomes whether more realistic balance sheet values or more realistic reported profits are preferred. There is a significant *cash flow* aspect involved, however. The choice of methods affects the amount of income taxes paid for the period. The higher earnings under FIFO are taxed as income from operations, even though they contain a profit made from old inventories. Therefore, one criterion in making the choice is the difference in tax payments, which *does* affect the company's funds. LIFO is preferable from this standpoint, even though with continued inflation, inventory values stated on the balance sheet will become more and more obsolete. Yet surprisingly, FIFO has remained a very common form of inventory costing, despite the fact that it can lead to a funds drain from higher tax payments. Apparently, the higher reported profit under FIFO costing is attractive enough to many managers to outweigh the actual tax disadvantage—a trade-off between reporting and economics.

In contrast to other permissible choices of accounting methods for tax purposes, current federal tax laws do not allow the use of one inventory costing method for tax calculation and another for bookkeeping and reporting. Thus, the ideal combination of LIFO for tax purposes and FIFO for reporting earnings cannot be employed. In fact, many firms employ an averaging method for inventory costing, or a combination of methods.

Trading firms, retailers, and companies experiencing significant fluctuations in the current values of inventories often adjust inventory values, usually at year-end, using the conservative method of restating inventories at cost or market value, whichever is lower, and writing off the difference against current profits. Such periodic adjustments tend to reduce stated values, not raise them, and allow the company to reflect the negative effects of changed conditions so as not to overstate inventory values. Under inflationary conditions, this practice does not, of course, assist in resolving the inventory costing issues we have just discussed.

Depreciation Methods

Depreciation is based on the accountant's desire to reflect as a charge against current operations some appropriate fraction of the cost of assets employed in producing revenues. Because physical assets other than land deteriorate with use and eventually wear out, the accounting challenge is to establish an appropriate period of time over which portions of the cost of the asset are charged against revenues. Moreover, the accountant has to decide on the pattern of the depreciation write-off, that is, level, declining, or variable depreciation. Another issue involves estimating any salvage value that may be realized at the end of an asset's useful life. Only the difference between asset cost and such salvage value is normally depreciated.

A similar rationale is applied to intangible assets such as patents and licenses, which are amortized and charged against operations over an appropriate period of years, and to specialized assets such as mineral deposits and timber, on which depletion allowances are calculated.

In the case of physical assets, the depreciation write-off is shown as a charge in the operating statement, and is accumulated on the balance sheet as an offset to the fixed assets involved, in an account called accumulated depreciation or reserve for depreciation. Thus, over time, the original asset value stated on the balance sheet is reduced, as periodic charges are made against operations. For performance assessment, the significance of depreciation write-offs is in the appropriateness of the charges in light of the nature of the assets and industry conditions, and thus, depreciation's impact on profits and balance sheet values. The significance for purposes of funds management is the tax impact of depreciation. Under normal circumstances, depreciation is a tax deductible expense, even though it is only an accounting allocation of past expenditures. The highest depreciation write-off legally possible will normally be taken by management to minimize the cash outlay for taxes, unless operating profits are insufficient over the taxable period (including tax adjustments like operating loss carryback and carryforward, which permit making use of losses to reduce the taxes of profitable periods) to take full advantage of the deductions.

The choice of depreciation methods is made easier by the provision in the current tax laws allowing the use of one method for bookkeeping and reporting purposes and another for income tax calculation. Recall that this was not possible for inventory valuation. Thus, a company can enjoy the best aspects of both depreciation concepts: slower depreciation for reporting higher profits, and faster depreciation for paying lower taxes.

The difference between the taxes actually paid versus what would be due had the book profit been taxed is accumulated on the balance sheet as a liability called deferred taxes, which we encountered earlier in our discussion. This liability will keep growing if a company continually adds to its depreciable assets and consistently uses faster write-offs for tax purposes. If the company stops growing or changes its depreciation policies, actual tax payments in future periods will increase and the differences will begin to reduce the deferred taxes account. There is no current consensus on how to treat this often significant amount in the calculation of performance assessment measures.

What are the most common choices for depreciation write-offs? Historically, accounting practice has favored *straight-line depreciation*. This is determined by dividing the cost of the asset (less the estimated salvage value) by its expected life. For example, an asset costing $10,000, with a salvage value of $400 and a six-year life, would be depreciated at the annual rate of $1,600 (one sixth, or 16⅔ percent of $9,600). A variant of this method is *unit depreciation*, in which the allocation is based on the total number of units estimated to be produced over the life of the asset and the annual depreciation is based on the number of units produced in that year.

Because many types of assets, such as automobiles, lose more of their value in early years, and also because allowing faster write-offs provides an incentive to reduce current income taxes, several methods of *accelerated depreciation* were developed over time. The two most common methods will be described here.

Double-declining balance depreciation is calculated by using twice the annual rate of straight-line depreciation (33 ⅓ percent for a six-year life), multiplying the full original cost of the asset for the first year with this factor, and the declining balance for each successive year. In other words, in our example, one-third of the remaining balance would be depreciated in each year (see Figure 3–5). The last year's depreciation is the remaining balance, and any salvage value is recognized by reducing the amount charged in the *final* year.

Sum-of-years-digits depreciation is calculated by adding the digits for all the years of the asset's life (1 + 2 + 3, etc.). The total is the denominator in a fraction (for a six-year life, this sum would be 21: 1 + 2 + 3 + 4 + 5 + 6). The numerators represent each year of useful life, in reverse order. (In our example, the fractions are 6/21, 5/21, 4/21, 3/21, 2/21, and 1/21). In a given year, the depreciation write-off is the asset's original cost (less salvage value) multiplied by the fraction for that year.

The depreciation methods permitted under prevailing IRS codes have changed frequently, especially during the 1980s. Under the 1986 revision of the tax code, the IRS lengthened the lives over which various classes of depreciable assets can be written off. Six asset classes were established for personal property, with lives of 3, 5, 7, 10, 15, and 20 years. For real property (e.g., buildings), two classes of 27.5 and 31.5 years were defined, which must be depreciated straight-line. The IRS stipulated the double-declining balance method for assets with up to ten years of life, and a variation of this method, the 150 percent declining balance method, for assets with a 15- and 20-year life.

In either case, a switch to straight-line depreciation in the latter years is permitted, when this becomes advantageous. These methods must be used if a company chooses to use accelerated depreciation for *tax* purposes, while *any* other method can be employed for bookkeeping and reporting. The specifics of the tax regulations applicable at the time of the analysis are best examined in the detailed materials provided by the Internal Revenue Service.

The different patterns of depreciation resulting from the use of the various methods are shown in Figure 3–5.

The Impact of Inflation

The extreme inflationary conditions in the United States beginning in the early 1970s resulted in significant distortions in many of the calculations we discussed. In recent years, inflationary trends have improved greatly in the United States, to the extent that inflation is now considered relatively benign. Many other countries have, of course, had to deal with far more insidious levels of inflation for much longer periods of time.

In the United States, the accounting profession and the Securities and Exchange Commission have expended much effort in developing new ways to account for and

FIGURE 3–5

Comparative Annual Depreciation Patterns
($10,000 Asset with Six-Year Life and $400 Salvage Value)

	Straight-Line Method	Double-Declining Balance Method*	150 Percent Declining Balance Method†	Sum-of-Years Digits Method
Year 1	$1,600	$3,333	$2,500	$2,743
Year 2	1,600	2,222	1,875	2,286
Year 3	1,600	1,482	1,407	1,829
Year 4	1,600	988	1,406	1,371
Year 5	1,600	658	1,406	914
Year 6	1,600	917	1,006	457
Total:	$9,600	$9,600	$9,600	$9,600

*Year 6 is shown net of salvage value of $400.

†Switch to straight line in Year four; required for 15- and 20-year IRS asset classes.

disclose the impact of changes in prices of goods and services and of fluctuating exchange rates due in part to inflation. However, the intricacies and arguments abundant in this difficult area are beyond the scope of this book. We are only mentioning a few of the basic mechanisms commonly employed to deal with price level changes where this is necessary to understand the impact on financial analysis. Thus, Chapters 2, 4, and 9 contain a brief discussion of essential price level adjustments pertaining to the subjects of operating funds management, projections, and valuation. Appendix I contains a discussion of the basic concepts underlying the inflation phenomenon.

In performance analysis, the main problem associated with inflation is the use of *historical costing* as a generally accepted accounting principle. The original cost of assets utilized in and charged to operations is reflected on the balance sheet. Depreciation and amortization reflect past values, which are often lower than current values. Financial statements of particularly heavily capitalized industries with long-lived depreciable assets and physical resources tend to reflect overstated profits and taxes, and understated asset values. This raises the issue of comparability of companies of different ages, and certainly of comparability of whole industries. Even short-term fluctuations in values will affect companies with high inventory turnover, such as wholesalers.

Another area of distortion affects the *viewpoint of the lender*. In inflationary times, the declining value of currency will affect borrowing/lending relationships, because eventual repayment will be made in less valuable dollars. Thus, the lender would be at a disadvantage unless the interest rate contracted for is high enough to offset this risk. The dramatic rise in the 1970s and subsequent fall in the 1980s and early 1990s of short- and long-term interest rates in response to growing and waning inflationary pressures will remain in the memories of long-term lenders in particular.

Among the many methods used to deal with price level changes are replacement cost accounting, new forms of inventory valuation, and partial or full periodic restatement of financial reports. In fact, inflation has turned the deceptively simple accounting principle of matching costs and revenues into an economic and intellectual challenge. As yet, there are no consistent ways of appraising the difference between this type of recast statement and the original accounting statements. A current proposal by the Financial Accounting Standards Board goes part way toward recasting financial statements for banks and financial institutions, asking that loans and investments be valued at current values. This raises a variety of issues that are far from resolved at the time of this writing.

SUMMARY

In this chapter, we discussed essential aspects of the main financial statements as a basis for appraising business performance. With this as background, we then demonstrated that the assessment of performance is made meaningful when seen from the points of view of the key groups interested in the company's success.

We chose to concentrate on the particular viewpoints of three groups— management, owners, and lenders—which are essential to the functioning of the business. The insights of these groups are used and expanded by others for their own particular needs. All three groups are concerned about the success of the business, each from its own standpoint.

It is management's prime duty to bring about stability, growth, and reliable earnings performance with the investment entrusted to it by the owners. We found that within the wide range of ratios displayed, the crucial test is the economic return on the capital employed in the business and its attendant effect on the value of the ownership stake. We also found that the ratios are linked by their common information base, and many are directly connected through the common use of certain elements. They are best interpreted when the business is viewed as a system of interdependent conditions responding to the decisions of management. To this end, modeling and computer simulation are increasingly accepted and meaningful, because many individual ratios are, by their nature, only static tests that cannot do justice to the dynamics of a business.

Shortcomings in the analysis relate to the limitations of the accounting principles commonly used, and we strongly suggested that managers and analysts take an economic (cash flow) viewpoint for decision-making, which will in the long run result in good accounting performance. Further distortions are introduced through price level changes stemming from inflation, currency fluctuations, and economic value changes. No definitive ways of compensating for these measurement problems have as yet been found to make financial analyses readily comparable and economically meaningful. As a result, the manager and analyst must use care and judgment at all times.

SELECTED REFERENCES

Anthony, Robert N. *Essentials of Accounting.* 5th ed. Reading, MA.: Addison Wesley, 1993.
Bandler, James P. *How to Use Financial Statements.* Burr Ridge, IL.: Irwin Professional Publishing, 1994.
Brealey, Richard, and Stewart Myers. *Principles of Corporate Finance.* 4th ed. New York: McGraw-Hill, 1991.
Dun & Bradstreet. *Industry Norms and Key Business Ratios* (annual). New York.
Merrill Lynch. *How to Read a Financial Report.* 7th ed. New York: Merrill Lynch, 1993.
Robert Morris Associates. *Annual Statement Studies.* Philadelphia.
Ross, Stephen; Randolph Westerfield; and Jeffrey Jaffe. *Corporate Finance.* 4th ed. Burr Ridge, IL: Richard D. Irwin, 1996.
Standard & Poor's Analysts Handbook (annual). New York.
Troy, Leo. *Almanac of Business and Financial Ratios.* Englewood Cliffs, N.J.: Prentice Hall (annual).
Weston, J. Fred, and Thomas E. Copeland. *Managerial Finance.* 10th ed. Hinsdale, Ill.: Dryden Press, 1992.

SELF-STUDY EXERCISES AND PROBLEMS

(Solutions Provided in Appendix V)

   1. Work the following exercises:
      a. A company's 1997 net profit represents 11.4 percent of net sales. What's the company's return on net worth if asset turnover is 1.34

and capitalization is 67 percent of total assets? How would faster asset turnover affect the result?

b. A company's gross margin on 1997 sales is 31.4 percent. Total cost of goods sold amounts to $4,391,300, and net profit is 9.7 percent of sales. What are the company's total assets if the ratio of sales to assets is 82.7 percent? What's the return on capitalization if current liabilities are 21 percent of total assets?

c. What's the change in a company's current ratio of 2.2:1 (current assets are $573,100) if the following actions are taken individually? Also, how does each item affect working capital? The company:

1. Pays $67,500 of accounts payable with cash.
2. Collects $33,000 in notes receivable.
3. Purchases merchandise worth $41,300 on account.
4. Pays dividends of $60,000, of which $42,000 had been shown as accrued (an unpaid current liability).
5. Sells machine for $80,000, on which book value is $90,000 and accumulated depreciation is $112,000.
6. Sells merchandise on account that cost $73,500. Gross margin is 33 percent.
7. Writes off $20,000 from inventory as scrap and amortizes $15,000 of goodwill.

d. From the following data, calculate the outstanding days' receivables and payables for a company, using the methods shown in the chapter. What's the inventory turnover, calculated in different ways? Discuss your assumptions.

Sales for three months	$437,500
Cost of sales	298,400
Purchases	143,500
Beginning inventory	382,200
Ending inventory	227,300
Accounts receivable	156,800
Accounts payable	69,300
Normal sales terms	2/10,n/30
Normal purchase terms	n/45

2. From the following financial statements of the ABC Company for 1996 and 1997, prepare the ratios and measures discussed in this chapter.
   a. Ratios from the viewpoint of management.
   b. Ratios from the viewpoint of owners.
   c. Ratios from the viewpoint of lenders.

   Comment on the changes shown between the two years, and discuss the results' significance from the three points of view. Indicate which additional kinds of comparison you'd like to make for this company (an electronics manufacturer) and the type of information you'd need.

ABC COMPANY
Balance Sheets
December 31, 1996 and 1997
($ million)

	1996	1997
Assets		
Current assets:		
Cash	$ 82.7	$110.9
Accounts receivable—net	92.6	146.2
Inventories	88.8	129.5
Prepaid expenses	2.8	6.2
Advances from government	5.3	2.8
Total current assets	272.2	395.6
Property, plant, and equipment	215.2	283.4
Less: Accumulated depreciation	101.2	119.6
Net property	114.0	163.8
Other assets	3.1	4.2
Total assets	$389.3	$563.6
Liabilities and Net worth		
Current liabilities:		
Accounts payable	*$ 43.4*	*$ 62.9*
Accrued income tax	*36.7*	*44.0*
Accrued pension and profit sharing	*27.1*	*38.4*
Other accruals	*21.9*	*31.2*
Current portion of long-term debt	*2.1*	*—*
Total current liabilities	*131.2*	*176.5*
Debentures (996 due 2000)	*—*	*94.0*
Other long-term debt	*7.8*	*4.1*
Deferred income tax	*5.2*	*7.6*
Common stock ($1 par)	*10.1*	*10.2*
Paid-in surplus	*25.1*	*27.2*
Retained earnings	*209.9*	*244.0*
Total liabilities and net worth	*$389.3*	*$563.6*

ABC COMPANY
Operating Statements for 1996 and 1997
($ millions)

	1996	1997
Assets		
Net sales	$655.1	$872.7
Cost of goods and services*	460.9	616.1
Gross profit	194.2	256.6
Selling, general, and administrative expenses	98.3	125.2
Employee profit sharing and retirement	26.9	38.7
	125.2	163.9
Operating profit	69.0	92.7
Other income	1.1	1.8
	70.1	94.5
Interest paid	1.0	7.4
	69.1	87.1
Provision for income taxes	31.8	40.1
Net profit†	$ 37.3	$ 47.0
*Depreciation and amortization	$ 28.2	$ 38.5
†Common dividends paid	5.5	6.0

3. Select a major manufacturing company, a retailing firm, a public utility, a bank, and a transportation firm. From an information source like Value Line, Moody's, or Standard & Poor's, develop a historical analysis of key measures you consider significant to appraise the effectiveness of management, the return to owners, and the position of the lenders. Develop significant industry comparisons and comment on the relative position of your chosen company Also comment on some of the assumptions and choices you have to make on the selection of specific accounts and data to work the analytical techniques.

FIGURE 3–6

TRW INC. AND SUBSIDIARIES

Selected Notes to Financial Statements

Principles of consolidation—The financial statements include the accounts of the company and its subsidiaries, except for an insurance subsidiary. The wholly-owned insurance subsidiary and the majority of investments in affiliated companies, which are not significant individually or in the aggregate, are accounted for by the equity method.

Use of Estimates—The preparation of financial statements in conformity with generally accepted accounting principles requires management to make estimates and assumptions that affect the reported amounts of assets and liabilities and disclosures of contingent assets and liabilities as of December 31, 1995 and 1994, respectively, and reported amounts of revenues and expenses for the years ended December 31, 1995, 1994 and 1993, respectively. Actual results could differ from those estimates.

Long-term contracts—The percentage-of-completion (cost-to-cost) method is used to estimate sales under fixed-price and fixed-price incentive contracts. Sales under cost-reimbursement contracts are recorded as costs are incurred. Fees based on cost, award fees, and incentive fees are included in sales at the time such amounts are reasonably estimable. Losses on contracts are recognized when determinable.

Accounts receivable—Accounts receivable at December 31, 1995 and 1994 included $507 million and $492 million, respectively, related to long-term contracts, of which $253 million and $269 million, respectively, were unbilled. Unbilled costs, fees, and claims represent revenues earned and billable in the following month, as well as revenues earned but not billable under terms of the contracts. A substantial portion of such amounts is expected to be billed during the following year. Retainage receivables and receivables subject to negotiation are not significant.

Inventories—Inventories are stated at the lower of cost, principally the first-in, first-out (FIFO) method, or market. Inventories applicable to long-term contracts are not significant.

Depreciation—Depreciation is computed over the assets' estimated useful lives, using the straight-line method for the majority of the company's depreciable assets. The remaining assets are depreciated using accelerated methods.

Intangible assets—Intangible assets are stated on the basis of cost. Intangibles arising from acquisitions prior to 1971 ($75 million) are not being amortized because there is no indication of diminished value. Intangibles arising from acquisitions after 1970 are being amortized by the straight-line method principally over 40 years. Capitalized data files are amortized by the straight-line method over periods not exceeding 15 years. The carrying value of intangible assets is assessed for impairment on a quarterly basis.

FIGURE 3–6

(continued)

Forward exchange contracts—The company enters into forward exchange contracts, the majority of which hedge firm foreign currency commitments and certain intercompany transactions. At December 31, 1995, the company had contracts outstanding amounting to approximately $219 million denominated in the German mark, the Italian lira, the British pound, the U.S. dollar, and the French franc, maturing at various dates through March 1997. Changes in market value of the contracts are included in the basis of the transactions. The company is exposed to credit loss in the event of nonperformance by the counterparties to the foreign exchange contracts. No collateral is held in relation to the contracts and the company anticipates that the counterparties will satisfy their obligations under the contracts.

Fair values of financial instruments

In millions	1995		1994	
	Carrying Value	Fair Value	Carrying Value	Fair Value
Cash and cash equivalents	$59	$59	$109	$109
Short-term debt	133	133	122	122
Floating rate long-term debt	74	74	171	171
Fixed rate long-term debt	547	632	680	673
Interest rate swaps—(liability)	—	(2)	—	(5)
Forward currency exchange contracts—asset	—	1	—	—

The fair value of long-term debt was estimated using discounted cash flow analysis, based on the company's current borrowing rates for similar types of borrowing arrangements. The fair value of interest rate and forward currency exchange contracts are estimated based on quoted market prices of offsetting contracts.

Environmental costs—TRW participates in environmental assessments and remedial efforts at operating facilities, previously owned or operated facilities, and Superfund or other waste sites. Costs related to these locations are accrued when it is probable that a liability has been incurred and the amount of that liability can be reasonably estimated. Estimated costs are recorded at undiscounted amounts based on experience and assessments, and are regularly evaluated as efforts proceed. Insurance recoveries are recorded as a reduction of environmental costs when fixed and determinable.

Earnings per share—Fully diluted earnings per share have been computed based on the weighted average number of shares of common stock outstanding during each year, including common stock equivalents (stock options), and assuming the conversion of the Serial Preference Stock II—Series 1 and 3. Primary earnings per share have been computed based on the weighted average number of shares of common stock outstanding during each year, including common stock equivalents.

Accounting change—Effective January 1, 1993, the company adopted Statement of Financial Accounting Standards No. 112, "Employers' Accounting for Postemployment Benefits." The company recognized the cumulative effect of this accounting change as of January 1, 1993, resulting in a one-time charge of $25 million (after a reduction for income taxes of $16 million).

Research and development

In millions	1995	1994	1993
Customer-funded	$1,387	$1,157	$1,223
Company-funded Research and development	422	412	378
Product development	154	140	136
	576	552	514
	$1,963	$1,709	$1,737

Company-funded research and development programs include research and development for commercial products and independent research and development and bid and proposal work related to government products and services. A portion of the cost incurred for independent research and development and

FIGURE 3–6

(continued)

bid and proposal work is recoverable through overhead charged to government contracts. Product development costs include engineering and field support for new customer requirements.

Restructuring

For balance sheet purposes, other accruals in 1995 and 1994 include $16 million and $33 million, respectively, relating to restructuring reserves. The decline in the reserve during 1995 resulted principally from the downsizing and streamlining of certain businesses in the automotive segment.

Restructuring expenses in 1993 consists of restructuring charges of $23 million, principally in the automotive segment, resulting from additional management decisions reduced by gains of $16 million from the sales of certain businesses in the automotive segment.

Other expense (income)—net

In millions	1995	1994	1993
Other income	$(42)	$(66)	$(69)
Other expense	47	60	42
Gain on sale of assets	(5)	(28)	(4)
Foreign currency translation	10	43	22
	$ 10	$ 9	$ (9)

Gain on sale of assets in 1994 includes a gain on the sale of a product line in the information systems and services segment.

Income taxes

Earnings before income taxes and cumulative effect of accounting change

In millions	1995	1994
U.S.	$511	$387
Non-U.S.	197	148
	$708	$535

Provision for income taxes

In millions	1995	1994
Current		
U.S. federal	$119	$106
Non-U.S.	57	40
U.S. state and local	19	24
	195	170
Deferred		
U.S. federal	32	28
Non-U.S.	14	5

U.S. state and local	21	(1)
	67	32
	$262	$202

Effective income tax rate

	1995	1994
U.S. statutory income tax rate	35.0%	35.0%
Restructuring benefits	—	—
Nondeductible expenses	1.3	1.6
U.S. state and local income taxes not of U.S. federal tax benefit	3.7	2.7
Non-U.S. tax rate variances net of foreign tax credits	(.1)	(.4)
Prior year adjustments	(2.7)	—
Other	(.2)	(1.1)
Effective income tax rate	37.0%	37.8%

Deferred Income taxes reflect the net tax effects of temporary differences between the carrying amounts of assets and liabilities for financial reporting purposes and the amounts used for income tax purposes. At December 31, 1995 and 1994, the company had unused tax benefits of $33 million and $40 million, respectively, related to non-U.S. net operating loss carryforwards for income tax purposes, of which $16 million and $23 million can be carried forward indefinitely and the balance expires at various dates through the year 2000. A valuation allowance at December 31, 1995 and 1994 of $27 million and $26 million, respectively, has been recognized to offset the related deferred tax assets due to the uncertainty of realizing the benefit of the loss carryforwards.

It is the company's intention to reinvest undistributed earnings of certain of its non-U.S. subsidiaries and thereby indefinitely postpone their remittance. Accordingly, deferred income taxes have not been provided for accumulated undistributed earnings of $325 million at December 31, 1995.

	Deferred tax assets		Deferred tax liabilities	
In millions	1995	1994	1995	1994
Pensions and post-retirement bene-fits other than pensions	$263	$259	$38	$43

FIGURE 3–6

(continued)

In millions	Deferred tax assets		Deferred tax liabilities	
	1995	1994	1995	1994
Completed contract method of accounting for long-term contracts	52	50	425	414
State and local taxes	22	29	9	9
Reserves and accruals	79	107	—	—
Depreciation and amortization	16	19	153	130
Insurance accruals	26	28	—	—
Non-U.S. net operating loss carryforwards	33	40	—	—
Other	133	109	48	49
	624	641	673	645
Valuation allowance for deferred tax assets	(27)	(26)	—	—
Total	$597	$615	$673	$645

Pension plans

The company has defined benefit pension plans (generally noncontributory except for those in the United Kingdom) for substantially all employees. Plans for most salaried employees provide pay-related benefits based on years of service. Plans for hourly employees generally provide benefits based on flat-dollar amounts and years of service.

Under the company's funding policy, annual contributions are made to fund the plans during the participants' working lifetimes, except for unfunded plans in Germany and certain non-qualified plans in the U.S., which are funded as benefits are paid to participants. Annual contributions to funded plans have met or exceeded ERISA's minimum funding requirements or amounts required by local law or custom.

The company sponsors a contributory stock savings plan for which a majority of its U.S. employees are eligible. The company matches employee contributions up to 3 percent of the participant's qualified compensation. The company contributions are held in an unleveraged employee stock ownership plan. The company also sponsors other defined contribution pension plans covering employees at some of its operations.

In millions	1995		1994		1993	
	U.S.	Non-U.S.	U.S.	Non-U.S.	U.S.	Non-U.S.
Defined benefit plans						
Service cost—benefits earned during the year	$55	$15	$60	$13	$52	$12
Interest cost on projected benefit obligation	157	27	149	24	150	23
Actual (return) loss on plan assets	(521)	(38)	40	11	(319)	(51)
Net amortization and deferral	314	19	(237)	(28)	126	35
Total pension cost of defined benefit plans	5	23	12	20	9	19
Defined contribution plans	1	5	1	3	1	2
Stock savings plan	38	—	36	—	36	—
	$44	$28	$49	$23	$46	$21

In millions	1995		1994	
	U.S.	Non-U.S.	U.S.	Non-U.S.
Actuarial present value of benefit obligations				
Vested benefit obligation	$1,961	$ 328	$1,546	$ 275
Overfunded plans	$1,995	$ 208	$1,565	$ 182
Underfunded plans	128	136	110	100
Total accumulated benefit obligation	$2,123	$ 344	$1,675	$ 282
Projected benefit obligation	$2,367	$ 378	$1,810	$ 311
Overfunded plans	$2,508	$ 249	$2,142	$ 220
Underfunded plans	78	28	65	25

FIGURE 3–6

(*continued*)

In millions	1995		1994	
	U.S.	Non-U.S.	U.S.	Non-U.S.
Total plan assets at fair value (primarily listed stocks and bonds)	2,586	277	2,207	245
Plan assets in excess of (less than) projected benefit obligation	219	(101)	397	(66)
Unrecognized net gain	(35)	(18)	(218)	(26)
Unrecognized net assets from January 1, 1986 (January 1, 1989 for non-U.S. plans)	(59)	(5)	(77)	(6)
Unrecognized prior service cost	30	9	42	9
Additional minimum liability	(26)	(8)	(18)	(6)
Net pension asset (liability) recognized in the balance sheet	$ 129	$ (123)	$ 126	$ (95)

Actuarial Assumptions:

	1995		1994	
	U.S.	Non-U.S.	U.S.	Non-U.S.
Discount rate	7%	7 – 8½%	8½%	8 – 8¾%
Rate of increase in compensation levels	3%	4½ – 5%	3%	5 – 5¾%
Long-term rate of return on plan assets	9%	7 – 9½%	9%	6 – 9½%

Postretirement benefits other than pensions

The company provides health care and life insurance benefits for a majority of its retired employees in the United States and Canada. The health care plans provide for cost sharing, in the form of employee contributions, deductibles, and coinsurance, between the company and its retirees. The postretirement health care plan, covering a majority of employees who retired since August 1, 1988, limits the annual increase in the company's contribution toward the plan's cost to a maximum of the lesser of 50 percent of medical inflation, or 4 percent. Life insurance benefits are generally noncontributory. The company's policy is to fund the cost of postretirement health care and life insurance benefits in amounts determined at the discretion of management. Retirees in certain other countries are provided similar benefits by plans sponsored by their governments.

In millions	1995	1994
Accumulated postretirement benefit obligation		
Retirees	$ 508	$ 420
Fully eligible active participants	38	37
Other active participants	232	194
	778	651
Plan assets at fair value (primarily listed stocks and bonds)	61	32
Accumulated postretirement benefit obligation in excess of plan assets	(717)	(619)
Unrecognized prior service cost	(7)	(7)
Unrecognized net (gain) loss	7	(89)

	1995	1994
Net liability recognized in the balance sheet	$(717)	$(715)

In millions	1995	1994	1993
Service cost	$10	$13	$13
Interest cost	55	53	59
Actual return on plan assets	(9)	—	(1)
Net amortization and deferral	4	(3)	(1)
Net periodic postretirement benefit cost	$60	$63	$70

The discount rate used in determining the accumulated postretirement benefit obligation as of December 31, 1995 and 1994 was 7 percent and 8½ percent, respectively. At December 31, 1995, the 1996 annual rate of increase in the per capita cost of covered health care benefits was assumed to be 10 percent for participants under age 65 and 9 percent for participants age 65 or older. The rates were assumed to decrease gradually to 6 percent and 5 percent, respectively, in the year 2009 and remain at that level thereafter. At December 31, 1994, the 1995 annual rate of increase in the per capita cost of covered health care benefits was assumed to be 10 percent for participants under age 65 and 9 percent for participants age 65 or older. The rates were assumed to decrease gradually to 6 percent and 5 percent, respectively, in the year 2021 and remain at that level thereafter. A 1 percent annual increase in these assumed cost trend rates would increase the accumulated postretirement benefit obligation at December 31, 1995 by approximately 8 percent, and the aggregate of the service and interest cost components of net periodic postretirement benefit cost for 1995 by approximately 9 percent. The weighted average expected long-term rate of return on plan assets was 8 percent for 1995 and 9 percent for 1994. The trust holding the majority of the plan assets is not subject to federal income taxes.

FIGURE 3–6

(continued)

Debt and credit agreements

Short-term debt

In millions	1995	1994
U.S. borrowings	$ 13	$ —
Non-U.S. borrowings	120	122
	$133	$122

Long-term debt

In millions	1995	1994
U.S. borrowings	$ —	$ 26
Non-U.S. borrowings	85	148
7.3% ESOP obligations due 1997	60	95
Medium-term notes:		
9.35% Notes due 2020 (due 2000 at option of note holder)	100	100
9⅜% Notes due 2021	100	100
Other medium-term notes	234	309
Other	42	73
Total long-term debt	621	851
Less current portion	80	157
	$541	$694

TRW maintains a committed U.S. revolving credit agreement with 17 banks. The agreement allows the company to borrow up to $550 million and extends through February 2000. The interest rate under the agreement is either a negotiated rate, the banks' prime rates, a rate based upon the banks' costs of funds in the secondary certificate of deposit market, or a rate based upon an Interbank Offered Rate. TRW's commercial paper borrowings are supported by this agreement. At December 31, 1995, there were no outstanding borrowings under the U.S. revolving credit agreement. The weighted average interest rate on short-term borrowings outstanding at December 31, 1995 and 1994 is 7.6 and 7.2 percent, respectively.

The company also maintains a committed multicurrency revolving credit agreement with 13 banks. The agreement allows the company to borrow up to $200 million and extends through February 2000. The interest rate under the agreement is based on various interest rate indices. At December 31, 1995, there were no outstanding borrowings under the multicurrency credit agreement. At December 31, 1995, $41 million of short-term non-U.S. borrowings have been reclassified to long-term non-U.S. borrowings,

because the company intends to refinance these borrowings on a long-term basis and has the ability to do so under its multicurrency revolving credit agreement.

As of December 31, 1995, the company has interest rate swap agreements for notional borrowings of $135 million, in which the company pays a fixed rate and receives a floating rate. The weighted average pay rate and receive rate under these agreements is 8.1 percent and 5.4 percent, respectively. These agreements mature at various dates through 1998.

The floating rates under the interest rate swap agreements are both based on commercial paper and LIBOR rates and have been calculated using these rates at December 31, 1995. Net payments or receipts under the agreements are recognized as an adjustment to interest expense. The company is exposed to credit loss in the event of nonperformance by the counterparties to the interest rate swap agreements. No collateral is held in relation to the agreements and the company anticipates that the counterparties will satisfy their obligations under the agreements.

The other medium-term notes bear interest rates ranging from 5.98 percent to 9.25 percent, and mature at various dates through 2020.

Non-U.S. borrowings bear interest, stated in terms of the local currency borrowing, at rates ranging from 2.13 percent to 12.5 percent at December 31, 1995, and mature at various dates through 2004.

The maturities of long-term debt are, in millions: 1996-$80; 1997-$76; 1998-$16; 1999-$16; 2000-$52; and $381 thereafter.

The indentures and other debt agreements impose, among other covenants, restrictions on funded debt and maintenance of minimum tangible net worth. Under the most restrictive interpretation of these covenants, the payment of dividends was limited to approximately $1,273 million at December 31, 1995.

FIGURE 3–6

(*continued*)

At December 31, 1995, approximately 800 employees were participants in the plans. As of that date, the average exercise price of options outstanding was $52.89 per share, and the expiration dates ranged from July 1996 to February 2005. The company is currently planning to adopt the disclosure provisions of Statement of Financial Accounting Standards No. 123, "Accounting for Stock-Based Compensation," in 1996.

TRW grants performance share rights to certain employees under which the employees are entitled to receive shares of the company's common stock based on the achievement of a certain return on assets employed. The rights specify a target number of shares which the employee would receive for each year that goals for returns on assets employed are met. If the goals are exceeded, the employee could receive up to 200 percent of the target shares, with the excess over 100 percent payable in cash (unless the compensation and stock option committee of the board of directors determines to pay the excess in shares). If the goals are not met, the employee would receive fewer than the target shares or no shares. At December 31, 1995 and 1994,

the target number of performance share rights granted to employees and still outstanding were .2 million and .4 million, respectively.

Stock options

TRW has granted incentive and nonqualified stock options to certain employees to purchase the company's common stock at the market price on the date of grant. TRW accounts for stock option grants in accordance with APB Opinion No. 25, "Accounting for Stock Issued to Employees." Subject to certain exceptions, incentive stock options become exercisable to the extent of one-half of the optioned shares for each full year of employment following the date of grant, and nonqualified stock options granted prior to 1987 become exercisable to the extent of one-fourth of the optioned shares for each full year of employment following the date of grant. Nonqualified stock options granted after 1986 become exercisable to the extent of one-third of the optioned shares for each full year of employment following the date of grant. Generally, both incentive and nonqualified stock options expire 10 years after the date of grant.

	1995		1994	
	Millions of shares	Option Price	Millions of shares	Option Price
Outstanding at beginning of year	4.7	$39.285 to $65.75	4.5	$31.44 to $64.07
Granted	.7	64.63	.9	65.75
Became exercisable	.3	44.125 to 65.75	.6	39.75 to 64.07
Exercised	.7	39.285 to 65.75	.6	31.44 to 56.94
Canceled, expired, or terminated	.1	39.285 to 65.75	.1	31.44 to 65.75
Outstanding at end of year	4.6	39.75 to 65.75	4.7	39.285 to 65.75
Exercisable	3.3	39.75 to 65.75	3.8	39.285 to 64.07

Contingencies

The company is subject to various investigations, claims, and legal proceedings covering a wide range of matters that arise in the ordinary course of its business activities. In addition, the company is conducting a number of environmental investigations and remedial actions at current and former company locations and, along with other companies, has been named a potentially responsible party for certain waste management sites. Each of these matters is subject to various uncertainties, and

some of these matters may be resolved unfavorably to the company. The company has established accruals for matters that are probable and reasonably estimable including $84 million for environmental matters at December 31, 1995. The company believes that any liability that may result from the resolution of environmental matters for which sufficient information is available to support cost estimates will not have a material adverse effect on the company's financial position. However, the company cannot predict the effect on the

FIGURE 3–6

(continued)

company's financial position of expenditures for aspects of certain matters for which there is insufficient information. In addition, the company cannot predict the effect of compliance with environmental laws and regulations with respect to unknown environmental matters or the possible effect of compliance with environmental requirements imposed in the future.

Further, product liability claims may be asserted in the future for events not currently known by management. Although the ultimate liability from these potential claims cannot be ascertained at December 31, 1995, management does not anticipate that any related liability, after consideration of insurance recovery, would have a material adverse effect on the company's financial position.

Lease commitments

TRW leases certain offices, manufacturing and research buildings, machinery, automobiles, and data processing and other equipment. Such leases, some of which are noncancelable and in many cases include renewals, expire at various dates. The company pays most maintenance, insurance, and tax expenses relating to leased assets. Rental expense for operating leases was $179 million for 1995, $164 million for 1994, and $162 million for 1993.

At December 31, 1995, future minimum lease payments for noncancelable operating leases totaled $388 million and are payable as follows: 1996-$98; 1997-$78; 1998-$52; 1999-$35; 2000-$28; and $97 thereafter.

Capital stock

Serial Preference Stock II—cumulative—stated at $2.75 a share; 5 million shares authorized.

Series 1—each share convertible into 4.4 shares of common; redeemable at $104 per share; involuntary liquidation price $104 per share; dividend rate of $4.40 per annum.

Series 3—each share convertible into 3.724 shares of common; redeemable at $100 per share; involuntary liquidation price $40 per share; dividend rate of $4.50 per annum.

Series 4—not convertible into common shares; redemption price and involuntary liquidation price of $125 per one one-hundredth of a share; annual dividend rate per one one-hundredth of a share of the lesser of $4.00 or the current dividend on common stock; no shares outstanding at December 31, 1995.

Common stock—$0.625 par value; authorized 250 million shares; shares outstanding were reduced by treasury shares of .6 million in 1995 and .4 million in 1994.

TRW has a shareholder purchase rights plan under which each shareholder of record as of January 6, 1989 received one right for each TRW common share held. Each right entitles the holder, upon the occurrence of certain events, to buy one one-hundredth of a share of Cumulative Redeemable Serial Preference Stock II, Series 4, at a price of $125. Should certain additional events occur, each right allows the shareholder to purchase $250 of the surviving entity's common shares at a 50 percent discount. The company may redeem these rights at its option at one cent per right under certain circumstances.

At December 31, 1995, 6.8 million shares of common stock were reserved for the exercise and issuance of stock options and conversion of the Serial Preference Stock II, Series 1 and 3. There were .7 million shares of Cumulative Redeemable Serial Preference Stock II, Series 4, reserved for the shareholder purchase rights plan.

Industry segments

TRW Inc. is a global manufacturing and service company based in the United States. It is strategically focused on providing products and services in the automotive, space and defense, and information systems and services markets. The principal markets for the company's automotive products are North American, European, and Asian original equipment

FIGURE 3–6

(continued)

manufacturers and independent distributors. Space and defense primarily provides products and services to the United States government, agencies of the United States government, and commercial customers. Information systems and services provides information and services to businesses, credit-granting organizations, financial institutions, and individual consumers.

Automotive—Occupant restraint systems, including sensors, air bag, and seat belt systems; electrical and electronic controls. Steering systems, including power and manual rack and pinion steering for light vehicles, hydraulic steering systems for commercial truck and off-highway vehicles and suspension components. Engine valves and valve train parts, pistons, engineered fasteners, stud welding and control systems.

Space & Defense—Spacecraft, including the design and manufacture of military and civilian spacecraft equipment, propulsion subsystems, electro-optical and instrument systems, spacecraft payloads, high-energy lasers and laser technology, and other high-reliability components. Software and systems engineering support services in the fields of military command and control, earth observation, environmental monitoring and nuclear waste management, air traffic control, telecommunications, security and counterterrorism, undersea surveillance, and other high-technology space, defense, and civil government support systems. Electronic systems, equipment and services, including the design and manufacture of space communication systems, airborne reconnaissance systems, unmanned aerial vehicles, avionics systems, and other electronic technologies for tactical and strategic space, defense, and selected commercial applications.

Information Systems & Services—Information systems and services, including consumer and commercial credit information and related services, direct marketing, real estate information and services, and imaging systems engineering and integration.

In millions	Year ended December 31	Automotive	Space & Defense	Information Systems & Services	Company Staff & Other	Total
Sales	1995	$6,468	$3,100	$604	$ —	$10,172
	1994	5,679	2,812	596	—	9,087
	1993	4,538	2,792	618	—	7,948
Operating profit by segment[1]	1995	$ 607	$ 192	$ 87	$(178)	$ 708
	1994	476	175	96	(212)	535
	1993	309	199	74	(223)	359
Identifiable assets by segment[2]	1995	$3,706	$1,113	$661	$ 410	$ 5,890
	1994	3,481	1,111	622	422	5,636
	1993	3,004	1,253	752	327	5,336
Depreciation and amortization of property, plant, and equipment	1995	$ 304	$ 102	$ 18	$ 9	$ 433
	1994	264	111	20	7	402
	1993	238	116	26	8	388
Capital expenditures	1995	$ 314	$ 114	$ 19	$ 38	$ 485
	1994	388	98	18	2	506
	1993	367	90	23	2	482

[1]The "Company Staff & Other" column includes: (1) company staff and other expenses of $84, $111, and $91 million, (b) interest expense of $95, $105, and $138 million, and (c) earnings from affiliates of $1, $4, and $6 million for each of the respective years. The total represents consolidated earnings before income taxes and cumulative effect of accounting change.
[2]The "Company Staff & Other" column includes: (1) company staff assets of $397, $380, and $317 million, (b) investment in affiliates of $49, $70, and $56 million, and (c) eliminations of $(36), $(28), and $(46) million for each of the respective years. The total represents the consolidated total assets of the company.

FIGURE 3–6

(continued)

At December 31, 1995 and 1994, accounts receivable in the automotive segment were $869 million and $774 million, respectively, and accounts receivable in the space and defense segment, principally from agencies of the U.S. Government, were $478 million and $491 million, respectively. The company generally does not require collateral from its customers.

Company staff assets consist principally of cash and cash equivalents, current deferred income taxes, and administrative facilities. Intersegment sales were not significant. Sales to agencies of the U.S. Government, primarily by the space and defense segment, were $2,899 million in 1995, $2,545 million in 1994, and $2,708 million in 1993. Sales to Ford Motor Company by the automotive segment were $1,474 million in 1995, $1,363 million in 1994, and $1,096 million in 1993.

Geographic segments

In millions	Year ended December 31	United States	Europe	Other Areas	Company Staff & Other	Total
Sales	1995	$6,816	$2,525	$831	$ —	$10,172
	1994	6,290	1,965	832	—	9,087
	1993	5,643	1,522	783	—	7,948
Operating profit by segment[1]	1995	$ 601	$ 220	$ 65	$(178)	$ 708
	1994	528	143	76	(212)	535
	1993	461	50	71	(223)	359
Identifiable assets by segment[2]	1995	$3,529	$1,465	$537	$ 359	$ 5,890
	1994	3,444	1,289	531	372	5,636
	1993	3,536	1,047	461	292	5,336

TRW's operations are located primarily in the United States and Europe. Interarea sales are not significant to the total revenue of any geographic area.

[1]The "Company Staff & Other" column includes: (1) Company Staff and other expenses of $84, $111, and $91 million, (b) interest expense of $95, $105, and $138 million, and (c) earnings from affiliates of $1, $4, and $6 million for each of the respective years. The total represents consolidated earnings before income taxes and cumulative effect of accounting change.

[2]The "Company Staff & Other" column includes: (a) Company Staff assets of $397, $380, and $317 million, (b) investment in affiliates of $49, $70, and $56 million, and (c) eliminations of $(87), $(78), and $(81) million for each of the respective years. The total represents the consolidated total assets of the company.

Stock prices and dividends

The book value per common share at December 31, 1995 was $32.97 compared to $27.91 at the end of 1994. Our directors declared the 230th consecutive quarterly dividend during December 1995. Dividends declared per share in 1995 were $2.10, up 7 percent from $1.97 in 1994. The following table highlights the market prices of our common and preferences stocks and dividends paid for the quarters of 1995 and 1994.

	Quarter	Price of traded shares				Dividends paid per share	
		1995		1994		1995	1994
		High	Low	High	Low		
Common stock	1	$ 70	$ 61¾	$ 77½	$ 65¾	$ .50	$ .47
Par value $0.625 per share	2	81¾	67	71¼	61	.50	.47
	3	82⅝	71⅜	75⅛	63⅝	.50	.50
	4	78⅝	64⅛	74¾	62	.55	.50
Cumulative Serial	1	350	225	326	320	1.10	1.10
Preference Stock II	2	349¼	348	350	250	1.10	1.10
$4.40 Convertible	3	336½	336½	325	325	1.10	1.10
Series 1	4	325⅝	300⅝	316	275	1.10	1.10
Cumulative Serial	1	236	236	256½	256½	1.125	1.125
Preference Stock II	2	292¼	265	244	232	1.125	1.125
$4.50 Convertible	3	288	283	272	272	1.125	1.125
Series 3	4	290	254	238	232	1.125	1.125

The $4.40 Convertible Series 1 was not actively traded during the first quarter of 1995. The prices shown represent the range of asked (high) and bid (low) quotations.

CHAPTER 4

Projection of Financial Requirements

Up to this point, we've discussed appraisal of performance and management of operating funds in the context of *past* decisions involving investments, operations, and financing. This chapter shifts the emphasis to a *forward* look, that is, forecasting likely future conditions, a critically important task in managing any business. We'll discuss the key concepts and techniques of projecting operating performance and expected financial requirements with which to support future operations. Such projections normally involve alternative plans developed for different sets of conditions, and testing of the sensitivity of the results to changes in key assumptions.

Projection of financial requirements is only part of the business planning process with which management positions the company's future activities relative to the expected economic, competitive, technical, and social environment. When business plans are developed, they are usually structured around specific goals and objectives cooperatively set by the organization and its subgroups. The plans normally spell out strategies and actions for achieving desired short-term, intermediate, and long-term results.

Eventually, such plans are quantified in financial terms, in the form of projected financial statements (pro forma statements) and a variety of operational budgets. Detailed cash budgets and cash flow statements are often included to provide greater insight into the funding implications of the projected activities. Also, key ratios are usually calculated and presented. The concepts and techniques discussed in Chapters 2 and 3 are the necessary tools for this quantification.

The scope of this book allows us to focus only on the major methods and formats of financial projection. We cannot explicitly take into account the broader strategic planning framework through which the future direction of the company should be explored before any financial quantification can become fully meaningful. Nor can we go into the details of various statistical methods which are at times used to support the judgments involved in estimating future conditions.

Nevertheless, financial projection techniques by themselves can be useful simulations of the likely results of broad assumptions made by management about a variety of future conditions. The ease with which pro forma financial statements and cash flow projections can be developed makes them attractive as convenient approximations—which can be refined with additional information and insights—especially as the number of alternatives for action is narrowed down.

The use of computer spreadsheets and planning models continues to grow rapidly, as does the selection of software packages offering financial simulation and projection capabilities. The speed and multiple tracking ability of computers has eliminated much of the drudgery of tracing investment, operational, and financing assumptions through the financial framework of a business. While commercial software offerings differ in their specific orientation and degree of sophistication, they are all built around the very concepts we will be discussing in this chapter.

The most important requirement for the successful analyst, however, is a solid understanding of basic financial techniques and relationships, because computer spreadsheets and analytical packages cannot remove the overriding need for judgment and consistency. Only with such understanding can the analyst take full advantage of the capabilities embodied within computer software and models. Therefore, this book doesn't focus on how to program spreadsheets or how to deal with specific software packages, but rather on explaining the financial concepts and techniques themselves in our decisional context.

The main techniques of financial projection fall into three categories:

■ Pro forma financial statements.

■ Cash budgets.

■ Operating budgets.

Pro forma statements, as the name implies, are projected financial statements embodying a set of assumptions about a company's future performance and funding requirements. Cash budgets are detailed projections of the specific incidence of cash moving in and out of the business. Operating budgets are detailed projections of companywide or departmental revenue and/or expense patterns, and they are subsidiary to both pro forma statements and cash flow statements.

All three categories involve organized arrays of financial and economic data for the purpose of assessing future performance and funds requirements. As we'll see, the three methodologies are also closely interrelated—a linkage that can be exploited to achieve consistent financial forecasts.

After discussing each category in detail, we'll also briefly examine basic financial modeling and the use of sensitivity analysis for testing the impact of changes in critical assumptions underlying the financial projections.

PRO FORMA FINANCIAL STATEMENTS

The most comprehensive look at the likely future financial performance of a company can be obtained by developing a set of pro forma statements. These are merely an operating statement and a related balance sheet extended into the future by a variety of assumptions. The pro forma operating statement represents an operational plan for the business, while the pro forma balance sheet reflects the anticipated cumulative impact of assumed future decisions on its financial condition. Both statements are prepared by taking the most readily available estimates of future activity and projecting, account by account, the assumed results and conditions. As we'll see, the approach is not based on detailed accounting transactions, but rather on a creative use of the financial statement framework as a structure on which to arrange future expectations.

Many times a third statement, the pro forma cash flow statement, is prepared to add further insight by displaying the funds movements expected during the forecast period, arranged into our familiar categories of operations, investments, and financing. It provides the most dynamic view of the expected changes in the company's funding picture, as we saw in Chapter 2.

Pro forma projections can be done for any time frame and at any level of detail desired. In summarized form, these statements are one of the most widely used ways of quickly making financial estimates. They are particularly favored by bank loan officers, who must assess the creditworthiness of the client company from a total financial standpoint. Detailed plans aren't needed to construct complete pro forma statements, even though using the results of a formal planning process would increase the degree of precision. Instead, selected ratios can be used to produce statements that are entirely satisfactory, particularly as a first look. As we'll demonstrate, an important aspect of pro forma analysis is the ability to find the company's net cash requirements as of the future date for which the pro forma balance sheet is prepared.

To show how pro forma statements are developed, we'll use the example of fictitious manufacturing company called XYZ Corporation. The company makes and sells three different products, has a seasonal pattern with the low point occurring in December, and it is currently profitable. The most recent actual results available are for the third quarter of 1996. This initial set of data allows us to project ahead, but we can also ask management for additional information as needed. The pro forma projection is to be made for the last quarter of 1996, and the objective is to determine both the level of profit for the quarter and the amount of additional funds that will be needed as of the end of the year. A quarterly pattern was chosen for this illustration because it permits us to consider seasonal changes in addition to simple period-to-period changes. There is no difference in the basic principles for projecting either annual or quarterly periods— only the length of the period.

Pro Forma Operating Statement

We begin the process with the pro forma operating statement for XYZ Corporation. The operating statement is normally prepared first, because the amount of aftertax profit developed there must also be reflected in the pro forma balance sheet as a change in retained earnings, in order to ensure consistency between the two statements.

The starting point for the operating statement, as shown on the first line in Figure 4–1, is a projection of the unit and dollar volume of *sales*. This can be estimated in a variety of ways, ranging from trend-line projection to detailed departmental sales forecasts by individual product, often built up from field estimates. In the absence of any other information we may, of course, make our own "guesstimates" based on past overall results. In the case of XYZ Corporation, we know that a seasonal pattern exists, and that sales can be expected to decline in the last quarter.

In Figure 4–1, we've shown the actual operating statement for the third quarter of 1996. Dollar amounts are given for key revenue and cost elements, as well as a breakdown into percent of sales, or common numbers. In making the necessary series of assumptions, we'll use the third-quarter experience as a guide, because we've been assured that the quarterly pattern over the years has been reasonably stable. Company statistics from past years suggest that during the fourth quarter, a drop of 18 to 20 percent in sales volume is normal. We'll take the midpoint of this range as a beginning assumption. After calculating a 19 percent drop in unit volume, we'll further assume that both prices and product mix will remain unchanged. It's possible, of course, to make different assumptions about volume, prices, and mix of the three individual products in order to reflect specific insights or to test the sensitivity of operating profit to the impact of "what if" questions. In our case, an inquiry to sales management will confirm that this set of assumptions about sales matches their own forecast.

Next we turn to *cost of goods sold*. The actual third-quarter operating statement provides details on the main components—labor, materials, overhead, and delivery—contained in cost of goods sold. The simplest approach is to calculate the proportion of cost that each of these elements represents, and assume that the same proportions will hold during the fourth quarter.

But we must also remember that the last quarter is the company's seasonal low point, and we can assume that overall production costs are likely to rise, because as operations slow down, some inefficiencies will likely occur. Without more data, we can probably assume a rise of something like one percentage point in the ratio of cost of goods sold to sales as a quick way to allow for the seasonal distortion. The dollar penalty of this assumption is a reduction in the gross margin—currently $10,250,000—by 1 percent, or $102,500. We could, of course, test the impact of other levels of the cost of goods sold ratio, using the detailed cost breakdown (labor, materials, etc.) given in the third-quarter operating statement. If more precision were desired, specific assumptions could be made about each of these components. This is a basic form of sensitivity analysis—testing the impact on the outcome from changes in one or more key assumptions.

The main expense categories can be estimated by again examining the actual statement for the third quarter. The figures provided there might simply be accepted and used as the base for our projection, or more detailed assumptions could be tested. For a quick first look, the overall approach is usually acceptable. *Selling expense* is shown as $875,000. Given that the fourth quarter has lower sales activity, we can probably assume a small decrease, such as $50,000. A

FIGURE 4–1

XYZ CORPORATION
Pro Forma Income Statement
For the Quarter Ended December 31, 1996
($ thousands)

	Actual Quarter Ended 9-30-96		Pro Forma* Quarter Ended 12-31-96		Assumption and Sources of Information
Units sold	137,000		111,000		Last quarter is seasonal low; past data show 18 to 20 percent decline from third quarter.
Net sales	$ 12,650	100.0%	$ 10,250	100.0%	Projected 19 percent lower volume with same price and mix.
Cost of goods sold:					
Labor	2,210		1,810		21.5% of cost of goods as before.
Materials	2,045		1,680		20.0% of cost of goods as before.
Overhead	5,685		4,660		55.5% of cost of goods as before.
Delivery	305		250		3.0% of cost of goods as before.
Cost of goods					Increase of 1 percentage point to
sold	10,245	81.0	8,400	82.0	simulate operating inefficiencies.
Gross margin . . .	2,405	19.0	1,850	18.0	
Expenses:					
Selling expense	875	6.9	825	8.0	Assume drop of $50, to show lower activity.
General and					Assume slight increase for year-end
administrative					costs.
expenses . . .	585	4.6	600	5.9	
Total expenses	1,460	11.5	1,425	13.9	
Operating profit . .	945	7.5	425	4.1	Shows effect of less efficient operations.
Interest	190	1.5	175	1.7	Based on outstanding debt.
Profit before taxes	755	6.0	250	2.4	
Income taxes . . .	272	2.2	90	0.9	Projected at 36%.
Net income	483	3.8	160	1.5	
Dividends	100	0.8	-0-	-0-	No payment of dividends scheduled.
Retained earnings	383	3.0%	160	1.5%	Carried to balance sheet.
Depreciation added					From fixed asset records. (Assume tax
back	575		600		and book depreciation are the same.)
Cash flow after	$ 958		$ 760		Rough measure of cash from
dividends					operations. (We should add back any dividends to reflect operations only.)

*All projections are rounded off.

reduction fully proportional to the 19 percent drop in volume would not be realistic, however, given that many of the costs, such as base salaries of sales and marketing personnel, are essentially fixed in the near term.

Administrative expenses should be rounded off a little higher for purposes of our projection because of expected nonrecurring year-end outlays. Note that both expense elements now represent a higher proportion of sales than was true for the actual prior quarter. If there's reason to believe that this result seems out of line, it may, of course, be modified. But we must remember that even if historical patterns were available in great detail, the projection has to deal with the future, and the purpose of the exercise is to make the most realistic assumptions possible. These will, of course, remain assumptions until actual experience supersedes them.

As a result of all our assumptions, the fourth quarter *operating profit* falls by half a million dollars, and the profit ratio drops to almost half its former level. This is due mostly to the 19 percent drop in sales volume and the associated loss in profit contribution. The volume reduction represents $2.4 million of lost sales which, with a normal cost of goods sold ratio of 81 percent, would have contributed $456,000 to profit. Moreover, we assumed certain inefficiencies in operations and expected only a partial ability to reduce what are mostly fixed expenses. As stated before, this result can and should be examined against the best available experience to judge its appropriateness.

Interest expense is charged according to the provisions of the company's outstanding debt, information which is provided to us by the financial organization. The operating statement will be complete once we calculate *income taxes* (assumed here at an effective rate of 36 percent) to arrive at *net income*. We note that net income has dropped significantly in response to the slowdown in operations.

A further assumption needs to be made about *dividends* to arrive at *retained earnings* for the period, which have to be reflected in the pro forma balance sheet. In XYZ's case, no dividends have been declared. As a last step, we have added back the depreciation for the period, to calculate the *cash flow* from operations. As we recall from Chapter 3, this is a quick approximation which we'll review later in the context of all other expected funds movements.

Pro Forma Balance Sheet

Armed with the data about expected operations, we can now develop the pro forma balance sheet, which is illustrated in Figure 4–2. Again, we must make specific assumptions about each account, using the actual balance sheet data at the beginning of the forecast period and applying any additional information we can obtain from management. Fortunately, we have relative freedom to make and vary our estimates—except that there must always be complete consistency between any assumptions affecting *both* the operating statement and the balance sheet. The objective is not accounting precision, of course, but rather to develop an indication of approximate funds needs three months hence and a look at the overall financial condition of the company at that time.

We'll start the process with the first account, *cash*, and assume that three months hence, the company would need to keep only the minimum working balance in its bank accounts. The information source for this figure ($1,250,000), again, is the finance department. In the absence of such specific data, we could assume a level of cash that is common among companies of this size. As we'll see later, the desired amount of cash on hand directly affects the amount of

FIGURE 4–2

XYZ CORPORATION
Pro Forma Balance Sheet as of December 31, 1996
($ thousands)

	Actual 9-30-96	Change	Pro Forma 12-31-96	Assumptions and Sources of Information
Assets:				
Cash	$ 1,450	–$ 200	$ 1,250	Cash set at estimated minimum balance.
Accounts receivable	4,250	1,200	3,050	Represents 30 days' sales (from December sales projection).
Raw materials . . .	1,500	-0-	1,500	Safety level; requirements purchased as needed.
Finished goods . .	4,050	– 750	3,300	Reduced production by 19 percent.
Total current assets	11,250	– 2,150	9,100	Drop reflects seasonal pattern.
Fixed assets:				
Land	2,500	-0-	2,500	No change assumed.
Plant and equipment	20,800	– 1,500	19,300	Sale of machines with original cost of $1,500 and accumulated depreciation of $950.
Less: Accumulated depreciation . . .	8,350	– 350	8,000	Depreciation for period $600, per income statement, less reduction of $950 from sale of machines.
Net plant and equipment . . .	12,450	– 1,150	11,300	
Total fixed assets	14,950	– 1,150	13,800	
Other assets	1,250	-0-	1,250	No change assumed.
Total assets	$27,450	–$3,300	$24,150	
Liabilities and net worth				
Current liabilities:				
Accounts payable	$ 1,120	–$ 410	$ 710	45 days' purchases (from November/ December purchase estimates).
Notes payable . . .	3,000	– 1,500	1,500	Repayment as scheduled.
Due contractor . . .	3,400	– 2,900	500	From payment schedule.
Accruals	1,250	– 310	940	Tax payments (–$400) and tax accrual (+$90).
Total current liabilities . .	8,770	– 5,120	3,650	Reflects heavy current repayments of obligations.
Long-term liabilities	8,500	-0-	8,500	No change.
Common stock	4,250	+ 250	4,500	Sale of stock under option.
Retained earnings . .	5,930	+ 160	6,090	Retained earnings per income statement (no payment of dividends).
Total liabilities and net worth	$27,450	– 4,710	22,740	
Funds required		+ 1,410	1,410	"Plug" figure representing financing need as of 12-31-96, the same as in Figure 4–4.
		–$3,300	$24,150	

funds the company may have to borrow. Also, we must not forget that any cash balance maintained as an ongoing requirement on the balance sheet represents an investment like any other commitment of resources.

Next we turn to *accounts receivable*. If the company sells its products on terms of net 30, it can expect to have at least 30 days' sales outstanding; more, if some of its customers are late in paying. Given no abnormal delays in collections, the accounts receivable balance on the December 31 balance sheet should represent the sales for the whole month of December. However, we do not have an exact December sales estimate, because our pro forma operating statement shows sales for the last three months combined. As a simple shortcut, we could assume that one third of the projected quarterly sales would be outstanding at the end of the quarter.

In our case, that would be one third of the sales of $10,250,000 in Figure 4–1, or $3,417,000. But we learn after some discussion with sales management that in view of the seasonal low in December, the company's sales force projects the month's sales at only $3,050,000. This amount thus represents the 30 days of sales we can assume to be outstanding in the form of accounts receivable at the end of the year, given normal collection experience.

Raw material inventory could be projected by using monthly withdrawal and purchase patterns, information that the company would be able to provide. However, manufacturing management informs us that for reasons of continuity, they like to keep $1,500,000 worth of raw materials on hand at all times, and frequent purchases are made as needed to maintain that level.

Finished goods inventory is likely to decline in concert with lower sales and production activity, and we have allowed for a 19 percent reduction. If we considered this an optimistic assumption, because of likely inefficiencies in adjusting production exactly to the seasonal low, a higher amount can, of course, be specified. This would necessarily mean, however, that a lesser amount of funds would be released from declining inventories.

When we add up all our changes in the *current asset accounts*, we find that the total is projected to decline by over $2 million, in effect releasing these funds for other uses in the company. Note that this pattern reflects the normal funds flow characteristics of seasonal operations, as discussed in Chapter 2.

Fixed assets are affected by several events. While *land* remains unchanged, we are told that some machines will be sold during the last quarter. Their original cost was $1.5 million, against which $950,000 of depreciation has been accumulated. They are to be sold for their book value of $550,000, involving no taxable gain or loss. To reflect this transaction, the *plant and equipment* account on our pro forma balance sheet must be reduced by the original cost, while *accumulated depreciation* must be reduced by the $950,000 of past write-offs recorded there. This effectively removes all traces of the machinery involved from the company's books, while cash in the amount of $550,000 will have been received.

We also know from the pro forma operating statement that the company's normal depreciation charges for the period will be $600,000. This amount has to be added to the accumulated depreciation account. As a net result of the two changes, accumulated depreciation will decline by $350,000. Overall, the combined effect of these fixed asset transactions will decrease the net plant and equipment account by $1,150,000. *Other assets* are assumed to be unchanged.

On the liability side, *accounts payable* are expected to decline in response to lower activity in the final quarter. We're told that payables are mostly related to purchases of raw material. We could approximate accounts payable, which have payment terms of net 45, by assuming that because the pro forma operating statement reflects 90 days of raw materials use, about one half of this amount would be outstanding ($840,000). But we have additional inside information on the actual level of *purchases* scheduled, and are able to refine our assumption to show all of December's purchases ($460,000) and one-half of November's ($250,000) as total accounts payable outstanding at year end ($710,000).

Other current liabilities must be analyzed in terms of specific payment schedules. We're informed that *notes payable* carry a provision for repayment of $1.5 million during the quarter. Moreover, the account *due contractor* requires XYZ Corporation to make a payment of almost $3 million owed on past construction, which will become due in the final quarter. *Accruals* largely involve income tax and other tax obligations. We already know from the pro forma operating statement that tax accruals projected for the quarter will be $90,000. We're also told that the company must make an estimated tax payment of $400,000 during the quarter. The two items cause a net reduction in accrued taxes of $310,000. Note that with all these changes, total current liabilities are estimated to be reduced by about $3.6 million, a significant drain of funds during the forecast period.

Long-term liabilities are assumed to remain unchanged, while the recorded value of *common stock* is expected to increase by $250,000, because stock options are about to be exercised. Finally, *retained earnings* should increase by the amount of net profit (income) of $160,000, calculated on the pro forma operating statement.

When all these results are added up, we find that the pro forma balance sheet doesn't balance! However, this shouldn't be surprising because we didn't use double-entry bookkeeping to balance our calculations. Instead, we made a variety of independent assumptions about many of the accounts, taking care only to be consistent with related projections in the pro forma operating statement. Having maintained this consistency, and given that we're reasonably satisfied with our assumptions, the balancing figure required to equalize assets and liabilities will represent either the company's net *funds need* or *excess funds* as of the pro forma balance sheet date.

This *plug* figure, as it's often called, serves as a quick estimate of what additional indebtedness the company will face on the date of the statement, or what uncommitted funds it will have at its disposal. But the plug won't indicate what peaks and valleys in funds requirements may have occurred during each of the three months. These fluctuations could, of course, be found by generating intermediate balance sheets more frequently than every 90 days.

In other words, we could find any major variations in funding conditions by taking financial "snapshots" in more closely spaced intervals. As we'll see shortly, however, preparing a detailed cash budget is a much more direct way of tracing the ups and downs of funds requirements within the forecast period. But before turning to the cash budget, we need to discuss the further interpretation of balance sheet changes by means of a cash flow analysis.

Pro Forma Cash Flow Statement

As we observed in Figure 4–2, some very significant changes took place between the beginning and ending balance sheets of the forecast period. A pro forma cash flow statement will help us highlight the cash movements caused by these changes and their impact on the company's financial condition. Using the techniques discussed in Chapter 2, we can take the changes in the balance sheet and selected information from the operating statement to construct the pro forma cash flow analysis shown in Figure 4–3.

Reflecting prevailing practice, we have separated the cash flows into funds from operations, funds for investment, and funds from financing. It becomes quite obvious that reduced operations are expected to release a significant net amount of

FIGURE 4–3

XYZ CORPORATION
Pro Forma Cash Flow Statement
For the Quarter Ended December 31, 1996
($ thousands)

	Sources	Uses
Funds from Operations:		
Net income	$ 160	$ —
Depreciation (noncash charge)	600	—
Working capital changes:		
Decrease in cash	200	—
Decrease in receivables	1,200	—
Decrease in finished goods	750	—
Decrease in payables	—	410
Decrease in accruals	—	310
Totals	2,910	720
Net funds from operations	2,190	
Funds from Investments:		
Proceeds from sale of machinery	550	—
Funds for Financing:		
Repayment of notes	—	1,500
Repayment of construction loan	—	2,900
Proceeds from stock options	250	—
Totals	250	4,400
Net funds for financing		4,150
Funding requirement as of 12/31/96	1,410	—
	$4,150	$4,150

working capital (sources of $2.15 million from cash, receivables, and finished goods less uses of $0.72 million, for a net of $1.43 million), of which $1.2 million comes from reduced accounts receivable alone. These working capital funds sources almost triple the basic operating cash flow (net income of $0.16 million plus depreciation of $0.6 million) into a total funds inflow from operations of $2.19 million.

Operating funds sources are far outweighed by significant funding needs for financing, however. To meet various financial obligations currently due, $4.4 million are scheduled for repayment during the quarter. Of this total, the notes payable of $1.5 million represents repayment of seasonal funding, made possible by the significant release of working capital as the seasonal low approaches. Cash received from the sale of machinery and the exercise of stock options assists somewhat in this, but there still remains a funding gap of $1.41 million.

It should be clear by now that any changes in the various assumptions for the pro forma cash flow projections will directly affect the size of the funding gap. In fact, it's often very helpful to test the sensitivity of the projected conditions to variations in key assumptions, such as sales volume, collection patterns, and major cost deviations.

The likely funding stresses falling within the three individual months of the forecast period still haven't been dealt with, however. These occur because the gradual release of operating funds caused by the seasonal slowdown during the quarter will likely lag the decline in operating volume. As a consequence, the exact scheduling of repayments within the three-month period could cause significant temporary shortfalls. For example, if all repayments came due in October, the funding gap would be much higher during that month than the pro forma statements suggest for the end of December. As we'll see shortly, only a detailed cash budget can reveal such hidden fluctuations.

To summarize, pro forma statements are a convenient and relatively simple way of projecting expectations about a company's performance. To create these statements requires maintaining consistent assumptions between the operating statement and the balance sheet, but otherwise, a great degree of subjective judgment is allowed. The balancing element in the pro forma balance sheet is the funds need or funds excess resulting from the conditions assumed. This plug will vary as assumptions are changed.

Pro forma cash flow statements help highlight the funds movements implied by changes in the balance sheet. Pro forma analysis is limited by the static nature of the balance sheet, which shows funds needs only at a specific point in time, and not their ebb and flow. A more dynamic intraperiod analysis requires either generating several short-term pro forma statements at key decision points, or making the detailed budgetary forecast embodied in the cash budget.

CASH BUDGETS

Cash budgets, or cash flow projections, are very specific month-by-month or even week-by-week planning vehicles normally prepared by a company's financial staff. They focus exclusively on the specific incidence of cash receipts and payments—as distinguished from the leads and lags embodied in the accrual accounting approach used by most enterprises. A financial analyst who develops a cash budget is very interested in observing the ongoing changes in the cash account as assumptions are made, with the objective of maintaining a level sufficient to allow timely payments of all obligations as they become due. Consequently, the analyst must plan cash activity in very specific detail, reflecting the exact timing of the inflows and outflows of cash in response to planned operational, investment, and financing decisions.

As we'll see, cash budgets again indicate the level of any funds needs or excesses. In fact, the amount at the end of the planning period will exactly match the funding need or excess shown on the pro forma balance sheet—if the cash budget was prepared with the same basic assumptions as those underlying the pro forma statements.

Cash budgeting is quite simple in principle. It is similar to personal budgeting, where bills due are matched with receipts from paychecks, dividend checks, bank interest payments, and so on. This matching is necessary, period by period, to align funds requirements and the cash available for payment. Normally, the cash balance will fluctuate from day to day, week to week, month to month, whether a personal or company budget is involved. If a company's collections from credit sales tend to lag for weeks while wages and purchases must be paid currently, serious cash shortages can occur. (The concept of lags in relation to funds flow patterns was demonstrated in Chapter 2.) Similarly, cash payments for nonrecurring items, such as outlays for capital equipment, may cause temporary funding problems that must be met. Given its focus, the cash budget is the ultimate expression of funds flow analysis, because in the end, all funds movements wind up as changes in the cash balance.

In preparing a cash budget, a time schedule of estimated receipts and payments of cash must be laid out. This schedule shows, period by period, the net effect of projected activity on the cash balance. The selection of the time intervals covered by the cash budget depends on the nature of the business and the trade terms under which it operates. If daily fluctuations are likely to be large, as in the banking business, day-by-day projections are necessary. In other cases, weekly, monthly, or even quarterly projections will suffice.

Let's now return to the data of XYZ Corporation and prepare a monthly cash budget for the last quarter of 1996. This will increase our understanding of the funds flow picture beyond that provided by the pro forma analysis alone. Figure 4–4 presents some of the basic data of the company's operations regarding sales, production, and purchases. We show two months of actual activities *prior* to the forecast period, because (due to the nature of the credit terms for sales and purchases) the cash lag from these past months will influence the three months being projected.

The lag effect can be clearly demonstrated in the first item of the *cash receipts*, collection of *receivables*. On the assumption that the company's customers will continue to remit within the 30-day terms, cash receipts for any month should be the sales made in the prior month. In contrast, if there were a 60-day

FIGURE 4–4

XYZ CORPORATION
Sample Cash Budget for the Quarter Ended December 31, 1996
($ thousands)

	August	September	October	November	December	Total for Quarter
Basic data:						
Unit sales	48,000	46,000	42,000	36,000	33,000	111,000
Unit production	50,000	50,000	35,000	34,000	31,000	100,000
Change in inventory	+2,000	+4,000	−7,000	−2,000	−2,000	−11,000
Sales volume (on credit)	$4,450	$4,250	$3,850	$ 3,350	$ 3,050	$ 10,250
Purchases (on credit)	760	740	520	500	460	1,480
Cash receipts:						
Collection of receivables—prior month's sales; normal terms of 30 days assumed			$4,250	$ 3,850	$ 3,350	$ 11,450
Proceeds from sale of stock options			-0-	250	-0-	250
Proceeds from sale of used machines at book value (original cost, $1,500)			-0-	-0-	550	550
Total cash receipts			4,250	4,100	3,900	12,250
Cash disbursements:						
Payment for purchases*			750	630	510	1,890
Production payroll (from operating budget)			560	545	500	1,605
Manufacturing expenses (from operating budget)			1,265	1,260	1,235	3,760
Selling and delivery expenses (from sales budget) . . .			350	345	335	1,030
General overhead expenses (from administrative budget)			200	200	200	600
Interest payment on debt			-0-	-0-	175	175
Principal payment on note payable			1,500	-0-	-0-	1,500
Federal tax payment			400	-0-	-0-	400
Payments on construction of new plant			-0-	2,000	900	2,900
Total cash disbursements			5,025	4,980	3,855	13,860
Net cash receipts (disbursements)			(775)	(880)	45	$ (1,610)
Cumulative net cash flow			$ (775)	$(1,655)	$(1,610)	
Analysis of cash requirements:						
Beginning cash balance			$1,450	$ 675	$ (205)	$ 1,450
Net cash receipts (disbursements)			(775)	(880)	45	(1,610)
Ending cash balance			675	(205)	(160)	(160)
Minimum cash balance			1,250	1,250	1,250	1,250
Cash requirements			$ 575	$ 1,455	$ 1,410	$ 1,410

*Normal terms of 45 days assumed. Payments therefore represent one month's purchases prior to last 1.5 months (e.g., half of August and half of September paid during October).

collection period, collections would represent the sales made two months earlier. Thus, any expected change in customer behavior or in the credit terms themselves must be reflected in a different receipts pattern.

It's often helpful to draw a scale of time periods on which the days, weeks, or months of dollar sales are first recorded when they occur. Using this scale, any assumed collection experience can be simulated by "staggering" (that is, delaying) the dollar receipts according to the appropriate number of days. For example, a schedule of sales and collections on 30-day credit would appear as follows:

	January	February	March	April	May	June
Credit sales	$25,000	$30,000	$40,000	$42,000	$35,000	$30,000
Collections	(Dec. sales)	25,000	30,000	40,000	42,000	35,000

The proceeds from the exercise of *stock options* and from the sale of used *machinery* have been budgeted in their respective months of incidence. The total cash receipts for each month show a diminishing pattern which lags the declining sales by a month. This reduction in collections is moderated somewhat by the non-operating proceeds from options and sale of used machinery.

As we turn to *cash disbursements*, we encounter another lag in payments for *purchases* made on credit. Under the normal credit terms of 45 days extended to XYZ Corporation, we can assume that the company's payments will lag by 45 days. Consequently, purchases made in the second half of August and the first half of September will be paid for in October, with a similar pattern repeating itself in November and December. In other words, one month's worth of purchases staggered by 45 days will be paid in a given month. Under these conditions, a time scale with 15-day intervals will help illustrate the payment pattern.

Inasmuch as the last quarter of 1996 is projected in a declining pattern, with a December seasonal low in sales and manufacturing activities, the staggered timing due to credit terms shifts somewhat higher cash receipts as well as payments into a period of low operating activity. Funds are released in the process, as we would expect when we recall Chapter 2's discussion of changes in operations and their funds impact. This funds result matches what we've observed in the totals provided by the pro forma analysis.

Had there instead been a rising volume of operations, more cash would have become tied up in working capital, requiring additional funds. In that case, the cash budget would have reflected the lag effect of the lower activities of the earlier months, with staggered collections rising. It should be apparent by now that there is a critical need for careful cash budgeting in any business where operating levels and payments tend to vary.

Other cash disbursements *(payroll, manufacturing expenses, selling and delivery, and general overhead)* are shown without lags, on the assumption that payments for these expenses and obligations will be made within the month they are incurred. This assumption could be slightly incorrect in the case of payroll disbursements and certain manufacturing expenses. Such items could indeed lag by one or two weeks. How precisely these lags are dealt with is a function of the relative importance of the cash flow problems they represent.

Production-related payments, such as payroll and manufacturing expenses, are based on the declining pattern of production shown in the basic data section of Figure 4–4, which also reflects a gradual inventory reduction. Yet, in the pro forma operating statement for the period, cost of goods sold are normally based on the pattern of *selling* activities for ease of projection. Thus, the pro forma statement and the more detailed cash budget may differ because the assumptions concerning sales and production are different. To ensure complete consistency, it is therefore necessary to determine carefully whether the pattern of production is projected on a different basis than the pattern of sales.

As an example of such a potential difference, it's entirely possible that the seasonal low could be used by management to build up inventories in advance of the expected resurgence of sales. If that were so, the inventory assumption for the pro forma balance sheet would have to be adjusted upward to show the buildup of inventories and the resultant additional funds need. The cash budget, in turn, would have to reflect the higher expenditures involved in producing for inventory. Recognizing differences in production and selling patterns is a key to refining the projection of company performance, and to making cash budgeting results consistent with the pro forma statements.

The final result of our cash budget exercise is a picture of the monthly cash effect of the operating plans on which it is based, and the net cash needs or excesses incurred each month. Note that the cash need at the end of December ($1.41 million) exactly matches the indication we received from the pro forma statements—not surprising, because the same assumptions were used throughout.

To summarize, cash budgets lay out in specific detail the exact timing incidence of cash receipts and disbursements. Like household budgets, they allow us to watch for peaks and valleys in cash availability and to schedule additional financing or repayments as needed. Unlike pro forma statements (which are limited to the beginning and end of a specific period or to its total net effects), cash budgets can be drawn up for as many intervals as desired within the period to simulate the fluctuations in cash flow. Given the same assumptions in terms of the volume of production and sales, and the handling of receipts, payments, and credit, etc., the cash budget and pro forma statements will agree in signaling the amount of funds need or excess at the end of the period covered.

OPERATING BUDGETS

The pro forma statements and cash budget we prepared for XYZ Corporation provide an overall view of the company's future performance. But in any sizable company, a whole hierarchy of more specific operating budgets are normally prepared. Operating budgets are essentially internal documents. As expressions of the details of ongoing operations, such budgets are linked closely to the organizational structure and to the type of performance measurement used by the particular company. Such budgets are part of the planning process we mentioned earlier, and are very useful as a background for pro forma and cash flow projections when a higher degree of detail and accuracy is desired.

Most managements structure their companies into manageable parts, for each of which an executive or manager is held responsible. The structure may be by *functions*, that is, sales, production, purchasing, and so on. In other cases, the organization may be composed of a set of smaller *profit centers*, each of which is expected to make a profit contribution to total company performance. More recently, cross-functional teams have been used for certain activities, with budgets to match. Even though there are countless variations of organizational structures, the principles of budgeting and financial projection are straightforward and commonly applicable.

Any projection of operating results must be done in a form that reflects the scope of the business unit involved. It must be related to the elements controllable by the responsible manager, and should be done on the same basis as the one with which the manager's performance is measured. These criteria obviously require that operating budgets be carefully designed to fit the particular unit's conditions and the management style of the company as a whole. This means that there's a great deal of difference in the approaches taken by various companies, even within the same industry, and there may be differences within the same company in the operating budgets used for different organizational units and processes. A growing body of literature has recognized the criteria and impact of what is called responsibility accounting within a given organization, more recently expanded to include team management and process management concepts.

For purposes of our discussion, a few illustrations of basic operational budgeting will suffice. Among the various internal operating budgets routinely prepared by XYZ Corporation are the *annual sales budget by quarters* and *a quarterly factory budget*. The sales budget is designed to show the sales unit's projected contribution to total corporate profits, while the factory budget reflects expected output and the total costs incurred in producing the forecast volume. There are many other types of profit and expense budgets, but we'll limit our discussion to these two, showing how they're used to provide background information for the financial analyst preparing and analyzing pro forma statements and cash budgets. The principles employed in our examples are the same for any other kind of budgeting arrangement.

Sales Budget

As is shown in Figure 4–5, the sales manager must first project the level of *unit sales* expected in the market territories served. The projection is made by major product line. Most likely, this forecast will be built up from the individual judgments of the persons closest to current and potential customers. Economic conditions will likely be factored in, as will the impact of marketing strategies XYZ Corporation and its competitors are likely to employ.

Next the *price levels* for each product must be estimated. Prices commonly are a function of three factors:

■ Industry pricing practices.

■ The competitive environment.

■ The cost effectiveness of the company's manufacturing operations.

Once the price has been established, *the sales revenue* can be calculated. Then the *cost of goods sold* for the products transferred internally or possibly

FIGURE 4–5

XYZ CORPORATION
Sample Quarterly Sales Budget
For the Year Ended December 31, 1996

	First	Second	Third	Fourth	Total
	Quarter				
Basic data:					
Unit sales (number of units):					
Product A	2,700	2,900	3,000	2,800	11,400
Product B	8,000	8,500	10,000	8,000	34,500
Product C	17,500	18,500	21,000	16,000	73,000
Price level (per unit):					
Product A	$ 145	$ 145	$ 150	$ 150	—
Product B	92	92	95	95	—
Product C	74	74	74	74	—
Number of salespersons	25	25	25	26	—
Operating budget ($000):					
Sales revenue	$ 2,423	$ 2,572	$ 2,954	$ 2,364	$10,313
Less: returns, allowances . . .	25	26	28	24	103
Net sales	2,398	2,546	2,926	2,340	10,210
Cost of goods sold	1,916	2,051	2,322	1,868	8,157
Margin before delivery	482	495	604	472	2,053
Delivery expense	56	60	68	54	238
Gross margin	426	435	536	418	1,815
Selling expense (controllable):					
Salespersons'					
compensation	94	94	94	98	380
Travel and entertainment . . .	32	32	32	33	129
Sales support costs	23	23	26	24	96
Total selling expenses . . .	149	149	152	155	605
Gross contribution	277	286	384	263	1,210
Departmental period costs	18	18	18	18	72
Net contribution	259	268	366	245	1,138
Corporate support (transferred):					
Staff support	23	25	25	27	100
Advertising	50	50	75	50	225
General overhead	63	63	63	63	252
Total corporate support . . .	136	138	163	140	577
Profit contribution (before					
taxes)	$ 123	$ 130	$ 203	$ 105	$ 561

purchased on the outside must be determined. The difference between the revenue and cost is the *margin before delivery* achieved by the sales unit. Next are the projected *delivery costs* to the customers, if these are borne by the company. Controllable *selling expenses* include *compensation* of sales personnel, *travel and entertainment*, and *sales support costs*.

The result is *gross contribution* from selling activities, which must be reduced by estimated *departmental period costs* (like rent, managers' salary, and other items that do not vary with short-term fluctuations in volume) to arrive at the *net contribution* provided by the department. After deducting allocated *corporate support costs*, which are staff support, advertising, and general overhead, the *profit contribution* for the period is established. In making all of these estimates, the sales manager can use past relationships and selected ratios, tempered by his or her judgment concerning changes in future conditions.

In our example, both basic data and dollar elements have been estimated and set out by the four quarters and for the full year of 1996. There's nothing unique about the format we have selected here, because many different arrangements of such information are possible to suit any specific organization. Generally, a company prescribes the format for its managers to follow in preparing projected activity budgets, both to maintain a degree of uniformity and to lessen the accounting problem of consolidating the projections when preparing overall financial forecasts. From the standpoint of financial projection, the sales and contribution data in our example are the raw material which goes into the company's total operating plan.

Factory Budget

The sales budget we just discussed is basically a projection of profit contribution. However, companies also must forecast for operations or activities that involve only costs or expenses. An example of this type of projection, a cost budget for a factory, is shown in Figure 4–6. This time the data are given for each month. We have included three months and the total for the quarter. The period shown is the second quarter, during which sales and production are expected to increase.

Again, the amount of detail included and the presentation format are chosen to suit the particular needs and preferences of the organization. This time we selected to arrange the headings and data to show that certain cost items (both direct and period costs) are under the control of the local manager. (Other costs, like allocated general overhead, are transferred in from corporate headquarters and thus are beyond the local manager's control.) This arrangement of the data will also be useful if the operating plan serves as a control device with which to measure the unit's performance.

Both sales and cost budgets commonly include additional columns in which *actual* as opposed to *projected* figures are recorded. In addition, *variance* columns are frequently used to measure deviations from plan. We'll not go into such refinements here, because our examples were only meant to show the type of internal budgeting and projection used formally or informally in most organizations preparatory to developing an overall financial forecast.

INTERRELATIONSHIP OF FINANCIAL PROJECTIONS

It should be obvious by now that the various types of projection presented in this chapter are closely related. If all three forecasts—pro forma statements, cash budgets, and operating budgets—are based on the same set of assumptions about

FIGURE 4–6

XYZ CORPORATION
Sample Factory Budget
For the Quarter Ended June 30, 1996

	April	May	June	Total
Basic data:				
Number of shifts (5-day week)	3	3	3	3
Days worked	20	21	22	63
Hourly employees per shift . . .	33	33	33	33
Number of machines	35	35	34	—
Unit production:				
Product A	1,000	1,050	1,100	3,150
Product B	2,400	2,510	2,640	7,550
Capacity utilization	94%	94%	96%	95%
Downtime for repairs (hours) . .	-0-	36	-0-	36
Operating budget:				
Direct costs (controllable):*				
Manufacturing labor	$ 57,600	$ 60,500	$ 63,400	$181,500
Raw materials	53,800	56,400	59,200	169,400
Operating supplies	6,500	6,900	7,300	20,700
Repair labor and parts	7,300	12,400	6,500	26,200
Power, heat, light	4,200	4,500	4,800	13,500
Total direct costs	129,400	140,700	141,200	411,300
Period costs (controllable):				
Supervision	5,500	5,500	5,500	16,500
Support labor	28,500	28,500	28,500	85,500
Insurance, taxes	8,700	8,700	8,700	26,100
Depreciation	20,500	20,500	20,500	61,500
Total period costs	63,200	63,200	63,200	189,600
Total controllable costs	192,600	203,900	204,400	600,900
General overhead (allocated) . .	72,000	72,000	72,000	216,000
Total cost	$264,600	$275,900	$276,400	$816,900

*Where appropriate, unit costs can be shown.

receipts and collections, repayment schedules, operating rates, inventory levels, and so on, they will all precisely fit together in the fashion illustrated in Figure 4–7.

The financial plans and the projected funds need or excess will differ only if different assumptions concerning the drivers affecting funds flows are used, particularly between the pro forma statements and the cash budget. It is quite easy to reconcile pro forma statements and cash budgets, however, by carefully thinking through the key assumptions to be made, one by one, and by laying out formats that contain sufficient detail and properly timed background data.

The diagram shows how the various operational budgets flow into a consolidated cash budget, which in turn is reinforced by specific data from the investment and financing plans. The combined information supports the pro

FIGURE 4–7

Interrelationship of Financial Projections

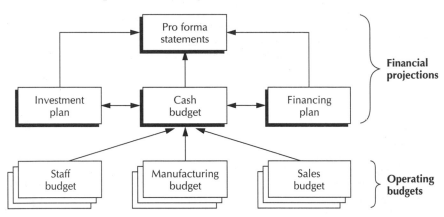

forma statements at the top of the diagram. Thus, pro forma statements are the all-encompassing expression of the expected conditions for the period ahead. As a consequence, if we choose to prepare pro forma statements with direct overall estimates, as we discussed (rather than building them up from the company's budgets and plans), they in effect will *imply* specific assumptions about all the other elements in the diagram.

We haven't yet discussed some of the elements shown in Figure 4–7. *Staff budgets* are spending plans based on the expected cost of operating various service functions of a company. These budgets are prepared and used in the same fashion as other expense budgets.

Investment plans (capital budgets) are projections of new outlays for land, buildings, machinery and equipment, and related incremental working capital, as well as major outlays for new products and services, expanding markets, new technology, etc. They may also spell out plans to divest any of the company's assets.

We recall that XYZ Corporation made a minor reduction in its fixed assets by selling some used machines. Also, a recently constructed plant was in the final stages of payment, as evidenced by the amount that had become due and payable to the contractor. This facility investment was already reflected on the actual balance sheet of September 30, 1996, largely supported by long-term debt raised earlier. Only the current payment due the contractor was properly scheduled as a pro forma cash disbursement. The company might consider raising some additional long-term debt to fund the new facility, as operations are not providing sufficient cash flow to pay off the contractor liabilities.

Financing plans are schedules of proposed future additions to or reductions in indebtedness or ownership funds during the forecast period. They may involve significant expansion or restructuring of a company's capital structure, depending on the projected capital requirements. XYZ Corporation planned no specific future financing, but provisions would have to be made for financing the sizable funds need revealed with the help of the pro forma analysis and to avoid having to strain its current funds as the plant is paid off.

A word about projection methodology should be added here. Any form of financial projection involves both an examination of past trends and specific assumptions about future behavior of revenues, costs, expenses, and other receipts and payments. Past trend analysis can range from simple "eyeballing" of obvious patterns to applying a variety of statistical methods to the available data in order to establish a trend line or curve as the basis for judging future conditions. The projection of key variables may start with such a trend, but hard, informed judgments about likely changes must override the temptation merely to extrapolate past conditions. The mathematical elegance of statistical methods should not be allowed to supplant the effort of making realistic future assumptions, both about specific company and market conditions, industry performance, and the national and world economic outlook affecting the likely financial performance of the business. The end-of-chapter references and Appendix V are sources of information on forecasting techniques and other processes that will assist the analyst in technical and judgmental aspects of financial projection.

FINANCIAL MODELING AND SENSITIVITY ANALYSIS

In recent years, computer software available or developed for financial modeling has vastly expanded the financial analyst's ability to explore the consequences of different assumptions, conditions, and plans. In principle, such software packages are no more than mathematical representations of key financial accounting relationships, ratios, and formats, supported by automatic subroutines which calculate, update, and display data and results in whatever form is desired. The process is based on the very same steps and reasoning discussed in this chapter.

The simplest form of financial modeling is found in the common use of spreadsheets to represent a particular set of relationships for analysis and manipulation. A full-fledged financial model, usually developed by a company's staff in collaboration with software vendors, encompasses many elements such as the company's accounting procedures, depreciation schedules, tax calculations, debt service schedules, debt covenants and restrictions, inventory policies, and so on. In many cases, the data, assumptions, and format can be "custom tailored" so that the financial analyst can reflect the specific characteristics of a given company. With the help of such a model, the analyst can calculate the projected results of conditions expected by the company. The ease of using computerized models allows the analyst to examine several sets of assumptions and assess alternative outcomes.

The major difference between the projection techniques discussed in this chapter and the use of spreadsheets and computer models is basically only the degree of automation of the process. A cash budget done by hand is essentially a model of the cash-flow pattern of the company. In constructing such a budget, the analyst must take into account corporate policies regarding accounting methods, tax reporting, and other detailed operating rules. These constraints can also be incorporated into a basic financial planning software package, or even a powerful spreadsheet program. The main difference is that the computer can run different options, while simultaneously tracking all important interrelationships (as indicated in Figure 4–8) much more easily and quickly than is possible when an analysis is done by hand.

The financial modeling software available on the market is constantly evolving, and the reader should familiarize him- or herself with the latest offerings available. In scope, the modeling packages range all the way from spreadsheets with which to calculate simple condensed pro forma statements to highly sophisticated representations of a company's financial accounting system and so-called enterprise models. In the latter case, a generalized model is extensively refined, with the help of the company's financial staff, to reflect the company's specific situation. Some companies have developed models that not only will calculate the results of specific sets of assumptions, but also contain optimizing routines that select the most desirable alternative investment and financing patterns according to criteria stipulated by management. Other models include statistical projection programs that can be used for initial trending of key variables from past experience. It is clearly beyond the scope of this book to detail the vast number of concepts and specialized techniques involved in the building and use of computerized financial models.

Figure 4–8 depicts a broad overview of the major relationships represented in a full-fledged model. The central element is the software program that governs

FIGURE 4–8

Financial Modeling: An Overview of Key Interrelationships

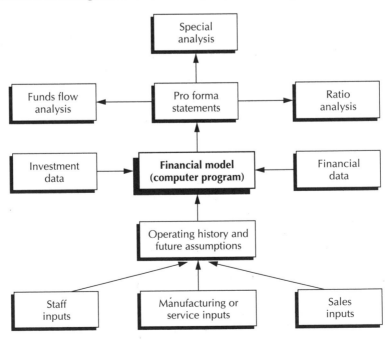

the calculations and displays, with the inputs coming from various sources and the outputs grouped into our familiar categories of analysis.

Sensitivity Analysis

One of the advantages of modeling is the ability to perform sensitivity analysis with considerable ease. This type of analysis involves selecting a few key conditions and altering them to determine the sensitivity of the result to such changes. For example, one of the key assumptions in our pro forma analysis of XYZ Corporation was the usual seasonal pattern of an 18 to 20 percent decline in sales volume in the last quarter. If there were reason to believe that a more serious drop might occur, the analyst could estimate the dollar decline in contribution from each additional 1 percent decrease in volume. If all other conditions were to remain the same, that dollar decline would be the lost contribution from the units left unsold.

The impact on cash needs would be traced by adjusting aftertax profits, and by recognizing that there would be a change in working capital because sales levels are lower, except in inventory where the unsold units might remain. If prices were considered unstable, a series of assumptions about the effect of lower prices for one or all of the product lines could be traced. In every case, the critical test would be the sensitivity of the cash needs to the changes in each of the three months. Clearly, many other tests could be applied and related to the altered result brought about by the change in any given assumption.

The key to this type of reasoning is the analyst's judgment as to which elements in the operating and financial patterns being projected are most subject to variability. Then the task is to simulate how sensitive the desired result is to each change. Given such a range of results, the decision maker using the analysis can judge the risk of the proposed course and adjust operating and financial policies accordingly. A computer model is not critical to making such sensitivity tests. Even our simple pro forma statements and cash budgets can be easily modified to answer basic questions of this sort.

Nonetheless, with appropriate software, the analyst can examine many more possibilities and determine the impact of a far greater number of assumptions. Sensitivity tests can be performed on more than one variable simultaneously, and whole scenarios can be developed with the financial impact reflected in the output. We'll return to the topic of sensitivity analysis again in later chapters.

SUMMARY

The principles of financial projection discussed in this chapter revolve around the use of *pro forma statements* and various types of *budgets*. We observed that financial projection is only part of the broader process of *business planning*. Financial projection can be expressed in the familiar form of financial statements and in many specifically tailored budget formats. The process is simple in that it represents an orderly way of sorting out the financial impact of investment, operating, and financing decisions. The process is difficult in that judgments about future conditions are fraught with uncertainty—as planning of any sort must be.

Here, the use of *sensitivity analysis*, the calculation of the impact of alternative assumptions, can narrow the range of uncertainty. Financial projection basically is a form of modeling the future within the context of operational and policy constraints. To the extent that more detail and more options for future plans are desired, automation of the process with the help of computer-based *financial modeling* can yield the significant benefits of speed, accuracy, and greater insight.

SELECTED REFERENCES

Anthony, Robert N. *Essentials of Accounting*. 5th ed. Reading MA: Addison Wesley, 1993.
Brealy, Richard A., and Stewart C. Myers. *Principles of Corporate Finance*. 4th ed. New York: McGraw-Hill, 1991.
Ross, Stephen; Randolph Westerfield; and Jeffrey Jaffe. *Corporate Finance*. 4th ed. Burr Ridge, IL: Richard D. Irwin, 1996.
Weston, J. Fred, and Eugene Brigham. *Essentials of Managerial Finance*. 10th ed. Hinsdale, IL: Dryden Press, 1992.

SELF-STUDY EXERCISES AND PROBLEMS

(Solutions are provided in Appendix V)

1. Complete the following exercises, based on these selected data about a company. Consider each exercise separately.

Total assets on 12-31-97	$2,750,000
Sales for the year 1997	9,137,000
Current assets on 12-31-97	1,315,000
Long-term debt on 12-31-97	210,000
Current ratio on 12-31-97	2.4:1
Cost of goods sold for 1997	83% of sales
Purchases during 1997	$5,316,000
Depreciation for 1997	174,000
Net profit after taxes for 1997	131,000
Taxes on income for 1997	112,000

a. Currently, the company's accounts receivable outstanding are 18 days' sales. To meet competitive pressures in 1998, the company must extend credit to an average of 40 days' sales to maintain operations and profits at 1997 levels. No other changes are contemplated for the next year, and sales and operations are expected to continue at 1997 rates. What's the impact of this change in credit policy on corporate funds needs? Will the company have to borrow? What if credit had to be extended to 60 days? Discuss.

b. The inventory levels maintained by the company have averaged $725,000 during 1997 with little fluctuation. If turnover were to slow to seven times (average inventory in cost of goods sold) due to a switch to a consignment policy, what would the financial impact be? Assume no change in sales levels. What other changes are likely to take place, and how would these affect the company's financial stance? What if turnover rose to 11 times? Discuss.

c. Payment for purchases has been made under normal trade terms of 2/10, n/30 with discounting done as a matter of policy. Suppliers anxious for business are beginning to offer 2/15, n/45 terms, which will become universal during the coming year. What would the financial impact of this change be if the company were to follow its policy of discounting purchases? What trade-off has to be considered? Discuss.

d. If the company is planning capital expenditures of $125,000 and simultaneously is planning to pay dividends at the rate of 60 percent of net profits, what are the financial implications, assuming all other elements are unchanged?

e. If sales are expected to grow 10 percent for the following year, with all *normal* relationships under (a) through (c) unchanged, what financial considerations arise? How would the intentions of (d) look then? Discuss.

2. In September 1998, ABC Company, a manufacturing firm, was making budget plans for the 12 months beginning November 1, 1998. Projected sales volume was $4,350,000, as compared to an estimated $3,675,000 for the fiscal year ended October 31, 1998. The best estimates of the operating results for the current year are shown in the operating statement.

   The projected increase in volume of operations was expected to bring improvements in efficiency, while at the same time some of the cost factors would continue to rise absolutely, in line with past trends. Following this statement are the specific working assumptions with which to plan financial results for the next year.

ABC COMPANY
Estimated Operating Statement
For the Year Ended October 31, 1998
($ thousands)

	Amount		Percent	
Net sales		$3,675		100%
Cost of goods sold:				
Labor	$919		25.0	
Materials	522		14.2	
Overhead	743		20.2	
Depreciation	133	2,317	3.6	63.0
Gross profit		1,358		37.0
Selling expense	305		8.3	
General and administrative expenses	323	628	8.8	17.1
Profit before taxes		730		19.9
Income taxes		336		9.1
Net income		$ 394		10.8%

Assumptions for fiscal year 1999:

Manufacturing labor would drop to 24 percent of direct sales because volume efficiency would more than offset higher wage rates.

Materials cost would rise to 14.5 percent of sales because some price increases wouldn't be offset by better utilization.

Overhead costs would rise above the present level by 6 percent of the 1998 dollar amount, reflecting higher costs. Additional variable costs would be encountered at the rate of 11 percent of the incremental sales volume.

Depreciation would increase by $10,000, reflecting the addition of some production machinery.

Selling expenses would rise more proportionately, by $125,000, because additional effort would be required to increase sales volume.

General and administrative expense would drop to 8.1 percent of sales.

Income taxes (federal and state) were estimated at 46 percent of pretax profits.

Develop a pro forma operating statement for the ABC Company and discuss your findings.

3. In December 1998, the DEF Company, a distributor of stationery products, was planning its financial needs for the coming year. As a first indication, the firm's management wished to have a pro forma balance sheet as of December 31, 1999 to gauge funds needs at that time. Estimated financial condition as of December 31, 1998 was reflected in this balance sheet:

DEF COMPANY
Estimated Balance Sheet
December 31, 1998

Assets

Current assets:

Cash	$ 217,300
Receivables	361,200
Inventories (pledged as security)	912,700
Total current assets	1,491,200
Fixed assets:	
Land, buildings, trucks, and fixtures	421,500
Less: Accumulated depreciation	217,300
Total fixed assets	204,200
Other assets	21,700
Total assets	$1,717,100

Liabilities and Net Worth

Current liabilities:

Accounts payable	$ 612,300
Note payable—bank	425,000
Accrued expenses	63,400
Total current liabilities	1,100,700
Term loan—properties	120,000
Capital stock	200,000
Paid-in surplus	112,000
Retained earnings	184,400
Total liabilities and net worth	$1,717,100

Operations for the ensuing year were projected using the following working assumptions to plan the financial results:

Sales were forecast at $10,450,000, with a gross margin of 8.2 percent.

Purchases were expected to total $9,725,000, with some seasonal upswings in May and August.

Accounts receivable would be based on a collection period of 12 days, while 24 days' accounts payable would be outstanding.

Depreciation was expected to be $31,400 for the year.

Term loan repayments were scheduled at $10,000, while bank notes payable would be allowed to fluctuate with seasonal needs.

Capital expenditures were scheduled at $21,000 for trucks and $36,000 for warehouse improvements.

Net profits after taxes were expected at the level of 0.19 percent of sales.

Dividends for the year were scheduled at $12,500.

Cash balances were desired at no less than $150,000.

Develop a pro forma balance sheet and discuss your findings.

4. In September 1998, the XYZ Company, a department store, was planning for cash needs during the last quarter of 1998 and the first quarter of 1999. The Christmas buying season always meant a considerable strain on finances, and the first planning step was development of a cash budget. The following data were available for this purpose:

Projected sales (half for cash, half charged on 90-day account):

October	$ 770,000	January	$ 650,000
November	690,000	February	580,000
December	1,010,000	March	720,000

Projected purchases (half on n/45; 40 percent on 2/10, n/30; 10 percent for cash):

October	$ 610,000	January	$ 320,000
November	535,000	February	450,000
December	290,000	March	480,000

Projected payments on purchases as of 9-30-98:

Due by October 10 (2% discount)	$ 60,000
Due by October 31 (net 45)	257,000
Due by November 15 (net 45)	113,000
Total	$430,000

Projected collections of receivables as of 9-30-98:

Due in October	$215,000
Due in November	245,000
Due in December	265,000
Total (bad debts negligible)	$725,000

Projected financial data:

Minimum cash balance required	$ 75,000
Beginning cash balance (October 1)	95,000
Mortgage payments (monthly)	7,000
Cash dividend due December 31	40,000
Federal taxes due January 15	20,000

Projected operations: salaries and wages average 19 percent of sales; cash operating expenses average 14 percent of sales.

Develop a monthly cash budget to show the seasonal funds requirements. Discuss your findings.

5. A newly formed space technology company, the ZYX Corporation, was in the early stages of planning for the first several months of operations. The initial capital put up by the founders and their associates amounted to 250,000 shares of $1 par value stock. Furthermore, patents estimated to be worth $50,000 were provided by two of the principals in exchange for 50,000 shares of common stock. Equipment costing $175,000 was purchased with the funds, and organization expenses of $15,000 were paid. Operations were to start February 1, 1998.

Orders already in hand amounted to $1,400,000 of electronic devices, which at an estimated monthly output of $400,000 (sales value), represented almost four months' sales. More orders were expected from contacts made. Monthly operating expenses and conditions were estimated as follows:

Manufacturing labor	$ 60,000
Rent for building	18,500
Overhead costs	76,000

Depreciation	6,000
Write-off of patents	500
Selling and administrative expenses	55,000
Purchases of materials, supplies	125,000
Sale terms	n/30
Collection experience expected	45 days
Purchase terms	n/30
Raw materials inventory level	$ 60,000
Finished goods inventory level	145,000
Prepaid expenses (average)	12,000
Accrued wages	1 week's
Accrued taxes (40% effective rate)	As incurred

If the company wanted to maintain a minimum cash balance of $40,000, what would the financial situation be after six months of operations? Develop pro forma statements and discuss the likely timing of any funds needs. How are the next six months likely to affect this picture? Discuss your findings.

6. The ABC Supermarket's management expected the next six months (January 1, 1998 through June 30, 1998) to bring a variety of cash requirements beyond the normal operational outflows. A monthly cash budget was to be developed to trace the specific funds needs. The following projections were available for the purpose:
   a. Cash sales projected:

January	$ 200,000	April	$200,000
February	190,000	May	230,000
March	220,000	June	220,000

   b. Cost of goods sold averages 75 percent of sales.
   c. Purchases closely scheduled with sales volume. Payments average a 15-day lag behind purchases. December purchases were $168,000.
   d. Operating expenses projected:
      1. Salaries and wages at 12 percent of sales, paid when incurred.
      2. Other expenses at an average 9 percent of sales, paid when incurred.
      3. Rent of $3,500, paid monthly.
      4. Income tax payments of $2,000 due in January, March, and June, and $3,500 due in April.
      5. Cash receipts from sale of property at $6,000 per month, due in March, April, and May.
      6. Payments on note owed local bank due as follows: $3,000 in February and $5,000 in May.
      7. Repayments of advances to principals of the firm due at $3,000 each in January, March, and May.

8. New store fixtures of $48,000 acquired, with four payments of $12,000 each due in February, March, April, and May.
9. Old store fixtures with a book value of $4,500 scrapped, to be written off in January.
10. Rental income from a small concession granted on the premises to begin at $300 per month in March.

Develop a cash budget as requested and show the effect of the operations and other elements described above on the beginning cash balance of $42,500. The principals of the firm would like to keep a cash balance of not less than $20,000 at any one time. Will additional funds be required? If so, when? Discuss your findings.

7. The XYZ Company, a fast-growing manufacturing operation, found its inventories in 1998 increasing faster than growth in sales. (As additional territories and customers had been developed, production schedules were stepped up in an effort to provide excellent service levels.) Also, collections had deteriorated, and the company's receivables represented two months' sales compared to normal 30-day terms. Because both conditions caused considerable pressures on the company's finances, a change to a level production schedule was considered beginning October 1, 1998, to allow inventories to be worked off while still providing employment to the company's full-time workers. Also, more effort would be expended on collections. A six-month trial of the new policy was to be analyzed in September before implementation, and the following assumptions and data were provided:

a. Current sales and forecast:

August	$1,925,000	December	$2,450,000
September (est.)	2,050,000	January	2,625,000
October	2,175,000	February	2,750,000
November	2,300,000	March	2,850,000

b. Current purchases and forecast (terms n/45):

August	$750,000	December	$650,000
September (est.)	675,000	January	650,000
October	650,000	February	650,000
November	650,000	March	650,000

c. Collection period, current and forecast:

August 31	63 days	December 31	40 days
September 30 (est.)	60	January 31	40
October 31	50	February 28	40
November 30	50	March 31	40

d. Materials usage, beginning October: $825,000 per month.

e. Wages and salaries, beginning October: $215,000 per month, paid as incurred.

f. Other manufacturing expenses, beginning October: $420,000 per month, paid as incurred.

g. Depreciation: $43,000 per month.

h. Cost of goods sold has consistently averaged 70 percent of sales.

i. Selling and administrative expenses: October and November, 15 percent of sales; December and January, 14 percent of sales; and February and March, 12 percent of sales.

j. Payments on note payable: $750,000 each in November and February.

k. Interest due in January: $300,000.

l. Dividends payable in October and January: $25,000 each.

m. Income taxes due in January: $375,000.

n. Most recent balance sheet (estimated) is shown below.

From the data given, develop a cash budget for the six months ended March 31, 1999, and pro forma statements for the quarters ended December 31, 1998, and March 31, 1999. Assume income taxes to be 50 percent, don't detail cost of goods sold, and assume no changes in accounts not specifically analyzed or projected here. What funds needs arise, and when? What if the collection speedup effort were unsuccessful and receivables stayed at 60 days? Discuss your findings about the policy changes being considered.

XYZ COMPANY
Estimated Balance Sheet
For September 30, 1998
($ thousands)

Assets

Current assets:		
Cash		$ 740
Accounts and notes receivable		3,975
Inventories:		
Raw materials	$ 2,725	
Finished goods	6,420	9,145
Total current assets		13,860
Plant and equipment	12,525	
Less: Accumulated depreciation	5,315	7,210
Other assets		1,730
Total assets		$22,800

Liabilities and net worth

Current liabilities:	
Accounts payable	$ 1,050
Notes payable	4,120
Accrued liabilities	2,875
Total current liabilities	8,045
Long-term debt	5,250
Preferred stock	1,750
Common stock	5,000
Retained earnings	2,755
Total liabilities and net worth	$22,800

CHAPTER 5

Dynamics of the Business System

At this point, we'll revisit the business system and demonstrate the key dynamic aspects of financial management and planning. In Chapter 1, we characterized the business system as a dynamic growth model and described in broad terms the interrelationship of decisions, financial yardsticks, and management policies. Now we need to become more specific about how the system's internal characteristics affect changes in the cash flow patterns that lead to shareholder value creation.

We'll demonstrate the major dynamics of the business system by first focusing on the concept of *leverage*—the impact of fixed elements on overall results—in two critical areas:

- Operating leverage.
- Financial leverage.

We'll explore in detail the impact of volume changes on profitability under a variety of assumptions about the nature and level of fixed elements in the company's cost pattern.

Then we'll turn to an integrated modeling approach that will demonstrate the financial implications of business growth in the system. The focus will be on testing the financial impact of policy changes in investment, operations, and financing. The vehicle will be financial growth plans, an integrated view of key financial dimensions which allows us to visualize the performance of the total business system. We'll cover the following concepts:

- The basic financial growth model.
- Determining sustainable growth.
- An integrated financial plan.

The broader concept of shareholder value creation will be dealt with extensively in Chapter 9.

The reader is encouraged to revisit the first section of Chapter 1, which describes the business system and its key interrelationships, many of which we'll test in this discussion.

LEVERAGE

Leverage, as previously mentioned, refers to the often favorable condition of having within the overall cost pattern of the business system a stable element which supports a wide range of profit levels. *Operating leverage* simply means that part of the ongoing costs of the business are fixed over a broad range of operating volume. As a result, profits are boosted or depressed more than proportionally for given changes in volume. Similarly, *financial leverage* occurs when a company's capital structure contains obligations with fixed interest rates. The effect is similar to operating leverage. Again, earnings after interest are boosted or depressed more than proportionally as operating volume and profitability fluctuate. Operating and financial leverage are one and the same in principle.

However, there are differences in the specific elements involved and in the methods of calculation of each type of leverage. Both operating and financial leverage can be present in any business, and their respective impact on net profit will tend to be mutually reinforcing.

Operating Leverage

Distinguishing between fixed and variable costs (those costs that vary with time and those that vary with the level of activity) is an old idea. This separation of costs is the basis for *break-even analysis.* The idea of "breaking even" is based on the simple question of how many units of product or service a business must sell in order to cover its fixed costs. Presumably, prices are set at a level high enough to recoup all direct (that is, variable) costs and leave a margin of contribution toward fixed (period) costs and profit. Once sufficient units have been sold to accumulate the total contribution needed to offset fixed costs, the margin from any additional units sold will become profit—unless a new layer of fixed costs has to be added at some future point to support the increased volume.

Understanding this principle will improve our insight into how the operational aspects of a business relate to financial planning and projections. But in a broader sense, it'll allow us to appreciate the distorting effect which significant operating leverage may exert on the measures and comparisons used in financial analysis.

A word of caution must be added here. There's nothing absolute about the concept of fixed costs, because in the longer run, every cost element becomes variable. Costs are a consequence of management decisions, and can therefore be altered by management decisions. As a result, the break-even concept must be handled with a degree of flexibility.

As we mentioned, introducing fixed costs to the operations of a business tends to magnify profits at higher levels of operation. This is due to the incremental contribution each additional unit provides over and above the strictly variable costs incurred in producing it. Depending on the proportion of fixed and variable costs in the company's cost structure, the total incremental contribution from the added units can result in a sizable overall jump in profit.

Once all fixed costs have been recovered through the cumulative individual contributions from a sufficient number of units, profits begin to appear as additional units are sold. Profits will grow proportionately faster than the growth in unit volume. Unfortunately, the same effect holds for declining volumes of operations, which result in a profit decline and accelerating losses that are disproportionate to the rate of volume reduction. Leverage is definitely a double-edged sword!

We can establish the basic definitions needed to analyze leverage as follows:

$$\text{Profit} = \text{Total Revenue} - \text{Total Cost}$$

$$\text{Total Revenue} = \text{Volume (Quantity)} \times \text{Price}$$

$$\text{Total Cost} = \text{Fixed Cost} + \text{Variable Cost}$$

The formal way of describing leverage conditions is quite simple. We're interested in the effect on profit (I) of changes in volume (V). The elements that bear on this are the unit price (P), unit variable costs (C), and fixed costs (F). The relationship is:

$$I = VP - (VC + F)$$

This formula can be rewritten as:

$$I = V(P - C) - F$$

which illustrates that profit depends on the number of goods or services sold times the difference between unit price and unit variable cost—which is the contribution to the constant element, namely fixed costs.

As unit volume changes, the unit contribution ($P - C$) multiplied by the change in volume will equal the total change in profit. Under normal conditions, the constant, fixed costs (F) will remain just that. The relative changes in profit for a given change in volume will be magnified because of this fixed element.

Another way of stating the leverage relationships is to use profit as a percent of sales (s), one of the ratios developed in Chapter 3. Using the previous notation,

$$s = \frac{I}{VP}$$

and defining I in terms of the components, the formula becomes:

$$s = \frac{V(p - C) - F}{VP}$$

and slightly rewritten:

$$s = \left[1 - \frac{C}{P}\right] - \frac{F}{VP}$$

The relationship indicates that the profit/sales ratio depends on the contribution per unit of sales, less fixed costs as a percent of sales revenue. We observe that, to the extent fixed costs are present, they cause a reduction in the profit ratio. The larger F is, the larger the reduction. Any change in volume, price, or unit cost, however, will tend to have a disproportional impact on s because F is constant.

Now let's examine how the process works, using some concrete examples. We'll use the cost/profit conditions of a simple business with relatively high fixed costs of $200,000 in relation to its volume of output and variable costs per unit. Our company has a maximum level of production of 1,000 units, and for simplicity, we assume there is no lag between production and sales. Units sell for $750 each, and variable costs of materials, labor, and supplies amount to $250 per unit. Every unit therefore provides a contribution of $500 toward fixed costs and profit.

Figure 5–1's *break-even chart* is a simple representation of the conditions just outlined. At zero volume, fixed costs amount to $200,000, and they remain level as volume is increased until full capacity has been reached. Variable costs, on the other hand, accumulate by $250 per unit as volume is increased until a level of $250,000 has been reached at capacity, for a total cost of $450,000. Revenue rises from zero, in increments of $750, until total revenue has reached $750,000 at capacity.

Where the revenue and variable cost lines cross (at 400 units of output), a break-even condition—no profit and no loss—has been reached. This means that the total cumulative revenue of $300,000 at that point is just sufficient to offset the fixed costs of $200,000, plus the total variable costs of $100,000 (400 units at $250 each). If operations increase beyond this point, profits are generated; at volumes of less than 400 units, losses are incurred. The break-even point can be found numerically, of course, by simply dividing the total fixed costs of $200,000 by the unit contribution of $500, which results in 400 units, as we expected:

$$\text{Break-even point } (I = O)\text{: } \frac{F}{P - C} = V$$

$$\text{Zero profit} = \frac{\$200,000}{\$500} = 400 \text{ units}$$

The most interesting aspect of the break-even chart, however, is the clear demonstration that increases and decreases in profit are not proportional. A series of 25 percent increases in volume above the break-even point will result in much larger percentage jumps in profit growth.

The relevant change data are displayed in the table under the chart. They show a gradual decline in the growth rate of profit from infinite to 51 percent. Similarly, as volume decreases below the break-even point in 25 percent decrements, the growth rate of losses goes from infinite to a modest 18 percent, as volume approaches zero. Thus, changes in operations *close* to the break-even point, whether up or down, are likely to produce *sizable* swings in earnings. Changes in operations well above or below the break-even point will cause lesser fluctuations.

We must be careful in interpreting these changes, however. As in any percentage analysis, the specific results depend on the starting point and on the

FIGURE 5–1

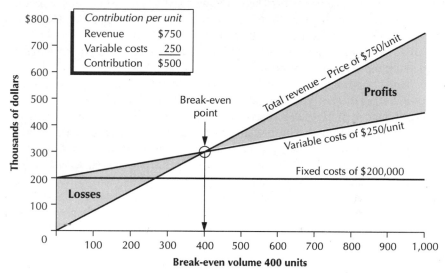

ABC CORPORATION
Simple Operating Break-Even Chart

Contribution per unit	
Revenue	$750
Variable costs	250
Contribution	$500

Break-even volume 400 units

Profits and Losses as a Function of Volume Changes of 25 Percent

Volume	Increase	Profits	Increase
400	—	-0-	—
500	25%	$ 50,000	Inflnite*
625	25	112,500	125%
781	25	190,500	69
976	25	288,000	51
Volume	Decrease	Losses	Increase
400	—	-0-	—
300	25%	$ 50,000	Infinite*
225	25	87,500	75%
169	25	115,500	32
127	25	136,000	18

*Infinite because the base is zero.

relative proportions of the components. In fact, managers will generally be much more concerned about the total amount of change in profit than about percent fluctuations. Moreover, it's easy to exaggerate the meaning of profit fluctuations unless they are viewed carefully in the context of a company's total cost structure and its normal level of operations.

Nevertheless, the concept should be clear: The closer to its break-even point a firm operates, the more dramatic will be the profit impact of volume changes. The analyst assessing a company's performance or making financial projections must attempt to understand where the level of its current operations is relative to normal volume and the break-even point, and then interpret the analytical results accordingly.

Furthermore, the greater the relative level of fixed costs, the more powerful the effect of leverage becomes. Therefore, we need to understand this aspect of the company's cost structure. In capital-intensive industries, such as steel, mining, forest products, and heavy manufacturing, most of the costs of production are fixed for a wide range of volumes. This tends to accentuate profit swings as companies move away from break-even operations.

Another example is the airline industry, which from time to time substantially increases the capacity of its flight equipment, e.g., from narrow body aircraft to jumbo jets. The fixed costs associated with owning and operating these expensive aircraft initially cause sharp drops in profit for many airlines. As business and private travel rise to approach the new levels of capacity, well-managed airlines experience dramatic improvements in profits. In contrast, service industries, such as consulting firms, can directly influence their major cost—salaries and wages—by adjusting the number of employees as demand changes. Thus, they're much less subject to the effects of the operating leverage phenomenon.

As we observed earlier, there are three main elements management can influence in the operating leverage relationship:

■ Fixed costs.
■ Variable costs.
■ Price.

All three are in one way or another related to *volume*. We'll demonstrate the effect of changes in all three by varying the basic conditions in our example.

Effect of Lower Fixed Costs

If management can lower *fixed costs* through energetic reductions in overhead, by using facilities more intensively, or by contracting out part of its production, the break-even point may be lowered significantly. As a consequence, the boosting effect on profits will start at a lower level of operations. Figure 5–2 shows this change.

Note that reducing fixed costs by one-eighth has led to a corresponding reduction in break-even volume. It will now take one-eighth fewer units contributing $500 each to recover the lower fixed costs. From the table we can observe that successive 25 percent volume changes from the reduced break-even point lead to increases or decreases in profit which are quite similar to our first example in Figure 5–1. Reducing fixed costs, therefore, is a very direct and effective way of lowering the break-even point to improve the firm's profit performance.

Effect of Lower Variable Costs

If management is able to reduce the variable costs of production (direct costs), thereby increasing the contribution per unit, the action can similarly affect profits at current levels and influence the movement of the break-even point itself. In

FIGURE 5–2

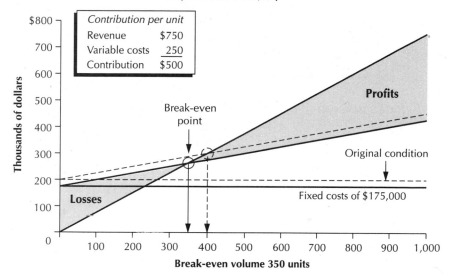

ABC CORPORATION
Simple Operating Break-Even Chart: Effect of Reducing Fixed Costs
(reduction of $25,000)

Profits and Losses as a Function of Volume Changes of 25 Percent

Volume	Increase	Profits	Increase
350.		0	
438.	25%	$ 44,000	Infinite*
547.	25	98,500	125%
684.	25	167,500	69
855.	25	252,000	51
Volume	*Decrease*	*Losses*	*Increase*
350.	—	-0-	—
262.	25%	$ 44,000	Infinite*
196.	25	77,000	75%
147.	25	101,500	32
110.	25	120,000	18

*Infinite because the base is zero.

Figure 5–3, we have shown the resulting change in the slope of the variable cost line, which in effect widens the area of profits. At the same time, loss conditions are reduced.

However, the change in break-even volume resulting from a 10 percent change in variable costs is not as dramatic as the change experienced when fixed costs were lowered by one-eighth. The reason is that the reduction applies only to a small portion of the total production cost, as variable costs are relatively low in

FIGURE 5–3

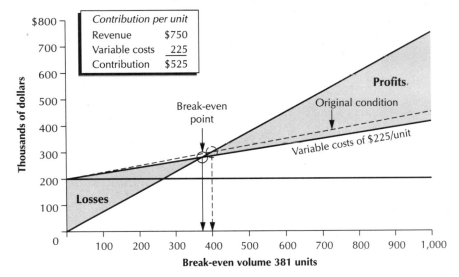

ABC CORPORATION
Simple Operating Break-Even Chart: Effect of Reducing Variable Costs
(reduction of $25 per unit)

Profits and Losses as a Function of Volume Changes of 25 Percent

Volume	Increase	Profits	Increase
381	—	-0-	—
476	25%	$ 49,900*	Infinite†
595	25	112,375	125%
744	25	190,600	69
930	25	288,250	51
Volume	Decrease	Losses	Increase
381	—	-0-	—
286	25%	$ 50,150	Infinite†
215	25	87,125	75%
161	25	115,475	32
121	25	136,475	18

*First 25 percent change not exactly equal due to rounding.
†Infinite because the base is zero.

this example. (This illustrates the point we made earlier about having to consider the relative cost proportions in this type of analysis.)

Only at the full capacity (1,000 units) does the profit impact of $25,000 correspond to the effect of the reduction of $25,000 in fixed costs in the earlier example. At lower levels of operations, lower unit volumes and the lesser impact of variable costs combine to minimize the effect. Nevertheless, the result is a clear improvement in the break-even condition, and a profit boost is achieved earlier on the volume scale. Again, 25 percent incremental changes are tabulated to show the specific results.

Effect of Lower Prices

Up to this point, we've concentrated on *cost* effects which are largely under management's control. In contrast, price changes are for the most part dependent on the firm's competitive environment. As a result, price changes normally affect the competitive equilibrium and will directly influence the unit volume a business is able to sell. Thus, it's not enough to trace the effect of raised or lowered prices on the break-even chart, but we must also anticipate the likely change in volume resulting from the price change.

In other words, raising the price may more than proportionately affect the unit volume the company will be able to sell competitively, and the price action may actually result in lower total profits. Conversely, lowering the price may more than compensate for the lost contribution per unit by significantly boosting the total unit volume which can be sold against competition.

Figure 5–4 demonstrates the effect of lowering the price by $50 per unit, a 6.7 percent reduction. Note that this change raises the required break-even volume by about 11 percent, to 444 units. In other words, the company needs to sell an additional 44 units just to recoup the loss in contribution of $50 from the sale of every unit.

For example, if the current volume was 800 units, with a contribution of $400,000 and a profit of $200,000, the price drop of $50 per unit would require the sale of enough additional units to recover 800 times $50, or $40,000. The new units required will, of course, provide the lower per-unit contribution of $450.

Under these conditions, as many as 89 additional units ($40,000÷$450) have to be sold at the lower price to maintain the $200,000 profit level, which represents a volume increase of 11 percent. Note that this results in a more than proportional change in unit volume (11 percent) versus the drop in price (6.7 percent). Price changes affect internal operating results, but they may have an even more pronounced and lasting impact on the competitive environment. If a more than proportional volume advantage, and therefore improved profits, can be obtained over a significant period of time after the price has been reduced, this may move. Otherwise, if price reductions can be expected to be quickly matched by other competitors, the final effect may simply be a drop in profit for everyone, because little if any shift in relative market shares would result. The repeated airline price wars are a prime example of this phenomenon.

This isn't the place to discuss the many strategic issues involved in pricing policy; the intent is merely to show the effect of this important factor on the operating area of the business system and to provide a way of analyzing likely conditions.

Multiple Effects on Break-Even Conditions

Up to now, we've analyzed cost, volume, and price implications and their impact on profit separately. In practice, the many conditions and pressures encountered by a business often affect these variables *simultaneously*. Cost, volume, and price

FIGURE 5–4

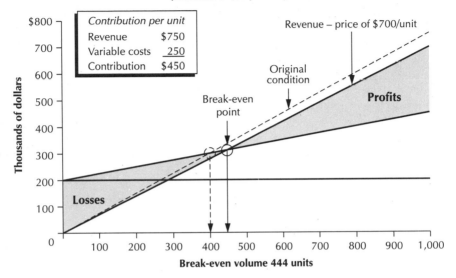

ABC CORPORATION
Simple Operating Break-Even Chart: Effect of Reducing Price
(reduction of $50 per unit)

Contribution per unit	
Revenue	$750
Variable costs	250
Contribution	$450

Revenue – price of $700/unit

Original condition

Profits

Break-even point

Losses

Break-even volume 444 units

Profits and Losses as a Function of Volume Changes of 25 Percent

Volume	Increase	Profits	Increase
444	—	-0-	—
555	25%	$ 49,750*	Infinite†
694	25	112,300	125%
867	25	190,150	69
1084	25	287,800	51
Volume	Decrease	Losses	Increase
444	—	-0-	—
333	25%	$ 50,150*	Infinite†
249	25	87,950	75%
187	25	115,850	32
140	25	136,000	18

*First 25 percent change not exactly equal due to rounding.
†Infinite because the base is zero.

for a single product may all be changing at the same time in subtle and often nonmeasurable ways. The analysis is further complicated when several products are involved, as is true of most major companies. In such cases, changes in the sales mix can introduce many additional complexities.

Moreover, our simplifying assumption which made production and sales simultaneous does not necessarily hold true in practice; the normal lag between production and sales has a significant effect. In a manufacturing company, sales and production can be widely out of phase. Some of the implications of this condition were discussed in Chapter 2, when we dealt with funds flow patterns under varying levels of operations, and in Chapter 4 when we examined the relationship of cash budgets and pro forma operating statements.

So far we've also assumed that operating conditions were essentially *linear*. This allowed us to simplify our analysis of leverage and break-even conditions. A more realistic framework is suggested in Figure 5–5. The chart shows potential changes in both fixed and variable costs over the full range of operations. Possible price–revenue developments are also indicated. In other words, changes in all three factors affecting operating leverage are reflected at the same time.

Figure 5–5 further shows that the simple straight-line relationships used in Figures 5–1 through 5–4 are normally only approximations of the "step functions" and the gradual shifts in cost and price often encountered under realistic circumstances. Inflationary distortions arising over time must also be considered. A few examples of the possible changes and likely reasons are described below the chart.

FIGURE 5–5

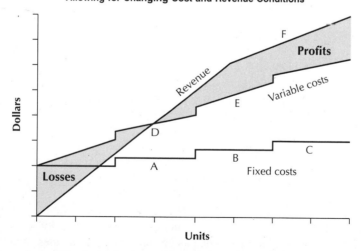

ABC CORPORATION
Generalized Break-Even Chart:
Allowing for Changing Cost and Revenue Conditions

A. A new layer of fixed costs is triggered by growing volume.
B. A new shift is added, with additional requirements for overhead costs.
C. A final small increment of overhead is incurred as some operations require overtime.
D. Efficiencies in operations reduce variable unit costs.
E. The new shift causes inefficiencies and lower output, with more spoilage.
F. The last increments of output must be sold on contract at lower prices.

Target Profit Analysis

An application of operational leverage is the use of target profit analysis as part of the planning process of a company. It takes into account the relative proportions of fixed and variable costs expected to occur in the company's system. Given projections of total fixed costs (F), estimates of variable costs (C), and expected price (P), the unit volume required to achieve any desired pretax target profit (TP) can be determined with the basic break-even formula:

$$\text{Volume for target profit: } V = \frac{F + TP}{P - C}$$

Similarly, if management wishes to test the level of variable costs (C) allowable for any desired pretax target profit (TP), with an estimated unit volume (V) and price (P) based on expected market conditions and projected fixed costs (F), the formula can be rewritten as:

$$\text{Variable unit cost for target profit: } C = P - \frac{(F + TP)}{V}$$

The reader is invited to rewrite the formula for the required price to achieve a desired pretax profit, and also to determine the change required to put the formula on an aftertax basis. Calculations of this kind serve well to scope the dimensions of the planning process, but cannot be substituted for detailed analysis and projections such as we discussed in Chapter 3. The approach is helpful for analysts and managers to recognize in broad terms the implications of the company's operating leverage.

Financial Leverage

The basic fixed/variable cost relationship can also be used to examine the effect of various proportions of debt in a firm's financial structure, that is, to analyze the company's financial leverage. A close similarity exists between operating and financial leverage in that both present an opportunity to gain from the fixed nature of certain costs in relation to increments of activity.

With financial leverage, the advantage lies in the possibility that funds borrowed at a fixed interest rate can be used for investment opportunities earning a rate of return higher than the interest paid. The difference, of course, accrues as profit to the owners of the business. Given the ability to make investments that consistently provide returns above the going rate of interest, it will be to a company's advantage to engage in "trading on equity," as the concept is sometimes called. This means borrowing as much as prudent debt management will permit, and thereby boosting the return on owners' equity by the difference between the rate of return achieved and the rate of interest paid. The opposite effect will, of course, apply if the company earns returns below the rate of interestpaid.

We must remember, of course, that over time the level of earnings on all investments must exceed not only the interest paid on debt but also meet the expectations of the holders of the company's equity. Shareholder value can only be created if the combined cost of capital is consistently exceeded, a principle we established early and will revisit in detail in Chapter 9. This requirement doesn't affect or alter the principles of leverage, however, it mainly establishes the level of effectiveness with which resources have to be employed.

Figure 5–6 shows the leverage effect on the return on equity measure under three conditions of return on net assets. All three curves are drawn with the assumption that funds can be borrowed at 4 percent per year after taxes.

If the normal return on the company's capitalization before interest, after taxes is 20 percent (curve A), growing proportions of debt cause a dramatic rise in return on equity. This return jumps to infinity as debt nears 100 percent—obviously a dangerous extreme in capital structure proportions. Curves B and C show the leverage effect under more modest earnings conditions. While somewhat lessened, the return on equity still shows sharp increases as the proportion of debt rises.

As we observed before, leverage unfortunately works also in the opposite direction. This effect is suggested by the increase in the distances between curves A, B, and C at higher debt levels. Should earnings drop, the plunge in return on equity can be massive.

FIGURE 5–6

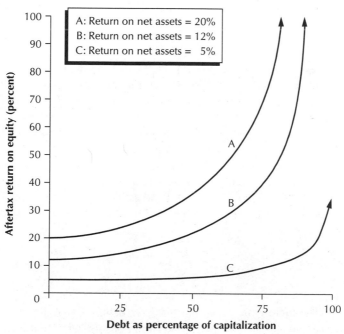

ABC CORPORATION
Return on Equity as Affected by Financial Leverage
(aftertax interest on debt is 4 percent)

A: Return on net assets = 20%
B: Return on net assets = 12%
C: Return on net assets = 5%

Aftertax return on equity (percent)

Debt as percentage of capitalization

To express financial leverage relationships formally, we begin by defining the components, as we did in the case of operating leverage. Profit after taxes (I) now has to be related to equity (E) and long-term debt (D). We also single out the return on equity (R), and the return on net assets (r) (capitalization) before interest and after taxes, and the aftertax rate of interest (i). First we define the return on equity as:

$$R = \frac{I}{E}$$

and the return on capitalization (the sum of equity and debt) as:

$$r = \frac{I + Di}{E + D}$$

We now restate profit (I) in terms of its components:

$$I = r(E + D) - Di$$

which represents the difference between the return on the total capitalization ($E + D$) and the aftertax cost of interest on outstanding debt (Di). We substitute this restated profit for R in our initial return on equity formula, which now reads:

$$R = \frac{r(E + D) - Di}{F}$$

and which can be further rewritten as:

$$R = r + \frac{D}{E}(r - i)$$

This formulation highlights the leverage effect, represented by the positive expression after r (that is, the proportion of debt to equity) multiplied by the difference between the earnings power of net assets and the aftertax cost of interest. Thus, to the extent that debt is introduced into the capital structure, the return on equity is boosted as long as interest cost doesn't exceed earnings power. This is the *net leverage contribution,* which we displayed in our systems view of key ratios in Chapter 3. Companies with different degrees of leverage will, even if their earnings power is the same, achieve different returns on equity due to the net leverage contribution (or detraction) caused by their capital structures. Analysts must therefore be careful in making direct comparisons of ROE results.

When we apply the formula to one set of conditions that pertained in Figure 5–6, the results can be calculated as follows. Given $i = 4$ percent, and $r = 12$ percent, if

(1) $D = 0$ and $E = \$100$, then R equals 12.0%
(2) $D = \$25$ and $E = \$75$, then R equals 14.7%
(3) $D = \$50$ and $E = \$50$, then R equals 20.0%
(4) $D = \$75$ and $E = \$25$, then R equals 36.0%

In this illustration, we have four different debt/equity ratios, ranging from no debt in the first case to a 3:1 debt/equity relationship in the fourth case. Given an aftertax cost of interest of 4 percent, and the normal opportunity to earn 12 percent after taxes on net assets invested, the return on equity in the first case is also 12 percent after taxes—because no debt exists, and the total capitalization is represented by equity.

As increasing amounts of debt are introduced to the capital structure, however, the return on equity is boosted considerably, because in each case, the return on investment far exceeds the cost of interest paid to the debt holders. This was, of course, demonstrated in the graph of Figure 5–6. The reader is invited to work through the opposite effect, that is, interest charges in excess of the ability to earn a return on the investments made with the funds.

We're also interested in the impact of leverage on the return on net assets, or capitalization (r), which we obtain first by reworking the formula

$$R = r + \frac{D}{E}\,(r - i)$$

into

$$r = \frac{RE + Di}{E + D}$$

Given $i = 4$ percent, and $R = 12$ percent, we can determine the minimum return on capitalization necessary to obtain a return on equity of 12 percent, for

(1) $D = 0$ and $E = \$100$, then R equals 12%
(2) $D = \$25$ and $E = \$75$, then R equals 10%
(3) $D = \$50$ and $E = \$50$, then R equals 8%
(4) $D - \$75$ and $E - \$25$, then R equals 6%

This is a useful way of testing the expected return from new investments. The approach simply turns the calculation around by fixing the return on equity and letting the expected return on investment vary. The process is straightforward. Note that the required amount of earnings on net assets, or capitalization, drops sharply as leverage is introduced, until it begins to approach the 4 percent aftertax interest cost. It will never quite reach this figure, however, because normally some amount of equity must be maintained in the capital structure to keep the company viable.

While it's simple to work out the mathematical relationships, the translation of these conditions into the appropriate financial strategies is much more complex. No management is completely free to vary the capital structure at will, and there are practical as well as legal and contractual constraints on any company to maintain some normalcy in the liability side of the balance sheet. While no absolute rules exist, the various tests of creditworthiness run the gamut of the ratios discussed in Chapter 2, particularly the measures oriented to the lenders' point of view.

With enlightened self-interest in mind, lenders will impose upper limits on the amount of debt capital to be utilized by any potential borrower. For manufacturing companies, the amount of long-term debt will normally range between 0 and 50 percent of their capitalization, while public utilities will range between 30 and 60 percent. Trading companies with highly liquid assets may have even higher debt proportions. The vast increase in leveraged buyouts during the 1980s introduced a far higher than normal level of debt into the capital structures of many companies. In these cases, financial leverage is used to the ultimate extent, which also vastly increases the exposure to the adverse effects of cash flow falling below expectations.

As stated before, we're interested in the effects of financial leverage on the broader area of financial planning for a company. As such, it is only one of several aspects affecting performance. In the next section, we will integrate financial leverage and the other key factors into a broader financial plan.

FINANCIAL GROWTH PLANS

Most managers aspire to building ever larger businesses, whenever the opportunities in the marketplace permit this. Typically, common shareholders also expect growing economic benefits to accrue from share ownership. Thus, it is not surprising that one important dimension of financial planning is continual testing of the effects of growth on investment, operations, and financing. The choices of financial policy open to management have different impacts on the expected results, and therefore must be tested along with the operational aspects of the plans.

Management can set a variety of financial objectives and financial policies to direct and constrain the company's planning effort and the specific financial projections based on these plans. The most commonly used financial objectives is the return on shareholders' equity. But this objective in turn is derived from specific objectives about:

- Growth in earnings per share.
- Growth in dividends per share.
- Growth in total profits.
- Growth in shareholders' equity.
- Growth in market value.

None of these objectives can singly be used as an overall standard, of course. In fact, the strong emphasis in recent years on shareholder value creation and total shareholder return achieved has put many of the accounting-based measures into a secondary role. As we'll discuss in more detail in Chapter 9, shareholder value creation is based on cash flows and market expectations, while total shareholder return takes into account the combined return to the investor from dividends and price changes in the market. The accounting measures remain important, however, because they are conveniently derived from published financial statements, and can be visibly linked to financial policies.

Foremost among these financial policies is the amount of financial leverage the company considers prudent, the subsidiary to it are the various measures of creditworthiness that management will wish to observe as constraints.

To demonstrate the buildup of an integrated financial plan that enables us to observe the effect of growth and its relationship to financial objectives and policies, we will begin by selecting just one of the objectives named above to work through a simple conceptual model of a hypothetical company. The format of this model is the basic framework that will allow us later to build a more detailed integrated financial plan. It will also serve to demonstrate the concept of sustainable growth.

Basic Financial Growth Model

A simple way of demonstrating the interrelated elements that affect growth in the business system is to use the objective of growth in owners' equity, as recorded on the balance sheet. Not only is this particular element easy to calculate, but it also encompasses the effects of profit growth and dividend payout—apart from any changes caused by issuing new shares or repurchasing existing shares in the market.

Figure 5–7 represents such a simplified financial model that allows us to trace the several aspects affecting equity growth in a company, namely, leverage, profitability, earnings disposition, and financing. With its help, we can demonstrate the effect different financial policies have on this objective.

Three cases have been worked out. The first represents an unleveraged company with $500,000 in equity, which pays no dividends and reinvests all of its profits in operations similar to its present activities. The second case shows the same company, but in a leveraged condition with debt at 50 percent of capitalization. In the third case, we take the conditions of the second case, but assume a dividend payout of 50 percent of earnings. All other financial conditions are assumed to remain constant.

Let's trace through the data for Case I. Given a gross return on net assets of 10 percent after taxes, the amount of net profit generated for the year is $50,000, all of which can be reinvested in the company's activities in the form of new investment for expansion, profit improvements, and so on. At the same time, we assume that, in addition, the amount of annual depreciation is spent on maintaining the present facilities in sound operating condition. (Recall a similar assumption from Figure 1–4, the business system diagram in Chapter 1.)

The results of Case I are a net return (after interest, which is zero in this example) on net assets, or capitalization, of 10 percent, a return on equity of 10 percent, and therefore growth in equity of 10 percent during the period. This condition holds because all profits are retained in the business for reinvestment.

In Figure 5–8, we've calculated three additional periods of operations for this particular company, without changing the assumptions. We can quickly observe that given stable policies and conditions, equity growth will indeed continue at 10 percent per year.

Case II differs only with regard to the use of debt financing. Because $250,000 has been borrowed at 4 percent after taxes, $10,000 of aftertax interest must be deducted from the amount of profit earned on net assets, which reduces

FIGURE 5–7

Financial Growth Model: Three Different Policies
($ thousands)

	Case I	Case II	Case III
Capital structure:			
Debt as a percentage of capitalization	-0-	50%	50%
Debt	-0-	$250	$250
Equity	$500	250	250
Net assets (capitalization)	$500	$500	$500
Profitability (after taxes):			
Gross return on net assets*	10%	10%	10%
Amount of profit	$ 50	$ 50	$ 50
Interest at 4%	-0-	10	10
Profit after interest	$ 50	$ 40	$ 40
Earnings disposition:			
Dividend payout	0%	0%	50%
Dividends paid	-0-	-0-	$ 20
Reinvestment	$ 50	$ 40	$ 20
Financing:			
Additional debt	-0-	$ 40	$ 20
New investment possible (next period)	$ 50	$ 80	$ 40
Results (in percent):			
Net return on net assets (capitalization)†	10%	8%	8%
Return on equity	10	16	16
Growth in equity‡	10	16	8

DIVIDEND

*Profits *before* interest, *after* taxes related to net assets (capitalization) as a measure of operational return on assets.
†Profits *after* interest and taxes related to net assets, as often shown in financial reports.
‡The growth in recorded equity based on earnings reinvested after payment of dividends.

the amount available for reinvestment to $40,000. If management wishes to maintain its policy of a 50 percent debt level, an additional $40,000 can be borrowed, matching the increase in equity. This raises the total funds available for new investment to $80,000.

Compared to Case I, the results have changed in several ways. Net return on capitalization has dropped to 8 percent because interest charges were introduced. As we expected, however, return on equity was boosted to 16 percent because of the leverage effect. Under these conditions, growth in equity can be similarly maintained at a level of 16 percent, as long as all of the internally generated funds are reinvested in opportunities returning 10 percent, and matching amounts of debt funds are obtained and similarly invested.

In Case III, the only change is the introduction of dividends. A 50 percent payout reduces the internal funds available for reinvestment to $20,000, and also reduces the available additional debt to $20,000, under a 50 percent debt policy. Total funds available for new investment have thus been reduced to $40,000. The

FIGURE 5–8

Financial Growth Model: Results of Three Different Policies Held Constant Over Three Periods ($ thousands)

	Case I			Case II			Case III		
	Period 1	Period 2	Period 3	Period 1	Period 2	Period 3	Period 1	Period 2	Period 3
Capital structure:									
Debt as a percentage of capitalization	-0-	-0-	-0-	50%	50%	50%	50%	50%	50%
Debt	-0-	-0-	-0-	$250	$ 290	$ 336.4	$250	$ 270	$291.6
Equity	$500	$550	$ 605	250	290	336.4	250	270	291.6
Net assets (capitalization)	$500	$550	$ 605	$500	$ 580	$ 672.8	$500	$ 540	$583.3
Profitability (after taxes):									
Gross return on net assets*	10%	10%	10%	10%	10%	10%	10%	10%	10%
Amount of profit	$ 50	$ 55	$60.5	$ 50	$58.0	$ 67.28	$ 50	$54.0	$58.32
Interest at 4%	-0-	-0-	-0-	$ 10	11.6	13.46	10	10.8	11.66
Profit after interest	$ 50	$ 55	$60.5	$ 40	$46.4	$ 53.82	$ 40	$43.2	$46.66
Earnings disposition:									
Dividend payout	0%	0%	0%	0%	0%	0%	50%	50%	50%
Dividends paid	-0-	-0-	-0-	-0-	-0-	-0-	$ 20	$21.6	$23.33
Reinvestment	$ 50	$ 55	$60.5	$ 40	$46.4	$ 53.82	$ 20	$21.6	$23.33
Financing:									
Additional debt	-0-	-0-	-0-	$ 40	$46.4	$ 53.82	$ 20	$21.6	$23.33
New investment possible (next period)	$ 50	$ 55	$60.5	$ 80	$92.8	$107.64	$ 40	$43.2	$46.66
Results (end of period)									
Net return on net assets (capitalization)†	10%	10%	10%	8%	8%	8%	8%	8%	8%
Return on equity	10	10	10	16	16	16	16	16	16
Growth in equity‡	10	10	10	16	16	16	8	8	8
Growth in total profit (after interest)	—	10	10	—	16	16	—	8	8

*Profits before interest, after taxes related to net assets (capitalization) as a measure of operational return on assets.

†Profits after interest and taxes related to net assets, as often shown in financial reports.

‡The growth in recorded equity based on earnings reinvested after payment of dividends.

dividend action seriously affects our objective of growth in equity, which is now only half the level in Case II.

This simple model illustrates the effects of a combination of decisions about investment, operations, earnings disposition, and financing strategy. It permits easy analysis of changes, and testing of the sensitivity of results in response to changed assumptions. Clearly we have oversimplified the conditions for illustrative purposes, but refinements in the assumptions about such items as return on net assets, dividend payout ratios, and increments of additional borrowing, to name but a few, will only be variations on the basic theme expressed here.

Sustainable Growth and the Sustainable Growth Formula

If growth in ownership equity were indeed considered to be the chief objective in our illustration, it would be useful to express the relationships on the basis of formulas similar to those used earlier.

In Case I, when no debt was employed and no dividends were paid, the following relationship held:

$$g = r$$

where g is growth in equity and r is the aftertax rate of return on capitalization. This formula simply expresses the fact that under these basic conditions, return on capitalization is *equal* to return on equity, and growth in equity is *equal* to return on equity.

In Case II, debt is introduced to the capital structure, and we must add the leverage effect to the formula as before to arrive at the growth formula:

$$g = r + \frac{D}{E}(r - i)$$

where D is debt, E is equity, and i is the aftertax interest rate. Leverage, as we discussed earlier, is a direct function of these two elements:

■ Proportion of debt in the total capital structure.

■ Difference between the return on investment and the interest cost of debt funds, both after taxes.

Because all earnings are assumed to be reinvested, the rate of growth in equity must again be equal to the *return* on equity—which in this case is a combination of the return on net assets and the net contribution from leverage.

In Case III, the introduction of dividend payments slows the growth in equity, because only the earnings retained can be reinvested. We have to adjust each of the two components of the formula to reflect this change. The factor p stands for the proportion of earnings retained as a percentage of total earnings. The resulting sustainable growth formula is:

$$g = rp + \frac{D}{E}(r - i)p$$

We now have a generalized formula for the rate of growth in equity that can be sustained by a business if stable conditions and policies hold. It is called the *sustainable growth formula*. If the business, over the long run, is managed within the following parameters, the growth in equity achieved will stabilize at the rate determined by the formula:

- Continually able to invest funds at the return indicated.

- Maintain the debt/equity proportion stable.

- Interest costs and the dividend payout ratio do not change.

As changes in policies are introduced, however, the fluctuations in year-to-year performance can be severe. The reader is invited to test the formulation for other conditions.

As we stated before, however, growth in equity is only one of several different types of financial objectives. Figure 5–8 indicates that such modeling is applicable to other objectives, such as growth in earnings. As the last line of the "Results" section indicates, under our stable sets of policies, growth in total earnings (profit after taxes) stabilizes at the same rate as growth in equity. In fact, the formula used for growth in equity applies to this objective as well, because profit growth depends on the same variables.

Similar models can be developed for the variables affecting earnings per share, dividends per share, debt service, or any other financial area of the business. We won't attempt to go into detail about these, but rather let growth in equity and growth in earnings serve as examples. The capabilities of computer spreadsheets are a natural assist in these types of analysis.

Integrated Financial Plan

We can now turn to an illustration of an integrated financial plan, which in concept and format is based on the models in Figures 5–7 and 5–8. This time, the focus is on taking a set of changing operating and financial assumptions and working them through this format. The XYZ Company is considering a number of modifications in its financial policies, and management wishes to study the impact of the combined operating projections and policy modifications on its rate of growth and profitability over the next five years. The resulting integrated financial plan (Figure 5–9) encompasses changes in debt proportions, return on net assets, interest cost (changing as debt proportions rise), and dividend payout.

One key benefit of displaying the interrelationships in this way is that any obviously inconsistent conditions will show up in the results. As undesirable effects occur, the analyst can explore them with more tenable assumptions and calculate the impact of such changes. Planning frameworks of this kind are now easily obtainable either in preprogrammed software or can be built with readily adaptable spreadsheets for use on personal computers. However, we must stress again that mere computing power doesn't obviate the need to understand the relationships we're demonstrating here.

FIGURE 5–9

XYZ CORPORATION
Integrated Financial Plan:
Sample Five-Year Projection of Effect of Policy Changes
($ thousands)

	Year 1	Year 2	Year 3	Year 4	Year 5
Capital structure:					
Debt as a percentage					
of capitalization	33.3%	43%	43%	50%	50%
Debt	$300.0	$ 470.7	$ 492.5	$ 688.9	$ 728.5
Equity	600.0	624.0	652.9	688.9	728.5
Net assets					
(capitalization) . . .	$900.0	$1,094.7	$1,145.4	$1,377.8	$1,457.0
Profitability (after taxes):					
Return on net assets	8%	7%	8%	8%	9%
Amount of profit	$ 72.0	$ 76.6	$ 91.6	$ 110.2	$ 131.1
Interest after taxes . . .	4%	4%	4%	4.5%	4.5%
Amount of interest . . .	$ 12.0	$ 18.8	$ 19.7	$ 31.0	$ 32.8
Profit after interest	$ 60.0	$ 57.8	$ 71.9	$ 79.2	$ 98.3
Earnings disposition:					
Dividend payout	60%	50%	50%	50%	40%
Dividends paid	$ 36.0	$ 28.9	$ 35.9	$ 39.6	$ 39.3
Reinvestment	$ 24.0	$ 28.9	$ 36.0	$ 39.6	$ 59.0
Financing and investment					
(next year):					
New debt, old ratio . . .	$ 12.0	$ 21.8	$ 27.2	$ 39.6	$ 59.0
New debt, revised ratio	158.7	-0-	169.2	-0-	-0-
New investment . . .	$194.7	$ 50.7	$ 232.4	$ 79.2	$ 118.0
Results (end of year):					
Net return on net					
assets*	6.7%	5.3%	6.3%	5.8%	6.8%
Return on equity	10.0	9.3	11.0	11.5	13.5
Growth in equity	4.0	4.6	5.5	5.8	8.1
Earnings per share					
(100,000 shares) . .	$ 0.60	$ 0.58	$ 0.72	$ 0.79	$ 0.98
Dividends per share . .	0.36	0.29	0.36	0.40	0.39

*Return after taxes and interest.

XYZ Corporation has a total capitalization of $900,000 and starts with a
debt proportion of 33.3 percent (every dollar of equity is matched by 50 cents of
long-term debt). The current return on net assets after taxes but before interest is
8 percent, which provides a profit of $72,000. Interest after taxes requires
$12,000, which leaves a net profit of $60,000. Depreciation is assumed to be
automatically reinvested in maintaining existing facilities, as we did in the financial systems discussion in Chapter 1.

With an assumed dividend payout of 60 percent, cash dividends of $36,000 are required, which leaves a balance of retained earnings of $24,000 for reinvestment in new assets, in addition to the amount of depreciation we assume to be automatically spent to keep facilities in good repair. If the debt proportion of 33.3 percent in Year 1 were to be maintained, new debt of $12,000 could be incurred and used for investment in Year 2, supported by the increased equity.

In anticipation of major expansion plans, XYZ management has decided to raise its debt proportion for Year 2 to 43 percent. This change would allow additional borrowing of $158,700 beyond the increase of $12,000 that would be possible under the old debt proportion. (The total amount of new debt is found by simply letting the increased equity of $624,000 represent 57 percent of net assets for Year 2.) For simplicity, we've assumed that all changes take place at year-end.

The results for the first year show a net return on capitalization of 6.7 percent, a return on equity of 10 percent, and growth in equity of 4 percent. Earnings per share are $0.60 and dividends per share are $0.36. The influx of new funds at the beginning of Year 2 raises the company's capitalization to almost $1.1 million.

For Year 2, the assumption about returns is lowered to reflect some normal inefficiencies as the new funds are invested; the overall return on net assets is expected to be 7 percent. After making proper allowance for interest payments, profits after taxes are $57,800. The assumed reduction in dividend payout to 50 percent requires only $28,900—which leaves $28,900 for reinvestment. Under the existing debt proportion of 43 percent, this amount is matched by $21,800 of new debt. These combined funds are added to the investment base for Year 3.

The process is repetitive as changes in policies are anticipated at the end of each year's operations. For example, we find a sizable new influx of capital in Year 4, as the debt proportion is again raised, this time to 50 percent. A small increase in the aftertax interest rate to 4.5 percent is assumed, because lenders will require higher interest as the capital structure becomes more leveraged and thus more risky. At the same time, however, the effectiveness of employing capital (aftertax return on net assets) has been left at 8 percent in Years 3 and 4, but was raised to 9 percent in Year 5, to allow some time for the new investments to become effective.

The results at the bottom of the table show some fluctuations in the net return on capitalization over the years, as either profitability or interest cost is changed. The return on equity, however, after dropping in Year 2, rises steadily to a sizable 13.5 percent in Year 5. Growth in equity jumps, after some intermediate boosts, to about double the original 4 percent rate in Year 5, that is, to 8.1 percent. Changes in total profit after interest are quite significant, as policy changes from year to year take effect. Similarly, growth in earnings per share fluctuates while dividends per share are somewhat diminished—showing little or no growth for most years as funds are reserved for investment.

The results from such a model raise some realistic questions. For example, it may not be prudent to change the dividend payout ratio in sizable steps as was done here. We observe a drop in dividends per share of almost 20 percent in the second year. In the absence of general economic problems, the corporation's directors might be very reluctant to make this change because a consistent dividend pattern is generally considered desirable. The main reason is that dividends represent part of the total shareholder return the investors have come to expect. Therefore, the dividend payout rate for Year 2 might be maintained near the original level with the purpose of avoiding a drop in dividends per share. The dividend payout percentage would be lowered only as total earnings rise sufficiently to permit paying a level or even growing dividend.

At the same time, it might be useful to refine the assumptions about return on net assets. We've used an overall percentage in this example. It would be more realistic if we split the analysis into

- Return on existing assets.
- Return on incremental assets.

specifically taking into account the lag in expected returns on the new investments made.

Such a refinement might be particularly useful if a company were diversifying its operations and expecting a highly different return from some of these new activities. More attention might also be paid to the assumption that depreciation will be reinvested without generating additional profits. A company with short life cycles of products or services, or one that's consolidating some of its ongoing operations to free funds for redeployment in more diversified lines of business, might not be willing to reinvest the equivalent of depreciation in old product lines.

The main purpose of this illustration is to show the usefulness of financial planning in the context of the overall business system. By observing how the key results respond to a variety of different inputs, the analyst can arrive at a set of assumptions and recommendations that fairly reflect management's desires and capabilities. Many more refined formats are, of course, possible, and the process is greatly enhanced by the use of computer spreadsheets.

SUMMARY

In this chapter we've attempted to integrate some key concepts discussed in the earlier parts of the book into the dynamic system framework established in Chapter 1. We added an expanded treatment of *operating* and *financial leverage* to demonstrate the important impact of fixed cost elements on changing operating conditions. Through the use of a simplified *financial modeling* approach, we demonstrated the need for consistency in operating and financial objectives and policies. We demonstrated the various implications of growth, and developed the policy rationale for *sustainable growth* over time. Finally, we applied the modeling approach to the needs and policies of a sample company and developed an *integrated financial* plan with which we tested the impact of changes in the policies on the company's growth and performance.

In the end, the key test of financial analysis is the viability of the methods and results as predictors of future activity, which was a major point made in the earlier chapters. Often the optimal approach requires use of quite detailed and sensitive financial models of the business. Yet the outside analyst, and even insiders, will often be well served with *simplified yardsticks and models* which can sufficiently approximate solutions to planning alternatives. In this sense, the chapter draws together many of the points of earlier materials to give the reader an overall, albeit simplified framework for analysis.

SELECTED REFERENCES

Donaldson, Gordon. *Strategy of Financial Mobility*. Boston: Division of Research, Graduate School of Business Administration, Harvard University, 1969 (a classic).

Donaldson, Gordon. *Corporate Restructuring: Managing the Change Process from Within*. Boston: Harvard Business School Press, 1994.

Donaldson, Gordon. *Managing Corporate Wealth: The Operation of a Comprehensive Financial Goals System*. New York: Praeger Publishers, 1984.

Drucker, Peter F., "The Information Executives Truly Need," *Harvard Business Review*, January/February 1995.

SELF-STUDY EXERCISES AND PROBLEMS

(Solutions are provided in Appendix V)

1. The ABC Corporation, a manufacturing company, sells a product at a price of $5.50 per unit. The variable costs involved in producing and selling the product are $3.25 per unit. Total fixed costs are $360,000. Calculate the break-even point and draw an appropriate chart.

   a. Calculate and demonstrate the effect of leverage by noting the profit impact of moving from the break-even point in 20 percent volume increments and decrements.

   b. Calculate and graph separately the impact of a 50-cent drop in price, a 25-cent increase in variable cost, and an increase of $40,000 in fixed cost.

   c. Draw a graph and discuss the implications if fixed costs increase $30,000 after 175,000 units of production, the average price drops to $5.25 per unit after 190,000 units are produced, and variable costs drop to an average of $3 after 150,000 units. How are the calculations for break-even affected?

2. Calculate the effect of financial leverage under the following two conditions:

   a. Interest rate is 5 percent after taxes; return on net assets is 8 percent after taxes.

   b. Interest rate is 6 percent after taxes; return on net assets is 5 percent after taxes.

Develop the effect of return on equity in each case for debt as a percentage of capitalization at 0 percent, 25 percent, 50 percent, and 75 percent. Discuss.

3. Develop a five-year financial plan for a company based on the following assumptions:

	Year 1	Year 2	Year 3	Year 4	Year 5
Net assets (000)	$1,500	—	—	—	—
Debt/equity	0.25:1	0.25:1	0.50:1	0.50:1	0.50:1
Return on net assets (after					
taxes)	8%	9%	10%	10%	10%
Interest rate (after taxes)	4.5	4.5	5.0	5.0	5.0
Dividend payout	⅔	⅔	⅔	½	½
Number of shares	200,000	—	—	—	—

a. Calculate all relevant financial results, such as earnings per share, return on equity, growth in equity, and growth in earnings. Discuss your assumptions and findings.

b. Demonstrate the sensitivity of earnings per share, return on equity, and growth in equity by varying the conditions in Year 5 as follows: debt/equity, 0.75:1; return on net assets, 11 percent; interest rate, 4.5 percent; and dividend payout, two thirds. Discuss your findings.

CHAPTER 6

Analysis of Investment Decisions

The decision to invest resources is one of the key drivers of the business financial system, as we established in Chapter 1. Sound investments that implement well-founded strategies are essential to creating shareholder value, and must be analyzed both in a proper context and with sound analytical methods. Whether the decision involves committing resources to new facilities, a research and development project, a marketing program, additional working capital, an acquisition, or to investing in a financial instrument, an economic trade-off must be made between the resources expended now and the expectation of future cash benefits to be obtained. Analyzing this trade-off is essentially a valuation process that makes an economic assessment of a combination of positive and negative cash flow patterns. The task is difficult because it deals with future conditions subject to uncertainties and risks—yet this valuation principle is common to all investments, large and small.

In this chapter, we'll examine in some detail both the key conceptual and the practical aspects of investment decisions, while in Chapters 7 and 8, we'll address the related issues of financing costs and the choice among financing alternatives. In Chapter 9, we'll expand on these concepts and demonstrate how the process applies to valuing a business and to the creation of shareholder value. From time to time, we'll introduce applicable portions of managerial economics and financial theory. In keeping with the scope of this book, however, we will avoid the esoteric in favor of the practical and useful. At the end of each chapter, we will summarize, in a separate list, the key conceptual issues underlying the analytical approaches covered, both as a reminder and as a guide for the interested reader in exploring the references listed.

The analysis of decisions about new investments, (as well as disinvestments) involves a particularly complex set of issues and choices that must be resolved by management. We'll discuss these in several categories:

- Strategic perspective.
- Decisional framework.

- Components of the analysis.
- Economic analysis methods.

Because business investments, in contrast to operational spending, are normally relatively long-term commitments of resources, they should always be made within the context of a company's explicit strategy.

In addition, financial analysis underlying the decisions and the trade-offs involved must be carried out within a consistent economic framework of accepted conceptual and practical guidelines.

Moreover, most business investment projects have in common several key components of analysis. These must be understood and made explicit, as well as comparable, in order to arrive at a proper choice among different investment alternatives.

Finally, the economic nature of the process requires that the analytical methods supporting the decisions focus on the cash flow impact of the investment or disinvestment.

We'll take up each area in turn, emphasizing in somewhat greater detail the analytical components and methodologies. Once we've demonstrated the fundamental concepts, we'll introduce certain refinements in the analytical process. Some comments about specialized topics will follow, and we'll close with a checklist of key issues affecting investment analysis.

STRATEGIC PERSPECTIVE

Investments in land, productive equipment, buildings, natural resources, research facilities, product development, employee development, marketing programs, acquisitions, and other resource deployments made for future economic gain should be the expression of a company's strategy—which management must establish and periodically reevaluate. Investment choices should always reflect the desired direction the company wishes to take, with due consideration of:

- Expected economic conditions.
- Outlook for the company's specific industry or business segment.
- Competitive position of the company.
- Core competencies of the organization.

An almost infinite variety of business investments are available to most firms. It does not matter how the resource commitment is reflected on the company's books, in the form of an asset or as an expense for the period—the critical point is that the outlay is being made with an expectation of future returns. A company may invest in new facilities for expansion, expecting that incremental profits from additional volume will make the investment economically desirable. Investments may also be made for upgrading worn or outmoded facilities to improve cost-effectiveness. Here, savings in operating costs are the justification.

Some strategies call for entering new markets, which could involve setting up entirely new facilities and associated working capital, or perhaps a major repositioning of existing facilities through rebuilding or through sale and reinvestment. In a service business, expansion strategies could involve significant employee training outlays and electronic infrastructure investments. Other strategic proposals might involve establishing a research facility, justified on the basis of its potential for developing new products or processes. Business investment could also involve significant promotional outlays, targeted on raising the company's market share over the long-term and, with it, the profit contribution from higher volumes of operation. At times, acquiring a company whose product or service lines fit into the company's strategy, or purchasing a supplier to integrate the technology base, may be appropriate.

These and other choices are conceived continuously by the organization. Typically, lists of proposals are examined during the company's strategic planning process within the context and constraints of corporate and divisional objectives and goals. Then the various alternatives are narrowed down to those options that should be given serious analysis, and periodic spending plans are prepared which contain those capital outlays that have been selected and approved.

The many steps involved in identifying, analyzing, and selecting capital investment opportunities—as well as opportunities for divestiture—are collectively known as *capital budgeting*. This process includes everything from a broad scoping of ideas to very refined economic analyses. In the end, the company's capital budget normally contains an acceptable group of projects that individually and collectively are expected to provide economic returns meeting long-term management goals in support of shareholder value creation.

In essence, capital budgeting is like managing a personal investment portfolio. In both cases, the basic challenge is to select, within the constraint of available funds, those investments that promise to yield the desired level of economic rewards in relation to the degree of acceptable risk. The process thus involves a conscious economic trade-off between exposure to potential adverse conditions and the expected profitability of the investment. As a general rule, the higher the profitability, the higher also will be the risk exposure. Moreover, the choice among alternatives in which to invest the limited funds available invariably involves opportunity costs, because committing to one investment can mean rejecting others, thereby giving up the opportunity to earn perhaps higher but riskier returns.

In an investment portfolio, cash commitments are made in order to receive future inflows of cash in the form of dividends, interest, and eventual recovery of the principal through sale of the investment instrument—which over time may have appreciated or declined in market value. In capital budgeting, the commitment of company funds is made in exchange for future cash inflows from incremental aftertax profits and from the potential recovery of a portion of the capital invested, or from the value of a going business at the end of the planning horizon.

However, the analogy carries only so far. In a typical company, managing investments is complicated by the need not only to select a portfolio of sound projects, but also to operate the facilities, service functions, or other assets deployed with effectiveness. In addition, analyzing potential investments in a business context is far more complex than selecting among stocks and bonds because the outlays often involve multiple expenditures spread over a period of time. The construction and equipping of a new factory and the gradual buildup of a service business and its infrastructure, are examples.

Determining the economic benefits to be derived from the outlay is even more complex. An individual investor generally receives specific contractual interest payments or regular dividend checks. In contrast, a business investment typically generates additional profits from higher volume, new products and services, or cost reduction. The specific incremental profit from a business investment may be difficult to identify, because it's intermingled in the company's financial reports with other accounting information. As we'll see, the analysis of potential capital investments involves a fair degree of economic reasoning and projection of future conditions that goes beyond merely using normal financial statements.

If we follow the analogy between a capital budget and an investment portfolio to its logical conclusion, capital budgeting would ideally amount to arraying all business investment opportunities in the order of their expected economic returns, and choosing a combination that would meet the desired portfolio return within the constraints of risk and available funding. The theoretical concepts that have evolved around these issues rely heavily on portfolio theory, both in terms of risk evaluation and in the comparison between investment returns and the cost of capital incurred in funding the investments.

These concepts are highly structured and depend on a series of important underlying assumptions. Not easy to apply in practice, they continue to be the subject of much learned argument. In simple terms, the theory argues that business investments—arrayed in declining order of attractiveness—should be accepted up to the point at which incremental benefits equal incremental cost, given appropriate risk levels.

This theory encounters several problems when applied in a practical setting. First, at the time the capital budget is prepared, it's simply not possible to forecast all investment opportunities, because management faces a continuously revolving planning horizon over which new opportunities keep appearing, while known opportunities may fade as conditions change even more rapidly.

Second, capital budgets are prepared only once a year in most companies. As various timing lags are encountered, actual implementation may be delayed or even canceled, because circumstances often change.

Third, economic criteria, such as rate of return and cost of capital, are merely approximations. Moreover, they are not the sole basis for the investment decision. Instead, the broader context of strategy, the competitive environment, the ability of management to implement the investment, organizational considerations, and other factors come into play as management weighs the risk of an investment against the potential economic gain. Thus, there is nothing automatic or simple in arriving at decisions about the stream of potential investments that are continuously surfaced within a business organization.

In this chapter, we'll explore the decisional framework and the analytical techniques that support the decision process for analyzing and choosing business investments. We won't delve into the broader conceptual issues of capital budgeting and portfolio theory, except to point out some of the key issues. Readers with further interest in these topics should check the references at the end of the chapter. The important question of the cost of capital as related to capital budgeting will be taken up in the next chapter, followed in Chapter 8 by the analytical reasoning behind the choice among types of potential funding of capital investments.

THE DECISIONAL FRAMEWORK

Effective analysis of business investments requires that both the analyst and the decision maker be very conscious of and specific about the many dimensions involved. We need to set a series of ground rules to ensure that our results are thorough, consistent, and meaningful. These ground rules cover:

- Problem definition.
- Nature of the investment.
- Estimates of future costs and benefits.
- Incremental cash flows.
- Relevant accounting data.
- Sunk costs.
- Time value of money.

A good rule of thumb to keep in mind is that of the total effort required to analyze a business investment, at least 90 percent should be spent on meeting these important requirements, and only 10 percent on "doing the numbers." Unfortunately, the proportions are often reversed in practice, resulting in costly mistakes.

Problem Definition

We should begin any evaluation by stating explicitly what the investment is supposed to accomplish. Carefully defining the problem to be solved (or the opportunity presented) by the investment, and identifying any potential alternatives to the proposed action, are critically important to proper analysis. This elementary point is often overlooked, at times deliberately, when the desire to proceed with a favorite investment project overrides sound judgment.

In most cases, at least two or three alternatives are available for achieving the purpose of an investment, and careful examination of the specific circumstances may reveal an even greater number. The simple diagram in Figure 6–1 can help us to visualize the key options for deciding on which alternatives to pursue in an investment proposal.

For example, the decision of whether to replace a machine nearing the end of its useful life at first appears to be a relatively straightforward either/or problem. The most obvious alternative, as in any case, is to do nothing, that is, to continue patching up the machine until it falls apart. The ongoing, rising costs likely to be incurred with that option are compared with the expected cost pattern of a new machine when we decide whether or not to replace it. But the alternative of doing nothing exists for any investment project, and sound analysis requires that its implications be tested before proceeding.

There are some not-so-obvious alternatives. Perhaps the company should stop making the product altogether! This "go out of business" option should at least be considered—painful as it may be to think about—before new resources are committed.

The reasoning behind this seemingly radical notion is quite straightforward. While the improved efficiency of a new machine or a whole new facility may raise the product's profit performance from poor to average, there may indeed be alternatives elsewhere in the company that would yield greater profit from the funds committed. By going ahead with the replacement, an opportunity cost from losing a higher profit option might be incurred. In the interest of shareholder value creation, it might be better to redeploy all resources now devoted to the product instead of prolonging its substandard performance.

Morever, even if the decision to continue making the product is economically sound under prevailing conditions, there still are several additional alternatives open to management. Among these, for example, are replacement with the same machine, or with a larger, more automated model, or with equipment using an

FIGURE 6–1

Alternatives for an Investment Decision

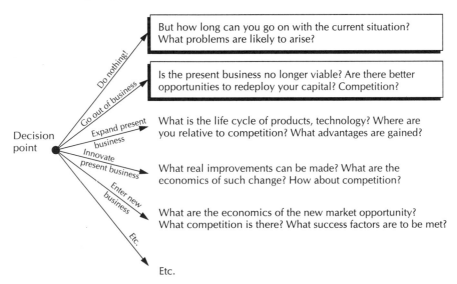

altogether different technology and manufacturing process—or outsourcing the manufacture and avoiding the investment.

It's crucial to select the appropriate alternatives for analysis and to structure the problem in such a way that the analytical tools are applied to the real issue to be decided. For decisions of major strategic importance, formal processes are available which use the disciplines of decision theory to aid in structuring the problem and in establishing an array of creative alternatives (see end-of-chapter references). As a general rule, however, no investment should be undertaken unless the best analytical judgment allows it to clear the hurdles implied in the first two branches of the decision tree.

Nature of the Investment

Most business investments tend to be independent of each other, that is, the choice of any one of them doesn't preclude also choosing any other—unless there are insufficient funds available to do them all. In that sense, they can be viewed as a portfolio of choices. The analysis and reasoning behind every individual decision will be relatively unaffected by past and future choices.

There are, however, circumstances in which investments compete with each other in their purpose so that choosing one will preclude the other. Typically, this arises when two alternative ways of solving the same problem are being considered. Such investment projects are called *mutually exclusive*. The significance of this condition will become apparent when we discuss the measures used to judge economic desirability. A similar condition can, of course, also arise when management sets a strict limit on the amount of spending, often called *capital rationing,* which will preclude investing in some worthy projects once others have been accepted.

Another type of investment involves *sequential outlays* beyond the initial expenditure. For example, any major capital outlay for plant and equipment usually also entails additional future outlays for major maintenance, upgrading, and partial replacement some years hence. These future outlays—to which the company is committing itself—should be considered when the initial decision is made. Another example is the introduction of a new product with high growth potential, where additional working capital and perhaps capacity expansions are a natural consequence of the decision to proceed.

The most logical evaluation of such investments comes from taking into account the whole pattern of major outlays recognizable at the time of analysis. If this isn't done, such a project may be viewed more favorably than a more straightforward one. Moreover, if the project is chosen, management may become trapped into having to approve unanticipated future outlays as they arise later—on the argument that these incremental funds are clearly justifiable because the project is "already in place." While that argument may be true given the earlier decision, the fact remains that the project was originally not judged on its full implications, and under those conditions might not have been justifiable.

Future Costs and Benefits

As we stated earlier, one of the key principles in making investment decisions is that the economic calculations used to justify any business investment must be based on projections and forecasts of *future revenues and costs*. It's simply not enough to assume that the past conditions and experience, such as operating costs or product prices, will continue unchanged and be applicable to a new venture. While this may seem obvious, there's a practical temptation to extrapolate past conditions instead of carefully forecasting likely developments. The past is at best a rough guide, and at worst irrelevant for analysis.

The success of an investment, whether the time horizon is two, five, ten, and even twenty-five years, rests entirely on future events and the uncertainty surrounding them. It therefore behooves the analyst to explore as much as possible the likely changes from present conditions in the key variables relevant to the analysis. If potential deviations in several areas are large, it may be useful to run the analysis under different sets of assumptions, thus testing the *sensitivity* of the quantitative result to changes in particular variables, such as product volumes, prices, key raw material costs, and so on. (Recall our references to this type of analysis in the earlier chapters.)

The uncertainty of future conditions affecting an investment is the *risk* of not meeting expectations and being left with an insufficient economic return or even an economic loss—the degree of risk being a function of the relative uncertainty about the key variables of the project. Careful estimates and research are often warranted to narrow the margin of error in the predicted conditions on which the analysis is based. Since the basic rationale of making investments relies on a conscious economic trade-off of risk versus reward, as we established earlier, the importance of explicitly addressing key areas of uncertainty should be obvious. Identifying key variables will also be helpful in judging the actual performance of the project after implementation, since tracking of these elements is usually much easier than trying to reconstruct the full scope of the project from the accounting records into which it has been merged.

Incremental Cash Flows

The economic reasoning behind any capital outlay is based strictly on the incremental changes resulting directly from the decision to make the investment, in other words, what is *different* between the current state of affairs and the situation introduced by the decision in the form of

- Incremental investment.
- Incremental revenues.
- Incremental costs and expenses.

Moreover, proper economic analysis recognizes only *cash flows*, that is, the cash effect of positive or negative funds movements caused by the investment.

Any *accounting* transactions related to the decision but not affecting cash flows are irrelevant for the purpose.

The first basic question to be asked is: What additional funds will be required to carry out the chosen alternative? For example, the investment proposal may, in addition to the outlay for new equipment, entail the sale or other disposal of assets that will no longer be used. Therefore, the decision may actually free some previously committed funds. In such a case, it's the *net outlay* that counts, after any applicable incremental tax effects have been factored in.

Similarly, the next question is: What additional revenues will be created over and above any existing ones? If an investment results in new revenues, but at the same time causes the loss of some existing revenues, only the *net impact,* after applicable taxes, is relevant for economic analysis.

The third question concerns the costs and expenses that will be added or removed as a result of the investment. The only relevant items here are those costs, including applicable taxes, that will go up or down as a consequence of the investment decision. Any cost or expense that is expected to remain the same before and after the investment has been made is not relevant for the analysis.

These three questions illustrate why we refer to the economic analysis of investments as an *incremental* process. The approach is relative rather than absolute, and is tied closely to carefully defined alternatives and the differences between them. The only data relevant and applicable in any investment analysis are the *differential* funds commitments as well as *differential* revenues and costs caused by the decision, all viewed in terms of *aftertax cash flows*.

Relevant Accounting Data

Investment analysis in large part involves the use of data derived from accounting records, not all of which are relevant for the purpose. Accounting conventions that don't involve cash flows must be viewed with extreme caution. This is true particularly with investments that cause changes in operating costs. There we must clearly distinguish between those cost elements that in fact vary with the operation of the new investment and those which only *appear* to vary. The latter are often *accounting allocations* which may change in magnitude but do not necessarily represent a true change in costs incurred.

For example, for accounting purposes, general overhead costs (administrative costs, insurance, etc.) may be allocated on the basis of a set operating volume expressed in units produced. At other times, direct labor hours are the basis for allocation. In the former case, the accounting system will charge a new machine having higher output with a higher share of overhead than the machine it replaces was charged.

Yet there was likely no actual change in the level of general overhead that can be attributed to the decision to substitute one machine for the other. Therefore, the reported change in the allocation is not relevant for purposes of economic analysis. The analyst must constantly judge whether there has been a change in the true cash outlays and revenues—not whether the accounting system is redistributing existing costs differently. A sound rule that helps avoid being trapped by allocations is to avoid unit costs whenever possible and to perform the analysis on the basis of annual changes in costs expected to be caused by the investment decision.

Sunk Costs

It's a common temptation to include in the analysis of a new investment all or some portion of outlays that occurred in the past, perhaps preparatory to making the new commitment. There's no basis in economic analysis, however, that justifies such backtracking to expenditures that have already been made and that are not recoverable in part or as a whole. Past decisions simply do not count in the economic trade-off underlying a current investment decision. The basic reason for this is that such *sunk costs,* even if they are connected in some way to the decision at hand, cannot be altered by making the investment now.

If, for example, significant amounts had been spent on research and development of a new product, the current decision about whether to invest in facilities to make the product should in no way be affected by those sunk costs. Perhaps the earlier decision to do research and development in retrospect was less rewarding than expected, and shouldn't have been made. But now the only point is: If the investment required to exploit the results of such past research appears economically justified on its own merits, it should be undertaken at the present time.

Economic decisions are always forward-looking and must involve only those things that can be changed by the action being decided. This is the essential test of relevance for any element to be included in the analysis.

The Time Value of Money

Given the future orientation of investment analysis, the proper application of economic reasoning requires us to recognize the intimate connection between two elements:

- Timing of incremental cash in-flows and outflows.
- The value of cash flows relative to the point of decision.

It's a simple axiom that a dollar received today is worth more than a dollar received one year hence, because we forgo the opportunity of profitably investing today the future dollar we have to wait for. Similarly, spending a dollar a year later is preferable to spending it now, because it can earn a return in the meantime. Thus, the time value of money is related both to the timing of receipt or expenditure, and the opportunity to earn a return on any funds invested.

Since the economic analysis of capital investments involves projecting a whole series and pattern of incremental cash flows, both positive and negative, we need a consistent method that will translate the respective values of these future flows into today's terms. Figure 6–2 shows the pattern of cash flows connected with a typical investment, consisting of an initial outlay, a series of positive benefits, an intermediate additional outlay, and ultimate recovery of part of the resources committed in the form of a terminal value.

FIGURE 6–2

Typical Cash Flow Pattern for a Business Investment

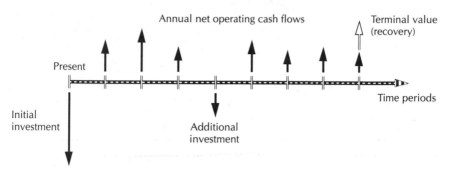

All of these future cash flows have to be brought back in time to the present point of decision by an appropriate methodology. The process of expressing future dollars in the form of *equivalent* present dollars is called *discounting*. It's the basis for all the modern techniques of investment analysis and valuation that will be discussed later in this chapter. We'll return to describing the key technical aspects of the time value of money shortly.

COMPONENTS OF ANALYSIS

Bearing in mind the strategic perspective and the ground rules just enumerated, we can now turn to the basic components common to all business investment proposals. In essence, capital is invested for one basic reason: to obtain sufficient future economic returns to warrant the original outlay and any related future outlays, that is, sufficient cash receipts over the life of the project to justify the cash spent. This basic trade-off of current cash outflow against expected future cash inflow must be recognized by the analytical methods in one way or another.

To judge the attractiveness of any investment, we must consider the following four elements:

- The amount expended—the *net investment.*
- The potential benefits—the *net operating cash inflows.*
- The time period of benefits—the *economic life.*
- Any final recovery of capital—the *terminal value.*

A proper economic analysis must take these four elements into account to be able to indicate whether the investment is worthwhile or not.

For Example

An outlay of $100,000 for equipment needed to manufacture a new product is expected to provide aftertax cash flow of $25,000 over a period of six years, without significant annual fluctuations. Although the equipment will not be fully worn out after six years, it is unlikely that more than scrap value will be realized at that time, due to technical obsolescence. The cost of removal is expected to offset this scrap value. Straight-line depreciation over the six years ($16,667 per year) was correctly adjusted for in the final cash flow fixture of $25,000 having been added back to the net aftertax improvement in profits of $8,333. ∎

Net Investment

The first element in the analysis, the net investment, normally consists of the gross capital requirements for the new assets, reduced by any funds recovered from the trade or sale of existing assets because of the decision. Such recoveries must be adjusted for any change in income taxes arising from a recognized gain or loss on the disposal of existing assets.

The basic rule for finding the investment amount committed to the decision is to calculate the net amount of outlays and recoveries caused by the decision to invest. In our simple case, no funds were recovered and therefore the net investment is the full outlay of $100,000.

When an investment is made to support a new product or to provide an increased volume of existing products, any additions to working capital required by the increased level of sales must be included in the analysis. Normally, such incremental working capital is added to the net investment. For our first example this refinement is ignored, but later in the chapter we'll demonstrate how working capital increments are handled.

Further capital outlays may also become necessary during the life of the investment project, and may be foreseeable enough to be estimated at the time of analysis. Any such potential consequences of the initial decision must be considered as part of the investment proposal. We'll also demonstrate the method of dealing with sequential elements later on.

Net Operating Cash Inflows

The operational basis for economic benefits over the life of the investment is the period-by-period *net change* in revenues and expenses caused by the investment, after adjusting for applicable income taxes. These incremental changes include such elements as operating savings from a machine replacement, additional profits from a new product line, increased profits from plant expansion, or profits created by developing land or other natural resources. Generally, they'll be reflected as increased profit reported in periodic operating statements, once the investment is in place and functioning. Our main focus, however, has to be on finding the estimated net impact on cash flow, adjusted for all applicable taxes. Later, we'll give numerous examples of how such project cash flows are derived.

For our simplified case, we'll assume that the net annual operating aftertax cash inflow will be a level amount of $25,000 over the project's life. This represents the sum of estimated net aftertax profits of $8,333 and depreciation of $16,667. As we'll see later, introducing a variable pattern of periodic cash flows can significantly influence the analytical results. Level periodic flows are easiest to deal with, but are quite rare in practice. Uneven cash flows are more common and make the analysis more complex—but they can be handled readily, as we'll soon demonstrate.

Economic Life

The third element, the time period selected for the analysis, is commonly referred to as the *economic life* of the investment project. For purposes of investment analysis, the only relevant time period is the economic life, as distinguished from the *physical* life of equipment, or the *technological* life of a particular process.

Even though a building or a piece of equipment may be perfectly usable from a physical standpoint, the economic life of the investment is finished if the market for the product or service has disappeared. Similarly, the economic life of any given technology is bound up with the economics of the marketplace—the best process is useless if the resulting product or service can no longer be sold. At that point, any usable resources will have to be repositioned, which requires another investment decision, or they may be disposed of for their recovery value. When redeploying such resources into another project, the net investment for that decision would, of course, be the estimated recovery value after taxes.

In our simple example, we have assumed a six-year economic life, the period over which the product manufactured with the equipment will be sold. The *depreciation life* used for accounting or tax purposes does not normally reflect an investment's true life span. As we discussed earlier, such write-offs are based on standard accounting and tax guidelines, and don't necessarily represent the investment's economic usefulness.

Terminal Value

Normally, if one expects a substantial recovery of capital from eventual disposal of remaining assets at the end of the economic life, these estimated amounts have to be made part of the analysis. Such recoveries can be proceeds from facilities and equipment (beyond the minor scrap value assumed in our example), as well as the release of any *working capital* associated with the investment. Again, we'll demonstrate the handling of these elements later on.

METHODS OF ANALYSIS

Up to this point, we've laid the groundwork for analyzing any business investment by describing the *strategic perspective*, the *decisional framework*, and the four essential *components* of the analysis. Our purpose was to demonstrate that analyzing a capital investment is not the simple matter it may appear to be, and we focused on *what* must be analyzed. We'll now turn to the question of *how* this is done—the methods and criteria of analysis that will help us judge the economics of the decision.

How do we relate the four basic components—

- ■ Net investment.
- ■ Operating cash inflow.
- ■ Economic life.
- ■ Terminal value.

—to determine the project's attractiveness? We'll first dispose quickly of some simplistic methods of analysis, which are merely rules of thumb that intuitively grapple with the trade-off between investment and operating cash flows. They are the *payback* and the *simple rate of return,* both of which occasionally are still used in practice despite their demonstrable shortcomings.

Our major emphasis in this section will be on measures employing the *time value of money,* enabling the analyst to deal with relevant cash flows in equivalent terms, that is, regardless of the timing of their incidence. Those key measures are *net present value,* the *profitability index,* and the *internal rate of return (yield).*

Thereafter, we'll turn to basic *risk analysis,* and discuss the *present value payback, annualized net present value, ranges of estimates, simulation, probabilistic reasoning,* and *risk-adjusted rates.*

Simple Measures

Payback

This crude rule of thumb directly relates assumed level annual cash inflows from a project to the net investment required. Using the data from our simplified example, the calculation is straightforward:

$$\text{Payback} = \frac{\text{Net investment}}{\text{Average annual operating cash flow}} = \frac{\$100,000}{\$25,000} = 4 \text{ years}$$

The result is the number of years required for the original outlay to be repaid, answering the question, How long will it be until I get my money back? It's a rough test of whether the amount of the investment will be recovered within its economic life span. Here, payback is achieved in only four years versus the estimated economic life of six years. Recovering the capital is not enough, of course, because from an economic standpoint, one would hope to earn a profit on the funds while they are invested.

Visualize a savings account in which $100 is deposited, and from which $25 is withdrawn at the end of each year. After four years, the principal will have been repaid. If the bank statement showed that the account was now depleted, the saver would properly demand to be paid the 4 or 5 percent that should have been earned every year on the declining balance in the account.

We can illustrate these basics of investment economics in Figure 6–3, where we've shown how both principal repayment and earnings on the outstanding balance have to be achieved by the cash flow stream over the economic life. We're again using the simple $100,000 investment, with a level annual aftertax operating cash flow. If the company typically earned 10 percent after taxes on its investments, part of every year's cash flow would be considered as normal earnings return, with the remainder used to reduce the outstanding balance.

The first column shows the beginning balance of the investment in every year. In the second column, normal earnings of 10 percent are calculated on these balances. In the third column, operating cash flows, reduced by these normal earnings, are applied against the beginning balances of the investment to calculate every year's ending balance. The result is an amortization schedule for our simple investment that extends into the sixth year—requiring about two more years of annual benefits than the simple payback measure would suggest. If the project ended in Year 4, an opportunity loss of about $30,400 would be incurred, and in Year 5, the loss would be about $8,400. Only in Year 6, will the remaining principal balance have been recovered and an opportunity gain of about $15,700 achieved. As we'll see shortly, all modern investment criteria are based on the basic economics underlying this example, with some refinements in the precise calculations used.

We can now quickly dispose of the payback measure as an indicator of investment desirability: It's insensitive to the economic life span and thus not a meaningful criterion of earnings power. It'll give the same "four years plus something extra" reading on other projects that have similar cash flows but 8 or 10-year economic lives, even though those projects would be clearly superior to our example. It implicitly assumes level annual operating cash flows, and cannot properly evaluate projects with rising or declining cash flow patterns—although these are very common. It cannot accommodate additional investments made during the period, or capital recoveries at the end of the economic life.

FIGURE 6–3

Amortization of $100,000 Investment at Ten Percent

	(1) Beginning Balance	(2) Normal Earnings at 10 Percent	(3) Operating Cash Inflow	(4) Ending Balance to Be Recovered
1	$100,000	$10,000	$25,000	$85,000
2	85,000	8,500	25,000	68,500
3	68,500	6,850	25,000	50,350
4	50,350	5,035	25,000	30,385*
5	30,385	3,039	25,000	8,424
6	8,424	842	25,000	(15,734)

*Payback.

The only situation where the measure has some applicability is in comparing a series of simple projects with quite similar cash flow patterns, but even there it is more appropriate to apply modern tools that are readily available on calculators and spreadsheets.

Simple Rate of Return

Again, only passing comments are warranted about this simplistic rule of thumb, which in fact, is the inverse of the payback formula. It states the desirability of an investment in terms of a percentage return on the original outlay. The method shares all of the shortcomings of the payback, because it again relates only two of the four critical aspects of any project, net investment and operating cash flows, and ignores the economic life and any terminal value:

$$\text{Return on investment} = \frac{\text{Average annual operating cash flow}}{\text{Net investment}} = \frac{\$25,000}{\$100,000}$$

$$= 25\%$$

All this result indicates is that $25,000 happens to be 25 percent of $100,000, because there's no reference to economic life and no recognition of the need to amortize the investment. The measure will give the *same* answer whether the economic life is one year, 10 years, or 100 years. The 25 percent return indicated here would be economically valid only if the investment provided $25,000 per year *in perpetuity*—not a very realistic condition!

Economic Investment Analysis

Earlier, we described business investment analysis as the process of weighing the economic trade-off between current dollar outlays and future net cash flow benefits which are expected to be obtained over a relevant period of time. This economic valuation concept applies to all types of investments, whether made by individuals or businesses. The time value of money is used as the underlying methodology in every case.

We'll begin this section by discussing in detail how the basic principles of *discounting and compounding* can be used to translate cash flows into equivalent monetary values irrespective of their timing. Then we'll explain and demonstrate the major measures of investment analysis that utilize these principles to calculate the quantitative basis for making economic choices among investment propositions.

Discounting, Compounding and Equivalence

We said earlier that common sense tells us a person will not be indifferent between two investment propositions that are exactly alike in all aspects except for a difference in timing of the future benefits. An investor will obviously prefer the one providing more immediate benefits. The reason, of course, is that funds available earlier give an individual or a company the opportunity to invest these funds at a profit, be it in a savings account, a government bond, a loan, a new facility, or any one of a great variety of other economic possibilities. Having to wait for a period of time until funds become available entails an opportunity cost in the form of lost earnings potential.

Conversely, common sense also dictates that given the choice between making an expenditure now versus making the same expenditure some time in the future, it's advantageous to defer the outlay. Again, the reason is the opportunity to earn a profit on the funds in the meantime. Stated another way, the value of money is affected directly by two aspects:

- Specific timing of its receipt or disbursement.
- Opportunity of earning a profit during the timing interval.

A simple example will help illustrate this point. If a person normally uses a savings account to earn interest of 5 percent per year, a deposit of $1,000 made today will grow to $1,050 in one year. (For simplicity, we ignore the practice of daily or monthly compounding commonly used by banks and savings institutions.) If for some reason the person had to wait one year to deposit the $1,000, the opportunity to earn $50 in interest would be lost. Without question, a sum of $1,000 offered to the person one year hence has to be worth less today than the same amount offered immediately. Specifically, today's value of the delayed $1,000 must be related to the person's normal opportunity to earn 5 percent. Given this earnings goal, we can calculate the *present value* of the $1,000 to be received in one year's time as follows:

$$\text{Present value} = \frac{\$1,000}{1.05} = \$952.38$$

The equation shows that with an assumed rate of return of 5 percent, $1,000 received one year from now is the *equivalent* of having $952.38 today. This is so because $952.38 invested at 5 percent today will grow into $1,000 by the end of one year. The calculation clearly reflects the economic trade-off between dollars received today versus a future date, based on the length of time involved and the available earnings opportunity. If we ignore the issue of risk for the moment, it also follows that our investor should be willing to pay $952.38 today for a financial contract that will pay $1,000 one year hence.

The longer the waiting period, the lower becomes the present value of a sum of money to be received, because for each additional period of delay, the opportunity to earn a return during the period is forgone. Principal and interest left in place would have compounded by earning an annual return on the growing balance. As we already pointed out, it'll also be advantageous to defer an expenditure as long as possible, because this allows the individual to earn a return during every period on the amount not spent plus the earnings left in place.

Calculating this change in the value of receipts or expenditures is quite simple when we know the time period and the earnings opportunity rate. For example, a sum of $1,000 to be received at the end of five years will be worth only $783.53 today, because that amount invested today at 5 percent compounded annually would grow to $1,000 five years hence, if the earnings are left to accumulate and interest is earned on the growing balance each year.

The formula for this calculation appears as follows:

$$\text{Present value} = \frac{\$1,000}{(1 + 0.05)^5} = \frac{\$1,000}{1.27628} = \$783.53$$

The result of $783.53 was obtained by relating the *future value* of $1,000 to the *compound earnings factor* at 5 percent over five years, shown in the denominator as 1.27628—which is simply 1.05 raised to the fifth power. When we divide the future value by the compound earnings factor, we have in effect *discounted* the future value into a lower *equivalent present value.*

Note that the mathematics are straightforward in achieving what we described in concept earlier: The value of a future sum is lowered in precise relationship to both the earnings opportunity and the timing incidence. The earnings opportunity is our assumed 5 percent compound interest, while the timing incidence of five years is reflected in the number of times the interest is compounded to express the number of years during which earnings were forgone.

We refer to the calculation of present values as discounting, while the reverse, the calculation of future values, is called compounding. These basic mathematical relationships allow us to derive the equivalent value of any sum to be received or paid at any point in time, either at the present moment, or at any specified future date.

The process of discounting and compounding is as old as money lending and has been used by financial institutions from time immemorial. Even though the application of this methodology to business investments is of more recent vintage, the techniques have become commonplace. Hand-held electronic calculators and ubiquitous computer spreadsheets with discounting and compounding capability have made deriving equivalent values and time-adjusted investment measures a routine matter.

The discount factors are also published in *present value tables,* which analysts used to calculate present values before computer-assisted methods were available. Two of these tables are provided at the end of this chapter as a reference. Even though they're no longer necessary for making the actual calculations, they provide a visual demonstration of the effect of discounting, which becomes ever more powerful the higher the rate and the longer the time period.

We can clarify a few points with the help of these tables. Table I (p. 239) contains the factors that translate into equivalent present values a single sum of money received or disbursed at the end of any period, under different assumptions about the rate of earnings. It's based on this general formula:

$$\text{Present value} = \frac{1}{(1 + i)^n}$$

where *i* is the applicable earnings rate (discount rate) and *n* is the number of periods over which discounting takes place. The table covers a range from 1 to 60 periods, and discount rates from 1 to 50 percent. The rates are related to these periods, however defined. For example, if the periods represent years, the rates are annual, while if months are used, the rates are monthly. The present value of a sum of money therefore can be found by simply multiplying the amount involved by the appropriate factor in the table:

$$\text{Present value} = \text{Factor} \times \text{Amount}$$

Note that the results from our savings account example on pages 203–204 can be found in Table II (p. 240) in the 5 percent column, lines 1 and 5, for the 1-year and 5-year illustrations, respectively.

Table II, a variation of Table I, allows the user to directly calculate the present value of a *series* of equal receipts or payments occurring over a number of periods. Such series are called *annuities*. The same result could, of course, be obtained by using Table I and repetitively multiplying the periodic amount with the appropriate series of successive factors and adding all of the results. Table II directly provides a set of such additive factors, however, which allow the analyst to obtain the present value of an annuity in the single step of multiplying the period receipt or payment by the appropriate factor:

$$\text{Present value} = \text{Factor} \times \text{Annuity}$$

These basic tables can be used for practically all investment problems normally encountered, and the factors in them precisely match those stored in calculators and computer spreadsheets. There are many possible variations and refinements in timing, such as more frequent discounting (monthly or weekly), or assuming that the annuity is received or disbursed in weekly or monthly increments rather than at the end of the period. The use of the continuous flow option introduces a forward shift in timing that leads to slightly higher present values, both for single sums and annuities. Refinements such as daily discounting or compounding are commonly applied to financial instruments, such as mortgages, bonds, charge accounts, etc., which involve contractual arrangements.

For the practical purpose of analyzing business capital investments, such refinements are not critical, because the imprecision of many of the economic estimates being made easily outweighs any incremental numerical precision that might be obtained. The periodic discounting embodied in the formulas of the two tables at the end of the chapter is quite adequate for most analytical needs, but if more precision is sought, the optional settings in calculators and spreadsheets easily accommodate such refinements.

We'll now turn to the discussion of the measures which employ these discounting and compounding principles. We'll cover the basic rationale on which the measures are based, and their applicability to economic investment analysis, as well as their shortcomings.

Net Present Value

The net present value (NPV) measure weighs the cash flow trade-off among investment outlays, future benefits, and terminal values in *equivalent* present value terms, and allows the analyst to determine whether the net balance of these values is favorable or unfavorable—in other words, the nature of the economic trade-off involved. To use the tool, a rate of discount representing normal earnings opportunities must first be specified. Appropriate present value factors are then applied to both inflows and outflows over the economic life of the investment proposal. Finally, the present values of all inflows (positive amounts) and outflows (negative amounts) are summed, and the difference between these sums represents the net present value. NPV can be positive or negative, depending on whether there is a net inflow or net outflow over the economic life of the project.

Used as a standard of comparison, the measure indicates whether an investment, over its economic life, will achieve the earnings rate applied in the calculation. Inasmuch as present value results depend on both timing and stated earnings opportunity, a positive net present value indicates that the cash flows generated by the investment over its economic life will:

■ Recover the original outlay (as well as any future capital outlays or recoveries considered in the analysis).

■ Earn the desired return standard on the outstanding balance.

■ Provide a cushion of excess economic value.

Conversely, a negative result indicates that the project is not achieving the earnings standard and thus will cause an opportunity loss if implemented. Obviously, the result will be affected by the level of earnings assumed, the specific timing pattern of the cash flows, and the relative magnitudes of the amounts involved.

A word should be said at this point about the rate of discount employed. From an economic standpoint, it should be the rate of return an investor normally enjoys from investments of similar nature and risk. In effect, this is an opportunity rate of return. In a corporate setting, the choice of a discount rate is complicated both by the variety of investment possiblities and by the types of financing provided by both owners and lenders. The corporate earnings standard normally used to discount investment cash flows should reflect the minimum return requirement that will provide the normally expected level of shareholder return, adjusted for any lower-cost financial leverage employed.

The standard most commonly employed is based on the overall corporate *cost of capital*, which takes into account shareholder expectations, business risk, and leverage. As we'll discuss in Chapter 7, shareholder value can be created only by making investments whose returns exceed the cost of capital. Therefore, the actual level of the standard established by a company will often reflect a specific management objective to achieve returns higher than the cost of capital. Sometimes a corporate earnings standard is separated into a set of multiple discount rates for different lines of business within a company, in order to recognize specific risk differentials. We'll deal with these concepts in greater depth in the next chapter.

For purposes of this discussion, we'll assume that management has chosen an appropriate earnings standard with which to discount investment cash flows, and we'll focus on how present value measures are used to assess potential investments on an economic basis.

As a first step, it's generally helpful to lay out the pertinent information period by period to give us a proper time perspective. A horizontal time scale can be used, on which the periods are marked off, as Figure 6–4 shows. Positive and negative cash flows are then inserted as arrows at the appropriate positions in time, scaled to the size of the dollar amounts. Note that the time scale begins at point 0, the present, and extends out as far as the project requires. Any events which occurred prior to the present (shown as negative periods) are not relevant to the analysis, unless the decision specifically causes a recovery of past expenditures, such as the sale of old assets.

To illustrate the process, let's return to the simple investment example we used earlier in the chapter. We'll show the numerical information as a table in Figure 6–5. Note the similarity in approach to the simple amortization process we used in Figure 6–3 (p. 201).

Figure 6–5 demonstrates that our sample net investment of $100,000 at point zero, together with the six annual benefit inflows of $25,000 from Years one through six, result in a net present value of almost $16,000, on the assumption that our company considers 8 percent after taxes a normal earnings standard.

The total initial outflow will have been recovered over the six-year period, while 8 percent after taxes will have been earned all along on the declining investment balance outstanding during the project life. An additional cushion of about $15,600 in equivalent present value dollars can be expected if the cash flow estimates are correct and if the project does live out its full economic life.

Note the similarity of this approach to the simple payback concept we discussed earlier, where we referred to the recovery of the original investment plus "something extra." The critical difference between payback and net present value, however, is the fact that net present value has a built-in earnings requirement in addition to full recovery of the investment. Thus, the cushion implicit in a positive net present value is truly a calculated economic value gain that goes beyond satisfying the required earnings standard.

If a higher earnings standard had been required, say 12 percent, the results would be those shown in Figure 6–6. The net present value remains positive, but

FIGURE 6–4

Generalized Time Scale for Investment Analysis

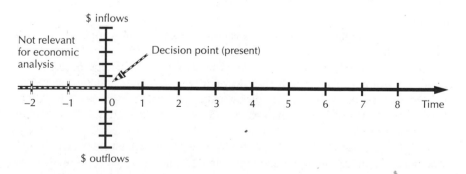

FIGURE 6–5

Net Present Value Analysis by Period at 8 Percent

Time Period	Investment (Outlays)	Benefits (Inflows)	Present Value Factor at 8 Percent*	Present Value	Cumulative Net Present Value
0	$100,000	—	1.000	−$100,000	−$100,000
1	—	$ 25,000	0.926	+ 23,150	− 76,850
2	—	25,000	0.857	+ 21,425	− 55,425
3	—	25,000	0.794	+ 19,850	− 35,575
4	—	25,000	0.735	+ 18,375	− 17,200
5	—	25,000	0.681	+ 17,025	− 175
6	—	25,000	0.630	+ 15,750	+ 15,575
	$100,000	$150,000		+$ 15,575	

*To illustrate the use of Table I, assuming that benefits occur at year-end. We could instead use a factor from Table II: 4.623 times $25,000, because the annual inflows are equal. The result for the total present value of the inflows is identical. (The factors for Years 1 through 6 total 4.623.)

the size of the cushion has dramatically decreased to only $2,800. We would expect such a decrease, because at the higher discount rate, the present value of the cash inflows must decline, with all other circumstances unchanged.

At an assumed earnings standard of 14 percent, the net present value shrinks even further. In fact, it is transformed into a negative result ($25,000 × 3.889 − $100,000 = − $2,775). These results illustrate the high sensitivity of net present value to the choice of earnings standards, especially at higher rates.

The importance of the length of the economic life of the investment is demonstrated in the last column of both Figures 6–5 and 6–6. There we can observe that the time required for the cumulative present value to turn positive was lengthened as the earnings standard was raised. At 8 percent, the economic life had to be about five years for the switch to occur (the net present value after the benefits of Year 5 is just about zero), while at 12 percent, most of the sixth year of economic life was necessary for a positive turnaround (about $10,000 of negative present value remaining at the end of Year 5 has to be recovered from the benefits of Year 6).

In our example, we assumed a level operating cash inflow of $25,000. Uneven cash flow patterns will have a notable impact on the results, although the method of calculation remains the same. The net present value approach can accommodate any combination of cash flow patterns without difficulty. The reader is invited to test this, using a cash inflow pattern that rises from, say, $15,000 to $40,000, and one that falls from $40,000 to $15,000, each totaling $150,000 over six years.

The best use of net present value is as a screening device that indicates whether a stipulated minimum earnings standard can be met over an investment

FIGURE 6–6

Net Present Value Analysis by Period at 12 Percent

Time Period	Investment (Outlays)	Benefits (Inflows)	Present Value Factors at 12 Percent*	Present Value	Cumulative Net Present Value
0	$100,000	—	1.000	–$100,000	–$100,000
1	—	$ 25,000	0.893	+ 22,325	– 77,675
2	—	25,000	0.797	+ 19,925	– 57,750
3	—	25,000	0.712	+ 17,800	– 39,950
4	—	25,000	0.636	+ 15,900	– 24,050
5	—	25,000	0.567	+ 14,175	– 9,875
6	—	25,000	0.507	+ 12,675	+ 2,800
	$100,000	$150,000		+$ 2,800	

*As in Figure 6–6, we could use 4.112 times $25,000 from Table II.

FIGURE 6 7

A Representation of Net Present Value

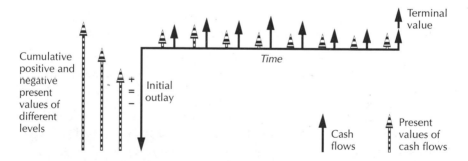

proposal's economic life. When net present value is positive, there is potential for earnings in excess of the standard and therefore economic value creation. When net present value is negative, the minimum earnings standard and capital recovery cannot be achieved with the projected cash flows. When net present value is close to or exactly *zero,* the earnings standard has just been met, on the assumption that the earnings estimates and the projected life are quite certain. The graphic representation in Figure 6–7 above demonstrates the various conditions.

While net present value is a useful tool in evaluating investment alternatives, it doesn't answer all our questions about the economic attractiveness of capital outlays. For example, when comparing different projects, how does one evaluate the respective size of the "cushion" calculated with a given return standard, particularly if the investment amount differs significantly? Also, to what extent is achieving the expected economic life a factor in such comparisons?

Furthermore, how does one quantify the potential errors and uncertainties inherent in the cash flow estimates, and how does the measure assist in investment choices if such deviations are significant? Finally, one can ask what specific return the project will yield if all estimates are in fact realized? Further measures and analytical methods are necessary to answer these questions, and we will show how a combination of techniques helps to narrow the choices to be made.

Profitability Index

After calculating the net present values of a series of projects, we may be faced with a choice that involves several alternative investments of different sizes. In such cases, we cannot ignore the fact that even though the net present values of the alternatives may be close or even equal, they involve initial funds commitments of widely varying amounts.

In other words, it does make a difference whether an investment proposal promises a net present value of $1,000 for an outlay of $10,000, or whether in another case, a net present value of $1,000 requires an investment of $25,000—even if we can assume equivalent economic lives and equivalent risk. In the first case, the cushion (excess benefit) is a much larger fraction of the net investment, which makes the first investment clearly more attractive, given all other conditions are comparable.

The profitability index (PI) is a formal way of expressing this relationship of benefits to cost, a ratio which is also called the *benefit cost ratio (BCR)*:

$$\text{Profitability index} = \frac{\text{Present value of operating inflows (\textit{benefit})}}{\text{Present value of net investment outlays (\textit{cost})}}$$

The present values in this formula are the same amounts we used earlier to derive the net present value, although then we subtracted inflows from outflows. In the case of the profitability index, the question is simply: How much in present value is being created for each dollar of net investment outlay?

The two cases we cited above would yield the following results:

$$1. \text{ Profitability index} = \frac{\$11,000}{\$10,000} = 1.10$$

$$2. \text{ Profitability index} = \frac{\$26,000}{\$25,000} = 1.04$$

The higher the index, the better the project. As we expected, the first project is much more favorable, given the assumption that all other aspects of the investment are reasonably comparable. If the index is 1.0 or less, the project is just meeting or is even below the minimum earnings standard used to derive the present values. An index of exactly 1.0 corresponds to a zero net present value.

Our simple machine example has a profitability index of 1.16 at 8 percent in Figure 6–5 ($115,575 ÷ $100,000), and 1.03 at 12 percent in Figure 6–6 ($102,800 ÷ $100,000).

The profitability index provides additional insight for the analyst or manager. As already mentioned, it allows us to choose between investment alternatives of differing size. But it still leaves several points unanswered, and there are some theoretical issues involved that we'll point out later in the chapter.

Internal Rate of Return (IRR, Yield)

The concept of a "true" return yielded by an investment over its economic life, also referred to as the *discounted cash flow return, or DCF,* was mentioned in our earlier discussion of net present value. The internal rate of return is simply the unique discount rate that, when applied to both cash inflows and cash outflows over the investment's economic life, provides a zero net present value—that is, the present value of the inflows is exactly equal to the present value of the outflows. Figure 6–8 visually presents this measure.

Stated another way, the principal can be amortized over the economic life, while earning the exact return implied by the underlying discount rate. Thus, the project may yield the earnings standard desired, but only if the underlying rate happens to coincide with the standard.

Naturally, the result will vary with changes in the economic life and the pattern of cash flows. In fact, the internal rate of return is found by letting it become a variable that is dependent on cash flows and economic life. In the case of net present value and profitability index, we had employed a specified earnings standard to discount the investment's cash flows. For the internal rate of return, we turn the problem around to find the discount rate that makes cash inflows and outflows equal.

We can again employ our basic formula (Present value = Factor × Annuity) if the project is simple enough to involve a single investment outlay and only level annual cash inflows. The formula can then be expressed as follows:

$$\text{Factor} = \frac{\text{Present value (net investment)}}{\text{Annuity}}$$

The factor can be located in the present value table for annuities (Table II). Because the economic life is a given, we can find the rate of return by moving

FIGURE 6–8

A Representation of Internal Rate of Return (DCF)

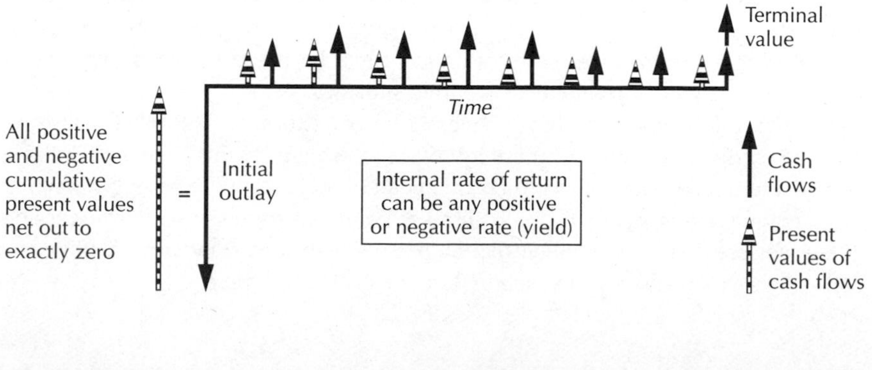

along the proper period row to the column containing a factor that approximates the formula result. Obviously, the result can be quickly obtained using a programmed calculator or a spreadsheet, but we're showing the details here to improve our understanding of the underlying mechanics.

To illustrate, our earlier investment example has a factor of 4.0 ($100,000 ÷ $25,000). On the line for period 6 in Table II we find that 4.0 lies almost exactly between 12 percent (4.112) and 14 percent (3.889). Approximate interpolation suggests that the result is about 13 percent.

When a project has a more complex cash flow pattern, a trial-and-error approach is needed if the analysis is done with the help of present value tables. Successive application of different discount rates to all cash flows over the investment's economic life must be made until a reasonably close approximation of a zero net present value has been found.

With some experience, an analyst will find that usually no more than two trials are necessary, because the first result will show the direction of any refinement needed. A positive net present value calls for applying a higher discount rate, while a negative one requires a lower rate. We observed this effect in 'our earlier example, when the net present value declined as the discount rate was raised from 8 to 12 percent (see Tables 6–5 and 6–6). Again, programmed calculators and computer spreadsheets will arrive at the result directly.

As a ranking device for investments, the internal rate of return isn't without problems. First, there's the mathematical possibility that a complex project with many varied cash inflows and outflows over its economic life may in fact yield two different internal rates of return. This is caused by the specific pattern and timing of the various cash inflows and outflows. While relatively rare, such a result can be an inconvenience.

More important, however, is the practical issue of choosing among alternative projects that involve widely differing net investments and have internal rates of return inverse to the size of the project (the smaller investment has the higher return). A $10,000 investment with an internal rate of return of 50 percent cannot be directly compared to an outlay of $100,000 with a 30 percent internal rate of return, particularly if the risks are similar and the company normally requires a 15 percent earnings standard. While both projects exceed the desired return, it may indeed be better to employ the larger sum at 30 percent than the smaller sum at 50 percent, unless both projects can be undertaken. If the economic life of alternative projects differs widely, it may similarly be advantageous to employ funds at a lower rate for a longer period of time than to opt for a brief period of higher return. This will be true if a choice must be made between two investments, both of which exceed the corporate standard.

It should be apparent that the internal rate of return, like all other measures, must be used with caution. Because it provides the analyst with a unique ("true") rate of return inherent to each project, the yield of an investment permits a ranking of potential alternatives by a single number. We recall from our earlier discussion of the net present value method that a specified earnings standard reflecting the company's expectations from such investments was used there.

In contrast, the internal rate of return approach solves for an earnings rate unique to each project. When the internal rates of return of different projects are compared, there's the implied assumption that the cash flows thrown off during each project's economic life can in fact be reinvested at their unique rates.

We know, however, that the company's earnings standard usually is an expression of the long-run earnings power of the company, even if only approximate. Thus, managers applying a 15 or 20 percent return standard to investments must realize that a project with its own internal rate of return of, say, 30 percent, cannot be assumed to have its cash flows reinvested at this unique higher rate. Unless the general earnings standard is quite unrealistic, funds thrown off by capital investments can only be expected to be re-employed over time at this lower average rate.

This apparent dilemma does not, however, invalidate the internal rate of return measure, because any project will certainly yield its calculated return if all conditions hold over its economic life. Therefore, it's appropriate to rank projects by their respective yields.

Later in this chapter, we'll return to a comparative overview of all measures and develop basic rules for their application. The reader is also invited to turn to the references listed at the end of the chapter for more extensive discussions of the many theoretical and practical arguments surrounding the use of present value techniques, particularly in the case of the internal rate of return.

Risk Analysis

The estimates used to analyze business investments are inevitably uncertain because of their future orientation. As we stated before, business investments involve risk because of the uncertainties surrounding the key variables used. The analyst who prepares the investment calculations and managers who use these results for decision making must allow for a whole range of possible outcomes. Even the best estimates can go wrong as events unfold, yet decisions always have to be made in advance of the actual experience.

The analytical and judgmental challenge is to assess the risk inherent in the key variables of the investment proposal. Such risk analysis can take many forms. In earlier chapters, we mentioned sensitivity analysis as a formal means of testing the impact of changes in key assumptions. This process can be very informal, such as back-of-the-envelope reasoning, or it can involve systematically working through the impact of assumed changes in revenues, operating savings, costs, size of outlays, recovery of capital, and so on, either singly or in combination, and testing the impact on the results.

We also mentioned using ranges of estimates, either for the total result, or for individual key variables. This approach allows management to examine the most optimistic and pessimistic cases as well as the most likely figures, and it is quite superior to single-point estimating, especially for significant investments.

In this section, we'll discuss two time-adjusted measures that help ascertain how much risk exposure is possible for a project while still meeting return standards. These measures, *present value payback* and *annualized net present value* are technically related to the net present value criterion. We'll also discuss the use of *ranges of estimates,* and their refined application in *probabilistic simulation.* Finally, we'll touch on the subject of *risk adjusted rates.* Only the first two measures will be taken up in detail, while the other areas will be covered just enough to indicate the potential value of further studying these concepts.

Present Value Payback

This measure establishes the *minimum life* necessary for an investment to operate as expected, and still meet the earnings standard of the present value analysis. In other words, present value payback is achieved at the specific point in time when the cumulative positive present value of benefits equals the cumulative negative present value of all the outlays. It's the point in the project's economic life when the original investment has been fully amortized and a return equal to the earnings standard has been achieved on the declining balance—the point at which the project becomes economically attractive. Figure 6–9 below provides a visual representation of this concept.

In Figures 6–5 and 6–6 (pages 208 and 209), we included a column for the cumulative net present value of the project. It served as a visual check for determining the point at which net present value turned positive. The present value payback for our example with a discount rate of 8 percent was about five years, while a 12 percent standard required almost six years, just about the full economic life of the investment. The minimum time needed to recover the investment and earn the return standard on the declining balance, when compared to the economic life, is a way of expressing the potential risk of the project. The measure does not specifically address the nature of the risk, but rather identifies any remaining part of the economic life as an overall risk allowance. One can then judge whether the risk entailed in the combination of elements of the project—or any one key variable in particular—is likely to outweigh the cushion of safety implied in the additional time the project may operate once it has passed the present value payback point. Remember, however, that the measure focuses only on the life span of the project, assuming implicitly that the estimated annual operating conditions will in fact continue to be achieved.

FIGURE 6–9

A Representation of Present Value Payback

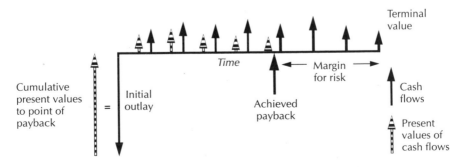

If uneven and more complicated cash flows are projected, a condition we'll examine later, the minimum life test of the present value payback requires a year-by-year accumulation of the negative and positive present values, as was done in simplified form in Figures 6–5 and 6–6.

If a project is a straightforward combination of a single outlay at point zero and level annual operating cash inflows, the analysis is quite simple and can be done readily on a programmed calculator or spreadsheet. To illustrate the concept, however, we'll again make use of the present value tables, this time using the annuity factors in Table II to quickly identify the present value payback. The following relationship is utilized:

$$\text{Present value} = \text{Factor} \times \text{Annuity}$$

We're looking for the condition under which the present value of the outflows is exactly equal to the present value of the inflows. Inasmuch as the net investment (outflow) must be recovered by the inflows, we can change the formula to:

$$\text{Net investment} = \text{Factor} \times \text{Annuity}$$

Because we know the level of the annuity, which is represented by the annual operating cash inflows, we can find the factor that satisfies the condition:

$$\text{Factor} = \frac{\text{Net investment}}{\text{Annuity}}$$

For our machine example, we can calculate the following results: $100,000 ÷ $25,000 = 4.0. We can look for the closest factor in the 8 percent column of Table II. The answer lies almost exactly on the line for period 5 (3.993), which indicates that the project's minimum life under the assumed operating conditions must be 5 years to achieve the standard 8 percent return. If the standard were 12 percent, the minimum life has to be approximately 5⅔ years (an interpolation between 3.605 and 4.112).

The test for present value payout (minimum life) at any given return standard thus becomes one more factor in assessing the margin for error in the project estimates. It sharpens the analyst's understanding of the relationship of economic life and acceptable performance, and is a much improved version of the simple payback rule of thumb. The measure is a useful companion to the net present value criterion. It does not, however, address specific risk elements and in fact leaves weighing of any favorable difference between minimum and economic life to the decision maker's judgment.

Annualized Net Present Value

Another way of testing for risk is to estimate how much of an annual shortfall in operating cash inflows would be permissible over the full economic life of the project, while still meeting the minimum return standard. We know that the net present value calculation normally results in either a cumulative excess or a cumulative deficiency of present value benefits vis-à-vis the net investment. We also know that if the net present value is positive, the amount can be viewed as a cushion against any estimating error contained in future cash inflows.

Unless a project has highly irregular annual flows, it's often useful to transform this net present value cushion into an *equivalent annuity* over the project's economic life. Such an annual equivalent, representing the allowable margin of error, can then be directly compared to the original estimates of annual operating cash inflow. This is possible because the present value cushion has in effect been "reconstituted" into level cash flows on the same basis as the estimates themselves, that is, in the form of annual cash flows unadjusted for time value. To illustrate, we can transform the net present value shown in Table 6–5, $15,575, into an annuity over the six-year life by simply using the familiar present value relationship:

$$\text{Present value} = \text{Factor} \times \text{Annuity}$$

Because we're interested in finding the annuity represented by the net present value, and wish to do so over a known economic life and at a specified discount rate—which is the earnings standard employed in the net present value calculation in the first place—we can transform the annuity formula as follows:

$$\text{Annuity} = \frac{\text{(Net) present value}}{\text{Factor}}$$

Our example has the following result:

$$\text{Annuity} = \frac{\$15,575}{4.623} = \$3,369$$

The annual operating cash inflows were originally estimated to be $25,000. Given the result above, the actual cash flow experienced could be lower by about $3,400 per year, and the project would still meet the minimum standard of 8 percent. Note, however, that the investment would have to operate over its full economic life for this condition to be true.

In this case, the risk allowance directly translates into a permissible downward adjustment of estimated operating cash inflows by 22 percent. We must remember from page 197, however, that the annual cash flow consists of an after-tax operating profit of $8,333, to which depreciation of $16,667 has been added back. In view of this sizable depreciation allowance—which is not subject to uncertainty—the permissible reduction in the aftertax profit alone ($8,333 − $3,369 = $4,964) amounts to a hefty 40 percent! As we can see, this type of analysis represents a more direct approach to judging the allowable risk in the key variables than did the present value payback.

Annualization can be more generally applied as a very practical and quick preliminary "scoping" of the attractiveness of an investment project that has not yet been fleshed out in detail. This method turns the normal investment analysis around by finding the approximate annual operating cash flow required to justify an estimated capital outlay, at a time when specific operating benefits have yet to be determined. Given an estimate of the economic life and an earnings standard, we can employ the formula

$$\text{Operating cash flow} = \frac{\text{Net investment}}{\text{Factor}}$$

to find the annual cash flow equivalent that, on average, will be the minimum target benefit. We can, of course, readily use electronic means to make this transformation.

We must be careful, however, to interpret this figure properly. Because by definition it is an aftertax cash flow, the result has to be correctly adjusted for the assumed annual depreciation in order to transform it into the minimum pretax operating improvement necessary to justify the outlay. The process simply involves working backward through the analysis, using the knowledge that cash flow consists of the sum of aftertax operating profit and annual depreciation. We can apply this to our example from Table 6–3 as follows:

First, we find the target cash flow benefits over six years at 8 percent, using the appropriate factor from Table II (or obtain the answer directly on a spreadsheet or calculator):

$$\frac{\$100,000}{4.623} = \$21,631$$

Next we transform this required aftertax cash flow into its equivalent pretax operating improvement:

Aftertax cash flow	$21,631
Less: Depreciation	16,667
Aftertax profit	$ 4,964
Tax at 34% of *pretax* profit	$ 2,557
Pretax profit	$ 7,521
Add back depreciation	16,667
Minimum pretax operating improvement	$24,188

Thus, our investment has to provide a minimum of about $24,200 in direct operating improvements such as lower costs, incremental revenues, and so on. Clearly, this method provides a quick look at the amount of pretax profit benefits required and allows the decision maker to think about the likely potential of the investment to achieve them. In other words, annualization applied in this way is a useful tool for making a first assessment of the chances that an investment will be in the ballpark.

Ranges of Estimates

Risk can be defined as the degree of variation in the actual versus estimated cash benefit levels of an investment. The wider the possible deviations, the greater the risk. Therefore, using a range of estimates is a more direct approach to investment risk analysis. It may not be necessary to do this for all types of investments, however, because degrees of risk vary widely among business and financial investments, as do the relative importance and magnitude of the investments themselves.

For example, the risk involved in holding a U.S. government bond is very small indeed, because default on the interest payments is extremely unlikely. Therefore, the range of possible benefits from the bond investment is narrowly focused on the contractual payments—in effect no range at all.

In contrast, the risk of a business investment for a product or service is a function of the whole range of possible benefit levels that may go from very positive cash flows to negative loss conditions. The uncertainty surrounding these outcomes poses a challenge to the analyst and the decision maker.

The "single-point" estimates of annual cash flow projections we've used so far are the expected results based on the best judgment of the analyst and the type of information available. In effect, they amount to an average of the possible outcomes, implicitly weighed by their respective probabilities. By introducing a range of high, low, and expected levels of annual cash inflows and outflows, the analyst can employ a form of sensitivity analysis to indicate the consequences of expected fluctuations in the annual results—and thus the degree of risk. At times, past experience can provide clues to the range of future outcomes, but essentially, the projection of future conditions has to be judgmental and based on specific forward-looking estimates.

The decision maker must assess the likelihood that the range of estimated outcomes fairly expresses the characteristics of the project, and decide whether the expected outcome is sufficiently attractive to compensate for the possibility that the actual results may vary as defined. Risk assessment in essence comes down to how comfortable the decision maker is with the possibility of experiencing adverse results—that is, a very personal risk preference or risk aversion. Stipulating a range helps the responsible person or group visualize the possible extremes in the expected results.

Probabilistic Simulation

A more refined approach to risk assessment consists of estimating ranges not only for the total annual cash flows, but also for the individual key variables that make up these cash flows. Probability distributions are then assigned to the likelihood of the outcomes for each of the variables. Any interdependencies between variables are defined and built into the analysis, and the possible outcomes of the project can then be simulated by running many iterations on the computer. The method is an extension of sensitivity analysis in that the potential changes in many variables are evaluated both simultaneously and in relation to each other.

The result is a range of possible annual cash inflows in the form of a probability distribution, or even a range of net present values or internal rates of return arrayed by probability. Such a risk profile allows the decision maker to think about the relative attractiveness of a project in terms of statements such as: "chances are 9 out of 10 that the project will meet the minimum standard of 10 percent," or, "there is a probability of 60 percent that the net present value of the project will be at least $1.0 million or better." Cumulative probability distributions such as those shown in Figure 6–10 can be drawn up as an aid.

The relative ease with which such simulations can be carried out does not eliminate the many practical issues involved in assigning specific probability distributions to the individual variables in the first place, or ease the problem of interpreting the final results.

As we said before, judging both the likelihood of an event and one's own attitude toward the risk expressed in this fashion is a highly personal response that often defies precise quantification. The amount of risk a decision maker will accept is largely a matter of personal experience and preference. In addition, investment decisions in a business setting are as much a function of complex personal and group dynamics as they are dependent on the pure analytical results, the quality of presentation, and examination of specific economic data.

Risk-Adjusted Return Standards

Another way of adjusting for risk is to modify the return standard itself to include a risk premium where warranted. In a sense, the concept is quite simple—the greater the risk, the higher the return desired from the investment. Also, this reasoning is intuitively attractive to business decision makers, because the process parallels the way we think about personal investments. At the same time, however, letting the return standard be an expression of riskiness deals only indirectly with the true source of risk, that is, the uncertainty about the investment cash flows and the specific variables they contain.

Investments in businesses subject to wide profit swings and competitive pressures would command a significant premium above the return standard, while fairly predictable businesses might find a lesser return acceptable. When

FIGURE 6–10

Cumulative Probability Distribution for Two Projects

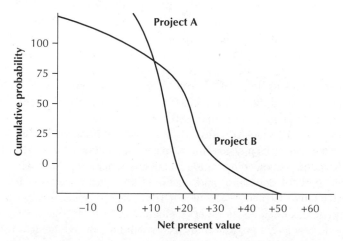

multiple return standards are employed, it is done on the assumption that a diversified company can use different standards which, in combination, will ensure an appropriate overall return to the shareholders and also fairly reflect the risk exposure of the individual lines of business. We'll return to the basis for earnings standards in the next chapter, and discuss both the conceptual and practical issues involved in deriving them.

REFINEMENTS OF INVESTMENT ANALYSIS

We'll now turn to some more realistic and complex examples in order to refine various aspects of both the components of analysis and the methodology itself. No new concepts or techniques will be introduced; instead, two expanded practical examples will help us work through the implications of many of the points we've so far only mentioned in passing. As we go through the projects step by step, the essentials of economic investment analysis should become firmly implanted in your mind.

At this point, we'll stress once more that it is always essential as the first step in economic analysis to carefully define the problem in all of its aspects. From this flows the rationale for deriving the net investment, operating cash flows, the economic life and any terminal values. Once these aspects have been properly established and understood, the actual calculation of the appropriate yardsticks becomes almost automatic.

Example One: A Machine Replacement

A company is analyzing whether to replace an existing five-year-old machine with a more automatic and faster model. Acquiring a new machine of some sort is viewed as the only reasonable alternative under the circumstances, because the product fabricated on the equipment is expected to continue to be profitable for at least 10 years. Moreover, the markets served could absorb additional output beyond the current capacity, as much as one-third more than the present volume.

The old machine is estimated to have at most five years' life left before it becomes physically worn out, while the new machine will operate acceptably for 10 years before it has to be scrapped. The old machine originally cost $25,000 and has a current book value of $12,500, having been depreciated straight-line at $2,500 per year. It can be sold for $15,000 in cash to a ready buyer.

The new machine will cost $40,000 installed. Also to be depreciated straight-line over 10 years, it will likely be salable at book value if it is disposed of prior to the end of its physical life. It has an annual capacity of 125,000 units (compared to the present equipment's 100,000 unit ceiling), and it will produce at lower unit costs for both labor and materials. In fact, the new machine will involve lower total labor costs because of fewer setups, releasing the time of the skilled mechanics required for other productive tasks in the plant. Two operators will be necessary as before. Materials usage will be reduced due to a lower level of rejects. The company expects no difficulty in selling the additional volume at the current price of $1.50, and will only incur modest incremental selling and promotional expense in the process.

Such a set of conditions is both common and fairly realistic except for the stable long-term market conditions assumed—yet the same analytical principles do apply in a shorter time frame. As we analyze this project, we'll expand on several aspects of economic capital investment analysis and draw generalized conclusions where appropriate.

Net Investment Refined

We recall that net investment was defined as the net change in funds committed to a project as a result of the investment decision. Two specific changes in funds must be considered in this case: (1) the initial outlay of $40,000 for the new machine, which is a straightforward cash commitment, and (2) the recovery of cash from the sale of the old machine.

Since the sale of the old machine is a direct consequence of the decision to replace it, the release of these funds is relevant to the analysis. The amount received, however, will have to be adjusted below the $15,000 cash value because the capital gain realized on the sale is a taxable event. We recall that the book value was only $12,500; thus the company will be taxed on the difference of $2,500. For simplicity, we'll assume that the applicable tax rate is the full corporate income tax rate of 34 percent, resulting in an incremental tax outlay of $850.

We now have all the components of the initial net investment figure relevant for this example:

Cost of the new machine	$40,000
Cash from sale of old machine	(15,000)
Tax payable on capital gain	850
Net investment	$25,850

In this economic analysis, we don't recognize the remaining book value on the old machine, except for its role in the income tax calculation. As we observed before, any funds expended in the past are irrelevant because they are sunk, and we're interested only in the changes caused by the current decision. Therefore, the proceeds from the equipment sale and the incremental tax due on the capital gain are the only relevant elements.

Had the old machine been unsalable despite its stated book value of $12,500, the only item of relevance would be the tax savings on the capital loss incurred with this condition. While there may be a temptation to include sizable book values in such analyses, doing so would confuse accounting with economics.

The net investment shown represents a balance between cash movements, both in and out, that are direct consequences of the investment decision. If we assume that the decision caused working capital (incremental receivables and inventories less incremental payables) to rise in support of the expected higher sales volume, any funds committed for this purpose would also become relevant for our analysis. Similarly, if the current decision were expected to directly cause further capital outlays in later years, such amounts would have to be recognized in the analysis. In our second example, we'll demonstrate how incremental working capital and sequential investments are handled.

Operating Cash Inflows Refined

As we established before, operating cash inflows are the net aftertax cash changes in revenue and cost elements resulting from the investment decision. In our replacement example, we must first carefully sort out the expected conditions to identify relevant *differential revenues and costs*. Each element should be carefully tested whether the decision to replace will make a cash difference in operating conditions.

The decision to replace has three significant effects:

■ The new machine will bring about greater efficiency that should result in operating savings vis-à-vis the old machine.

■ The additional volume of product produced will provide an incremental profit contribution, if we assume the sales efforts are successful.

■ There'll be a tax impact from the change in the amount of depreciation charged against operations.

The calculations in Figure 6–11 illustrate how to deal with these elements in clearly labeled successive stages.

Stage 1: Operating Savings. Operating savings for the existing level of output (100,000 units) are found by simply comparing the annual costs of operating the two machines at that volume. While each requires two operators, the new machine will incur $1,000 less in setup costs because the time of the skilled mechanics involved can be employed elsewhere in the plant. We were also told earlier that the new machine uses materials more efficiently, and this attribute will save about $2,000.

Overhead changes, in contrast, are not relevant for this comparison, because overhead costs are represented by allocations at the rate of 120 percent of direct labor. The fact that direct labor cost has declined does not automatically mean that spending on overhead has changed. The only change is in the basis of allocation, which in this case happens to be a lower labor cost against which an unvarying percentage rate is applied. Clearly, the plant manager and the office staff still receive the same salaries, and other overhead costs are not affected.

Only if the decision to replace directly caused an actual change in overhead spending, such as higher property taxes, insurance premiums, additional maintenance, and technical support, would a change have to be reflected in the calculation. Under those conditions, we'd estimate the annual overhead expenditures before and after the installation of the new machine, and calculate the differential cost to be included in the analysis, just as we did for the other differential operating cash inflows.

FIGURE 6–11

Differential Cost and Revenue Analysis

	Old Machine	New Machine	Relevant Annual Differences
1. Operating savings from current volume of 100,000 units:			
Labor (2 operators plus setup)	$ 31,000	$ 30,000	$ 1,000
Material	38,000	36,000	2,000
Overhead (120% of direct labor)	37,200	36,000	—*
	$106,200	$102,000	$ 3,000
2. Contribution from additional volume of 25,000 units:			
25,000 units sold at $1.50 per unit . .		$ 37,500	
Less:			
Labor (no additional operators) . . .		—	
Material cost at 36¢/unit		(9,000)	
Additional selling expense		(11,500)	
Additional promotional expense . . .		(13,000)	$ 4,000
Total savings and additional contribution			$ 7,000
3. Differential depreciation (additional expense; for tax purposes only)	$ 2,500	$ 4,000	$(1,500)
Taxable operating improvements			5,500
Income tax at 34%			1,870
Aftertax profit improvement			3,630
Add back depreciation			1,500
Aftertax operating cash flow			$ 5,130

*Not relevant, because it represents an allocation only.

Whenever we're comparing operating costs, it's usually more appropriate to use annual totals rather than to rely on per-unit figures. The latter may cause the analyst to inadvertently apply accounting allocations, which as a rule are irrelevant for economic analysis—even though they are necessary and appropriate for cost accounting (determining cost of goods sold, inventory values, price estimating, etc.) in line with generally accepted accounting principles.

Stage 2: Contribution from Additional Volume. Now we're ready to determine the incremental contribution from the increased output. This change must be counted as an additional benefit from the decision to replace, because the old machine had a ceiling of 100,000 units of production. The additional sales revenue from the extra 25,000 units available for sale at $1.50 each is relevant, as are any additional costs which can be attributed to the higher sales volume.

We know that the two existing operators are able to produce the higher output, and thus there will be no additional labor cost. The higher volume will require additional materials, however, which are charged at the usage rate of the more efficient machine, i.e., 36 cents per unit. We've also been told that additional selling and promotional expenses of $24,500 will be incurred to move the higher volume, and these are relevant as well. The combination of operating savings and incremental product profit totals $7,000.

Stage 3: Differential Depreciation. The only remaining relevant item is the tax impact of differential depreciation. As we discussed in Chapters 1 and 2, depreciation as such is not relevant to funds flows. For purposes of our analysis, it merits attention only because depreciation is tax deductible. Because depreciation charges normally reduce income tax payments, they're called a tax shield. If an investment decision causes higher or lower depreciation charges than before, such a difference must be reflected as a change in the tax shield.

For our replacement example, the differential depreciation for the next five years will be $1,500, an increase due to the higher cost basis of the new machine. We're assuming that straight-line depreciation is also used for tax purposes, to keep the calculations simple.

As shown in Figure 6–11 (p. 223), the analysis results in taxable operating improvements of $7,000, an incremental tax of $1,870, and a change in aftertax profit of $3,630. The applicable tax rate is normally the rate a company would be paying on any incremental profit. As the final step, the differential depreciation is added back to arrive at the aftertax operating cash flow of $5,130.

In following these steps, we have correctly reflected a tax reduction due to the differential depreciation, but then removed depreciation itself from the picture to leave us with the economic cash effect of the investment.

We could have obtained the same result by doing the analysis in two steps: (1) determining the tax on the operating improvement before depreciation, and (2) directly determining the tax shield effect of the differential depreciation. This would appear as shown below, and as we might expect, the result is exactly the same.

Taxable operating improvement	$7,000
Tax at 34%	2,380
Aftertax operating improvement	$4,620
Tax shield at 34%* of depreciation of $1,500	510
Aftertax operating cash flow.	$5,130

*Each dollar of depreciation provides a tax shield of $1 times the applicable tax rate.

Economic Life Refined

Earlier, we defined economic life as the length of time over which an investment yields economic benefits. Now we find that a complication has been introduced because of the expected difference in the physical lives of the two machines. Inasmuch as the old machine is assumed to wear out in 5 years while the new one will last for 10, the two investments are comparable only over the next 5 years. After that, the original alternative no longer exists, and a decision would have to be made at that point in any case. The situation is illustrated in Figure 6–12.

Differential revenues and costs can be defined only as long as both alternatives exist together. After five years, the old machine would be gone, which

FIGURE 6–12

Overlapping Economic Life Spans

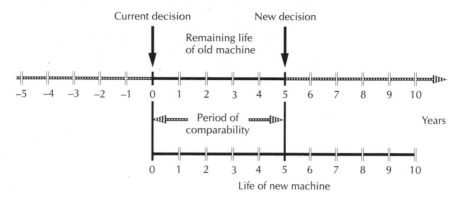

means that we can't analyze the situation beyond five years without making some assumptions about the remaining life of the new machine. While we have estimates that the product is likely to be salable for at least the total 10-year life of the new machine, the economic comparison for the replacement decision can be made only over 5 years.

There are two ways of handling this problem. First, we can cut off the analysis at the end of Year 5 and assign an assumed recovery value to the new machine at that point, because it should be able to operate well for another 5 years. This *terminal value estimate* must be counted as a capital recovery in Year 5, that is, its present value should be recognized as a benefit. This approach is widely used in practice, and usually the amount of terminal value is considered to be at least the amount of the remaining book value. But if the asset's value is quite predictable (as is the case with automobiles or trucks), the estimated sales value (adjusted for any tax consequences) is entered in the present value analysis as a benefit.

An alternative way of dealing with the problem is to assume that the old machine would be replaced by a new one in Year 5, and that a similar replacement would be made in Year 10 when the current new machine wears out. This approach involves a great deal of sequential guessing about possible replacement options 5 and 10 years hence. Moreover, in spite of such analytical effort, the economic lives of the two machines would still not be the same. Admittedly, the power of discounting would make the estimates of the later years almost immaterial. On balance, unless there are compelling reasons to develop such a series of replacement assumptions, the cutoff analysis described earlier is far more straightforward and less fraught with judgmental traps.

Capital Additions and Recoveries

The treatment of terminal values deserves a few more comments here. It's quite common for larger projects to require a series of additional capital outlays over time, and eventually provide likely recoveries of at least part of these funds. As a practical matter, any increments of capital committed or recovered should be entered in the present value framework as cash outflows or cash inflows at the point in time when they occur. This also applies to incremental working capital commitments, which should be shown as outflows as incurred, and which can be assumed to be recovered in total or in part at the end of the economic life of the project.

In our replacement example, we have made no provision for additional working capital in order to keep the problem focused on other basic refinements. The assumed terminal value of the new machine after five years, however, would be treated as a capital recovery and entered as a positive cash inflow at the end of Year 5. For simplicity, we'll assume that its economic value (realizable through sale or trade) will be equal to its book value. This would amount to $20,000 ($40,000 less five years' depreciation at $4,000 per year), with no taxable capital gain or loss expected.

We would have to modify this amount, of course, if circumstances indicated a higher or lower value due to changes in technology or other conditions. Book value is frequently used because it is easy to do, causes no taxable gains or losses, and also because the need for precision in terminal values is diminished by the exponential impact of discounting in later years.

Analytical Framework for Example 1

With all the basic data at hand, we can now lay out the framework for a present value analysis. We'll assume a 10 percent return standard and again set up the figures in a tabular format. The result in Figure 6–13 indicates a sizable net present value of $6,013—that is, of course, if all of our assumptions are borne out in fact! It would suggest that the replacement is desirable, at least on a numerical basis.

Note that the analysis is significantly affected by the assumed recovery of the book value of $20,000 in Year 5, which amounts to a present value inflow of

FIGURE 6–13

Present Value Analysis of Machine Replacement

Time Period	Investment	Operating Cash Inflow	Present Value Factors at 10 Percent*	Present Value of Net Investment	Present Value of Operating Inflows
0	−$25,850	—	1.000	−$25,850	—
1	—	+$ 5,130	0.909	—	+$ 4,663
2	—	+ 5,130	0.826	—	+ 4,237
3	—	+ 5,130	0.751	—	+ 3,853
4	—	+ 5,130	0.683	—	+ 3,504
5	—	+ 5,130	0.621	—	+ 3,186
5 (end)	+ 20,000	—	0.621	$ 12,420	—
	−$ 5,850	+$25,650		−$13,430	+$19,443
				Net present value	+$ 6,013

*For Years 1 to 5, we could use 3.791 from Table II.

$12,420. In effect, this terminal inflow reduces the net investment to only $13,430 in present value terms. Remember, economic analysis requires that this value be counted at the end of Year 5, even though there is no intention of actually selling the machine at that point.

This inclusion is relevant because the company would have the option of selling at the end of Year 5 and thereby realizing this economic value. After the five years are over, the alternative of selling could, of course, be compared with the alternative of recommitting the realizable value of $20,000 in order to preserve the profitable business at the level of 125,000 units. But these latter considerations deal with a future set of decisions and therefore are not relevant today.

The profitability index of the project is positive, as we might expect from the sizable net present value of about $6,000. Dividing $13,430 (net investment less recovery) into the operating benefits of $19,443 results in an index of 1.45, which should give the project a favorable ranking against an average return of only 10 percent from the company's investment opportunities. Some analysts prefer to express the profitability index by relating the original net investment to the total of all inflows, including capital recoveries. In our example, the result would be $31,863 ÷ $25,850 = 1.23, again a very favorable showing when this more stringent test is applied. While we could argue for and against either method, consistent application of one of them will be satisfactory.

The internal rate of return has to be found by trial and error using the present value tables, because the capital recovery at the end of Year 5 complicates an otherwise straightforward annuity. The problem can be handled as shown in Figure 6–14. The trial at 15 percent indicates a positive net present value of $1,286, but at 16 percent it is reduced to $466. Thus, the precise result is somewhat above 16 percent. Again, we've used the present value tables for illustration of the process; electronic calculation will obtain the result directly.

FIGURE 6–14

Present Value Analysis to Find Internal Rate of Return

Time Period	Cash Flow	Present Value Factors at 15 Percent	Present Value at 15 Percent	Present Value Factors at 16 Percent	Present Value at 16 Percent
0	−$25,850	1.000	−$25,850	1.000	−$26,510
1					
2					
3	+ 5,130/yr.	3.352*	+ 17,196	3.274*	+ 16,796
4					
5					
5 (end)	+ 20,000	0.497	+ 9,940	0.476	+ 9,520
	+$19,800		+$ 1,286		−$ 466

*From Table II.

A risk analysis can be carried out by calculating the present value payback (minimum life) and the annualized net present value. For the former, we must cumulate the present values of operating cash inflows until they approximate the net investment of $13,430 (Figure 6–13). A quick addition shows that this will happen after slightly more than three years, leaving a cushion of almost two years of economic life against risk.

A minor technical question arises here as to whether we should bring the assumed recovery at the end of Year 5 forward in time to obtain a more precise calculation of minimum life. This would involve a process of iteration, because not only would the present value of the recovery rise, but the sales value of the machine would also be higher in earlier years. Such a refinement is normally not called for even though it can readily be handled through computer simulation.

The annualized net present value can be found when we divide the net present value in Figure 6–14 by the 10 percent annuity factor in Year 5 from Table II, or $6,013 ÷ 3.791, which is $1,586 per year. All other aspects being equal, the project would still be acceptable if the annual operating cash inflows over the five years dropped from $5,130 to only $3,544, a possible shrinkage of over 30 percent. If we remove the depreciation tax shield of $510 from this test, the allowable drop in the pure aftertax operating improvement could be better than 34 percent ($1,586 against $4,620).

Another way of looking at the net present value cushion is to ask how sensitive the result would be to a reduced expected capital recovery at the end of Year 5. This answer can be readily found by reconstituting at the end of Year 5 a dollar amount that has the equivalent present value of the cushion of $6,013. To find this future dollar amount, we simply divide the net present value of $6,013 by the single sum factor given in Table 6–I for 10 percent in period 5, which is 0.621, to obtain a required amount of $9,683. We can see that if the expected recovery of $20,000 were reduced by about $10,300, the project would still be acceptable, given that all other conditions hold.

While perhaps a little complex, the step-by-step process we've just completed has exposed most of the practical issues encountered in the methodology of investment analysis. Let's turn to one more illustration which additionally shows the handling of working capital as well as successive investments.

Example Two: Business Expansion

The cash flow patterns in Figure 6–15 reflect the kinds of commitments and recoveries normally associated with a major business expansion. In the early life of the project, we find not only an outlay for facilities, but also a buildup of working capital during the first and second years. Additional equipment outlays are required at the end of Years 4 and 6, while recoveries of equipment and working capital are made as the economic life comes to an end. All cash flows are assumed to have been adjusted for tax consequences along the lines we discussed in our first example. The operating cash flows show a growth stage, peak in the middle years, and decline toward the end.

FIGURE 6–15

Present Value Analysis of Complex Expansion Project ($ thousands)

Time Period	Investments	Operating Cash Inflow (All Tax Adjustments Made)	Present Value Factors at 12%	Present Value of Investments	Present Value of Operating Inflows
0	–$130,000 (facilities)		1.000	–$130,000	—
1	– 25,000 (working capital)	+$ 20,000	0.893*	– 22,325	+$ 17,860
2	– 20,000 (working capital)	+ 40,000	0.797*	– 15,940	—
3	—	+ 40,000	} 2.144†	—	+ 85,760
4	—	+ 40,000			
4 (end)	– 15,000 (additional equipment)‡	—	0.636*	– 9,540	—
5	—	+ 50,000	} 1.075†	—	+ 53,750
6	—	+ 50,000			
6 (end)	– 10,000 (equipment overhaul)‡	—	0.507*	– 5,070	—
7	—	+ 20,000	0.452*	—	+· 9,040
8	—	+ 10,000	0.404*	—	+ 4,040
8 (end)	+ 25,000 (equipment recovery)	—	} 0.404*	+ 24,240	—
	+ 35,000 (working capital recovery)§	—		—	—
	$110,000	⌐$270,000		–$158,635	+$170,150
				Net present value	+$ 11,815

*From Table I.

†From Table II, representing the difference between the annuity factors applicable: 3.037 – 0.893 = 2.144 and 4.112 – 3.037 = 1.075, respectively.

‡Additional depreciation has been reflected in cash inflows.

§Assume loss in liquidation of $10,000.

No new concepts are required for us to deal with this investment example. Working capital (incremental inventories and receivables less new trade obligations) represents a commitment of capital just as definite as an expenditure for buildings and equipment, except that no depreciation write-off is involved. If all inventories and receivables can be expected to be successfully liquidated at the end of the economic life, these funds (net of payables) will be an inflow at that point, a capital recovery. If we assume some fraction of this investment to be unsalable or uncollectible, the figure must be lowered.

Additional capital expenditures for equipment during the life of the project are simply recognized as cash outflows when incurred. Care must be taken, however, to reflect the additional depreciation pattern in each case as a tax shield during future operating periods. Uneven cash flows present no problems when programmed calculators or spreadsheets are used to find the present value of each period's flows. But to demonstrate how the calculations are made, we have again employed the present value tables to find the factors, including those for partial annuities.

As was shown in Figure 6–15, the expected result of the project is a positive net present value of almost $12 million. The profitability index is 1.07, while the internal rate of return is approximately 13 percent. These results leave little margin for error. The annualized net present value suggests that the annual operating cash inflows can be reduced by $11,815 ÷ 4.968, or at most, by about $2.4 million per year. The minimum life (present value payback) is about six years, when all capital recoveries are included.

This is as far as we can carry the financial aspects of the analysis with the data at hand. The various judgments leading to the final decision call for much more insight into the nature of the product, the technology, the requirements and outlook of the market place, the competitive setting, etc., as we outlined in the first section of this chapter.

Mutually Exclusive Alternatives

So far we've dealt with individual investment projects without regard to the broader question of how these projects fit into the whole range of possibilities open to a company. We assumed that our examples were independent investment projects that could be evaluated and ranked against other independent projects. At times, however, managers face the issue of evaluating projects that are not independent of each other. Such is the case with sets of different alternatives which may be available for achieving the same purpose. These are called mutually exclusive alternatives, because if one is chosen, the others are eliminated by that very decision.

Dealing with such a situation is merely a special case of economic analysis which uses the same underlying concepts as before but emphasizes incremental reasoning. To illustrate, let's assume that a company has developed three alternatives to investing in facilities and working capital to produce and sell a modified product over the next seven years. The company's return standard is 14 percent. The first alternative represents existing technology, the second a more costly but advanced process, while the third provides higher capacity as well as the advanced process. Let us assume further that both the quality of the estimates and the uncertainty about the outcomes are the same in all three cases.

The key dimensions of the three alternatives are presented as follows:

Alternative	Net Investment	Annual Inflows	Terminal Value
(1) Standard	$500,000	$112,000	$150,000
(2) Advanced	600,000	128,000	150,000
(3) Expanded	750,000	169,000	200,000

The major investment measures were calculated and appear as follows:

Alternative	Net Present Value (NPV)	Internal Rate of Return (IRR)	Present Value Index (PVI)
(1) Standard	$40,256	16.3%	1.08
(2) Advanced	8,864	14.4	1.01
(3) Expanded	54,672	16.1	1.07

The first observation is that all three alternatives meet the company standard by every measure, although to different degrees. The issue is to select the best of the three alternatives, however, and we have to contend with somewhat different signals. From a net present value standpoint, Alternative 3 is clearly best, while the IRR and PVI results favor Alternative 1.

We must remember that the objective of successful investment is to create an economic trade-off that will increase shareholder value. If only one alternative can be chosen, this would argue for number 3 with the highest net present value. But Alternative 3 is also the most expensive one, and its creation of value per dollar invested (PVI) is somewhat less than number 1.

A useful way of thinking through the economic aspects of mutually exclusive alternatives is to examine the incremental benefits obtained as one moves from the least expensive to the most expensive one. In our example, the incremental investment for Alternative 2 is $100,000, but it reduces net present value from $40,256 to $8,864. This is clearly not desirable, and the lower IRR and PVI measures for Alternative 2 confirm this. Going from Alternative 1 to Alternative 3, however, results in an incremental investment of $250,000, which improves net present value by $14,416.

The incremental investment certainly exceeds the company standard of 14 percent, because its IRR can be calculated at 15.7 percent. This result is not quite as attractive as Alternative 1 with an IRR of 16.3 percent—but then the question becomes whether the company has any other projects that might give a better return than 15.7 percent. If not, Alternative 3 should be favored, assuming that all other judgmental aspects are comparable among the three alternatives—especially that the higher volume of business can in fact be counted on.

Actual Results Below Estimates

Throughout this discussion we have dealt with estimates of future costs and benefits largely as givens. In practice, estimates are more often than not proven wrong by actual experience—in either direction. When projects are performing better than expected, all is well. When actual results are disappointing, however, economic analysis becomes important if it can be decided to terminate the project in midstream. This is particularly important if a project contains another decision point for additional investment.

Figure 6–16 illustrates such a situation, where the first four years of the project's life have passed with disappointing results, and management is faced with the decision whether to fund the second investment phase.

The cardinal rule of economics to remember here is that past investments and cash flows are *sunk,* and that only *present* and *future cash flows* affect the decision to continue or quit. The economic trade-off, therefore, is between

- The net present value of the additional investment and the revised future cash flows on the one hand, and
- Any recovery value of the investment in place on the other.

FIGURE 6–16

Actual Results Lower - New Decision

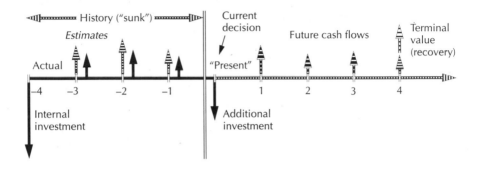

If no additional investment were required, the trade-off is between the present value of expected future cash flows and the recovery value. In either case, the view taken must be from the decision point onward into the future.

The same argument can be made when a company is faced with the decision to produce a product or service after having spent much more than planned on research and product development. With hindsight, the past decision to invest in the total project was a poor one. But the current decision to proceed with funding production may very well remain a sound economic choice, if the estimates about future price, volume, and cost continue to be favorable.

The weight of past mistakes must not be allowed to suppress sound judgment based on the only relevant factors: present and future conditions that can be affected by a current decision. At the same time, it should be obvious that any management must be careful not to make a series of such investments each of which as a whole is unsatisfactory, thereby creating sunk costs. Remember, sunk costs were future costs at one time, and should have been properly taken into account when they were relevant to the initial decision.

When to Use the Investment Measures

During our discussion of the different investment analysis measures, we cautioned the reader about various shortcomings and issues of interpretation. We will now review and expand some of these caveats.

Basically, investment analysis measures exist to help analysts and managers determine whether a project meets the earnings standard established for the business. Also, they assist in ranking the relative desirability of a group of proposals during the capital budgeting process. If the projects being considered are independent of each other, the time-adjusted measures of net present value, profitability index, discounted payback, and internal rate of return will singly or in combination properly reflect the projects' relative economic attractiveness and result in an appropriate ranking sequence.

Shown below in Figure 6–17 is a comparative view of the consistent readings of net present value, internal rate of return, and present value payback as applied to three types of independent projects. Project A exceeds the company standard, Project B falls short, and Project C just meets the standard.

Uneven lives of capital investments pose complications that are handled by adjusting the analysis to equalize the time spans for purposes of comparison. This can be achieved by truncating the life of a project with an assumed recovery of funds from disposal at an earlier point, as we did in the replacement example, or by extending the shorter alternative by assuming repeated investment. Mutually exclusive projects with different lives can also be compared by annualizing their net present values over their respective economic lives to determine their respective annual equivalent benefits or cost. This process simply calls for dividing the net present value by the relevant annuity factor, or using an appropriate computer program.

For mutually exclusive projects, the profitability index will normally give a fair assessment, but the choice has to be considered in terms of the relative size and length of the commitment as well—the risk/reward trade-off. As we discussed earlier, a larger investment with a somewhat lower profitability index and yield may be preferable to a smaller investment, if both alternatives show benefits well above normal.

If a company's identified projects exceed the limits of its funding potential—a fairly common condition—management has to apply what is called *capital rationing*. This involves spending the company's limited funds on the best selection of projects from the larger list of acceptable projects. The investment

FIGURE 6–17

Investment Measures Applied to Three Projects

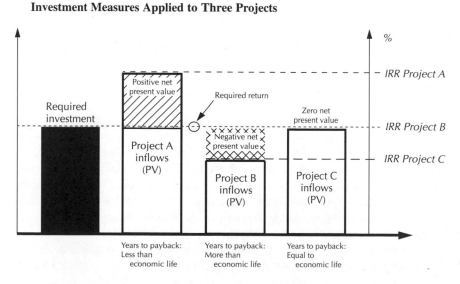

measures used have to provide an economic ranking, that is, optimize the benefits obtained from the investment dollars spent. Essentially, the company should choose that group of projects within the budget limit that will generate the highest aggregate net present value.

To do this, projects can be ranked in declining order of their profitability index until the budgeted amount has been exhausted. This amounts to maximizing the present value benefits achieved per dollar of investment, because investment funds are the limiting factor. This concept ties closely to the principles of shareholder value, as will be discussed in Chapter 9. In practice, however, capital budgets are rarely so precise that truly attractive projects that were initially rejected for lack of funds, or that appeared during the budget period could not at least be considered at another point in time.

Let's also remember that there should be nothing automatic about the use of any of the investment measures. The seemingly precise results achieved with present value calculations can tempt us to "let the numbers decide." Many more elements have to be weighed in even fairly straightforward projects, as we observed at the beginning of the chapter. Besides the obvious constraints imposed by uncertainty in the economic estimates, management must also consider competitive, technical, human, societal, and other constraints within the company's strategic context, before significant investment or divestment decisions are made.

SOME FURTHER CONSIDERATIONS

Several specialized aspects of business investment analysis have been mentioned only briefly so far. A detailed treatment would go beyond the scope of this book. Yet, for completeness, we'll add some further comments on how *leasing* affects the economics of investment, on the impact of accelerated depreciation on present value analysis, and on the impact of inflation. Finally we'll once more put into perspective the degree of accuracy warranted in the calculations.

Leasing

Leasing is a popular means of obtaining a wide variety of capital assets for businesses as well as individuals, in exchange for making a pattern of periodic payments. For our purposes, however, the main point to consider is that leasing represents merely one form of financing, as we'll discuss in Chapter 8. Therefore, it's only *after* economic investment analysis has shown a project to be acceptable that alternative ways of financing should be considered. This principle is consistent with the business systems approach we have taken, where we clearly separated the decisions on investment, operations, and financing. While funding for business investments should come from appropriate sources—matching their long-term nature—the specific alternatives of financing, including leasing, must remain independent from the economic justification of the investment itself.

All along we've viewed investment analysis as a cash flow trade-off which is independent of the compensation paid for the funds that finance the asset. The cost of capital or a return standard related to it automatically takes into account the expectations of the various providers of capital for appropriate compensation. If such an economic analysis is favorable, a separate test can then be applied whether the company is better off leasing or owning the assets involved. This involves comparing various funding methods, where the question clearly becomes "lease versus buy" not "invest versus not invest." A number of specialized software applications exist, which permit analysts and managers to make the necessary calculations and tests for comparing financing alternatives. Because of the special complexities involved in these analytical methods, the reader is directed to the references at the end of the chapter for detailed discussion and illustration.

Accelerated Depreciation

For simplicity, we've used straight-line depreciation in this chapter to derive the tax shield effect of depreciation charges as they affect economic analysis. However, we've also referred to the accelerated write-offs allowed under the Internal Revenue Code (see Chapter 3), which are periodically modified by Congress. Rather than focus on any one of the several methods permitted, we'll make only a few generally applicable comments.

Remember, when doing investment analysis we're interested in depreciation, whatever pattern it may take, only insofar as it changes the tax expenditures of the company. From a present value standpoint, accelerated depreciation provides an advantage because it moves the favorable tax impact of the write-offs forward in time. In other words, in the early years of a project, the tax shield effect will be greater than under straight-line conditions.

Similarly, shorter lives permitted by the ever-changing Internal Revenue Code will also place more tax benefits into the early stages of a project. Project benefits will be increased in the present value context, assuming, of course, that the company has sufficient taxable profits to take advantage of higher early write-offs. The calculations required to take account of accelerated depreciation in economic investment analysis can be easily handled with computer spreadsheets, just as any other uneven cash flow pattern can be accommodated.

The reader is encouraged to seek out the most current information published by the IRS to ascertain the proper depreciation class and write-off patterns for the assets being analyzed, and also to be aware of the particular tax management circumstances of the company that may affect its election of write-off patterns for tax purposes.

Inflation and Investment Analysis

The most important point to remember about the impact of inflation on investment analysis is the need for consistency between the measures used and data being analyzed. As we'll see in the next chapter, company return standards are commonly based on the weighted cost of capital. This cost specifically embodies inflation expectations both in the interest rate ascribed to debt, and the investors' return expectations on which the cost of shareholder equity is based.

The analysis of business investment projects should therefore be carried out with revenue and cost estimates that contain the same inflation expectations as the return standard employed. In other words, reasonable assumptions about price level changes affecting every part of the investment cash flow analysis should be built in, in order to make the discounting process meaningful. For example, using a return standard which contains an inflation allowance in discounting constant dollar projections would give a result biased against the project. Similarly, using a constant dollar return standard to discount inflated cash flows would unduly improve the project's measures. The reader is referred to Appendix III on inflation for a more detailed discussion of the underlying concepts.

Accuracy

At all times we must remember that the great precision implied by the mathematical basis of the investment analysis tools should be viewed with extreme caution. As we've pointed out before, the very nature of cash flow estimates—to which the tools are applied—is uncertain because they're based on expectations, forecasts, projections, and sometimes plain guesses. Only rarely does the analyst deal with contractual sums, such as interest or lease payments, and even these are subject to a degree of uncertainty. It therefore makes no sense to generate deceptively precise results or to allow highly specific numerical rankings to take on undue importance.

In our examples, we've been more precise than we needed to be. Our intention was mainly to give the reader enough specific details to be able to follow the various methods step by step. In practice, liberal rounding of calculations, and certainly the final results, is highly advisable to keep the mathematical process from overwhelming the realistic business judgments required.

Keeping accuracy in proper perspective is even more important when we realize that the power of discounting is such that even widely different estimates for distant time periods can be so severely reduced in present value terms that they have relatively minor effects on the final result. A glance at the present value tables will confirm the rapid shrinkage of factors as discount rates rise and periods are more remote.

KEY ISSUES

The following is a recap of the key issues raised directly or indirectly in this chapter. They're enumerated here to help the reader keep the analysis tools and methods within the perspective of both financial theory and business practice.

1. Business investment decisions are made continuously within the larger context of business strategy. This context evolves over time, and the portfolio of potential investments never remains constant or visible in its entirety.

2. The trade-off between outlays and benefits must be made with the objective of increasing shareholder wealth, that is, the return standards employed in measuring this trade-off must reflect the earnings potential and risks expected from a given business.

3. Shareholder expectations are incorporated into relevant earnings yardsticks through the concept of a weighted cost of capital, which reflects the appropriate level of future compensation to all providers of capital.

4. To permit an economic judgment to be made, investment measures must take into account the timing of inflows and outflows of an investment and relate economic attractiveness to defined return expectations.

5. Economic analysis of investment decisions must be based on differential revenues and costs in the form of cash flows that are caused by the decision, and not on changes that are merely due to accounting conventions.

6. Risk is inherent in all estimates of future conditions because of the uncertainty about most variables affecting an investment project. It must be expressed consistently in developing the expected cash flows and in applying the investment measures.

7. Inflation and specific price changes in revenues and costs can complicate both the estimating process and the level of the investment standards, and they must be handled consistently in both.

8. Capital budgets in practice are neither absolute ceilings on the amount of investments for a company, nor are they automatically affected by purely quantitative project ranking.

9. Financing patterns affect both the capability to invest and management's risk tolerance because of the impact of leverage and the need to cover fixed obligations.

10. Analytical techniques can provide ranges of results and quantitative insights of considerable sophistication, but they can't supplant qualitative business judgments that reflect the broader context of strategy and risk assessment.

SUMMARY

In this chapter, we've presented the basic analytical framework for investment analysis in the broad context of capital budgeting. The strategic backdrop of this activity was highlighted before the techniques themselves were discussed. We focused on time-adjusted concepts and measures because they reflect the economic nature of the analysis and decisions.

All along we've stressed, however, that the most critical aspect of the process was thoughtful structuring of the problem in all of its dimensions before any quantitative techniques are applied. We discussed the need to define the problem, including development of relevant alternatives, careful preparation of all relevant data about the investment and the changes in the operating conditions introduced by the decision, and any capital recoveries—all done in an economic cash flow context. We found conceptual problems in all of these aspects, particularly in the use and meaning of the investment measures themselves. Working through increasingly complex examples, we provided the reader with a basic ability to perform investment analysis. But we cautioned that numerical results were only inputs to the broader management task of strategic positioning of the business—the selection and matching of appropriate long-term capital commitments with appropriate funding sources, within the framework of defined corporate objectives and goals, and with the ultimate purpose of creating shareholder value.

SELECTED REFERENCES

Analytical Process

Garrison, Raymond H. and Erick W. Noreen. *Managerial Accounting: Concepts for Planning, Control, Decision Making.* 7th ed. Homewood, IL.: Richard D. Irwin, 1994.

Grant, Eugene, L., et al. *Principles of Engineering Economy.* 8th ed. New York: John Wiley & Sons, 1990. A classic.

Weston, Fred, and Eugene Brigham. *Essentials of Managerial Finance.* 10th ed. Hinsdale, IL.: Dryden Press, 1992.

Framework of Capital Budgeting

Aggarwal, R. (editor). *Capital Budgeting under Uncertainty: Advances and New Perspectives.* Englewood Cliffs, NJ.: Prentice Hall, 1991.

Bierman, Harold Jr., and Seymour Smidt. *The Capital Budgeting Decision.* 6th ed. New York: Macmillan, 1984. A classic.

Dixit and Pindyck. "The Options Approach to Capital Investment," *Harvard Business Review,* May-June 1995.

Levy, Haim, and Marshall Sarnat. *Capital Investment and Financial Decisions.* 4th ed. Englewood Cliffs, NJ.: Prentice Hall, 1990.

Shank and Govindarajan. "Strategic Analysis of Technological Investments." *Sloan Management Review,* Fall 1992.

Specialized Areas

Hertz, David B. "Risk Analysis in Capital Investment." *Harvard Business Review* September-December 1979. A classic.

McNamee, Peter, and John Celona. *Decision Analysis with Supertree.* 2nd ed. South San Francisco, CA.: The Scientific Press, 1990.

Perlman, Kalman I. *The Leasing Handbook.* Chicago; Cambridge, England: Probus Publishing Co., 1992.

Thorndike, David. *The Thorndike Encyclopedia of Banking and Financial Tables, 1995 Yearbook.* Boston: Warren, Gorham & Lamont.

TABLE 6–1

Present Value of Single Sum of $1 Received or Paid at End of Period

Period of Receipt or Payment	1%	2%	4%	5%	6%	8%	10%	12%	14%	15%	16%	18%	20%	22%	24%	25%	26%	28%	30%	35%	40%	45%	50%
1	0.990	0.980	0.962	0.952	0.943	0.926	0.909	0.893	0.877	0.870	0.862	0.847	0.833	0.820	0.806	0.800	0.794	0.781	0.769	0.741	0.714	0.590	0.667
2	0.980	0.961	0.925	0.907	0.890	0.857	0.826	0.797	0.769	0.756	0.743	0.718	0.694	0.672	0.650	0.640	0.630	0.610	0.592	0.549	0.510	0.476	0.444
3	0.971	0.942	0.889	0.863	0.840	0.794	0.751	0.712	0.675	0.658	0.641	0.609	0.579	0.551	0.524	0.512	0.500	0.477	0.455	0.406	0.364	0.328	0.296
4	0.961	0.924	0.855	0.823	0.792	0.735	0.683	0.636	0.592	0.572	0.552	0.516	0.482	0.451	0.423	0.410	0.397	0.373	0.350	0.301	0.260	0.226	0.198
5	0.951	0.906	0.822	0.784	0.747	0.681	0.621	0.567	0.519	0.497	0.476	0.437	0.402	0.370	0.341	0.328	0.315	0.291	0.269	0.223	0.186	0.156	0.132
6	0.942	0.888	0.790	0.746	0.705	0.630	0.564	0.507	0.456	0.432	0.410	0.370	0.335	0.303	0.275	0.262	0.250	0.227	0.207	0.165	0.133	0.108	0.088
7	0.933	0.871	0.760	0.711	0.665	0.583	0.513	0.452	0.400	0.376	0.354	0.314	0.279	0.249	0.222	0.210	0.198	0.178	0.159	0.122	0.095	0.074	0.059
8	0.923	0.853	0.731	0.677	0.627	0.540	0.467	0.404	0.351	0.327	0.305	0.266	0.233	0.204	0.179	0.168	0.157	0.139	0.123	0.091	0.068	0.051	0.039
9	0.914	0.837	0.703	0.645	0.592	0.500	0.424	0.361	0.308	0.284	0.263	0.225	0.194	0.167	0.144	0.134	0.125	0.108	0.094	0.067	0.048	0.035	0.026
10	0.905	0.820	0.676	0.614	0.558	0.463	0.386	0.322	0.270	0.247	0.227	0.191	0.162	0.137	0.116	0.107	0.099	0.085	0.073	0.050	0.035	0.024	0.017
11	0.896	0.804	0.650	0.585	0.527	0.429	0.350	0.287	0.237	0.215	0.195	0.162	0.135	0.112	0.094	0.086	0.079	0.066	0.056	0.037	0.025	0.017	0.012
12	0.887	0.788	0.625	0.557	0.497	0.397	0.319	0.257	0.208	0.187	0.168	0.137	0.112	0.092	0.076	0.069	0.062	0.052	0.043	0.027	0.018	0.012	0.008
13	0.879	0.773	0.601	0.530	0.469	0.368	0.290	0.229	0.182	0.163	0.145	0.116	0.093	0.075	0.061	0.055	0.050	0.040	0.033	0.020	0.013	0.008	0.005
14	0.870	0.758	0.577	0.505	0.442	0.340	0.263	0.205	0.160	0.141	0.125	0.099	0.078	0.062	0.049	0.044	0.039	0.032	0.025	0.015	0.009	0.006	0.003
15	0.861	0.743	0.555	0.481	0.417	0.315	0.239	0.183	0.140	0.123	0.108	0.084	0.065	0.051	0.040	0.035	0.031	0.025	0.020	0.011	0.006	0.004	0.002
16	0.853	0.728	0.534	0.458	0.394	0.292	0.218	0.163	0.123	0.107	0.093	0.071	0.054	0.042	0.032	0.028	0.025	0.019	0.015	0.008	0.005	0.003	0.002
17	0.844	0.714	0.513	0.436	0.371	0.270	0.198	0.146	0.108	0.093	0.080	0.060	0.045	0.034	0.026	0.023	0.020	0.015	0.012	0.006	0.003	0.002	0.002
18	0.836	0.700	0.494	0.416	0.350	0.250	0.180	0.130	0.095	0.081	0.069	0.051	0.038	0.028	0.021	0.018	0.016	0.012	0.009	0.005	0.002	0.001	0.001
19	0.828	0.686	0.475	0.396	0.331	0.232	0.164	0.116	0.083	0.070	0.060	0.043	0.031	0.023	0.017	0.014	0.012	0.009	0.007	0.003	0.002	0.001	
20	0.820	0.673	0.456	0.377	0.312	0.215	0.149	0.104	0.073	0.061	0.051	0.037	0.026	0.019	0.014	0.012	0.010	0.007	0.005	0.002	0.001	0.001	
21	0.811	0.660	0.439	0.359	0.294	0.199	0.135	0.093	0.064	0.053	0.044	0.031	0.022	0.015	0.011	0.009	0.008	0.006	0.004	0.002	0.001		
22	0.803	0.647	0.422	0.342	0.278	0.184	0.123	0.083	0.056	0.046	0.038	0.026	0.018	0.013	0.009	0.007	0.006	0.004	0.003	0.001	0.001		
23	0.795	0.634	0.406	0.326	0.262	0.170	0.112	0.074	0.049	0.040	0.033	0.022	0.015	0.010	0.007	0.006	0.006	0.003	0.002	0.001			
24	0.788	0.622	0.390	0.310	0.247	0.158	0.102	0.066	0.043	0.035	0.028	0.019	0.013	0.008	0.006	0.005	0.004	0.003	0.002	0.001			
25	0.780	0.610	0.375	0.295	0.233	0.146	0.092	0.059	0.038	0.030	0.024	0.016	0.010	0.007	0.005	0.004	0.003	0.002	0.001	0.001			
26	0.772	0.598	0.361	0.281	0.220	0.135	0.084	0.053	0.033	0.026	0.021	0.014	0.009	0.006	0.004	0.003	0.002	0.002	0.001				
27	0.764	0.586	0.347	0.268	0.207	0.125	0.076	0.047	0.029	0.023	0.018	0.011	0.007	0.005	0.003	0.002	0.002	0.001	0.001				
28	0.757	0.574	0.333	0.255	0.196	0.116	0.069	0.042	0.026	0.020	0.016	0.010	0.006	0.004	0.002	0.002	0.002	0.001	0.001				
29	0.749	0.563	0.321	0.243	0.185	0.107	0.063	0.037	0.022	0.017	0.014	0.008	0.005	0.003	0.002	0.002	0.001	0.001	0.001				
30	0.742	0.552	0.308	0.231	0.174	0.099	0.057	0.033	0.020	0.015	0.012	0.007	0.004	0.003	0.002	0.001	0.001	0.001	0.001				
35	0.706	0.500	0.253	0.181	0.130	0.066	0.036	0.019	0.010	0.008	0.006	0.003	0.002	0.001									
40	0.672	0.453	0.208	0.142	0.097	0.046	0.022	0.011	0.005	0.004	0.003	0.001	0.001										
45	0.639	0.410	0.171	0.111	0.073	0.031	0.014	0.006	0.003	0.002	0.001												
50	0.608	0.372	0.141	0.087	0.054	0.021	0.009	0.003	0.001	0.001	0.001												
60	0.550	0.305	0.095	0.054	0.030	0.010	0.002	0.001															

1. To find present value (PV) of future amount: PV = Factor × Amount
2. To find future amount representing given PV: Amount = PV/Factor
3. To find period given future amount, PV and yield: Factor = PV/Amount; locate in column
4. To find yield given future amount, PV and period: Factor = PV/Amount; locate in row

239

TABLE 6–II

Present Value of $1 per Period Received or Paid at End of Period (Annuity)

Number of Periods	1%	2%	4%	5%	6%	8%	10%	12%	14%	15%	16%	18%	20%	22%	24%	25%	26%	28%	30%	35%	40%	45%	50%
1	0.990	0.980	0.962	0.952	0.943	0.926	0.909	0.893	0.877	0.870	0.862	0.847	0.833	0.820	0.806	0.800	0.794	0.781	0.769	0.741	0.714	0.690	0.667
2	1.970	1.942	1.886	1.859	1.833	1.783	1.736	1.690	1.647	1.626	1.605	1.566	1.528	1.492	1.457	1.440	1.424	1.392	1.361	1.289	1.224	1.165	1.111
3	2.941	2.884	2.775	2.722	2.673	2.577	2.487	2.402	2.322	2.283	2.246	2.174	2.106	2.042	1.981	1.952	1.923	1.868	1.816	1.696	1.589	1.493	1.407
4	3.902	3.808	3.630	3.545	3.465	3.312	3.170	3.037	2.914	2.855	2.798	2.690	2.589	2.494	2.404	2.362	2.320	2.241	2.166	1.997	1.849	1.720	1.605
5	4.853	4.713	4.452	4.329	4.212	3.993	3.791	3.605	3.433	3.352	3.274	3.127	2.991	2.864	2.745	2.689	2.635	2.532	2.436	2.220	2.035	1.876	1.737
6	5.795	5.601	5.242	5.075	4.917	4.623	4.355	4.112	3.889	3.784	3.685	3.498	3.326	3.167	3.020	2.951	2.885	2.759	2.643	2.385	2.168	1.983	1.824
7	6.728	6.472	6.002	5.786	5.582	5.206	4.868	4.564	4.288	4.160	4.039	3.812	3.605	3.416	3.242	3.161	3.083	2.937	2.802	2.508	2.263	2.057	1.883
8	7.652	7.325	6.733	6.463	6.210	5.747	5.335	4.968	4.639	4.487	4.344	4.078	3.837	3.619	3.421	3.329	3.241	3.076	2.925	2.598	2.331	2.108	1.922
9	8.566	8.162	7.435	7.108	6.802	6.247	5.759	5.328	4.946	4.772	4.607	4.303	4.031	3.786	3.566	3.463	3.366	3.184	3.019	2.665	2.379	2.144	1.948
10	9.471	8.983	8.111	7.722	7.360	6.710	6.145	5.650	5.216	5.019	4.833	4.494	4.192	3.923	3.682	3.571	3.465	3.269	3.092	2.715	2.414	2.168	1.965
11	10.368	9.787	8.760	8.307	7.887	7.139	6.495	5.937	5.453	5.234	5.029	4.656	4.327	4.035	3.776	3.656	3.544	3.335	3.147	2.752	2.438	2.185	1.977
12	11.255	10.575	9.385	8.863	8.384	7.536	6.814	6.194	5.660	5.421	5.197	4.793	4.439	4.127	3.851	3.725	3.606	3.387	3.190	2.779	2.456	2.196	1.985
13	12.134	11.343	9.986	9.393	8.853	7.904	7.103	6.424	5.842	5.583	5.342	4.910	4.533	4.203	3.912	3.780	3.656	3.427	3.223	2.799	2.468	2.204	1.990
14	13.004	12.106	10.563	9.898	9.295	8.244	7.367	6.628	6.002	5.724	5.468	5.008	4.611	4.265	3.962	3.824	3.695	3.459	3.249	2.814	2.477	2.210	1.993
15	13.865	12.849	11.118	10.379	9.712	8.559	7.606	6.811	6.142	5.847	5.575	5.092	4.675	4.315	4.001	3.859	3.726	3.483	3.268	2.825	2.484	2.214	1.995
16	14.718	13.578	11.652	10.838	10.106	8.851	7.824	6.974	6.265	5.954	5.669	5.162	4.730	4.357	4.033	3.887	3.751	3.503	3.283	2.834	2.489	2.216	1.997
17	15.562	14.292	12.116	11.274	10.477	9.122	8.022	7.120	6.373	6.047	5.749	5.222	4.775	4.391	4.059	3.910	3.771	3.518	3.295	2.840	2.492	2.218	1.998
18	16.398	14.992	12.659	11.690	10.828	9.372	8.201	7.250	6.467	6.128	5.818	5.273	4.812	4.419	4.080	3.928	3.786	3.529	3.304	2.844	2.494	2.219	1.999
19	17.226	15.678	13.134	12.086	11.158	9.604	8.365	7.366	6.550	6.198	5.877	5.316	4.844	4.442	4.097	3.942	3.799	3.539	3.311	2.848	2.496	2.220	1.999
20	18.046	16.351	13.590	12.463	11.470	9.818	8.514	7.469	6.623	6.259	5.929	5.353	4.870	4.460	4.110	3.954	3.808	3.546	3.316	2.850	2.497	2.221	1.999
21	18.857	17.011	14.029	12.821	11.764	10.017	8.649	7.562	6.687	6.312	5.973	5.384	4.891	4.476	4.121	3.963	3.816	3.551	3.320	2.852	2.498	2.221	2.000
22	19.660	17.658	14.451	13.163	12.042	10.201	8.772	7.645	6.743	6.359	6.011	5.410	4.909	4.488	4.130	3.970	3.822	3.556	3.323	2.853	2.498	2.222	2.000
23	20.456	18.292	14.857	13.489	12.303	10.371	8.883	7.718	6.792	6.399	6.044	5.432	4.925	4.499	4.137	3.976	3.827	3.559	3.325	2.854	2.499	2.222	2.000
24	21.243	18.914	15.247	13.799	12.550	10.529	8.985	7.784	6.835	6.434	6.073	5.451	4.937	4.507	4.143	3.981	3.831	3.562	3.327	2.855	2.499	2.222	2.000
25	22.023	19.523	15.622	14.094	12.783	10.675	9.077	7.843	6.873	6.464	6.097	5.467	4.948	4.514	4.147	3.985	3.834	3.564	3.329	2.856	2.499	2.222	2.000
26	22.795	20.121	15.983	14.375	13.003	10.810	9.161	7.896	6.906	6.491	6.118	5.480	4.956	4.520	4.151	3.988	3.837	3.566	3.330	2.856	2.500	2.222	2.000
27	23.560	20.707	16.330	14.643	13.211	10.935	9.237	7.943	6.935	6.514	6.136	5.492	4.964	4.524	4.154	3.990	3.839	3.567	3.331	2.856	2.500	2.222	2.000
28	24.316	21.281	16.663	14.898	13.406	11.051	9.307	7.984	6.961	6.534	6.152	5.502	4.970	4.528	4.157	3.992	3.840	3.568	3.331	2.857	2.500	2.222	2.000
29	25.066	21.844	16.984	15.141	13.591	11.158	9.370	8.022	6.983	6.551	6.166	5.510	4.975	4.531	4.159	3.994	3.841	3.569	3.332	2.857	2.500	2.222	2.000
30	25.808	22.396	17.292	15.372	13.765	11.258	9.427	8.055	7.003	6.566	6.177	5.517	4.979	4.534	4.160	3.995	3.842	3.569	3.332	2.857	2.500	2.222	2.000
35	29.408	24.999	18.665	16.374	14.498	11.654	9.664	8.176	7.070	6.617	6.215	5.539	4.992	4.541	4.164	3.998	3.845	3.571	3.333	2.857	2.500	2.222	2.000
40	32.835	27.355	19.793	17.159	15.046	11.925	9.779	8.244	7.105	6.642	6.234	5.548	4.997	4.544	4.166	3.999	3.846	3.571	3.333	2.857	2.500	2.222	2.000
45	36.094	29.490	20.720	17.774	15.456	12.108	9.863	8.282	7.123	6.654	6.242	5.552	4.998	4.545	4.166	4.000	3.846	3.571	3.333	2.857	2.500	2.222	2.000
50	39.196	31.424	21.482	18.256	15.762	12.234	9.915	8.304	7.133	6.661	6.246	5.554	4.999	4.545	4.167	4.000	3.846	3.571	3.333	2.857	2.500	2.222	2.000
60	44.955	34.761	22.623	18.929	16.161	12.376	9.967	8.324	7.140	6.665	6.249	5.555	5.000	4.545	4.167	4.000	3.846	3.571	3.333	2.857	2.500	2.222	2.000

1. To find present value (PV) of series of equal receipts or payments: PV = Factor × Annuity
2. To find annuity representing given PV: Annuity = PV/Factor
3. To find number of periods to recover investment: Factor = Investment/Annuity; locate in column
4. To find yield of annuity given investment: Factor = Investment/Annuity; locate in row

SELF-STUDY EXERCISES AND PROBLEMS

(Solutions are provided in Appendix V)

1. An investment proposition costing $60,000 is expected to result in the following aftertax cash inflows over seven years:

Year	
1	$10,000
2	15,000
3	15,000
4	20,000
5	15,000
6	10,000
7	5,000

   a. Calculate the net present value at 10 percent and at 16 percent.
   b. Determine the internal rate of return (yield) of the proposition.
   c. If the annual cash flows were an even $13,000 per year for seven years, what would be the net present value at 10 percent?
   d. What level of annual cash flows would be required to yield a 16 percent return?
   e. How would the results of (a) and (b) change if there were a capital recovery of $10,000 at the end of Year 7?
   f. How would the result of (d) change if there were a capital recovery of $10,000 at the end of Year 7?

2. After having spent and written off against expenses of past periods an estimated $1,150,000 of R&D funds on a new product, the ABC Company must decide whether to invest a total of $1,500,000 in a large-scale initial promotional and advertising campaign to bring the product to market. The campaign will be conducted over a six-month period, and all costs will be charged off as expenses in the current year. The effect of the campaign is an estimated average incremental profit of $400,000 per year for at least the next five years, before taxes and without the initial promotional costs. The likely pattern of profits is estimated to be $200,000 in the first year, $300,000 in the second, $600,000 in the third, $500,000 in the fourth, and $400,000 in the fifth year.

   Assume that income taxes on incremental profits are paid at the rate of 36 percent and that the company normally has the opportunity to earn 14 percent after taxes. Calculate the various measures of investment desirability, first on the average profit and then on the annual pattern expected. Determine the simple payback and return on investment, average return, net present value, present value index, present value payback, annualized net present value, and internal rate of return (yield). What's the effect of the R&D expenditures on these results? Discuss your findings.

3. After careful analysis of a number of possible investments, a trustee of a major estate is weighing the choice between two $100,000 investments considered to be of equal risk. The first (a) will provide a series of eight year-end payments to the estate of $16,500 each, while the second (b) will provide a single lump sum of $233,000 at the end of 11 years. Which proposition provides the higher yield? If the normal return experienced by the estate for investments of this risk category is 6 percent, which investment is preferable? Should the pattern of cash flows be a consideration here, and how would this affect the choice? Ignore taxes and discuss your findings.

4. In an effort to replace a manual operation with a more efficient and reliable automatic process, the DEF Company is considering the purchase of a machine that will cost $52,800 installed and has an expected economic life of eight years. It will be depreciated over this period on a straight-line basis for both book and tax purposes, with no salvage value foreseen. The main benefit expected is a true reduction in costs due to the elimination of two operator positions and less materials spoilage. There will be some additional costs such as power, supplies, and repairs. The net annual savings are estimated to be $12,100, and the machine will be scrapped at the end of its life.

Assume that income taxes on incremental profits are paid at the rate of 36 percent and that normal opportunities return 12 percent after taxes. Calculate the simple payback and return on investment, average return, net present value, present value index, present value payback, annualized net present value, and internal rate of return (yield). Discuss your findings.

5. The XYZ Corporation's strategy includes the periodic introduction of a new product line, which involves investments in R&D, promotion, plant, equipment, and working capital. Now the company has readied a new product after an expenditure of $3.75 million on R&D during the past 12 months. The decision to be made is whether to invest $6.3 million for the production of the new line. The economic life of the product is estimated at 12 years, while straight-line depreciation will be taken over 15 years. At the end of 12 years, the equipment's book value is expected to be recovered through sale of the machinery. Working capital of $1.5 million must be committed to the project during the first year, and $1.25 million of this amount is expected to be recovered at the end of the 12 years. An expenditure of $1 million for promotion must be made and expensed in the first year as well.

The best estimate of profits before depreciation, promotion expenses, and income taxes is $1.9 million per year for the first three years, $2.2 million per year for the fourth through eighth years, and

$1.3 million per year for years 9 through 12. Assume that income taxes on incremental profits are paid at the rate of 36 percent and that the company normally earns 12 percent after taxes on its investments. Calculate the various measures of investment desirability. Which of these best indicates the project's attractiveness? Should the company plan to develop similar opportunities by spending research and development funds? How much margin for error exists in this project? Discuss your findings.

6. The ZYX Company has found that after only two years of using a new machine for a semiautomatic production process, a more advanced and faster model has arrived on the market, which not only will turn out the current volume of products more efficiently but will allow an increased output of the item. The original machine had cost $32,000 and was being depreciated straight-line over a 10-year period, at the end of which time it would be scrapped. This machine's market value currently is $15,000, and a buyer is interested in acquiring it.

   The advanced model now available costs $55,500 installed, and because of its more complex mechanism is expected to last eight years. A scrap value of $1,500 is considered reasonable.

   The current level of output of the old machine, now running at capacity, is 200,000 units per year, which the new machine would boost by 15 percent. There's no question in the minds of the sales management that this additional output could be sold. The current machine produces the product at a unit cost of 12 cents for labor, 48 cents for materials, and 24 cents for allocated overhead (at the rate of 200 percent of direct labor). At the higher level of output, the new machine would turn out the product at a unit cost of 8 cents for labor (because one less operator is needed), 46 cents for materials (because of less spoilage), and 16 cents for allocated overhead. Differences in other operating costs, such as power, repairs, and supplies, are negligible at both volume levels.

   If the new machine were run at the old 200,000-unit level, the operators would be freed for a proportionate period of time for reassignment in other operations of the company.

   The additonal output is expected to be sold at the normal price of $0.95 per unit, but additional selling and promotional costs are expected to amount to $5,500 per year.

   Assume that income taxes are paid at the rate of 36 percent and that the company normally earns 16 percent after taxes on its investments. Calculate the various measures of investment desirability and select those that are most meaningful for this analysis. What major considerations should be taken into account in this decision? Discuss your findings.

7. The UVW Company, a small but growing oil company, was about to invest $275,000 in drilling development wells on a lease near a major

oil field with proven reserves. Since other companies were also drilling in the vicinity, the volume of the flow of oil expected couldn't be predicted except within wide limits. Nevertheless, some oil would be obtained for a period of 12 years, in the best judgment of the geologists. After careful evaluation of the market and distribution aspects, company management decided that the major uncertainty lay in the physical yield, with lesser risk in the other areas. Consequently, an assessment was made of the range of aftertax cash flows (after considering depletion, depreciation, etc.) at various levels of production, and the likelihood of occurrence of these levels was estimated. There was believed to be a 5 percent chance that the cash flow would be $15,000 yearly over the life of the project, a 15 percent chance that it would be $35,000 yearly, a 40 percent chance that it would be $45,000 yearly, a 25 percent chance that it would be $50,000, and a 15 percent chance that it would be $60,000 per year. It was expected that oil would flow at any given level for the full life of the project, although there was the risk that the wells could run dry sooner. Would this be a worthwhile project if the company normally earned 10 percent after taxes? What considerations are critical? Discuss your findings.

CHAPTER 7

The Cost of Capital and Business Decisions

$\mathbf{A}$ common theme of this book is to view business decisions as economic cost/benefit trade-offs. Up to this point, however, we've focused mainly on the economic benefits obtained from investing in and operating a business. Now we'll deal in more specific terms with the economic costs caused by business decisions.

For example, in Chapter 5, during our discussion of financial leverage, we encountered the special profit impact that is caused by the cost of long-term debt funds. We demonstrated how such fixed-cost obligations introduce magnified earnings fluctuations at different levels of profitability. In Chapter 6, we referred to the overall cost of long-term capital as a main criterion by which to judge the desirability of business investments. We established that only projects providing a time-adjusted cash flow return above the cost of capital will create value for the company's shareholders.

In this chapter, we'll discuss in greater detail the cost of various types of capital employed in a business, examine how this cost is measured, and in what form and for which purposes this economic reality should affect business decision making. We'll begin by sketching out the types of decisions for which cost of capital considerations are important. Then we'll discuss the cost of the different types of capital used, including *operating funds, long-term debt,* and *owners' equity* (*preferred stock* and *common equity*).

Given the specific costs of each of these types of capital, we'll derive an approach to determining the overall corporate *weighted cost of capital,* and discuss the use of this cost concept in relation to the various *return standards* for business investments. The chapter will end with a list of *key issues.*

COST OF CAPITAL AND FINANCIAL DECISIONS

The decisional context we used in the first five chapters stressed the interrelationship of investment, operations, and financing. We observed that, over time, most management decisions cause funds movements in one form or another.

However, we didn't deal directly with the sources of these funds and their respective costs.

The dynamics of the business system are such that at any time, funds are used—temporarily or permanently—from a variety of sources, either internal (e.g., retained earnings from profitable operations or shifts in existing uses of funds) or external (e.g., through borrowing or raising new equity). Because the basic purpose of investing in, operating, and funding a business is to increase the economic value of the owners' stake over time, management decisions should create economic value for the shareholders through benefits that are higher than the cost of the inputs. Among these inputs is the cost of capital obtained from various long-term sources.

Investment Decisions

Chapter 6 discussed the various economic measures used to judge the desirability of an investment. All of these had in common the basic requirement that the project provide an economic return. This implies that all costs must be recovered, including compensation to the providers of all types of funds. We also established that minimum standards for investments had to be set high enough to compensate both for the project's specific risk and for the opportunity loss of forgoing the returns from alternative uses of the funds invested. Such alternative investments in the company's normal activities were assumed to adequately compensate both shareholders and lenders for providing their capital. We then suggested that the company's overall cost of capital, when used as a minimum standard for the economic desirability of investments, implicitly embodied all of these requirements.

The analytical methods discussed in Chapter 6 didn't directly include any financing costs; rather, the cash outflows and inflows as defined represented only capital outlays on the one hand, and incremental aftertax operating benefits and capital recoveries on the other. These cash flows were then discounted at a return standard that *implicitly* allowed for the recovery of all actual costs and opportunity costs combined. Very importantly, we didn't take into account the cost of the *specific* funds to be used for financing the project, instead letting at all times a broad overall standard represent the *combined* cost of all types of funding employed by the company.

Accordingly, the economic results from a business investment have to be sufficiently attractive to justify allocation of part of the various long-term funds available to the company. Here we must recognize an important principle, derived from our systems discussion in Chapter 1: Normally, the funds for new investments come from a pool of different sources, none of which can or should be specifically identified with any particular project under review. Instead, all funds used for investment purposes should carry the overall cost of the company's pool of funds, as suggested by Figure 7–1.

Given the long-term nature of capital expenditures for working capital, facilities, technology, etc., these funds commitments are normally backed by the long-term capital structure of a company. This structure may include different

FIGURE 7–1

Long-term Funds Commitments vs. Long-term Sources

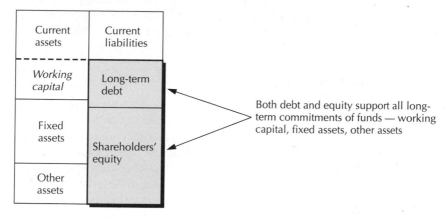

degrees of leverage and a whole range of financial instruments, and it may change over time as the company's business patterns develop. This pool of funds is the relevant source of funding—not any particular increment of financing the company may be using at a given point in time to augment its capital structure. Therefore, the *weighted* cost of capital measure, which we'll discuss shortly, is the most significant criterion of cost in the capital budgeting and investment analysis context.

Operational Decisions

The time horizon for operational decisions is generally shorter than that of the typical business investment. Nonetheless, operational funds movements, such as increases or decreases in trade credit—both used and extended—and swings in cash balances and accruals as described in Chapter 2 do involve costs, both in the form of out-of-pocket charges and opportunity costs. For example, a near-term decision to take purchase discounts may involve significant economic benefits when weighed against any incremental borrowing necessary to take advantage of the discount. Cash management decisions to minimize bank balances can eliminate the opportunity costs inherent in idle funds. In fact, there are myriad circumstances in which near-term decisions can cause or eliminate the cost of employing funds, as these decisions are often directly linked to incremental sources that entail specific costs. We'll discuss some of these shortly.

Financing Decisions

There are costs connected with obtaining financing and compensating providers of various sources of funds, both short-term and long-term, which must be considered by management in making any financing decision. Clearly, using any type of funds entails an economic cost to the company in one form or another. One of management's obligations is to develop a pattern of funding that both matches the risk/reward profile of the business and is sufficiently adapted to meeting the evolving needs of the company. We'll discuss the financing choices and the framework of analyzing them in the next chapter.

COST OF OPERATING FUNDS

In the course of its operations, a business commonly employs many types of debt, including trade obligations (in the form of accounts and notes payable), short- and intermediate-term credit, notes payable to banks or individuals, tax accruals owed various government agencies, wages due employees, payments due on installment purchases, and lease obligations. For all types of debt, including long-term obligations in the company's capital structure, the *specific cost* of borrowing can be determined rather easily. Normally, debt arrangements carry stated interest provisions that call for interest payments during the debt period, at its end, or as an advance deduction from principal. The last of these provisions is called discounting. In all cases, the specific cost of debt is simply the direct cost of the interest commitment.

We must also remember that under current IRS guidelines, interest payments of all kinds are tax deductible for corporations. Because of this feature, the net cost of interest to corporations (at least for those with sufficient profits to be liable for taxes or able to apply tax-averaging provisions) is the annual interest multiplied by a factor (f) of one minus the applicable tax rate.

For example, if a corporation pays 9 percent per year on the principal of a note and its effective tax rate (t) for any incremental revenue or cost is 34 percent, the net annual effective interest cost (i) of this note will be:

$$f = 1 - t$$
$$f = 1 - 0.34 = 0.66$$
$$i = 9\% \times 0.66 = 5.94\% \text{ (after taxes)}$$

Tax deductibility effectively reduces the cost of debt to a net amount after the prevailing tax rate is applied, if the company is in a position where changes in net income affect the amount of taxes due. This tax advantage may also be enjoyed by individuals in some circumstances, such as in the case of home mortgage interest deductions. However, the specific cost of other forms of capital (such as dividends on preferred stock) is not tax deductible for corporations at this time, as we'll see later.

We can define operating debt as short- or intermediate-term revolving obligations incurred in the ordinary daily operations of most businesses. Some of these debt funds are provided by creditors free of charge for short periods, under trade terms generally accepted in the industry or service in which the company operates.

Foremost in this category are accounts payable, which are the amounts owed vendors for goods or services purchased. Depending on the terms of the purchase agreement, the company being billed for goods and services can hold off payment for 10 or 15 days, or as long as 45 or even 60 days. In the interim, it can make use of the funds without incurring any specific cost. Recall from Chapter 2 that such trade credit is in fact a significant funds source that is rolled over continuously, and which grows or declines with the volume of operations.

In many cases, suppliers offer their customers a discount for early payment. For example, the supplier's terms may provide for a 2 percent reduction in the invoice amount if payment is received within 10 days (2/10), or 3 percent within 15 days (3/15) of the date of the invoice. This practice, common in many business sectors, allows the customer effectively to reduce the original cost of the goods or service by the specified discount. The incentive is intended to speed up the vendor's collections and thus reduce the level of the vendor's funds tied up in customer credit.

If the buyer lets the discount period lapse, however, the invoice amount becomes due and payable in full at the end of the period specified (n/30, n/45, etc.). Failure to take advantage of the trade discount, and thereby prolonging the time during which the buyer can make alternative use of the funds, results in a very definite opportunity cost. While often ignored, this cost can be quite sizable.

For instance, if the credit terms are 2/10, n/30, the cost of using the funds for the extra 20 days amounts to a loss of 2 percent of the invoice amount, or an annual rate of 36 percent! The calculation is quite simple:

$$\frac{360 \text{ days}}{20 \text{ days}} \times 2\% = 36\% \text{ (before taxes)}$$

In effect, the company loses, as taxable income, the cash discount it would otherwise have earned. To arrive at the net cost, the cash discount must be reduced by the taxes that would have been paid on the lost income. If we assume taxes to be 34 percent, the net cost for using the creditor's funds for the extra 20 days amounts to

$$1 - 0.34 = 0.66$$
$$2\% \times 0.66 = 1.32\% \text{ (after taxes)}$$

The annualization is calculated as

$$\frac{360 \text{ days}}{20 \text{ days}} \times 1.32\% = 23.76\% \text{ (after taxes)}$$

This cost is very high, especially when compared to the aftertax cost of the prime interest rate, which is the rate normally charged large corporations of impeccable credit rating—or even relative to the aftertax cost of much higher interest rates smaller companies pay to borrow operating funds.

Some companies, especially small and rapidly growing enterprises, make it a practice to use accounts payable as a convenient source of credit, often unilaterally exceeding the outside limits of credit terms by significant periods. The longer the funds are kept, of course, the lower the specific cost of accounts payable becomes, as trade creditors normally do not charge interest unless the receivable has to be renegotiated. In extreme cases, trade creditors may convert unpaid amounts into notes payable due on specific dates, with or without interest. This is usually done— albeit reluctantly—by vendors who wish to establish a somewhat stronger claim against the customer's resources.

It is clearly a poor practice for any borrower to violate stipulated trade credit terms, both from the standpoint of business reputation and continuing cred- itworthiness. Prospective creditors will take such tardy performance into account when evaluating the customer's credit history, as such information is readily available from the databases of credit rating agencies. This is an *implicit* eco- nomic cost which must be considered in addition to the specific monetary cost incurred with trade credit.

Another form of operating debt includes short-term notes and installment contracts, where interest is either charged ahead of time or is added to the amount of principal stated in the contract. For example, a one-year, $1,000 note which carries an interest rate of 9 percent will provide the debtor with only $910 in ready cash if the note is "discounted" by deducting the interest in advance. The effective cost before taxes is higher than the stated interest, because the company is in effect paying $90 for the privilege of borrowing $910 for one year:

$$\frac{\$90}{\$910} = 9.89\% \text{ (before taxes)}$$

The adjustment for income taxes is handled exactly as shown in the last example.

In the case of an installment contract for, say, $1,000 payable in four equal quarterly installments, with annual interest of 10 percent on the original balance, the effective cost of interest is far higher than stated, because decreasing amounts of principal will be outstanding over the term of the contract as the quarterly payments amortize the principal, while providing interest on the rapidly declining balance. The precise cost of 15.7 percent can be easily calculated with a calcula- tor or spreadsheet, using the present value approach discussed in Chapter 6.

We can use an averaging process as a quick method of determining the approximate effective cost. Over the term of the contract, the amount of principal will decline from $1000 to zero, with the average outstanding balance of roughly one-half of this range, or $500. The contractual interest was 10 percent on $1,000, or $100, one-quarter of which was added to each of the four payments. When we relate the total interest paid to the average amount of funds used by the borrowing company during the term of the contract, the approximate cost dou- bles, as follows:

$$\frac{\$100}{\$500} = 20\% \text{ (before taxes)}$$

The actual result of 15.7 percent was lower because in our example, inter- est in effect is also paid on the installment basis. (The adjustment for income taxes is the same as before.) If the contract ran for more than one year, the interest cost must be annualized, that is, the amount of interest must be allocated to the specific time period involved to derive the true cost per year, which is the normal period of comparison.

More complex financial arrangements are normally handled with present value techniques. Banks and other lending institutions routinely use computers to precisely calculate the payments and charges, and they are legally bound to disclose the effective cost of the arrangement on an annualized basis. The simple averaging technique shown earlier is useful as a quick check in many circumstances, including personal finance, to approximate the effective cost of credit for rough initial comparisons.

The discussion so far has focused on the specific cost of operational debt, which can range from zero to substantial annual rates of interest. This specific cost is not the only aspect of debt, however. As already mentioned in earlier chapters, repayment of the loan is required, which commits part of the company's future cash flows to that purpose. The obligation to repay the loan principal in a timely fashion forces the financial manager to forecast and plan cash receipts and disbursements with care. The projections could indicate that refinancing may be desirable when the amount becomes due. The basic techniques of making cash flow projections as discussed in Chapter 4 are applicable here.

Another element of the burden of debt, as already mentioned, is the impact various forms of debt obligations have on a company's creditworthiness in relation to current and future funding requirements. In other words, the balance between owners' equity and other peoples' money may become precarious and forestall borrowing of any kind for some time until the company has worked itself out from under its debt obligations. Highly debt-leveraged operations can be costly, both in terms of the risk of not meeting obligations as they fall due, and in having to turn to much more expensive sources of credit or equity funds as additional needs arise.

COST OF LONG-TERM DEBT

Most companies employ at least some form of long-term debt obligation to support part of their permanent financing needs arising from major capital outlays, growth of operations, or replacement of other types of capital. This type of debt becomes integral to the long-term capital structure of the company. Examples are bonds of various types issued by a company and traded in the financial markets, or long-term borrowing arrangements with banks and other financial institutions.

As we'll discuss in Chapter 8, management must make well-planned decisions when determining an appropriate level of debt in the capital structure, weighing the cost, risk, and debt service involved relative to the prospective uses of the funds. Long-term debt commitments by their very nature have a much more lasting impact on a company's situation than do short-term, working capital, financing, or intermediate-term loans.

The *specific cost* of long-term debt is expressed in the stated annual interest rate of the financial instrument involved. For example, a 12 percent debenture bond, which is an unsecured (no specific assets are pledged) general debt obligation of the company, has a specific aftertax cost of

$$12\% \times (1 - .34) = 7.92\%$$

if we assume that the company is able to take advantage of the interest deduction. An incremental tax rate of 34 percent was used. In addition, we'll assume that the bond had been sold at a price that nets the company its *par value* (face value). The stated annual interest rate (coupon rate) of a bond is based on the par value, that is, 100 percent of the principal due at a specified future date—regardless of the actual proceeds received by the issuing company. These proceeds often vary because marketable debt securities are generally sold at the best possible price obtainable in the market through underwriters who take some or all of the risk of marketing the issue for a small percentage of the gross receipts. Legal and registration expenses are also borne by the company. Therefore, depending on the issue price, which is related to prevailing interest yields and the quality of the company's credit rating, the company may actually receive net proceeds at a *discount* (below par value), or it may receive a small *premium* over par.

In either case, the specific cost has to be adjusted to take the actual proceeds into account. The effect is similar to the short-term loan discussed earlier, on which the interest was due in advance and that therefore entailed a specific cost somewhat higher than the stated rate. If we assume that instead of 100 percent of par value, the company received 95 percent for its debentures after all expenses and commissions, the effective aftertax cost with a 12 percent coupon rate is as follows:

$$0.12 \,(1 - .34) \times \frac{1}{.95} = 8.34\% \qquad \frac{7.92}{.95} = 8.34\;).$$

Apart from the specific cost of interest, long-term debt also again involves repayment of the principal. There are many types of repayment provisions, generally structured to fit the nature of the company and the type of risks the debt holder visualizes. Periodic repayment requirements may be met through a *sinking fund* set aside for that purpose and held in trust by a depository institution. Partial or full principal payments due at the end of the lending period are called *balloon payments*.

The basic point to remember is that debt instruments, even if long-term, must in some form and at some time be repaid. The cost of this repayment is implicit in the need to carefully plan future cash flows, and also to consider the company's ability to achieve future refinancing if the funds needs are likely to continue or even grow. Recall Chapter 4's discussion of funds projections.

Another implicit cost of long-term debt involves the nature and degree of restrictions normally embodied in the debt agreement (*indenture*). Such provisions may limit management's ability to use other forms of credit (e.g., leasing), they may specify minimum levels of some financial ratios (e.g., working capital proportions or debt burden coverage), or they may limit the amount of dividends that can be paid to shareholders. At times, specific assets may have to be pledged as security. Any set of such provisions carries an implicit cost in that it limits management's freedom of choice in making decisions. The greater the perceived risk of the indebtedness, the greater the restrictions are likely to be.

The rationale for these restrictions was presented in the discussion of financial ratios from the point of view of lenders (Chapter 3). Not to be overlooked is the introduction of *financial leverage* into the capital structure, as discussed in Chapter 5. The implicit cost of this condition again depends on the degree of risk exposure caused by specific company and industry conditions.

COST OF OWNERS' EQUITY

Preferred Stock

This form of equity ownership is conceptually at the midway point between debt and common stock. Although subordinated to the various creditors of the corporation, the preferred shareholder has a claim on corporate earnings that ranks ahead of the common shareholders' position up to the amount of the stated preferred dividend. In liquidation, the preferred shareholders' claims are satisfied prior to the residual claims of the holders of common stock.

The *specific cost* of preferred stock is normally higher than that of debt with a similar quality rating. Because of the near-equity status of preferred stock, preferred dividends at this writing are not tax deductible for the issuing corporation and are therefore an outflow of aftertax funds. For instance, a 14 percent preferred stock, issued at par (net of expenses), costs the corporation 14 percent after taxes. For each dollar of dividends to be paid on this preferred stock, the corporation must therefore earn, before taxes:

$$\$1.00 \times \frac{1}{1 - .34} = \$1.52$$

as compared to $1 for every dollar of interest paid on a long-term debt obligation. Where the 12 percent bond in the previous section had an aftertax cost of 7.92 percent, the 14 percent preferred bond has an aftertax cost of 14 percent. The stated dividend rate of a preferred stock is therefore directly comparable to the tax-adjusted interest rate of a bond.

We can easily compare the cost to the company of long-term debt and preferred stock if we assume that they were issued at prices that result in proceeds exactly equal to the par (face) value. When proceeds do not equal par value, as often happens because of market conditions, the cost must be based on the proceeds to obtain the effective cost as discussed above.

The additional *implicit* cost of preferred stock lies in the fact that it is a security senior to common stock, and the dividend claims of its holders rank ahead of common dividends. In addition, the essentially fixed nature of preferred dividends (they can be omitted only under serious circumstances) introduces a degree of financial leverage with varying earnings levels. Preferred stock being closer in concept to owners' equity than to debt, however, makes the implicit costs of its encumbrances far less serious than those of debt.

Common Equity

The holder of common shares is the residual owner of the corporation, with a claim extending to all assets and earnings not subject to prior claims. Common shareholders provide long-term funds with the expectation of being rewarded with both dividends and an increase in the economic value of their shares. This value accretion consists of the interlocking impact of (hopefully) growing earnings and growing dividends on the market value of the shares. In turn, the market value is impacted by general economic conditions and by risks specific to the industry and to the individual company.

In other words, in the case of common stock, we are dealing with more variables, while contractual provisions for compensation, such as coupon interest or the stated preferred dividend rate, are absent. As a result, the *specific cost* of common equity requires a more complex evaluation than we encountered with either debt or preferred stock.

The cost of common equity has to be viewed in an opportunity framework. The investor has provided funds to the corporation expecting to receive the combined economic return of dividends declared by the board of directors and future appreciation in market value. The investment was made—presumably on a logical basis—because the level and nature of the risk embodied in the company and its business reasonably matched the investor's own risk preference. In addition, the investor's expectations about earnings, dividends, and market appreciation were considered satisfactory.

The investor made this choice, however, by forgoing other investment opportunities. Moreover, the commitment was made under a condition of uncertainty about future results, because the only hard data available to any investor are *past* performance statistics. Therefore, measuring the cost of the shareholders' funds to the corporation is a challenge that must address investor expectations about the risk/reward trade-off made by investing in this opportunity. In other words, the company must strive to compensate the shareholder with an economic return implicit in its past performance as well as its future outlook, and relative to the potential returns from the stock market as a whole.

Several approaches to measuring the cost of common equity are used in practice; all involve many assumptions and a great deal of judgment. The greatest difficulty lies in finding a specific linkage with the collective risk/reward judgments continuously made in the security markets, judgments that drive the market value of the common shares. We'll discuss two major methods:

(1) the dividend approach, and the

(2) risk assessment approach based on the capital asset pricing model (CAPM).

The dividend approach is fairly straightforward; in effect it directly values expected future streams of dividends. But it's limited by highly simplifying assumptions. The risk assessment method, in contrast, approximates shareholder return expectations by adding to a *"normalized"* rate of return on securities in general a calculated numerical *risk premium* that is *company-specific*. As we'll see, it's the only approach that arrives at an economic return for the specific security relative to average yields experienced in the securities markets.

Dividend Approach to Cost of Common Equity

A way of dealing with at least one of the measurable benefits obtained by the shareholder is to use annual dividends to estimate the cost of common equity. This is a cash flow method that parallels the measures for the other forms of capital. Yet the approach suffers from serious oversimplification, because companies vary greatly in their rate of dividend payout, and the method does not specifically address the effect of reinvestment of retained earnings. Remember, common shareholders are the residual owners of all earnings not reserved for other obligations, and dividends paid are usually only a portion of the earnings accruing to common shares.

In its simplest form, the dividend approach is the same as the dividend yield we discussed as one of the market indicators in Chapter 2:

$$\text{Cost of common equity} = \frac{\text{Projected dividend per share}}{\text{Current market price per share}}$$

$$k_e = \frac{dps}{P}$$

Introducing estimated growth in dividends into the formula is an improvement that implicitly recognizes the effect of reinvestment on the value received by shareholders. The assumption here is that over time, successful reinvestment of retained earnings will lead to growing earnings and thus growing dividends. The mathematics of the formula allow us simply to add the assumed rate of growth in dividends to the equation shown above. We begin with the dividend yield and add a stable percentage rate of dividend growth (g) to simulate the overall expectations of the shareholders:

$$k_e = \frac{dps}{P} + g$$

The difficulty, however, lies in determining the specific dividend growth rate, which must be based on our best assumptions about future performance, tempered by past experience. Many estimating processes can be used. In Chapter 5, we discussed the concept of sustainable growth, which assumed stable investment, payout, and financing policies. This may yield clues to the growth rate that would be appropriate for the dividend approach, but the process really requires projecting expected future dividend policies as set by the company's directors. If significant changes in dividend policy can be expected, the analyst may want to modify the approach, making a series of year-by-year assumptions and in effect calculating a composite of future dividend growth patterns from these yearly forecasts.

A word about taxes is necessary here. In the dividend approach, we're dealing with aftertax cash flows from the company's viewpoint. Common dividends, like preferred dividends, are not tax deductible and must be paid out of aftertax earnings. No adjustment is therefore necessary in the result to make it comparable with the aftertax cost of debt and preferred stock.

The shareholder is judging the opportunity to earn an economic return on the same basis. However, interest and dividends are taxable income to the recipient. Because personal tax conditions vary greatly, one more adjustment is necessary from the investor's point of view to assess investment options objectively. Yet the business analyst cannot perform the calculation for the shareholder without knowledge of the individual's tax status. Consequently, the only working assumption we can make in this context is that most investors are subject to some taxation; we can arrive at financial results that are consistent up to the point at which the individual investor must calculate the personal tax impact.

Risk Assessment Approach to Cost of Common Equity

As we said earlier, the risk assessment method doesn't rely on specific estimates of present and future earnings or dividends. Instead, a *normal market return* is developed from published data on financial returns and yields, which is adjusted by a *company-specific risk premium or discount.* The rationale is based on the assumption that a company's cost of equity in terms of shareholder return expectations is related to the *relative risk* of its common stock. The greater this relative risk, the greater the premium—in the form of an additional economic return over and above a normalized return—that should be expected by an investor. This approach makes intuitive sense and can also be demonstrated statistically.

At any time, the securities markets yield a spread of rates of return ranging from those on essentially risk-free government securities at the low end of the scale (6 to 8 percent), to the sizable returns from highly speculative securities, including high-yield but risky junk bonds (18 to 20 percent or more). The risk/return trade-off inherent in the many classes of security investments is reflected in this spread. Risk is defined as the *variability* of returns inherent in the type of security, while return is defined as the total *economic* return obtained from the security, including both interest or dividends and changes in market value.

A number of specific methods have been developed over the years to express the risk premium concept of return on common equity—which reflects the cost of common equity to the corporation—as a methodology both theoretically acceptable and practically usable. While no individual method is totally satisfactory in these terms, the most widely accepted is the *capital asset pricing model (CAPM).* We'll discuss some of its salient features here, but the conceptual and theoretical underpinnings are extensive and far beyond the scope of this book. The reader is encouraged to explore the references at the end of the chapter for more extensive treatments of the evolution, theory, and validation of the CAPM.

Three elements are required in applying the capital asset pricing model approach, and each must be carefully estimated:

■ Level of return from a risk-free investment.

■ Level of return from securities of average risk.

■ Expression of relative risk of the company's security.

The first element is a judgment about the basic return of a security from which all risk has been excluded. The purpose is to find the lowest part of the range of yields currently experienced in the securities markets as the starting point from which to build up the higher, risk-adjusted return specific to the particular common stock. Long-term U.S. government obligations are commonly used as a surrogate for such a risk-free return. The yields on U.S. government obligations are widely quoted and accessible, both for the present and for historical periods. For our purposes, current yields can be used, possibly adjusted for expected changes, such as the inflation outlook during the next several years. Precision is not possible here, and reasonable approximations supported by the analyst's judgment are quite workable.

The second element is an estimate of the return from a comparable type of security of average risk. This is needed because the CAPM approach develops a specific adjustment for the *relative* riskiness of the particular security as compared to an average or baseline. For our purposes, we can use an estimate of the total expected return for the Standard & Poor's 500 Index, a broad-based measure of the price levels of the common stocks of 500 widely traded companies. Such projections of the total return—a combination of dividends and market appreciation—that is expected from the companies represented in the index, are frequently made by security analysts and published in financial services and newsletters (see Appendix II). While the S&P 500 Index provides a broad-based estimate of return, more specific indexes could be chosen. Again, the analyst must exercise judgment in using projections of future economic returns. The main point is to obtain a reasonable approximation of the average return from average investments of the type being evaluated.

The third element required is an expression of relative risk, which is based on the *variability of returns* of the particular security being analyzed. The definition of risk is very specific in the CAPM approach, and this has caused some controversy. Risk is not defined as total variability of returns, but rather, as the *covariance* of the particular stock's returns with those of assets of average risk. The assumption here is that an investor does not focus on the total variability of return experienced with each individual security, but rather on how each security affects the variability of the total return from the portfolio held by the investor. Note, however, that significant changes in a company's capital structure will tend to affect the company's relative risk as well as its covariance with the portfolio.

Risk, therefore, is a very relative concept in the CAPM, and its specific definition may not be acceptable to everyone. We'll ignore the arguments for and against this risk definition in our discussion, and concentrate instead on how risk is recognized in the CAPM approach to arrive at a company-specific return. This risk measure, in the form of the covariance of an individual stock's returns with that of the portfolio of stocks of average risk, is called beta (β). It is found by linear regression of past monthly total returns of the particular security against a baseline such as the S&P 500 Index. Services like *Value Line* list the current β for publicly traded securities as a matter of course.

How are these three elements combined to arrive at an expected return and the company's cost for a particular equity security? As we stated earlier, the CAPM method defines the cost of common equity as the combination of the risk-free return and a risk premium that has been adjusted for the specific company risk.

The CAPM formula is   *CAPITAL ASSET PRICING MODEL*

$$k_e = R_f + \beta(R_m - R_f)$$

where

k_e is the cost of equity capital.

R_f is the risk-free return. *(LONG TERM GOVERMENT ISSUES)*   "*BETA*"

β is the company's covariance of returns against the portfolio. ↳ *RISK FACTOR*

R_m is the average returns on common stocks.

The company's β is expressed as a simple factor that is used to multiply the difference between the expected return on the average portfolio and the expected risk-free return. This difference, of course, equals the risk premium inherent in the portfolio. The β factor adjusts this average risk premium to reflect the *individual* stock's higher or lower relative riskiness. β goes above 1.0 as the relative risk of the stock exceeds the average, and drops below 1.0 when the relative risk is less than average.

The calculation itself is quite simple, while deriving the inputs isn't, as we've already observed. To illustrate, let's arbitrarily choose a risk-free rate of return of 9 percent, an S&P 500 return estimate of 13.5 percent, and a company with a fairly "risky" β of 1.4. The cost of equity in this hypothetical example would be

DIFF = 6.3 %

$$k_e = 9.0 + 1.4(13.5 - 9.0) = 15.3\%$$

↑ HIGH RISK

1.0%. = LOW RISK

composed of the risk-free return of 9 percent plus the calculated company-specific risk premium of 6.3 percent, for a total of 15.3 percent.

A large number of issues surface when the CAPM or related measures are used to derive the cost of securities. One of these, already mentioned, is the quality of the estimate of both the risk-free return and the average return on a portfolio of common stocks. While the return on long-term U.S. government securities is a reasonable surrogate for the former, estimating an average portfolio return is fraught with conceptual problems. If β is the sole indicator of relative risk, the nature of the portfolio against which covariance is measured is clearly important. Broad averages such as the S&P 500 may or may not be appropriate under the circumstances. Also, there is the problem of using past data, particularly for variability of returns, in estimating the future relationships that indicate shareholder

Finally, there is the issue of the effect of changes in a company's
rage.

uently, the results of these calculations, as with most types of finan-
should be used with caution and a great deal of commonsense

Inflation

So far we've been talking about the cost of capital without specific reference to the impact of inflation. We could do this because *no* adjustment is in fact needed. The risk-free return on a government bond does implicitly allow for the expected level of inflation, inasmuch as expectations about future inflationary conditions affect the yield from such securities. When inflation abates, the yields decline— as dramatically occurred in the mid-1980s and early 1990s. When inflation expectations rise, so do bond yields. The same is true of the yields from other financial instruments.

If no inflation existed, risk-free returns would probably be in the range of 3 to 4 percent, the basic interest rate. In fact, not just the CAPM, but all of the measures of cost of capital we've been discussing include expected inflationary effects in that estimates of future returns take these expectations into account. The spectrum of returns ranging from risk-free bonds to those on speculative securities is also consistent in reflecting the effects of inflation.

To summarize, it should be obvious by now that the cost of common equity, apart from the specific method of calculation, is generally higher than the cost of interest-bearing securities or preferred stocks. As we said at the beginning of this section, the residual claim represented by common shares involves the highest risk/reward trade-off. Thus, returns expected of common shares are higher, which in turn, must translate into the highest cost of capital from the corporation's standpoint. This fact will become even more important when we examine the alternative choices of financing new funds requirements, the subject of the next chapter.

WEIGHTED COST OF CAPITAL

Having determined the specific costs of the various types of capital individually, we now have all the specific cost inputs needed to make some of the funding decisions listed earlier. But because most companies use more than one form of long-term capital in funding investments and operations, and because the mix of sources used for long-term financing may change over time, it's necessary to examine the cost of the company's capital structure as a whole. The result we're looking for is a cost of capital figure that is weighted to reflect the mix of the various capital sources used as a matter of policy. It encompasses the cost of compensating long-term creditors and preferred shareholders in terms of the specific provisions applicable to them, and of rewarding the holders of common stock in terms of the risk-adjusted return they expect.

Several issues have to be resolved in determining an overall corporate cost of capital. The first is generating appropriate costs for the different types of long-term capital employed, which we have already done conceptually. The second is a decision about the weights, or proportions, of each type of capital in the structure to be analyzed. The third is the question of whether to apply market values versus book values of the various categories of capital in arriving at the weighting. It's only then that we can calculate a weighted cost of capital that is meaningful for the intended purpose.

Cost

First to be resolved is the question of whether it is relevant to consider the *past* costs of existing securities in a company's capital structure, or alternatively, the *incremental* costs involved in adding newly issued securities. Quite often the debt and preferred stock section of the balance sheet lists a whole array of past issues, many of which carry interest or dividend rates that differ significantly from current experience. Obligations that are 5, 10, or 15 years old likely carry stated costs that are no longer relevant today. Moreover, the various methods of arriving at the cost of common equity were based on future expectations, which are not necessarily consistent with past debt or preferred costs. To solve this dilemma, we must again apply the principle established early in this book: The purpose of the analysis always determines the choice of data and methodology.

Normally, the key purpose of calculating a weighted cost of capital is for use in decisions about new business investments, serving as a standard of return that will adequately compensate all providers of capital. Unless a company undergoes significant restructuring, the funds for new capital commitments are likely to come from current internal cash flow, augmented by new debt, new equity, or both. This is an *incremental* condition, because the choices for adding new investments are still being made. Consequently, the cost of capital measure most appropriate here is based on the incremental costs of the various forms of capital employed by the company. As we already know, past decisions on investments and financing are *sunk costs,* and not relevant here.

Weighting

As we mentioned, we're deriving a weighted cost that reflects the normal proportions of the different types of capital in a company's capital structure. Again, significant issues arise. The current capital structure as reflected on the balance sheet is the result of past management decisions on funding both investments and operations. The question to be asked here is whether the types and proportions of capital in this structure are likely to hold in the future, i.e., whether they match the strategic plans of management. The intended capital budget supporting the company's future strategy, particularly when calling for sizable outlays, may indeed cause significant changes in the long-term financing pattern. Also, management may choose to make gradual modifications to its financial policies which, over time, can cause sizable shifts in the capital structure. (Recall Chapter 5's discussion of the impact of policy changes.)

In other cases, management may well be satisfied with the current proportions of the company's capital structure as a long-term objective. Yet the incremental capital required from time to time is normally raised in blocks limited to one form of security, that is, debt, preferred stock, or common equity. Therefore, in the near term, any one type of capital may be emphasized more than the long-term proportions desired would suggest. Capital must be raised in response to market conditions, and the choice of which type is appropriate at any given point is based on a series of considerations that we'll explore in the next chapter.

The analyst has to resolve the dilemma caused by such divergences with judgment. Given the fact that a company's conditions never remain static in the long run, the choice of capital structure proportions has to be a compromise intended to approximate the conditions relevant for purposes of analysis. Precision becomes secondary to common sense. Current proportions are a good starting point, but should normally be modified by specific assumptions about the future direction of the company's long-term financing. It may also be useful to generate a range of assumptions to bracket the findings, which as we know is a form of sensitivity analysis.

Market versus Book Values

The weights to be assigned to different types of capital are clearly going to be different if we choose to apply current market values as contrasted with the stated values on the right-hand side of the balance sheet. Again, we must be guided by the purpose of the analysis to decide which value is relevant. If we're interested in a criterion against which to judge expected returns from future investments, we should use the current market values of the various types of capital of the company, because these values reflect the expectations of both creditors and shareholders. The latter certainly didn't invest in the book value of common equity, which usually differs significantly from the current share value as traded in the market. Further, it's management's obligation to meet the expectations of the shareholders in terms of the future economic value to be created by investments and operations, and to compensate creditors out of future earnings. Stated book values, as we observed before, are static and not responsive to changing performance or values.

The choice of market values also complements the use of incremental funding in that both are expressed in current market terms. The market value of common equity automatically (and implicitly) includes retained earnings as reported on the balance sheet. Although many people feel that retained earnings bear no cost, this is a misconception. In fact, retained earnings represent part of the residual claim of the shareholders, even if they are imperfectly valued on the balance sheet because of required accounting conventions.

In this area, there are again conceptual issues and arguments that can be raised for and against market value weights. One of these has to do with a company that is experiencing financing requirements rather different from the historical pattern reflected in its capital structure. There it can be argued that a book value approach may be more suitable. Again, we must leave the in-depth exploration of these concepts to the reader, because they go beyond the scope of this book.

Calculating the Weighted Cost of Capital

Let's now turn to a simplified example of calculating a weighted cost of capital for a hypothetical company. This will allow us to demonstrate the basic mechanics of what we now understand to be a process that involves a great deal of judgment.

We'll use the condensed balance sheet of ABC Corporation in Figure 7–2, augmented by some additional data and assumptions.

The company has three types of long-term capital, that is, debt, preferred stock and common equity. We assume that it could issue new bonds at an effective cost of 12 percent, and new preferred stock at an effective cost of 13 percent, based on proceeds from expected pricing in the market and after applicable underwriting and legal expenses. Note that these current costs are above the rates the company has been paying on its long-term capital as stated in the balance sheet. ABC's common stock is currently trading between $63 and $67, and the most recent earnings per share were $4.72. Dividends per share last year were $2.50. The company's β, as calculated by security analysts, is 1.1, a fairly average risk. We further assume that the estimated risk-free return is 8.5 percent, and the best available forecast for the total return from the S&P 500 is 15 percent.

Overall company prospects are assumed to be satisfactory, and security analysts are forecasting normal growth in earnings at about 6 percent. Given this background, it's possible to calculate a weighted cost of capital. As we proceed, the choices to be made will be highlighted.

The respective costs of the three types of capital employed can be derived as shown below. Note that we are employing the *incremental* cost of funds in each case, rather than the *past* costs as reflected in the balance sheet, where outstanding bonds carry a rate of 10 percent and preferred stock a dividend rate of 12 percent. The calculations for each type of capital appear as follows, using the methods discussed earlier:

Long-term debt: $k_d = 12.0 \times (1 - .34) = 7.92\%$ after taxes

Preferred stock: $k_p = 13.0\%$ after taxes

Common equity: $k_e = 8.5 + 1.1\ (15.0 - 8.5) = 15.65\%$ after taxes

FIGURE 7–2

ABC CORPORATION
Condensed Balance Sheet
($ thousands)

Assets		Liabilities and Net worth	
Current assets	$27,500	Current liabilities	$ 9,500
Fixed assets (net)	35,000	Bonds (10%)	12,000
Other assets	1,500	Preferred stock (12%) . .	6,000
Total assets		Common stock	
	$64,000	(1.0 million shares) . .	10,000
		Retained earnings	26,500
		Total liabilities and net worth	$64,000

The cost of debt was based on the effective cost of 12 percent, adjusted for taxes, while the effective cost of preferred stock required no tax adjustment. The CAPM was used for the common equity calculation. The CAPM figure can be compared to the less satisfactory answer obtained using the dividend approach, which provides an alternative lower result. This is a function of the current dividend rate and the expected dividend growth rate:

$$\text{Common equity: } k_e = \frac{\$2.50}{\$65} + 6.0\% = 9.85\% \text{ after taxes}$$

It's not uncommon to find that the two approaches to determining the cost of equity provide rather different results, as the data and assumptions going into the calculations are not comparable. We already highlighted the most significant issues when we discussed each measure earlier.

The weights to be used in calculating the corporate cost of capital depend both on the relative stability of the current capital structure and the relevance of market values to the results. Let's assume that management is satisfied with the current capital structure and is likely to raise funds in the same proportions over time. Let's further assume that the existing bonds of the company are currently trading at 83⅜, (a $1,000 bond with a coupon rate of 10 percent is worth a discounted price of about $837.50, in view of the increase in bond yields), while the existing preferred stock with a $12 dividend rate is trading at 92¼ because of the increase in yields (each share with a nominal value of $100 is currently worth about $92.25).

As Figure 7–3 shows, the following proportions result when we list both book value and market value for each type of capital. Depending on the way management assesses its future needs, the proportions could remain as shown in the table, or they could be altogether different.

Assuming that no significant change is foreseen, we can calculate the weighted cost of capital for both the market and book value (Figure 7–4). The results don't differ materially in this case. Differences would become significant only after more than one percentage point.

Given that all the assumptions and choices needed to make the calculations involved some margin of error, the results should be liberally rounded off in all cases before the measure is used as a decision criterion. We can say that under

FIGURE 7–3

Capital Structure of ABC Corporation

	Book Value	Proportion	Market Value	Proportion
Bonds	$12,000	22.0%	$10,050	12.5%
Preferred stock	6,000	11.0	5,535	6.9
Common equity	36,500	67.0	65,000	80.6
Totals	$54,500	100.0%	$80,585	100.0%

FIGURE 7–4

Weighted Cost of Capital for ABC Corporation

	Book Value Weighting			Market Value Weighting		
	Cost	Weight	Composite	Cost	Weight	Composite
Bonds	7.92%	.22	1.74%	7.92%	.12	0.95%
Preferred stock	13.00	.11	1.43	13.00	.07	0.91
Common equity	15.65	.67	10.48	15.65	.81	12.68
Totals		1.00	13.65%		1.00	14.54%

the stipulated conditions for ABC Corporation, the weighted cost of incremental capital is approximately 14 to 15 percent.

If the measure is used to judge the expected return from new investments, it should be viewed as a minimum standard of return from investments with comparable risk characteristics. The weighted cost of capital becomes the discount rate to determine net present values as discussed in Chapter 6. It represents the boundary between projects that create value and those that destroy value for the shareholders.

COST OF CAPITAL AND RETURN STANDARDS

We've stated all along that the basic purpose of deriving a weighted cost of capital was to find a reasonable criterion for measuring new investments. This amounts to establishing a level of return high enough to compensate all providers of funds according to their expectations. By definition, projects with a positive net present value when their cash flows are discounted at this return standard would create economic value for the shareholders in the form of growing dividends and market appreciation.

However, using the weighted cost of capital for this purpose warrants further discussion. In this section, we'll examine more closely the notion of this measure as a *cutoff rate,* and then discuss the question of projects in different *risk categories.* We'll also review the problem of the *multibusiness firm,* in which a variety of business risks are combined. Finally, we'll touch on the issue of modified standards using *multiple discount rates.* In all of these areas, a balance has to be found between the theoretically desirable and the practically doable.

Cost of Capital as a Cutoff Rate

ess company with fairly definable risk characteristics, the apital as calculated here can well serve as a cutoff rate in assessment projects ranked in declining order of economic desirability.

If consistent analytical methods and judgments are applied to projecting the project cash flows, and if the risks inherent in the projects are similar and have been consistently estimated and tested through sensitivity analysis, then acceptance or rejection can be decided with this minimum return standard. We're assuming that the company can finance all of the projects being considered at the same incremental cost of capital and without significantly changing the capital structure.

The weighted cost of capital works well in this idealized condition because the risk premium built into the measure, the proportions of the sources of new funds, and the range of risks embodied in the projects are all consistent with each other as well as the business risk inherent in the company. When some of these conditions change, however, managerial judgment must be exercised to modify the cost of capital and its application.

One common problem, even in the single-business firm, is the real possibility that the amount of potential capital spending will exceed readily available financing to some degree. If the list of projects contains many investments that more than meet the standard, they may be attractive enough for management to modify the company's capital structure to accommodate them—if the management team has the capacity to implement all of them. Then the weighted cost of capital will likely change.

Increasing leverage may introduce additional risk, thus exerting upward pressure on the cost of both debt and equity. A significant increase in the equity base will result in near-term dilution of earnings per share, thus affecting the market value of the stock and possibly the β of the company's common stock as judged by security analysts. While the changes may be manageable, the point is that the process of business investment and the selection of appropriate standards is never a static exercise. .

Another practical issue is management's attitude toward taking business risks. Knowing that the analyses underlying business investment projects contain many uncertainties, management may wish to set the cutoff rate arbitrarily higher than the weighted cost of capital, to allow for estimating errors—and even for deliberate bias in the preparation of the estimates, which is not at all uncommon in most organizations where managers compete for funds. There may also be a desire to play it a little safer in view of the limited reliability of the return standard itself. This adjustment, however, shouldn't be considered a substitute for using the best possible analytical effort and decision analysis tools to sharpen and test the cash flow patterns underlying the investment proposals. As we observed in Chapter 6, risk and uncertainty are a function of the many variables of an investment, which must be understood, quantified, and subjected to sensitivity analysis before appropriate return standards are applied to expected outcome.

From a theoretical standpoint, using cutoff rates significantly higher than the cost of capital may cause opportunity losses, because potentially worthwhile projects are likely to be rejected. From a practical standpoint, however, it may be deemed prudent to leave a margin for error by adding some points to the cost of capital before using it as a cutoff rate. Of course, it's still possible at any time to reach below such a higher standard if a project has many other strategic or operational advantages that mitigate the effects of its marginal economic performance.

Finally, we must reiterate that capital budgeting and project selection are not merely numerical processes. Even in the most tightly focused single-product company, where all levels of management have firsthand knowledge about the intricacies of the business and its competitive setting, the decision process is always a combination of judgments affected by personal preferences, group dynamics, and the pressures of organizational realities.

Risk Categories

By definition, the weighted cost of capital represents a company's unique relative risk and particular capital structure. Yet, in a sense, this is misleading because even in the single-business company, different investment projects do involve different degrees of risk. Normally, a company encounters a variety of classes of investments ranging from replacement of equipment and facilities to expansion in existing markets, and beyond that to ventures into new products or services and new markets.

The degree of risk inherent in these classes of investments will differ, sometimes materially, even though the products and services involved are within the scope of a single industry with a definable overall risk. Replacement of physical assets to continue serving a proven market where the company holds a strong position clearly is far less risky and permits more reliable estimates of cash flow benefits than entering a new domestic or even international market.

A common way of handling such divergences is to set a higher discount standard for projects that are perceived to be riskier, A hierarchy of minimum rates of return can be established, somewhat arbitrarily, that ranges upward from the weighted cost of capital cutoff point. For example, if the weighted cost of capital is, say, 15 percent, that standard may be applied to ordinary replacements and expansion in markets where the company has a position. A standard of 16 or 17 percent may be applied to entering related markets, while a new venture may be measured at a premium standard of even 20 percent or higher.

As we've demonstrated earlier in discussing the power of discounting, particularly at the higher rates, the chances of riskier projects being acceptable will be severely tested under such conditions. Yet such a demanding risk/reward trade-off standard may be appropriate if management's risk preferences are conservative.

On the other hand, it's often argued—particularly in a single-business company—that the weighted cost of capital implicitly embodies the whole range of risks normally encountered while participating and growing in that business. Consequently, it is argued that the range of discount standards should be grouped around the weighted cost of capital. In effect, this allows the less risky projects to be discounted at a return standard *below* the weighted cost of capital, while riskier ones would be tested at or above that level. When all projects are combined, the result should be an average return at or above the weighted cost of capital.

This approach would require, however, that the proportions of projects being approved in the various risk classes be carefully monitored to ensure that the overall average will achieve the desired result over time. Otherwise, the company could encounter significant deviations from expected performance. Moreover, we must remember that shareholder value can grow only if investment returns exceed the cost of capital in the long run.

An additional practical issue tends to support raising the return standards for the different classes of capital projects. Every company faces a certain percentage of capital expenditures that yield no definable cash flow benefits. Among these are mandated outlays for environmental protection, investments for improved infrastructure of facilities, expenditures for office space and equipment, etc.

A strong argument can be made that funds required for these purposes must in fact be economically carried along by the expected cash flow benefits obtained from all other productive investments. By definition, therefore, the total amount of capital invested should provide a return sufficient to meet or exceed the weighted cost of capital. If some part of the capital budget is economically neutral, the returns from the economically positive projects will have to be higher to make up for such "nonproductive" investments. If management chooses to adjust its return standards for this condition, the modification will likely involve a fair degree of judgment about the mix and characteristics of the expected project portfolio.

Our discussion has gone beyond the purely analytical aspects of the subject and we've pointed out many practical issues involved in choosing and using economic measures for business decisions, of which discount standards are only one form. It's important to remember that the actual procedures employed by a company are likely to allow for a fair degree of judgmental override of the quantitative results of any financial analysis. This includes the specific return standards for capital investments, which are likely to be modified from time to time, to assist not only in project-specific economic assessment, but also in shifting the strategic emphasis between classes of investments. Senior management must, of course, continuously monitor and guide the pattern of investments they wish to undertake so that shareholder expectations are met. The pattern of investments suggested by the economic analyses and the return standards can and should be modified to fit the changing strategic direction of a company.

Cost of Capital in Multibusiness Companies

The issues involved in setting appropriate return standards become even more complex when a company has several divisions or subsidiaries engaged in rather different businesses and markets that vary greatly in their risk characteristics. While it's possible to calculate an overall cost of capital for the company with the help of a β that reflects the company's covariance of consolidated returns with the market return, it's far more difficult to derive equivalent cost of capital standards for the individual operating divisions. Most commonly, a multibusiness company has a single capital structure that supplies funds for the various

businesses. Therefore, capital cannot be apportioned to the different risk categories on the basis of individual cost of capital standards that employ specific betas
and debt ratings. These would be available only if the divisions were autonomous
companies whose shares are traded in the securities markets.

The approach often used under such conditions is to estimate a series of
surrogate costs of capital based on costs for independent companies that are comparable to the various businesses, if that's at all possible. From this background, a
group of individual standards can be developed for the multibusiness company—
modified with a great deal of judgment—that are similar to the array of risk categories in a single-business company.

Obviously, the apportionment of capital in a multibusiness setting is also
complicated by the practical issue of divisional managements competing for limited funds while having to meet different standards. Corporate management must
be very careful first to establish broad allocations of funds to the various operating divisions that match the desired corporate strategic emphasis. Then projects
can be ranked within those individual blocks of allocated funds according to the
different discount rates, and decisions can be made to accept or reject specific
investments.

A predictable consequence of such an approach, however, is the dilemma
of having to refuse specific higher return (and perhaps higher risk) opportunities
in one division, whose overall allocation is exhausted, in favor of lower return
(and perhaps lower risk) opportunities in another division. This dilemma has to
be resolved by corporate management, who are responsible for developing and
monitoring the strategic direction of the total company. The main point to remember is that top management needs to shape the company's overall capital
investment portfolio in line with shareholder expectations, so that the sum of the
parts can be expected to meet or exceed the corporate weighted cost of capital
standard.

As we'll discuss in Chapter 9, the cost of capital is also used to determine
whether individual lines of business in a diversified company are contributing to
or detracting from shareholder value creation. Here the point is to test past and
prospective overall cash flows from each business unit as a whole in relation to a
minimum cash flow return standard based on the cost of capital.

Multiple Rate Analysis

One additional technical observation should be made here. Some practitioners argue for applying different discount rates to different portions of the cash flow pattern of a single project when calculating the measures of economic desirability, in
order to reflect the relative riskiness of the various elements of the project. In effect, this is one more risk adjustment beyond the risk premium already inherent in a
particular discount standard. For example, an investment can be separated into elements that carry a business risk, such as products or services, and elements that
carry an investment risk, like land or other resources underlying the former. There
are many variations of this approach, although it is not widely used in practice.

It should be apparent that the uncertainties inherent in project analysis and the complexities of establishing the standards multiple rate analysis may not be warranted in most normal business investment situations. At the same time, they may indeed be necessary in assessing specialized projects, such as real estate investments, complex leasing proposals, and other uniquely structured cash flow proposals. Such special conditions may involve financial contracts integral to the projects themselves.

In those cases, it is warranted to discount portions of project cash flows at rates that reflect their contractual nature, as compared with other portions of the cash flow pattern that are subject to the uncertainties of operating in the business environment. These analytical refinements are too specific to be covered here, but are dealt with in the reference materials listed at the end of the chapter.

KEY ISSUES

The following is a recap of the key issues raised directly or indirectly in this chapter. They are enumerated here to help the reader keep the techniques discussed within the perspective of financial theory and business practice:

1. The specific costs to a company of various types of indebtedness and preferred securities are readily apparent in the tax-adjusted cash obligations involved, but it's difficult to measure the secondary costs implicit in debt service, credit rating, and market assessment.

2. Determining the cost of equity capital is intricately linked to the risk/ reward expectations of the financial markets, because the cost must be expressed in terms of an expected economic return for the shareholders of the company.

3. Simple surrogates for the cost of equity capital, such as earnings and dividend models, suffer from both variability of underlying conditions, which can distort their results, and from conceptual shortcomings.

4. The conceptual link established by modern financial theory between general financial market expectations and the value of an individual company's equity securities remains an approximation based on a series of simplifying assumptions.

5. The use of a company-specific risk factor (β) to adjust average return expectations is a valid theoretical concept, but both definition and measurement of this factor remain open to disagreement and continue to pose practical problems.

6. The development of a weighted cost of capital raises significant questions regarding not only the elements comprising the various costs, but also regarding the weights to be used and the concept of measuring incremental funding.

7. The use of a weighted cost of capital in setting business investment return standards is conceptually useful for projects within a company's normal range of risk, but the measure may need modification for business investments of dissimilar risk.

8. The theory of finance continues to evolve, but as new concepts generated are introduced and refined in the decision-making process, careful linkages to both data sources and to the organization have to be established in order to make practical application both understandable and feasible.

9. Objective analytical approaches to business investment assessment are only one important input in the choices management must make. Individual and group attitudes, preferences, and judgments exert significant influences over interpretation and decision processes in the areas of investment, operations, and financing.

10. The precision implied in the calculations of economic measures like cost of capital or net present value must be tempered by the knowledge that the data and assumptions underlying them are potentially subject to a wide range of error.

SUMMARY

In this chapter, we've sketched out the rationale for determining the costs of various forms of financing as an input in making different types of financial decisions. We found that the specific cost of debt, both short-term and long-term, was relatively easy to calculate, given the nature of the contracts underlying it in most cases. The same was true for preferred stock. We also found that the fixed nature of the obligations incurred with debt and preferred stock raised a host of secondary considerations that exact an economic cost from the company in terms of debt service and restrictive covenants. Establishing the cost of common equity was particularly challenging because of the residual claim common shareholders have on the company, and because of their risk/reward expectations, which are reflected in the market's valuation of the shares.

After discussing techniques for calculating the respective costs of the three basic types of financing, and pointing out the theoretical and practical caveats, we developed the weighted cost of capital as an input to investment analysis. It was characterized as the dividing line between projects that added value and those that destroyed value for the shareholders. We found that use of the weighted cost of capital as a minimum standard for discounting investment cash flows is affected by the way project and business risks are interpreted within the corporate portfolio, and by the attitudes of corporate decision makers. At the same time, we found the approximate weighted cost of capital to be a conceptually appropriate target around which to build a series of return standards befitting a particular company's range of businesses and the investments and risks connected with them.

SELECTED REFERENCES

Brealey, Richard, and Stewart Myers. *Principles of Corporate Finance*. 4th ed. New
    York: McGraw-Hill, 1991.
Ross, Stephen A.; Randolph W. Westerfield; and Jeffrey Jaffe. *Corporate Finance*. 4th
    ed. Burr Ridge, IL.: Richard D. Irwin, 1996.
Weston, J. Fred, and Eugene Brigham. *Essentials of Managerial Finance*. 10th ed.
    Chicago, IL: The Dryden Press, 1992.

SELF STUDY EXERCISES AND PROBLEMS

(Solutions are provided in Appendix V)

1. The GHI company has three types of capital in its capital structure:

    Long-term debt at 12%. (Current yield is 10%.)
    14 % preferred stock. (Current yield is 12%.)
    Common stock with a book value of $67.50 per share.

    Currently, the company's common stock is trading in the range of $75
    to $82; the most recent closing price was $77. The most recent annual
    earnings per share were $9.50, while dividends paid over the past year
    were at the rate of $4.50 per share. The company's earnings have been
    growing on average about 7 percent per year. *Value Line* lists the com-
    pany's β at 1.25, while the risk-free return is estimated to be 9 percent.
    Forecasts for returns from the S&P 500 are currently about 15 percent.
    Calculate the specific cost of capital for each type of capital of GHI
    Company. Assume a tax rate of 34 percent. Discuss your findings.

2. The KLN Company has the following capital structure:

	Proportion	Existing Conditions	Current (Incremental)
Long-term debt	$250	7% average rate	11% yield
Preferred stock	50	6% stated rate	9% yield
Common equity	400	—	Price range $45–$60
(10 million shares)			(Recent price $50)
Total capitalization	$700		

    The company's β is currently estimated at 1.2, while the risk-free
    return is considered to be 7.5 percent. The most recent estimate of the
    return from the S&P 500 is 13.5 percent. Develop the weighted
    corporate cost of capital for KLN Company for both the existing
    conditions (original costs) and incremental conditions. Also use both a
    book value and a market value weighting for each case. Assume a tax
    rate of 34 percent. Discuss your findings and the range of results
    achieved.

CHAPTER 8

Analysis of Financing Choices

Let's now turn to analyzing the third aspect of the three-part decisional systems context introduced in Chapter 1: investment, operations, and *financing*. We'll concentrate on the choices available in arranging a company's long-term financing, while setting aside the incremental operational funds sources used routinely by companies in keeping with the customs of a particular industry or service. We choose this focus because, as was observed in earlier chapters, the nature and pattern of long-term funding sources is intricately connected with the types of business investments made and is critical to the growth, stability, or decline of operations. As we've said before, management must fund its strategic design with an appropriate mix of capital sources that will assist in bringing about the desired increase in shareholder value.

This chapter will deal with the main considerations in assessing the basic financing options open to management. While the choice among debt, preferred, and common equity is blurred by a bewildering array of modifications and specialized instruments in each category, we'll only discuss the main characteristics of the three basic types of securities. Because our emphasis is on quantitative analysis, you must keep in mind that many other considerations enter into these choices. For example, the specific types of business and the industry in which it operates will affect the long-term capital structure chosen at various stages of a company's development, as will the preferences and experiences of senior management and the board of directors. These aspects cannot be adequately covered within the scope of this book.

We'll begin with a framework for analysis that defines the key areas to be analyzed and weighed in choosing sources of long-term financing. Next, we'll look at the techniques of calculating the impact on a company's financial performance from introducing new capital supplied by each of the three basic sources. Then we'll turn to a graphic representation of these results, the *EBIT break-even chart*, in order to demonstrate the dynamic impact funds choices have on changing company conditions. After touching on leasing as a special source, we'll briefly discuss capital structure issues, and list the key issues involved in the area of funds choices.

FRAMEWORK FOR ANALYSIS

Several key elements must be considered and weighed when a company is faced with raising additional (incremental) long-term funds. We'll take up five of these in some detail:

- Cost.
- Risk exposure.
- Flexibility.
- Timing.
- Control.

This framework will serve as a conceptual checklist to ensure that the most important considerations have been covered.

Cost of Incremental Funds

One of the main criteria for choosing from among alternative sources of additional long-term capital is the cost involved in obtaining and servicing the funds. In Chapter 7, we discussed in detail the specific and implicit costs a company incurs in using debt, preferred stock, or common equity.

As a general rule, we found that funds raised through various forms of debt are least costly in specific terms, in part because the interest paid by the borrowing company is tax deductible under current laws. The actual rate of interest charged on incremental debt will depend, of course, on the credit rating of the company and on the degree of change introduced into the capital structure by the new debt. In other words, the specific cost will be affected not only by current market conditions for all long-term debt instruments, but also by the company-specific risk as perceived by the underwriters and investors. As was mentioned earlier, other costs are also implicit in the raising of long-term debt, including legal and underwriting expenses at the time of issue, and the nature and severity of any restrictions imposed by the creditors.

The stated cost of preferred stock is generally higher than debt, partly because preferred dividends are not tax deductible, and partly because preferred stock has a somewhat weaker position on the risk/reward hierarchy, so that holders of these shares expect a higher return. The comparative specific cost of preferred stock is relatively easy to calculate. The dividend level is clearly defined, and legal and underwriting costs incurred at the time of the issue are reflected in the net proceeds to the company. However, at times a variety of specific provisions can involve implicit costs to the company.

Determining the cost of common equity turned out to be a fairly complex task. It involved constructing a theoretical framework within which to assess the risk/reward expectations of the shareholder. Direct approaches (shortcuts) to measuring the specific cost of common equity were found wanting because they didn't address the company's relative risk as reflected in common share values. We had to use a more complex framework involving some surrogates and approximations to arrive at a practical result based on the theoretical model.

The cost of common equity based on the CAPM approach could be directly compared to the specific costs of debt and preferred stock, and it could also be used to arrive at a weighted overall cost of the company's capital structure. As we'll see shortly, however, increasing common equity in the capital structure by issuing new shares involves additional considerations. The incremental shares dilute earnings per share, require additional and even growing dividends where these are paid, and also change the capital structure proportions. These effects introduce implicit economic costs or advantages into the funding picture.

Risk Exposure

If we use *variability of earnings* as a working definition of risk, we find that a company's risk is affected by the specific cost commitments, such as interest on debt or dividends on preferred shares, that each funding source entails. These commitments introduce financial leverage effects in the company's earnings performance, or will heighten any financial leverage already existing. As we've discussed in Chapter 5, the use of instruments involving fixed financial charges will widen the swings in earnings as economic and operating conditions change.

Being responsible for providing holders of common shares with growing economic value, management must therefore expend much thought and care in determining the appropriate mix of debt and equity in the company's capital structure. This balance involves providing enough lower-cost debt to boost the shareholders' returns, but not so much debt as to endanger shareholder value creation during periods of low earnings.

The ultimate risk, of course, is that a company will not be able to fulfill its debt service obligations. The proportion of debt in the capital structure, and similarly, the proportion of preferred stock, affects the degree of risk of partial or total default. Analyzing risk exposure is based on establishing a historical pattern of earnings variability and cash flows from which future conditions are projected. These must take into account the extent to which a company's strategy is changing, any shifts in exposure to the business cycle, shifting competitive pressures, and potential operating inefficiencies.

Clearly, company-specific risk (earnings variability) and the company's ability to service its debt burden are intimately related to the particular characteristics of the business or businesses in which the company operates. Moreover, they're affected by general economic conditions—apart from management's ability to generate satisfactory operating performance.

The degree of financial leverage advisable and prudent will therefore differ greatly for different industries and services, and will also depend on the firm's relative competitive position and maturity stage. A business just starting up entails a far different risk exposure for the creditor than does the established industry leader, apart from the specific industry situation.

Flexibility

The third area we must consider is the question of flexibility, defined here as the range of future funding options that remain once a specific alternative has been chosen. As each increment of financing is completed, the choice among future alternatives may be more limited on the next round. For example, if long-term debt obligations are chosen as a funding source, the level of total debt, restrictive covenants, encumbered assets, and other constraints that impose minimum financial ratios may mean that the company can only use common equity as a future source of capital for some time ahead.

Flexibility essentially requires forward planning. Careful consideration must be given to strategic plans and matching corporate financial policies. Potential acquisitions, expansion, and diversification all are affected by the degree of flexibility management has in choosing proper funding, and by the funds drain resulting from servicing debt commitments. To the extent possible, management must match its planned future funds flows and investment patterns to the pattern of successive rounds of financing that will support them. Having future funds sources limited to only one option because of present commitments can pose a significant problem. Changing conditions in the financial markets for different types of securities may make this single option unappealing or even infeasible when funds needs become critical.

Timing

The fourth element in choosing long-term funding is the timing of the transaction. Timing is important in relation to the movement of prices and yields in the securities markets. Shifting conditions in these markets affect the specific cost a company will incur with each option, in terms of the stated interest rate on new debt or the preferred dividend rate carried by new preferred stock, as well as the proceeds to be received from each of the alternatives. The timing of the issue will therefore affect the cost spread between the several funding alternatives. Specific market conditions may in fact either preclude or distinctly favor particular choices.

For instance, in times of depressed stock prices, bonds may prove to be the most suitable alternative from the standpoint of both cost and market demand. Inasmuch as the proceeds from any issue depend on the success of the placement—public or private—of the securities, the conditions encountered in the stock or bond markets may seriously affect the choice. Uncertainty in financial markets is therefore a strong argument for always maintaining some degree of flexibility in the capital structure.

Control

Finally, the degree of ownership control of the company held by existing shareholders is an important factor as funding choices are considered. Obviously, when new shares of common stock are issued to new shareholders, the effect is a dilution of both earnings per share and the proportion of ownership of the existing shareholders. Such dilution becomes a significant issue for the owners of companies that could be subject to potential raids. In the past decade, the issue of control has been raised to new heights in the many battles over control during the corporate takeover boom.

Even if debt or preferred stock is used as the source of long-term funding, existing shareholders may be indirectly affected because restrictive provisions and covenants may be necessary to obtain bond financing, or because concessions must be made to protect the rights of the more senior preferred shareholders.

Dilution of ownership is a very important issue in closely held corporations, particularly new ventures. In such situations, founders of the company or the major shareholders may exercise full effective control over the company. Issuing new shares will dilute both control over the direction of the company and the key shareholders' ability to enjoy the major share of economic value growth from successful performance. Dilution of earnings and possible retardation of growth in earnings per share brought about by diluting common equity ownership is, of course, not limited to closely held companies. Rather, it's a general phenomenon that we'll discuss shortly.

Finally, dilution of control and earnings is a major consideration in *convertibility,* a very common feature found in certain bonds and preferred stocks. This provision allows conversion of the security into common stock under specified conditions of timing and price. In effect, such instruments are hybrid securities, as they represent delayed issues of common stock at a price higher than the market value of the common stock at the time the convertible bond or preferred stock is issued. We mentioned this feature in earlier chapters in terms of its effect on financial ratios, particularly when discussing the concept of fully diluted earnings per share, and we'll return to it later in this chapter.

Control becomes an issue in convertible financing options because the eventual conversion of the bond or preferred stock will add new common shares to the capital structure and thus cause dilution. The ultimate effect is just like a direct issue of new common stock.

The Choice

It should be clear from this brief résumé of the considerations involved that a decision about alternative sources of long-term funding can't be made alone, even though cost is a most important factor and must be an the decision-making process. Unfortunately, there are no hard spelling out precisely how the final decision should be made, becau depends so much on the circumstances prevailing in the compan securities markets at the time. The best approach is to consider carefully the five areas we've presented above and to examine the pros and cons of each as an input to the decision. Needless to say, a very significant consideration is the effect of each funding source on a company's future earnings performance. In the section that follows, we'll examine methods of calculating this effect.

TECHNIQUES OF CALCULATION

For purposes of illustration, we'll employ the basic statements of a hypothetical company, ABC Corporation. The company is weighing alternative ways of raising $10 million to support the introduction of a new product. After analyzing the corporation's current performance, we'll successively discuss the impact on that performance level caused by introducing long-term debt, preferred stock, and common equity, in equal amounts of $10 million each.

ABC's abbreviated balance sheet is shown in Figure 8–1. The company currently has 1 million shares of common stock outstanding, with a par value of $10 per share. From the company's operating statement (not shown), we learn that ABC Corporation has earned $9 million before taxes on sales of $115 million in the most recent year. Income taxes paid amounted to $3.06 million, an effective rate of 34 percent.

Current Performance

We begin our appraisal of the current performance of ABC Corporation by calculating the earnings per share (EPS) of common stock. Throughout the chapter, this format of calculating EPS and related measures will be used. It is a step-by-step analysis of the earnings impact of each type of long-term capital.

First, we establish the earnings before interest and taxes (EBIT), a measure which was discussed in Chapter 3. From that figure we must subtract a variety of charges applicable to different long-term funds. The first of these is interest charges on long-term debt. Normally short-term interest can be ignored unless it's a

FIGURE 8–1

ABC CORPORATION
Balance Sheet
($ millions)

Assets		Liabilities and Net Worth	
Current assets	$15	Current liabilities	$ 7
Fixed assets (net)	29	Common stock	10
Other assets	1	Retained earnings	28
Total assets	$45	Total liabilities and net worth . .	$45

significant amount, because we assume—given the temporary nature of short- term obligations that arise from ongoing operations—that the related interest charges have been properly deducted from income before arriving at the EBIT figure.

The calculations of earnings per share are shown in Figure 8–2. A provision is made in the table for both long-term interest and preferred dividends. No amounts are shown for these as yet, however, because our hypothetical company at this point has neither long-term debt nor preferred stock outstanding. The calculations result in earnings available to common stock of $5.94 per share. From that figure we must subtract $2.50, which represents a cash dividend voted by the board of directors. We assume that this level of dividend payout (between 40 and 50 percent of earnings) has been maintained for many years. We further assume that earnings have steadily grown by about 4 percent on average over the past decade.

The stock is widely held and traded, and currently commands a market price ranging from about $38 to $47, which means it's trading at roughly seven to eight times earnings. The latest security analyst's report suggests a β of 0.9, while the risk-free rate of return is judged to be 6.5 percent, and the average expected return from the S&P 500 is forecast at 14.0 percent.

Long-term Debt in the Capital Structure

As debt is introduced into this structure, both the financial condition and the earnings performance of ABC Corporation are significantly affected. To raise the $10 million needed to fund the new product, management has found that it's possible, as one alternative, to issue debenture bonds. Debentures are unsecured by any

FIGURE 8–2

ABC CORPORATION
Earnings per Share Calculation
($000, except per share figures)

Earnings before interest and taxes (EBIT)	$9,000
Less: interest charges on long-term debt	-0-
Earnings before income taxes	9,000
Less: Federal income taxes at 34%	3,060
Earnings after income taxes	5,940
Less: Preferred dividends	-0-
Earnings available for common stock	$5,940
Common shares outstanding (number)	1 million
Earnings per share (EPS)	$ 5.94
Less: Common dividends per share	2.50
Retained earnings per share	$ 3.44
Retained earnings in total	$3,440

specific assets of the company; instead they are issued against the company's general credit standing. These bonds, under assumed market conditions, will carry an interest (coupon) rate of 11.5 percent, will become due 20 years from date of issue, and entail a sinking fund provision of $400,000 per year beginning with the fifth year. The balance outstanding at the end of 20 years will be repaid as a balloon payment of $4 million. The company expects to raise the full $10 million from the bond issue after all underwriting expenses, in effect receiving the par value.

Once the new product financed with the proceeds has been successfully introduced, the company projects incremental earnings of at least $2.0 million before taxes. Little risk of product obsolescence or major competitive inroads is expected by management for the next 5 to 10 years, because the company has developed a unique process protected by careful patent coverage.

We can now trace the impact of long-term debt on the company's performance, observing both the change in earnings and dividends, and the specific cost of the newly created debt itself. We'll analyze two contrasting conditions:

■ The immediate impact of the $10 million debt without any offsetting benefits from the new product.

■ The improved conditions expected once the investment has become operative and the new product has begun to generate earnings, probably after one year.

The results of the two calculations are shown in Figure 8–3. The instantaneous effect of adding debt is a reduction of the earnings available for common stock. This is caused by the stated interest cost of 11.5 percent on $10 million of bonds, or $1,150,000 before taxes. Earnings after interest and taxes drop by $759,000 as compared to the initial conditions in Figure 8–2. The reduction represents, of course, the aftertax cost of the bond interest, or $1,150,000 times $(1 - .34)$.

As a consequence, earnings per share decline to $5.18, a drop of 76 cents, or an immediate dilution of 12.8 percent from the prior level. This change is purely due to the incremental interest cost, which on a per share basis amounts to the same 76 cents, that is, the aftertax interest of $759,000 divided by one million shares. In Chapter 7 we discussed the stated annual cost of debt funds, defined as the tax-adjusted rate of interest carried by the debt instrument. Assuming an effective tax rate of 34 percent in our example, the stated cost of debt for ABC Corporation is therefore 7.59 percent. We also explained in Chapter 7 that the specific annual cost of debt is found by relating the stated annual cost to the actual proceeds received. If these proceeds differed from the par value of the debt instrument, the *specific* annual cost of the debt will, of course, be higher or lower than the stated rate.

In the case of ABC Corporation, we assumed that net proceeds were effectively at par, and therefore the specific cost of ABC's new debt is also 7.59 percent, a figure which we'll compare with the specific cost of the other alternatives for raising capital.

FIGURE 8–3

ABC CORPORATION
Earnings per Share with New Bond Issue
($ thousands, except per share figures)

	Before New Product	With New Product
Earnings before interest and taxes (EBIT)	$9,000	$11,000
Less: Interest charges on long-term debt	1,150	1,150
Earnings before income taxes	7,850	9,850
Less: Federal income taxes at 34%	2,669	3,349
Earnings after income taxes	5,181	6,501
Less: Preferred dividends	-0-	-0-
Earnings available for common stock	$5,181	$ 6,501
Common shares outstanding (number)	1 million	1 million
Earnings per share (EPS)	$ 5.18	$ 6.50
Less: Common dividends per share	2.50	2.50
Retained earnings per share	$ 2.68	$ 4.00
Retained earnings in total	$2,681	$ 4,001
Original EPS (Figure 8–2)	$ 5.94	$ 5.94
Change in EPS	−0.76	+0.56
Percent change in EPS	−12.8%	+9.4%

When we turn to the second column of Figure 8–3, we find that the assumed successful introduction of the new product will more than compensate ABC Company for the earnings impact of the interest paid on the bonds. In other words, the investment project is earning more than the specific cost of the debt employed to fund it. Aftertax earnings have risen to $6,501,000, a net increase of $561,000 over the original $5,940,000 in Figure 8–2. As a consequence, earnings per share rose 56 cents above the original $5.94, an increase of almost 10 percent.

By more than offsetting the total aftertax interest cost of the debentures of $759,000, the successful new investment is projected to boost the common shares' earnings. Incremental earnings of $1,320,000 ($2 million pretax earnings less tax at 34 percent) significantly exceed the incremental cost of $759,000. Therefore, the investment—if ABC's earnings assumptions prove realistic—has made possible an increment of economic value. In effect, the financial leverage introduced with the debt alternative is positive.

Yet, several questions might be asked. For example, suppose the investment earned just $759,000 after taxes, exactly covering the cost of the debt supporting it and maintaining the shareholders' position just as before in terms of earnings per share. Would the investment still be justified? Would this mean that the investment was made at no cost to the shareholders?

At first glance, one might believe this, but a number of issues must be considered here. First of all, no mention has been made of the sinking fund obligations which will begin five years hence and which represent a cash outlay of $400,000 per year. Such principal payments are not tax deductible and must be paid out of the aftertax cash flow generated by the company. Thus, debt service (burden coverage) will require 40 cents per share over and above the interest cost of 76 cents per share, for a total of $1.16 per share. The $400,000 will no longer be available for dividends or other corporate purposes, because it is committed to the repayment of principal. If we suppose that earnings from the investment exactly equaled the interest cost of the debt, how would the company repay the principal? At what point are the shareholders better off than they were before?

There's an obvious fallacy in this line of discussion. It stems from the use of accounting earnings to represent the benefits of the project and comparing these to the aftertax cost of the debt capital used to finance it. This isn't a proper economic comparison, as we pointed out in Chapters 6 and 7. Only a time-adjusted cash flow analysis can determine the true economic cost/benefit trade-off. We could say that the project was exactly yielding the specific cost of the debt capital associated with it only if the net present value of the project was exactly zero when we discount the incremental annual cash flows at 7.59 percent.

This result would then represent an internal rate of return of 7.59 percent, a level of economic performance that would scarcely be acceptable to management. Yet even under that condition, the project's cash flows (as contrasted to the accounting profit recorded in the operating statement) would have to be higher than the $759,000 aftertax earnings required to pay only the interest on the bonds. This must be so because under the present value framework of investment analysis, the incremental cash flows associated with a project must be sufficient not only to provide the specified return but also to amortize the investment itself.

Let's now return to the real purpose of this analytical framework. Our analysis isn't designed to judge the desirability of the investment; we must assume that this has been adequately done by management. Instead, we're interested only in which alternative form of financing is most advantageous for the company under the circumstances presented. In this context, the impact of each alternative on the company's earnings is just one of several aspects in deciding on new funding.

In the case of debt, which under normal conditions is the lowest cost alternative, we would indeed expect a financial leverage effect in favor of the shareholder. When the project was chosen, it must have met a return standard based approximately on the weighted cost of capital—a return which far exceeds the cost of debt capital alone.

The introduction of debt, in summary, immediately dilutes earnings per share, but this impact is followed by a boost in earnings per share as the project's reported accounting earnings exceed the interest cost as reflected in the company's income statement. The company must allow for the future sinking fund payments from a cash planning standpoint, because beginning with the fifth year, 40 cents per share of the company's cash flow will be committed annually to repayment of principal.

It's generally useful to examine the implications of these facts under a variety of conditions, that is, the risk posed by earnings fluctuations in both the basic business and in the new products' incremental profit contribution, which all along we've assumed to be successful. We'll take such variations into account later.

Preferred Stock in the Capital Structure

ABC Corporation could also meet its long-term financing needs with an alternative issue of $10 million of preferred stock, at $100 per share, which carries a stated dividend rate of 12.5 percent. For simplicity, we'll again assume that the net proceeds to the company will be equivalent to the nominal price of $100, after legal and underwriting expenses. Figure 8–4 analyzes the conditions before and after the introduction of the new product project.

This time we find a more severe drop in the earnings available for common stock, due to the impact of the preferred dividends of $1.25 million per year. Not only is the stated cost (as well as the specific cost, given that the net proceeds were again at par) of the new preferred stock higher by one full percentage point than the stated cost of the bonds, but also the dividends paid on the preferred stock are not tax deductible under current laws. In fact, we are dealing with an

FIGURE 8–4

ABC CORPORATION
Earnings per Share with New Preferred Stock Issue
($000, except per share figures)

	Before New Product	With New Product
Earnings before interest and taxes (EBIT)	$9,000	$11,000
Less: Interest charges on long-term debt	-0-	-0-
Earnings before income taxes	9,000	11,000
Less: Federal income taxes at 34%	3,060	3,740
Earnings after income taxes	5,940	7,260
Less: Preferred dividends	1,250	1,250
Earnings available for common stock	$4,690	$ 6,010
Common shares outstanding (number)	1 million	1 million
Earnings per share (EPS)	$ 4.69	$ 6.01
Less: Common dividends per share	2.50	2.50
Retained earnings per share	$ 2.19	$ 3.51
Retained earnings in total	$2,190	$ 3,510
Original EPS (Figure 8–2)	$ 5.94	$ 5.94
Change in EPS	-1.25	+0.07
Percent change in EPS	-21.0%	+1.2%

alternative which costs, in comparable terms, 12.5 percent after taxes versus 7.59 percent after taxes for the bonds.

Therefore, the immediate dilution in earnings with the preferred issue is $1.25 per share, or 21 percent, when compared to the initial situation. Over time, as the earnings from the new product are realized, the eventual increase in earnings per share amounts to only 7 cents, or a slight improvement of 1.2 percent. The $1.25 million annual commitment of aftertax funds for dividends leaves very little room for any net gain in reported profit from the earnings generated by the investment—which we know are estimated as $2.0 million before taxes and $1,320,000 after taxes.

In this situation, the assumed conditions allow for very limited financial leverage. Only little more than a 1 percent rise in earnings per share is achieved over the starting level, inasmuch as the fixed aftertax financing costs introduced have nearly doubled when compared to the bond alternative. Earnings per share would be unchanged if the product were to achieve minimum earnings in the amount of the pretax cost of the preferred dividends:

$$\frac{\$1,250,000}{(1-.34)} = \$1,894,000$$

At that level, the incremental earnings from the new product would just offset the incremental financing cost—a break-even situation. Note that the sizable earnings requirement of almost $1.9 million is two-thirds larger than the $1,150,000 pretax interest cost with the bond alternative.

Common Stock in the Capital Structure

A new issue of common stock as the third alternative for raising $10 million has an even more severe impact on earnings. Let's assume that ABC Corporation will issue 275,000 new shares at a net price to the company of $36.36 after underwriters' fees and legal expenses are met. Such a discount from the current market price of $40 should help ensure successful placement of the issue. The number of shares outstanding thus increases by 27.5 percent over the current 1.0 million shares. Figure 8–5 shows the impact on earnings in the same way as was done for the other two alternatives.

We observe that immediate dilution is a full $1.28 per share, a drop of 21.5 percent, which is the highest impact of the three choices analyzed. Common stock, in terms of this comparison, is the costliest form of capital—if only because it results in the greatest immediate dilution in the earnings of current shareholders.

Moreover, there will also be an annual cash drain of at least $687,500 in aftertax earnings from the 275,000 new shares, if the current $2.50 annual dividend on common stock is maintained. Further, we can project that this cash drain could grow at the historical earnings growth rate of 4 percent per year. This assumption will hold if the directors continue their policy of declaring regular cash dividends at a fairly constant payout rate from future earnings that continue

FIGURE 8–5

ABC CORPORATION
Earnings per Share with New Common Stock Issue
($000, except per share figures)

	Before New Product	With New Product
Earnings before interest and taxes (EBIT)	$9,000	$11,000
Less: Interest charges on long-term debt	-0-	-0-
Earnings before income taxes	9,000	11,000
Less: Federal income taxes at 34%	3,060	3,740
Earnings after income taxes	5,940	7,260
Less: Preferred dividends	-0-	-0-
Earnings available for common stock	$5,940	$ 7,260
Common shares outstanding (number)	1.275 million	1.275 million
Earnings per share (EPS)	$ 4.66	$ 5.69
Less: Common dividends per share	2.50	2.50
Retained earnings per share	$ 2.16	$ 3.19
Retained earnings in total	$2,752	$ 4,072
Original EPS (Figure 8–2)	$ 5.94	$ 5.94
Change in EPS	-1.28	-0.25
Percent change in EPS	-21.5%	-4.2%

growing. For the present, the pretax earnings required to cover the $2.50 per share dividend amount to:

$$\$2.50 \times 275{,}000 \text{ shares} = \$687{,}500 \text{ (after taxes)}$$

$$\frac{\$687{,}500}{(1 - .34)} = \$1{,}042{,}000 \text{ (before taxes)}$$

We can directly compare this earnings requirement of about $1.05 million to the alternative bond requirement of $1.15 million and the preferred stock requirement of $1.90 million. From both an earnings and a cash planning standpoint, these amounts and the differences between them are clearly significant.

The effect of immediate dilution of earnings is only part of the consideration. There will be the second-stage effect of *continuing dilution,* because in contrast to the other two types of capital, the new common shares created represent an ongoing residual claim on corporate earnings on a par with that of the existing shares. Thus, the rate of growth in earnings per share experienced to date will be slowed in the future, merely because more shares will be outstanding— unless, of course, the earnings provided by the investment of the proceeds are superior in level and potential growth to the existing earnings performance.

When we turn to the second column of Figure 8–5, it's apparent that despite the incremental earnings from the new product, the net dilution of earnings per share in the amount of 25 cents, or 4.2 percent, will in fact continue. The contribution of the new product to reported earnings wasn't sufficient to meet the earnings claims of the new shareholders and maintain the old per share earnings level. The negative impact on earnings of the common stock alternative thus is greater than the earnings generated by the new capital raised.

Up to this point, we've dealt with the earnings impact of common stock financing. To find a first rough approximation of the specific cost of this alternative, we can establish as a minimum condition the maintenance of the old earnings per share level, and relate this to the proceeds from each new share of common stock. The current EPS of $5.94 (Figure 8–2) and the proceeds of $36.36 result in a cost of about 16 percent:

$$\frac{\$5.94}{\$36.36} = 16.34\% \text{ (after taxes)}$$

Recall from the discussion in Chapter 7, however, that using accounting earnings in measuring the cost of common equity is not appropriate. If we employ the dividend approach to find the specific cost of the incremental common stock, as discussed in Chapter 7, we must relate the current dividend per share to the net price received, and add prospective dividend growth. We know that the company has experienced fairly consistent growth in earnings of 4 percent per year, and we'll assume that, given a constant rate of dividend payout, common dividends will continue to grow at the same rate. The result is a cost of about 11 percent:

$$\frac{\$2.50}{\$36.36} + 4.0 = 10.9\%$$

As we stated in Chapter 7, however, the dividend approach is limited in concept and usefulness. Therefore, let's now use the background data provided to test the specific cost of capital for ABC's common equity with the CAPM approach explained in Chapter 7.

The resulting cost of common equity, k_e, is approximately 13.25 percent when we put into the CAPM formula the risk-free return, R_f, of 6.5 percent, the β of 0.9, and the expected average return, R_m, represented by the S&P 500 estimate of 14 percent:

$$k_e = R_f + \beta \ (R_m - R_f)$$
$$k_e = 6.5 + 0.9(14.0 - 6.5)$$
$$k_e = 13.25\%$$

This result is the most credible one for judging the specific cost of the common stock. It can be compared to the specific cost of the bonds of 7.59 percent, and to the specific cost of the preferred stock of 12.5 percent.

Clearly, the common equity alternative is the most expensive source of financing, and we have already established that the dilution effect is also serious.

In addition, the cash flow requirements for paying the current dividend of $2.50 per share plus any future increases in the common dividend have to be planned for. Because it's difficult to keep all of these quantitative aspects visible in our deliberations, let's now turn to a graphic representation of the various earnings and dilution effects to compare the relative position of the three alternatives.

EBIT BREAK-EVEN CHART

We've referred several times to changes in the earnings performance of a company and the different impact the three basic financing alternatives have under varying conditions. The static format of analysis we've used so far does not readily allow us to explore the range of possibilities as earnings change, or to visualize the sensitivity of the alternative funding sources to these changes. It would be quite laborious to calculate earnings per share and other data for a great number of earnings levels and assumptions. Instead, we can exploit the direct linear relationships that exist between the quantitative factors analyzed.

A graphic break-even approach can be used to compare the earnings impact of alternative sources of financing. In this section, we'll show how such a model, keyed to fluctuations in EBIT and resulting EPS levels, can be employed to display important quantitative aspects of the relative desirability of the choices available. As we'll see, the break-even model allows us to perform a variety of analytical tests with ease.

To begin with, we've summarized the data for ABC Corporation in Figure 8–6. Variations in these data can then be displayed graphically in a simple break-even chart which shows earnings per share (EPS) on the vertical axis and EBIT on the horizontal axis. This EBIT chart allows us to plot on straight lines the EPS for each alternative under varying conditions, and to find the break-even points between them.

Commonly, one of the reference points is the intersection of each line with the horizontal axis, that is, the exact spot where EPS is zero. These points can easily be found by working the EPS calculations backward, that is, starting with an assumed EPS of zero and deriving an EBIT that just provides for this condition. The calculation is shown in Figure 8–7 for the original situation and for each of the three alternatives. The data in Figures 8–6 and 8–7 give us sufficient points with which to draw the linear functions of EPS and EBIT for the various alternatives, as shown in Figure 8–8.

We can quickly observe that the conclusions about the earnings impact of the alternatives we drew from the two EBIT levels previously analyzed, $9 million and $11 million, hold true over the fairly wide range of earnings presented. That is, every alternative considered causes a significant reduction in earnings per share relative to the original condition.

There's a major new observation, however. Under the common stock alternative, the slope of the EPS line is different. In fact, the line for common stock intersects both the debt and the preferred stock lines. The latter two lines are parallel with each other and also with the line representing the original situation,

FIGURE 8–6

ABC CORPORATION
Recap of EPS Analyses with New Product
($ thousands, except per share figures)

	Original	Debt	Preferred	Common
EBIT	$9,000	$11,000	$11,000	$11,000
Less: Interest	-0-	1,150	-0-	-0-
Earnings before taxes	9,000	9,850	11,000	11,000
Less: Taxes at 34%	3,060	3,349	3,740	3,740
Earnings after taxes	5,940	6,501	7,260	7,260
Less: Preferred dividends	-0-	-0-	1,250	-0-
Earnings available for common stock	$5,940	$ 6,501	$ 6,010	$ 7,260
Common shares outstanding (number)	1 million	1 million	1 million	1.275 million
EPS	$ 5.94	$ 6.50	$ 6.01	$ 5.69
Less: Common dividends	2.50	2.50	2.50	2.50
Retained earnings	$ 3.44	$ 4.00	$ 3.51	$ 3.19
Retained earnings in total	$3,440	$ 4,001	$ 3,510	$ 4,072
Original EPS change		−12.8%	−21.0%	−21.5%
Final EPS change		+9.4%	+1.2%	−4.2%
Specific cost		7.59%	12.5%	13.25%

FIGURE 8–7

ABC CORPORATION
Zero EPS Calculation
($ thousands, except per share figures)

	Original	Debt	Preferred	Common
EPS	-0-	-0-	-0-	-0-
Common shares	1 million	1 million	1 million	1.275 million
Earnings to common	-0-	-0-	-0-	-0-
Preferred dividends	-0-	-0-	$1,250	-0-
Earnings after taxes	-0-	-0-	1,250	-0-
Taxes at 34%	-0-	-0-	644	-0-
Earnings before taxes	-0-	-0-	1,894	-0-
Interest	-0-	$1,150	-0-	-0-
EBIT or zero EPS	-0-	$1,150	$1,894	-0-

FIGURE 8–8

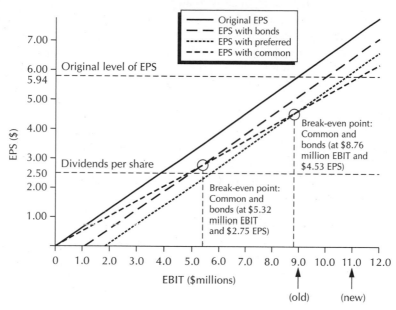

ABC CORPORATION
Range of EBIT and EPS Chart

both appearing to the right of that line. The lesser slope of the common stock line is easily explained. Introducing new shares of common stock results in a proportional dilution of earnings per share at all EBIT levels. As a consequence, the incremental shares cause earnings per share to rise less rapidly with growth in EBIT.

In contrast, the parallel shift by the debt and preferred stock lines to the right of the original line is caused by the introduction of fixed interest or dividend charges, while at the same time the number of common shares outstanding remains constant over the EBIT range studied.

The significance of the intersections should now become apparent. They are break-even points at which, for a given EBIT level, the EPS for the common stock alternative and one of the other two alternatives are the same. Note that the break-even point of common stock line with the bond alternative occurs at about $5.3 million EBIT, while the break-even point of common stock with preferred stock occurs at about $8.8 million EBIT.

Below $5.0 million EBIT, therefore, the common stock alternative causes the least EPS dilution, while above $9 million EBIT, it causes the worst relative dilution in EPS. Recall that ABC's current EBIT level is $9.0 million, and is expected to be at least $11 million once the new product is fully contributing its projected earnings. Both break-even points thus lie below the likely future EBIT performance, which makes the common stock alternative the costliest in terms of earnings dilution.

Therefore, it's not possible to assess the three alternatives without defining a "normal" range of EBIT for the company's expected performance, given that relative earnings effects of the three alternatives are different over the wide range of EBIT shown. If future EBIT levels could in fact be expected to move fairly well within the two break-even points, common stock looks more attractive than preferred stock from the standpoint of EPS dilution, but worse than debt. If EBIT can be expected to grow and move fairly well to the right of the second break-even point, as is almost certain in the case of ABC Corporation, new common stock is not only least attractive from the standpoint of EPS dilution, but will remain so.

All of these considerations depend, of course, on unchanging assumptions about the terms under which the three forms of incremental capital could be is-sued. If we can expect any of these terms to change significantly, such as the offering price of the common stock, or the terms of the bond, an entirely new chart must be drawn up, or we must at least reflect any possible discontinuities in cost or proportions of the alternatives as EBIT levels change.

The intersections between the EPS lines that represent the EBIT break-even points for the common stock alternative with the other two choices can be quite easily calculated. For this purpose, we formulate simple equations for the conditions underlying any intersecting pair of lines. EPS are then set as equal for the two alternatives, and the equations are solved for the specific EBIT level at which this condition holds. To illustrate, let's first establish the following definitions:

E = EBIT level for any break-even point with common stock alternative.
i = Annual interest on bonds in dollars (before taxes).
t = Tax rate applicable to the company.
d = Annual preferred dividends in dollars.
s = Number of common shares outstanding.

The equation for any of the EPS lines can be found by substituting known facts for the symbols in the following generalized equation:

$$\text{EPS} = \frac{(E - i)\,(1 - t) - d}{s}$$

We can now find the EBIT break-even levels for bonds and common stock at the point of EPS equality. For this purpose, we fill in the data for the two expressions and set them as equal:

$$\begin{array}{cc}
\textit{Bonds} & \textit{Common} \\
\dfrac{(E - \$1,150,000).66 - 0}{1,000,000} = & \dfrac{(E - 0).66 - 0}{1,275,000}
\end{array}$$

When we solve for E we obtain the following result:

$$0.66E - \$759,000 = \frac{0.66E}{1.275}$$

$$0.842E - \$967,725 = 0.66E$$

$$E = \$5,317,000$$

This break-even level of $5.32 million can easily be verified graphically in Figure 8–8.

When the same approach is applied to the preferred and common stock alternatives, the following result emerges:

$$\begin{array}{cc} Preferred & Common \end{array}$$

$$\frac{(E - 0).66 - \$1,250,000}{1,000,000} = \frac{(E - 0).66 - 0}{1,275,000}$$

$$\frac{0.66E - \$1,250,000}{} = \frac{0.66E}{1.275}$$

$$0.842E - \$1,593,750 = 0.66E$$

$$E = \$8,757,000$$

Again, the chart can be used to verify the break-even level of $8.76 million.

We can also use the EBIT chart to show the impact of different assumptions about common dividends on the three alternatives. For example, the horizontal line at $2.50 in the chart represents the current annual common dividend. Where this line intersects any alternative EPS line we can read off the minimum level of EBIT required to supply this dividend. Similarly, it's possible to reflect in the chart the earnings requirements for sinking funds or other regular repayment provisions. In effect, such annual provisions commit a portion of future earnings for this purpose.

We can develop the effect of these requirements by carrying the calculations one step further and arriving at the so-called *uncommitted earnings per share (UEPS)* for each alternative after provision for any repayments. We simply subtract the per share cost of such repayments (that require aftertax dollars) from the respective EPS of the alternative thus affected, and redraw the lines in the chart. The result will be a parallel shift of the affected line to the right of its prior position.

For example, the sinking fund requirement of $400,000 per year in the bond alternative would represent 40 cents per share, and the new line for bonds would move to the right by this amount over its whole range. Similarly, the intersection at the zero EPS point, currently $1,150,000 EBIT, would move right to a zero UEPS point of $1,756,000. This shift reflects the sinking fund requirement of $400,000 per year, which translates into an incremental pretax earnings requirement of $400,000 ÷ (1 − 0.34), or $606,000. In this case, the UEPS line for bonds would move very close to the EPS line for preferred stock in Figure 8–8.

By now the usefulness of this earnings framework for a dynamic analysis of the various financing alternatives should be clear. The reader is invited to think through the implications of the variety of tests that can be applied. It's possible, for example, to determine the minimum EBIT level under each alternative which would cover the current common dividend of $2.50 per share, while assuming a variety of different payout ratios, such as 50 percent or 40 percent. For example, with an assumed 50 percent payout, EPS would have to be $5. A horizontal line would be drawn at the $5 EPS level, and its intersection with the lines of the various alternatives would represent the minimum EBIT levels for the $2.50 dividend. The analyst would have to assess the likelihood of EBIT declining to this level, and judge whether this endangers the current dividend payout. Other tests can be applied, of course, depending on the particular circumstances of the company.

While we have concentrated on the earnings implications of the choice, it should be clear that the framework can also be used to work through the cash flow implications of each of the results, by translating the respective EBIT levels into equivalent cash flow from operations, as discussed in Chapters 2 and 3. This would bring the analysis closer to the valuation concepts we'll take up in the final chapter—recognizing that cash flows are the ultimate drivers of company performance and value. Among the extra steps required are calculating the tax shield effect of depreciation and depletion write-offs, elimination of other accounting adjustments, and recognition of new investment requirements. Computer spreadsheet analysis can be used to make the multiple calculations required.

Again we must emphasize, however, that any one specific EBIT chart works only under fixed assumptions about proceeds received and about stable interest and preferred dividend rates. If there's reason to believe that any of the key assumptions might change, the positions of the EPS lines on the graph must be adjusted.

Obviously, any changes in the relative cost of the various alternatives will also have an effect. As the spread between the alternatives increases, for example, the differences in earnings impact will widen, and thus the distance between the parallel lines will increase. This simply reflects that imposing higher-cost fixed obligations depresses EPS.

Enlarging the amount of capital issued also has an effect, because the slope of the line is determined by the amount of leverage already present in the existing capital structure. In other words, if there's already some debt and preferred stock in the capital structure, the basic EPS would rise and fall much more sharply with changes in EBIT. Any increases in the fixed-cost alternatives would simply magnify this leverage. At the same time, the slope of the EPS line for common equity is governed by the relative number of shares issued, which in turn is related to the degree of earnings dilution, as demonstrated in the example.

Financial planning models and computer spreadsheets can be used to enhance the basic analysis demonstrated here. The point to remember, however, is that this analysis in essence quantifies the relative impact of the alternatives on reported accounting earnings. This effect is but one of the many factors that have to be weighed in making funding choices. As we mentioned in the beginning of this chapter, the conceptual and practical setting for the eventual decision is far more inclusive than this graphic expression of respective break-even conditions suggests. Strategic plans for the future, risk expectations, market factors, the specific criteria we listed, and current company conditions all have to enter the final judgment.

SOME SPECIAL FORMS OF FINANCING

Our earlier discussion focused on the very basic choice between debt, preferred stock, and common stock, setting aside the many variations often found in these instruments as well as in other specialized forms of financing. We'll now briefly cover several more specialized areas of financing choices, namely *convertible* bonds and preferred stocks, *rights offerings, warrants,* and *leasing.*

Convertible Securities

As we stated earlier, convertibility into common shares is a feature sometimes added to issues of bonds or preferred stocks for reasons of marketability and timing. The essence of convertibility is simply that the issuing company is in effect able to sell common shares at prices higher than those prevailing at the time the bond or preferred stock is issued. This is due to the fact that the *conversion price* for the common stock it represents is set at an expected future level, based on the company's value growth experience and expectation.

The conversion price is the basis for the *conversion ratio* set for the bond or preferred issue. For example, a new $100 convertible preferred may have a conversion ratio of 3, that is, each share of preferred stock is convertible into three shares of common stock. This represents a conversion price of $33.33 per common share, while the company's shares may currently be trading in the $25 to $27 range. The difference between current price and the conversion price is called the *conversion premium.* The same approach applies to bonds, which are usually denominated in thousand-dollar units.

Given the expectation that the company's common stock will in time exceed the conversion price, the bond or preferred stock will trade at values that reflect both the underlying interest or dividend yield, and the *conversion value* itself. Initially the stated yield will predominate, but when common share prices begin to exceed the conversion price, the price of the bond or preferred stock will be boosted to reflect the current market value of the underlying common shares. This is the point at which conversion becomes increasingly attractive to the investor. If share prices remain below the conversion price, however, the conversion value will always be the floor value for the bond or preferred—while the actual price will depend on the yield provided by the stated interest rate or the preferred dividend.

Given the potential attraction of conversion to the investor, the issuing company usually pays a somewhat lower rate of interest or preferred dividend on these instruments. To limit the time period over which these securities are outstanding, the company can usually force conversion—once the market price of common stock has reached the conversion price—by exercising the *call provision* (the right of the company to redeem all or part of the issue) included in most convertible issues. This provision is usually based on a predetermined price close to the conversion price.

Convertibility adds a number of considerations to the three basic choices we discussed earlier. Because successful convertible issues eventually result in an increase in common shares, the delayed impact on control, earnings per share, and the amount of future common dividends must be taken into account in the analysis. The graphic display we used earlier can be applied by showing this alternative in two forms:

- The convertible bond or preferred as a straight bond or preferred.

- The additional common shares from eventual conversion.

As long as significant convertible issues remain outstanding, companies are required to calculate fully diluted earnings per share, as discussed in Chapter 3.

Stock Rights

A so-called *rights offering* is a form of common stock financing that minimizes the dilution of existing shareholders' proportional holdings. Also referred to as a *privileged subscription,* such an offering provides to each existing shareholder a proportional number of rights to purchase a specified number of new common shares from the company at an advantageous *subscription price* during a limited time period, after which the rights expire. The number of rights issued matches the number of shares of common stock outstanding, and a defined number of rights are necessary to purchase each share of new stock. Rights are issued as special certificates and are often traded on securities exchanges or in the over-the-counter market.

To illustrate, if the XYZ Company has 1 million common shares outstanding and wishes to sell 250,000 new shares, 1 million rights will be issued to existing shareholders with the provision that four rights are required to purchase a new share of stock at the subscription price. If the subscription price is $30, while the current market price is $40, a shareholder has to surrender 4 rights and $30 to the company to receive another share currently worth $40.

The attraction to a company of this course of action is, apart from limiting the potential for dilution of control, a direct appeal for funds to a group of investors already familiar with its history and outlook. If so inclined, a shareholder will exercise the rights by purchasing directly from the company the number of shares specified at the set subscription price. If the shareholder isn't interested, the rights can be sold as such, because they'll reflect the value differential between the subscription price and the market price of the stock. We'll return to determining the value of rights to the investor in Chapter 9.

The analytical implications of this alternative are quite similar to those of a public offering, which we assumed to be the case earlier in the chapter. The subscription price may differ somewhat from the price the underwriters provide in a public offering, but otherwise the analysis will parallel the common stock alternative we explored.

Warrants

Warrants are a form of corporate security that entitle the holder to purchase a specified number of common shares at a fixed *exercise price* over a stated period of time. Some warrants even have no expiration date. They are issued as an added incentive for investors to purchase a new public issue of bonds, or a private placement of loans or bonds. Sometimes warrants are even issued as part of an offering of common stock. The proportion of warrants issued with the new offering will vary depending on the exercise price and the degree of incentive desired to move the new debt issue into the hands of investors. Warrants are attached to these new securities as part of the offering, but in most cases, they can be detached by the holder and sold separately if desired. Numerous warrants are traded at any time in the securities markets.

In effect, a warrant gives the holder the option to buy common stock if it's advantageous to do so; i.e., if the exercise price is below the market price. Just as in the case of rights, when a warrant is exercised, the funds go directly to the company. Since warrants, in contrast to rights, are valid for relatively long time periods, there is the potential for earnings dilution from unexpired warrants. Companies with significant numbers of warrants outstanding must calculate fully diluted earnings per share, just as in the case of convertible issues outstanding (Chapter 3).

The main implication for analysis of a new debt offering with attached warrants is the need to recognize the potential funds inflow from new shares as warrants are exercised, and the earnings dilution from these shares. Our graphic analysis has to be modified to allow for the combination of these effects. We'll return to the value of warrants in Chapter 9.

Leasing

We've referred to leasing at several points in this book. Leasing is a special form of financing that gives a company access to a whole range of assets, from buildings to automobiles, without having to acquire these items outright. The lessee pays an agreed upon periodic fee that covers the lessor's ownership costs, financing and tax expenses, and also provides an economic return. The lessee can use the asset for a specified period, assumes none of the risks of ownership or technical obsolescence, and can replace or upgrade the asset while the lessor assumes the task of disposing of the old items. The latter provision is particularly appealing in the case of computers or technical equipment. The lessee, in effect, only incurs a tax-deductible periodic expense.

Long-term lease contracts, particularly for buildings, can extend over many years and thus become, in fact, part of a company's financial structure. Current accounting practice requires the disclosure of lease obligations in a company's published financial statements if such leases represent a commitment of material size. While leases are not normally included as liabilities in the balance sheet itself, footnotes to the balance sheet must disclose the amount of periodic payments and an estimated capitalized value of the lease obligations.

Such disclosure recognizes the fact that lease obligations represent a financial burden that must be serviced just like any other form of financing. Any company that leases a significant portion of its assets has less flexibility in its financing choices. The effect is the same as that of a large outstanding long-term debt. Fixed leasing charges introduce a degree of leverage into the company's operations that is quite comparable to leverage resulting from other sources.

There are many considerations involved in the choice of leasing versus ownership. Very importantly, this comparison must not be made until after the cash flow economics of the project involved indicate that it will add value to the company. Thereafter, leasing can properly be considered as merely one form of financing. When comparing the leasing cash flow pattern to that of ownership, the specific financing cost embodied in the periodic lease payments must be separated or removed. Remember, all cash flow analyses must be made before the specific financing costs involved, because the cost of capital discount standard represents the overall cost of funding. We'll not deal with the techniques of analyzing the cash flow implications of the many types of leasing arrangements, because they are too specialized and complex to be covered here. But we must recognize that leasing involves an economic cost, because the lessor must be compensated for providing, financing, servicing, and replacing the asset. By definition, leasing charges must be high enough to make leasing attractive for the lessor. At the same time, the lessor is often able to use economies of scale in acquiring the assets that may favorably affect the cost of leasing, as is the case with major equipment leasing companies, for example.

The comparative analysis necessary to make the final choice between leasing and ownership has to weigh such elements as the periodic expense to the lessee, any technological advantages from being able to use the latest in facilities and equipment, services received as part of the contract, the flexibility of not being tied down by ownership, and the impact on the company's financial position. As in all financial analyses, the choice is based on both quantifiable data and management judgment. In some industries, leasing is part of the normal way of doing business. For example, in wholesaling, warehouses are commonly leased, and in the transportation industry, leasing of rolling stock, trucks, and aircraft prevails. In other areas, the choice of leasing is wide open and depends on what financing alternative is considered advantageous at the time.

THE OPTIMAL CAPITAL STRUCTURE

A great deal of theoretical and practical effort continues to be expended on determining the optimal mix of different long-term capital sources in a company's capital structure. This book is not the place to explore the many intricate conceptual issues involved, but a few comments are in order. We referred many times to the fact that financial decision making involves a series of economic trade-offs as well as the personal judgments and risk preferences of the key managers and directors. Such is the case with the design and modification of capital structure proportions.

The key trade-off is one of risk versus reward. Introducing leverage into a capital structure will, as we've observed before, tend to lower the overall cost of capital because of the least-cost nature of debt. This is not a static condition, however, because increasing amounts of debt expose the company to greater risk of earnings (and cash flow) variability, as well as potential default on the principal. Theoretical models of finding the optimal cost of capital take into account the dynamics of changing proportions of debt, preferred stock, and equity. Many studies have shown that, as a general rule, the cost of capital will tend to be lowest at debt proportions of around one-third versus two-thirds of equity in various forms. The specific risk characteristics of the company and its industry clearly will affect this general result.

The evidence also shows that the overall cost of capital generally moves in a relatively narrow band between the extremes of leverage conditions, usually no more than two percentage points. This is due in part to the tax-deductibility of interest which moderates the impact of higher rates as leverage increases. But as we said before, the cost involved in financing is but one of many other considerations entering the complex trade-offs in capital structure planning.

It should be added here that the effect of restructuring and more successful performance by many companies in the first half of this decade has led to a definite shift toward more conservative capital structures. Strong cash flows obtained from disposals of underperforming businesses and leaner ongoing operations have often been applied to reducing the debt proportions of many major companies. This was in part a reaction to the heavy—at times extreme—use of leverage during the eighties, which apart from greater risk exposure had not been justified by the results of the investments made with these funds. The drive to create value has included a rethinking of sustainable capital structure proportions.

Another effect of this return on economic performance focus has been the surge in stock repurchases and its attendant effect on the capital structure. Here the trade-off is simply between the quality and risk of perceived reinvestment opportunities on the one hand, and the impact of returning excess cash to the shareholders on the other. The latter effect will generally be a rise in the value of the stock as fewer shares are left outstanding, and a proportional lessening of the dividend payments maintained as a matter of policy. As the equity base shrinks, the proportions in the capital structure shift as well, and the overall balance has to be reconsidered in line with the company's long-range strategy.

Ultimately we must view the optimal capital structure in the broad context of our financial systems model as discussed in Chapter 1. It cannot be separated from the variables we identified in all parts of the system.

KEY ISSUES

The following is a recap of the key issues raised directly or indirectly in this chapter. They are enumerated here to help the reader keep the analysis techniques discussed within the perspective of financial theory and business practice:

1. The choice among different types of long-term financing is inextricably connected with the business strategy of a company. The final choice must match the risk/reward characteristics inherent in both strategy and financing.

2. The cost of different types of capital is only one element on which a decision about new funding is based. While debt is generally the lowest-cost alternative and common equity the highest-cost alternative, the need to build and maintain an appropriate balance in the capital structure often overrides the cost criterion.

3. Noncost elements, such as risk, flexibility, timing, and shareholder control as well as management preferences have to be weighed in relation to both changing market conditions and the company's future policies.

4. New financing at times may represent a significant proportion of the existing capital structure. How these funds are raised can cause shifts away from a firm's ideal target capital structure. Because a block of one form of long-term capital was chosen at one point in time, management may be limited in the choices for the next round of financing. To compensate for this imbalance, a compromise mix of funds may have to be used.

5. The specific provisions of a new issue of securities are generally tailor-made for the situation. Investment bankers, underwriters, and management collaborate to negotiate the design and price of a financial instrument that reflects market conditions, the company's credit rating and reputation, risk assessment, the company's strategic plans, and current financial practices.

6. As a company's capital structure changes, so does its weighted cost of capital. However, temporary shifts resulting from adding blocks of new capital should not affect the return standards based on cost of capital, unless there is a deliberate and permanent change in the company's policies.

7. New common equity has the long-term effect of diluting both ownership and earnings per share. This is true whether the new shares are directly issued or brought about by conversion of other securities, or by exercise of warrants. The decision of whether to issue new common shares thus must be closely tied to the expected results from the strategic plans in place. It also involves weighing the advantages of introducing new permanent equity capital into the capital structure.

8. Leasing as a form of financing is based on a series of trade-offs that must be weighed in relation to both the company's capital structure and its business direction. It doesn't serve as a means of justification for obtaining the asset involved; only economic analysis can.

SUMMARY

This chapter reviewed both the decisional framework and some of the techniques used to analyze the different types of long-term funds. We focused on the three basic alternatives open to management: long-term debt, preferred stock, and common equity, leaving the discussion of the many specialized aspects of funding instruments to be pursued in the reference materials at the end of the chapter.

We found that the choice of financing alternatives is a complex mixture of analysis and judgment. Several areas of consideration were highlighted. We reviewed the cost to the company, the relative risks, and the issues of flexibility, timing, and control with respect to the various funding sources. We found that many of the aspects involved in choosing types of capital went beyond quantifiable data.

We also focused on the impact of each financing alternative on the reported earnings of a company, and then developed a break-even graph relating EPS and EBIT. This simple model allowed us to test visually the earnings impact of the alternatives over the whole dynamic range of potential earnings levels. The graph suggested the potential use of broader financial models or computer spreadsheets with which to simulate more fully the impact of alternative financing packages or changing conditions. We briefly examined the key aspects of some more specialized forms of financing, convertible securities, rights, warrants, and leasing and suggested the kind of analytical considerations applicable to these modified conditions. Last, we touched on some of the key issues surrounding capital structure planning.

SELECTED REFERENCES

Brealey, Richard, and Stewart Myers. *Principles of Corporate Finance.* 4th ed. New York: McGraw-Hill, 1991.

Hull, John. *Options, Futures and Other Derivative Securities.* New York: Prentice-Hall, 1993.

Ross, Stephen; Randolph Westerfield; and Jeffrey Jaffe. *Corporate Finance.* 4th ed. Burr Ridge, IL: Richard D. Irwin, 1996.

Weston, J. Fred, and Eugene Brigham. *Essentials of Managerial Finance.* 10th ed. Chicago, IL: Dryden Press, 1992.

SELF-STUDY EXERCISES AND PROBLEMS

(Solutions are provided in Appendix V)

1. The ABC Corporation is planning the financing of a major expansion program for late 1997. Common stock has been chosen as the vehicle, and the 50,000 shares to be issued in addition to the 300,000 shares outstanding are to bring estimated proceeds of $5 million. The current

price range of common stock is $120 to $140 per share. The new program is expected to raise current operating profits of $14.7 million by 18 percent. The company's capital structure contains long-term debt of $10 million, with an annual sinking fund provision of $900,000 to begin in 1998 and interest charges of 11 percent. The most recent estimated operating statement of the company, which includes the additional profit, appears as follows:

ABC CORPORATION
Pro Forma Operating Statement
For the Year Ended December 31, 1998
($ thousands)

Net sales	$66,000
Cost of goods sold*	42,000
Gross profit	24,000
Selling and administrative expenses	9,300
Operating profit	14,700
Interest on debt	1,100
Profit before taxes	13,600
Federal income tax (34%)	4,600
Net income	$ 9,000

*Includes depreciation of $2,250.

The company's β was calculated at 1.4, while the risk-free return was estimated to be 8 percent, and the expected return from the stock market 14.5 percent.

   a. Develop an analysis of earnings per share, uncommitted earnings per share, and cash flow per share, and show the effects of dilution in earnings.

   b. Develop the same analysis for an alternative issue of $5 million of 10 percent preferred stock, and an alternative issue of $5 million of 9 percent debentures due in full after 15 years.

   c. Develop the specific comparative cost of capital for all three alternatives and discuss your findings.

2. XYZ Corporation is planning to raise an additional $30 million in capital, either via 240,000 shares of common at $125 per share net proceeds, or via 300,000 shares of 9 percent preferred stock. Current earnings are $12.50 per share on 1 million shares outstanding, $2.5 million in interest is paid annually on existing long-term debt, and dividends on existing preferred stock amount to $1.5 million per year. The current market price is $140 per share, the β is 1.2, and risk-free return is 8 percent. The expected return from the stock market is 13 percent.

   a. Develop the specific cost of capital for each alternative and show calculations (long form). Assume income taxes are 46 percent.

    b. Develop the point of earnings per share equilvalence between the common and preferred alternatives. Assuming a common dividend of $8 per share, calculate the EPS/dividends per share break-even point for the common stock alternative.

    c. Assuming EBIT levels of $10 million, $15 million, $22.5 million, and $33.75 million, demonstrate the effect of leverage with the preferred stock alternative, by graph and calculation. Discuss your findings.

3. The DEF Company was weighing three financing options for a diversification program that would require $50 million and provide greater stability in sales and profits. The options were as follows:

    a. One million common shares at $50 net to the company.

    b. 500,000 shares of 9.5 percent preferred stock.

    c. $50 million of 8.5 percent bonds (entailing a sinking fund provision of $2 million per year).

The current capital structure contained debt on which $1 million per year was paid into a sinking fund and on which interest of $1.2 million was currently paid. Preferred stock obligations were dividends of $1.8 million per year. Common shares outstanding were 2 million, on which $2 per share was paid in dividends. The current market price range was $55 to $60, and the company's β was 1.2. The risk-free rate of return was 7.5 percent, while expectations about the returns from a portfolio of stocks were 14 percent. EBIT levels had fluctuated between $22 million and $57 million, and earnings before interest and taxes from diversification were expected to be about $8 million. The most recent EBIT level of the company had been $34 million.

Assume that proceeds to the company after expenses would equal the par value of the securities in the second and third alternatives; also, disregard the obvious exaggerations in the relationships that were made for better contrast. Income taxes are 36 percent.

Develop a graphic analysis of the data given and establish by calculation the earnings per share, uncommitted earnings per share, dilution, specific costs of capital, break-even points, dividend coverage, and zero earnings per share. Discuss your findings.

CHAPTER 9

Valuation and Business Performance

Throughout this book, we have stressed that managers must primarily focus their decision making about investment, operations, and financing on the creation of economic value for the company's shareholders. Let's now put value creation into a broader context by examining the key concepts of value and relating them to successful business performance. Earlier we discussed such categories as the stated values reflected in a company's financial statements, the economic values represented by the cash flows generated through capital investments, and the market value of common equity. In each case, value was viewed in a specific context of analysis and assessment, but not necessarily against the full dynamics of management strategies and decisions that underlie the performance of any business.

We'll discuss the meaning of value in a variety of common situations where valuation is required. We'll not only define several concepts of value in more precise terms, but also once again use some of the now familiar analytical approaches that can be applied to the process of valuation. Foremost among these, of course, is the present value analysis of future cash flows (the main subject of Chapter 6), which is a common underpinning of modern valuation principles and shareholder value creation.

We'll begin with some basic definitions of value found in business practice. Next, we'll take the point of view of the investor assessing the value of the main forms of securities issued by a company. Finally, we'll discuss the key issues involved in valuing an ongoing business as the basis for determining shareholder value—the principal objective of modern management. As we've emphasized throughout this book, the linkage between cash flows and the creation of economic value is the ultimate expression of success or failure of business decisions on investment, operating, and financing. Recognition of this linkage spurred the wave of takeovers and restructuring activities of the 1980s—essentially a reassessment of the effectiveness with which resources were employed by target companies—leading to redeployment of those resources in alternative ways expected to generate higher cash flows and returns to the shareholders.

DEFINITIONS OF VALUE

It will be useful briefly to refresh our memory about the different types of value we've encountered so far, and to state as clearly as possible what they represent and for what purposes they may be appropriate.

Economic Value

This concept relates to the basic ability of an asset—or a claim—to provide a stream of aftertax cash flows to the holder. Such cash flows may be generated through earnings, or contractual payments, or partial or total liquidation at a future point. As earlier chapters said, economic value is essentially a cash flow trade-off concept. The value of any good is defined as the amount of cash a buyer is willing to give up now—its present value—in exchange for a pattern of future expected cash flows. Therefore, economic value is also a future-oriented concept. It's determined by estimating and assessing potential future cash flows, including proceeds from the ultimate disposal of the good itself. Remember that costs and expenditures caused by past decisions are sunk costs and thus irrelevant from an economic standpoint.

As we'll see, economic value underlies some of the other common concepts of value because it's based on a trade-off logic that is quite natural to the process of investing funds. Calculating economic value is not without practical difficulties, however. Recall that a representative discount rate (return standard) has to be selected and applied to the expected positive and negative cash flows over a defined period of time. These cash flows also include the terminal value assumption about any recoverable cash or any ongoing value at the termination point of the analysis. The process in effect determines the equivalence of the cash flow amounts occurring in different parts of the time spectrum.

Recall also the need for risk assessment, both of the cash flow pattern itself and in setting the appropriate return standard. In other words, economic value isn't absolute; it's a result of the relative risk assessment of future expectations. In fact, economic value is closely tied to individual risk preferences. Yet, economic value principles are at the core of all business decisions on investment, operating, and financing, whether or not these aspects are made explicit.

Market Value

Also referred to as *fair market value,* this is the value of any asset, or collection of assets, when traded in an organized market or between private parties in an unencumbered transaction without duress. The securities and commodity exchanges are examples of organized markets, as are literally thousands of regional and local markets and exchanges that enable buyers and sellers to find mutually acceptable values for all kinds of tangible and intangible assets. Market value is, of course, also established through transactions between individuals when no organized market is conveniently available.

Again, there's nothing absolute in market value. Instead, it represents a momentary consensus of two or more parties. In a sense, the parties to a transaction adjust their respective individual assessments of the asset's economic value sufficiently to arrive at the consensus. The market value at any one time can therefore be subject to the preferences and even whims of the individuals involved, the psychological climate prevalent in an organized exchange, the heat of a takeover battle, economic variations, industry developments, economic and political conditions, and so forth. Moreover, the current volume of trading in the asset or security will influence the value placed on it by buyers and sellers.

Despite its potential variability, market value is generally regarded as a reasonable criterion in estimating the current value of individual balance sheet assets and liabilities as recorded. It's frequently used in inventory valuation and in capital investment analysis in the form of future recovery values. Mergers and purchases of going concerns are also based on market values established by the parties.

As was the case with economic value, there are practical problems associated with establishing market value. A true market value can be found only by actually engaging in a transaction. Thus, unless the item is in fact traded, any market value assigned to it remains merely an estimate, which will tend to shift as conditions change and the perceptions of the parties are altered.

But even if market quotations are readily available, certain judgments apply. For example, popular common stocks traded on the major exchanges have widely quoted market prices, yet there frequently are significant price fluctuations even within a day's trading. Thus, market value based on many similar transactions can be fixed only within a given range, which in turn, is tied to the trading conditions of the day, week, or month. For items that are traded infrequently, estimating a realistic transaction value can become even more difficult.

Book Value

Recall from Chapter 1 that the book value of an asset or liability is the stated value on the balance sheet, which has been recorded according to generally accepted accounting principles. While book value is generally handled consistently for accounting purposes, it usually has little relationship to current economic value. It's a historical value that, at one time, may have represented a market value, but the passage of time and changes in economic conditions increasingly distort it. This is especially true of the frequently quoted book value of common shares, which represents the shareholder's proportional claim on the composite residual of all past transactions in assets, liabilities, and operations. Its usefulness for economic analysis is therefore questionable under most circumstances.

Liquidation Value

This value relates to the special condition when a company needs to liquidate part or all of its assets and claims. In essence, it's an abnormal situation where time pressures and even duress distort the value assessments made by buyers and sellers.

Under the cloud of impending business failure or intense pressure from creditors, management will find that liquidation values generally are considerably below potential market values. The economic setting is adversely affected by the known disadvantage under which the selling party must act in the transaction. As a consequence, liquidation value is really applicable only for the limited purpose intended. Nevertheless, it's sometimes used to value assets of unproven companies to perform ratio analysis in assessing creditworthiness.

Breakup Value

A variation of liquidation value, breakup value is related to corporate takeover and restructuring activities, as discussed later in this chapter. On the assumption that the combined economic values of the individual segments of a multibusiness company exceed the company's value as an entity—because of inadequate past management or current opportunities not recognized earlier—the company is broken up into salable components for disposal to other buyers. Any redundant assets, such as excess real estate, are also sold for their current values.

Note that breakup value is usually realized on business segments with ongoing operations, and less frequently through forced liquidation of individual assets supporting these business segments, as would be the case in a bankruptcy sale, for example. Any redundant assets may, of course, be liquidated as such. Estimates of breakup value are a critical element in the analysis preceding takeover bids.

Reproduction Value

This is the amount that would be required to replace an existing fixed asset in kind. In other words, it is the like-for-like replacement cost of a machine, facility, or other similar asset. Reproduction value is, in fact, one of several yardsticks used in judging the worth of an ongoing business. Determining reproduction value is an estimate largely based on engineering judgments.

There are several practical problems involved. The most important is whether the fixed asset in question could, or would, in fact be reproduced exactly as it was constructed originally. Most physical assets are subject to some pattern of technological obsolescence with the passage of time, in addition to physical wear and tear. There's also the problem of estimating the currently applicable cost of actually reproducing the item in kind. For purposes of analysis, reproduction value often becomes just one checkpoint in assessing the market value of the assets of a going business.

Collateral Value

This is the value of an asset used as security for a loan or other type of credit. The collateral value is generally considered the maximum amount of credit that can be extended against a pledge of the asset. With their own security in mind, creditors usually set the collateral value lower than the market value of an asset. This provides a cushion of safety in case of default, and the risk preference of the individual creditor will determine the size of the often arbitrary downward adjustment. Where no market value can be readily estimated, the collateral value is set on a purely judgmental basis, the creditor being in a position to allow for as much of a margin of safety as deemed advisable in the particular circumstances.

Assessed Value

This value concept is established in local legal statutes as the basis for property taxation. The rules governing assessment vary widely, and may or may not take market values into account. The use of assessed values is limited to raising tax revenues, and therefore such values bear little relationship to the other value concepts.

Appraised Value

Appraised value is subjectively determined and used when the asset involved has no clearly definable market value. An effort is usually made to find evidence of transactions that are reasonably comparable to the asset being appraised. Often used in transactions of considerable size—especially in the case of commercial or residential real estate—appraised value is determined by an impartial expert accepted by both parties to the transaction, whose knowledge of the type of asset involved can narrow the gap that may exist between buyer and seller, or at least establish a bargaining range. The quality of the estimate depends on the expertise of the appraiser and on the availability of comparable situations. Again, individual ability and preference enter into the value equation. Only rarely will different appraisals yield exactly the same results.

Going Concern Value

This is an application of the economic value concept because a business viewed as a going concern is expected to produce a series of future cash flows that the potential buyer must value to arrive at a price for the business as a whole. Note that the same concept applies to valuing ongoing business segments of a company in terms of breakup value, as discussed earlier. Apart from the specific valuation technique applied here, the concept requires that the business be viewed as an ongoing "living system" of operating parts rather than as a collection of assets and liabilities.

Recall our earlier strong emphasis on the fact that business value is created by a positive trade-off of future cash flows for present commitments and outlays. As we'll see later in the chapter, the going concern value is useful when comparative cash flow analyses, singly and in combination, are developed for setting value management goals and for acquisitions and mergers. The continuing challenge to the analyst is to properly weigh this pattern of cash flows.

Shareholder Value

As we've stated a number of times, shareholder value is created when the returns generated from existing and new investments consistently exceed the cost of capital of the company. It's the total increase in the economic value of the business, which in turn is reflected in a growing periodic total return to shareholders as measured by the combination of dividends and capital gains or losses achieved. Shareholder value is closely tied to cash flow trade-offs and return expectations that are the basis of economic value, and we'll discuss the concept in more detail later.

In summary, we've discussed a number of value definitions. Some were specialized yardsticks designed for specific situations. Many are directly or indirectly related to economic value. We defined economic value as the present value of future cash flows, discounted at the investor's risk-adjusted standard. This value concept is broadly applicable as the underpinning of shareholder value creation, and we'll use it extensively as we examine various decision areas where value measures are needed.

VALUE TO THE INVESTOR

As in Chapters 5, 7, and 8, we'll concentrate only on the three main types of corporate securities—bonds, preferred stock, and common stock—in discussing the techniques involved to assess *value* and *yield*. As used here, value is defined as the current value of the investment to the investor in present value terms, while yield represents the internal rate of return (IRR) earned by the investor on the price paid for the investment. We'll discuss major provisions in the basic securities types only insofar as they may affect their value and yield. The techniques covered should appear quite familiar to the reader because they closely relate to the analytical approaches presented in earlier chapters.

Bond Values

Valuing a bond is normally fairly straightforward. A typical bond issued by a corporation is a simple debt instrument. Its basic provisions generally entail a series of contractual semiannual interest payments, defined as a fixed rate based on the bond's stated par (face) value (usually $1,000). The legal contract, or *indenture,* promises repayment of the principal (nominal value) at a specified maturity date a number of years in the future. The two basic characteristics, defined interest payments and repayment stipulations, are encountered in most normal debt arrangements. Complicating aspects are sometimes found in provisions such as conversion into common stock at a predetermined exchange value, or payment of interest only when earned by the issuing company. We'll review some of these specialized features briefly.

A bond's basic value rests on the investor's assessment of the relative attractiveness of the expected stream of future interest receipts and the prospect for eventual recovery of the principal at maturity. Of course, there's normally no obligation for the investor to hold the bond until maturity because most bonds can be readily traded in the securities markets. Still, the risk underlying the bond contract must be considered here in terms of the issuing company's future ability to generate sufficient cash with which to pay both interest and principal. The collective judgment of security analysts and investors about the issuing company's prospects influences the price level at which the bond is publicly traded. Also, the bond is likely to be rated by financial services like Moody's and Standard & Poors and placed in a particular risk category relative to other bonds.

To determine a bond's value, we must first calculate the present value of the interest payments received up to the maturity date and add to this the present value of the ultimate principal repayment. You'll recognize this method as comparable with the process of calculating the present value of capital expenditures in Chapter 6. The discount rate applied is the risk-adjusted interest rate that represents the investor's own standard of measuring debt investment opportunities within a range of acceptable risk. For example, an investor with an 8 percent annual interest return standard would value a bond with a coupon interest rate of 6 percent annually significantly lower than its par value. The calculation is shown in Figure 9–1. The investor's annual standard of 8 percent is equivalent to a semiannual standard of 4 percent, a restatement for purposes of calculation that's necessary to match the semiannual interest payments paid by most bonds.

The resulting value, $832.89, represents the maximum price our investor should be willing to pay—or the minimum price at which the investor should be willing to sell if the investor normally expects a return (yield) of 8 percent from this type of investment. This particular bond should therefore be acquired only at

FIGURE 9–1

Bond Valuation

Date of analysis:	July 1, 1997		
Face value (par) of bond:	$1,000		
Maturity date:	July 1, 2011		
Bond interest (coupon rate):	6% per year		
Interest receipts:	$30 semiannually		

	Total Cash Flow	Present Value Factors, 4 Percent*	Present Value
28 receipts of $30 over 14 years (28 periods)	$ 840	16.663 (× $30)	$499.89
Receipt of principal 14 years hence (28 periods)	1,000	0.333	333.00
Totals	$1,840		$832.89

*From Tables II and I (Chapter 6), respectively.

a price considerably below (at a discount from) par. Note that the stated interest rate on the bond is relevant only for determining the semiannual cash receipts in absolute dollar terms.

Actual valuation of the bond and the cash flows it represents therefore depends on the investor's opportunity rate (return standard). In other words, the desired yield determines the price, and vice versa. This relationship also applies, of course, to the market quotations for publicly traded bonds. The quoted price, or value, is a function of the current yield collectively desired by the many buyers and sellers of these debt instruments.

If our investor were for some unrealistic reason satisfied with the very low annual yield of only 4 percent from holding the same bond (equivalent to 2 percent per six-month period), the value to the investor would rise considerably above par, as shown in Figure 9–2. Under these assumed conditions, the investor should be willing to pay a premium of up to $212.43 for the $1,000 bond, because the personal return standard is lower than the stated interest rate. If the investor's own standard and the coupon interest rate were to coincide precisely, the value of the bond would, of course, match exactly the par value of $1,000.

In fact, the quoted market price of any bond will tend to approach the par value as it reaches maturity, because at that point, the only representative value will be the imminent repayment of the principal—assuming, of course, that the company is financially able to pay as the amount becomes due.

Bond Yields

A related but common problem for the analyst or investor is the calculation of the yield produced by various bonds, when quoted prices differ from par value. The key to this analysis again is the relationship of value and yield as discussed above, and the technique used is a present value calculation that in effect determines the internal rate of return (IRR) of the cash flow patterns generated by the bond over its remaining life.

FIGURE 9–2

Bond Valuation with Lower Return Standard (4 percent per year)

	Total Cash Flow	Present Value Factors, 2 Percent*	Present Value
28 receipts of $30 over 14 years (28 periods)	$ 840	21.281 (× $30)	$ 638.43
Receipt of principal 14 years hence (28 periods)	1,000	0.574	574.00
Totals	$1,840		$1,212.43

*From Tables II and I (Chapter 6), respectively.

The method is identical to that used for assessing the cash flows of any business investment proposal. The key difference in the data is that the individual investor's calculations are based on pretax cash flows that must be adjusted in each case by the investor for his or her personal tax situation. Other minor differences are the cash incidence in a semiannual pattern, and the form in which bond prices (the net investment) are quoted. Published prices are normally stated as a percentage of par. For example, a bond quoted at 103⅜ has a price of $1,033.75.

Bond yield tables have long been employed to determine a bond's internal rate of return, or yield. While today's computers and calculators have financial routines that allow direct calculation, we'll nevertheless take a quick look at a yield table, if only to help the reader understand the examples by visual inspection of the relationships. Bond yield tables are finely graduated present value tables that list the whole potential range of stated interest rates, subdivided into fractional progressions of as little as ¹/₃₂ of a point. They're far more detailed than the present value tables we used in Chapter 6.

For example, Figure 9–3 is a small segment of such a yield table, in this case for a bond with a coupon interest rate of precisely 6 percent. The columns show the number of 6-month periods remaining in the life of the bond, while the rows display the yield to maturity. The yield to maturity simply refers to the yield obtained by the investor if the bond is actually held until its par value is repaid at the maturity date. If the investor were to sell at an earlier date, the market price of the bond received at that time would be substituted for par value in calculating the return. As a result, the yield achieved for the period up to the date of sale may differ from the

FIGURE 9–3

Bond Yield Table (sample section for a 6 percent rate)

	Price Given Years or Periods to Maturity					
Yield to Maturity	13 Years (26 periods)	13½ Years (27 periods)	14 Years (28 periods)	14½ Years (29 periods)	15 Years (30 periods)	15½ Years (31 periods)
3.80%	1.224 043	1.230 661	1.237 155	1.243 528	1.249 782	1.255 919
3.85	1.218 284	1.224 709	1.231 012	1.237 196	1.243 263	1.249 215
3.90	1.212 559	1.218 793	1.224 907	1.230 904	1.236 787	1.242 557
3.95	1.206 868	1.212 913	1.218 841	1.224 654	1.230 354	1.235 944
4.00	1.201 210	1.207 068	1.212 812*	1.218 443	1.223 964	1.229 377
4.05	1.195 585	1.201 260	1.206 821	1.212 273	1.217 616	1.222 853
4.10	1.189 993	1.195 486	1.200 868	1.206 142	1.211 310	1.216 375
4.15	1.184 434	1.189 747	1.194 952	1.200 051	1.205 046	1.209 940
4.20	1.178 908	1.184 043	1.189 073	1.193 999	1.198 823	1.203 549
4.25	1.173 414	1.178 374	1.183 230	1.187 985	1.192 642	1.197 201

*This example was used in Figure 9–2 (slight difference due to rounding of present value factors). Note that prices are given in the form of a 7-digit multiplier, which is applied against a $1,000 par value.

yield to maturity if the bond were trading above or below par. We can quickly find the bond's yield to maturity at any given purchase price in the bond yield tables.

Conversely, it's also possible to find the exact price (value) that corresponds to any particular desired yield to maturity. Our example of the 6 percent bond used in the previous section (Figure 9–1) is represented on the 4 percent yield line and in the 28-period column of the bond yield table segment reproduced in Figure 9–3. Bond yield tables provide a visual impression of the progression or regression of prices and yields which is, of course, based on their mathematical relationship. A calculator or spreadsheet goes through the same steps and formulas used to generate the tables.

Yield to maturity can be approximated by using a shortcut method, if neither a computer nor a bond table is handy. If we assume that our 6 percent bond was quoted at a price of $832.89 on July 1, 1997, (which was the result of our earlier calculation), the discount from the par value of $1,000 is $167.11. The investor will thus not only receive the coupon interest of $30 each for 28 periods, but will also earn the discount of $167.11, if the bond is held to maturity and if the repayment of $1,000 is received.

The shortcut method approximates the true yield by adjusting the periodic interest payment with a proportional amortization of this discount. The first step reflects the common accounting practice of amortizing discounts or premiums over the life of the bond. In our example, the discount of $167.11 is therefore divided by the remaining 28 periods, and the resulting periodic value increment of $5.97 is added to the periodic interest receipt of $30. The adjusted six-month earnings pattern is now $35.97 per period.

The next step relates the adjusted periodic earnings of $35.97 to the average investment outstanding during the remaining life of the bond. The price paid by the investor is $832.89, while the investment's value will rise to $1,000 at maturity. The average of the two values is one-half of the sum, or $916.45. We can then calculate the *periodic* yield to maturity (based on the six-month interest period) by relating the periodic earnings of $35.97 to the average investment outstanding, or we can find the *annual* yield to maturity by relating two six-months earnings amounts of $35.97 each to the average investment:

$$\text{Yield} = \frac{2 \times \$35.97}{\$916.45} = 7.85\% \text{ per year}$$

This result is slightly below the precise yield of 8 percent per year on which our original calculation was built. The averaging shortcut will always introduce some error, because it imperfectly simulates what is in fact a progressive present value structure. As yield rates and the number of time periods increase, larger errors will result. Yet the rough calculation provides a satisfactory result for use as an initial analytical check.

Had a premium been involved (i.e., had the purchase price been above the par value of the bond), the shortcut calculation would, in contrast, reduce the periodic interest earnings by the proportional amortization of the premium. The second example discussed in the previous section (Figure 9–2) posed such a condition.

The result would appear as follows, again representing a close approximation of the true 4 percent solution:

$$\text{Yield} = \frac{(\$30.00 - \$7.59)2}{(\$1,212.43 + \$1,000) \div 2} = 4.05\% \text{ per year}$$

In summary, bond yield calculations involve a fairly straightforward determination of the internal rate of return of future cash flows generated by the bond investment at a known present price. As in the case of a business capital investment, a trade-off of current outlays for future cash flows under conditions of uncertainty is involved. Yield and value are mathematically related and this relationship can be utilized to locate either result in preset bond yield tables, or to solve the analysis directly with a programmed calculator or personal computer.

Bond Provisions and Value

The simple value and yield relationships discussed so far are, of course, affected by the specific conditions surrounding the company and its industry, and also by additional provisions in the specific bond indenture itself. The issuer's ability to pay must be assessed through careful analysis of the company's earnings pattern and projections of expected performance. The techniques discussed in the early chapters of this book are helpful in this process. Ability to pay is a function of the projected cash flows and how well these flows cover debt service of both interest and principal. Sensitivity analysis based on high and low estimates of performance can be useful here.

Variations in the bond indenture will also affect the value and the yield earned. We'll refer only to the major types of bond variations here. *Mortgage bonds* are secured by specific assets of the issuing firm. Because of this relationship, the bondholders have a cushion against default on the principal. Because of the reduced risk, the coupon interest rate offered with mortgage bonds may be somewhat lower than that of unsecured debenture bonds, resulting in a reduced yield to the investor. *Income bonds* are at the other extreme on the risk spectrum because they are not only unsecured, but also pay interest only if the earnings of the company reach a specified minimum level. Their yield levels will be correspondingly high.

Convertible bonds, as we already observed, add the attraction of the holders' eventual participation in the potential market appreciation of common stock for which the bond can be exchanged at a set price. Therefore, the coupon rate of interest may be somewhat lower than that of a straight bond. As we discussed in Chapter 8, the value of convertible bonds is affected by

- The market's assessment of the likely performance of the common stock.
- The gap between the stipulated conversion price and the current price of the common stock.
- The coupon interest it pays semiannually.

Normally, the conversion price is set higher than the prevailing market value of the common stock at the time of issue, to allow for expected value growth of the common stock over time. Conversion is essentially at the investor's discretion when found advantageous, although the indenture usually stipulates a time limit as a well as the right of the issuing company to call the bonds for redemption at a slight premium price after a certain date, thus forcing the investor to act. As common share prices approach and surpass the conversion price, the bond's value will rise above par because of the growing value of the equivalent common shares it represents.

A more recent phenomenon in the bond markets is the use of so-called *junk bonds,* extensively promoted by some investment bankers to support company takeovers, using very high levels of debt, or for *leveraged buyouts* by groups of managers or investors that similarly use extremely high financial leverage to finance the purchase of the company involved. These securities are in effect *subordinate* to (ranking below) the claims of other creditors in case of default and are sold under often highly risky circumstances, because the amount of indebtedness involved in some of these transactions exceeds what are normally considered prudent levels. The yields provided by these unsecured instruments are usually commensurate with the high risk perceived by investors, and defaults are not uncommon.

Many other modifications and provisions are possible to tailor bonds of various types to the needs of the issuing company and to the prevailing conditions in the securities markets. The many variations in bond provisions and their impact on value and yield call for careful judgments that go beyond the direct analytical techniques we discussed. We repeat that the calculations described are but the starting point, and no hard-and-fast rules exist for mechanically weighing all aspects of bond valuation. In the final analysis, value and yield must be adjusted with due regard to the investor's economic and risk preferences, in line with the specific objectives in owning debt instruments. The references at the end of the chapter cover these aspects in greater detail.

Preferred Stock Values

By its very nature, preferred stock represents a middle ground between debt and common equity ownership. The security provides a series of cash dividend payments, but normally has no specific provision (or expectation) for repayment of the par value of the stock. However, at times preferred stock carries a call provision, which allows the issuing company to retire part or all of the stock during a specific time period by paying a small premium over the stated value of the stock.

While the investor enjoys a preferential position over common stock with regard to current dividends and also to recovery of principal in the case of liquidation of the enterprise, preferred dividends may not be paid if company performance is poor. Such an event will, of course, affect the value of the stock adversely.

Preferred dividends, like common dividends, are declared at the discretion of the board of directors and might not be made up if missed, unless the preferred issue carries specific legal requirements to the contrary. Such provisions, for example, may call for *cumulating* past unpaid dividends until the company is in a position to afford declaring dividends of any kind. At other times, particularly in new companies, preferred stocks may carry a *participation* feature, which requires the board of directors to declare preferred dividends higher than the stated rate if earnings exceed a stipulated minimum level. But these two special situations are infrequent.

The task of valuing preferred stock, therefore, has to be based on less definite conditions than was the case with bonds, because the only reasonably certain element is the stated annual dividend, which was set as a percentage of stated value. For example, an 8 percent preferred stock usually refers to a $100 share of stock which is expected to pay a dividend of $8 per year, most likely in quarterly installments, a pattern normally matching that for common stocks. The investor is faced with valuing this stream of prospective cash dividends. If the price paid for a share of preferred stock was $100, and the stock is held indefinitely, the yield under these circumstances would be 8 percent, assuming that the company is likely to be able to pay the dividend regularly.

If the price was more or less than the stated value, the yield could be found by relating the amount of the dividend to the actual price per share:

$$\text{Yield} = \frac{\text{Annual dividend per share}}{\text{Price paid per share}}$$

If the investor could expect to sell the stock at $110 five years hence, the exact yield can be determined by using either present value techniques or the shortcut methods discussed earlier in the section on bonds.

However, estimating a future recovery value involves a good deal of conjecture. In contrast to bonds, preferred shares have no specific maturity date or par value to be paid at maturity. The actual price of a preferred stock traded in the securities markets depends on both company performance and on the collective value the securities markets place on the given preferred issue. In turn, this price level reflects the risk/reward trade-off demanded for the whole spectrum of investments at the time. The value range will depend not only on the respective risk premiums assigned to individual securities, but also on the inflationary expectations underlying the economy that are reflected in the risk-free rate on which risk premiums are based. Value may be a little easier to estimate if the stock carries a mandatory call provision applicable at a specific future date and price, especially if the date of analysis is close to that time.

When we look at preferred stock values from the viewpoint of investing, we should use the investor's own return standard to arrive at the maximum price the investor should be willing to pay for the stock, or the minimum price at which the investor should be willing to sell. We simply relate the stipulated dividend rate to our investor's required return—relevant for the level of risk implicit in the preferred issue—to arrive at the answer. If the return standard were 9 percent against which to test the 8 percent preferred, we would determine the investor-specific value as follows:

$$\text{Value per share} = \frac{\text{Stated dividend rate}}{\text{Required return}} = \frac{0.08}{0.09} = \$88.89$$

If the investor were satisfied with only a 7 percent return, the value would be:

$$\text{Value per share} = \frac{0.08}{0.07} = \$114.28$$

The judgments that remain to be made, of course, relate to any uncertainty in the future dividend pattern, and any likely material change in the future value of the stock, either due to changing market conditions, or because of a scheduled call for redemption at a premium price.

Preferred Stock Provisions and Value

As in the case of bonds, there are many modifications in the provisions of preferred stocks that may affect their value in the market. We mentioned earlier that some preferred stocks, particularly in newly established companies, contain a *participation* feature, which entitles the preferred holder to higher dividends, if corporate earnings exceed a set level. This feature can favorably affect the potential yield, and thus the valuation of the stock, depending on how likely it is that the company will reach this higher earnings level.

A much more common feature, similar to some bonds, is *convertibility,* the possibility of changing the preferred ownership position into that of common stock, as discussed in Chapter 8. As in the case of convertible bonds, however, the value of this feature can't be calculated precisely. Yet, as the price of common stock reaches and exceeds the stated conversion price, the price of the convertible preferred stock will tend to reflect the market value of the equivalent number of common shares. Before this point is reached, the convertible preferred stock's value will largely be considered the same as a regular preferred, and based essentially on the stated dividend. Convertibility is generally accompanied by a call provision, at a premium price, which enables the company to force conversion when conditions are right.

In summary, the challenge of preferred stock valuation also goes beyond the simple techniques we have shown. In the end, decisions should be made only after careful assessment of the relative attractiveness of the specific features and conditions surrounding a particular company's preferred stock.

Common Stock Values

The most complex valuation problem is encountered when we turn to common stock, because by definition common stock represents the residual claim of owners on the total performance and outlook of the issuing corporation. We found this to be true when we examined the cost of capital from the point of view of the corporation in Chapter 7.

Common stock valuation is especially difficult because shareholders carry full ownership risks, yet have residual claims on both assets and earnings only after all other claims have been satisfied. An investment in common stock thus involves sharing both risks and rewards. This heightens the uncertainty about potential dividend receipts and any gain or loss in recovering the principal. As a consequence, measurement techniques have to deal with variables subject to a high degree of judgment.

The rewards of successful common stock ownership are several: *cash dividends* (and sometimes additional *stock distributions* in lieu of cash), *growth in recorded equity* from growing earnings, whose underlying cash flows are reinvested by management in total or in part, and past and prospective *cash flow performance,* which is the basis for potential appreciation (or decline) of the stock's market price. As we observed in Chapter 7, there are many practical and theoretical issues surrounding the interpretation and measurement of these elements. Here we'll focus on ways of developing reasonable approximations of common share values, and similarly, approximations of the yield an investor derives from a common stock investment.

Earnings and Common Stock Value

The quickest—if simplistic—way to approach the valuation of a share of common stock is to estimate the likely future level of earnings per share, and to capitalize these earnings at an appropriate earnings multiple (price/earnings ratio) that reflects expectations about the company and its industry:

$$\text{Value per share} = \text{Earnings per share} \times \text{Price/earnings ratio}$$

There are, of course, serious shortcomings in using projected accounting earnings as a measure of shareholder expectations. Since ultimately all value derives from cash flows, the surrogate of earnings per share can't capture the full impact on value. Moreover, the approach is static unless any potential growth or decline in earnings is built in. Finally, there remains the basic problem of forecasting the earnings pattern itself, both for the company and its industry.

A more specific, cash-based approach to estimating common share value is to capitalize expected dividends. The size, regularity, and trend in dividend payout to shareholders has an important effect on the value of a share of common stock, being one of the elements of shareholder value creation. Yet there's also a degree of uncertainty about the receipt of any series of future dividends. Not only will such dividends depend on the ability of the company to perform successfully, but also dividends are declared at the discretion of the corporate board of directors.

No general rule applies in this area—dividend policies can range from no cash payment at all to regular payments of 75 percent or more of current earnings. At times, dividends paid may even exceed current earnings, because the company is unwilling to cut the current dividend per share during a temporary earnings slump. Most boards of directors see some value in a consistent pattern of dividend payments, and major adjustments in the size of the dividend, up or down, are made very reluctantly.

The approach to valuation via dividends involves projecting the expected dividends per share and discounting them by the return standard appropriate for the investor. Several major issues arise here.

First, the current level of dividends paid is likely to change over time. For example, in a successful, growing company the dividend is likely to grow as well. The problem is to make the projection of future dividends realistic, even though past performance is the only guide. If a company has been paying a steadily growing dividend over many years, an extrapolation of this past trend may be reasonable, but must be tempered by subjective judgments about the outlook for the company and its industry. Companies with more erratic patterns of earnings and dividends, however, pose a greater challenge.

The second issue is the method of calculation. The most common format is the so-called *dividend discount model,* or *dividend growth model,* which appears below in its simplest form. The formula is a restatement of the dividend approach we used as one way of calculating the cost of equity in Chapter 7. In that approach, we defined the cost of common equity as the ratio of the current dividend to the current market price plus the expected rate of growth of future dividends. Here, instead of solving for the cost of equity, which is the investor's expectation of return, we solve for the value, or price, of the stock:

$$\text{Value per share} = \frac{\text{Current dividend}}{\text{Discount rate (Investor's expectation of return)} - \text{Dividend growth rate}}$$

This particular formula is based on the idea that the value of a share of stock is the sum of the present values of a series of growing annual dividend payments, discounted at the investor's return expectation for this class of risk. The formula also permits using the less realistic assumption of a constantly declining dividend. But either way it implies an ongoing series of payments in perpetuity, and it also implies a constant annual rate of growth or decline in the dividend payment.

Note, however, that this model would give an invalid answer for a company paying dividends expected to grow as fast or faster than the discount rate, because then the denominator would become zero or even negative. Clearly, under such a happy condition, the investor's return expectation should be reexamined and raised, or the stock should be considered outside the investor's risk/reward spectrum.

The dividend discount model is related mathematically to an annuity formula which assumes a constant growth rate and constant discount rate. The valuation it provides implicitly includes any appreciation in the stock's future market value as management reinvests the retained portion of the growing earnings. This condition holds because in the model, the market value of the stock at any future time is defined as the present value at that point of the ensuing stream of growing dividends.

The simplifying assumption of a constant rate of growth in dividends can be modified if a more erratic pattern of future dividends is expected. The calculation then becomes a present value analysis of uneven annual cash flows up to a selected point in the future. If the analyst wishes to assume that the dividend growth rate will stabilize at some future time, the basic formula can then be inserted and its result discounted to the present. Remember, however, that forecasting a precise pattern of dividends is problematic under most circumstances and the analyst should look for reasonable approximations.

The dividend discount model (and earnings multiples) does not take into account the general trends and specific fluctuations in the securities markets. Obviously, the market value of specific shares can't be independent of movements in the securities markets as a whole, which are caused by economic, industry, political, and myriad other factors. Therefore, the economic returns a company achieves on the resources invested tend to be recognized in the *relative market value* of its shares, that is, relative to share values of its peers and within the context of overall market movements. Moreover, the value of a company's shares reflects the collective performance assessments by security analysts and institutional investors, and the resulting demand for, or lack of interest in, those shares. While very important, these considerations are beyond the scope of this book.

Common Stock Yield and Investor Expectations

In Chapter 3, we presented two simple yardsticks for measuring the owners' return on investment in common stock. One of these was the *earnings yield,* a simple ratio of current or projected earnings per share to the current market price. The other was the inverse relationship, the so-called *price/earnings ratio.* As we pointed out, these simple ratios are static expressions based on readily available data and should only serve as temporary rough indicators of the real investor's yield created by a company's economic performance, that is, the cash flow pattern generated and projected.

The two yardsticks are useful mainly for a comparative analysis of companies or industry groupings, but must be supplemented by more insights if the analyst wishes to approximate the actual economic yield of a stock. Any serious examination of value or yield relative to the expectations of the shareholder should use more sophisticated techniques, such as the capital asset pricing model (CAPM), which take into account market risk, specific company risk, portfolio considerations, and investors' risk preferences.

A third measure we discussed in Chapter 3 was *total shareholder return,* or *TSR.* This is an expression of the actual yield achieved over a period of time when a share of stock is acquired at the beginning of the period and sold at the end. The combination of dividends received during the period and the gain or loss achieved from the change in the share price is then related to the initial investment. This calculation, which is published widely for publicly held companies in statistical compilations such as the Fortune 500 represents a direct approach to measuring the yield for the investor.

Yield, of course, is a function of the risk exposure chosen by an investor. A great deal of research has improved our understanding of the relative performance of common stocks within the broad movements of the security markets. This has resulted in refined definitions of the *systematic risk* underlying a diversified portfolio of stocks traded and the *unsystematic (avoidable) risk,* of a particular security. As we discussed in Chapter 7, the CAPM relates the relative risk of a security to the risk of the market portfolio through a calculated factor, β, which indicates the difference in the risk characteristics of the stock versus the risk characteristics of the portfolio. These are defined in terms of the historical trend in returns earned over and above the *risk-free return* from the safest type of investment, such as long-term U.S. government bonds.

Thus, the expected yield of a particular common stock is the sum of the risk free return plus a risk premium, which is the risk premium earned in the total portfolio of stocks, adjusted by the inherent riskiness of the particular security. We described the formula in Chapter 7:

$$\text{Yield} = R_f + \beta(R_m - R_f)$$

where

     R_f is the risk-free return.
     β is the particular stock's covariance of variability in returns (the specific measure of riskiness).
     R_m is the average return expected on common stocks.

Fortunately, the β for publicly traded companies is published routinely in financial services such as *Value Line*. Current indications of the risk-free rate prevalent at the time and estimates of the return from groups of common stocks are also available in published sources.

We've only touched on some of the techniques used to determine value and yield for common stocks. Much more practical and theoretical insight is needed to deal confidently with the complex issues involved. The references listed at the end of this chapter provide greater depth.

Other Considerations in Valuing Common Stock

The book value per share of common stock is often quoted in financial references and company reviews. As we observed before, this figure is the recorded residual claim of the shareholder as stated on the balance sheet. Book value is an accumulation of past transactions and values and does not reflect current economic value based on potential earnings or dividends. Only under unusual circumstances will book value per share be reasonably representative of anything approximating the economic value of a share of common stock.

This might be true, for example, if a company has either just been started, or is about to be liquidated. Under normal conditions, however, book value per share will become increasingly remote from current values, because under current accounting rules, positive changes in the values of existing assets are rarely, if ever, reflected on the books. The *book to market* ratio discussed in Chapter 3 is used as a rough indicator of this divergence, and a book value that is close to or even exceeding market value may suggest the issuing company is underperforming, a situation that could invite takeover attempts by aggressive investors or corporations.

Market values of common stocks have been treated very lightly in our discussion, because a book on financial analysis techniques is not the place in which to explore the complex workings of the securities markets. We earlier established the principle that in the broadest sense the stock market values expected future cash flows, which are implicitly discounted by a rate of return reflecting the current outlook for the economy and the market as a whole. Key factors driving this rate of return are inflation expectations and projected tax rates. A rise in either of these will tend to lower the stock market, while lower inflation and tax rates will boost it.

Within the general market trends the share prices of individual companies are similarly driven by cash flow expectations. The relative performance of a company's shares depends largely on these cash flows, but also to a significant extent on the trading pattern and volume of the particular stock. Suffice it to say here that if the following several basic conditions are met, quotations of a stock in the securities markets can reasonably be assumed to represent the underlying economic value based on the current and prospective performance of a company.

■ The stock should be *traded frequently* and in fairly sizable volume.

■ Share ownership should ideally be *widespread* so that trading does not involve moving large blocks of shares between a small number of concerned parties.

■ The stock should be *publicly traded* on one or more exchange, or be part of the increasingly important over-the-counter market.

Even if all of these conditions are met, the market value of a stock at any point may not necessarily reflect the true potential of the company, because external factors, such as changes in the economy, publicity about the company and its industry, or takeover attempts may affect the price at which the stock is traded. To help them understand this context, analysts will study the range within which market values have moved, preferably over at least one year and usually longer, and will chart the behavior of specific share prices relative to market averages and composite averages for the industry grouping. One example is the historical and projected charting found in the *Value Line* company analyses.

Specialized Valuation Issues

In Chapter 7 we discussed the main aspects of *rights* and *warrants* from the perspective of the issuing company. We'll now turn briefly to illustrating the value of these specialized forms of financing to the investor.

Rights values arise from the fact that these securities entitle the holder to purchase common shares at a price often significantly below the prevailing market price. For example, an investor holding five common shares has received five rights that represent the opportunity to purchase one new share of common at $30. The current market value of the existing common stock is $40.

Our investor's initial position is as follows:

Number of shares	5
Number of rights	5
Value of five shares @ $40	$200
Subscription price	$ 30

After exercising the rights and paying $30 to the company, the shareholder's position will be:

```
Number of shares . . . . . . . . . .         6
Value of investment  . . . . . . . .   $230.00
Investment per share  . . . . . . .    $ 38.33
Value of a right  . . . . . . . . . . .  $   1.67 (Old value – new value)
```

The market value of the company's shares after all rights have been exercised will in fact approximate $38.33, because the new shares were offered at a significant discount, in the ratio of one new share for each five old shares held. When a rights offering is announced, the shares of the company will trade *cum rights* from the effective date (holder-of-record date) until the specified date at which the stock becomes *ex rights*. At that time, the decline in price reflecting the value of the now separate rights will take place.

The value to the investor of each right is therefore the proportionate discount provided by the rights offering, as related to the ratio of old and new shares. Rights are often traded in the market at the approximate level of the calculated value. Both the value of common stock ex rights, and the value of rights themselves will, of course, be influenced by general movements in the securities markets that are independent of the particular company's circumstances.

Warrants have value directly related to the market price of the common shares of the company. Unlike rights, warrants are not issued proportionally to all common shareholders, but are most frequently attached to issues of new debt and occasionally to new issues of common. Moreover, warrants tend to have expiration dates far longer than rights, and in some cases have no expiration at all. In effect, warrants are options entitling the holder to purchase a new share of common at a fixed exercise price for an extended period of time.

The value of the warrant therefore will be directly related to the difference between the exercise price and the expected market value of the common during the usually lengthy exercise period. If the common stock continually trades at or below the exercise price, the value of the warrant will be zero. If the market value of the common rises above the exercise price, and especially if it's expected to grow in the future during the remainder of the exercise period, the value of the warrant will rise in concert.

BUSINESS VALUATION

Managers, investors, and investment bankers need to know how to measure the total value of a business as an ongoing entity. Whether it's a multibusiness-business global corporation or any of its individual lines of business, or a small single-business company, there are many occasions when obtaining a current valuation is necessary. The most obvious use for such a valuation arises when purchase or sale of a company or a line of business is being considered. The wave of acquisitions, mergers, and hostile takeovers in the past decade involved thousands upon thousands of valuations.

A similar type of valuation is useful when a company, for purposes of internal restructuring, disposes of certain product lines or operating divisions. The buyers may be other companies, groups of investors, or even the existing management who may want to acquire the division financed through a leveraged buyout (a purchase based on using a high proportion of debt in excess of normal capital structure proportions). Regardless of the form of the purchase, sale, or restructuring, both the buyer and the seller need to arrive at a reasonable approximation of the economic value of the company or line of business as a going concern.

Another important use of business valuation—related to the ones mentioned—stems from the growing recognition of value management as the critical focus for successful performance. Managing for shareholder value has become a key strategic objective for corporate managers. Many successful companies measure economic value creation for the company as a whole and for its major businesses and reward the management team accordingly. In this context, the business is periodically valued with various techniques to determine progress against planned performance, and to set the appropriate incentive compensation awards.

We'll first discuss the basic concepts of *valuing the equity of a company,* then *valuing the company* as a whole. In each case, we'll use cash flow techniques which apply to most valuation situations. Next we'll touch on the more specialized cases of *restructuring* and the values driving corporate takeovers, and end the chapter by reviewing the broad implications of managing for *shareholder value*—the concept with which we started the book.

Valuing the Equity

The value of a company's equity can be calculated by estimating the future cash flows to the shareholders. The process is quite comparable to the business investment techniques we developed in Chapter 6. In essence, the stake of the shareholders in the company is the present value of the total expected common dividends paid during an analysis period that is reasonable for the type of industry—three to five years for fast-changing industries like computers, and ten to twenty years for resource-based industries like forest products or oil—plus the present value of the expected worth of the equity at the end of the analysis period. We can express this definition in a formula:

$$V_E = PV(\text{Expected cash dividends}) + PV \text{ (Value of equity at end of period)}$$

Note that these cash flows are expectations, just as they are in all types of business investments. Note also that this approach differs from the dividend discount model in that it establishes a definite time period and substitutes a direct estimate of the future value of the equity at the end of the period for the assumption about a perpetually growing dividend.

The process is carried out by discounting the pattern of annual dividends and the ending equity value at the company's cost of *equity* capital, which reflects the risk to the owners of the equity. This cost is *not* the weighted average cost of capital, based on a combination of debt and equity in the company's capital structure, but the higher cost of the equity alone.

The pattern of estimated dividend cash flows can rise or decline, depending on the analytical assumptions underlying the expectations of the analyst. Similarly, the estimate of the ending value of the total equity may be based on a variety of assumptions, ranging from a simple dividend multiple to a detailed assessment of the company's competitive viability.

In the attempt to focus specifically on the value of the company's equity, however, this approach blurs the contribution from the successful use of leverage. Remember, the dividend cash flow to shareholders is made possible not only through successful investment of equity funds, but also from earnings exceeding the cost of long-term financing used in the capital structure. In fact, the common theme established early in the book was that the economic success of any company had to come from exceeding the weighted cost of capital in its present and future investments. As we'll see in a moment, it's far more useful to approach valuing shareholder equity by first valuing the total company and then subtracting the value of the debt.

Valuing the Total Company

As we've said before, any ongoing business represents a series of expected future cash flows. To arrive at the total value of the company, we must therefore transform past and projected earnings performance into a net cash flow framework, just as if we were calculating the desirability of a capital investment project. The cash flow employed for this purpose is *free cash flow,* which we've defined earlier as the aftertax cash flow from operations before interest, reduced by required funding of additional working capital and net new business investments. This cash flow represents the cash available for investors and creditors after the ongoing investment needs of the business have been met. Note that this definition matches the principles we employed in Chapter 6, where the cash flow pattern of any investment was developed independent of any compensation to the providers of the funds, because the cost of capital used for discounting embodied the weighted average of shareholder and creditor expectations.

Several steps are normally used to arrive at the free cash flow pattern. The first is to forecast the operating earnings of the business for a reasonable number of years in the future. The definition of operating earnings relevant for this purpose is EBiAT, that is, earnings before interest, but after taxes, or EBIT $(1 - \text{tax rate})$, as was discussed in Chapter 3. The reason for using tax-adjusted EBIT is that we are looking for the cash flows generated *before* any financing considerations—just as we did in the case of analyzing business investments in Chapter 6.

Developing the expected earnings pattern calls for a variety of assumptions and judgments. The simplest way to project, of course, would be to keep the current level of earnings constant. Under most circumstances, however, such a simplification would not be realistic. If operating earnings can be expected to grow or decline, or follow a pronounced cyclical pattern, it's necessary to make a year-by-year projection for as far in the future as possible. Any significant nonoperating earnings after applicable taxes, such as investment income, should be recognized and added in the period they occur, as they represent part of the value of the total company.

The second step is to convert the operating earnings pattern into cash flows, by adjusting the aftertax earnings for noncash elements such as depreciation and amortization, and for deferred taxes, as we discussed in Chapters 3 and 6.

The third step is to estimate the future investment outlays deemed necessary to support both the present level of earnings and any anticipated changes in operations. These include spending on new property, plant, and equipment, major programs such as research and development projects, and all incremental working capital requirements. The outlays will be reduced by any planned disposals of existing investments.

While such estimates can be quite speculative, it's normally unrealistic to assume that earnings of an ongoing business will continue at current levels. Unquestionably, there will have to be periodic infusions of capital for replacement and upgrading of existing equipment, not to mention the requirements to support growing volume (or capital releases from volume declines), as discussed in Chapter 2. There we observed that a simplifying assumption commonly used to project these capital expenditures is that in order to maintain the present level of earnings, an amount close or equal to annual depreciation must be reinvested each year. The additional investments for expansion or new products and services and their effect on earnings are estimated as separate, distinct outlays with ensuing periodic cash inflows. We made such an assumption in the business models in Chapters 1 and 5.

The final step in setting up the pattern for valuing an ongoing business involves truncating the analysis after an appropriate number of years and deriving an estimate for the ongoing value (market value) of the business at that point. By definition, this ongoing value would be the sum of the present values of all future cash flows from that point on. Some analysts assume level cash flows (an annuity) for the foreseeable future, while others assume a declining pattern reflecting competitive and technological uncertainty. The difficulty of forecasting operations beyond the end of the chosen analysis period suggests that we find an acceptable shortcut answer for the ongoing value.

A common way of dealing with the problem is to use a simple earnings multiple at that point, i.e., to set the value of the business in year 6 or 10, or whatever cutoff point is desired, at 8, 10, or 15 times the aftertax earnings in that year. The multiple chosen will depend on the nature of the business and the trends in the industry it represents. Because of the power of discounting, such an approximation of terminal value will generally suffice.

Once all the cash flow elements have been estimated, they can be assembled in the form of a spreadsheet in this generalized format, which parallels the various examples we gave in Chapter 6:

Cash Flow Element	Year 1	Year 2	Year 3	Year i	Year j
Aftertax operating earnings*	+	+	+	+	+
Add: write-offs and other noncash items	+	+	+	+	+
Less: Net capital investments including working capital	−	−	−	−	−
Plus: Terminal value					+
Net cash flows	y_1	y_2	y_3	y_i	y_j

* plus any significant *nonoperating* earnings after taxes.

The resulting annual net cash flows (free cash flow) represent the cash available to the company to support its obligations to all providers of the long-term funds, i.e., the payment of interest, dividends, and potential repayment of debt or even repurchase of its own shares.

After discounting the pattern of annual cash flows over the chosen time frame at the appropriate return standard, normally the weighted cost of capital, the resulting net present value will be a fair approximation of the value of the total business. The quality of the result depends, of course, on the quality of the estimates that were used in deriving it. The analyst should employ extensive sensitivity analysis to test the likely range of outcomes.

It'll be useful to demonstrate visually how this present value relates to a company's capital structure. What we've developed by discounting the net cash flow stream and the assumed terminal value is the approximate fair market value of the company's *capitalization.* Figure 9–4 demonstrates that the total recorded value of a business is the sum of its working capital, fixed assets, and other assets, which are financed by the combination of long-term debt and equity. The present value approach has enabled us to express this accounting value in current

FIGURE 9–4

Present Value of Business Cash Flows and the Capital Structure

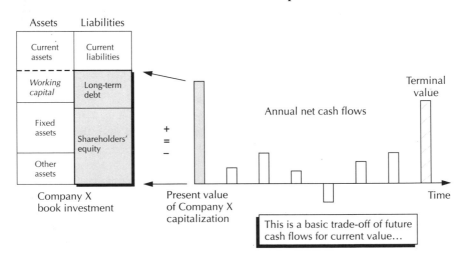

economic terms—a present value which may be higher or lower than the recorded values on the balance sheet. Only by coincidence will the two values be precisely equal, because as we discussed in Chapter 1, recorded values on the balance sheet reflect historical transaction values which may become obsolete with the passage of time.

It should be evident that to arrive at the market value of the shareholders' equity, we must subtract the value of the long-term debt from the present value result—which was the market value of the total business, also called *value of the firm* or *enterprise value*. It may be necessary to restate the value of long-term debt based on the current yields prevailing for debt of similar risk, as we discussed earlier in this chapter, rather than the recorded values on the balance sheet. For example, if current interest rates are higher than the stated rates for the company's debt, the value of the debt will be lower than recorded, and vice versa. By observing this principle, we remain consistent with the weighted average cost of capital yardstick applied in discounting the cash flow pattern, a measure which contains the cost of incremental debt, as we recall from Chapter 7. A similar deduction must be made for any preferred stock contained in the capital structure.

We've now achieved a direct valuation of the company's common equity by means of an economic approach which is superior to the simpler devices discussed in the common stock section of this chapter. This concept is the basis for much of the analytical work underlying modern security analysis, where the use of cash flow analysis has begun to overshadow most other methodologies.

In a multibusiness company, the approach can be refined by developing operating cash flow patterns for each of the business units, and discounting these individual patterns at the corporate cost of capital or, if the businesses differ widely in their risk/reward conditions, by applying different discount standards that reflect these differences. In recent years, testing the present value of individual business units' cash flow patterns to determine the relative contribution to the total value of the corporation has become widely accepted.

Yet given the nature of the estimates underlying the analysis, there's nothing automatic about the use of such values in an actual transaction involving the sale of a company or any of its parts. Different analysts and certainly buyers and sellers will use their own sets of assumptions in developing their respective results. There will also be efforts to test the analytical results against comparable transactions, to the extent these are available and relevant. The actual value finally agreed upon in any transaction between a buyer and a seller will depend on many more factors, not the least of which is the difference in the return expectations of the parties involved, and the negotiating stance and skills used by them.

Shortcuts in Valuing an Ongoing Business

In the previous approach, an earnings multiple was used to derive the terminal value for the business. This multiple simply indicated what a particular level of current or projected earnings was "worth" at the end point of the analysis. Closely related to the price/earnings ratio, this rule of thumb is often applied to quickly value the company, and the result can be an "opener" in initial negotiations. Never precise, the earnings multiple is derived from rough statistical comparisons of similar transactions, and from a comparative evaluation of the performance of the price/earnings ratios of companies in the industry.

When the measure is turned into a ratio of estimated earnings to value, it provides a rough estimate of the rate of return on the purchase or selling price, assuming that the earnings chosen are representative of what the future will bring. When taken as only one of the indicators of value within a whole array of negotiating data, the earnings multiple and the related crude rate of return have some merit.

Other shortcuts in valuing an ongoing business involve determining the total market value of common and preferred equity from market quotations—in itself somewhat of a challenge in view of stock market fluctuations—and adjusting this total for any long-term debt to be assumed in the transaction. One issue involved in this approach is the question of how representative the market quotations are depending on the trading pattern and volume of the particular stock. At times, when no publicly traded securities are involved, the book value of the business is examined as an indicator of value. Needless to say, the fact that recorded values don't necessarily reflect economic values can be a significant problem.

All of these results may at one time or another enter into the deliberations, but considerable judgment must be exercised to determine their relevance in the particular case. In most situations, the discounted cash flow approach will be the conceptually most convincing measure.

Value in Restructuring and Combinations

We'll now apply the concepts of cash flow analysis of an ongoing business and related measures to the specific issue of restructuring a company for higher value, or for seeking higher value in a combination of two or more companies.

Restructuring and Value

The opportunity to restructure arises from the perception—by management or by interested outside parties—that a *value gap* exists between the value actually being created by a company, and the potential value achievable under changed circumstances. In simple terms, this value gap is the difference between the present value of the projected cash flows under existing conditions, and the present value of a different and usually higher cash flow pattern from the restructured company. The attraction in a corporate takeover is for the acquirer to realize the potential benefits implicit in the value gap. Depending on the circumstances, the value gap can support very sizable premiums in the price bidding usually encountered in takeover situations—even though at times the final result may be a reverse gap due to an excessive premium paid in the heat of the contest.

It's beyond the scope of this book to develop all aspects of the rationale and the special considerations and techniques employed by corporate takeover specialists, leveraged buyout consultants, and investment bankers using a large variety of instruments, including junk bonds, to achieve the restructuring of large and small companies. Instead, we'll briefly discuss the economic rationale and basic analytical approach to determining the value gap. For this purpose, the most common reasons that explain the value gap should be listed first.

Underperformance by parts or all of a company is likely to be the most important cause of lowered values. In thousands of situations, the historical record and projected performance by existing management using existing strategies and policies was demonstrated to be inferior to peer companies. Such a record is usually directly reflected in relative share price levels. Whether restructuring is initiated by the board of directors from within, or through friendly or hostile initiatives by outsiders, the aim is to raise lagging performance and cash flow expectations. Revision of business strategies, improved cost-effectiveness and technology, reduction of unnecessary expenses, and more aggressive management of the company's resources are commonly used to achieve such results.

Disposal of selected lines of business is an extension of the improvement strategies mentioned above. Here the considerations may involve the sale of poor performers and reinvesting the proceeds in more promising parts of the company, distributing the cash to owners in the form of special dividends—or even repurchasing shares, which in recent years has become an increasingly popular way of creating value with excess cash. Successful lines of business may also be sold with the idea of realizing the economic gains from such a "star," and using the proceeds to fund remaining potential successes. Another consideration is to more sharply focus the attention of management on lines of activity it can competently manage for long-term success. Not to be overlooked is the fact that proceeds from the sale of part of a company can help finance the takeover transaction itself.

Eliminating redundant assets is often used as a means of freeing economic value that tends to remain hidden, such as unused real estate, investments, and even excessive amounts of cash bearing only minimal returns. The restructuring analysis in effect focuses on separating those economic values that are necessary to carry on the desired activities, while "cashing in" on all resources not relevant to the core purposes of the new company.

It should be clear that the point of view of restructuring is to develop, in essence, a breakup value of the company under study, carefully examining each business unit and all major assets held, and looking for ways of not only improving operating cash flows but also realizing the economic values of resources that can be stripped away without affecting the chosen direction.

From an analytical standpoint, the approach is quite similar to the present value cash flow valuation discussed earlier. The main difference is that a set of estimates is used that identifies specific enhancements in the cash flow pattern, as well as disposal values from businesses or redundant resources.

If our earlier analysis can be stated as

$$\text{Value} = PV(\text{Free cash flow} + \text{Terminal value})$$

the restructuring approach can be stated as

$$\text{Value} = PV(\text{Free cash flow} + \text{Terminal value}) + PV(\text{Enhancements})$$
$$+ PV(\text{Disposal proceeds} - \text{Cash flow lost from disposals})$$

and the value gap will be the difference between the two results. A key attraction to the restructurer is, of course, obtaining control of the higher cash flows involved.

It should be noted that two other aspects enter the picture. First, if a company changes hands in a restructuring, the depreciation basis for the assets involved is usually increased because of the higher values involved in the transaction, which under the purchase method of accounting are then recorded on the new set of books. This recorded value increase translates directly into a stream of future cash flows because of the tax shield effect of depreciation. For example, if the acquired company's depreciable assets have a book value of $500 million, but are written up to $650 million because of the premium paid during the acquisition, the acquiring company will gain the cash value of the tax shield on the $150 million differential during the remaining life of the assets. If the company's tax rate is 40 percent, a total of $60 million in cash flow spread over the asset lives will be created, assuming the company has sufficient earnings to take advantage of these write-offs. The present value of this cash flow pattern is a direct offset to the price premium the acquiring company is paying. In effect, the U.S. government is helping to finance the transaction.

Second, if the restructuring introduces higher financial leverage, as is usually the case, the impact on return on shareholders' equity should be favorable, even though the cash flow valuation may be adversely affected. As the risk exposure increases, the cost of debt in the company's weighted cost of capital will rise, causing the discount standard to rise and thereby lowering the present value. This is another example of the different signals given by accounting and economic measures.

Combinations and Synergy

Another form of restructuring is found in the combination of two or more hitherto independent companies. The rationale often claimed for acquisitions and mergers is that synergy between the entities will bring real economic benefits. While many empirical studies have cast serious doubt on whether business combinations are as mutually beneficial as hoped, it's tempting to assume that joining two separate businesses, particularly in the same industry, will tend to bring about some operating efficiencies. Examples might include the potential to fully engage partially utilized manufacturing facilities or warehousing space, eliminating duplicate railway tracks or delivery routes, or consolidating certain activities, such as marketing and selling, support staff, and administration. Many of these benefits are also expected when complementary companies or even those in different businesses are combined.

The impact of synergy can be felt in two major ways. The more *direct* benefits are identifiable cash flow improvements, i.e., lower expenses that result from consolidation and reduction of facilities and staffs, and higher contribution from improved market position and coverage. The specific levels of such cash flow benefits must be estimated when an acquisition or merger is considered. Such estimates will, of course, vary in quality depending on how quantifiable the various opportunities for improvement are. There are also likely to be the kinds of tax shield and leverage effects we discussed in the previous section.

A more *indirect* benefit is that the stock of the combined company may become more attractive to investors and will achieve a higher market price, reflecting improved cash flows. Security analysts and the investment community generally expect combinations that are considered synergistic to result not only in a more profitable company, but possibly one poised for faster growth, one with a stronger market position, or one subject to lesser earnings fluctuations as the cycles of the individual businesses offset each other. This reassessment may in time lower the company's risk premium, its cost of capital, and also improve the expected price/earnings ratio.

Possible profit improvements resulting from a business combination can be displayed to the extent they are quantifiable. To do this, the analyst uses two sets of pro forma statements. One set shows the projected net profits and cash flows from each company separately, while the other reflects the combined company and includes the envisioned improvements. These statements then become the basis for comparative ratio analysis, for calculating value with various methods, including present value analysis, and for highlighting the estimated annual amount of synergistic effect included in the second set of statements.

At times it may be useful to determine separately the present value of all the synergistic cash flow benefits contained in the combined pro forma statements. This present value can then be used as a rough guide in negotiating the terms of the merger, as the value of these benefits may have to be considered in setting the value premium the acquirer has to pay. In the end, the basis for valuation is likely to be a combination of present value analysis, rules of thumb, and the effect of a large variety of conditions both tangible and intangible.

Combinations and Share Values

When an exchange of common stock is involved in an acquisition or merger agreement, the valuation challenge is extended beyond the economic valuation of the cash flow patterns themselves. The problem of valuing two different securities arises, as well as having to find an appropriate ratio of exchange which reflects the respective values of the shares. Moreover, in most cases, the acquirer has to pay a significant premium (between 15 and 25 percent is the usual range) over the objective value of the acquired company.

This premium will, of course, not only affect the cash flow results, but also impact the actual ratio of exchange of shares agreed on. While in the end a numerical solution is applied, the underlying values and the premium will be the result of extensive negotiation and a certain amount of "horse trading."

As the two stocks are valued, any differences in the quality and breadth of trading in the securities markets can be an important factor. If, for example, a large, well-established company acquires a new and fast growing company, the market value assessment of the acquirer's stock is likely more reliable than that of the candidate, whose stock may be thinly traded and unproven. But even if they had comparable market exposure, the inherent difference in the nature performance of the two companies may exhibit itself in, among other indi a pronounced difference in price/earnings ratios. In effect, this m company's performance is valued less highly in the market than the other. This difference will tend to influence valuation of the stocks and the final price negotiated—apart from the specific cash flow patterns that have been developed for economic valuation.

We'll demonstrate just a few key calculations needed to arrive at the basis of exchange, using a simplified example. Let's assume that Acquirer Corporation and Candidate, Inc. have the following key dimensions and performance data at the time of their merger negotiations:

Key Data	Acquirer Corporation	Candidate, Inc.
Current earnings	$50 million	$10 million
Number of shares	10 million	10 million
Earnings per share	$5.00	$1.00
Current market price	$60.00	$15.00
Price/earnings ratio	12 X	15 X

Negotiations between the management teams have reached a point where, after Candidate had rejected several offers, Acquirer now considers a price premium of about 20 percent over the current market value of Candidate's stock necessary to make a deal. This would call for an exchange ratio of $18/$60, or about 0.3 shares of Acquirer stock for each share of Candidate stock. The impact on Acquirer would be as follows, at the combined current levels of earnings that include no synergistic benefits:

	Acquirer Corporation
Combined earnings	$60 million
Number of shares (10.0 + 3.0 million)	13 million
New earnings per share	$4.62
Old earnings per share	$5.00
Immediate dilution	$0.38

Under these conditions, Acquirer would suffer an immediate dilution of 38 cents per share from the combination. Yet the fact that the stock of Candidate had a higher price/earnings ratio suggests that the smaller company enjoys desirable attributes which may include high growth in earnings, a technologically protected

therefore consider two points. First, are the earnings of Can-
 at a rate that will close the gap in earnings per share rela-
 by any synergistic benefits available now? Second, is the
late likely to change the risk/reward characteristics of the
 so as to improve the price/earnings ratio—and thus help
on?

In our example, the earnings gap to be filled is 13 million shares times 38 cents, or almost $5 million in annual earnings—just to return to the current level of Acquirer's earnings per share. How much in synergistic benefits can be expected? Perhaps the ratio of exchange has to be reconsidered in this light. But would the smaller company even be interested in being acquired at less than a 20 percent premium over market, a not uncommon inducement?

Note that if we assume a reversal of the price/earnings ratios in the example, both the terms of the offer and the reported performance of the combined companies would change dramatically. At 15 times earnings, the price of Acquirer would be $75 per share, while at 12 times earnings, Candidate would sell at $12 per share. Given a 20 percent acquisition premium for Candidate's stock, the exchange ratio would be $14.40 ÷ $75, or 0.192 shares of Acquirer for each share of Candidate. This would call for 1.92 million new shares of Acquirer, and the new earnings per share would amount to $60,000,000 − 11,920,000, or $5.03 per share, a slight net improvement even before any synergistic benefits are realized. In this changed situation, both parties would be better off immediately, simply because we assumed the price/earnings ratios to be reversed. It's possible, of course, that a company acquired at a premium—which has caused the combined earnings per share to drop initially—may more than offset the gap with higher growth and synergistic benefits later. This would depend on the relative size of the two companies as well as on the value and exchange considerations discussed.

We've given but one simplified example, and therefore only a quick glimpse of the nature of the deliberations involved in exchanges of stock, which usually are superimposed on the detailed cash flow economics used in valuing the companies. At the same time we have attempted to alert the reader to the many issues underlying the valuation process in mergers and acquisitions. Analysis of such transactions always involves careful projections of the separate and combined earnings and cash flow patterns, the calculation of dilution, and an assessment of the likely risk/reward market response—in effect, a potential change in the β—as an input to the negotiation process.

INTEGRATION OF VALUE ANALYSIS

We've discussed a large variety of value concepts and valuation approaches in this chapter, ranging all the way from simple rules of thumb to economic cash flow models. We've used some illustrative examples from time to time in using the formulas, but also recognized that valuation is one of the more difficult areas of financial analysis which must be practiced with more integrative problems. Such complex cases go beyond the scope of this book, but they can be readily found in more extensive finance texts and case books, such as we've listed at the end of each chapter.

For our purposes, it'll be useful to touch on a series of key areas that are commonly found in the valuation process, and to provide a broad framework within which to view the practice. We'll address the following points:

- Perspectives in valuation.
- Dealing with expectations.
- Choosing the time period.
- Developing the pattern.
- Estimating ending values.
- Using comparables for validation.
- Results and negotiation.

Perspectives

No value judgment can be derived without a proper perspective on the nature of the issue being addressed. Early in the chapter we presented a variety of definitions of value, each of which was based on a particular perspective that made it relevant. But even within a particular category, such as deriving the economic value of a business, there are different perspectives that must be defined and understood before the methodology and framework for analysis are chosen. For example, are we establishing the value of equity for purposes of an exchange of shares, or are we determining the total business value? Are we attempting to value a business unit in order to set incentive plan targets for its management? Is the purpose of the analysis to establish a negotiating basis for a contested acquisition, or are we contemplating the sale of a successful business unit? In each case, there will not only be differences in the specific inputs and even the methodology chosen, but also differences in the interpretation of the results.

As we've observed before, solid preparatory thinking for any analytical task is much more important than the application of the tools themselves. This is particularly true in business valuation analysis, because most issues in this area usually have to be viewed within a very complex framework and with a strategic background. When a business entity is valued in part or as a whole, the judgments required extend directly or indirectly to all success factors that drive the business—within a future-oriented mindset. To ensure that the appropriate elements are considered and the proper tools chosen, the specific purpose of the analysis and its likely implications must be understood from the outset.

Expectations

These are the basis for most valuation approaches, because it is fair to say that the economic value of an object or a business entity reflects the benefits to be obtained from owning it. These benefits, whether stated in the form of earnings, cash flows, or future recoveries will always be estimates of future events. We've encountered this principle in earlier chapters, and observed that depending on the importance of the analytical task, a degree of sensitivity analysis should be performed. Given the importance of valuing businesses as a whole or in major segments, the need for at least developing ranges of estimates should be obvious. This requires that the drivers behind earnings and cash flows be understood and the major variables tested for changes in projected conditions. It is simply not sufficient to project current earnings or cash flow levels.

Time Period

The period chosen for a business valuation most often depends on the nature of the industry of the company or unit being analyzed, unless there is a time horizon specific to the company, such as planned strategic change or a limited life cycle in a particular product or service. For example, the changes occurring in high technology industries are so frequent and extensive that time horizons of more than three years can be unrealistic. In cyclical industries, the time horizon should extend for at least one business cycle, while multibusiness companies with a portfolio mix of ascending, declining, and new venture business units can likely be valued over a five- to eight-year period. The main point is that the time horizon has to be a function of the circumstances, not the apparent neatness of a five- or ten-year pattern.

Cash Flow Pattern

The economic valuation process depends greatly on establishing a realistic pattern of expected cash flows, just as we discussed in Chapter 6 for business investments. It is critical that the earnings stream expected during the time period under analysis reflect not only the ongoing operations of the company or business unit, but is also adjusted for planned strategic investments, divestments, potential synergies from combinations, major research outlays, and planned restructuring. In other words, the pattern of inflows and outflows should as closely as possible represent a strategic plan for the business under review.

Just as important is the need to be consistent in the adjustments for accounting processes, such as depreciation, amortization, and other elements that may or may not affect cash flows. This includes the tax shield benefits that may arise from revaluing assets in the case of a purchase. In most analyses, the data will be expressed in a form closely related to free cash flow, while in simpler situations earnings-based approaches may be used.

It's good practice to base the analysis on cash flows at some point in the process. This allows the analyst to deal consistently with the cash-in, cash-out trade-offs that underlie value, which can then be alternatively tested and expanded through earnings-based analyses.

Ending Values

This aspect of value analysis is probably the least comfortable for analysts to deal with. The ending or terminal value at the point where the analysis is truncated on the time scale is in itself a business valuation of an ongoing operation—but several years removed from the present. Obviously, the shorter the time period, the more this value can affect the result because of the effect of discounting. But more important is the issue of how to set a realistic figure, when the pattern of expected cash flows leading up to this value was already difficult enough to establish. We discussed using price/earnings ratios, capitalizing the last year's cash flows, or using growth formulas.

Any one of these processes doesn't substitute for the careful judgment required to assess, from a broad strategic standpoint, whether the company or business unit will be viable at the end point, and whether it's realistic to assume steady growth, continued competitive strength, and repeated technological success. For example, it's probably a sound assumption that performance far above a company's peers cannot be sustained indefinitely, because competitive pressures will inevitably moderate such results. The analyst must address these issues in the valuation process and not let the convenience of simple rules of thumb or multiples take over. Ending values are also a place where ranges of estimates and sensitivity analysis should be employed, to scope the possible variations and their impact on the results.

Comparables

Part of the analytical challenge is the calibration of the results obtained. In other words, the value derived from a thorough analysis of a particular company or business unit should be tested against comparable companies or business units as a matter of course. In fact, it's sound practice to attempt to calibrate the major assumptions used during the process of developing the time pattern and ending values. At the same time, we must be realistic about the amount and quality of data available for this purpose, and about the differences that invariably affect the matching of the subject company or business unit with peers.

The very effort of developing comparable values and indicators, however, forces the analyst to be thoughtful about the realism of the assumptions used in the analysis. If profit margins, growth rates, investment patterns, and research outlays differ materially from comparable companies, the resulting cash flow pattern should be assessed critically. Furthermore, comparable companies or businesses are likely to be competitors, and trying to bring their dimensions into the analysis necessarily introduces a strategic perspective. Finally, if the valuation results are to be used in negotiation, there's every reason to believe that comparables will be brought up in one form or another.

Negotiations

Inevitably, negotiations affect the extent and direction of any valuation process. While objectivity for any analytical task is a worthwhile goal, the pressure of securing advantageous negotiation positions at the outset and during the deliberations will spur the parties to interpret the data and results from this perspective. Here the notion of using ranges as well as minimum and maximum acceptable results becomes commonplace. The practical implication for analysis is simply that the perspective of the analyst must change to take into account the tactics and strategies by the parties involved, and that the analysis should be made from more than one viewpoint. The analytical tools will likely be the same, but it's also to be expected that the parties will emphasize those approaches that favor their position. This should not be surprising, for as we've said many times, financial/economic analysis is not a freestanding activity, but intricately related to the specific needs and issues surrounding it.

MANAGING FOR SHAREHOLDER VALUE

We now return to the primary concept we established at the beginning of this book, namely, that the basic obligation of the management of any company is to make investment, operating, and financing decisions that will enhance shareholder value over the long term. Our discussion of valuing business cash flows and the issues involved in restructuring strongly suggest that management should periodically re-examine the policies and strategies followed to test whether its basic obligation of creating shareholder value is being met. We recall that increasing shareholder value depends on making new investments that exceed the cost of capital—an expression of investor expectations—as well as managing existing investments for cash flow results that similarly exceed investor expectations.

Despite the upheavals caused by the takeover boom of recent years, its most beneficial aspect has been the widespread rediscovery of management fun-damentals—even if under threat of dismissal by hostile raiders. In fact, testing the efficiency with which all resources are employed and defining the relative contribution from various business segments with an objective "outside" orien-tation has become commonplace in many companies. One could argue that this approach should have been commonplace all along, because the economic basis of all business decisions should have been recognized.

In recent years, a number of valuation methodologies have been developed which aim to link past and expected cash flow patterns to the market value of a company as a whole and to the relative price level of its common shares. Referred to as *value management,* such approaches are used by various consulting firms to establish a firm connection between management actions and shareholder value results. Moreover, such programs relate cash flow thinking and results to man-agement incentive pay, and are designed to provide a coherent set of economic principles that should guide a company's planning processes, investment poli-cies, financing choices, operational decisions, and management incentives toward increasing shareholder value.

The most sophisticated and empirically grounded methodology of this kind has been developed by HOLT Value Associates, a subsidiary of The Boston Consult-ing Group (see the reference at the end of the chapter). Its value-based management system is based on translating a company's financial results through a variety of ad-justments into a current-dollar cash flow return on investment (CFROI) measure, which expresses the company's economic performance. This concept, when applied to expected cash flows and combined with projected growth in the company's asset base, can be used to calculate the company's market value. The HOLT model recog-nizes the adjusted cash flow contributions from existing assets and combines them with new investment cash flows, all on a comparable economic basis. This culmi-nates in the concept of *cash value added (CVA),* that amounts to finding the eco-nomic value created by successful business strategies and investments.

In effect, HOLT transforms a company's financial data into a consistent series of economic "project" cash flows that, when discounted at an empirically derived investor's return standard, permits calculation of the relative market value of the company's capitalization. In most cases, the calculated share values not only track very closely with historical price patterns but also become solid predictors for expected value if the assumed cash flows are realized in the future. The model is a highly integrated and sophisticated application of the economic cash flow principles we've discussed throughout this book.

Another approach that has gained wide publicity in recent years is the concept of *economic value added (EVA),* developed by Stern Stewart & Company (see the reference at the end of the chapter). This is not a new principle, because in its basic form, EVA simply states that a company or a business unit is adding value when aftertax earnings before interest are higher than the weighted cost of capital of the resources employed. The calculation is a straightforward subtraction of the cost of capital from earnings:

$$EVA = EBIT\,(1 - t\,) - Ck$$

where

> t = effective tax rate.
> C = total recorded long-term capital employed (net of depreciation).
> k = weighted average cost of capital.

Note that the formula as stated relies on reported earnings and the recorded capital base supporting these earnings, not on cash flows. In effect, EVA is determined by subtracting from earnings a capital charge for the book value of the money invested in the company by owners and creditors. For a business unit, the capital charge is usually based on the net assets employed. EVA therefore appears to be more of an accounting-based than economic measure. In practice, however, Stern Stewart makes a large series of adjustments when working with client companies to calibrate the measure closer to an economic cash flow basis, paralleling the economic valuation concepts we've discussed earlier. Moreover, the EVA approach is applied not only to measuring current performance but also to measuring new investments and to developing incentive compensation.

Let's now turn to a summary overview of the major elements of shareholder value creation and their relationship to the three areas of management decisions: investments, operations, and financing. The diagram in Figure 9–5 will be useful in tying together the various concepts we've discussed. It's designed to assist the reader in visualizing the linkage between management decisions and shareholder value. The diagram shows the three basic types of decisions on the left and identifies their key impacts on the cash flows that are the drivers for creating value. The combination of investment and operating decisions generates cash flow from operations after taxes, or free cash flow, while the financing decisions will influence the capital structure and the level of the weighted cost of capital of the company.

Applying the cost of capital—which of course reflects expected investor returns—as a discount rate to the free cash flow determines the shareholder value, as we discussed earlier. At the same time, product life cycles, competition, and many other influences will affect the size and variability of the cash flow from operations. In turn, the capital markets will influence the investor's return expectation.

Alternatively, the last part of the diagram shows that shareholder value can also be viewed as a combination of cash dividends and realized capital gains, when seen through the eyes of the shareholder. This investor viewpoint is inseparable from the basic driving force of the business—cash flow patterns—for it is positive free cash flow that will permit the company to pay dividends in the first

FIGURE 9–5

An Overview of Shareholder Value Creation

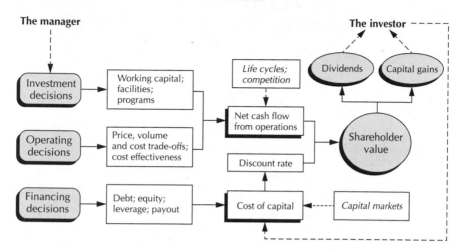

place, and will also boost the market value of the shares, enabling the investor to realize capital gains.

What are the implications of this overview? Note that we have once more returned to a systems view of the corporation, driven by the same three basic management decisions, but stressing the cash flow patterns that are the economic underpinning of performance and value. All financial analysis techniques and methodologies in the end are related to the business system as viewed here and in Chapter 1.

The basic message of managing for shareholder value is nothing more than management's obligation to base all of its investment, operating, and financing decisions on an economic—cash flow—rationale, and to manage all resources entrusted to its care for superior economic returns. Over time, consistency in this approach will generate growing shareholder value, and relative growth in share price performance.

If this sounds fundamental, it's intended to be, for the challenge left by the waning 20th Century is competitive survival through managing better in a world arena—where economic fundamentals are gaining dominance over ideology. Financial analysis in its many forms, as it was introduced in Chapter 1 and specifically explained in the remainder of this book, is an essential tool kit for analytically oriented persons of any viewpoint, as they judge the financial/ economic performance and outlook of any business.

KEY ISSUES

The following is a recap of the key issues raised directly or indirectly in this chapter. They are enumerated here to help the reader keep the techniques discussed within the perspective of financial theory and business practice.

1. The challenge of valuation involves the dual problems of forecasting the economic benefits derived from an asset, and of selecting an economic standard against which to measure these benefits.

2. Value takes many forms, but in the end, valuation in business must rest on an attempt to express an economic risk/reward trade-off in the form of cash flows committed and cash flows generated.

3. Investors approach the valuation of an investment proposition in terms of their individual risk preferences. Thus, market values are a function of individual and collective risk assessments.

4. Valuation techniques are essentially assessment tools that attempt to quantify available objective data. Yet such quantification will always remain in part subjective, and in part impacted by forces beyond the individual parties' control.

5. While the securities markets provide momentary indications, the relative value of a share of common stock in the market at any time is a combination of future expectations, residual claims, and assessments of general and specific risk, subject to economic and business conditions and the decisions of management and the board of directors.

6. Valuation is distorted by the same elements that distort other types of financial analysis: price-level changes, accounting conventions, economic conditions, market fluctuations, and many subjective intangible factors.

7. Valuing a business for sale or purchase is one of the most complex tasks an analyst can undertake. It calls for skills in projection of earnings and cash flows, assessment of risk, strategic insight and interpretation of the impact of combining management styles, operations, and resources.

8. Shareholder value is the ultimate result of successful investments, operations and financing carried out by management within an economic framework. However, the link between a company's current and prospective performance in these areas and the market value of its common stock at a particular time is not necessarily direct or directly measurable, because of the combination of forces acting on the stock market.

SUMMARY

In this chapter, we have brought together a whole range of concepts and techniques to provide the reader with an overview of how to value assets, securities, and business operations. To set the stage, we discussed key definitions of value, and then took the viewpoint of the investor assessing the value of the three main forms of securities issued by a company. After covering both value and yield in these situations, we expanded our view to encompass the value of an ongoing business. Our purpose was to find ways of setting the value in transactions such as sale of a business, restructuring, or the combination of companies in the form of a merger or acquisition.

We found that methods were available for deriving such values, but that the specific assumptions and the background of the transaction added many dimensions to the basic calculations. Finally, we reviewed the concept of managing for shareholder value, returning to a systems overview that linked management decisions on investment, operations, and financing to the present value of a business, and in turn linked shareholder value to dividends and capital gains. Ultimately, value will always remain partially subjective and will be settled in an exchange between interested parties—but managing for economic performance and value will always remain the basic obligation of management.

SELECTED REFERENCES

Brealey, Richard and Stewart Myers. *Principles of Corporate Finance.* 4th ed. New York: McGraw Hill, 1991.

Copeland, Tom; Tim Koller; and Jack Murrin. *Measuring and Managing the Value of Companies.* McKinsey & Company, Inc. New York: John Wiley & Sons, 1991.

Cornell, Bradford. *Corporate Valuation: Tools for Effective Appraisal and Decision Making.* Homewood, IL: Business One Irwin, 1993.

McTaggart, James M., Peter W. Kontes, and Michael C. Mankins. *The Value Imperative.* New York: The Free Press, 1994.

Pratt, Shannon P. *Valuing a Business: The Analysis and Appraisal of Closely Held Companies.* 2nd ed. Homewood, Ill.: Dow Jones-Irwin, 1989.

Rappaport, Alfred. *Creating Shareholder Value.* New York: Free Press, 1986.

Ross, Stephen; Randolph Westerfield; and Jeffrey Jaffe. *Corporate Finance.* 4th ed. Burr Ridge, IL: Richard D. Irwin, 1996.

Stewart, G. Bennett, III. *The Quest for Value.* New York: Harper Business, 1991. (Stern Stewart & Co. EVA concepts).

The Boston Consulting Group. *Value Based Management: A Framework for Managing Value Creation.* Chicago, IL: 1993. (Holt value concepts)

Weston, J.F., and Eugene Brigham. *Essentials of Managerial Finance.* 10th ed. Hinsdale, IL: Dryden Press, 1992.

SELF-STUDY EXERCISES AND PROBLEMS

(Solutions provided in Appendix V)

1. Using the present value tables in Chapter 6, develop the value (price) of bonds with the following characteristics:

   a. A bond with a face value of $1,000 carries interest of 8 percent per year, paid semiannually. It will be redeemed for $1,075 at the end of 14 years. At what price would the bond yield a return of 6 percent? A yield of 10 percent?

b. A bond with a face value of $1,000 carries interest of 8.5 percent per year, paid semiannually. It's callable at 110 percent of face value beginning October 1, 2006, and will be redeemed (unless called) on October 1, 2016. What price on October 1, 1997, would yield a prospective investor a return of 6 percent? What price would yield 9 percent? (Use interpolation.)

2. Develop the approximate yield (return) of bonds with the following characteristics:

a. A bond with a face value of $1,000 carries interest at 7 percent per year, paid semiannually on January 15 and July 15. It will be redeemed at 110 percent on July 15, 2008. The market quotation on July 15, 1997, is 124⅛. What's the approximate yield to an investor who purchases the bond on this date? What's the exact yield given in an appropriate bond table?

b. The same bond is quoted at 122½ on September 1, 1997. In addition to the market price, accrued interest is paid by the purchaser if the trade takes place between interest dates. What's the exact yield given in an appropriate bond table?

c. A bond with a face value of $500 carries interest at 8 percent per year, paid annually. It will be redeemed at par on March 1, 2018. The bond was purchased on August 20, 1997, for $487.50, including accrued interest. What's the approximate yield? What's the exact yield, using an appropriate bond table or a computer?

3. Develop and discuss the value of individual rights to subscribe to shares of stock under the circumstances of (*a*) and (*b*), and calculate the subscription price in (*c*).

a. A company is offering its common stockholders the right to subscribe to one share of common at $65 for each 12 shares held. At the time of the offering, the common is trading at $89. What's the likely market value of the common going to be after the offering period (ex rights)?

b. A company is offering its common stockholders the right to purchase one share of 7 percent convertible preferred at $82 for each six shares of common stock held. A reasonable expectation is that the preferred will be trading at $105, once issued. What would the rights value be if the offer were made for each four shares of common held?

c. If the value of a right is expected to be $2, and the market price is expected to be $123 after exercise of the rights, what's the subscription price under a subscription ratio of 11:1?

4. The following information is available about two different common stocks, Company A and Company B:

	Company A	Company B
Earnings per share:	$2.50	$7.25
Dividends per share	1.00	5.00
Growth in earnings	8%	4%
Price range	$26–$20	$60–$56
β	1.3	0.8
Risk-free return	7.0%	7.0%
Expected return, S&P 500	13.5%	13.5%

On the assumption that the companies' growth rates will continue, develop an estimate of the value of the common stock and its yield for each. Discuss.

5. The following estimates about the next five years' performance of GHI Company have been provided to you. Based on this information and the current data available to you, calculate the value of the company as a going business, assuming that the expected return from such a business investment would be 12% after taxes. Test the present value calculation against other yardsticks of value. Discuss.

GHI Company Projections
($ millions)

	Year 1	Year 2	Year 3	Year 4	Year 5
Projected earnings (after taxes)	$2.7	$2.9	$3.2	$3.6	$4.0
Projected investments (including working capital)	$0.5	$2.5	$1.5	$1.5	$2.0
Projected depreciation	$1.0	$1.1	$1.4	$1.6	$1.8

The terminal value at the end of the period can be estimated at between ten and twelve times earnings. The company's earnings for the past year were $2.5 million, and the price/earnings ratio for its industry is currently 11.0.

6. The MNO Company's stock was closely held, and the volume of stock traded over the counter represented only a small fraction of the total shares outstanding. You've been asked to develop as many valuation approaches as possible in preparation for the disposition of a 25 percent block of common stock held by the estate of one of the founders. The estate's executor will be interested in the possible viewpoints to be taken in arriving at a fair value. The following data have been made available for the purpose:

MNO COMPANY
Balance Sheet, December 31, 1997
($ thousands)

Assets

Current assets:

Cash	$ 230	(working balance, $150)
Marketable securities	415	(held for payment of taxes and investment in equipment)
Accounts receivable	525	(94% collectible, net of expenses)
Inventories	815	(quick disposal value two-thirds of book, normal sale 95%)
Total current assets	1,985	
Fixed assets	1,715	(quick sale value $225, replacement value, $2,500)
Less: Accumulated depreciation	820	
Net fixed assets	895	
Prepaid expenses	40	(insurance, licenses, etc.)
Goodwill	175	(based on previous acquisitions)
Organization expense	20	(legal fees, taxes)
Total assets	$3,115	

Liabilities and Net Worth

Current liabilities:

Accounts payable	$ 370	($350 current, $20 overdue)
Notes payable	125	(due 60 days hence)
Accrued liabilities	290	(wages, interest, etc.)
Accrued taxes	150	(income taxes, withholding)
Total current liabilities	935	
Mortgage payable	175	(80% of fixed assets as security)
Bonds, net of sinking fund	520	(unsecured)
Deferred income taxes	55	
Reserve for self-insurance	110	(contingency surplus reserve)
Preferred stock	300	(7% preferred, 3,000 shares)
Common stock	525	(52,500 shares, $10 par)
Capital surplus	110	(excess paid in for common)
Retained earnings	385	(accumulated earnings less dividends)
Total liabilities and net worth	$3,115	

The company's β is estimated at 1.2 while the spread between a risk-free return of 7 percent and S&P 500 returns is expected to be about 6 percent.

Operating History, MNO Company

	1993	1994	1995	1996	1997	3-31-98*
Profit after taxes (000) . . .	$92	$110	$126	$139	$118	$34
Depreciation	62	63	66	70	72	19
Earnings per share	1.75	2.10	2.40	2.65	2.25	0.64
Dividends per share	1.20	1.60	1.60	1.80	1.80	0.45
Market price, high	31⅜	33¼	37⅞	34⅛	29¾	30⅞
Market price, low	13⅞	19¾	23⅝	22⅛	19¼	19⅜
Market price, average	22⅝	26½	31¾	28⅛	24½	25⅛
Industry price/earnings ratio	14X	15X	16X	12X	11X	—

*Quarter.

Develop valuation approaches based on book values, market values, past trends, and projections (no significant changes are expected in the operations of the company and the industry), taking into account redundant assets and limited trading of the stock. Stipulate your assumptions and list additional information you would consider necessary for a recommendation. Discuss your findings.

6. Two companies are discussing a potential merger. Company A has a price/earnings ratio of 12 ×, with current EPS of $8, a dividend of $2, and a market price range of $90 to $100, with a recent price of $98. Ten million shares are outstanding. Company B has a price/earnings ratio of 20 ×, and is growing at twice the 6 percent rate of Company A. Its current EPS are $3, it pays no dividend, and its market price is ranging between $45 and $70. One million shares are outstanding. Company A is assessing the impact of a potential offer to Company B at a price of $65, as compared to Company B's current price of $54. Calculate the appropriate measures to assess the impact of these terms, and discuss potential implications.

APPENDIX I

Glossary of Key Concepts*

Accelerated depreciation Patterns of *depreciation* write-offs that place larger proportions into the early years of an *asset's* book life, rather than into the later years, either for accounting or for tax deduction purposes.

Accounting earnings The difference between recognized *revenues* and *expenses* during an accounting period, based on generally accepted accounting principles.

Accounts payable (payables) Obligations owed to trade creditors and suppliers as incurred in the normal course of business; also called *trade credit*.

Accounts receivable (receivables) Obligations owed by customers and other parties as incurred in the normal course of business.

Accruals Recognition of *revenues* or *expenses* when earned or incurred, without regard to the actual timing of the cash transactions; used in the accrual method of accounting.

Acid test A stringent measure of *liquidity* relating current cash *assets* (cash, cash equivalents, and receivables) to *current liabilities*.

Activity-based analysis A form of *economic analysis* that develops the specific *costs* and *benefits* generated by an activity, product line, or business segment.

Aftertax cash flow Cash generated from *operations* or from an *investment* net of income taxes, derived by adding back noncash charges like *depreciation* to aftertax earnings.

Aftertax value Net *revenue*, net *cost*, or net *investment* after adjusting for the effect of applicable income taxes.

Allocation An assignment or distribution of *costs* or *revenues* to products, activity centers, or other entities using a common basis.

Amortization A periodic charge reflecting the decline in the recorded value of an *intangible asset* over a specified number of years.

Annualized net present value The transformation of a *net present value* into an equivalent series of annual cash flows over the life of the project, used in judging the proposal's margin of *risk*.

Annuity A uniform series of payments or receipts over a specified number of periods.

Asset A physical or intangible item of value to a company or an individual.

Asset turnover An expression of the effectiveness with which *assets* generate sales, defined as the ratio of *net sales* to total assets.

Balance sheet A *financial statement* reflecting the recorded values of all *assets, liabilities*, and *owners' equity* at a point in time.

Balloon payment A significant *principal* payment due at the end of the term of a financial obligation.

---

*Items shown in italics are defined separately.

Bankruptcy   A legal process of disposing of the *assets* of a business or individual to satisfy creditors' claims in total or in part, and protecting the debtor(s) from further legal action.

Benefit (cost/benefit)   The positive element in an *economic trade-off* which relates *economic earnings* to *economic costs* in an *investment, operating,* or *financing* decision.

Beta (β)   A calculated form of expressing the specific (systematic) risk of a company's *common stock* relative to the stock market as a whole. (Cf. *volatility.*)

Bond   A financial instrument representing a form of corporate *long-term debt* issued to investors; a variety of different types of bonds exist.

Bond rating   A published ranking of a *bond* developed by financial organizations to express its relative soundness on a defined scale.

Book value   The recorded value of an *asset* or *liability* as reflected in the *financial statements* of a company or individual.

Book value of equity   The recorded value of *owners' equity* on a company's *balance sheet*, representing the owners' residual claim on the *assets*.

Break-even analysis   Determining the level of sales at which a company will just recover *fixed* and *variable costs*; a zero-profit condition.

Breakup value   The value realized from separating the parts of a multibusiness company and disposing of them individually.

Burden   The combination of interest charges and current *principal* payments required by a financial obligation.

Burden coverage   The ratio of periodic *income* before taxes to the corresponding amount of *burden*, adjusted for income taxes; a test of the ability to service a *debt* obligation.

Business risk   The risk inherent in the *cash flows* from *investments* and *operations*, apart from the risk inherent in the form of *financing* used.

Call provision   A provision permitting the issuing company to redeem in part or in total a *bond* or *preferred stock* issue at a date determined by the company.

Capital   The *funds* committed to an enterprise in the form of ownership *equity* and long-term *financing*.

Capital budget   A selected group of *investment* projects approved in principle for implementation, pending individual approval, and related closely to a company's business strategies.

Capital investment   A relatively long-term commitment of funds to a project expected to generate positive net *cash flows* over time.

Capital rationing   The allocation of limited *investment* funds to a selection of investment projects smaller than all currently acceptable projects; a fairly common condition.

Capital structure   The relative proportions of different sources of *capital* used in the long-term funding of the *investments* and *operations* of a company.

Capitalization   The sum of all long-term sources of *capital* of a company, also derived by subtracting *current liabilities* from total *assets*.

Cash accounting   A method of accounting in which *revenues* and *expenses* and all other transactions are recognized when cash changes hands, in contrast to the *accrual* method of accounting.

Cash budget   A periodic projection of cash receipts and cash disbursements over a specified length of time. (Cf. *cash flow forecast.*)

Cash flow   The positive (inflow) or negative (outflow) movements of cash caused by an activity over a specific period of time.

Cash flow analysis   An economic method of analysis that employs the positive (inflow) and negative (outflow) movements of cash caused by an activity to determine the relative desirability of the activity; usually involves *discounted cash flow* methodology.

Cash flow cycle   The periodic movement of cash through an enterprise, caused by *investment, operating*, and *financing* decisions.

Cash flow forecast   A periodic forecast of cash movements through an enterprise, recognizing sources and uses of funds.

Cash flow from operations   Cash generated or used by a business over a specified period of time; usually derived by adjusting aftertax profit for *noncash* charges and noncash receipts.

Cash flow return on investment (CFROI)   A ratio relating operational cash flows to the cash value of the assets employed in generating them. In its most sophisticated form, it employs present value techniques.

Cash flow statement   A *financial statement* listing the cash impact of the activities of a business over a specified period of time, separating the *cash flows* into the areas of *operations, investments*, and *financing*. (Cf. *funds flow statement*.)

Cash value added (CVA)   A form of *net present value* analysis expressing the increase in present value caused by a business investment, a strategic plan, or the operations of a business unit.

Collection period   The average number of days over which *accounts receivable* are outstanding, either in total or by defined categories; a measure of the effectiveness with which customer *credit* is managed.

Common stock (common shares)   Securities representing a direct ownership interest in a corporation and a residual claim on the *assets*.

Common-size financial statements   A ratio analysis of *balance sheets* and *income statements* in which all elements are represented as a percentage of *assets* or *net sales*, respectively. Used in analyzing trends and in comparing statements from different companies.

Comparables   Selected *assets* or business entities chosen by analysts to establish comparability with an asset or business being valued; used in determining the *fair market value* in the absence of market transactions.

Compounding   The process of calculating the growing value of a sum of money over time, caused by the periodic interest earned and by the reinvestment of such interest.

Constant-dollar analysis   The adjustment of financial magnitudes for inflation to reflect a common dollar value basis (using dollar values of a specified point in time), and the use of these adjusted values in accounting or *economic analysis*.

Consumer price index (CPI)   An index provided by the U.S. government that represents the periodic change in the cost of a selected group of items purchased by consumers; used as a measure of *inflation*.

Contribution analysis   A method of analysis that determines the relative excess of revenue over variable costs of product lines, business segments, and activities, and judges the contribution made toward meeting *fixed costs*, overhead, and *profits*.

Conversion ratio   The stated number of *common shares* or other securities into which a *convertible security* may be exchanged.

Conversion value   The *market value* represented by the *common shares* or other *assets* into which a *convertible security* may be exchanged.

Convertible security   A financial security that may be exchanged into another security or *asset* with a prescribed *conversion ratio* at the option of the holder.

Cost   The transaction value at which an *asset* was acquired; also, any periodic *expense* recognized against matching periodic *revenue*.

Cost of capital (weighted average cost of capital, hurdle rate)   The weighted average of the aftertax cost to a company of all forms of long-term financing used; employed as a minimum standard for the return to be earned on new *investments*.

Cost of debt   The *cost* to a company of employing *debt*, developed from the aftertax interest charges of various forms of debt.

Cost of equity   The *cost* to a company of employing common shareholders' funds, developed from the investors' expectations about the return from holding such shares, usually in the form of dividends and capital gains.

Cost of goods (services) sold (cost of sales)   The total of all *costs* and *expenses* incurred in producing or acquiring goods or services for sale.

Coupon rate   The stated interest rate specified on the interest coupons attached to *bonds*, as contrasted with the *yield* obtained on a bond, which relates the coupon rate to the *market value* of the bond.

Covenant   Provision in the *bond* agreement specifying restrictions or other requirements that the issuer has to observe to maintain the bond's *credit* rating.

Coverage   Relationship of fixed requirements, such as interest or *burden* connected with *debt*, to operating income before or after taxes. (Cf. *times interest earned, times burden covered*.)

Credit (creditworthiness)   The recognized ability of an individual or company to assume indebtedness with the prospect of properly servicing such *debt*.

Cumulative preferred stock   A form of *preferred stock* that carries the provision that any unpaid dividends accumulate for later payment, and must be paid in full before common dividends may be declared.

Current asset   Any *asset* on the *balance sheet* with a short-term expectation of being turned into cash, such as cash, *receivables*, and inventories; usually considered as having a one-year time horizon or less.

Current liability   Any *liability* on the *balance sheet* with a short-term maturity, usually payable within one year, such as *accounts payable* and accrued taxes.

Current portion of long-term debt   The proportion of a long-term *liability* that is due and payable within one year.

Current ratio   A common measure of *liquidity* that relates the sum of *current assets* to the sum of *current liabilities*.

Current-dollar accounting   The adjustment of historical financial magnitudes for inflation to reflect current-dollar values (adjusting for price changes) and the use of these adjusted values in accounting or economic analysis. (Cf. *constant-dollar analysis*.)

Current-value basis   The restatement of the recorded values of selected *assets* in current dollar terms to reflect price changes. (Cf. *current-dollar accounting*.)

Cutoff rate   The minimum *rate of return* (*hurdle rate*) that *capital investment* projects have to meet, usually based on the *cost of capital* or a judgmentally adjusted standard.

Cyclical variations   The impact on a company's *funds flows* from the operational changes caused by business cycles.

Day's sales   A measure of the credit quality of *accounts receivable*, which expresses outstanding receivables in terms of average daily *sales*; can be compared with the *credit* terms under which sales were made.

Debt (liability)   An obligation to pay amounts due (and interest if required) under specified terms, or to provide goods or services to others.

Debt to assets   A ratio relating outstanding *debt* obligations (usually *long-term debt* but at times all types of debt) to total *assets*; used as a measure of *financial leverage*. (Cf. *debt to equity*.)

Debt to capitalization   A ratio relating *long-term debt* to a company's *capitalization*; used as a measure of *financial leverage* as found in the *capital structure*. (Cf. *debt to equity*.)

Debt to equity   A ratio relating outstanding *debt* obligations (usually *long-term debt* but at times all types of debt) to *shareholders' equity*; used as a measure of *financial leverage*.

Default   Failure to make a payment on a *debt* obligation when due.

Deferred taxes   A provision for income tax *liabilities* or income tax *assets* recorded on the *balance sheet*, arising from timing differences between recognized tax liabilities in a company's accounting system and tax liabilities reported to the tax authorities.

Deflation   A decline in general price levels. (Cf. *inflation*.)

Depreciation   The decline in an *asset's* value, from use or obsolescence, that's recognized in the accounting system and for income tax purposes as a periodic allocation (*write-off*) against income of a portion of the original *cost* of the *asset*. (Cf. *accelerated depreciation; noncash charges*.)

Dilution   The proportional reduction of *earnings per share* or *book value* per share from an increase in the number of shares outstanding, either from a new issue or from conversion of *convertible securities* outstanding.

Discount rate   The earnings rate used in calculating the *present value* of future *cash flows* using the *discounting* process.

Discounted cash flow   The *discounting* methodology employed in determining the economic attractiveness of *capital investment* projects.

Discounted cash flow rate of return (DCF)   The *earnings* rate (*yield*) that equates a project's cash inflows and outflows over its economic life; also called *internal rate of return*.

Discounting   The process of calculating the reduced value of a future sum of money in proportion to the opportunity of earning interest and the distance in time of payment or receipt. (Cf. *compounding, present value*.)

Disinvestment   The act of disposing of assets or whole business segments, caused by a reassessment of the strategic fit of these assets; the opposite of *investment*.

Diversification   The process of investing in a number of unrelated or partially interdependent *assets* or activities to achieve a more stable *portfolio*.

Dividend coverage   Relationship of the amount of common and/or preferred dividends to aftertax *earnings* of a company; a test of the ability of the company to pay the current level of dividends.

Dividend discount model   A valuation method for *common stock* that employs the *present value* of expected future dividends and any change in the expected level of dividends.

Dividend payout   A ratio relating the amount of dividends distributed to the aftertax *earnings* of a corporation to derive the percentage of earnings paid to shareholders.

Dividend yield   The current return to shareholders from dividends received over a specified period, derived by dividing dividends per share by the current average market price of the *stock*. (Cf. *yield*.)

Dynamic analysis   A method of analyzing business decisions that incorporates the effect of likely changes in key variables, as contrasted with fixed assumptions. (Cf. *sensitivity analysis*.)

Earnings (income, net income, profit, net profit)   The difference between all recorded *revenues* and all related *costs* and *expenses* for a specified period, using generally accepted accounting principles.

Earnings before interest and taxes (EBIT)   An expression of a company's earning power before the effects of financing and taxation; used in a variety of *financial analyses*.

Earnings per share (EPS)   The proportional share of a corporation's *earnings* that can be claimed by each share of *common stock* outstanding, derived by dividing aftertax earnings after payment of preferred dividends by the average number of common shares outstanding during the period. (Cf. *fully diluted earnings per share*.)

Earnings yield   The current return to shareholders from *earnings* recorded for a specified period, derived by dividing periodic earnings by the *stock's* current or average market price. (Cf. *yield*.)

Economic analysis   The development of the economic impact of a business decision that determines the actual *trade-off* between *economic costs* and *benefits* independent of accounting conventions.

Economic benefit   The consequence of a decision that causes an ultimate increase in present and future *cash flows*.

Economic cost   The consequence of a decision that causes an ultimate reduction in present and future *cash flows*.

Economic earnings (loss)   The net result of a *trade-off* between *economic benefits* and *economic costs*.

Economic life   The time over which a current or future *investment* can be expected to provide *economic earnings*, which is independent of the physical life of any *assets* involved.

Economic return   A measure of the earnings power of an *investment* in terms of net *cash flows* generated by the *capital* committed. (Cf. *discounted cash flow*.)

Economic trade-off   The comparison of the *economic benefits* and *economic costs* caused by a business decision.

Economic value   The *net present value* of all future *economic benefits* and *costs* expected from an existing or prospective *investment*.

Economic value added (EVA)   A form of expressing the value created by investing in projects whose returns exceed the company's *cost of capital*. The simplest way is to show the difference between annual *profits* (or *cash flow*) and the weighted cost of the assets employed.

Enterprise value   The *net present value* of all estimated future *cash flows* to be generated by a business.

Equity (owners' equity, net worth, shareholders' equity)   The recorded ownership claim of common and preferred shareholders in a corporation as reflected on the *balance sheet*. Also defined as total *assets* less all *liabilities*.

Equivalence A point of indifference at which the *present value* of future *cash flows* reflects the return expectations of a prospective investor.

Expected return A weighted average of alternative outcomes of an *investment*, using the respective probabilities as weights.

Expense A periodic offset against *revenue* recognized under generally accepted accounting principles, representing either a direct cash outlay or an *allocation* or *accrual* of past and future outlays.

Fair market value (FMV) The price for an *asset* on which two rational parties with sufficient information would agree in the absence of negotiating pressure.

Financial Accounting Standards Board (FASB) The official rule-making institute of the accounting profession, which is privately funded by the profession.

Financial analysis The process of determining and weighing the financial impact of business decisions.

Financial flexibility The ability to maintain alternative choices for raising additional *capital* while preserving a *capital structure* appropriate to the risks and conditions of a company's business.

Financial growth plans A model of future financial flows that tracks the results of key *investment, operational*, and *financing* dimensions under a variety of assumptions about strategies, policies, and business conditions.

Financial leverage The magnifying (or diminishing) effect on *return on equity* from the use of *debt* in the *capital structure*, caused by introducing fixed interest charges against the returns obtained from the incremental funds invested. (Cf. *operating leverage.*)

Financial model The representation in a computer program of key financial dimensions of a business system for purposes of simulating the impact of management decisions. (Cf. *financial growth plans.*)

Financial statements Key periodic statements prepared under generally accepted accounting principles, which represent the financial condition of a company (*balance sheet*), *the operating results* (*operating statement*), the changes in funds flows (*funds flow statement*), and the changes in *owners' equity* (statement of changes in *owners' equity*).

Financial system A dynamic representation of the key elements and relationships governing *investments, operations*, and *financing* of a business entity. (Cf. *financial model.*)

Financing The provision of *funds* from internal or external sources to fund the *investments* and *operations* of a business.

First-in, first-out (FIFO) A method of accounting for inventory in which the oldest item is assumed to be used or sold first. (Cf. *last-in, first-out.*)

Fixed assets Any *asset* on the *balance sheet* considered to have a life or usefulness for a business in excess of one year, such as land, buildings, and machinery. (Cf. *current assets.*)

Fixed costs Any *cost* that doesn't vary with changes in the volume of operations over time.

Fixed-income security Any security that provides an unchanging stream of interest or dividends to the holder over its life.

Foreign exchange exposure The potential loss from an unexpected change in currency exchange rates affecting *investments* or *operations*.

Free cash flow   The net *cash flow* available to a company after providing for all acceptable new *investments* to support its strategy, before any dividend payments or changes in *financing*.

Fully diluted earnings per share   *Earnings per share* which are calculated on the assumption that all outstanding *convertible securities* and *warrants* have been converted into the appropriate number of common shares, raising the denominator and reducing *earnings per share*.

Funds   A general term denoting means of payment, often equated with cash.

Funds flow   The movement of *funds* of all types through a business over time, ultimately resulting in changes in cash.

Funds flow statement   A *financial statement* prepared to display the *funds* movements in a business over a specified period of time, separated into sections on *operations, investment, financing*, and cash balances. (Cf. *funds flow statement.*)

Going-concern value   The *net present value* of the expected future *cash flows* generated by a business from its normal operations. (Cf. *economic value, enterprise value.*)

Gross margin   The difference between *net sales* and *cost of goods sold* (or *cost of services provided*), generally expressed as a ratio of this difference divided by net sales.

Growth/decline variations   The impact on a company's *funds* flows from the operational changes caused by growth or decline in the volume of business.

Hedge   A strategy to neutralize the risk of an *investment* by engaging in offsetting contracts whereby potential gains and losses will cancel each other.

Historical cost principle   An accounting principle requiring the recording of transactions and the maintenance of recorded values at the actual level incurred, regardless of any subsequent changes in the value of the *assets* or *liabilities* involved.

Hurdle rate   A minimum standard for the return required of an *investment*, used in selecting from alternative investment choices.

Income   The difference between the *revenues* and the matching *costs* and *expenses* for a specified period. (Cf. *earnings.*)

Income statement (operating statement, profit and loss statement)   A *financial statement* reporting the periodic *revenues* and matching *costs* and *expenses* for a specified period, and deriving the *income* for the period.

Incremental analysis   A method of analysis that focuses on the changes caused by a business decision.

Inflation   An increase in general price levels.

Inflation premium   The increased *return on investment* required to compensate the holders for expected inflation.

Insolvency   The condition where an individual's or company's *liabilities* exceed the realizable value of the *assets* held.

Interest coverage   Relationship of periodic interest expense to operating *income* before or after taxes, used to judge a company's ability to pay interest charges. (Cf. *times interest earned.*)

Internal rate of return (IRR) The *discount rate* that equates the cash inflows and cash outflows of an *investment* project, resulting in a *net present value* of zero. (Cf. *rate of return, yield.*)

Inventory turnover A ratio that relates ending inventory or average inventory to the *cost of goods sold* for a specified period of time; used in judging the effectiveness with which inventories are controlled.

Inventory valuation Any adjustment to recorded inventory values to correct for differences between historical *costs* and current prices, also affecting *cost of goods sold*.

Investment The commitment of *funds* for purposes of obtaining an *economic return* over a period of time, usually in the form of periodic *cash flows* and/or a *terminal value*.

Investment value The value of a *convertible security* based strictly on its characteristics as a *fixed-income security*, without regard to its conversion provision.

Junk bond Any *bond* issued by corporations with risk characteristics higher than what's normally rated as investment-grade risk (normal risk exposure).

Last-in, first-out (LIFO) A method of accounting for inventory in which the newest item is assumed to be used or sold first. (Cf. *first-in, first-out.*)

Leasing The process of contracting for the use of *assets* owned by others over a specified period of time, in exchange for a stipulated pattern of periodic payments.

Leverage The magnifying effect from volume changes on *profits* caused by fixed elements in a company's *cost* structure, or the magnifying effect from profit changes on *return on equity* caused by *fixed-cost debt* obligations in the *capital structure*. (Cf. *financial leverage, operating leverage.*)

Leveraged buyout (LBO) The acquisition of a business by investors using a high percentage of *debt* carried by the business itself.

Liability An obligation to pay a specified amount or to perform a service; at times also the recognized potential obligation to pay or perform a service (contingent liability).

Liquid asset An *asset* that can be rapidly converted into cash without suffering a significant reduction in value, usually classified as a *current asset*.

Liquidation The process of terminating a business entity by selling its *assets*, paying off its *liabilities*, and distributing any remaining cash to its owners.

Liquidation value The estimated value of a business based on *liquidation* of its *assets*.

Liquidity The degree to which a company is readily able to meet its current obligations from *liquid assets*. (Cf. *acid test, current ratio.*)

Long-term debt Any *debt* obligation of a company with a maturity of more than one year.

Managerial economics The methodology underlying the analysis and resolution of the *economic trade-offs* involved in making management decisions.

Marginal costs (revenues) Increments of *costs* and *revenues* attributable to changes in a variable affecting an issue being decided.

Market to book value The relationship between the current market price of *common stock* and its recorded *book value*, a ratio often used in judging the performance of a company's *stock*.

Market value   The value of an *asset* as determined in an unconstrained market of multiple buyers and sellers, such as a securities exchange.

Market value added (MVA)   The difference between the recorded value of shareholders' equity and the current market value of the shares involved.

Market value of equity   The combined value of all *common shares* of a company at current market prices. (Cf. *book value of equity*.)

Market value of firm   The *market value* of a company's *equity* plus the market value of its *debt*.

Monetary asset   Any *asset* defined in terms of units of currency, such as cash and *accounts receivable*.

Multiple hurdle rates   A set of minimum return standards in a company that are used to judge the desirability of *investments* in activities or lines of business with widely different risk characteristics.

Mutually exclusive alternatives   Alternative *investments* for achieving the same objective, of which only one can be undertaken.

Net assets   Total *assets* less *current liabilities*, as recorded on the *balance sheet*.

Net income (loss)   The difference between periodic *revenues* and matching *costs* and *expenses*. (Cf. *earnings, net profit, profit*.)

Net investment   The commitment of new *funds* to an *investment* project, net of any funds recovered due to the decision to invest, adjusted for tax implications.

Net present value (NPV)   The difference between the *present values* of cash inflows and outflows from an *investment*, representing the net gain or loss in value expected relative to the earnings standard applied.

Net profit   The difference between periodic *revenues* and matching *costs* and *expenses*. (Cf. *earnings, net income, profit*.)

Net sales   Total *revenue* from sales for a specified period, less adjustments such as returns, allowances, and sales discounts.

Net worth   The recorded value of *shareholders' equity* on the *balance sheet*.

Nominal amount   Any quantity not adjusted for changes in the purchasing power of the currency in which it's recorded. (Cf. *real amount*.)

Noncash item   An *expense* or *revenue* recognized in the accounting process that doesn't represent a *cash flow* during the period, such as *depreciation* or unrealized income or gains.

Operating cash flow   The net *cash flow* caused by the operations of a business during a specified period.

Operating funds   *Funds* required to support current operations, such as *working capital* items.

Operating leverage   The magnifying (or diminishing) effect of volume changes on *profits* caused by the *fixed costs* in the company's operations.

Operating statement (income statement)   A *financial statement* reporting the *revenues* and matching *costs* and *expenses* for a specified period, and deriving the *net income*.

Operational analysis   The various methods of analyzing the specific and comparative aspects of a company's operating performance.

Operations   The activities in a company that support the basic purpose of the business, generating *revenues* and managing related *costs* and *expenses* for profitable results.

Opportunity cost   *Economic benefits* forgone by selecting one alternative course of action over another.

Opportunity rate of return   A rate of return standard reflecting the long-term level of returns expected in a business, often based on a company's *cost of capital*.

Option   A contractual opportunity to purchase or sell an *asset* or security at a predetermined price, without the obligation of doing so.

Over-the-counter market (OTC)   A market network among security dealers that permits electronic trading of securities not listed on a formal securities exchange.

Owners' equity   The recorded value of *preferred* and *common* shareholders' claims against the *assets* on a company's *balance sheet*; also, the proprietors' recorded claims in the case of an unincorporated business or partnership. (Cf. *equity, shareholders' equity*.)

Paid-in capital   The recorded amount of *capital* provided by shareholders on the *balance sheet*, as contrasted with *retained earnings*.

Par value   The *nominal* value established by the issuer of a security, as contrasted with the *market value* of the security. In the case of a *bond*, the issuing company will pay the par value at maturity.

Payables   See *accounts payable*.

Payables period   A translation of *accounts payable* into the days of average purchases outstanding at a point in time; used as an indicator of the effectiveness with which *trade credit* is employed.

Payback period   The period of time over which the *cash flows* from an *investment* are expected to recover the initial outlay.

Perpetuity   A series of level periodic receipts or payments (*annuity*) expected to last forever.

Plug figure   A common term used to represent an unknown variable in a financial analysis, such as the amount of *financing* required in a pro forma projection. (Cf. *pro forma statement*.)

Portfolio   A set of diverse *investments* held by an individual or a company.

Preferred stock   A special class of capital stock, usually with a dividend provision, that receives a form of preference over *common stock* in its claims on *earnings* and *assets*.

Present value   The value today of a future sum or series of sums of money, calculated by *discounting* the future sums with an appropriate rate.

Present value payback   The point in the *economic life* of an *investment* project at which the cumulative *present value* of *cash inflows* equals the present value of the *cash outflows*.

Price to earnings (P/E)   The relationship of the market price of a share of *stock* to the most recent *earnings per share* over 12 months; used as a rough indicator of what investors are willing to pay for $1 of a company's *earnings*.

Primary earnings per share   A company's *earnings per share* calculated on the basis of all *common shares* actually outstanding, without regard to any *convertible securities* or *warrants* yet to be converted. (Cf. *fully diluted earnings*.)

Principal   The original amount of a loan or *bond*, also called face value, on which the rate of interest to be paid is based.

Private placement   The sale of securities to a selected group of investors rather than through a *public offering.*

Profit   The difference between periodic *revenues* and matching *costs* and *expenses.* (Cf. *earnings, net profit.*)

Profit center   A portion of a business in which *revenues, costs,* and *expenses* can be recognized separately, allowing the activity to be managed for *profit* performance.

Profitability index (PI)   A measure of *investment* desirability, defined as the *present value* of all cash inflows expected over the *economic life* of a project divided by the present value of the cash outflows.

Pro forma statement   A projected *financial statement* reflecting the financial impact of a set of assumed conditions for a specified future period.

Projection   A forecast of the quantitative implications of a set of assumed conditions.

Public issue (public offering)   The sale of newly issued securities to the public through underwriters. (Cf. *private placement.*)

Purchasing power parity   A condition in which commodities in different countries cost the same amount when prices are expressed in a given currency, due to expected adjustments in foreign exchange rates.

Quick ratio (acid test)   A stringent measure of *liquidity* relating current cash *assets* (cash, cash equivalents, and *receivables*) to *current liabilities.*

Quick sale value   The value of an asset or business when assumed to be sold under hurried conditions, resulting generally in a lower valuation than *market value.*

Range of earnings chart (EBIT chart)   A graphic representation of the related changes in *earnings before interest and taxes (EBIT)* and *earnings per share* under various financing alternatives.

Rate of return   The level of *earnings* attained or expected from an *investment* over a period of time. (Cf. *yield.*)

Ratio analysis   The use of a variety of ratios in analyzing the financial performance and condition of a business from various viewpoints, such as managers', owners', and creditors'.

Real amount   Any quantity that has been adjusted for changes in the purchasing power of the currency in which it's recorded. (Cf. *nominal amount.*)

Realized income   *Earnings* or gains that are recognized as the result of a transaction, as contrasted with earnings or gains that exist on paper only.

Receivables   See *accounts receivable.*

Recovery value (terminal value)   The value of any *assets* or future *profits* expected to be realized at the end of the *economic life* of an *investment,* net of taxes.

Redundant assets   Any *assets* held by a company that don't contribute returns appropriate for the lines of business principally engaged in; these are candidates for *disinvestment* (divestiture).

Relevant costs   Identifiable *cost* or *expense* elements that are expected to change in response to a decision being analyzed.

Relevant revenues   Identifiable *revenue* elements that are expected to change in response to a decision being analyzed.

Residual profits A measure of *profit center* performance, defined as *income* less the estimated annual *cost* of the *capital* supporting the profit center.

Retained earnings (earned surplus) The cumulative amount of past and current *earnings* retained and reinvested in a corporation, instead of being distributed to shareholders in the form of dividends.

Return on assets (ROA) The relationship of annual aftertax *earnings* to total *assets* (average or ending balance), used as a measure of the productivity of a company's assets. At times aftertax earnings are adjusted for interest to eliminate the impact of *financing*.

Return on capitalization (invested capital) (ROC) The relationship of annual *earnings* before interest, after taxes to the *capitalization* (average or ending balance); used as a measure of the productivity of a company's invested *capital* regardless of the amount of *financial leverage* employed. (Cf. *return on net assets.*)

Return on equity (net worth) (ROE) The relationship of annual aftertax *earnings* to the recorded *shareholders' equity*. Used as a measure of the effectiveness with which shareholder funds have been invested.

Return on investment (ROI) The relationship of annual aftertax *earnings* to the *book value* (average or ending balance) of the *asset*, business, or *profit center* generating these earnings. Used as a measure of the productivity of the *investment*. (Cf. *return on assets.*)

Return on net assets (RONA) The relationship of annual *earnings* before interest, after taxes to total *assets* less *current liabilities* (*net assets*) (average or ending balance), used as a measure of the productivity of a company's invested *capital* regardless of the amount of *financial leverage* employed. (Cf. *return on capitalization.*)

Revenue (sales) The recorded incidence of a sale of goods and/or services as recognized in the accounting system.

Risk allowance A provision for risk in an analysis, such as lowering a project's expected *cash flows* or using a *risk-adjusted return standard.*

Risk analysis A process of integrating risk dimensions into an analysis, such as using *sensitivity analysis* or modeling outcomes that have been adjusted by probabilistic methods.

Risk aversion A subjective unwillingness to accept a given level of risk unless a significant *economic trade-off* can be realized.

Risk-adjusted return standard (discount rate, hurdle rate, cost of capital) A minimum *discount rate* that has been adjusted upward to include a specified risk premium.

Risk-free interest rate The assumed *yield* obtainable on a guaranteed security in the absence of *inflation.*

Risk premium The increased *return* required from an *investment* to compensate the holder for the level of risk involved.

Sales (revenue) The recorded incidence of a sale of goods and/or services as recognized in the accounting system.

Seasonal variations The impact on a company's *funds* flows from the operational changes caused by seasonal business conditions.

Secured creditor A creditor whose claim is backed by the pledge of a specified *asset*, whose proceeds will go to the creditor in case of *liquidation.*

Securities and Exchange Commission (SEC) The regulatory body established by the federal government to oversee securities markets.

Senior creditor   Any creditor with specific claims on *income* or *assets* that rank ahead of that of general (unsecured) creditors.

Sensitivity analysis   The process of testing the impact on the results of an analysis from changes in one or more of the input variables.

Sequential outlays   One or more future *investment* outlays expected during the *economic life* of an investment project, which should be taken into account in judging the project's overall desirability.

Shareholder return   The *economic return* to shareholders in the form of dividends and capital gains or losses from *share price appreciation* or declines realized during a specified period.

Shareholder value   The economic value created by successfully investing in activities whose returns exceed the company's *cost of capital,* which will cause growth in total *shareholder return.*

Shareholders' equity   The recorded value of the residual claims of all shareholders as reflected on the *balance sheet.*

Share price appreciation   The change in the *market value* of preferred and common shares over time.

Shelf registration   The filing, under *SEC* rules, of a general-purpose prospectus outlining possible financing plans for up to two years, to speed up the actual issue when the timing is considered appropriate.

Short-term liabilities   *Debt* obligations due within 12 months of the date of a *balance sheet.* Generally listed under *current liabilities.*

Simulation   The process of modeling the potential outcomes of a financial plan or *investment* proposal, taking into account alternative assumptions about key variables and policies, and calculating the results using computer programs.

Sinking fund   A separate pool of cash into which periodic payments are made for the future redemption of an obligation.

Solvency   The condition of an individual or company in which obligations can be paid when due.

Sources and uses statement   A *financial statement* that separates all *funds* inflows and outflows for a given period of time, derived from changes in *balance sheet* accounts and supplemented with *operating statement* data.

Spot market   A market in which prices of securities or commodities are determined for immediate transactions.

Spread   The difference between the issue price of a new security and the net amount received by the issuing company, caused by underwriting commissions and *expenses.*

Standard deviation   A statistical measure of variability.

Statement of changes in financial position   A variation of the *funds flow statement* focusing on changes in *working capital* for the period.

Stock   General term used in referring to *common stock*; also applied to *preferred stock.*

Stock buyback   The purchase by a company of its own shares in the market, using available funds to reduce the number of shares outstanding versus investing those funds internally or paying an increased dividend.

Stock option   A contractual arrangement allowing selected corporate employees to purchase a specified number of shares at a set price within a specified period of time; used as an incentive for key personnel.

Straight-line depreciation   A pattern of *depreciation* write-offs that charges level amounts during the *asset's* book life, for either accounting or tax deduction purposes.

Subordinated creditor   A creditor whose claim is specifically designated as ranking below the claims of other creditors of a company.

Sunk cost   A past outlay of *funds* that can't be recovered or changed by a current or future decision, and that's therefore irrelevant in the analysis of future actions.

Sustainable growth rate   The rate of growth in *equity* or *sales volume* that a company can maintain without changing its *return on assets, asset turnover, debt to equity*, and *dividend payout*, and while keeping its *capital structure* proportions at their current levels.

Synergy   The assumed *economic benefits* to be obtained from a successful combination of two businesses due to increased efficiency, economies of scale, and mutual reinforcement of business effectiveness.

Tax shield   The impact on a company's income tax obligations from a change in a tax-deductible expense, such as *depreciation* or interest, defined as the amount of change times the applicable tax rate. It assumes that the company has sufficient taxable income to offset the change in the *expense*.

Terminal value (recovery value)   The value of any *assets* or future *cash flows* expected to be realized at the end of the *economic life* of an *investment*, net of taxes.

Time lags   The elapsed time between the recorded incidence of a transaction and its actual cash impact.

Time value of money   The *discounted* or *compounded* value of a sum of money over a specified period of time, using a specified discount or compound rate. (Cf. *present value*.)

Times burden covered   The relationship of the amount of debt *burden* during a period to *earnings* before interest and taxes. Used as a measure of a company's ability to service its *debt*.

Times interest earned   The relationship of the amount of periodic interest expense to *earnings* before interest and taxes. Used as a measure of a company's ability to make regular interest payments.

Total shareholder return (ISR)   The *economic return* to shareholders in the form of *dividends* and capital gains or losses from *share price appreciation* or decline realized during a specified period.

Trade credit   Credit extended to a company in the course of normal business operations by its suppliers. (Cf. *accounts payable*.)

Trade-off   The process of judging the relative advantage or disadvantage from making a decision that involves identified *economic benefits* and *costs*.

Trade payables   Amounts owed to a company's suppliers of goods and services. (Cf. *accounts payable*.)

Transfer price   An internally established price level at which units of a company trade goods or services with each other.

Trend analysis   A method of analysis that applies judgmental or statistical methods to historical series of data for the purpose of judging performance or making informed projections of future conditions.

Uncommitted earnings per share (UEPS)   *Earnings per share* adjusted for the effect of future *sinking fund* payments and other repayment provisions, used in judging alternative financing possibilities.

Underwriter   Investment banker or a group (syndicate) of investment bankers used by a corporation in marketing new securities issues to the public, guaranteeing a specific price to the issuing company. (Cf. *public offering.*)

Unrealized income (gain)   *Earnings* or gains that are recognized on paper without the benefit of a transaction, as contrasted with earnings or gains that are realized through actual transactions. (Cf. *realized income.*)

Variable cost   Any *cost* or *expense* that varies with operating volume over a specified period. (Cf. *fixed cost.*)

Volatility   The risk introduced by past and expected fluctuations in a company's *earnings*, often expressed as β (*beta*).

Warrant   A financial instrument issued to investors giving them the option to purchase additional shares at a specified price. Usually issued in connection with a new security issue.

Weighted average cost of capital   Overall *cost of capital* derived by weighting the respective *costs* of different parts of a company's *capital structure* by their proportions.

Working capital (net working capital)   The difference between *current assets* and *current liabilities* as recorded on the *balance sheet*, representing the amount of *operating funds* that are financed by the company's *capital structure*.

Working capital cycle   The periodic transformation of *working capital* components into cash inflows and outflows.

Write-offs   Accounting entries that allocate portions of past outlays into appropriate operating periods, such as *depreciation* and *amortization*.

Yield   The *rate of return* earned by an *investment's* cash inflows and outflows during a specified period. (Cf. *internal rate of return.*)

Yield to maturity   The *internal rate of return* earned by a *bond* when held to maturity.

Some International Issues in Business Analysis

In Chapter 3 we developed the principles of performance analysis and stressed the need for management to derive an economic return from the resources entrusted to them. The analysis involved such measures as profit margins, return on assets, and return on net worth, seen from different points of view. We also related the various measures within a system of ratios to show the different levers management can use to improve the profitability of the business and to create shareholder value. We will briefly discuss some of the challenges generally encountered in measuring multibusiness companies, and then turn to the particular issues arising from operating with different national currencies.

GENERAL PERFORMANCE ANALYSIS CHALLENGES

Performance measures work best when applied to a total business entity, where investment, operations, and financing are collectively controlled and managed by a management team. It's possible to derive both return on investment (ROI) and return on equity (ROE)—the latter allowing for the effect of financial leverage. Recall the expanded formula for return on equity,

$$\text{ROE} = \frac{\text{Net profit}}{\text{Sales}} \times \frac{\text{Sales}}{\text{Assets}} \times \frac{\text{Assets}}{\text{Assets} - \text{Liabilities}}$$

where the first element represents operations, the second element investment, and the third financial leverage. Also, as we discussed in Chapter 9, various cash flow analysis approaches can be applied to judge the performance and the value of the company.

Complications arise when the measures are applied to segments of a multi-unit company, where individual units are responsible for investment and operations only, and financing remains a corporate headquarters function. In this case, the units are normally measured on a return on investment basis only, employing concepts such as return on total assets (ROA), return on net assets (RONA), or return on average assets employed (ROAA), modified to suit the needs of the particular company. The management of financial leverage doesn't enter in here. Recall the formula for return on assets,

$$\text{ROA} = \frac{\text{Net profit}}{\text{Sales}} \times \frac{\text{Sales}}{\text{Assets}}$$

which when applied to an operating unit, relates the unit's net profit (before or after taxes) to the unit's sales and its identifiable assets. Again, we can use cash flow measures to judge the performance and the value of business units, but these require a variety of adjustments to make sure that all relevant cash flow elements have been considered, and that the appropriate return standards are applied.

Further complications arise when units within a large corporation supply goods and services to each other. The most difficult aspect is the issue of setting appropriate transfer prices for the value of the goods and services moving between units of the corporation. At times, readily available, clearly established market prices can be used to value these transfers. More often than not, however, transfer prices have to be set through negotiation or even by corporate decree. There are no entirely satisfactory approaches to resolving this often vexing issue, which cannot only cause serious distortions in the results of individual units, but—even more significantly—may distort the decisions of unit managers and cause them to over- or underinvest, or to suboptimize their operations.

INTERNATIONAL PERFORMANCE ANALYSIS CHALLENGES

The issue of measuring the performance of a business becomes particularly challenging when operations extend into the international arena, either when divisions are operating entirely within a foreign country, or when organizational entities perform transactions in several currencies. In the former situation, the division usually can be viewed as a rather independent entity—albeit operating with a foreign currency—while in the latter case, the flow of goods and services across borders introduces significant measurement problems. All of the measurement issues we mentioned earlier usually apply to foreign operations as well, but in addition there's the problem of measuring the impact of absolute and relative changes in the different currencies involved.

Foreign Subsidiaries Operating in a Single Country

The simplest case involves a wholly owned subsidiary, which for all practical purposes acts as part of the host country, and which keeps its books and financial statements in the local currency. The key measurements in which the U.S. parent company will be interested are current earnings performance and the valuation of the subsidiary.

Given that all transactions and cost accounting steps are carried out in the local currency, the calculation of earnings performance through various ratios will be internally consistent and unaffected by currency fluctuations and exchange rates. Whether the subsidiary operates in German marks, English pounds, or Brazilian cruzeiros, performance measures will indicate the effectiveness with which the subsidiary's assets are employed, and various ratios used to measure performance will give appropriate readings.

Since the U.S. parent company will also be interested in viewing the level of earnings as expressed in U.S. dollars, particularly for purposes of consolidating the earnings, exchange rates must be brought into play. We can represent the situation in the form of some simple formulas, revisiting the discussions of Chapters 3 and 5. If we simulate the subsidiary's earnings in dollars $(E_\$)$ by denoting unit price (P), variable costs (C), fixed costs (F), unit volume (V), and exchange rate (R), and denote all relevant components in terms of the foreign currency (f), the simple equation is

$$\text{Subsidiary } E_\$ = R \left[(P_f - C_f) V - F_f \right]$$

Clearly the exchange rate R affects all financial terms in the formulation, and the dollar earnings reported will be a function of the level of exchange between the dollar and the foreign currency involved. There's nothing the subsidiary management can do about the exchange rate, which may fluctuate wildly or may be very stable. The subsidiary's earnings as such aren't affected—only their expression in dollar terms will be altered. The U.S. parent, on the other hand, may be quite affected by rising or falling exchange rates that will change the subsidiary's dollar earnings.

When we wish to develop the dollar return on investment (return on assets) of the subsidiary $(ROI_\$)$, the only additional item needed to complete the formula is the amount of the subsidiary's assets denoted in the foreign currency (A_f):

$$ROI_\$ = \frac{R \left[(P_f - C_f) V - F_f \right]}{R \times A_f} = \frac{(P_f - C_f) V - F_f}{A_f} = ROI_f$$

Note that the exchange rate R drops out of the equation and the return on investment in dollar terms is equivalent to the return in foreign currency terms. As we stated earlier, ratio analysis performed on an entity with consistent accounting in a single currency will provide meaningful results independent of exchange rate concerns. Only the distortions inherent in the accounting system itself, as discussed in Chapters 2 and 3, will affect the stated amount of the division's assets.

The implications of this discussion are rather straightforward. The management of a subsidiary operating as a unit completely within a given country can be judged by using all standard ratios expressed in the local currency. But the inclusion of the subsidiary's foreign currency earnings in consolidated U.S. financial statements will be affected by any movement in the dollar exchange rates, as will the recording of foreign assets in U.S. dollar terms. The U.S. parent's financial statements may have to be adjusted frequently to account for exchange rate differences alone.

Distortions arising from significant inflationary trends will affect a foreign subsidiary in much the same way as businesses experienced inflation in the United States during the 1970s. In essence, recorded asset values will tend to be understated over time. To the extent that inflationary conditions in the foreign country exceed U.S. levels, it may be desirable to revalue the foreign subsidiary's balance sheet elements for analysis purposes to make sure that ratios derived from the statement are internally consistent.

Valuation of the subsidiary in cash flow terms can be done by expressing the expected cash inflows in the foreign currency and discounting these to arrive at the present value, as we did in Chapter 9. Note that the issues of price, volume, and cost as well as terminal value will remain consistent through the use of the foreign currency in which they occur. All of the issues surrounding the estimates of future conditions in markets, costs, economic developments, and so on will apply here as they would in the United States. The final result can then be translated into U.S. dollars at the prevailing exchange rate, if desired.

Subsidiaries Operating Across Foreign Borders

A more common consequence of the continued expansion of international trade is the need for a corporate entity to do business in several countries and in their respective currencies. Now the issue of exchange rates begins to loom large, for both earnings calculations and performance measures will be affected by the mix of currencies on the company's books. Let's take the simplified example of a so-called *cross-border subsidiary* that imports goods from the U.S. parent company and sells these goods within the foreign country in which it operates. Let's further assume that the U.S. parent requires payment for the goods in dollars, while the subsidiary quotes and sells the goods in the local currency. Moreover, all other costs of the subsidiary will be incurred in the local currency as well.

We can again write the equation for the dollar earnings of the subsidiary ($E_\$$), taking into account the fact that its variable costs are incurred in dollars:

$$\text{Subsidiary } E_\$ = R \left[(P_f - \frac{C_\$}{R}) V - F_f \right]$$

This equation simply describes the subsidiary's condition in which prices and fixed costs have to be converted into dollars, while variable costs are already incurred in dollars.

The complications that can arise from this situation are apparent. No longer does the exchange rate simply apply to earnings as it did in the case of the single-country subsidiary. Now the exchange rate additionally affects a highly significant cost element in the subsidiary's cost structure. Any movement in the exchange rate during a period of operations will directly affect the subsidiary's cost of goods sold. For example, if the foreign currency weakens from four units per U.S. dollar to six, the subsidiary has suffered a 50 percent increase in its cost of goods sold because it must obtain dollars for payment to its U.S. parent that have become 50 percent more expensive. This could severely affect the subsidiary's competitive position in the local market unless it can readily pass on this price increase. An opposite effect will, of course, occur if the exchange rate moves in favor of the local currency, such as from four units per U.S. dollar to three.

The impact on the subsidiary's performance measures of exchange rate movement depends on a number of factors. If significant price changes in the subsidiary's cost of goods sold due to the U.S. dollar exchange rate don't affect its market position because it can adjust the price of the goods based on the change in cost—a highly unrealistic assumption—the performance ratios are likely to be unaffected. In reality, changes in the cost of goods sold will normally impact the subsidiary's ability to compete locally, and attempts to price according to cost will not only affect the volume of units sold, but also change operational costs because of these volume changes.

It's not possible to develop a simple formula approach here, because the total operating system of the subsidiary will be affected in largely unpredictable ways. For example, any attempted price changes are likely to be less than proportional to the change in the cost of goods sold, in order to minimize the competitive impact. Market reactions to these price changes will largely depend on the subsidiary's market position, the quality and price of competitive goods, the availability of competitive substitutes from sources not subject to similar exchange rate fluctuations, and so on. It will usually be best to model the major dimensions of the subsidiary's business system and to simulate a variety of assumptions about price, volume, and cost changes.

The basic calculation in Figure II–1 shows the type of analysis that will help gauge the effect on the subsidiary's earnings and ROA under several assumed conditions. Clearly, more specific knowledge about local market conditions would have to be applied to refine the range of estimates, and more of the underlying variables would have to be modeled to obtain a clearer picture of the impact of currency exchange rates.

FIGURE II–1

Impact on Subsidiary Earnings and ROA Using Several Assumed Exchange Rate Conditions

		Current Period		
Variable	Prior Period	Constant Exchange Rate	Dollar Strengthens	Dollar Weakens
Exchange Rate (R)	$0.25	$0.25	$0.17	$0.33
(U.S. dollars/foreign currency)				
Selling price per unit (P_f)	f50.00	f55.00	f75.00	f50.00
Purchased cost per unit (C_s)	$10.00	$10.00	$10.00	$10.00
Purchased cost per unit (C_f)	f40.00	f40.00	f60.00	f30.00
Number of units sold (V)	1,000	1,000	750	1,100
Subsidiary assets (A_f)	f30,000	f30,000	f36,000	f27,000
Earnings, ROI in foreign currency:				
Revenues	f50,000	f55,000	f56,250	f55,000
Cost of goods sold	40,000	40,000	45,000	33,000
Fixed costs	5,000	5,000	5,000	5,000
Earnings	5,000	10,000	6,250	17,000
ROI	17%	33%	17%	63%
Earnings in U.S. dollars	$1,250	$2,500	$1,063	$5,610

This set of assumptions reflects conditions in two time periods, with exchange rates allowed to move significantly in the current period away from the conditions of the prior period. The foreign selling price was assumed to increase slightly in the current period under stable exchange rates (second column). The impact of this 10 percent price increase is a doubling of foreign earnings from f5,000 to f10,000, and a parallel doubling of the dollar earnings. Note that the ROI reflects this doubling as well.

As the dollar strengthens in the third column, the foreign purchase cost per unit jumps 50 percent, and the subsidiary tries to increase the price to recover the extra cost. This is likely to depress the volume sold—here it's assumed to drop by 25 percent. Higher-cost inventories will also increase the subsidiary's asset base by an assumed f6,000. While earnings in the foreign currency decline by 37.5 percent, the ROI is cut in half because of the impact of higher-cost inventories on the asset base. The dollar earnings, however, suffer an even greater decline due to the strengthening of the dollar exchange rate.

The fourth column reflects a weakening of the dollar, which makes U.S. goods cheaper to import. In fact, the cost to the subsidiary drops to 50 percent of the stronger dollar condition in the third column. We assume that the subsidiary will pass on much of this in the form of a lower price, which raises the number of units sold by 10 percent, to 1,100. Revenues are now the same as in the case of the stable exchange rate in the second column. Note, however, the impact of the reduction in costs on the foreign earnings, which soar to f17,000 and are reflected in the ROI of 63 percent—which in turn is boosted by the drop in assets due to lower-cost inventories. In addition, the weaker dollar exchange rate escalates the dollar earnings to more than twice the level of the second column, an increase of 124 percent!

It should be clear from this highly simplified example that we must thoroughly analyze the dynamics of the foreign markets and conditions in addition to assessing the mere reflection of currency exchange rates as changes occur. You're invited to trace through a variety of assumptions in this simple model to gain further insight into the dynamics at play.

More complexity is introduced when differing inflation rates in various countries are taken into account. As was experienced in the United States during the 1970s, inflationary conditions don't necessarily increase operating earnings proportionately, as the prices of inputs like materials, labor, and fuel don't necessarily move in concert. Thus, a detailed analysis of the impact of foreign operations requires much more insight than this brief exposure could provide.

We should briefly mention another aspect of foreign currency transactions here. Companies engaged in buying, selling, and operating in various foreign currencies will use, whenever possible, the concept of *hedging* to protect themselves from even temporary exposure to currency fluctuations. In simple terms, hedging involves the simultaneous purchase or sale of foreign currency contracts that offset the amounts of the commercial transaction undertaken. For example, if a U.S. company sold goods into a foreign market and expects to be paid in the foreign currency some 30 or 60 days hence, the company's treasurer may execute a simultaneous contract to sell an equivalent amount of foreign currency at that time, but based on today's exchange rate. Such a currency contract, called a *forward trade*, exemplifies a common transaction in the worldwide market for currencies. The purpose of currency hedging is in effect to lock in the prevailing exchange rate and to avoid the risk of fluctuations. Again, there are many more aspects of foreign currency management than we can cover in a book of this scope. Readers should turn to specialized materials on these subjects for in-depth coverage.

Basic Inflation Concepts

Throughout this book we've referred to inflation's distorting effects on financial decisions and analysis. In this appendix, we'll offer a brief commentary on the basic nature of the often misunderstood phenomenon of inflation. Financial transactions are carried out and recorded with the help of a common medium of exchange, such as U.S. dollars. Variations in this medium will affect the numerical meaning of these transactions. But we know that underlying the transactions are economic trade-offs; that is, values are given and received. We must be careful not to confuse changes in economic values with changes in the medium used to effect and account for these transactions. We'll examine the ramifications of this important distinction in several contexts below.

PRICE LEVEL CHANGES

The economic values of goods and services invariably change over time. The reason for this is as basic as human nature: The law of supply and demand operates, in an uncontrolled market environment, to increase the value of goods and services that are in short supply, and to decrease the value of those available in abundance. This shift in relative values takes place even in a primitive barter economy that doesn't utilize any currency at all. The ratio of exchange of coconuts for beans, for example, will move in favor of coconuts when they're scarce, and in favor of beans when these are out of season. Many seasonal agricultural products go through a familiar price cycle, beginning with their temporary unavailability, on to the first arrivals in the market place, and eventually to an abundance before they become unavailable again. This phenomenon is not limited to seasonal goods, however. Natural resources go through cycles of availability, be it from the need to set up the expensive infrastructure to exploit new sources as old ones expire, or from extreme concerted actions such as OPEC's moves to limit production in the 1970s and 80s that caused world oil prices to surge through the cartel's control of over half the world's production. As alternative sources of oil and other energy were stimulated by the high prices, the cartel's power began to wane, hastened by inevitable squabbles among the member countries trying to look out for their own interests—and oil prices settled on a much lower, more sustainable level.

We know that the economic value of manufactured goods is similarly subject to the law of supply and demand. For example, as new technology emerges in the market, such as the first digital watches or compact disk players, or successive waves of innovation in electronic chips and other components, the price commanded by the early units will be well above the prices charged later on, after many suppliers have entered the market and competed for a share of industrial or consumer demand. The same is true of all goods and services for which there are present or potential alternative suppliers, domestic or international.

Our point here is that the economic value underlying personal, commercial, and financial transactions is determined by forces that are largely independent of the monetary expression in which they're recorded. As we'll see, an analysis of price level changes ideally should separate the change in price levels caused by shifts in economic value from those caused by changes in the currency itself. Accurate separation of the two is difficult in practice, but necessary for understanding the meaning of financial projections.

MONETARY INFLATION

Another phenomenon affecting transaction values is any basic change in the purchasing power of the currency. There are many reasons underlying the decline or strengthening of a currency's value as a medium of exchange. One of the most important factors causing inflationary declines in purchasing power is the amount of currency in circulation relative to economic activity. If the government raises the money supply faster than required to accommodate the growth in economic activity, there will literally be more dollars chasing relatively fewer goods and services, and thus the stated dollar prices for all goods and services will rise—even though the basic demand for any specific item may be unchanged.

This description is oversimplified, of course. A great many more factors affect currency values. One of these is the impact of government deficits and the way they are financed. Another is the value of the dollar relative to other currencies and the impact of exchange rates on international trade. In addition, international money flows and investment in response to more attractive investment opportunities cause shifts in the values of national currencies over and above the effects of the individual countries' fiscal and economic conditions. Union negotiations, wage settlements, and cost of living adjustments in wages, pensions, and social security are also related to changing currency values. Every nation's central bank—the Federal Reserve bank in the case of the United States—is vital in the process because its policies affect both the size of the money supply and the level of interest rates. These in turn affect government fiscal policies, business activity, international trade and money flows, etc. And ultimately, serious declines in the value of a currency can also affect the basic supply and demand of goods and services, as, for example, customers and businesses buy ahead to beat anticipated price increases.

The point here isn't to systematically analyze inflation and its causes, but rather to make the basic distinction between economic and monetary changes influencing price levels. Suffice it to say that price level changes due to monetary effects are largely the ones that distort economic values of personal and commercial transactions. If monetary conditions remained stable (that is, if the amount of currency in circulation always matched the level of economic activity), price level changes would only reflect changes in economic values—something we've agreed is at the core of management's efforts to improve the shareholders' economic condition. Because monetary stability is an unrealistic expectation, however, the challenge remains to make the analysis of the actual conditions affecting prices and economic values truly meaningful.

NOMINAL AND REAL DOLLARS

Business and personal transactions are expressed in terms of *nominal* dollars, also called current dollars, that reflect today's prices, unadjusted or altered in any way. For accounting purposes, nominal dollars are used every day to record transactions. However, when dollar prices change over time, the amounts recorded in the past no longer reflect current prices, either in terms of the underlying economic values or in terms of the value of the currency at the moment.

To deal with changes in the value of the currency, economists have devised *price indexes* intended to separate, at least in part, monetary distortions from fluctuations in economic value. Such an index is constructed by measuring the aggregate change in the prices of a representative group of products and services as a surrogate for the change in the value of the currency. Yet we already know that any goods and services chosen for this purpose are themselves also subject to changes in supply and demand, apart from mere currency fluctuations. But there's no direct way to measure changes in currency values as such. Inevitably, therefore, the price index approach involves mixing demand/supply conditions and currency values, and the only hope is that the selection of goods and services employed in a given index is broad enough to compensate somewhat for the underlying demand/supply conditions.

The *consumer price index*, a popular index of inflation, is calculated in this fashion. It's based on frequent sampling of the prices of a "market basket" of goods and services purchased by U.S. consumers, including food, housing, clothing, and transportation. The composition and weighting of this basket is changed gradually to reflect changing habits and tastes, although there is much room for argument about how representative and up-to-date the selection is. Another popular index applicable to business is the *producer price index*, based on a representative weighted sampling of the wholesale prices of goods produced. Other indexes deal with wholesale commodity prices and a variety of specialized groupings of products and services.

The broadest index in common use is applied to the gross national product as a whole, the so-called *GNP deflator*, which expresses the price changes experienced in the total range of goods and services produced in the U.S. economy. Based on broad statistical sampling, the current level of the GNP deflator is announced frequently throughout the year in connection with other economic statistics about business and government activity. All of these indexes are prepared by calculating the changes in prices from those of a selected base year, which is changed only infrequently to avoid having to adjust comparative statistical series whenever the base year is changed.

The price indexes are used to translate nominal dollar values in government statistics and business reports into *real dollar values*. This involves converting nominal dollar values to a chosen standard so that past and present dollar transactions can be compared in equivalent terms. For example, to compare this year's performance of the economy to that of last year, we may choose to express current economic statistics using last year's dollars as the standard. Last year's dollars are then called real, and today's data are expressed in these real terms. To do this, we simply adjust today's dollars by the amount of inflation experienced since last year. If inflation this year was 3.0 percent over last year as expressed in the GNP deflator, every nominal dollar figure for this year would be adjusted downward by 3.0 percent. The result would be an expression of this year's results in terms of real dollars, which are based on the prior year.

A real dollar is thus simply a nominal dollar that has been adjusted to the price level of a particular stated base year, using one of the applicable price indexes. The base chosen can be any year, as long as past or future years are consistently stated in terms of the currency value for the base year. In fact, real dollars are often called *constant dollars*, a name that simply recognizes that they're derived from a constant base. The process of adjustment has the following effect: During inflationary periods, the real dollars for the years preceding the base year will be adjusted upward, while the real dollars of future years will be adjusted downward. The reverse is true, of course, if the period involves deflation instead.

To illustrate, let's assume that the following price developments took place during a five-year period. We're using the producer price index (PPI). This index was constructed on the basis of Year 0. In the following table, we've set Year 3 as the base year for our analysis.

	Year 1	Year 2	Year 3	Year 4	Year 5
Producer price index (Year 0)	1.09	1.15	1.21	1.25	1.33
Producer price index (Year 3)	0.90	0.95	1.00	1.03	1.10
Real value of $100 (Base Year 3)	$111	$105	$100	$97	$91

Note that two steps were involved. First, the producer price index had to be adjusted for our chosen base, Year 3. That is, the index had to be set at 1.00 for Year 3 and then all index numbers were divided by the value of the index for the base year, which is 1.21. (However, the index could have been constructed on any other year because an index measures price changes year by year from whatever starting point is chosen.) The next step was to divide the adjusted index values on the second line into the nominal dollars of each year. We chose to use the amount of $100 for all years, but the process applies, of course, to any amount of nominal dollars in any one of the years. Using a single round figure permitted us to illustrate the shifts in value with a same dollar amount.

The example clearly shows that a dollar's purchasing power in Year 4 versus Year 3 declined by 3 percent. The implication from a business point of view is that a company must increase its nominal earnings power by 3 percent in order to keep up with inflation in the prices it must pay for goods and services. Anything less than that will leave the owners worse off.

This simple process allows us to convert nominal dollars into inflation-adjusted real dollars. Problems arise in choosing the proper index for a business situation, and also from the fact that the index embodies changes in economic value as well as in currency value, as we discussed earlier. Much thought has been expended on refining the process of inflation adjustment, but in the end, the judgment about its usefulness depends on the purpose of the analysis and the degree of accuracy desired.

APPLICATIONS OF INFLATION ADJUSTMENT IN FINANCIAL ANALYSIS

Restatement of company data or projections in real dollar terms is at times useful to assess whether the company's performance has kept up with shifts in currency values. Such restatement may be used to value a company's assets and liabilities, or to show the real growth or decline in sales and earnings. As we observed, publicly traded companies are obligated to include an annual inflation-adjusted restatement of key data in their published shareholder reports.

Much effort goes into adjusting financial projections for inflation, particularly in the area of capital investment analysis. There are no truly satisfactory general rules for this process, however. When an analyst must project cash flows from a major capital investment, the easiest approach continues to be projection in nominal dollars, taking into account expected cost and price increases of the key variables involved, tailored specifically to the conditions of the business. The discount standard applied against the projection must also be based on nominal return expectations that, of course, embody the inflationary outlook.

To refine the analysis, many companies prepare projections in real dollars, attempting to forecast the true economic increases or decreases in costs and prices. Then an appropriate inflation index is applied to the figures to convert them into nominal dollars. The problem is, however, that the margin between revenues and costs may widen unduly, simply because the same inflation index is applied to the larger revenue numbers and to the smaller cost numbers. Often arbitrary adjustments have to be made to keep the margin spread manageable.

Another approach involves developing projections expressed in real dollars and discounting these with a return standard that has also been converted into real returns. The result will be internally consistent as far as the project is concerned. However, the result is not readily comparable with the current overall performance of the business—recorded and expressed in nominal dollar terms—unless the company has also found a way to convert and measure ongoing performance in real dollar terms. Some companies are beginning to experiment with such restated reports and measures, but the approach involves a massive effort, both in terms of data preparation and education of personnel generating and using the projections and performance data. It's instinctively easier to think about business in nominal dollars than real dollars, and progress in this area is being made only gradually. The complexities are such that the financial and planning staffs of companies wishing to use this approach face a lengthy conceptual and practical conversion problem.

IMPACT OF INFLATION

To restate quickly, the basic impact of inflation—and the much less common opposite situation, deflation—is a growing distortion of recorded values on a company's financial statements, and an ongoing partial distortion of operating results. Accounting methods discussed in Chapters 1 and 2 are designed to make the effect of the inflationary distortion at least consistent. In terms of cash flows, inflation distorts a company's tax payments if the taxes due are based on low historical cost apportionment, and it results in a cash drain if dividends are higher than they would be if real-dollar earnings were considered, to name two examples. Inflation also affects financing conditions, particularly the repayment of principal on long-term debt obligations. As we observed before, however, the mediating influence of interest rates—which respond to inflation expectations—tends to prevent windfalls for the borrower looking to repay debt with "cheap" dollars. Normally, over the long run, distortions from inflation affect lenders and borrowers alike. Relative advantages gained by one over the other are only temporary.

Overall, the subject of inflation adjustments continues to evolve in financial analysis. It's unlikely that totally consistent methods that are generally applicability will be found.

Sources of Financial Information

While this book's orientation is techniques of financial analysis, many of the applications we've discussed implied the use of information beyond that stipulated or available directly. Thus, you must be familiar with at least the main sources of financial information to obtain the necessary input for analysis. For this reason, we've devoted this appendix to a brief review of common data sources; where required we give guidelines for interpreting the financial data presented. The information provided gives you the background needed to make more sophisticated decisions about company performance, new financing, temporary borrowing, investments, credit, capital budgeting, and so on.

Again, in keeping with the nature of this book, this appendix is meant only as an introduction to sources of current financial, periodic financial, and background company and business information. Additional references for further study and data are provided at the end of this appendix.

CURRENT FINANCIAL INFORMATION

The most common and convenient way to keep abreast of financial developments is through the daily financial pages of national, metropolitan, and regional newspapers. The most complete and widely read financial coverage is found in *The Wall Street Journal* and *The New York Times*, which contain detailed information on securities and commodity markets; news, feature articles, and statistics on economic and business conditions; news and earnings reports for individual companies; dividend announcements; currency, commodity, and trading data; and a great deal of coverage of international business and economic conditions. Major U.S. and Canadian dailies also carry key financial and economic data, but their coverage and emphasis vary greatly. Smaller and regional papers often provide only selected highlights tailored to the area and the readership.

The bulk of the materials shown in the financial pages involve securities transactions and current financial data. This information isn't entirely self-explanatory. We'll describe the meaning of some of the abbreviations and symbols used in *The Wall Street Journal* listings for stock transactions (traded on exchanges and over the counter), bond transactions, and other key financial data. Other newspapers generally present data in a fairly comparable fashion, but in less detail.

Stock Quotations

Stock Exchanges

Transactions executed on organized exchanges—New York Stock Exchange (NYSE), American Stock Exchange (AMEX), and several regional exchanges—and the electronic network of the National Association of Securities Dealers

FIGURE IV–1

New York Stock Exchange—Sample of Stock Transactions, Tuesday, March 5, 1996

| | 52 Weeks | | | | | Yield | P/E | Sales in | | | | Net |
	High	Low	Stock	Sym.	Div.	%	Ratio	100s	High	Low	Close	Change
	19	12	Abitibi	ABY	.40 e	...	...	706	14 1/8	13 7/8	14	– 1/8
s	45 7/8	28 1/4	Bell South	BLS	1.44	3.6	31	10852	39 7/8	38 7/8	39 7/8	+ 5/8
▲	36700	21160	Berk Hathwy	BRK	...	...	78	z 430	37300	36450	37200	+ 600
s	12 3/4	1 1/4	vj Edison Bros	EBS	m	...	...	2275	1 3/4	1 1/2	1 1/2	– 1/4
n▼	29 1/4	15 3/4	Mafco Cnsl	MFO	...	...	...	737	16	15 5/8	15 3/4	– 1/4
	27 1/2	24 3/4	IBM dep pf		1.88	7.0	...	30	27 1/8	27	27	– 1/8
	12 1/4	6	Lone Star wt		...	...	...	52	11 1/4	11 1/8	11 1/4	+ 1/4
n	21 1/4	20 1/2	Natwd Hlth wi		...	...	...	3	21	21	21	–
	70 1/2	36 5/8	Travelers	TRV	.90 f	1.3	12	15014	68 3/8	67	67 5/8	–1
	15	10 7/8	Wiser Oil	WZR	.12 m	1.0	49	269	12 1/8	11 3/4	12 1/8	+ 1/4
	259 1/2	155 1/4	Wells F	WFC	5.20 f	2.1	12	3825	253 1/4	248 3/8	252 5/8	+3 3/4
	62 7/8	42 7/8	Wrigley	WWY	.68 a	1.1	31	721	60 7/8	59 1/2	60 3/8	+ 1/4

(NASDAQ) generally include the kind of information shown in Figure IV–1. It shows the day's transactions in 12 stocks out of the 3,139 individual stocks traded on the New York Stock Exchange on Tuesday, March 5, 1996, as reported the next day in *The Wall Street Journal*. The total volume of shares traded for the day was about 435 million, an above-average volume in a year in which daily volumes well over 400 million were quite common and in which a slow day involved trading volumes under 300 million shares. Daily trading statistics for the NYSE, AMEX, and NASDAQ are summarized in *The Wall Street Journal* under overall headings "Stock Market Data Bank" and "The Dow Jones Averages."

The first stock listed in Figure IV–1, Abitibi, had a high value of 19 and a low of 12 over the previous 52 weeks. This is the range in which the shares closed at the end of the trading day in the previous 52 weeks, but not including the closing value of March 5, 1996. The quotations are given in dollars per share and fractions of a dollar not smaller than 1/8 ($0.125). Next to the name is the company's symbol, ABY, used in the electronic stock quotations flashed all over the world. This is followed by the annual dividend paid. While Abitibi paid dividends of $.40 during the past 12 months, the notation "e" indicates that there is no regular dividend rate. Therefore, no dividend yield is indicated for Abitibi in the next column, which normally reflects the annual dividend yield based on current market quotations. The special symbol "g" next to the company name indicates that Abitibi, a major pulp and paper company headquartered in Canada, paid its dividends in Canadian dollars. The next column reports the price/earnings ratio based on current reported earnings (12-month period) and the current closing price. Abitibi's P/E isn't shown because of losses, but it is listed for most other companies.

The day's transactions in Abitibi stock totaled 70,600 shares, as indicated in the eighth column, where sales are listed in multiples of 100 shares. This convention is used because stocks are ordinarily traded in round lots of 100 shares, while fewer than 100 shares is considered an odd lot, and brokers usually charge a premium for trading in the latter.

The next four columns indicate the stock's price movements based on actual transactions during March 5, 1996. Trade in Abitibi reached a high for the day of 14 1/8 and a low of 13 7/8, closing at 14. The net change of −1/8 in the last column indicates the difference between its price at the close of trading on March 5 and the price at the close of the previous trading day.

Unless otherwise indicated, the transactions listed involve common stocks. If a preferred stock is traded, the symbol "pf" is added right after the name. In our example, the IBM issue traded is a preferred stock. The dividend quoted for preferred stock is the annual rate, as is the case with common stock. IBM's preferred paid a dividend of $1.88, providing a yield of 7.0 based on its current price.

The symbol "s" next to the high for Bell South and Edison Brothers indicates a stock dividend or split, while the "n" with Mafco and Nationwide Healthcare indicates a stock newly issued in the past 52 weeks. The upright black arrow with Berkshire Hathaway indicates that a new 52-week high has been reached, while the inverse arrow with Mafco indicates a new low. Berkshire Hathaway, the most expensive stock in the market (which pays no dividends but focuses on capital gains) sold only 430 shares that day, as indicated by the "z" (sales in full) with the sales figure. Edison Brothers, where the symbol "vj" ahead of the name indicates a state of bankruptcy, isn't paying a dividend, and the letter "m" signals that the dividend was omitted during the past 52 weeks. Its low price compared to the 52-week high indicates the company's severe difficulties. The symbol "f" with Travelers Insurance and Wells Fargo reflects recent dividend increases, while the "m" with Wiser Oil indicates a recent dividend reduction. Finally, "wt" with Lone Star's name designates the issue as a warrant (trading separately from its related stock), while the new Nationwide Healthcare stock "wi" is trading on a "when issued" basis.

A number of additional symbols and abbreviations are commonly used and explained briefly in footnotes on the financial pages of most papers. Among these are extra dividends ("a"), an initial dividend ("p"), trading ex-dividend ("x") after the date the dividend was declared, and ("b"), the annual rate of cash dividends plus a stock dividend.

Apart from notations for dividend exceptions, symbols are also used to show when a company's P/E ratio can't be calculated because a deficit was reported for the period ("dd"), or a company's calling for redemption of a particular stock ("cld"), various conditions of rights and warrants (which represent options to purchase additional shares), and the first day of trading of a new stock ("FD").

The individual listings of stock transactions in *The Wall Street Journal* are supplemented by various summaries of overall trading figures in the so-called *Stock Market Data Bank*. One of these is the list of the day's most active stocks. On March 5, 1996, the two stocks with by far the highest turnover of shares on the

NYSE were Micron Technology (12.5 million shares) and Hanson Corp. (10.9 million shares). Both stocks were very volatile over the past 52 weeks.

Another market summary—the "diary" for the past two trading days and for trading one week ago, covering the NYSE, NASDAQ, and AMEX—showed that on March 5, 1996, among the 3,139 different issues traded on the NYSE, 1,220 advanced and 1,123 declined, leaving 796 issues unchanged. The number of new highs achieved was 148, while there were 12 new lows—reflecting the record surge in the market during the first part of 1996. The volume of advancing issues outpaced declining issues by 255 million to 159 million in the total trading volume of 435 million shares. The diary also lists price percentage gainers and losers for the day, which on March 5, 1996, were Nashua (up 15.6 percent) and Sizzler International (down 18.5 percent). Among the volume percentage leaders, Watsco took first place at 887,000 shares, which represented a surging 8,000 percent increase over its average trading volume during the past 65 days.

Also included are graphic displays of four months of the movements of the Dow Jones averages, for industrials, transportation, and utilities, and a table of the opening, closing, and hourly values of the averages for five trading days. For example, on Tuesday, March 5, 1996, the Dow Jones Industrial Average closed at 5,642.42, up 42.27 from Monday, March 4. Briefer listings of other major market indicators (such as the Standard & Poor's 500 Index, the NASDAQ Composite Index, and the London and Tokyo indexes) are shown in an overview table. These and other indicators collectively provide an impression of the market's "mood" and direction.

Quotations of transactions on the American Stock Exchange are similar. Transactions on regional exchanges, such as the Pacific Stock Exchange in San Francisco and the Midwest Stock Exchange in Chicago, are often listed together with the most important quotations on the major Canadian stock exchanges in Toronto and Montreal. These transactions are quoted in less detail. Normally, only the number of shares traded, the high and low prices, and the closing prices with changes from the previous close are listed. At times, the quotations are limited to volume and closing prices only.

Reference was made earlier to the various stock price averages, which are popular and important clues to the stock market's behavior in general. These averages are calculated daily and in some cases continuously from on-line databases. The averages are followed by analysts, investors, and financial managers who interpret market movements to decide on purchase or sale of securities, or to assess various types of new securities. Because the various averages involve a selected and relatively small number of stocks, their upward or downward movement over time isn't necessarily a predictor of the likely movement of any particular stock or of the overall market.

As discussed earlier, there are many factors underlying the value and market position of a particular security, the most important being the current and prospective operating circumstances of the company and the cash flows generated in response to these. The market's atmosphere and general economic conditions will certainly influence the particular stock's behavior, but we must caution against the adage that a "rising tide lifts all ships in the harbor" (a gross oversimplification of stock market behavior). The limitations of stock indexes are those of averages in general, which can only be broad indicators of a likely trend against which all particulars of a security have to be compared.

The most commonly quoted and publicized stock price averages are the Dow Jones averages of 30 industrial, 20 transportation, and 15 utility stocks, and the composite average of all those 65 securities. The Dow Jones Industrial Average contains most well-known companies in the United States, such as IBM, General Motors, General Electric, 3M, Coca-Cola, and Procter & Gamble. Because it's heavily weighted toward these "blue-chip" securities—many of which have performed poorly in the past decade—the Dow Jones average isn't particularly applicable for analysis of securities of lesser known companies, specialized "growth situations," and conglomerates.

The New York Times average of 50 stocks includes 25 transportation issues and 25 industrial stocks. This average is also somewhat weighted in favor of blue chips. The Standard & Poor's averages—composite indexes of 425 industrial stocks, 50 utilities, and 25 transportation companies, and a combination of all these averages in the S&P 500—are more broadly based and more closely approximate the average price level of all stocks listed on the New York Stock Exchange because the S&P 500 includes about one quarter of the issues actively traded there. The NASDAQ composite average is a broad sampling of the many issues traded electronically through a wide network of security dealers. These quotations have achieved growing recognition over the past decade and represent a vast grouping of new, emerging, and fast growing securities as well as securities of large numbers of smaller, well-established companies.

As pointed out before, the various stock averages, including daily ranges and average price levels, are available for each trading day. Because transactions are electronically tracked, the current level of these averages is always available almost instantaneously during the trading day. Continuous adjustments are made for stock splits, stock dividends, and many changes in the corporate structure of the companies in the index. Some references at the end of this appendix detail how the indexes are calculated.

NASDAQ National Market Issues

A huge volume of securities is traded outside the organized exchanges in an auction market consisting of hundreds of security dealers and individuals in all parts of the country. They're electronically linked via extensive computer networks. This over-the-counter (OTC) market is an amazingly flexible arrangement which allows trading between prospective buyers and sellers of such securities as government bonds, state and municipal bonds, stocks and bonds of smaller and newer companies, bank stocks, mutual funds, insurance companies, small issues, and infrequently traded issues.

On Tuesday, March 5, 1996, the NASDAQ Composite Index climbed 11.93, or .1.1 percent, to 1096.81. Advances topped declines 1,881 to 1,765 on a total volume of 492 million shares, which exceeded the NYSE's volume by about 60 million shares. Financial listings for the NASDAQ national market issue transactions are similar to stock exchange transaction listings, except that notations indicating special conditions are incorporated into the four- or five-letter listing symbol. If a fifth letter is used, its special meaning is keyed to a symbol explanation below the NASDAQ listing.

Figure IV–2 from the March 6, 1996, *The Wall Street Journal* provides a sample listing of eight NASDAQ quotations for March 5, 1996. The format is the same as that for the New York Stock Exchange listings in Figure IV–1 except that the symbol specifying the company is composed of four letters, with a fifth added as needed to denote a special situation.

The notations with NASDAQ transactions parallel the New York Stock Exchange quotations, but some additional (fifth) letters occur in our sample of companies. The "F" with Abacan Resources indicates a foreign stock, the "A" with Ben & Jerry's denotes a Class A stock, while the "Z" with Diacrin signals a special situation in this new ("n") stock yet to be issued. The "S" with National Insurance Co. denotes shares of beneficial interest.

Foreign Exchanges

Some of the larger newspapers carry limited quotations from major foreign stock exchanges. Trading of internationally recognized securities on the Paris, London, Tokyo, or Frankfurt stock exchanges is reported in the currency of the country involved. At times, the financial pages may contain current stock averages for foreign countries, supplemented by accounts of major activities there. *The Wall Street Journal* presents the Dow Jones World Stock Indexes, which reflect market trends in major regions of the world. Closing prices and changes from the prior trading day are provided for many industrial groupings and for major regions such as the United States, the Americas, Europe, and Asia-Pacific.

FIGURE IV–2

NASDAQ National Market—Sample of Stock Transactions, Tuesday, March 5, 1996

	52 Weeks High	Low	Stock	Sym.	Div.	Yield %	P/E Ratio	Sales in 100s	High	Low	Close	Net Change
n	3 7/16	2 1/8	Abacan Res	ABACF		...	...	325	3 7/8	3 1/5	3 1/4	+1/16
	20 3/4	10 1/2	Ben Jerry A	BJICA		...	19	70	16	15 3/4	15 3/4	–
n	10 1/4	8	Diacrin un	DCRNZ		...	...	322	10 1/8	9 1/2	10 1/8	+3/4
	31 1/4	24 1/2	Fst Hawiin	FHWN	1.18	4.2	12	45	28 1/2	28	28	–3/8
	13 21/64	5 7/16	Hahn Autmtve	HAHN	stk	...	dd	16	8 3/4	8 1/4	8 1/4	–1/2
▲	34	26 1/4	Keystn Fnl	KSTN	1.44f	4.2	13	532	34 1/4	33 1/4	34 1/4	+ 3/8
s	13 3/8	10 7/16	Natl Inco	NIRTS	.80r	6.2	dd	3	13	13	13	–3/8
▼	25 15/16	11 1/4	Sequent Cptr	SQNT		...	11	8330	11 5/8	10 3/4	11 1/8	–5/8

Mutual Funds

Mutual funds are professionally managed investment pools. A share of a mutual fund represents an investment in a portfolio of different securities, which may be oriented toward a variety of investment objectives such as earnings or capital appreciation. These funds have gained in importance in recent years, and mutual fund trading is quoted in most major newspapers. Price ranges are provided by the National Association of Securities Dealers.

The quotes normally show the investment objectives incorporated in the name of the specific fund under the heading to the management company, defined in many categories, including capital appreciation (CAP) and growth and income (G&I) for stock funds, short-term (BST) and high-yield taxable (BHI) for taxable bond funds, and intermediate-term (IDM) and high-yield municipal (HYM) for municipal bond funds. Next is given the net asset value per share (NAV), followed by the net change in NAV from the previous day. Finally, the total return is provided in percent for the year to date.

A variety of mutual fund indexes developed by Lipper are quoted to show daily trends in major categories, such as growth funds, small company growth funds, and gold funds, as well as bond indexes for different funds such as world income or general municipals.

Options

Options (which are essentially contracts to buy or sell a security on a future date and at a stipulated price) are traded on various exchanges and are listed in terms of closing prices for "puts" (sales prices) and "calls" (purchase prices) for several months in the future. This specialized market has grown rapidly in recent years as has the market for commodity futures, which similarly represent contracts for future sales and purchases of certain commodities and are quoted in the financial pages.

Option quotations provide the option and strike price, the expiration date, volume of trades during a given day, and the last trade in dollars plus fractions. The 40 most active contracts the exchange traded on is identified, as is the net change from the prior trading day, the closing price, and the "open interest" (options outstanding) from the prior trading day.

Bond Quotations

The three major types of bonds—corporate, state and municipal, and federal government—represent a huge market involving both the organized exchanges and the NASDAQ market. In fact, the overwhelming majority of government bonds of both types are traded in the NASDAQ market, while the majority of corporate bond issues are traded on the stock exchanges. It will be useful to discuss how bond transactions are listed. Figure IV–3 shows a sample listing for the NYSE; trading on other exchanges is handled similarly.

The first line gives not only the name of the issuing company, but also the coupon interest rate and the maturity date by the last two digits of the year. Thus,

FIGURE IV–3

New York Stock Exchange Bond Transactions, Tuesday, March 5, 1996 (volume $24,592,000)

Bonds	Current Yield	Volume	Close	Net Change
Am T&T 8 1/8 22	7.7	27	106 1/8	...
BBN 6s 12	cv	25	114	–2
duPnt dc 6s 01	6.0	740	99 1/2	+1/8
Motrla zr 13 13	...	27	73 1/2	+1/2
OldRep 5 3/4 cld	cv	15	130 1/2	...
Unisys na 15s 97	...	155	106 3/4	–3/8

the first line is an American Telephone and Telegraph issue with a stated interest rate of 8 1/8 percent and due date of 2022. Note that the issue is trading at a price above par to yield 7.7 percent, a yield more in keeping with the lower long-term interest conditions of 1996 compared to 1992, when the bond was issued.

The most important difference to remember vis-à-vis stock quotations is that bonds are quoted in percentages of par value, expressed in fractions no smaller than one-eighth of a percent. For example, the AT&T bonds closed at a price of 106 1/8, which represents $1,072.25 for each $1,000 of par value. Sales volumes are given in thousands of dollars because $1,000 is the most common denomination of a single bond. In contrast to stocks, only the closing price and the change from the prior day's closing price are listed.

The symbols used with the individual bonds parallel those discussed earlier. For example, "cv" with the BBN and Old Republic bonds indicates that these securities are convertible into common stock, and their prices will reflect the share values of the common they represent. This is especially true for the Old Republic bond, which has just been called ("cld") for redemption, and is trading at a considerable premium over par. The DuPont bond is selling at a deep discount ("dc"), while the Motorola is a zero coupon bond, which means that the bond is sold at a discount deep enough to provide the investor at maturity with both recovery of principal and an earnings yield commensurate with prevailing interest rate conditions. The symbol "na" with the Unisys bond indicates that there is no interest accrual, and the low price of the bond relative to the high 15 percent coupon rate indicates that investors expect little recovery beyond the principal in 1997, the year of maturity.

A slightly different method is used to list current quotations for government agency bonds and miscellaneous securities traded over the counter. Again, we'll use an example from *The Wall Street Journal* for the trading day of Tuesday, March 5, 1996. Figure IV–4 gives quotes for U.S. Treasury bonds, U.S. Treasury bills, Federal Home Loan Bank bonds, and World Bank bonds.

FIGURE IV–4

Government Agency and Miscellaneous Securities Quotations, Tuesday, March 5, 1996 (over the counter)

Rate	Maturity	Days to Maturity	Bid	Asked	Bid Change	Ask Yield
U.S. Treasury Bonds and Notes (n):						
12 3/8	May 04		141:07	141:11	–11	5.93
5 1/2	Sep 97 n		100:13	100:15	–3	5.18
10 5/8	Aug 15		145:28	145:30	–25	6.45
7 1/4	Aug 96 n		100:31	100:01	–1	5.05
U.S. Treasury Bills:						
	Apr 04, '96	28	4.95	4.85	...	4.95
	Feb 06, '97	336	4.83	4.81	+0.06	5.06
Federal Home Loan Bank:						
8.10	3-96		100:05	100:07	...	3.59
9.50	2-04		120:14	120:20	...	6.18
World Bank Bonds:						
7.25	10-96		101:04	101:06	...	5.08
8.13	5-01		110:14	110:18	...	5.66

We find that the securities are listed in terms of bid and asked quotations, which represent the price desired for purchase or sale on the trading day but don't necessarily denote specific transactions. Another important difference reflected in this example is the custom of quoting prices in percentage of par value, this time stated in terms of fractions of a percent in 32ds of a point. Thus, a quote of 141:07 means a price of 1,410 7/32 percent or $1,412.19 per $1,000 of par value. The final column shows the yield to maturity, which reflects the return on investment earned at the current price if the bond is held to its maturity date and redeemed at par.

Note that the yield on the 12 3/8 percent Treasury bond due in 2004 is well below the relatively high coupon rate, while the 5 1/2 percent bond due in September 1997 is yielding 5.18 percent, very close to the coupon rate. These differentials reflect the relatively low interest levels prevailing in 1996, which were far below the inflation-driven conditions of the late 1970s and early 1980s. The slightly higher yield on the 10 3/4 percent bond is due to the fact that its maturity is not until 2015, while the 5.05 percent yield on the 7 1/4 coupon note is due to the fact that it will mature in a few months.

U.S. government securities as well as other debt instruments will be affected by the general outlook for interest rates. U.S. government securities will tend to yield a lower return than most corporate and other public bonds, because the likelihood of default is extremely remote and the purchaser is normally looking for a safe investment with an assured long-term or short-term yield. Also, they generally are exempt from state income taxes.

As we found in the case of the stock market quotations, bond market listings are supplemented by a variety of reports on the volume of trading, bonds averages, summaries of advancing and declining conditions, highs and lows for the year, and so on. Again, these provide the investor with a general feel for the daily movements of the bond markets and interest rate conditions. The most commonly used averages are the Dow Jones Bond Averages (20 bonds, including 10 public utilities and 10 industrials), Merrill Lynch Corporate Debt Issues, and Lehman Brothers U.S. Securities Indexes. Bond averages are calculated in percentages of par, as were the quotations themselves.

On Tuesday, March 5, 1996, the NYSE bond volume was $24,592,000 for all issues, with the 20-bond average rising slightly to 104.88, up 0.07 from the prior trading day. Issues traded numbered 328, of which 123 staged advances, 138 declined, and 67 remained unchanged. New highs for the year were achieved by 13 issues, and new lows by 2 issues.

Other Financial Data

Most papers list, in one form or another, so-called leading, coincident, and lagging business and economic indicators—such as indexes of industrial production, freight car loadings, prices, output in the automotive industry, and steel production—both in feature stories and in tabular form. When supplemented by reports of earnings and dividend declarations of individual corporations, news about corporate management, analysis and announcement of new financing, and industry analysis, this information can provide a broad background for financial analysis.

Among the more specialized data in the financial pages are listings of transactions in the commodities markets. Commodities include a great variety of basic raw materials such as cotton, lumber, copper, and rubber as well as foods such as coffee, corn, and wheat. The best-known exchange for commodity trading is the Chicago Board of Trade. More specialized exchanges include the New York Cotton Exchange or international exchanges such as the London Metal Exchange. Commodities may be traded on a spot basis; that is, the commodity is purchased outright at the time. Commodities futures are also traded. These are contracts to buy or sell a commodity at a specified price at some point in the future. The commodities market is far too varied to describe here, but we should take a quick look at how commodities are quoted.

The information on commodities trading provided by most sources usually involves opening and closing transactions as well as highs and lows for the trading day and the season. Changes from the previous trading day are also often listed. A variety of indexes are available, such as the Dow Jones Spot Index, Dow Jones Futures Index, and Reuters United Kingdom Index. A company whose operations depend to a large extent on raw materials traded in a spot or futures market can be severely influenced by fluctuations in spot or futures prices.

Because fluctuations in commodities markets can be severe, traders in these markets often hedge. This involves arrangements to both buy and sell the same commodity, which will "cover" the trader for shifts in prices. References at the end of this appendix provide detailed information on commodities trading.

Foreign Exchange

Most newspapers list the major currencies of the world in equivalents of U.S. dollars. Normally the quotations represent selling prices of bank transfers in the United States for payment abroad, and quotations are given for the current trading day as well as for the previous day. Also, prices for foreign bank notes are often quoted in equivalents of U.S. dollars on both buying and selling bases.

PERIODIC FINANCIAL INFORMATION

Apart from the financial data contained in daily newspapers, a wealth of information is provided by various financial, economic, and business periodicals. Furthermore, readily available reference works contain periodic listings and analyses of financial information oriented toward the investor and financial analyst. The advent of the computer has made possible the rapid collection and analysis of company and economic data, and current information can now be obtained on-line through database access or in hard copy on a timely basis. The most important sources of periodic financial and business information are discussed next.

Magazines

Major Periodicals

For general business coverage, *Business Week* remains one of the most useful and widely read publications. It covers current developments in business and economics, both national and international. It analyzes major events and reports on individual companies, stock markets, labor, business education, and so on with a selective listing of economic indicators as well as a special index of business activity.

For more detailed coverage of stock quotations, security offerings, banking developments, and financial, industrial, and commodity trends, the *Commercial and Financial Chronicle* is the most comprehensive source available. *The Wall Street Transcript* analyzes securities of a great variety of individual companies, on both a financial and economic basis, and assesses the technical indications of stock market charts. It discusses major corporate presentations to security analysts about past performance and future plans, and features roundtable discussions on industry groups by security analysts.

Barron's covers business trends in terms of individual companies as well as major industries, and provides much information about corporate securities. The section "Stock Market at a Glance" is a useful and detailed picture of the securities markets. *Fortune* offers biweekly comments on national economic trends. It profiles major U.S. and international executives in addition to giving detailed articles on industry, company, and socioeconomic trends. The magazine's annual listing and ranking of the Fortune 500 (the best-performing U.S. companies) and similar listings of banks and major foreign companies are useful references.

Semimonthly *Forbes* magazine takes the investor's viewpoint, providing detailed and searching analyses of individual companies and their managements. The annual January issue, which reviews the performance of major U.S. industries, is an excellent source of information on industry trends and ranks companies by a series of criteria.

For an international outlook, the weekly British magazine *The Economist* surveys international and United Kingdom developments in politics, economics, and business, and discusses U.S. developments in depth. It can be considered an international *Business Week*, as can *World Business*.

Economic and business trends are covered in considerable detail in publications of major commercial banks such as the *National City Bank Monthly Letter* and *New England Letter* of the First National Bank of Boston. The various Federal Reserve banks' general bulletins and regional bulletins contain regional economic data.

The bimonthly *Harvard Business Review* (a highly regarded forum for discussion of management concepts and tools) includes financial insights from practitioners and academicians for an extensive worldwide readership of business executives. Several other major business schools publish journals of similar orientation.

Dun's Review presents trade indexes, data on business failures, and key financial ratios in addition to articles about industry and commerce. *Nation's Business*, a publication of the U.S. Chamber of Commerce, presents general articles on business subjects. The *Federal Reserve Bulletin* contains much statistical data on business and government finances, both domestic and international. The *Survey of Current Business* also provides extensive business statistics.

Detailed stock exchange quotations and data about many unlisted securities (those not traded on a recognized exchange), foreign exchange, and money rates are contained in the *Bank and Quotation Record*. The quarterly *Journal of Finance* presents articles on finance, investments, economics, money, and credit, including international aspects of these topics.

Other Periodicals

Many specialized periodicals are published by trade associations and banking, commercial, and trading groups too numerous to mention. Also useful are the great variety of U.S. government surveys and publications, statistical papers provided by the United Nations and its major agencies, and the various analyses and reviews in academic journals. The end of this appendix lists several books that provide detailed guidelines on and descriptions of the type of information available from various sources.

Listed below are some major periodicals that deal directly with, or relate to, corporate finance. Many other relevant publications are also available. Some publications are specialized and oriented toward a specific community of interest; others deal with financial conditions in foreign countries. The titles are largely self-explanatory:

Banker's Magazine	*Financial World*
CFO Magazine	*Journal of Commerce*
Corporate Financing	*Management Accounting*
Credit and Financial Management	*Mergers and Acquisitions*
Finance	(U.S. and British editions)
Journal of Banking and Finance	*National Tax Journal*
Financial Analysts Journal	*Managerial Finance*
Financial Executive	*World Financial Markets*
Financial Management	

Financial Manuals and Services

Most current financial and economic information is now available through various on-line services and information subscription services. This includes information available in published manuals and services. The most popular and best-known set of these is provided by Moody's, with Standard & Poor's a close second. Moody's publishes several volumes: *Industrials; Banks and Finance; Insurance; Public Utilities; Transportation; Municipals;* and *Government; OTC* (over the counter); and *International.* These manuals are published each year and contain up-to-date key historical data, financial statements, securities price ranges, and dividend records for a large number of companies, including practically all publicly held corporations. Moody's manuals are updated through semiweekly supplements with detailed cross-references.

Moody's *Quarterly Handbook* gives one-page summaries of key financial and operating data for major publicly held corporations. Furthermore, Moody's weekly stock and bond surveys analyze market and industry conditions. Besides its semiweekly *Dividend Record*, a semimonthly *Bond Record* contains current prices, earnings, and ratings of most important bonds traded in this country.

Standard & Poor's publications include the *Standard Corporation Records.* This financial information about a large number of companies is published in loose-leaf format and is updated through daily supplements. A useful S&P publication, the *Analysts Handbook*, provides industry surveys with key financial data on individual companies and some industries. Standard & Poor's other services include several dealing with the bond market, weekly forecasts of the security markets, securities statistics, and a monthly earnings and stock rating guide.

Financial services similar to Moody's and Standard & Poor's are provided by Fitch's *Corporation Manuals* and by more specialized manuals such as Walker's *Manual of Pacific Coast Securities.* An almost overwhelming flow of information, judgments, and analyses of individual companies from an investor's standpoint is provided by the major brokerage houses. Furthermore, services available to individuals on a subscription basis provide up-to-date financial analyses and evaluations of individual companies and their securities. The most important among these services are *Value Line, United Business Service, Babson's,* and *Investor's Management Sciences.* The *Value Line* investment survey provides ratings and reports on companies, with selections and opinions for the investor, while *Investor's Management Services* concentrates on providing a great deal of standardized statistical information as the basis for making analytical judgments. *Dun & Bradstreet's* credit information services help in evaluating small or unlisted companies.

BACKGROUND COMPANY AND BUSINESS INFORMATION

Annual Reports

The most commonly used reference source about the current affairs of publicly held corporations is the annual report furnished to shareholders, supplemented by briefer quarterly reports. The formats used by individual corporations vary widely from detailed coverage (that may even include current corporate, industry, and national issues) to a bare minimum disclosure of financial results. Nevertheless, the annual report is generally an important direct source of financial information. Because the disclosure requirements of the Securities and Exchange Commission (SEC), the recommendations of the accounting profession, and state laws have become more and more demanding over time, the analyst can usually count on annual reports presenting a fairly consistent set of data.

Government Data

More specific details about company operations can often be found in the annual statement that corporations must file with the SEC in Washington, D.C. This information is filed on Form 10-K and is available upon request for public inspection. Furthermore, when a corporation wants to issue new securities in significant amounts or alter its capital structure in a major way, the detailed proposal that must be filed with the SEC, the *prospectus*, is generally a more complete source of company background data than is the normal annual report. It will cover the history of the company, ownership patterns, directors and top management, financial and operating data, products, facilities, and information regarding the intended use of the new funds.

If a company is closely held (most of the shares are held by founders, their families, and key employees) or too small to be listed by the key financial services, information about its financial operations can often be obtained from the corporation records departments of the states in which the company does business. Again, these reports are open to the public for inspection.

Trade Associations

Trade associations, which number in the hundreds, are a prime source of information about their respective industries. A great deal of statistical information is available annually or more often and covers products, services, finances, and performance criteria applicable to the industry or trade group. Often financial and performance data are grouped by types and sizes of firms to make overall statistics on the industry more applicable to a particular operation. Trade associations include the American Electronics Association, Association, American Paper Institute, and National Lumber Manufacturers Association to name but a few. Sources for listings and addresses of these associations and their publications can be found in the references at the end of the appendix.

Econometric Services

Many forecasts of U.S. and international economic conditions are available to the financial analyst. Based on so-called econometric models developed by a variety of academic institutions and economic advisory services, these forecasts of the U.S. economy and more recently of other countries' economies as well can provide valuable clues regarding the likely movement of the economy within which financial conditions must be viewed. Among the widely quoted and used econometric models are those developed by the Wharton School at the University of Pennsylvania, Data Resources Inc., and Chase Econometric Associates. Many corporations subscribe to such forecasting services and use the projections in their operational and financial planning. Increasingly, corporate and academic economists are testing their own assumptions about economic trends with the help of econometric models. Another feature of these services is the growing variety of on-line data bases containing a vast array of statistical and financial information for immediate access.

While we've merely touched on the major sources of specific or general information on financial business affairs, the reader is encouraged to make use of the sources discussed as well as the references at the end of this appendix. In addition, a great deal of information is available from various business libraries in corporations, colleges, and universities as well as from local institutions. The problem facing a financial analyst, whether student or professional, isn't a lack of data; rather, it's selecting what's truly relevant.

SELECTED REFERENCES

Ibbotson, Roger G., and Rex A. Sinquefield. *Stocks, Bonds, Bills and Inflation.* Chicago: Ibbotson Associates. (Annual Yearbook).

Lehmann, Michael B. *The Dow Jones-Irwin Guide to Using The Wall Street Journal.* Homewood, Ill.: Dow Jones-Irwin, 1990.

Novallo, Annette. *Information Industry Directory.* 14th ed. Detroit: Gale Research, 1993.

Pierce, Phyllis S., ed. *The Dow Jones Averages 1885-1990.* Homewood, Ill.: Business One-Irwin, 1991.

Way, James, ed. *Encyclopedia of Business Information Sources.* 9th ed. Detroit: Gale Research, 1992.

Solutions to Self-Study Problems Plus Questions for Discussion

This appendix contains solutions to all problems at the end of Chapters 2 through 9. A series of questions for discussion is provided following each chapter's solutions. These questions should help stimulate your thoughts about key aspects of the chapter and serve as a basis for group discussions.

CHAPTER 2

Solutions to Problems

1.

CBA COMPANY
Changes in Balance Sheet ($ thousands)

Assets		Liabilities	
Cash	$(12.2)	Accounts payable	$ 11.8
Marketable securities	10.0	Notes payable	90.0
Accounts receivable	(8.8)	Accrued expenses	2.9
Inventories	60.7	Total current liabilities . . .	$104.7
Total current assets	49.7		
Land	-0-	Mortgage payable	$(15.2)
Plant and equipment (net) . . .	19.6	Common stock	5.0
Total fixed assets	19.6	Retained earnings	(17.0)
Other assets	8.2	Total net worth	$(27.2)
		Total liabilities and	
Total assets	$ 77.5	net worth	$ 77.5

Cash Flow Statement, 1997

Sources		Uses	
Depreciation	$32.2*	Loss from operations . .	$ 2.0*
Decrease in cash	12.2	Dividends paid	15.0†
Decrease in accounts receivable . .	8.8	Increase in securities . .	10.0
Increase in accounts payable	11.8	Increase in inventories	60.7
Increase in notes payable	90.0	Investment in plant . . .	51.8‡
Increase in accrued expenses	2.9	Increase in other assets	8.2
Increase in common stock	5.0	Decrease in mortgage	15.2
Total	$162.9	Total	$162.9

The results were built up from:

*Taken from 1997 operating statement.

†Change in retained earnings matches the combination of loss from operations ($2,000) on the 1997 operating statement and dividends paid ($15,000). No extraordinary items appear and no assumptions are necessary.

‡Since net plant and equipment increased by $19,600, and the only known element affecting the account is depreciation ($32,200), the amount of investment must have been the sum of these amounts ($51,800).

Observations

The biggest single use is a drastic rise in inventories, even though sales volume changed little. Are inventory controls failing? Dividends were wisely cut as profits plummeted. The key funds source was borrowing (short-term) of $90 which provides more than half of funds needs. Sizable capital investment (almost twice depreciation) points to optimistic future plans—any problems in sight? Is the company beginning to lean on suppliers? (Accounts payable is up somewhat.) Is equity capital called for?

2. *a.*

ABC COMPANY

Beginning balance, retained earnings (12/31/96)		$167,300
Less:		
Net loss for 1997 (incl. loss from abandonment)	$14,100	
Common dividends paid	12,000	
Inventory adjustment	24,000	
Amortization of goodwill, patents	15,000	65,100
Ending balance, retained earnings (12/31/97)		$102,200

Cash Flow Items

Sources		Uses	
Depreciation	$21,400	Net *operating* loss	$10,100
Total	$21,400	Loss from abandonment	4,000
		Dividends paid	12,000
		Investment in fixed assets	57,500
		Amortization	15,000
		Inventory adjustment	24,000
		Total	$122,600

Depreciation (noncash) should be reflected as a source as it reduced operating profit/loss; loss conditions don't change its basic character. Loss from abandonment can be separated from profit/loss; it was offset by reduction in assets. A gain could be shown as a separate source, offset by the increase in cash. Amortization and inventory adjustments are assumed to have been retained earnings reductions here; they can be separated out as shown, unless they've been offset by a decrease in patents and inventories, or they can be eliminated on both sides of the statement.

b. DEF Company

The layout of the data is:

	Beginning Balance	Additions	Reductions	Ending Balance	Change
Gross property and fixed assets	$8,431,500*	$1,250,500*	$1,252,000†	$8,430,000*	$ (1,500)
Accumulated depreciation	3,513,000†	1,613,000*	1,252,000‡	3,874,000*	361,000
Net property and fixed assets	$4,918,500	$ (362,500)	$ -0-	$4,556,000	$(362,500)
					(Result)

The result is built up from:

*Given information.

†Forced figures.

‡Assumption that fully depreciated assets were abandoned.

Observations

Any assumption about a gain or loss on sale and/or abandonment would be handled as in Item 2a. Any disposition of partially depreciated assets would cause greater "reductions" in assets than in accumulated depreciation, which in turn would raise the derived asset additions.

c. XYZ Company

The layout of the data is:

	Beginning Balance	Additions	Reductions	Ending Balance	Change
Gross fixed assets	$823,700*	$236,100†	$ 2,500‡ 110,000*	$947,300	$123,600
Accumulated depreciation	N.A.	78,500*	2,500‡ 81,000*	N.A.	(5,000)*
Net fixed assets . . .	$ N.A.	$157,600	$ 29,000†	$ N.A.	$128,600
		(result)			(result)

The result was built up from:

*Information available.

†Forced figures.

‡Assumption that fully depreciated assets of $2,500 were written off.

Gain on sales of assets:

Recorded value	$110,000
Accumulated depreciation	81,000
Book value	$ 29,000
Cash received	45,000
Gain on sale	$ 16,000

Cash Flow Items

Sources		Uses	
Depreciation	$78,500		
Net write-off of assets . .	29,000*	Investments	$236,100
	$107,500		

*Could be split into gain ($16,000) and cash received ($45,000).

Note that sources and uses net out to $128,600.

3.

FED COMPANY
Cash Flow Statement, 1997

Sources		Uses†	
Net income	$ 6*	Increase in accounts	
Depreciation	26*	receivable	$ 5
Increase in deferred income		Increase in notes	
taxes	2	receivable	20
Gain from sale of asset	4†	Increase in inventories	7
Decrease in cash	12	Investment in plant and	
Overdraft	4	equipment	38†
Decrease in securities	18	Increase in prepaids	2
Increase in accounts payable	24	Decrease in notes payable	30
Increase in accrued expenses	9	Decrease in secured notes	
Increase in preferred stock . .	4	payable	20
Increase in common stock		Dividends (preferred and	
and capital surplus	20	common)	7
Total	$129	Total	$129

The results were built up from:

*Taken from 1997 operating statement.

†The fixed property conditions are as follows:

	Beginning Balance	Additions	Reductions	Ending Balance	Change
Gross property and expenses	$268	$38←	$23	$283	$15
Accumulated depreciation . .	157	26	23	160	3
Net property and expenses . .	$111	$12	$-0-	$123	$12

The key element is the forced figure of $38, which is based on the stated assumptions. The gain from sale of assets in the retained earnings account should be reflected as a source, just like net income.

Patent and other amortization of $3 is adjusted for in the retained earnings account; thus it is not a funds item.

This format clearly shows the important financial and investment movements, which leave operations strapped.

4. ZYX Company

A variety of cash flow statements are possible here:

From peak to trough of season (two seasons).
From peak to peak, or trough to trough.

From April to April, or any other month.

Two-year span, July to July, to provide a long-term perspective.

Samples of these possible cash flow statements are:

	1/31/97 to 4/30/97	1/31/98 to 4/30/98	4/30/96 to 1/31/98	1/31/96 to 1/31/98	4/30/96 to 4/30/98	7/31/96 to 7/31/98
Sources of Cash						
Profit from operations	$ 10	$ 17	$ 67	$ 77	$ 84	$172
Depreciation	6	7	21	27	28	54
Decrease in cash	—	—	1	—	—	5
Decrease in receivables	191	237	—	—	—	11
Decrease in inventories	184	253	—	—	33	—
Decrease in other assets . . .	1	—	—	—	—	—
Increase in payables	—	—	85	67	—	16
Increase in notes	—	—	342	48	—	45
Increase in common	—	—	25	25	25	25
Total sources	$392	$514	$541	$244	$170	$328
Uses of Cash						
Capital Investments	$ 48	$ 50	$ —	$ 48	$ 50	$ 98
Increase in cash	17	13	—	16	12	—
Increase in receivables	—	—	260	69	23	79
Increase in inventories	—	—	220	36	—	—
Increase in other assets	—	—	3	2	3	2
Decrease in payables	18	91	—	—	6	—
Decrease in notes	294	342	—	—	—	—
Decrease in mortgage	—	—	10	10	10	20
Dividends paid	15	18	48	63	66	129
Total uses	$392	$514	$541	$244	$170	$328

Observations

This strong seasonal pattern from January to April shows up vividly in the peak to trough and trough to peak comparisons, where receivables and inventories are matched with payables and sizable short-term notes. There's a lag effect in the buildup of inventories and receivables, as expected. Growth shows up in like-to-like comparisons, with no undue strains. This is a good example of the effect of careless placement of cash flow analysis over alternative time periods.

Questions for Discussion

1. Differentiate between cash flow and funds movements. What is "cash flow from operations"?

2. In what ways does a cash flow statement correspond to the operating statement for a period? In what ways does it differ? Can the two be readily reconciled?

3. In what ways are the concepts of debit and credit related to cash uses and sources? On the basis of a simple balance sheet, derive the principles of this relationship. Discuss.

4. Does a sizable profit for a period necessarily mean an increase in a company's cash account? If not, why not?

5. Does a company whose operations are shrinking always throw off cash? If not, why not? What assumptions must be made?

6. Why is depreciation a "source of cash" when it's clear that a mere bookkeeping entry is involved?

7. If a company incurred an operating loss for a period, is depreciation still treated as a cash inflow?

8. What's the tax impact of depreciation? Are there any cash movements involved?

9. Why is it necessary to "reverse" such transactions as write-down of goodwill and amortization of patents?

10. What is the cash impact of accelerated depreciation, and why?

11. By what criteria is the selection of the proper time period for cash flow analysis made? Can you derive any rules?

12. What are the major ways in which inflation distorts the cash flow picture? Should adjustments be made?

CHAPTER 3

Solutions to Problems

1. a. $\dfrac{\text{Net profit}}{\text{Sales}} = 11.4\%; \dfrac{\text{Sales}}{\text{Assets}} = 1.34$

$\text{Assets} = \dfrac{\text{Sales}}{1.34}$ (Sales > Assets); $\text{Sales} = 1.34 \times \text{Assets}$

Thus

$$\frac{\text{Net profit}}{\text{Assets}} = \frac{\text{Net profit}}{\dfrac{\text{Sales}}{1.34}} = 11.4\%(1.34) = 15.28\%$$

If we assume no debt in the capitalization, then net worth equals capitalization. Thus

$$\frac{\text{Net profit}}{\text{Capitalization}} = \frac{\text{Net profit}}{\text{Net worth}} = \frac{1}{.67} \times \frac{\text{Net profit}}{\text{Assets}}$$

Return on net worth is

$$\frac{15.28}{.67} = 22.8\%$$

A faster asset turnover means a smaller asset base and smaller capitalization relative to sales. Thus, return figures go up.

b. Gross margin is 31.4 percent; thus the cost of goods sold of $4,391,300 must represent sales of

$$\frac{\$4,391,300}{1.0 - .314} = \$6,401,312$$

Net profit must be 9.7 percent of $6,401,312, or $620,927. Total assets must be derived from

$$\frac{Sales}{Assets} = .827; \; Assets = \frac{Sales}{.827} = \frac{\$6,401,312}{.827} = \$7,740,401$$

Return on capitalization must be

$$\frac{Net\ profit}{Assets - Current\ liabilities} = \frac{Net\ profit}{.79\ (Assets)} = \frac{\$621,927}{6,114,917} = 10.15\%$$

c. Changes in current ratio and effect on working capital:

$$Current\ ratio:\ 2.2\ to\ 1 = \frac{\$573,100}{\$260,500}$$

(The $260,500 is derived from the relationship.)

Working capital: $573,100 − $260,500 = $312,600

(1) Payment of accounts payable:

Decrease in cash $67,500
Decrease in payables $67,500

Both current assets and current liabilities are reduced by the same amount; this improves current ratio but leaves working capital unaffected:

$$\frac{\$573,100 - \$67,500}{\$260,500 - \$67,500} = \frac{\$505,600}{\$193,000} = 2.62\ to\ 1$$

This is a common action taken by small companies at year-end to improve their current ratio.

(2) Collection of note:

Increase in cash $33,000
Decrease in notes receivable $33,000

Both elements are within current assets; thus there's no net effect on either the current ratio or the working capital.

(3) Purchase on account:

Increase in inventory $41,300

Increase in payables $41,300

Both current assets and current liabilities are increased; thus
the opposite effect of exercise (1), with working capital
unaffected:

$$\frac{\$573,100 + \$41,300}{\$260,500 + \$41,300} = \frac{\$614,400}{\$301,800} = 2.04 \text{ to } 1$$

(4) Dividend payment:

Decrease in cash $60,000

Decrease in accrued dividends $42,000

Decrease in retained earnings . . . . $18,000 (no effect)

The effect on the two elements is uneven; thus changes
occur in both the current ratio and working capital:

$$\frac{\$573,100 - \$60,000}{\$260,500 - \$42,000} = \frac{\$513,100}{\$218,500} = 2.35 \text{ to } 1$$

The current ratio is slightly improved, while working capital
drops by $18,000.

(5) Machine sale:

Increase in cash . . . . $ 80,000

Decrease in fixed assets . . . . $202,000 (no effect)

Decrease in accumulated depreciation . . . . $112,000 (no effect)

Loss on sale of assets . . . . $ 10,000 (no effect)

The only effect is an increase in current assets, which
increases both the ratio and working capital:

$$\frac{\$573,100 + \$80,000}{\$260,500} = \frac{\$653,100}{\$260,500} = 2.51 \text{ to } 1$$

The current ratio rises to 2.51, while working capital
improves by $80,000.

(6) Sale of merchandise:

Increase in receivables $109,700*

Decrease in inventory . . . . $ 73,500

Increase in retained earnings . . . . $ 36,200 (no effect)

*Derived from $\frac{73,500}{1.0 - .33}$ = $109,700.

There's a net increase in current assets, which improves the current ratio and working capital:

$$\frac{\$573,100 + \$109,700 - \$73,500}{\$260,500} = \frac{\$609,300}{\$260,500} = 2.34 \text{ to } 1$$

The current ratio rises to 2.34, while working capital improves by $36,200.

(7) Write-offs:

Decrease in inventory $20,000

Decrease in goodwill . . . . $15,000 (no effect)

Decrease in retained earnings . . . . $35,000 (no effect)

There's a reduction of current assets, which affects both the current ratio and working capital:

$$\frac{\$573,100 - \$20,000}{\$260,500} = \frac{\$553,100}{\$260,500} = 2.12 \text{ to } 1$$

The current ratio drops slightly to 2.12, while working capital is reduced by $20,000.

d. Days' receivables and payables:

$$\frac{\text{Net sales}}{\text{Days}} = \frac{\$437,500}{90} = \$4,861 \text{ per day}$$

$$\frac{\text{Purchases}}{\text{Days}} = \frac{\$143,500}{90} = \$1,594 \text{ per day}$$

$$\text{Days' receivables} = \frac{\text{Accounts receivable}}{\text{Daily sales}}$$

$$= \frac{\$156,800}{\$4,861} = 32.3 \text{ days}$$

$$\text{Days' payables} = \frac{\text{Accounts payable}}{\text{Daily purchases}}$$

$$= \frac{\$69,300}{\$1,594} = 43.5 \text{ days}$$

The company's collections are fairly slow in view of the discount period of 10 days, while its payments are slightly faster than needed against the 45-day terms.

Inventory turnover:

$$\text{Average inventory:} \quad \frac{\$382,200 + \$227,300}{2} = \$304,750$$

Turnover on sales:

$$\frac{\text{Average inventory}}{\text{Sales for quarter}} = \frac{\$304,750}{\$437,500} = 69.7\% \text{ (quarterly)}$$

or

$$\frac{\text{Average inventory}}{\text{Annual sales}} = \frac{\$304,750}{4(\$437,500)} = 17.4\% \text{ (annualized)}$$

or

$$\frac{\text{Sales for quarter}}{\text{Average inventory}} = \frac{\$437,500}{\$304,750} = 1.44 \text{ times (quarterly)}$$

or

$$\frac{\text{Annual sales}}{\text{Average inventory}} = \frac{4(\$437,500)}{\$304,750} = 5.74 \text{ (annualized)}$$

Turnover on cost of sales:

$$\frac{\text{Average inventory}}{\text{Cost of sales for quarter}} = \frac{\$304,750}{\$298,400} = 102.1\% \text{ (quarterly)}$$

$$\frac{\text{Average inventory}}{\text{Annual cost of sales}} = \frac{\$304,750}{4(\$298,400)} = 25.5\% \text{ (annualized)}$$

or

$$\frac{\text{Cost of sales for quarter}}{\text{Average inventory}} = \frac{\$298,400}{\$304,750} = .98 \text{ times (quarterly)}$$

or

$$\frac{\text{Annual cost of sales}}{\text{Average inventory}} = \frac{4(\$298,400)}{\$304,750} = 3.92 \text{ times (annualized)}$$

Turnover on ending inventory:

$$\frac{\text{Ending inventory}}{\text{Cost of sales for quarter}} = \frac{\$227,300}{\$298,400} = 76.2\% \text{ (quarterly)}$$

$$\frac{\text{Cost of sales for quarter}}{\text{Ending inventory}} = \frac{\$298,400}{\$227,300} = 1.31 \text{ times (quarterly)}$$

The cost of sales figures are more useful as a rule. Ending inventory should be used in relation to the quarterly cost of sales if there are significant seasonal swings. Annualization on a simple "4×" basis is problematic if a strong seasonal or growth/ decline pattern is suspected.

2. ABC Company

The various ratios are grouped by point of view:

   a. Management's view:

	1996	1997
Cost of goods sold	70.4%	70.6%
Gross margin	29.6%	29.4%
Profit margin	5.7%	5.4%
Profit before interest and taxes	10.7%	10.8%
Profit after taxes, before interest	5.8%	5.8%
Selling and administrative expenses	15.0%	14.4%
Employee profit sharing	4.1%	4.4%
Other income	.2%	.2%
Tax rate . . . . . . , ...	46.0%	46.0%
Contribution	N.A.	N.A.
Gross asset turnover $\left(\dfrac{\text{Assets}}{\text{Sales}}\right)$	59.5%	64.6%
Net asset turnover $\left(\dfrac{\text{Assets}}{\text{Sales}}\right)$	39.4%	44.4%
Ending inventory turns $\left(\dfrac{\text{Cost of sales}}{\text{Inventory}}\right)$	5.2×	4.8×
Days' receivables	51.1 days	60.7 days
Days' payables (cost of sales)	34.0 days	37.0 days
Net profit to total assets	9.6%	8.3%
Net profit to capitalization	14.4%	12.1%
Net profit before interest and tax to total assets . . .	18.0%	16.8%
Net profit before interest and tax to capitalization . .	27.2%	24.4%
Net profit after tax, before interest, to total assets . .	9.7%	9.0
Net profit after tax, before interest, to capitalization	14.6%	13.2%

   b. Owner's view:

	1996	1997
Net profit to net worth (including deferred tax)	15.1%	16.3%
Net profit to common equity (w/o deferred tax)	15.2%	16.7%
Earnings per share	$3.69	$4.61
Cash flow per share	$6.48	$8.38
Dividends per share	$ .54	$ .59
Dividend coverage—earnings	6.8×	7.8×
Dividend coverage—cash flow	11.9×	14.2×

c. Lender's view:

	1996	1997
Current ratio	2.1:1	2.2:1
Acid test (excluding advances)	1.3:1	1.4:1
Total debt to assets	35.7%	48.7%
Long-term debt to capitalization	3.0%	25.3%
Total debt to net worth	55.5%	95.0%
Long-term debt to net worth	3.1%	32.9%
Interest coverage (pretax)	70×	13×
Cash flow before taxes—interest coverage	98×	18×
Full interest coverage ($8.5 million)	—	11×

Observations

A slight worsening is shown in operating performance, at the same effective tax rate, which makes 1996 the better year. More investment has been committed both in working capital and fixed assets—collections are slowing, inventories are up, and profits on assets are down by every measure.

Leverage has improved the profit on net worth, however, and earnings per share are up sharply. No problems exist in covering dividends on interest, even if a full year's interest is assumed.

Comparisons should be made with companies in similar product lines, particularly on capital structure, return on net worth, and coverages. High-low analysis of good and bad years should highlight risk of earnings fluctuations. A two-year static picture isn't enough for good perspective.

Questions for Discussion

1. Explain the relationships of the four basic financial statements. Which statement encompasses the results of all decisions? Why?

2. Why does the balance sheet have to balance at all times? What does the statement signify?

3. What are the key factors that allow comparison of industry ratios to the ratios of an individual company?

4. List several accounting practices that can result in changes in the ratios that measure profitability. What's their effect?

5. List several accounting practices that can result in changes in the ratios that measure liquidity and debt exposure. What's their effect?

6. What measurement issues arise when two different divisions of a company are compared on the basis of management ratios, given widely divergent conditions in age, markets, and costs?

7. A commonly used ratio from the standpoint of the lender is "times interest earned." How meaningful is this ratio in assessing the quality of the indebtedness involved?

8. Does operating cash flow represent the majority of funds movements caused by operations? If not, why not?

9. What key questions would you ask if you were a banker reviewing a loan request from a small, rapidly growing company?

10. What's the impact of inflation on ratio analysis? What key distortions can be expected, and in which ratios?

11. What are the major problems encountered in the process of adjusting for inflation?

12. If you were general manager of a division, which key ratio would you choose to be evaluated on for your unit's financial performance, and why? What conditions would you stipulate?

CHAPTER 4

Solutions to Problems

1. *a.* Change in credit policy:
     40 days' sales developed as follows:

$$\text{Daily sales: } \frac{\$9,137,000}{360} = \$25,381/\text{day}$$

18 days' sales: $18 \times \$25,381 = \$456,858$

40 days' sales: $40 \times \$25,381 = \$1,015,240$

Increase in receivables: $558,382

60 days' sales:

60 days' sales: $60 \times \$25,381 = \$1,522,860$

Increase in receivables: $1,066,002

Observations
Funds needs increase with 40 days is over $500,000. Cash flow per year available from operations is only $305,000. Likely the company must secure other funds. Need is doubled if policy is changed to 60 days.

b. Inventory consignment:
     Average inventory: $725,000.

$$\text{Current turnover: } \frac{\text{Cost of goods sold}}{\text{Average inventory}} = \frac{.83 \times \$9{,}137{,}000}{\$725{,}000}$$

$$= 10.5 \text{ times}$$

$$\text{Turnover slowdown: } \frac{\text{Cost of goods sold}}{7.0} = \frac{\$7{,}583{,}700}{7.0}$$

$$= \$1{,}083{,}400$$

Inventory increases by $1,083,400 less $725,000 = $358,400

$$\text{Turnover increase: } \frac{\text{Cost of goods sold}}{11.0} = \frac{\$7{,}583{,}700}{11.0} = \$689{,}400$$

Inventory decreases by $725,000 less $689,400 = $35,600

Observations

Funds needs change as indicated. The company likely will require increased production operations to achieve higher supply (about 5 percent), and also some increased purchases, which will provide some funds through higher payables. But the slowdown must be financed by other funds sources.

c. Change in payment terms:
Company now has 10 days' purchases outstanding:

$$\text{Payables} = \frac{\text{Purchases}}{360} \times 10 = \frac{\$5{,}316{,}000}{36} = \$147{,}667$$

Change in terms means 5 more days' extension, which provides funds of $73,833 (1/2 of above) for no additional cost.

Observations

Company earns 2 percent now to pay 20 days sooner; it will earn 2 percent to pay 30 days sooner (from day 15 to day 45). Annual interest thus 12 times 2% = 24%. If company can obtain funds for less, it's desirable to discount. (See Chapter 7.)

d. Capital expenditures and dividends:

Funds needs	$125,000 for equipment
Plus 60% of $131,000	79,000
Total	$204,000

Against cash from operations:

Profits	$131,000
Depreciation	174,000
Total	$305,000

Observations

Can be handled by internal funds unless significant changes in working capital needs occur (such as in earlier examples).

e. Sales growth:
10 percent increase in sales ($913,700) requires:

Funds for receivables: 18 days of increased sales	$ 45,700
Funds for inventories: 10 percent increase	72,500
Funds from payables: 10 days of increased purchases	(14,800)
Total funds need	$103,400
Against additional profits of 10% (assume no efficiency of scale):	$ 13,100

Observations
Unless there are significant improvements in operations, the increase in sales requires funds of about $90,000. This makes dividends and capital expenditures under (*d*) barely possible from internal funds, and leaves no room for inefficiency.

2.

ABC COMPANY
Pro Forma Operating Statement
For the Year Ended October 31, 1999
($ thousands)

	Amount		Percent	
Net sales		$4,350		100.0%
Cost of goods sold:				
Labor	$1,044		24.0	
Materials	631		14.5	
Overhead*	862		19.8	
Depreciation	143		3.3	
	2,680		61.6	
Gross profit	$1,670		38.4	
Selling expense	430		9.9	
General and administrative	352	782	8.1	18.0
Profit before taxes		$ 888		20.4
Income taxes (46%)		408		9.4
Net income		$ 480		11.1%

*$743 + $45 + $74.

Observations

A slight increase in the rate of profit is due to higher efficiency in labor and overhead, which combine to overcome a rise in selling expense.

3.

DEF COMPANY
Pro Forma Balance Sheet
December 31, 1999

Cash . . . . $ 150,000 (desired level)
Receivables . . . .   348,300 (12 days on $10.45 mil.)
Inventories* . . . .   1,044,600 (as calculated below)
   Total current assets $1,542,900
Land, buildings, etc. . . . . $ 478,500 (plus $57,000)
   Accumulated depreciation . . .   248,700 (plus $31,400)
                                       $ 229,800
Other assets . . . .   21,700 (no change)
   Total assets $1,794,400
Accounts payable . . . . $ 648,300 (24 days' purchases)
Note payable—bank . . . .   468,900 (plug figure—up by $43,900)
Accrued expenses . . . .   63,400 (no change)
   Total current liabilities $1,180,600
Term loan—properties . . . . $ 110,000 (minus $10,000)
Capital stock . . . .   200,000 (no change)
Paid-in surplus . . . .   112,000 (no change)
Retained earnings . . . .   191,800 ($184,400 + $19,900 – $12,500)
   Total liabilities and net worth $1,794,400

*Beginning inventory $912,700
Purchases   9,725,000
                                                       $10,637,700
Cost of goods sold . . . .   9,593,100 (91.8% of $10,450,000)
Ending inventory $1,044,600

Observations

The main difference appears to be a rise in inventories that requires about $130,000, while receivables drop slightly. Apparently sales are leveling off or dropping. (If 12 days' sales are assumed outstanding in 1996, sales for the year must have been $10,836,000, while purchases keep going up.) Repayment of note and high dividend payout cause need for extra borrowing (plug figure) of about $44,000 even if cash is drawn down to $150,000.

4.

XYZ COMPANY
Cash Budget for Six Months
October 1998 through March 1999
($ thousands)

	Oct.	Nov.	Dec.	Jan.	Feb.	Mar.	Total
Cash receipts:							
Collections from credit	$ 215	$ 245	$ 265	$ 385	$ 345	$ 505	$1,960
Cash sales	385	345	505	325	290	360	2,210
Total receipts	$ 600	$ 590	$ 770	$ 710	$ 635	$ 865	$4,170

	Oct.	Nov.	Dec.	Jan.	Feb.	Mar.	Total
Cash disbursements (see breakdown of purchases below):							
Cash purchases	$ 61	$ 54	$ 29	$ 32	$ 45	$ 48	$ 269
Credit purchases—							
10 days (less 2% discount)	218	220	146	121	160	184	1,049
Credit purchases—							
45 days	257	266	286	205	153	192	1,359
Salaries and wages . .	146	131	192	124	110	137	840
Operating expenses . .	108	97	141	91	81	101	619
Cash dividend	—	—	40	—	—	—	40
Federal income tax . . .	—	—	—	20	—	—	20
Mortgage payment . . .	7	7	7	7	7	7	42
Total cash disbursements	$ 797	$ 775	$ 841	$ 600	$ 556	$ 669	$4,238
Net cash receipts (disbursements)	$(197)	$(185)	$ (71)	$ 110	$ 79	$ 196	$ (68)
Cumulative net cash flow	$(197)	$(382)	$(453)	$(343)	$(264)	$ (68)	
Analysis of cash requirements:							
Beginning cash balance	$ 95	$(102)	$(287)	$(358)	$(248)	$(169)	
Net cash receipts (disbursements)	(197)	(185)	(71)	110	79	196	
Ending cash balance . .	$(102)	$(287)	$(358)	$(248)	$(169)	$ 27	
Minimum cash balance	75	75	75	75	75	75	
Cash requirements . . .	$ 177	$ 362	$ 433	$ 323	$ 244	$ 48	

Observations

In spite of sizable cash needs, which reach a peak of $433,000 in December, the pattern of cash movements winds up not far below the minimum cash balance six months hence. Seasonal short-term borrowing is indicated here to cover inventory buildup and lag in collection pattern.

5. Pro forma statements developed from data given:

Initial cash	$250,000
Less: Equipment	175,000
	$ 75,000
Organization expenses	15,000
Cash remaining	$ 60,000

ZYX CORPORATION
Breakdown of Monthly Purchases

Terms	Aug.	Sept.	Oct.	Nov.	Dec.	Jan.	Feb.	Mar.
Cash	N.A.	$45	$61*	$54	$29	$32	$45	$48
2/10, n/30	N.A.	60/60/60*	81*/81*/82	71/71/72	38/39/39	42/43/43	60/60/60	64/64/64
n/45	145/145*	112*/113	153/152	134/133	72/73	80/80	112/113	120/120
Total	—	$450	$610	$535	$290	$320	$450	$480

*Due for payment in October. (September purchases are reconstructed from $60 amount to 2/10, n/20, which must be one third of 40 percent of total purchases.)

ZYX CORPORATION
Pro Forma Operating Statement
Six Months Ended July 31, 1998
($ thousands)

Sales revenue		$2,400	(6 × $400,000)
Cost of goods sold:			
Labor	$ 360		(6 × $ 60,000)
Materials purchased	750		(6 × $125,000)
Rent	111		(6 × $ 18,500)
Overhead	456		(6 × $ 76,000)
Depreciation	36		(6 × $ 6,000)
Amortization	3		(6 × $ 500)
Total	$1,716		
Less: Prepaids	$ 12		
Inventories	205		
	$ 217	1,499	
Gross margin		$ 901	
Selling and administrative expenses		330	(6 × $ 55,000)
Profit before taxes		$ 571	
Taxes at 40%		228	
Aftertax profit		343	

ZYX CORPORATION
Pro Forma Balance Sheet
July 31, 1998
($ thousands)

Cash	$ 40	(minimum balance)
Accounts receivable	600	(45 days' sales)
Inventories	205	(given)
Total current assets	$ 845	
Equipment	$175	
Less: Depreciation	36	139
Prepaid items	12	(given)
Patents	47	(net of amortization)

Organization expense	15 (given)
Total assets	$1,058
Accounts payable	$ 125 (30 days' purchases)
Accrued expenses	15 (1 week's wages)
Accrued taxes	228 (from operating statement)
Total current liabilities	$ 368
Capital stock ($1 par)	300 (given)
Retained earnings	343 (from operating statement)
	$1,011
Plug figure	47 (funds needs 7/31/98)
Total liabilities and net worth	$1,058

Observations

The figures appear quite optimistic; no allowance is made for start-up problems. Profitability thus seems excessive. There are likely to be greater funds needs early in the period, as collections lag and production problems appear. Also, if taxes have to be prepaid, a major funds source will be affected. Moreover, growth will require additional funds:

10% increase in sales requires:	
10% increase in receivables, inventories	$80
Less: 10% increase in payables, accruals	34
	$46
10% increase in cash flow from operations	38
Need	$ 8

This need will increase drastically if any key assumptions are off.

6.

ABC SUPERMARKET
Cash Budget
For Six Months Ended June 30, 1998
($ thousands)

	Jan.	Feb.	Mar.	Apr.	May	June	Total
Receipts:							
Cash sales	$200.0	$190.0	$220.0	$200.0	$230.0	$220.0	$1,260.0
Cash from sale of property	—	—	6.0	6.0	6.0	—	18.0
Rental income . . .	—	—	.3	.3	.3	.3	1.2
Total receipts . . .	$200.0	$190.0	$226.3	$206.3	$236.3	$220.3	$1,279.2
Disbursements:							
Purchases recorded	$150.0	$142.5	$165.0	$150.0	$172.5	$165.0	$ 945.0
Payment for purchases (15-day lag)	$159.0	$146.3	$153.7	$157.5	$161.3	$168.7	$ 946.5

	Jan.	Feb.	Mar.	Apr.	May	June	Total
Salaries (12% of sales)	24.0	22.8	26.4	24.0	27.6	26.4	151.2
Other expenses (9% of sales)	18.0	17.1	19.8	18.0	20.7	19.8	113.4
Rent	3.5	3.5	3.5	3.5	3.5	3.5	21.0
Income taxes	2.0	—	2.0	3.5	—	2.0	9.5
Note payment . . .	—	3.0	—	—	5.0	—	8.0
Repayment to principals	3.0	—	3.0	—	3.0	—	9.0
Payments on fixtures	—	12.0	12.0	12.0	12.0	—	48.0
Total disbursements	$209.5	$204.7	$220.4	$218.5	$233.1	$220.4	$1,306.6
Net cash flow	$ (9.5)	$ (14.7)	$ 5.9	$ (12.2)	$ 3.2	$ (.1)	$ (27.4)
Cumulative net cash	$ (9.5)	$ (24.2)	$ (18.3)	$ (30.5)	$ (27.3)	$ (27.4)	
Analysis of cash requirements:							
Beginning cash balance	$ 42.5	$ 33.0	$ 18.3	$ 24.2	$ 12.0	$ 15.2	
Net cash flow	(9.5)	(14.7)	5.9	(12.2)	3.2	(.1)	
Ending cash balance	$ 33.0	$ 18.3	$ 24.2	$ 12.0	$ 15.2	$ 15.1	
Minimum cash balance	20.0	20.0	20.0	20.0	20.0	20.0	
Cash need (excess)	$ (13.0)	$ 1.7	$ (14.2)	$ 8.0	$ 4.8	$ 4.9	

Observations

The cash pattern indicates excess funds needs in four out of the six months if a $20,000 minimum balance is desired. The greatest funds need is in April 1998, but even by the end of the period no cleanup of required borrowing will have been achieved.

7.

XYZ COMPANY
Cash Budget by Month
Six Months Ended March 31, 1999
($ thousands)

	Oct.	Nov.	Dec.	Jan.	Feb.	Mar.	Total
Cash receipts:							
Collections (see next table) . . .	$2,608	$2,092	$2,983	$2,400	$2,567	$2,708	$15,358
Cash disbursements:							
Payments for purchases (see below)	712	663	650	650	650	650	3,975
Wages	215	215	215	215	215	215	1,290
Other expenses	420	420	420	420	420	420	2,520
Selling and administrative expense	326	345	343	368	330	342	2,054

	Oct.	Nov.	Dec.	Jan.	Feb.	Mar.	Total
Note repayments	—	750	—	—	750	—	1,500
Interest	—	—	—	300	—	—	300
Dividend payments	25	—	—	25	—	—	50
Tax payment . . .	—	—	—	375	—	—	375
Total disbursements	$1,698	$2,393	$1,628	$2,353	$2,365	$1,627	$12,064
Net cash receipts (disbursements)	$ 910	$ (301)	$1,355	$ 47	$ 202	$1,081	$ 3,294
Cumulative cash flow	$ 910	$ 609	$1,964	$2,011	$2,213	$3,294	

Collection Pattern—Sales

Timing	Aug.	Sept.	Oct.	Nov.	Dec.	Jan.	Feb.	Totals
Oct. 1–10	$ 641							
Oct. 11–20	642							$2,608
Oct. 21–31	642	$ 683*						
Nov. 1–10		683						
Nov. 11–20		684						$2,092
Nov. 21–30			$ 725					
Dec. 1–10			725					
Dec. 11–20			725	$ 766*				$2,983
Dec. 21–31				767				
Jan. 1–10				767				
Jan. 11–20					$ 816			$2,400
Jan. 21 31					817			
Feb. 1–10					817			
Feb. 11–20						$ 875		$2,567
Feb. 21–29						875		
Mar. 1–10						875		
Mar. 11–20							$916	$2,708
Mar. 21–31							917	
Totals	$1,925	$2,050	$2,175	$2,300	$2,450	$2,625	—	

*Change in collection pattern assumed.

Accounts Receivable

Sept. 30, 1998:	August sales	$1,925
	September sales	2,050
		$3,975 (60 days)
Dec. 31, 1998:	1/3 of November sales	$767
	December sales	$2,450
		$3,217 (40 days)
March 31, 1998:	1/3 of February sales	$917
	March sales	2,850
		$3,767 (40 days)

Purchase pattern: Forty-five days' payables throughout; thus there's a lag of 3/2 months.

Pro forma statements developed from data given and calculated:

XYZ COMPANY
Pro Forma Income Statements
Three Months Ended 12/31/98 and Six Months Ended 3/31/99
($ thousands)

	1998 Three Months	1998/99 Six Months	
Sales	$6,925	$15,150	(given)
Cost of sales	4,848	10,605	(70 percent of sales)
Gross margin	$2,077	$ 4,545	
Selling and administrative	$1,014	$ 2,054	(from cash budget)
Interest	75	150	(developed)
	$1,089	$ 2,204	
Profit before taxes	$ 988	$ 2,341	
Income taxes	494	1,171	(50 percent of profit)
Net income	$ 494	$ 1,170	(to balance sheet)

XYZ COMPANY
Pro Forma Balance Sheets
December 31, 1998 and March 31, 1999
($ thousands)

	12/31/98	3/31/99
Cash	$2,704 (+$1,964)	$4,034 (+$3,294)
Accounts receivable	3,217 (see above)	3,767 (see above)
Raw materials	2,200 (see below)	1,675 (see below)
Finished goods	6,081 (see below)	4,833 (see below)
Plant and equipment (net)	7,081 (–$129 depr.)	6,952 (–$258 depr.)
Other assets	1,730 (no change)	1,730 (no change)
Total assets	$23,013	$22,991
Accounts payable	$975 (45 days)	$975 (45 days)
Notes payable	3,370 (–$750)	2,620 (–$1,500)
Accrued liability	3,444 (see below)	3,521 (see below)
Long-term debt	5,250 (no change)	5,250 (no change)
Preferred stock	1,750 (no change)	1,750 (no change)
Common stock	5,000 (no change)	5,000 (no change)
Earned surplus	3,224 (–$25, +$494)	3,875 (–$50, +$1,170)
Total liabilities	$23,013	$22,991

INVENTORY ANALYSIS

	12/31/98	3/31/99
Raw materials:		
Beginning balance	$ 2,725	$ 2,725
Purchases @ $650/month	1,950	3,900
	$ 4,675	$ 6,625
Withdrawals @ $825/month	2,475	4,950
Ending balance	$ 2,200	$ 1,675
Finished Goods:		
Beginning balance	$ 6,420	$ 6,420
Materials @ $825/month	2,475	4,950
Wages @ $215/month	645	1,290
Other expenses @ $420/month	1,260	2,520
Depreciation @ $43/month	129	258
	$10,929	$15,438
Cost of goods sold reported	4,848	10,605
Ending balance	$ 6,081	$ 4,833

Assume interest of $300 covers one year. Thus, by 9/31/98, $225 must have been accrued. Also, assume liabilities to accrue until paid in cash.

ACCRUED LIABILITIES

	12/31/98	3/31/99
Beginning balance	$2,875	$2,875
Accrued interest	75	150
Accrued taxes (income statement)	494	1,171
	$3,444	$4,196
Interest payment	—	(300)
Tax payment	—	(375)
Balance shown	$3,444	$3,521

Observations

The key change is the transformation of receivables and inventories into cash, due to the change in policies. Note the dramatic drop in inventories by 3/31/99, if the policies work as expected. No funds needs arise during the period, and the main collection impact is felt in October and December. If collections don't come in as expected, $1,833 will be deferred and not available by 3/31/99, and $1,533 by 12/31/98:

Receivables 12/31/98	$3,217
60 days	4,750
Difference	$1,533
Receivables 3/31/99	$3,767
60 days	5,600
Difference	$1,833

Management must make sure inventories go down, and this depends on quality and nature of goods on hand.

Questions for Discussion

1. As we can balance a pro forma balance sheet with a plug figure representing cash or a loan, must we be very careful with accounting conventions?

2. Given the freedom to project pro forma balance sheets and plugging them in the end, what limitations are there to this freedom? Explain.

3. Name key assumptions that have to agree for both a pro forma balance sheet and the matching pro forma operating statement.

4. Differentiate between a cash budget and a pro forma operating statement.

5. Should depreciation ever appear on a cash budget? If not, does it have any direct impact?

6. Must a cash budget and a corresponding set of pro forma statements always tie together so that they can be reconciled?

7. Differentiate between an operating budget (sales, manufacturing, service) and a cash budget.

8. Is it permissible to show an increase in finished goods inventories on a pro forma balance sheet, while at the same time reflecting a production level less than current unit sales in the cost of goods sold area of the operating statement?

9. In what ways is a pro forma cash flow statement helpful to understand projected conditions?

CHAPTER 5

Solutions to Problems

1. ABC Corporation

Break-even point calculation:

Price per unit	$5.50
Variable costs per unit	$3.25
Contribution	$2.25

Fixed costs: $360,000.

Units required to recover fixed costs with contribution:

$$\frac{\$360,000}{\$2.25} = 160,000 \text{ units}$$

a. Leverage

Units	Profit	Change	Units	Profit	Change
Units	Profit	Change	Units	Profit	Change
160,000	$0	—	160,000	$0	—
192,000	72,000	infinite	128,000	(72,000)	infinite
230,400	158,400	120.0%	102,400	(129,600)	80.0%
276,480	262,080	65.5%	81,920	(175,680)	39.8%
331,776	386,496	47.5%	65,536	(212,544)	21.0%

*(Left group header: **Profit Effect from Volume Increases (20%)**; Right group header: **Profit Effect from Volume Decreases (20%)**)*

Note the declining rate of change as we move away from the break-even point.

b. Changes in conditions:
Price drop of 50 cents:
Change in contribution from $2.25 to $1.75:

$$\text{Break-even point: } \frac{\$360,000}{\$1.75} = 205,715 \text{ units}$$

Cost increase of 25 cents—variable:
Change in contribution from $2.25 to $2.00:

$$\text{Break-even point: } \frac{\$360,000}{\$2.00} = 180,000 \text{ units}$$

Cost increase of $40,000—fixed:
Change in fixed cost from $360,000 to $400,000:

$$\text{Break-even point: } \frac{\$400,000}{\$2.25} = 177,778$$

c. Changing conditions by operating level:
Calculations must be made step by step to take account of changing conditions:
(1) Contribution from first 150,000 units:

Price	$5.50
Variable costs	3.25
Contribution	$2.25 × 150,000 = $337,500

(2) Contribution from next 25,000 units:

Price $5.50

Variable costs 3.00

    Contribution . . . . $2.50 × 25,000 = $62,500

The break-even point will lie between 150,000 and 175,000
units, since the combined contribution of $400,000 exceeds fixed
costs by $40,000. Thus the break-even point is based on fixed
costs remaining after 150,000 units, i.e., $22,500 ($360,000 –
$337,500).

$$\frac{\$22,500}{\$2.50} = 9,000 \text{ units added to } 150,000, \text{ or } 159,000 \text{ units}$$

The contribution from units after 175,000 units and after 190,000
does not come into play unless fixed costs were raised earlier.

ABC CORPORATION
Break-Even Chart

Original condition and price drop

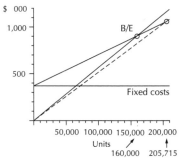

Original condition and variable cost increase

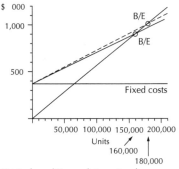

Original condition and fixed cost increase

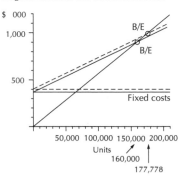

Original condition and step-wise changes

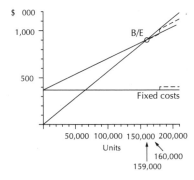

2. Financial leverage

a. For $i - 5\%$ and $R - 8\%$:

No debt: $r = 8\%$
25% debt: $0.08 + 25/75(.08 - .05)$; $r = 9\%$
50% debt: $0.08 + 50/50(.08 - .05)$; $r = 11\%$
75% debt: $0.08 + 75/25(.08 - .05)$; $r = 17\%$.

b. For $i = 6\%$ and $R = 5\%$:

No debt: $r = 5\%$
25% debt: $0.05 + 25/75(.05 - .06)$; $r = 4.7\%$
50% debt: $0.05 + 50/50(.05 - .06)$; $r = 4\%$
75% debt: $0.05 + 75/25(.05 - .06)$; $r = 2\%$

Observations

The leverage effect is less dramatic as the difference between interest rates paid and return on assets earned decreases. Still, at high leverage, a more than proportional push on ROE is achieved, as Figure 5–6 in the chapter suggests. The negative leverage resulting from poor performance achieved by investing the capital is just as powerful as in the positive case.

3. Five-year financial plan ($ thousands)

	Year 1	Year 2	Year 3	Year 4	Year 5	Revised Year 5
Capital structure						
Debt as a percent of capitalization	20%	20%	33%	33%	33%	43%
Debt	$300	$309	$638	$664	$706	$1,059
Equity	1,200	1,235	1,277	1,330	1,413	1,413
Net assets (capitalization) . . .	$1,500	$1,544	$1,915	$1,994	$2,119	$2,472
Profitability (after taxes):						
Return on net assets . .	8%	9%	10%	10%	10%	11%
Amount of profit	$120	$139	$192	$199	$212	$272
Interest rate (after taxes)	4.5%	4.5%	5.0%	5.0%	5.0%	4.5%
Amount of interest	$ 14	$ 14	$ 32	$ 33	$ 35	$ 48
Profit after interest and taxes	$106	$125	$160	$166	$177	$224
Earnings disposition:						
Dividends payout	2/3	2/3	2/3	1/2	1/2	2/3
Dividends paid	$ 71	$ 83	$107	$ 83	$ 88	$149
Reinvestment	$35	$42	$53	$83	$89	$75
Financing and investment:						

	Year 1	Year 2	Year 3	Year 4	Year 5	Revised Year 5
New debt, old ratio . . .	9	10	26	42	44	56
New debt, new ratio . . .	—	319	—	—*	—	—
New investment	$ 44	$ 371	$ 79	$125	$133	$131
Results (end of year):						
Net return, net assets . .	7.1%	8.1%	8.4%	8.3%	8.4%	9.1%
Return on equity	8.8	10.1	12.5	12.5	12.5	15.8
Growth on equity	2.9	3.4	4.2	6.2	6.3	5.3
Growth in earnings . . .	—	17.9	28.0	3.8	6.6	34.9
Earnings per share . . .	$0.53	$0.62	$0.80	$0.83	$0.88	$1.12
Dividends per share . . .	$0.36	$0.42	$0.54	$0.42	$0.44	$0.74

*For revised Year 5, this item should be $353.

Observations

The results displayed are self-explanatory and show a rising level as both operating and financial conditions are changed. The higher dividend payout in the revised Year 5 situation causes a drop in equity growth, even though operating conditions are more favorable.

Questions for Discussion

1. Derive a simple formula to express the break-even point in relation to volume and cost.

2. What influence does depreciation, as a fixed cost, have on a company's break-even characteristics?

3. Draw parallels and distinctions between operating and financial leverage, and cite examples from your own experience.

4. Why isn't it possible, at the same time, to have high growth in equity and a high dividend payout?

5. What are the key levers management can apply to bring about high growth in equity?

6. What relevant growth areas can you name as modeling targets, and why are they relevant?

7. Is it realistic to assume a continuous rollover of debt in the growth model? Are there any likely limitations?

8. What are the potential lags involved in attaining sustainable growth targets, such as were discussed in Chapter 2?

9. How does funds flow analysis relate to the business systems diagram (Figure 1–4) in Chapter 1?

10. Which are the most important assumptions in a growth model?

CHAPTER 6

Solutions to Problems

1. *a.* Net present value at 10 percent and 16 percent (factors from Table I in Chapter 6):

Amounts	PV Factors at 10%	Present Value	PV Factors at 16%	Present Value
$10,000 ×	.909	$ 9,090	.862	$ 8,620
15,000 ×	.826	12,390	.743	11,145
15,000 ×	.751	11,265	.641	9,615
20,000 ×	.683	13,660	.552	11,040
15,000 ×	.621	9,315	.476	7,140
10,000 ×	.564	5,640	.410	4,100
5,000 ×	.513	2,565	.354	1,770
		$63,925		$53,430
Outlay		60,000		60,000
Net present value		$ 3,925		$ (6,570)

b. Internal rate of return (yield):
Must be between 10 and 16 percent; closer to the lower end. Trial at 12 percent (factors from Table 6–I):

Amounts	PV Factors at 12%	Present Value
$10,000 ×	.893	$ 8,930
15,000 ×	.797	11,955
15,000 ×	.712	10,680
20,000 ×	.636	12,720
15,000 ×	.567	8,505
10,000 ×	.507	5,070
5,000 ×	.452	2,260
		$60,120
Outlay		60,000
Net present value		120

c. Even cash flows:
$13,000 per year at 10 percent (factor from Table II):

$$\$13,000 \times 4.868 = \$63,284$$
$$\text{Net investment} = \underline{60,000}$$
$$\text{Net present value} = \$ \ 3,284$$

d. Cash flows to yield 16 percent:

Annualize the investment of $60,000 at 16 percent:

$$A = \frac{PV}{f}$$

$$= \frac{\$60,000}{4.039} = \$14,855$$

The required amount over seven years is slightly under $14,900.
e. Net present valucs at 10 and 16 percent, given recovery of
$10,000:
Recovery of $10,000 at end of Year 7 (factors from Table I):

at 10 percent: $10,000 × .513 = $5,130

at 16 percent: $10,000 × .354 = $3,540

Original values in *a*:

At 10 percent: $3,925 plus recovery of $5,130 = $9,055

At 16 percent: $(6,570) plus recovery of $3,540 = $(3,030)

IRR must now be somewhat under 16 percent since net present
value turns negative below that rate.
f. Cash flows to yield 16 percent, given recovery of $10,000:
Present value of recovery at 16 percent: $3,540 (from *e*)
Present value of investment:
Outlay less present value of recovery:

$60,000 less $3,540 = $56,460

Cash flows required based on annualizing present value of
investment (see *d*):

$$A = \frac{\$56,460}{4.039} = \$13,979$$

Note that the recovery of $10,000 in Year 7 reduced required
cash flows by about $900 per year. This can, of course, be shown
directly by developing the annual equivalent of the recovery:

$$A = \frac{\$3,540}{4.039} = \$876$$

2. ABC Company

Net investment: 64% of $1,500,000 = $960,000

Past research and development: Not relevant here.

Profit improvement:

Year 1: 64% of $200,000 = $128,000
Year 2: 64% of $300,000 =   192,000
Year 3: 64% of $600,000 =   384,000
Year 4: 64% of $500,000 =   320,000
Year 5: 64% of $400,000 =   256,000
 Total $1,280,000
 Average yearly
  amount $256,000

Measures calculated (000 omitted):

a. Payback (on average amount):

$$\frac{\$960}{\$256} = 3.75 \text{ years—Almost four years on actual pattern}$$

b. Return on investment:

$$\frac{\$256}{\$960} = 26.7 \text{ percent—Can't calculate on actual pattern}$$

c. Average return:

$$\frac{\$256}{\$480} = 53.3 \text{ percent—Can't calculate on actual pattern}$$

d. Net present value (at 12 percent):

Based on average: 3.605 × $256 (Table II) . . . . +$922,800
Outlay . . . . − 960,000
Net present value . . . . −$ 37,120

Based on actual pattern (factors from Table I):

Amounts	PV Factors		Present Value	Cumulative
$128,000 ×	.893	=	$114,304	$114,304
192,000 ×	.797	=	153,024	267,328
384,000 ×	.712	=	273,408	540,736
320,000 ×	.636	=	203,520	744,256
256,000 ×	.567	=	145,152	889,408
			+$889,408	
	Outlay		− 960,000	
	Net present value		−$ 70,592	

(Note that the actual pattern causes worsening of the result!)

e. Present value index:

$$\text{Based on average: } \frac{\$922,880}{960,000} = .96$$

$$\text{Based on pattern: } \frac{\$889,408}{960,000} = .93$$

f. Internal rate of return:
Due to the closeness of the present value results, the IRR is approximately 12 percent in either case, slightly lower on the average basis, and somewhat lower on the actual pattern.

g. Present value payback:
Just about five years; a little less on the average basis, a little more on the pattern.

h. Annualized net present value (factors from Table II):

$$\text{Based on average: } \frac{+\$37,120}{3.605} = +\$10,297 \text{ each year}$$

$$\text{Based on pattern: } \frac{-\$70,592}{3.605} = -\$19,582 \text{ each year}$$

Observations
The project barely meets current standards. If the data had been available *before* the R&D expenditures were made, the expenditures then and now shouldn't be made. If no other preferable investments are available now, however, the investment is OK since past outlays are *sunk* costs.

3. Trustee of major estate:
Net investment: $100,000 in *a* and *b*.
Yield:

a.
$$\text{Yield factor: } \frac{\$100,000}{\$16,500} = 6.06$$

In Table II, on the eight-year line this corresponds to a yield of about 7 percent if a rough interpolation is made.

b.
$$\text{Yield factor: } \frac{\$100,000}{\$233,000} = .429$$

In Table I, on the 11-year line this corresponds exactly to a yield of 8 percent. Thus, the second proposition is preferable.

Net present value (6 percent):
a. Benefits: 8 × $16,500.
Present value of benefits: 6.210 × $16,500 (Table II) = $102,465.
Net present value: +$2,465.
b. Benefits: Lump sum in 11 years is $233,000.
Present value of benefits: .527 × $233,000 (Table I) = $122,791.

Net present value: +$22,791.

* *Observations*

If a higher discount factor were used, the results would be reversed since proposition (*a*) provides continuous early benefits. The question of risk looms large here—11 years is a long time. Also, some argue that reinvestment of the cash flows makes (*a*) preferable—but the effect has been taken into account in the discount procedure. It's worthwhile to calculate a *compounding* of all cash flows to 11 years to prove this point. The question of changing earnings opportunities over time can be raised.

4. DEF Company

Net investment: $52,800.

Life: Eight years, no salvage.

Depreciation: $6,600/year straight-line.

Annual operating cash flow:

Net labor and material savings	$12,100
Less depreciation	6,600
	$5,500
Taxes at 36%	1,980
Aftertax savings	$3,520
Add back depreciation	6,600
Operating cash flow	$10,120

a. Payback:

$$\frac{\$52,800}{\$10,120} = 5.2 \text{ years}$$

b. Return on investment:

$$\frac{\$10,120}{\$52,800} = 19.2\%$$

c. Average return:

$$\frac{\$10,120}{\$26,400} = 38.3\%$$

d. Net present value (at 12 percent):

Present value of operating cash flow:

4.968 × $10,120 (Table II):	+$50,276
Present value of net investment	−52,800
Net present value	−$2,524

e. Present value index:

$$\frac{\$50,276}{\$52,800} = .95$$

f. Internal rate of return: Approximately 11%.

g. Present value payback: Just about eight years. A small gap exists. There's no cushion.

h. Annualized net present value:

$$\frac{-\$2,594}{4.968} = -\$508 \text{ each year}$$

(This shows the annual gap that has to be overcome to meet the standard!)

Observations

This example introduces depreciation and its importance as a tax shield. This is an opportunity to demonstrate various ways of calculating the tax shield effect. Accelerated depreciation available under the tax laws would tend to boost considerably the benefits of the project in the early years. You should work through different depreciation patterns and develop present values using Tables I and II.

5. XYZ Corporation

Past investment: $3.75 million (sunk).

Net investment data:

Original outlay: $6,300,000.
Recovery in 12 years: $1,260,000 (book value).
Working capital:

Initial . . . . $1,500,000.
Recovery in 12 years . . . . $1,250,000.

Promotion expenditure ($1.0 million × .64): $640,000 (aftertax).
Life of proposition: 12 years.
Profit improvements:

	Years 1–3	Years 4–8	Years 9–12	Total
Profit improvement	$1,900	$2,200	$1,300	$21,900
Less: Depreciation	420	420	420	5,040
	$1,480	$1,780	$ 880	$16,860
Tax at 36% (rounded)	533	640	317	6,070
	$ 947	$1,140	$ 563	$10,790
Add back depreciation	420	420	420	5,040
Operating cash flow	$1,367	$1,560	$ 983	$15,830

Present value analysis at 12 percent:

Time Period	Investments	Operating Cash Flows	PV Factors at 12%*	Present Values	PV Factors at 15%*	Present Values
0	−$6,300 −$1,500 −$640		1.000	−$8,440	1.000	−$8,440
1 2 3		+$1,367/yr.	2.402	+3,284	2.283	+3,120
4 5 6 7 8		+$1,560/yr.	4.968 −2.402 2.566	+4,003	4.487 −2.283 2.204	+3,438
9 10 11 12		+$983/yr.	6.194 −4.968 1.226	+1,205	5.421 −4.487 .934	+918
12 †	+$1,260 +$1,250		.257	+645	.187	+469
Net present values				+$697		−$495

*From Table II, except year-end of Year 12, which is from Table I.
†Year end.

Net *present value* at 12 percent is about $700,000, indicating a bet-ter-than-standard result. In fact, the recovery of working capital and book values of equipment in Year 12 could be forgone and the proj-ect would still meet standards.

Present value index at 12 percent:

Based on initial investment:

$$\frac{\$9,137}{\$8,440} = 1.08$$

Based on net investment:

$$\frac{\$8,492}{\$7,795} = 1.09$$

Present value payback:

Just about 12 years because the recovery represents the excess present value.

Internal rate of return (IRR):

By trial and error a little under 14 percent. (See PV analysis above.)

Annualized net present value:

$$\frac{\$697}{6.194} = \$122,500 \text{ per year (narrow margin for error)}$$

Observations

Project is close to standard; it shows problems of handling uneven cash flows. Can't recover past (sunk) R&D. Therefore similar future projects will be of doubtful value to the company.

6. ZYX COMPANY

Net Investment

Original machine	$32,000
Current book value	$25,600
Market value	15,000 (relevant)
Loss on sale	$10,600
Tax savings on loss @ 36%	3,816 (relevant)
Net loss	$ 6,784
Net investment	$55,500
Value in eight years	$ 1,500

Calculation of Net Investment

New machine	$55,500
Less cash on old	15,000
	$40,500
Less tax savings	3,816
Initial investment	$36,684

To be adjusted for recoveries in Year 8.

COMPARISON OF LIVES

Only eight years are comparable. If the new machine lasted longer, its life would have to be cut off for purposes of comparison.

Operating Savings and Benefits

	Old Machine	New Machine	Annual Difference
Operating savings—current volume:			
Labor	$ 24,000	$ 16,000	$ 8,000
Materials	96,000	92,000	4,000
Overhead (200% of labor)	48,000	32,000	(not applicable)
	$168,000	$140,000	$12,000
Contribution—additional volume:			
30,000 units @ $.95		$ 28,500	
Less: Labor @ $.08		(2,400)	
Materials @ $.46		(13,800)	
Selling and promotion		(5,500)	6,800
Total savings and contribution			$18,800
Depreciation	$ 3,200	$ 6,750*	(3,550)
Taxable benefits			$15,250
Taxes at 36%			5,490
Aftertax benefits			$ 9,760
Add back depreciation			3,550
Aftertax cash flow			$13,260

*$55,500 new machine
 −1,500 scrap
 $54,000 + 8 = $6,750/year

Payback:

$$\frac{\$36,684 - \$1,500}{\$13,260} = 2.65 \text{ years}$$

Return on investment:

$$\frac{\$13,260}{\$35,184} = 37.7\%$$

Net present value:

Time Period	Amounts	PV Factor 16%	Present Values
0	−$36,684	1.00	−$36,684
1–8	+$13,260/yr.	4.344	+$57,601
8	+$1,500	.305	+$458
		Net present value	+$21,375

Present value index:

• Net investment basis:

$$\frac{\$57,601}{\$36,684 - \$458} = 1.59$$

- Without terminal value:

$$\frac{\$57,601 + \$458}{\$36,684} = 1.58$$

Present value payback:

This is determined through use of the annuity table:

$$\text{Annuity factor} = \frac{\$36,226}{\$13,260/\text{yr.}} = 2.732$$

Interpolation in the 16 percent column of Table II indicates a little under four years is required. The terminal value could be a problem if it were significantly larger than assumed here, because it has been discounted for receipt in Year 8, which is much later than the payback period of 4 years. If precision is required, year-by-year trial-and-error approaches can be made.

Annualized net present value:

$$\frac{\$21,375}{4.344} = \$4,920$$

This is a sizable cushion for error in the performance estimates.

Internal rate of return (IRR):

Trial and error necessary; result is about 32%.

Time Period	Amounts	PV Factors at 35%	Present Values	PV Factors at 30%	Present Values
0	−$36,684	1.000	−$36,684	1.000	−$36,684
1–8	+$13,260/yr.	2.598	+$34,449	2.925	+$38,786
8	+$1,500	.091	+$136	.123	+$184
			−$2,098		+$2,286

Observations

This is the best example, among the ones provided, with which to practice your mastery of problem structure, differential costs, different lives, and accounting allocations. Questions could be raised concerning a 10-year life of the new machine, and also whether the product is worthwhile per se—which is the assumption on which the differential cost analysis rests. The improvement could merely raise product profitability from poor to mediocre!

7. UVW Company

Net investment: $275,000.

Life: 12 years.

Operating cash flows:

Amount	Probability	Expectation
$15,000	.05	$ 750
35,000	.15	5,250
45,000	.40	18,000
50,000	.25	12,500
60,000	.15	9,000
	1.00	$45,500

a. Net present value at 10% (on expectation):

Investment outlay	−$275,000
12 years at $45,500 (6.814)	+ 310,040
Net present value	+$ 34,960

This is also approximately the same as the net present value based on the most likely outcome ($45,000):

Investment	−$275,000
6.814 × $45,000	306,630
Net present value	+$ 31,630

b. Annualized net present value:
  • On expectation:

$$\frac{\$34,960}{6.814} = \$5,130$$

  • On most likely value:

$$\frac{\$31,630}{6.814} = \$4,640$$

In either case there's a sizable cushion against estimating error.

c. Internal rate of return:

$$\frac{\$275,000}{\$45,500} = 6.044; \text{ or } \frac{\$275,000}{\$45,000} = 6.111$$

Yield over 12 years is about 12 percent (12-year life in Table II) in either case.

d. Minimum life at $45,000/year:

$$\frac{\$275,000}{\$45,000} = 6.111 \text{ at } 10\%$$

This requires a little under 10 years (10 percent column in Table II), a cushion of about 2 years.

e. Minimum cash flow to achieve 10 percent:

$$\frac{\$275,000}{6.814} = \$40,360 \text{ per year for 12 years}$$

The chances of achieving this level of cash flow are better than 80 percent. Is this good enough?

Observations

This example serves to illustrate analysis by elements of probabilistic reasoning, holding a lot of assumptions stable. It appears that the project has a reasonable chance of success, but the final answer rests on the judgment of the people involved.

Questions for Discussion

1. Define the difference between cash flows, differential costs, and relevant costs.

2. Why should we study the various alternatives before making a capital investment decision?

3. Are sunk costs always to be ignored in capital investment analysis? Can't such a practice lead to financial difficulties?

4. Do past investments in large support facilities count when considering production investments that will make use of this unused capacity?

5. Do accounting allocations ever become relevant in investment analysis?

6. Define the difference between present value payback and annualized net present value.

7. What's the difference between an annualized net present value and an annuity?

8. Why might the internal rate of return (yield) provide two answers at the same time?

9. Why is it necessary to adjust for uneven lives in alternative capital investments when discounting reduces the importance of future cash flows anyway?

10. Is it possible to make an annual charge for working capital in a capital investment proposal, in lieu of specifying an outflow for the

amount of working capital at point zero and an inflow for its recovery at the end of the past year?

11. Differentiate between capital budgeting and capital investment analysis. Which additional questions need to be resolved in the former?

12. Which aspects of capital investment analysis and capital budgeting lend themselves to modeling?

CHAPTER 7

Solutions to Problems

1. GHI Company

   Calculations of cost of capital:

Existing debt:	$12\% \times (1 - .36) = 7.7\%$
Incremental debt:	$10\% \times (1 - .36) = 6.4\%$
Existing preferred:	14.0%
Incremental preferred:	12.0%
Common equity:	
Earnings basis:	$\dfrac{\$\,9.50}{\$77.00} = 12.3\%$
Dividend basis:	$\dfrac{\$\,4.50}{\$77.00} + 7\% = 12.8\%$
CAPM:	$k_e = 9\% + 1.25\,(15.0 - 9.0) = 16.5\%$

   Observations

   We need to define the purpose of the analysis, and the figures by themselves are only the beginning. The cost of common equity shows a large differential between the shortcuts and the CAPM approach. It would be useful to be able to review recent company performance. Apparently the risk premium implicit in the β suggests that more volatility can be expected.

2. KLN Company

   Weighted cost of capital:

   Existing conditions:

Debt cost 7.0(1 – .46)	3.78%
Preferred cost	6.00%
Common equity cost—(CAPM 7.5 + 1.2 [13.5 – 7.5])	14.70%

   Incremental conditions:

Debt cost 11.0(1 − .46)	5.94%
Preferred cost	9.00%
Common equity (CAPM)	14.70%

Assignment of weights:

Book value basis:

Debt	$250	35.8%
Preferred	50	7.1
Common equity	400	57.1
	$700	100.0%

Market value basis:

Debt (7.0/11.0 × 250)	$159	23.0%
Preferred (6.0/9.0 × 50)	33	4.8
Common equity $50/share	500	72.2
	$692	100.0%

Weighted cost (incremental):

	Book Value			Market Value		
Debt	35.8% ×	5.94 =	2.13%	23.0% ×	5.94 =	1.37%
Preferred	7.1 ×	9.00 =	0.64	4.8 ×	9.00 =	0.43
Common equity	57.1 ×	14.70 =	8.39	72.2 ×	4.70 =	10.61
	100.0%		11.16%	100.0%		12.41%

Weighted cost (existing):

	Book Value			Market Value		
Debt	35.8% ×	3.78 =	1.35%	23.0% ×	3.78 =	0.87%
Preferred	7.1 ×	6.00 =	0.43	4.8 ×	6.00 =	0.26
Common equity	57.1 ×	14.70 =	8.39	72.2 ×	14.70 =	10.61
	100.0%		10.17%	100.0%		11.74%

Observations

The range of results is narrow, within two percentage points. If we ignore the book value basis as not relevant, the market value results are even closer. If any use is made of the concept for future investments, the existing conditions aren't relevant either. Thus, the weighted cost is about 12 percent, perhaps a little higher.

Questions for Discussion

1. Why can't we speak of "*the* cost of capital" as an absolute figure?

2. What indirect costs can be ascribed to a long-term loan or to a convertible debenture?

3. Why are shareholder expectations important in developing the cost of common equity when the company has no control over the behavior of the stock market?

4. If beta, as defined in the CAPM, isn't a fully satisfactory measure of risk, what alternative concepts can you suggest?

5. How important is the choice of weights in developing the weighted cost of capital as a minimum return standard?

6. If weighted cost of capital is a useful standard with which to assess prospective returns from new capital investments, how should the return on existing investments be judged?

7. If a company's financial policies are changing (e.g., the use of leverage increases), does this mean its return requirements must change also?

8. If you were president of a multidivision company with rather different businesses, how would you answer the argument that some divisions should use lower return standards than others?

9. How critical is it that a capital investment project exactly meet the weighted cost of capital standard? What questions would you ask?

10. What major elements would you consider in developing a broad allocation of capital to the rather different divisions of a company? Which would be most important?

CHAPTER 8

Solutions to Problems

1. *a.*

ABC CORPORATION
Per Share Analysis
($ thousands, except per share amounts)

	Old Level	New Level
EBIT	$14,700	$17,400 (118%)
Interest (same)	1,100	1,100
Profit before taxes	$13,600	$16,300
Taxes at 34%	4,625	5,540
Profit after taxes	$8,975	$10,760
Number of common shares	300,000	350,000
Earnings per share	$29.91	$30.74

	Old Level	New Level
Sinking fund	$900	900
Sinking fund per share	$3.00	$2.57
Uncommitted earnings per share	$26.91	$28.17
Depreciation per share	$7.50	$6.43
Cash flow per share	$37.41	$37.17

Immediate dilution: $\dfrac{\$8,975,000}{350,000} - \$29.41 = (\$3.77)$ dilution (12.8%).

Net dilution (strengthening): $30.74 − $29.41 = $1.33 strengthening
(4.5%).
  b. $5.0 million preferred stock (10%)
      or $5.0 million debentures (9%), due in 15 years.

Per Share Analysis
($ thousands, except per share amounts)

	Preferred		Debentures	
	Old Level	New Level	Old Level	New Level
EBIT	$ 14,700	$ 17,400	$ 14,700	$ 17,400
Interest—old	1,100	1,100	1,100	1,100
Interest—new	—	—	450	450
Profit before taxes	$ 13,600	$ 16,300	$ 13,150	$ 15,850
Taxes at 34%	4,625	5,540	4,475	5,390
Profit after taxes	$ 8,975	$ 10,760	$ 8,675	$ 10,460
Preferred dividends . . .	500	500	—	—
Profits to common	$ 8,475	$ 10,260	$ 8,675	$ 10,460
Number of common shares	300,000	300,000	300,000	300,000
Earnings per share . . .	$ 28.25	$ 34.20	$ 28.92	$ 34.86
Sinking fund	$ 900	$ 900	$ 900	$ 900
Sinking fund per share	$ 3.00	$ 3.00	$ 3.00	$ 3.00
Uncommitted earnings per share	$ 25.25	$ 31.20	$ 25.92	$ 31.86
Depreciation per share	$ 7.50	$ 7.50	$ 7.50	$ 7.50
Cash flow per share . . .	$ 35.75	$ 41.70	$ 36.42	$ 42.36

Immediate dilution:

Preferred: $28.25 − $29.91 = (1.06); $\dfrac{\$\ 1.66}{\$29.91} = 5.9\%$ dilution

Debentures: $28.92 − $29.91 = ($.99); $\dfrac{\$.99}{\$29.91} = 3.4\%$ dilution

Net dilution (strengthening):
  Preferred: $34.20 − $29.91 = $4.29; 14.3% strengthening
  Debentures: $34.86 − $29.91 = $4.95; 16.5% strengthening

c. Comparative cost of capital:

Common stock:

$5 million represents 50,000 shares, or $100 per share, far below the current average price of $130. EPS required to keep stockholders as well off as before: $29.91. Thus, the apparent "cost" of this issue is

$$\frac{\$29.91}{\$100.00} = 29.9\% \text{ after taxes, a very low P/E ratio, indeed.}$$

Based on the CAPM, the cost of common stock is

$$8.0 + 1.4\ (14.5 - 8.0) = 17.1\% \text{ after taxes}$$

This is obviously a risky company, from which the market is demanding a high risk premium.

- Preferred stock: 10% after taxes.
- Debentures: 5.9% after taxes.

Observations

Note the apparent attractiveness of the new investments, and the leverage effect of lower-cost preferred or debt. (The example has been exaggerated with a low P/E to make the differences more apparent.)

2. XYZ Corporation

a. Comparative cost of capital:

(1) Determine the EBIT level:

EPS (current)	$	12.50
Number of common shares		1,000,000
Profit to common		$12,500,000
Preferred dividends (existing)		1,500,000
Profit after taxes		$14,000,000
Taxes (46%)		11,925,000
Profit before taxes		$25,925,000
Bond interest (existing)		2,500,000
EBIT		$28,425,000

(2) Determine profit to common at current EBIT level:

	Common	Preferred
EBIT	$28,425	$28,425
Interest	2,500	2,500
Profit before taxes	$25,925	$25,925
Taxes (46%)	11,925	11,925
Profit after taxes	$14,000	$14,000
Preferred dividends	1,500	4,200
Profit to common	$12,500	$ 9,800
Number of shares	1,240,000	1,000,000
EPS	$10.08	$ 9.80

(3) Determine profit to common needed to maintain current EPS:

	Common	Preferred
EPS	$12.50	$12.50
Number of shares	1,240,000	1,000,000
Profit to common	$15,500	$12,500
Profit to common—current EBIT	12,500	9.800
Incremental profit (after taxes)	$3,000	$2,700
Incremental investment	$30,000	$30,000
Specific cost of capital	10.0%	9.0%
Specific cost before taxes	18.5%	16.7%

The cost of preferred stock is the same as the stated dividend rate, of course, assuming the stock was issued at par.

(4) Calculation of cost of common equity based on CAPM:

$$k_e = 8.0 + 1.2 \ (13.0 - 8.0)$$
$$= 8.0 + 6.0 = 14.0\%$$

b. Equivalency between common and preferred alternatives:

$$\text{Formula: } \frac{(E - i) \ .54 - p}{n}$$

$$\overset{\text{(common)}}{\frac{(E - \$2,500) \ .54 - \$1,500}{1,240}} = \overset{\text{(preferred)}}{\frac{(E - \$2,500) \ .54 - \$4,200}{1,000}}$$

$$540E - 1,350,000 - 1,500,000 = 669.6E - 1,674,000 - 5,208,000$$
$$129.6E = 4,032,000$$
$$E = 31,111$$

Earnings equivalency thus is at $31,111,000 EBIT.
Earnings per share/dividend per share equivalency:

EPS needed for $8.00 dividend	$	8.00
Number of common shares		1,240,000
Profit to common	$	9,920,000
Preferred dividends		1,500,000
Profit after taxes		$11,420,000
Taxes (46%)		9,728,000
Profit before taxes		$21,148,000
Interest		2,500,000
EBIT for $8.00 dividend		$23,648,000

c. Leverage effect of preferred alternative:

	Level 1	Level 2	Level 3	Level 4
EBIT (current $28,425)	$10,000	$15,000	$22,500	$33,750
Interest	2,500	2,500	2,500	2,500
	$ 7,500	$12,500	$20,000	$31,250
Taxes (46%)	3,450	5,750	9,200	14,375
	$ 4,050	$ 6,750	$10,800	$16,875
Preferred dividend . . .	4,200	4,200	4,200	4,200
Profit to common	$ (150)	$ 2,550	$ 6,600	$12,675
Common shares	1,000,000	1,000,000	1,000,000	1,000,000
EPS (current $12.50)	$ (.15)	$ 2.55	$ 6.60	$12.68
Percent increase in EBIT		50%	50%	50%
Percent increase in EPS		Infinite	159%	92%

This is a highly leveraged situation, but the rate of increase drops as earnings move away from the EBIT break-even level (coverage of fixed charges = zero EPS, or EBIT level of $10.28 million).

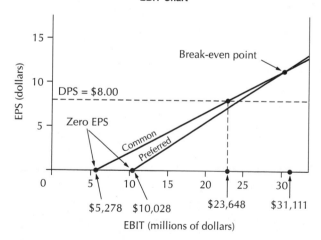

XYZ CORPORATION
EBIT Chart

Observations

Again, some exaggeration is used to make the points involved. The example can be used for a good drilling of concepts—by working the data in both directions.

3.

DEF COMPANY
EPS Calculations
($ thousands, except per share amounts)

	Common		Preferred		Debentures	
	Current*	Low	Current*	Low	Current*	Low
EBIT	$42,000	$22,000	$42,000	$22,000	$42,000	$22,000
Interest—old ...	1,200	1,200	1,200	1,200	1,200	1,200
Interest—new ...	—	—	—	—	$ 4,250	$ 4,250
Profit before taxes	$40,800	$20,800	$40,800	$20,800	$36,550	$16,550
Taxes (46%)....	18,768	9,568	18,768	9,568	16,813	7,613
Profit after taxes	$22,032	$11,232	$22,032	$11,232	$19,737	$ 8,937
Preferred dividend—old	1,800	1,800	1,800	1,800	1,800	1,800
Preferred dividend—new	—	—	4,750	4,750	—	—
Profit to common	$20,232	$ 9,432	$15,482	$ 4,682	$17,937	$ 7,137
Number of common shares (millions).....	3.0	3.0	2.0	2.0	2.0	2.0
EPS	$6.74	$3.14	$7.94	$2.34	$8.97	$3.57
SFPS	$.33	$.33	$.50	$.50	$1.50	$1.50
UEPS	$6.41	$2.81	$7.24	$1.84	$7.47	$2.07
Dividend coverage (EPS).......	3.37 ×	1.57 ×	3.87 ×	1.17 ×	4.49 ×	.79 ×

*Current EBIT plus incremental earnings on new capital.

Dilution Analysis

	Common	Preferred	Debentures
EBIT (old)	$34,000	$34,000	$34,000
Interest	1,200	1,200	5,450
Profit before taxes	$32,800	$32,800	$28,550
Taxes (46%).................	15,088	15,088	13,133
Profit after taxes	$17,712	$17,712	$15,417
Preferred dividends	1,800	6,550	1,800
Profit to common	$15,912	$11,162	$13,617
Number of shares (millions)	3.0	2.0	2.0
EPS (old = $7.96)	$ 5.30	$ 5.58	$ 6.81

Immediate dilution:

> Common: $7.96 − $5.30 = $2.66; drop of 33.4%
>
> Preferred: $7.96 − $5.58 = $2.38; drop of 29.9%
>
> Debentures: $7.96 − $6.81 = $1.15; drop of 14.4%

Net dilution (strengthening):

Common: $7.96 − $6.74 = $1.22; drop of 15.3%
Preferred: $7.96 − $7.74 = $(.22); drop of 2.8%
Debentures: $7.96 − $8.97 = $(1.01); drop of 12.7%

Cost of capital (after taxes):

Common: $7.96 per share for $50.00—apparent "cost" = 15.9%*
Preferred: 9.5 percent stated rate   = 9.5 %
Debentures: 9.5 percent before tax $(1 − .46) \times 8.5\%$ = 4.6 %
*Based on the CAPM, the cost of common is 7.5 + 1.2(14.0 − 7.5) = 15.2%.

Break-even points:
- Common versus preferred:

$$\frac{(E − 1,200).54 − 1,800}{3,000} = \frac{(E − 1,200).54 − 6,550}{2,000}$$
$$\text{(common)} \qquad\qquad \text{(preferred)}$$

$$1,080E − 1,296,000 − 3,600,000 = 1,620E − 1,944,000 − 19,650,000$$
$$540E = 16,698,000; \; E − 30,922; \text{EBIT} = \$30,922,200$$

- Common versus debentures:

$$\frac{(E − 1,200).54 − 1,800}{3,000} = \frac{(E − 5,450).54 − 1,800}{2,000}$$

$$1,080E − 1,296,000 − 3,600,000 = 1,620E − 8,829,000 − 5,400,000$$
$$540E = 9,333,000; \; E = 17,283; \text{EBIT} = \$17,283,300$$

- Dividend coverage:
Shown in the EPS calculations above.

Zero EPS:
- Common:

$$(E − 1,200).54 − 1,800 = 0;$$
$$.54E − 648 − 1,800 = 0;$$
$$E = \$4,533,300 \text{ EBIT}.$$

- Preferred:

$$(E − 1,200).54 − 6,550 = 0;$$
$$.54E − 648 − 6,550 = 0;$$
$$E = \$13,329,600 \text{ EBIT}.$$

DEF COMPANY
EBIT Chart

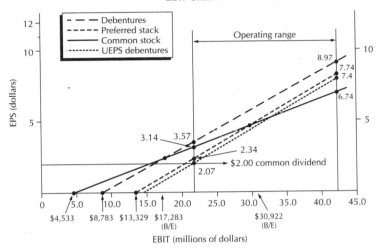

EBIT (millions of dollars)

- Debentures:

$$(E - 5,450).54 - 1,800 = 0;$$
$$.54E - 2,943 - 1,800 = 0;$$

$$E = \$8,783,300 \text{ EBIT.}$$

Observations

The example allows full treatment of the technical aspects of the three alternatives, and the display is useful in its exaggeration. Please review the key points beyond those represented by the figures, which are also necessary for choice. Otherwise the data are self-explanatory.

Questions for Discussion

1. List the key conditions that would affect the relative importance of the areas of cost, risk exposure, flexibility, timing, and control.

2. Why is it important to look ahead to the potential next stage of financing when deciding the choice among current alternatives for new funds?

3. Relate the weighted cost of capital of a company to the costs of the respective alternatives for incremental funds. Are they based on the same reasoning?

4. How does the immediate dilution of earnings caused by alternative ways of raising additional funds relate to the return standards required for new investments?

5. Why are calculations of the comparative cost of alternative financing choices based on the proceeds and not on the face value?

6. What are the key assumptions underlying the EBIT chart, and under what conditions is it necessary to redraw the lines?

7. How does prospective inflation affect the choice among alternative methods of raising additional funds?

8. When leasing is an alternative, what are the key considerations that would make it attractive?

9. Is there such a thing as an ideal long-term capital structure, and should blocks of incremental capital be tailored to fit such a structure?

CHAPTER 9

Solutions to Problems

1. Bond price examples:
   a. Price at 6%:

Principal due after 28 periods at 3%, plus premium of $75 (using preprogrammed calculator) $1,075 × 0.437	$ 469.78
PV of 28 semiannual interest payments of $40, at 3% per period (factor from calculator) $40 × 18.764	750.56
Price to yield 6% per annum	$1,220.34
Price at 10%	
$1,075 × 0.255 (Table I in Chapter 6)	$ 274.12
$40 × 14.898 (Table II in Chapter 6)	595.92
Price to yield 10% per annum	$ 870.04

   b. Price at 6%:

Principal due after 44 periods at 3% if not called:	
$1,000 × 0.31 (interpolation, Table I)	$ 310.00
44 semiannual interest receipts of $42.50:	
$42.50 × 24.0 (interpolation, Table II)	1,020.00
Price to yield 6% per annum	$1,330.00
If called at 110 on 10/1/96:	
Principal plus call premium due after 24 periods at 3%:	
$1,100 × 0.50 (interpolation, Table I)	$ 550.00
24 semiannual interest receipts of $42.50:	
$42.50 × 16.9 (interpolation, Table II)	718.25
Price to yield 6% per annum	$1,268.25

c. Price at 9%:

$1,000 × 0.13 (interpolation, 4.5%) $130.00

$42.50 × 18.7 (interpolation, 4.5%) 794.75

Price to yield 9% per annum $924.75

If called:

$1,100 × 0.33 (interpolation, 4.5%) $363.00

$42.50 × 14.3 (interpolation, 4.5%) 607.75

Price to yield 9% per annum $970.75

2. Bond yield examples:
   a. No interest accrued because the interest date coincides with the purchase date.

Market price 7/15/97 . . . . $1,241.25

Redemption price 7/15/98 . . . .   1,100.00

                                                                             $2,341.25

Average investment (1/2) $1,170.63

Number of periods: 28.

Interest per period: $35.00.

Amortization of premium: $141.25 ÷ 28 = $5.04.

Average periodic income: $35.00 − $5.04 = $29.96, or $59.92 per year.

$$\text{Yield: } \frac{\$59.92}{\$1,170.63} = 5.12\%$$

Exact yield from bond
table: 4.65%

   b. Exact yield from bond table: 4.85%.
   c. Annual interest: $40.00.
   Accrued interest on August 20, 1997:

$$5 \text{ months} + 20 \text{ days} = 170 \text{ days}$$

or

$$\frac{170}{360} \times \$40 = \$18.89$$

Net price on August 20:

$$\$487.50 - \$18.89 = \$468.61$$

Market price 8/20/97 . . . . $468.61
Redemption price 3/1/98 . . . .   500.00
$968.61
Average investment (1/2) $484.30
23 ½ (approximately) periods of interest @ $40.00.
Amortization of discount: $31.39 + 23.5 = $1.34.
Annual income: $40.00 − $1.34 = $38.66.

Approximate yield: $\dfrac{\$38.66}{\$484.30} = 7.98\%$

Exact yield from bond table: 8.62%

3. Value of rights and subscription price:
   a. Market value ex rights:

$$\text{Subscription price } (S) = \$65.00$$
$$\text{Market price } (M) = \$89.00$$
$$\text{Number of rights } (N) = 12$$

The following relationship holds where R = value of a right:

$$R = \frac{M - S}{N + 1}; \; R = \frac{89 - 65}{13} = \$1.85$$

The market value ex rights will be approximately $89.00 − 1.85 = \$87.15$, reflecting the removal of the rights value.

   b. Rights value for purchase of convertible preferred:

$$\text{Value of preferred } (V) = \$105.00$$
$$\text{Subscription price } (S) = \$82.00$$
$$\text{Number of rights } (N) = 6$$

The following relationship holds where R = value of a right:

$$R = \frac{V - S}{N*} = \frac{105 - 82}{6} = \$3.83$$

*Number of common shares isn't affected.

   if $N = 4$, $R = \$5.75$
   c. Subscription price:

$$\text{Market price } (M) = \$123.00$$
$$\text{Number of rights } (N) = 11$$
$$\text{Value of a right } (R) = \$2.00$$
$$R = \frac{M - S}{N + 1}; \; 2 = \frac{123 - S}{12}; \; S = \$99.00$$

4. Calculation of common stock value:
   a. Expected yield using the CAPM:

Company A: $7.0 + 1.3(13.5 - 7.0) = 7.0 + 8.45 = 15.45\%$
Company B: $7.0 + 0.8(13.5 - 7.0) = 7.0 + 5.2 = 12.2\%$

b. Valuation (dividend discount model):

$$\text{Company A: } P = \frac{D}{I - g} = \frac{\$1.00}{.154 - 0.08} = \$13.50$$

$$\text{Company B: } P = \frac{\$5.00}{0.122 - 0.04} = \frac{\$5.00}{.082} = \$61.00$$

c. Other yardsticks:

	Company A	Company B
Earnings yield:	$\dfrac{\$2.50}{\frac{1}{2}(26 + 18)} = 11.4\%$	$\dfrac{\$7.25}{\frac{1}{2}(60 + 56)} = 12.5\%$
Dividend yield:	$\dfrac{\$1.00}{\$22.00} = 4.5\%$	$\dfrac{5.00}{\$58.00} = 8.6\%$

Observations

Company A is the more volatile company, while it is growing faster. The market is apparently awarding it a premium at the moment. It would be useful to check out public expectations about the company's future performance. Company B seems stable and properly priced; no surprises are expected here.

5. Valuation of GHI Company as an ongoing business:

Calculation of Present Values

	Year 1	Year 2	Year 3	Year 4	Year 5	Terminal Value
Earnings after taxes	$2.7	$2.9	$3.2	$3.6	$4.0	—
Add: Depreciation	1.0	1.1	1.4	1.6	1.8	—
Aftertax cash flow	$3.7	$4.0	$4.6	$5.2	$5.8	—
Less: Investments	0.5	2.5	1.5	1.5	2.0	—
Net cash flow	3.2	1.5	3.1	3.7	3.8	$40.0
Present value factors (from Table I)	.893	.797	.712	.636	.567	.567
Present values	$2.86	$1.20	$2.21	$2.35	$2.15	$22.68
Cumulative	$2.86	$4.06	$6.27	$8.62	$10.77	$33.45

Based on current P/E ratio, the company is worth about $11 \times \$2.5$ million ($27.5 million). Building in the projected growth raises the value.

Observations

Quality of estimates is a question, as is the choice of the discount rate. If the rate is raised, the value drops, of course. We would need to know more about financial condition, debt to be assumed, nature of business, and so on. Many more questions must be asked. This is just the start.

6. MNO Company valuation:

Book value (based on balance sheet):

Common equity:

Common stock	$525
Capital surplus	110
Earned surplus	385
Total	$1,020
Number of shares	52,500
Book value per share	$19.43

If we assume surplus reserves and deferred taxes to be part of equity, the total rises to $1,185, and the value per share to $22.57. The redundant cash is minimal in this picture and should probably be applied to accounts payable.

Liquidation value:

Assets	Fast Liquidation	Normal Sale
Cash....................................	$ 230	$ 230
Securities	415	415
Receivables (94%)	494	494
Inventories (2/3; 95%)	543	774
Fixed assets	225	225+
Prepaids (assume 25%).....................	—	10
Goodwill	—	—
Organization expense	—	—
Total	$ 1,907	$2,148
Less:		
Current liabilities	$ 935	$ 935
Mortgage payable	175	175
Bonds	520	520
Preferred stock	300	300
Total deduction	$ 1,930	$1,930
Value of common	$ (23)	$ 218
Per share	$ (.44)	$ 4.15

Market value:

Most recent: $25⅛, but thinly traded.

Based on average of past 3 years: $28⅛.

Based on recent industry P/E of 11: $.65 × 4 × 11 = $28.60.

Based on average P/E of 13: $.65 × 4 × 13 = $33.80.

Based on long-term profit growth, EPS should be about $3.00, and P/E of 11 would be $33.00.

Observations

Because no forced liquidation is intended, the value should be based on a going concern concept, and the main argument should be on the breadth of the market, the use of industry P/E ratios, and the expectation of future cash flows.

Additional information should be sought about nature of the industry, long-term product trends, profitability of similar companies, dividend policies of other companies, product line changes and threats, competitive abilities, and so on.

7. Potential merger:

	Company A	Company B
P/E ratio	12X	20X
Earnings per share	$8.00	$3.00
Dividends per share	$2.00	none
Aftertax earnings	$80.0 million	$3.0 million
Price range	$90 to $100	$45 to $70
Current price	$98.00	$54.00 ($65.00 offered)
Growth rate	6% per year	12% per year
Number of shares	10 million	1 million

a. Exchange ratio:

65 ÷ 98 = ⅔ share of A for 1 share of B = 667,000 shares

b. Impact on earnings:

$80.0 million plus $3.0 million = $83.0 million

10.0 million shares plus 667,000 = 10,667,000 shares

$83.0 ÷ 10,667,000 = $7.78 per share (22¢ dilution)

c. Impact on dividends: Each share of Company B now receives the equivalent of $1.33 per share in dividends versus none before.

d. Impact on earnings growth: Three years hence the situation is expected to be:

Company A @ 6 percent growth will earn $95.3 million ($9.53 EPS).

Company B @ 12 percent growth will earn $4.2 million ($4.20 EPS).
Total company earnings thus will grow to $99.5 million, and EPS will be $99.5 ÷ 10,667,000 = $9.33.

Observations

The dilution in earnings of 22 cents immediately isn't likely to be overcome in the foreseeable future inasmuch as in three years the earnings per share of the combined company will be 20 cents lower than what Company A alone could have achieved. On the other hand, synergy, if any, hasn't been considered. In view of the sizable annual dividends now paid them, the holders of Company B stock might perhaps consider a somewhat lower offer.

Questions for Discussion

1. Differentiate between economic value and market value. Are both concepts absolute?

2. Is value in the eye of the beholder or can conditions be quantified sufficiently to allow objective choices?

3. Discuss the relationship between yield and value. Are both concepts based on the same conditions?

4. Is it possible to allow specifically for the effect of such provisions as participation, convertibility, callability, and other special covenants in valuing preferred stocks or bonds?

5. Why should we attempt to value an ongoing business via cash flow analysis when in the end the decision is based on many other factors as well?

6. List major considerations affecting valuation in an inflationary environment.

7. If price/earnings ratios are so important in setting the ratio of exchange in a merger based on a share swap, how can such a volatile measure give reasonable indications of value?

8. Synergy is an argument for business combinations, but it's hard to measure and achieve. Why?

9. With vast increases in computer capabilities, will valuation likely become more quantified?

10. If there's so much uncertainty in estimates of future cash flows, why does it make sense to apply even more sophisticated valuation formulas?

INDEX